John,
Proof text without
Index

Ed

THE NEWMAN-SCOTUS READER

THE NEWMAN-SCOTUS READER

CONTEXTS AND COMMONALITIES

Edited by Edward J. Ondrako, OFMConv.

ACADEMY OF THE IMMACULATE
New Bedford, MA
2015

The Newman-Scotus Reader is a book prepared for publication by the Academy of the Immaculate [academyoftheimmaculate.com], POB 3003, New Bedford, MA, 02741-3003.

© Franciscan Friars Conventual
All rights reserved

Cum permissu superiorum
Very Rev. James McCurry, OFMConv.
Minister Provincial

The permission of the superiors is a declaration of the Roman Catholic Church that a work is free from error in matters of faith and morals; but in no way does it imply that she endorses the contents of the book.

Epiphany, January 2015.

ISBN: 978-1-60114-069-2

COVER CREDITS: Design by Mary Flannery, Flannery Studios. Portrait sketch of Bl. John Duns Scotus by Mariola Paini, Artist of the Saints [www.saintsgallery.com]. Bl. John Henry Newman portrait, cortesy of the Birmingham Oratory, England. Icon on back by Friar Matthew Bond, OFMConv. Underlay of stained glass from Saint Mary the Virgin, Oxford.

He who beholds that light is so enthralled
that he would never willingly consent
to turn away from it for any other sight.
Comedia, Paradiso 33, 100–02

To my greatest teacher, my sister Margie,
who helps me to contemplate the Infinite Being.
Her Down Syndrome is God's hidden gift beyond price!

Dedicated to all with Down Syndrome and Special Needs

Contents

Foreword xxiii
Friar Marco Tasca, OFMConv.

Acknowledgments xxv

List of Abbreviations xxvii
   Primary Sources. xxvii
   Versions, Translations, and Series. xxviii

General Introduction 1
   Is Scotus a *Progenitor* of Newman?. 2
   From condetermination to certitude 6
   Part One. Foundations in the Contours. 9
   Part Two. Contextualizing the Theological Consistency. 12
   Part Three. The Implications for the Church and the Modern World 12
   Three assumptions before engaging *The Newman-Scotus Reader* 16
   Further research. 19

PART 1
FOUNDATIONS IN THE CONTOURS BETWEEN JOHN DUNS SCOTUS AND JOHN HENRY NEWMAN

INTRODUCTION
KEY CONCEPTS
Edward Ondrako

Intuition and Certitude: A Preparatory Position to Study Contours in the Thought of Bl. Scotus and Bl. Newman 25
   Précis. 25
   Excursus: On Intuition and Certitude. 25
   Introduction: Four objectives. 27
   Format: Ten defining elements. 28
   A concise definition of epistemology and metaphysics 28
   The panorama or landscape of our subject. 30
   Element 1. Scotus, Vatican II, and recent Popes.. 30
   Element 2. St. Francis inspires Scotus. 31

Element 3. Recognizing Scotus's Mariology. 33
Element 4. Mary as memory of the Church.. 34
Element 5. God merited our salvation vicariously.. 35
Element 6. The Franciscan thesis: what God has done. 36
Element 7. The Franciscan thesis and ontotheology. 37
Element 8. Scotus, Newman and Kantianism.. 40
Element 9. The Franciscan anthropology of Scotus.. 41
Element 10. "Mary and Theology: Scotus Revisited." 50
Summary: Scotus on the primacy of Christ and the motive of the
     Incarnation. 51
Summary: Newman and the complex process of apprehension and
     argumentation.. 52
Conclusion to the excursus: using an anthropological 'arc' to love in an
     orderly way 53

CHAPTER I

NEWMAN'S REASONABLE APPROACH TO FAITH

John T. Ford

Reasoning as Inferential Process 57

Personal Inference 59

"Three Protestants". 61

Christian Initiation as Inferential Process 64

The Illative Sense 66

The Reasonableness of Faith 67

CHAPTER 2

AN OVERVIEW OF THE SCOTISTIC SCHOOL

Edward Ondrako

Scotus's Life 71

Excursus on Pope Benedict XVI's Papal Audience July 7, 2010. 74

Scotus's Works 75
     The Franciscan Studium at Paris and Oxford. 76
     Conclusion 77

The Perdurance of the Scotist School 78

The Scotistic Tradition, Modern Secularism, and the Redemption 88

CHAPTER 3

John Duns Scotus on Intuitive Cognition, Abstractive Cognition, Scientific Knowledge, and our Knowledge of God

Timothy B. Noone

Standard Aristotelian-Scholastic Psychology .97

Scotus's Philosophical Psychology: Intuitive and Abstractive Cognition 98

Scientific Knowledge 103

Knowledge of God 105

CHAPTER 4

Mary and Theology: Scotus Revisited

Peter Damian Fehlner

Sedes Sapientiae, ora pro nobis 111

I. Magisterium Theologicum: Teaching and Learning 115

II. I Am the Immaculate Conception 136

III. Theology and Theological Method: Mary as Teacher 149
    Authoritative 150
    Metaphysical 158
    Practical. 164

Conclusion. 170

Editor's Note 173

Study Questions for Part 1 176

PART 2

Contextualizing the Theological Consistency of Newman and Scotus

INTRODUCTION

Secular Christianity and Modern Voluntarism

Précis 181

Excursus: Scotus Unites Metaphysics and Theology 181
    Metaphysics and theology lean on each other to exist 182

Three caveats when studying modern voluntarism and secular or liberal Christianity 186

The contra-distinction between Scotus and Newman from Kant on the will. 196

    Secular or liberal Christianity and first principles.. 196

    Epistemology and metaphysics assist an orderly voluntarism. 198

    Scotus's anthropology differs from naturalistic anthropology. 200

Recapitulation: The autonomous will of Kant vs. Scotus's primacy of the will. 201

    Point 1. The rationality of the will as a pure perfection. 201

    Point 2. The causes of the deformation of 'private judgment.' 201

    Point 3. Newman's thought on illumination is close to Bonaventure. 202

Conclusion to the excursus: a reply to runaway autonomy of the will. 203

CHAPTER 5

NEWMAN'S PERSONALIST ARGUMENT FOR BELIEF IN GOD

John T. Ford

Real Assent to the Existence of God 211

    Conversion as Catalyst 213

God's Existence: Notional or Real? 215

    Conscience and Conversion. 217

    Newman's Codicil on Conscience 220

    Papal Authority and Conscience. 222

    Conscience in the Twenty-First Century 224

CHAPTER 6

BL. DUNS SCOTUS AND BL. CARDINAL JOHN NEWMAN ON KNOWLEDGE, ASSENT, AND FAITH

Timothy B. Noone

Tenent philosophi perfectionem naturae. 227

Newmanesque Intimations: Scotus on Faith and Pedestrian Knowledge 230

Points for Comparison and Contrast 234

An Effort at Drawing some Comparison and Contrasts 236

CHAPTER 7

Scotus and Newman in Dialogue

Peter Damian Fehlner

Excursus: Table of Parallel Thought Patterns in Bonaventure, Scotus, and Newman 243

Prima Pars: Essential Components 244
  Newman Metaphysician and Scotus Phenomenologist 244
    The Will, the Critical Question and Faith 247
    Scotus, Newman and Onto-theology. 250
    Scotus and Newman on the Definition of Free Will: Integration of
    Discretion and Choice. 252
    Interiorizing and Anthropological Theology: Natural Faith
    in Newman. 254
    Integration of Knowledge and Love or Wisdom: scientia
    in quantum transit in affectum 264
    Franciscan Epistemology, Newman and Kant 270
    Newman Metaphysicus in via Bonaventurae et Scoti. 277
  The Metaphysical-Dogmatic Thread during the Course of Newman's
    Life 284
    Two Luminously Self-evident Beings 285
    Butler's Analogy 288
    The Person and the Church 292
    Love of Learning and Desire for God 296

Secunda Pars: Examples of Scotistic Affinities in Newman. 298
  Writings Dealing with the Motive of the Incarnation 299
  Memorandum on the Immaculate Conception 302
  The Idea of a University. 306
  Apologia pro vita sua. 333

Tertia Pars: The *Grammar of Assent* and *Oxford University Sermons* . . .337
  The *Grammar of Assent* 337
  The *Oxford University Sermons* and the *Grammar of Assent* in a Scotistic
    Framework. 373

Conclusion. 383

Concluding Remarks 385

Study Questions for Part Two 390

PART 3

THE IMPLICATIONS FOR THE CHURCH AND MODERN WORLD

INTRODUCTION

SCIENTIFIC FORM AND REAL ASSENT

Edward Ondrako

Précis 395

Excursus: Seven Themes about the Light 395

    Finding the 'light that lights.' 396

    From inference to real assent: the road to interiorization.. 397

    'Setting the table' for scientific form and wisdom. 399

    Caveats about the approaches to the history of philosophy. 401

        Caveat about Newman's style. 401

        Caveat about the weak state of Catholic philosophy. 402

        Caveat about the Syllabus of Errors. 403

        Caveat about the pairing of Thomas and the Franciscan traditions. 404

    Testing three approaches to the history of philosophy. 404

        The 'stakes' in the approach of Ockham, Hume and Kant. 407

        Keeping the meta in meta-ethics and meta-physics. 410

    Conclusion to the excursus: an outcome of the anti-metaphysical

    mindset 412

CHAPTER 8

THE BASE AND THE SUMMIT: THE NOBILITY OF THE WILL ACCORDING TO DUNS SCOTUS

Olivier Boulnois

CHAPTER 9

THE SCOTIST DOCTRINE OF THE INCARNATION AND THE ANGLICAN TRADITION: NEWMAN IN FRAME AND CONTEXT

Geoffrey Rowell

CHAPTER 10

COR AD COR LOQUITUR: RE-FASHIONING THE IMAGINATION AROUND LOVE

Mary Beth Ingham

A moral vision centered on love 448

An ethics of beauty and moral artistry 452

An ethics of right loving and right use 454

CHAPTER 11

NEWMAN, SCOTUS, AND CATHOLIC HIGHER EDUCATON: A WORTHWHILE CONVERSATION

Patricia Hutchison

Higher Education, Undergraduate Students, and the Journey
of Faith. 460

The Importance of Companions on the Journey. 462

The Notional and the Real: Service and the Power of the Personal
Encounter 463

The Incarnation and the Call to Love. 465

Contemplation and Conversion: From Awareness to Reflection to
Transformation. 465

Conscience Formation and Ethical Living 466

Newman, Scotus, and Curricular Integration 467

Catholic Studies and the Catholic Imagination 470

Sacred Spaces: The Impact of Sacred Space. 471

A Call for Further Research on Newman, Scotus, and their Influence on
Higher Education. 472

Conclusion. 473

CHAPTER 12

HOLINESS IN JOHN HENRY NEWMAN'S THEORY OF DOCTRINAL DEVELOPMENT: THE HARMONY OF THE INTELLECT AND AFFECTIVE SPIRIT

Robert C. Christie

CHAPTER 13

THE STORY OF A MIRACLE

Deacon Jack Sullivan

My Early Life and Carol. 483

Obstacles and Challenges. 484

The Mystery of Redemptive Suffering. 486

The Miracle 489

Reflection after the Beatification. 490

What I Think this May Mean for the Church and the Modern World 491

CHAPTER 14

RETRIEVING OF SCOTUS AND NEWMAN BY IMITATING GERARD
MANLEY HOPKINS
Edward Ondrako

Metaphysics and experience are not mutually exclusive. 497

From Scotus's metaphysics to the metaphysical English in Hopkins's
poetry. 509

Recapitulation 514

Conclusion. 517

Supplemental Materials 519
   Franciscan Metaphysics 519
   Instress and inscape 520
   Views of four critics. 521

CHAPTER 15

UNCOUPLING SCOTUS AND KANT WITH THE HELP OF NEWMAN
Edward Ondrako

Précis 525

Introduction. 525
   General Points of Comparison. 528
     Necessity and contingency in Scotus vs. duty in Kant 528
     Aristotle, Scotus and Kant on the will. 530
     The foundations of Scotus's priority of the will and Kant's sense of duty
     530
     Metaphysics in Scotus vs. the mathematical physics of Kant 531
     The will as a pure perfection and the univocity of the concept of being
     vs. Kant's noumena 532
     Freedom and the univocity of the concept of being 533
     Scotus on revealed, natural and physical theology vs. Kant's anti-
     metaphysical take 534
     Scotus is Newman's role model rather than Kant 535
     Firm assent in faith vs. the gap between the mental and extra-mental

. . . . 536
Scotus and the epistemological-theological vs. Kant and the
epistemological-scientific 537
Special Points of Comparison 538
The seductive appeal of the Kantian form of modern idealism vs. Scotus's
equilibrium 538
The Church at Vatican II and attempts to 'Christianize' Kant 540
The disjunctive transcendentals in Scotus and the phenomenal-
noumenal in Kant 542
The nature of theology for Scotus differs from reason and Revelation
in Kant 545
The primacy of charity for Scotus and the categorical imperative
for Kant. 547
The anthropology of Scotus, ethics, and hermeneutical turn for Kant.
. . . . 548
The absolute primacy of Christ in Scotus and Kant's Savior figure. . 551
The "meta-pedagogical ground" in Scotus and Kant's autonomous self
. . . . 553
Scotus, the intellectually mature person and holiness for the
21st century 555
Uncoupling Scotus and Kant and the new structure of metaphysics. 556
Recapitulation: personal convictions about de-linking Scotus
and Kant 559

Conclusion. 561
Appendix A: The Disjunctive Transcendentals of Being 564

CHAPTER 16

BEING AND BECOMING: HEGEL'S INVERSION AND NEWMAN'S CONSISTENCY WITH SCOTUS

Edward Ondrako

Précis. 567

Prefatory Note 567

Part I: The Problem of Being and Becoming 570
Introduction 570
Romanticism and modernity as a crisis. 571
Hegel and Kant vs. the theory of the person and the will in Scotus . 574
Patripassion connections: an attempt to reduce the gap between human
and divine 577
Scotus's formalitas, Butler's Analogy, Hegel's Lectures, Newman's

Grammar of Assent 580

Part II: The theological center is the charity that is God 583

   Introduction 583

     Scotus's primacy, creation, and salvation vs. the non-being and becoming
     of Hegel. 584
     Scotus's providence and predestination in Christ vs. Hegel's theory of
     history as mediated logic 586
     Scotus's sharing in the glory of the Blessed Trinity vs. the modern
     idealism of Hegel 589
     Disputed Question:. 592

   Recapitulation. 597

Conclusion. 606

CHAPTER 17

SCOTUS THE NEFARIOUS: UNCOVERING GENEALOGICAL SOPHISTICATIONS

Cyril O'Regan

Standard Misprisonings of Scotus and Scotism. 615

Balthasar and the Metaphysical Guilt of Scotus 628

Conclusion. 634

Study Questions for Part Three. 636

CONCLUSION

Outer circle: General Contributions. 642

Inner Circle: Specific Contributions. 643

   Part One 643
   Part Two 645
   Part Three 646

Grace, Freedom and Bridge Building 652

Watching for the Shoals of an Evolutionary or pantheistic Unitarianism
. 653

Afterword: John Jukes, Bishop of Strathearn. 657

Contributors 659

Bibliography. 661

Index 687

For private consultation and not distribution without the consent of E Ondrako

Foreword

Friar Marco Tasca, OFMConv.

Prot. N. 345/10   Rome, October 14, 2010

Dear Participants in the Newman-Scotus Symposium,

I greet you with great joy as you meet at Washington Theological Union this weekend to launch a carefully prepared academic study of the contours in the thought of the newly beatified Bl. John Henry Newman and the theologian disciple of St. Francis of Assisi, Bl. John Duns Scotus. Both scholars labored in England and, as I understand it, until now, little research has been done to not only suggest but to prove several significant similarities in their thought which is your goal. This past spring, when I was first alerted that this Symposium was to take place on October 22-24, my immediate reaction was to encourage the conveners and to pray for its success.

One of my most ardent passions is to look for ways to creatively put into practice the authentic spirit of the Second Vatican Council, to show the continuity in tradition even as we read the signs of the times with openness to the promptings of the Holy Spirit. Bl. Newman and Bl. Scotus anticipated the questions raised at the Council. It is up to the presenters and participants to demonstrate convincingly how they did so and the perennial wisdom in their replies. May your labors extend not only for the time of the Symposium but afterword with sound follow up in the formation of many loyal devotees to the thought of Bl. Newman and Bl. Scotus. May you ignite a fire to demonstrate convincingly how their ideas speak to our secularized world about the primacy of the Christ and the primacy of love.

In his beatification homily, the Holy Father recognized Bl. Newman in the long line of saints and scholars who graced the islands making up the United Kingdom today. He mentioned Bl. Scotus specifically. May the day come soon when you can bring your conclusions to our scholarly Holy Father who has spoken about Bl. Scotus several times during his

For private consultation and not distribution without the consent of E Ondrako

pontificate. In fact, his addresses this past March reminded our brother Dominicans and us Franciscans not to forget in the midst of many ministerial responsibilities that there is an intellectual component to our vocations from the time of our founders. May we, clerics, professed, and laity, respond to his clarion call under the protection of the Mother of God, the Mother of beautiful love.

Affectionately,

Friar Marco Tasca, OFMConv.
Minister General

Acknowledgments

Most Reverend Marco Tasca, OFMConventual, Minister General of the Conventual Franciscans, gave his blessing and encouragment to the inaugural Newman-Scotus Symposium, October 22-24, 2010 at Washington Theological Union, as a creative response to the forward looking spirit of Vatican II.

The Very Reverend James McCurry, OFMConventual, Minister Provincial of the Province of Our Lady of Angels in the USA, with its Custody in England and Ireland, intuited the need for the Newman-Scotus Symposium to retrieve the thought of Bl. John Duns Scotus (1265-1308), in line with the beatification of Bl. John Henry Newman, September 19, 2010. His encouragement for more interest and study along the lines of The Newman-Scotus Reader is constant.

In gratitude to the esteemed contributors to Newman-Scotus Symposium and its development into The Newman-Scotus Reader who have undaunting confidence that they are planting seeds for a new century in which scholarship has changed the textual landscape.

In gratitude to Friar John, F.I., manager, and Mary Flannery, designer, of the Academy of the Immaculate for their expertise in producing this volume.

In gratitude to the University of Notre Dame, Shari Hill Sweet of the Graduate Office, and Tanya Pokrym, Electronic Resources librarian, whose skills also contributed to this volume.

The technological skills of Friar Martin Breski, OFMConv., and Friar Roderick Burke, FI, made the proceedings of the Newman-Scotus Symposium available on youtube.com. The marketing was in the capable hands of Nicole R. Hanley. Sr. Kathy Kandefer and staff of Washington Theological Union managed the Conference logistics. The Franciscan Friars Conventual students provided liturgical accompaniment.

In gratitude for the constant loving support of my sister and brother in law, Frances and Ronald Simkulet.

In memory of the faithful example of my loving parents.

In memory of Sr. Theresa Higgins, friend and devotee of Bl. Newman, from Mr. and Mrs. Al Kaneb.

In memory of Bishop John Jukes, OFMConv., Bishop of Strathearn.

In gratitude for the gift of faith and blessings upon their family, from Mr and Mrs. Walter Poland.

In recognition of the philosophical scholarship of their brother, Dr. John Boler, Fr. Martin Boler, OSB, of Pine City, N.Y. and his sister, Maureen Boler, were happy to hear that their brother, Dr. John Boler, a medieval philosopher, who died September 9, 2009, received recognition for his quiet work on the thought of Bl. Scotus.

For private consultation and not distribution without the consent of E Ondrako

List of Abbreviations

Primary Sources

Augustine

Aug	*Works of St. Augustine.* Edited by John E. Rotelle, OSA. Hyde Park, N.Y.: New City Press, 1991-.

Anselm of Canterbury

AC	*Anselm of Canterbury: The Major Works.* Edited by Brian Davies and G. R. Evans. Oxford and New York: Oxford University Press, 1998.

Aquinas, Thomas

ST	*Summa theologiae*

Bonaventure

Brev	*Breviloquium*
CUOM	*Christus Unus Omnium Magister*
Hex.	*Collationes in Hexaemeron, Sermons on the Six Days of Creation*
Itin	*Itinerarium mentis in Deum*

Duns Scotus, John

DPP	*De primo rerum principio*
Lect.	*Lectura*
Op Ox	*Opus Oxoniense*
Ord	*Ordinatio*
Quod	*Quodlibitum*
Rep Par	*Reportata Parisiensia*
Vatican	*Opera Omnia Scoti*, ed. C. Balič and others
Vivès	*Opera Omnia Scoti*, ed. Vives

Lombard, Peter

Sent	*Sententiae in quatour libros distinctae*

For private consultation and not distribution without the consent of E Ondrako

Migne *PG*   *Patrologia cursus completus. Series graeca.*
Edited by J.P. Migne. Paris, 1857–66. 161 volumes.

PL   *Patrologia cursus completus. Series latina.* Edited
by J.P.Migne. Paris. 1844–64. 221 volumes.

Versions, Translations, and Series

Être   Olivier Boulnois, *Être et représentation*

Dialogue   Peter Damian Fehlner, *Scotus and Newman in Dialogue*

Durham   *Acts of the Symposium on Scotus' Mariology*, Durham,
             England, 2008

MFC   *Mary at the Foot of the Cross* in nine vols. 2001-2010

Newman   John Henry Newman

Apologia   *Apologia pro vita sua*, 1864

Athanasius   *Selections*, 1840

Biglietto   *Speech* on becoming a Cardinal in May, 1879

Consulting   *On Consulting the Faithful in Matters of Doctrine*, 1859

Essay   *Essay on the Development of Doctrine*, 1845

Grammar   *Grammar of Assent*, 1869–1870

Idea   *The Idea of a University*, 1852

LD   *Letter and Diaries* in 32 vols.

Justific   *Lectures on Justification*, 1836

Memo   *Memorandum on the Immaculate Conception*, 1849

Norfolk   *Letter to the Duke of Norfolk*, 1874

OUS   *Oxford University Sermons*

PPS   *Parochial and Plain Sermons* in 8 vols.

Scotus

Wolter   ed. Wolter, Allan Bernard, *A Treatise on God as First
             Principle*, 1982; *The Transcendentals and Their Function
             in the Metaphysics of Duns Scotus*, rpt. 2008.

For private consultation and not distribution without the consent of E Ondrako

General Introduction

L'intuition est un flamboiement de certitude qui déchire la nuit des sens.[1]
Intuition is a blaze of certitude which tears the night of the senses. This is a
fitting template for the subtle view of Bl. John Duns Scotus (1265–1308)
on intuition and certitude. It is one of the most substantive points that link
him to the world of theology of Bl. John Henry Newman (1801–1890).
The premise is that there is a coherent whole between the primary object
of theology, the Trinity, and secondary object of theology, the economy of
salvation. This Trinitarian perspective is at work in the contributions to
this innovative *Newman-Scotus Reader*. The scholarly analyses that follow
are cognizant that there is no real abyss between the intra and extra mental.
If there is an abyss, its cause is how one uses one's freedom, and one's will,
whether co-operating with grace or not, that may create an abyss. It is with
such a perspective that Newman recognizes freedom as foremost for every
mind, the freedom to be holy, and the consequent perfection of freedom.
It is a choice every person makes from the shadows and images of the
natural order, and is fully realized in the ability to assent in faith which is
aided by divine grace.

This original and comprehensive reader reflects a new discovery, the
indications that, although living in two different cultural ambients, there
is something more than mere chance between the thought of two Oxford
luminaries, one who inspired the other. The contributors are convinced
that this new discovery has enormous purchase in an age of autonomy, in
the light of advances in human knowledge, and an age when it is common
to refer to the 'crisis of faith' in the Church. On being named a Cardinal,
Newman gave a *Biglietto Address* where he poured from his heart a lifetime
of reflection on the *analogical*[2] meaning of 'crisis,' the consequences of the
repudiation of the dogmatic principle he held dearly, and the manipulation
of a pragmatic mindset to take the place of virtue, an ethics without faith.
Newman saw the cynicism and rapidly depleting authority of Christianity
in modernity. The invitation to believe in the divinity of Christ and His
redemptive sacrifice, and to the obedience of faith, is in the context of the
secularization of Western Christendom and its appeal to practicality and
utilitarianism. Newman got to the heart of the matter. He intuited that
it is rarely thought about that all development of human knowledge is a
reflection of the eternal generation of the Word by the Father.

---

[1] OLIVIER BOULNOIS, *Être et représentation* (Paris : Presses Universitaires de France, 2008), 134.
[2] Newman was an expert in using analogy. To describe crisis analogically is not to describe it
univocally. Scotus uses analogy as Newman does.

1

For private consultation and not distribution without the consent of E Ondrako

This trenchant insight identifies the Trinitarian perspective as the significant link between the two Oxford theologians and why Scotus and Newman came to understand that the human idea first formed is called a concept and is related to divine begetting. Moreover, once Newman learned about the Virgin Mary from Hurrell Froude, it was a small step for him to make the connection that the one who was so loved by the Trinity should also have loved us. Scotus inherited the love of the *Theotokos* from St. Francis of Assisi who calls her Spouse of the Holy Spirit. Scotus reasoned that in making God's will her cause, she has made our cause her cause. God loved the world most perfectly and commanded his Son to be born of the woman to save us in the most perfect way possible in any possible world however perfect. He reasoned: Mary is "the perfect fruit of a perfect redemption by a most perfect Redeemer."[3]

Au contraire, Hegel reflects the secularized mind and captures the imagination in his modification of the Trinitarian landscape. It is noteworthy, however, that Hegel does not capture the intellect as Scotus and Newman have done. Kant, on the other hand, by changing the pre-given borders of reason, neutralizes religion in a manner that has contemporary endurance and contributes to the crisis of faith viewed *analogically*. His focus is on the individual, but not the individuation of Scotus and Newman in the context of the community of believers. On this critical point, Kant's sense of community, continuity between past, present and future, and above all certitude is left wanting.

Is Scotus a *Progenitor* of Newman?

The definition of a *projenitor* is a person or thing that first indicates a direction, originates something, or serves as a model; predecessor, precursor; such as the projenitor of modern painting. A precursor is a person who precedes, as in a job, a method, etc.; predecessor. A *precursor* is a person that goes before and indicates the approach of someone or something else; harbinger; forerunner.[4] There are several nuances to person, direction, and method that have a bearing on our thesis. Bishop Joseph Butler (1692–1752), preceded Newman at Oriel College. His *Analogy of Religion, Natural and Revealed, to the Constitution and Course of Nature* (1736), was a defense of revealed religion, which Newman first read in 1823. This gave him a method, an approach that is visible in his works for the rest of his

---

3 SCOTUS, III *Sent.*, d. 3, q.1. In a similar vein, Thomas Aquinas refers to three quasi-infinites, the Incarnation, divine maternity, and salvation. ST I, q. 25, a. 4.

4 Websters Encyclopedic Unabridged Dictionary of the English Language, 1996.

For private consultation and not distribution without the consent of E Ondrako

life. Behind Butler there are some aspects of the great scotistic tradition in England that continued during the Reformation. By 1836 one finds a presence of scotistic thought in Newman's *Lectures on Justification* in the reference in the Appendix to the Conventual Cornelius Musso, Bishop of Bitonto, who was present at the Council of Trent. By 1840, explicit references to the absolute primacy are in Newman's *Select Treatises of Athanasius* and *The Arians of the Fourth Century*. On December 9, 1849, Newman wrote to Faber: "Certainly, I wish to take the Scotist view on that point [the motive of the Incarnation]. As I understand the Scotist view it simply is that He would have become incarnate, even had man not sinned—but when man sinned it was for our redemption; in matter of fact, the end was to make satisfaction."[5]

If one looks for a person that first indicates a direction to the absolute primacy of Christ, and the absolute primacy of the will, it is the thought of Scotus and the statements of recent Pontiffs that have affirmed this. There is clearly a larval presence of that thinking in Newman as early as 1836 thanks to the careful research of Fehlner. Newman used the principle of antecedent probability with extraordinary respect, for he thought it was the way one could teach truth to anyone who desired to know it and to embrace it. I am convinced that there is an antecedent probability that Newman refers to Scotus in *The Idea of a University*[6] because he gradually discovered Scotus as a role model for his approach to life and once he found the sure guidance of Scotus's method, he never parted from it.

Newman began Discourse VII of the *Idea* with a reference to the previous two discourses, i.e., that the cultivation of the intellect as an end may reasonably be pursued for its own sake and the nature of that cultivation. It is truth! His memorable quote is: "Truth of whatever kind is the proper object of the intellect; its cultivation then lies in fitting it to apprehend and contemplate truth."[7] Newman goes on to explain what he means by the process of training, and the real worth of a liberal education is practical and not merely utilitarian. It is in this context that he mentions Scotus.[8] Newman then turns his sights on Locke's utilitarianism through

---

[5] JOHN HENRY NEWMAN, *Letters and Diaries* (Oxford: Oxford University Press, uniform edition), 13, 335, 342. See FEHLNER, "Scotus and Newman in Dialogue," ch. 7 in this volume.

[6] The full title of Newman's work was edited, with an introduction, and notes by MARTIN J. SVAGLIC, *The Idea of a University Defined and Illustrated in Nine Discourses Delivered to the Catholics of Dublin in Occasional Lectures and Essays Addressed to the Members of the Catholic University* (1960). By this lengthy title, Svaglic preserves the metaphysical focus on the essence of a university. The epistemological counterpart is the *Grammar of Assent*.

[7] SVAGLIC, *Idea of a University*, Discourse VII, 114.

[8] SVAGLIC, *Idea of a University*, Discourse VII, 117. Newman mentions Occam [sic] as "something of a disciple of Scotus." In his notes as editor, Svaglic says that "it is not altogether clear why Newman mentions him in this particular context apart from the fact that he studied and

For private consultation and not distribution without the consent of E Ondrako

the end of the Discourse VII. He challenges what he calls the fallacy of Locke and his disciples. In a manner that underscores the approach of Bonaventure on making a judgment, the *dijudicatio*, and anticipates his own 'illative sense,' Newman is implicitly following the approach to making a judgment that is fully in accord with the approach of Scotus.[9] Newman concludes "that training of the intellect, which is best for the individual himself, best enables him to discharge his duties in society."

> University training is the great ordinary means to a great but ordinary end; it aims at raising the intellectual tone of society, at cultivating the public mind…. It is education which gives a man a clear conscious view of his own opinions and judgments, a truth in developing them, an eloquence in expressing them, and a force in urging them.[10]

Newman opens his address: "A Form of Infidelity of the Day" (1858), with his concern for the "subtle, silent, unconscious perversion and corruption of Catholic intellects." He contrasts the problems of the medieval age with the present, when "universal toleration prevails, and it is open to assail revealed truth (whether Scripture or Tradition, the Fathers or the Sense of the Faithful)." He adds another quotable: "I prefer to live in an age when the fight is in the day, not in the twilight; and think it again to be speared by a foe, rather than to be stabbed by a friend."[11]

This context in which Newman refers to Scotus is crystal clear. He refers to "a seat of learning that had been home to Scotus and Alexander of Hales." Then he asks the pivotal question: "What envious mischance put an end to those halcyon days, and revived the *odium theologicum* in the years that followed?"[12] Halcyon means calm, peaceful, tranquil, as halcyon weather. It means rich, wealthy, prosperous, as halcyon times of peace. It means happy, joyful, and carefree, as halcyon days of youth.[13] The *odium theologicum* is the hatred of theology. Newman is masterful in addressing

---

taught at Oxford," 413–414. My interpretation is that in 1852 when these discourses were being written, Newman was just getting his feet on solid ground in regard to Scotus. There is a perception that since Ockham is a Franciscan, he is to be considered simply as a disciple of Scotus. It is no surprise that Newman may have thought this. Svaglic seems to be saying the same. Boulnois gives the same impression in *Être et représentation*. POPE BENEDICT XVI's Regensburg Address, September 12, 2006, prior to his later writings on Scotus, implies the same view. Our answer is that Ockham is an innovator in regard to Scotus. See E. ONDRAKO, Introduction to part 2, 204; Introduction to part 3, 408; Study Questions, no. 2, 637.

9   SVAGLIC, *Idea of a University*, Discourse VII, 132.

10 SVAGLIC, *Idea of a University*, Discourse VII, 134–135.

11 SVAGLIC, *Idea of a University*, "A Form of Infidelity of the Day," 286.

12 SVAGLIC, *Idea of a University*, "Infidelity of the Day," 297.

13 Webster's Encyclopedic Unabridged Dictionary.

For private consultation and not distribution without the consent of E Ondrako

the contest with faith in his time. Physical Science has a better temper, he says, if not a keener edge, for this purpose than the medieval philosopher who had no weapon against Revelation, but metaphysics. His solution is to recognize the reality of the mischief that has been done and the wisest course for the interests of infidelity is to leave it to itself, to let the fever gradually subside, for treatment would irritate it.[14]

In the twenty-first century, these problems seem to have a greater purchase. Newman's wise insight is: "Not to interfere with Theology, not to raise a little finger against it, is the only means of superseding it. The more bitter is the hatred which such men bear it, the less they must show it. Such is the tactic which a new school of philosophers adopt against Christian Theology. They have this characteristic, compared with former schools of infidelity, viz., the union of intense hatred with a large toleration of Theology."[15]

In 1858, in "Discipline of Mind: an Address to the Evening Classes," Newman refers to John Scotus Erigena at Paris and Duns Scotus at Oxford.[16] The context is to argue that the seat of a great intellectual progress is from Ireland in contrast with skepticism and insubordination in religion even in Catholic countries in Europe. His point was to show the importance of study and speculation in contrast to any other motive, and to combine it with Catholic devotion.[17] Newman addresses the importance of keeping a harmony between a life of study and entering into the heart.

This is the context for Newman to recognize Scotus as one, if not the greatest theological luminary that Oxford ever knew. There is a convergence of probabilities that the series of resemblances between Scotus and Newman, being meticulously developed in these essays, show common convictions in Scotus and Newman about the nature of theology and how to conduct it. The critical question is *interiorization*, or entering the heart, and that is where evidence abounds that there are striking similarities in their thought patterns. For example, Newman explicitly agrees with Scotus's absolute primacy of Christ (and with it the Immaculate Conception), the sacramentality of creation, and the primacy of charity. It is the basis for similarities in their epistemology. The idea of progenitor finds support in Newman's preferred method of combining antecedent probability, evidence and the convergence of probabilities in searching for truth. Newman was extremely attentive to the argument from antecedent prob-

---

14 SVAGLIC, *Idea of a University*, "Infidelity of the Day," 297–298.

15 SVAGLIC, *Idea of a University*, "Infidelity," 297–303.

16 SVAGLIC, *Idea of a University*, "Discipline of Mind," 366. There was still a popular idea that Scotus was Irish.

17 SVAGLIC, *Idea of a University*, "Discipline of Mind," 364–365.

For private consultation and not distribution without the consent of E Ondrako

ability as his starting point. From this vantage point, one can juxtapose the univocity of the concept of being, the disjunctive transcendentals, and the formal distinction *a parte rei*, which makes up the core of Scotus's method.

In sum, these are some of the reasons for placing Newman and his approach in line with the approach of Bonaventure and Scotus. After reading *The Newman-Scotus Reader*, the judgment about progenitor will be up to the discerning reader. Today Newman's method together with Scotus's method have promise in dealing with Pope Benedict's question about liberty in relation to the intellect and will which is rooted in the conviction that metaphysical necessity and freedom are not opposed. The definition of will, freedom and necessity or independent being in the Franciscan school is the heart of the debate and clarity seems as urgent today in the wave of Kantian voluntarism and Hegelian psychologism as it was in the beginning of the fourteenth century. What do we do with the freedom of the human will? What do we do with the freedom of the human will under grace? What is God's part in the salutary act of the human person acting under efficacious grace? To answer with Thomists that the human person must will what God already wills necessarily and so is deprived of freedom is a failure to see that metaphysical necessity and freedom are not opposed. To answer with the Franciscan school is to recognize that the human will should be elevated by grace to the point where the human person by way of *condetermination* necessarily wills the absolute good which does not deprive man of freedom, but perfects it.

From condetermination to certitude

In the *Grammar of Assent*, Newman wrote: "Certitude does not admit of an interior, immediate test, sufficient to discriminate it from false certitude."[18] If "certitude is indefectible, will not that indefectibility itself become at least in the event a criterion of the genuineness of the certitude?"[19] Newman was worried because certitude is not an assent of the first order and is more reflexive, while assent as given to a judgment as true, is given on rational grounds, with a sense of finality, and with permanence. Certitude is somewhat more of a second order affair, but follows investigation and proof, invokes a sense of intellectual satisfaction, and is irreversible.[20] The question about certitude for Scotus is linked to

---

[18] JOHN HENRY NEWMAN, *Grammar of Assent* (London: uniform edition), 255. Henceforth, NEWMAN, *Grammar*.

[19] NEWMAN, *Grammar*, 255.

[20] NEWMAN, *Grammar*, 258.

For private consultation and not distribution without the consent of E Ondrako

the light guiding all of our thought, a unique formulation to keep logic linked to reality, which is the univocity of the concept of being. Intuition and abstraction work together for Scotus as real and notional apprehension and assent for Newman to reach the blaze of certitude. This is an important coupling which leads to the proposition that Newman puts Scotus into modern English.

Newman is anxious about certitude in matters of religion because of the post Lockian ethos prevalent in British culture and even more the problem of how to protect oneself against skepticism in a post Hume world. The Lockian turn is against metaphysics in favor of individuality which tends to reduce objective truth to little or nothing of much value, because Locke judges the relative firmness of strong or weak logic in relation to an inference and to its premises. An inference lacks permanence and that is the problem for Newman and Scotus who are very mindful of the reflexivity involved in the quest for certitude. In his writings, Newman explains why he thinks there is a difference between ordinary knowledge that centers about an assent and salutary or saving knowledge to accept Christ as Savior that one accepts on the authority of God as it is properly exercised by God's ministers. The latter is impossible without the gift of the Spirit. The first is assent or natural faith, an act of the will that is supported by evidence, but not dependent on it. The second is different. It is complex assent usually made conscious of a previously made assent. It is infused faith, a leap from assent based on evidence to assent without that support. An assent (natural faith) to the real is what accounts for the real difference between assent and inference or reasoning. It is in this context, the dynamic of moving from simple to complex assent where the process is not automatic and a person may lose or weaken one's faith. However, it is here in this profound phenomenological activity that Newman is very ascetic and clear: "philosophical discoveries cannot really contradict divine revelation."[21] In a related way for the psychology of Scotus, the image of a still pond posits that there is an entrance and exit, even the quietest trickle. The entrance is where the unconscious begins to influence the conscious mind, while the exit is where the soul remains unsatisfied after exercising all of its intellectual powers. It is following upon investigation, the lack of repose and intellectual satisfaction in the mind that evokes a critical point from Augustine.[22] There is a need to return to the hierarchy of memory, understanding and will that form the ambiance for contemplation.

---

[21] NEWMAN, *Grammar*, 258.

[22] CHRISTOPHER DEVLIN, *The Psychology of Scotus* (Oxford: 1950), 3–4. This is a very rare pamphlet that I discovered by accident in the Cambridge University Library.

For private consultation and not distribution without the consent of E Ondrako

Newman delivered nine discourses which explain his theory of education, *The Idea of a University* between 1852 and 1854. He refers to Scotus (1265–1308) as one of the distinguished persons under whose shadow he once lived, and laments the loss of those halcyon days, and identifies him as one of the boldest and most subtle of disputants.[23] With the long list of theological luminaries in the history of Oxford and their contributions to the civility and nobility of humanity, why might Newman have thought so highly about Scotus? Did Newman read and know Scotus all that well and what did he actually say? How strong a background did Newman have in the thought of other scholastic metaphysician-theologians such as Thomas Aquinas whose analysis of faith was not the evidentialism or evangelicalism of his 19th century contemporaries? These questions have a bearing on inculturation or how individuals learn the ideas, behavior, and internalize the values of their culture. Scotus's concern with analogical reasoning in life is in relation to religious values and how to demonstrate the reasonableness of Christianity as a true religion, its practical and not its theoretical dimension, its emphasis on the practical wisdom of Aristotle, *phronesis*. Scotus's concern is the deeper level of the meaning of the person and one's relation with the incommunicability of the Trinity. He anticipates Newman's concern of how analogical reasoning leads one to the knowledge of religious truth, but his is not a zero sum game. Newman's claim to Christian truth as absolute truth is by way of Butler's *Analogy*, a work that opened many ideas for Newman's approach to fit into the form of 19th century British philosophy. Late in life Newman lamented that he did not have the training in scholastic metaphysics, but his thinking resonates with the profundity of the metaphysics of Thomas and Scotus, which gives the foundation for building our argument that Scotus may be a progenitor of Newman.

Although Newman understood what he called notional apprehension and assent, the mind's gift of abstraction, he has to be read on his own terms and in light of his own methodology. Newman has an empirical point of departure and makes the claim that propositions correspond to doubts, inferences, and assents, which is an approach intended to be personal and apologetical, not abstract and theoretical. In other words, Newman recognizes that a proposition may be notional for one person and real for another. Newman's life is a profoundly personalist quest for truth. In that quest he exemplifies the drive to find both implicitly and explicitly a role model that touched every fiber of his being. He looked for a systematic consistent theologian to inspire his own desire to be consis-

---

[23] JOHN HENRY NEWMAN, *The Idea of a University*, ed. Martin J. Svaglic (Notre Dame: University of Notre Dame Press, 1982), 117, 297, 366, and fn. 117.7, 413–414. *396*

For private consultation and not distribution without the consent of E Ondrako

tent. He was not afraid to change his mind in conformity with principles of Aristotelian science at the highest level. For example, following upon his Oxford University Sermons, especially sermon fifteen with its Mary-Eve typology, he discovered something that he longed for, something basic to the whole of theology, that is, seven creative notes on the development of doctrine. The Mary-Eve typology is linked to his first note, the preservation of type. Typological thinking led him to change his mind from the preservation of an idea to the preservation of type. For Newman, to alter the type is to destroy it. Yes, to live is to change, and to be perfect is to have changed often. It may seem like a contradiction, and why his thinking is not a contradiction in the midst of the changes in his life, and changes called for by living in a changing world, will unfold in the works in this volume.

Newman joins the chorus of those who anticipate contemporary sensitivities of inculturation with full awareness of the need to proceed along lines of formal equivalency and not dynamic equivalents, which is a chorus sung from the time of the Fathers of the Church and by those faithful to interpreting the Fathers without overtones of ideology incompatible with the Catholic faith and dogma. Reading Clement of Alexandria, for example, kept Newman from ultra-rationalism and naturalism. Since Scotus is influenced by the Alexandrian school, this opens a relationship with Newman that is more than a kindred spirit. The Alexandrian view can apply synchronically and diachronically. Newman understands that theological conclusions are often made by antecedent reasoning, but theological reasoning claims to be sustained by more than human power, and it is that more than human power that brings him into the closest proximity with Scotus. Newman concludes: "When a number of antecedent probabilities confirm each other, it may make it a duty for a prudent person to not only act as if the statement were true, but to accept and to believe it."[24]

There are three parts to *The Newman-Scotus Reader*.

Part One. Foundations in the Contours

The *Newman-Scotus Reader* has three parts: "Foundations in the Contours between John Duns Scotus and John Henry Newman; Contextualizing the Theological Consistency of Newman and Scotus; and, The Implications for the Church and Modern World." Our book opens with the inspiring, confident and forward looking words of the Most Reverend Marco Tasca, Minister General of the Conventual Franciscans. He invites

---

[24] NEWMAN, *Grammar*, 383.

For private consultation and not distribution without the consent of E Ondrako

the reader to continue the new venture and discoveries of the Newman-Scotus Symposium.[25] He exhorts scholars to labor with intensity and intellectual rigor in order to reply to Pope Benedict XVI's profound and perplexing modern question about freedom in relation to the will and intellect.[26] After an introductory excursus by the editor of some key concepts and defining elements that will be developed in the chapters ahead, John Ford, historical theologian at the Catholic University of America, sets the critical tone with "Newman's Reasonable Approach to Faith." In an especially touching manner, he unfolds the completely diverse journeys of the three Newman brothers in their faith pursuits. He is uncanny in his ability to convince the reader how the practical and theoretical are at work in a person. Ford gently unfolds the historical context of Britain in the 19th century that is not the Britain that welcomed the first Franciscans in 1224, or the Oxford of Scotus as described by Gerard Manley Hopkins: "that fired France for Mary without spot."[27] Ford uses what is familiar to Catholics, the Rite of Christian initiation of Adults, as a contemporary example of applying Newman's reasoning as an inferential process. He makes it easy to understand the meaning of personal inference and Newman's creative explanation of the illative sense in making judgments.

A short but inclusive overview of the Scotistic School from the time of his death in 1308 to the present demonstrates the formation of Scotus, the work of his immediate followers, the perdurance of the Scotistic School, and the application of his thought to the principal question of redemption. An account of the critical contribution of the English friars to scotistic thought is particularly important because it enables the historian to follow the pre-Reformation thought of Scotus which finds its way into the eighteenth century work of Butler and later, Newman. The works of the Italian Conventuals of the 17th century were important, in a similar way as Butler, for a comprehensive summary of Scotus's philosophical and theological thought. Of note, B. Mastrius coined the term *condetermination* to describe the workings of freely bestowed efficacious grace and how an individual exercises freedom. It differs from the Thomists after Banez and the Molinists, and this difference is decisive. Condetermination in fidelity

---

25 The Newman-Scotus Symposium was inaugurated on Oct 22–24, 2010, at Washington Theological Union, Washington, D.C. The proceedings were requested and several additional scholars found the premises convincing and offered to contribute which made *The Newman-Scotus Reader* possible. At the request of the participants and sponsors, plans are under way for the next Newman-Scotus Symposium, which will be at various educational settings.

26 POPE BENEDICT XVI, Papal Audience on the Thought of Bl. John Duns Scotus, July 7, 2010. Henceforth, Benedict XVI, Scotus Audience.

27 From the sonnet, "Duns Scotus Oxford," by Gerard Manley Hopkins, a reference to the poet's recognition of Scotus's role in contributing to the development of the doctrine of the Immaculate Conception.

For private consultation and not distribution without the consent of E Ondrako

to Scotus's thought has at the opposite pole from Pelagian naturalism and Kantian autonomism, which are very significant themes for modernity and post-modernity to be developed in our *Scotus- Newman Reader.*

Accounts of contemporary Scotism are more readily available, especially the five congresses held in 2008,[28] which have a storehouse of information for the researcher. However, in preparation for reading them, familiarity with older works such as the collection by Juniper Carol and George Marcil are helpful for a broad historical perspective. More recently, Thomas Williams offers an excellent introduction to the study of Scotus. Three volumes edited by Mary Beth Ingham and Oleg Bychkov offer the proceedings of four of the congresses in 2008. One volume from the Friars of the Immaculate gives the Acts of the Symposium on Scotus's Mariology, held at Durham, England,[29] which was the fifth congress and first to be published. These selected works are a modicum of the wealth of data now easily accessible for serious study. In addition, there is a *Bibliography* for future research at the end of our book. The intention of *The Newman-Scotus Reader* is to provide more than an introduction for the scholar. It has a readable road map, ample resources, and contains the formula of joy in discovering the practical wisdom in Scotus and Newman. Theirs is a wisdom that has been either forgotten because of historical challenges to its continuity, or misunderstood by superficial analyses, or impaired by bigotry, because both thinkers require extra effort to read well, and that is our primary concern, to make it easier.

The first conference of Timothy Noone, Professor at the Catholic University of America: "Scotus, Intuitive and Abstractive Cognition," develops "Scotus's Philosophical Psychology, Scientific Knowledge, and Knowledge of God." Peter Damian Fehlner, emeritus professor from several Franciscan seminaries, writes in fidelity to the Marian metaphysics of Scotus and sets the stage with "Mary and Theology: Scotus Revisited" and develops the themes of the Nature of Theology, Learning and Teaching,

---

[28] The first Congress was at St. Bonaventure, N.Y., October 2007; second at Oriel College, Oxford, July 2008; third at Thomas Institute, Cologne, November 2008; and fourth at the University of Strasbourg, France. The fifth Congress was originally planned to follow the Oriel Congress but was held at Durham, England, from 9–11 September 2008.

[29] JUNIPER B. CAROL, *Why Jesus Christ? Thomistic, Scotistic and Conciliatory Perspectives* (Manasses, VA, 1986); GEORGE MARCIL, "The Franciscan School through the Centuries," ed. Kenan B. Osborne, *The History of Franciscan Theology* (St. Bonaventure, N.Y.: The Franciscan Institute, 1994), 311–330; ed. THOMAS WILLIAMS, *The Cambridge Companion to Duns Scotus* (Cambridge; Cambridge University Press, 2003); MARY BETH INGHAM and OLEG BYCHKOV, eds., *Archa Verbi: Proceedings of The Quadruple Congress on John Duns Scotus* (St. Bonaventure, N.Y.: The Franciscan Institute, 2010), 3 volumes; and the fifth congress in 2008, eds. FRANCISCANS OF THE IMMACULATE, *Bl. John Duns Scotus and His Mariology, Grey College, Durham, England, Sept. 9–11, 2010, Mariologia Franciscana* (New Bedford, MA: Academy of the Immaculate, 2009). Henceforth, Durham 2008 and the name of the contributor.

For private consultation and not distribution without the consent of E Ondrako

Mary as Teacher and Witness Section, and the Metaphysical Subtlety and Practicality of studying Scotus. Mary has a place which was designed from eternity. Because of her preservative redemption, which is in view of the foreordained merits of her Son and Savior, Mary is the active personal instrument of our liberative redemption. Study questions follow.

Part Two. Contextualizing the Theological Consistency

The second part, "Contextualizing the Theological Consistency of Newman and Scotus" begins with an introduction-excursus by the editor on secular Christianity and voluntarism and the unique gift of Scotus who unites metaphysics and theology without destroying either. John Ford addresses "Newman's Personalist Argument for Belief in God." Ford asks: What does real assent to the existence of God mean? How does change or conversion serve as a catalyst? Is the existence of God real or notional? Ford is keenly alert to Newman's subtle apologetic aim in his famous Apologia because of his wish that his contemporaries would understand the history of his religious opinions and make those religious opinions their own. In his codicil, Ford brilliantly analyzes the famous reply of Newman in the Letter to the Duke of Norfolk about toasting conscience and the Pope. Timothy Noone addresses "Scotus and Newman on Knowledge, Assent and Faith." He explains Newmanesque Intimations, Scotus on Faith and Pedestrian Knowledge, and offers Points for Comparison and Contrast. If one is looking for a shortcut, so to speak and not to disparage any of the contributors, Peter Damian Fehlner addresses "Scotus and Newman in Dialogue" in such a manner, which one reader suggests, is the marrow of the argument to offer convincing reasons to the critical reader that Scotus is a progenitor of Newman. This is his second venture and develops the themes of Newman *vis a vis* nominalism and voluntarism, that Newman's early theological consistency is scotistic, and lists the scotistic affinities in Newman's mature works. Study questions follow.

Part Three. The Implications for the Church and the Modern World

The third part: "The Implications for the Church and Modern World," begin with an introduction-excursus by the editor on scientific form and certitude, which raises questions that are beneath the rationalism and arbitrary voluntarism of western secularism, and the relation of

For private consultation and not distribution without the consent of E Ondrako

scientific form to intellectual certainty. Does every speculative proof for God's existence mean that it is merely a proof from ontotheology, a proof with no relation to reality? With these questions in mind, our intention is to examine the substratum beneath the influence of Bl. Newman and Bl. Scotus and to bring their originality into persuasive contemporary language and purchase. Colonization is another way to refer to the contemporary influences of Scotus and Newman, actual and potential. We are aware of a discursive colonization in the modern period, a hermeneutical turn with Kant, and his assumption that his philosophy is superior to theology and to biblical interpretation. In that sense, his is a hermeneutics of ingratitude. Kant does not have Paul Ricoeur's hermeneutic of charity or hermeneutic of retrieval. The crucial underlying question is: Can any theory of inculturation take precedence over the absolute character of metaphysical truth?

In chapter eight, "The Nobility of the Will according to Duns Scotus," Olivier Boulnois, emeritus professor at the Sorbonne, contributes Scotus's quintessential thought on the nobility of the will as the 'base and summit,' a compelling image for the Newman-Scotus project. Beatitude consists in more than the vision of God which is the intuitive act of the intellect, but in a more principal act, the one of the will. Our end is supreme happiness and we unite to it by an act of willing. Since beatitude is an act of will, it is a free act. The will takes the initiative with a spontaneous necessity while it remains free in the presence of God. Boulnois recognizes that never before Scotus had the autonomy of metaphysics been proclaimed by such force by a theologian. He has given permission for this key text to be included from *Être et représentation*. Agnes Deferluc, doctoral candidate, translates.[30]

In chapter nine, "The Scotistic Doctrine of the Incarnation in the Anglican Tradition—Newman in Frame and Content," Geoffrey Rowell, retired Anglican Bishop of Gibraltar, offers an original analysis of the central theme of the motive of the Incarnation from the Anglican and Reformed Traditions, which brings 'new' scholarly and ecumenical promise, centers on the motive of the Incarnation and what has always been true and reflected on in the Anglican tradition and Reformed Traditions and may be forgotten or never reflected upon. His years at Keble College Oxford and responsibilities as Anglican Archbishop of Europe equipped him with a scholarly and pastoral sensitivity.

---

[30] In May 2011, Olivier Boulnois told Agnes Deferluc that he has a team translating *Être et représentation* into English, which will be a complement to this volume, especially chapters 3, 4, 7, and Boulnois's conclusion. See chapter 8 in this volume.

For private consultation and not distribution without the consent of E Ondrako

In chapter ten, "*Cor ad Cor Loquitur*: refashioning the imagination around love," Mary Beth Ingham, a prolific writer and teacher of Scotus from Loyola Marymount, Los Angeles, develops Newman's ethical thought in relation to Scotus that is founded on the premise that there is no abyss between the intra and extra mental in the pilgrimage to beauty and right loving in the world. This was a major theme in her keynote address at our first Newman-Scotus Symposium, an address with a vision of the ethics of beauty and rationality of love. Her eye is on the future of the planet and she challenges future contributors, in a most inviting manner, to do the hard work of understanding Scotus and Newman well, without falling into the contemporary attraction of pantheism or animism.

In chapter eleven, "Newman, Scotus, and Catholic Higher Education: A Worthwhile Conversation," Patricia Hutchison from Neumann College, Aston, PA, educator and facilitator in Franciscan higher education, offers a vision for Catholic education that is in the trajectory with the founding of the medieval universities. Scotus incorporates the *De Doctrina Christiana* of St. Augustine and recognizes that theology determines metaphysics simply by liberating it to allow it to accomplish its proper ends. She presents a very inviting approach because she knows how to listen to students, teachers, and administrators by inviting them to understand the faith that is preserved within the Church. She has a personal response to be imitated in the quest for insights for creative contemporary education that is born in and the fruit of her responsibilities associated with Franciscan Education Conferences. Her goal is to draw teachers and students towards the theory of education in Newman's *The Idea of a University*, by linking Scotus's ethical influence and Newman's personal influence.

In chapter twelve, "Holiness in John Henry Newman's Theory of Doctrinal Development: The Harmony of the Intellect and Affective Spirit," Robert Christie, researcher for Devry University, unfolds the validity of the universal call to holiness as it was rediscovered by Newman and at the reforms of Vatican II. Christie addresses the critical problem of the relation between intellectual pursuits and prayer, that of intellect and will, the search for wisdom predicated on pride or humility, in the spirit of St. Augustine, *De Trinitate*. Bl. Newman pursued learning with a priority to charity.

In chapter thirteen, "The Story of a Miracle," Deacon Jack Sullivan begins with the profound human account of what happened to him through the intercession of Bl. Newman. By the faithful example of his wife Carol, he became aware of how he was breathing a secular air, that the intellect was a gift from God, but the greatest gift is faith and that faith needs protection, education, and defense. Like Bl. Newman, he came to

For private consultation and not distribution without the consent of E Ondrako

see that faith is preserved in the Church as the "gift of gifts" from God and that everyone is called into an intimate relationship with God. He gives an account of his extraordinary gift which contributed to Bl. Newman's beatification on September 19, 2010.

In chapter fourteen, "Retrieving Scotus and Newman by Imitating Gerard Manley Hopkins," Edward Ondrako, visiting scholar in the department of theology at Notre Dame, develops the hidden inter-relationship of the metaphysical content of Newman and Scotus that is put into modern English in the poetry of Hopkins. In 1866 Hopkins was received into the Roman Church by Newman and in 1872 discovered a manuscript on the thought of Scotus that influenced his spirituality and entire poetical career. In sum, theology does not dictate its contents, but simply requires metaphysics to be a distinct science of itself and this is accomplished by liberating metaphysics to perfect its proper ends. Metaphysics disengages itself from theology, while theology lets itself find ballast by metaphysics. Hopkins subtly replies to the critical contemporary problem of novelty and continuity in the context of change.

In chapter fifteen, "Uncoupling Scotus from Kant with the Help of Newman," Ondrako addresses several of the difficulties and serious consequences of the erroneous linking of Scotus with Kant. The thought of Kant (d. 1804), which will likely remain as influential as it is for some time, is linked to Scotus in an uncritical manner, as if Scotus were Kant's precursor. Kant writes with an axiom of absolute freedom. He is anti-metaphysical, while Scotus, more than his predecessors, allows metaphysics and theology to be united more profoundly. Each science leans on the other to exist, but both need understanding of the intellect with its transcendental powers to be sciences. The essay analyzes some of the major difficulties with the line of thinking that assumes, or hypothesizes, or maintains that there are arguable threads to link Scotus and Kant. In the next essay we will see that Ockham may be the better candidate for such a linkage.

In chapter sixteen, "Being and Becoming: Hegel's Inversion and Newman's Consistency with Scotus," Ondrako tackles a problem that is probably less perilous than Kant's discursive colonization, but still a worry, i.e., how it is that Hegel (d. 1831) captures imaginations? It is a serene reflection on how far Scotus's 'metaphysics of being as being' is from the consequences of Hegel's equating of being and nothing. Hegel shares some assumptions with Kant especially that there is a recognized turn to the subject that is non-negotiable. He accepts criticisms against Kant especially Kant's epistemology. Hegel develops a view of Christianity as dialectical which is the bottom line of how he redesigns the Trinitarian

For private consultation and not distribution without the consent of E Ondrako

landscape and offers a conceptual smoothing of dualistic kinks rather than captures the intellect.

Finally, in chapter seventeen, "Scotus the Nefarious: Uncovering Genealogical Sophistications," Cyril O'Regan offers a compelling x-ray of 'misprisonings' of Scotus and Scotism from several earlier perspectives and more recent ones including that of Heidegger, Balthasar, and the school of Radical Orthodoxy. To misprison means the offering of readings in a literary oeuvre that are forceful, highly interesting, and seem forceful, which O'Regan applies to Scotus. He makes the reader, stop, look, and think about Scotus as he really was and what he thought, not the way he has been interpreted. He begins with an original and unprecedented analysis of the importance of the philosophical and theological stature of Scotus to command respect and sophisticated analysis as other medieval figures as Thomas Aquinas. One of Notre Dame's senior theologians and world's foremost experts on Hegel, O'Regan offers an evocative, erudite and comprehensive analysis of several difficulties in misreading Scotus and takes the form of a plea for the unaligned to open up the plurality of the tradition of the metaphysics and theology of Scotus. Scotus establishes the independence of metaphysics within interdependence. Philosophy and theology establish each other in their own order, in their gaps and in their reciprocal relations.

Three assumptions before engaging *The Newman-Scotus Reader*

At the outset, it warrants repeating to work with three important assumptions. The first has to do with style; the second with resemblances on how to conduct theology; and the third on how the mind actually works. The assumptions help the reader to hear, to converse with, and especially to answer Newman and Scotus. How does change relate to the unchangeableness of certitude in Newman's thought? What is understanding in Scotus's thought? How does the "illative sense" of Newman relate to Scotus's "understanding?"

> The first assumption is that Newman's is a more phenomenological style while Scotus's is a more metaphysical style but both deal with the real and spiritual in life. Several of the essays in this *Newman-Scotus Reader* examine the presuppositions which Newman understands and demonstrate reasons for a remarkable series of resemblances between Scotus and Newman without suggesting that there is a trajectory between them. Rather, the cultivated instinct, or illative sense of Newman, enables the mind

For private consultation and not distribution without the consent of E Ondrako

to converge probabilities into a view. The probabilities indicate genuine unity of approach to the nature of theology. For example, the dogma of the Trinity is paradigmatic for the assent of faith, but one that is an object of notional assent because it is difficult to view the Trinity as a systemic whole. The sum of the propositions that define the Trinity is the object of real assent. Newman must have been familiar with Hegel's Trinity, a conceptual smoothing between the eternal and temporal, with its result in a tragic depersonalization and loss of the sense of awe.

The second assumption is that the resemblances between Newman and Scotus and how to conduct theology has a bearing on one of the most sensitive questions of the day, liberty in relation to the will and intellect.[31] It is a small step to suggest that this groundbreaking view might have a significant bearing on the future of Catholic theology. The contributed work that follows engages pertinent historical, philosophical, and theological ideas that will define key concepts in Newman's project and relate them to Scotus's project. Their thought addresses the urgency felt today to engage subtle related issues on the surface and the still waters that run deep, such as having convictions and living by them. At the core, the human idea is first formed in order to know and is a concept related to divine begetting, as the eternal generation of the Word by the Father. This is not Hegel's marginality of the Trinitarian landscape, or Kant's noumenal and phenomenal orders, for there is no critical problem in terms of an abyss between the intra and extra mental for Newman and Scotus. Their problem is with the refusal to engage the contemplative aspect of knowing.

The third assumption is that Newman's project is to demonstrate how the mind actually works, the unconditionality of assent by the wise person who routinely makes right judgments, and how one reaches certitude in matters of religion. Newman suggests that a judgment is not self-grounded but has antecedent grounding. This is a reply to Lockian formal logic, strong or weak, and its reduction of assent and judgment to inference and probability without the possibility of assent. The relative firmness of formal logic strong or weak, in the relation of an inference to its premises, both imply weak alone, the critical problem of Kant. It is a reply to the indefectibility of certitude and how a person protects one's certitude about assents and judgments against skepticism in a

---

[31] BENEDICT XVI, Scotus Audience.

For private consultation and not distribution without the consent of E Ondrako

post Hume age. Newman is a phenomenologist of judgment and judgment is a first order matter. Certitude is a second order matter. Certitude follows from investigation and proof, is accompanied by an intellectual *tranquilitas*, and is irreversible.[32] Newman is constantly alert to how the mind actually works in relation to any form of the rationalist trap, or rash judgment, or prejudice. The essential safeguard is to look for a light to guide one's thought and to keep formal inference securely linked to reality. The contributions of Scotus keep Newman from falling into the rationalist trap. The key concept is that Scotus's univocity of the concept of being is a unique incomparable formulation of divine illumination in logical form which helps Newman to keep formal inference at bay, i.e. from securely linking his thought to reality or being, and the disjunctive transcendentals are his metaphysics.[33]

The three assumptions inform the critical question for Newman: how does change relate to the unchangeableness of certitude? The celebrated criticism of Charles Kingsley was, in substance, against Newman's decision to be received into the Roman Church because, in retrospect, Kingsley pointed out that prior to 1845 Newman had articulated convincingly all of the criticisms of Anglicans against the Church of Rome. Newman responded to Kingsley in 1864 with his theory of faith, the *Apologia pro vita sua*, which was composed with a rare burst of adrenalin. The *Grammar of Assent* was written more serenely in 1869–1870 after reflecting for a lifetime on liberalism in religion and integrating assent, judgment and certitude into his theory of epistemology. Here is where Newman's genius is to be self-referential, not to continuously reconstruct the self but to recognize that the self is capable of change.

In sum, the three assumptions define one side of the project to demonstrate striking similarities in the thought patterns of Newman and Scotus when, on face value, the employment of 19th century British philosophy seems far removed from the scholastic method of Scotus and Thomas. The other, the complementary side of the project, consists in defining sixteen significant terms that make up the repeated references to the theological-metaphysical views in discussing the parallel thought patterns in Scotus and Newman throughout the essays. In sum, Scotus reflects the theological and philosophical tradition of Bonaventure which was inspired by St. Francis of Assisi. A further dimension is acknowledg-

---

[32] NEWMAN, *Grammar*, 258.
[33] The disjunctive transcendentals are in an outline form as the Appendix to E. ONDRAKO, *Uncoupling Scotus from Kant with Newman's Help*, chapter 15 in this volume.

For private consultation and not distribution without the consent of E Ondrako

ment that Kant and Hegel receive considerable attention in regard to the critical question of interiorization. Kant receives even more attention because it is his exercise of hermeneutics that receives more contemporary "currency and prestige."[34]

The contributions in *The Newman-Scotus Reader* address this thesis about interiorization and related questions by thoroughly defining, comparing and contrasting the major terms. For example, Newman's 'illative sense' is related to Scotus's 'understanding,' and Bonaventure's *dijudicatio* or judgment. Newman's will is defined as the power to be good or holy. Scotus's will is essentially rational, the core of a person's life. Bonaventure's will is the *liberum arbitrium*[35] of discretion and choice. Newman's natural or anthropological is related to Scotus's *perfectio simpliciter simplex*[36] and Bonaventure's image. These similarities form the convergence of probabilities[37] that there is a unity of approach to the nature of theology and how to conduct it in Scotus and Newman. Newman demonstrates a correct appreciation for Scotistic Franciscan theology and Catholic theology in general. For Newman, they go hand in hand as a response to the spread of Kantianism and its generative power.

Further research

1. *The Newman-Scotus Reader* provides a point of reference for appreciating and discussing further what has been said and some more ideas that could be said about Bl. Scotus as a progenitor of Bl. Newman, but it does not stop there. To many, this may sound totally new, even strange, and may seem to be an artificially forced thesis. However, as one reads the essays in this volume, our thesis will come alive, not as a novelty, but as a scholarly thesis that can be substantiated. Several of the essays that follow will demonstrate the grounding of our thesis, even as we have and are open to competing views. Thanks to the on-going labors of the Scotus Commission since 1950, the authenticity of the critical edition of Scotus's works are now more readily available. This has made

---

34 CYRIL O'REGAN, "Kant: Boundaries Blind Spots and Supplements," in Jeffrey Bloechl, ed., *Christianity and Secular Reason*. Notre Dame: University of Note Dame Press, 2012, 87–126. Here p. 89. "Kant's logic of supplementarity, which sets limits to both the range and depth of critical reason, can be exploited by modern and postmodern thought with a view to trimming Hegel's promethean ambitions."

35 Free will.

36 A pure perfection cannot be reduced any simpler.

37 See the *Grammar of Assent* and understand it as a tying together of any loose ends in Newman's lifelong quest for certitude in matters of religion.

For private consultation and not distribution without the consent of E Ondrako

the work of modern researchers much easier even as Scotus requires a disciplined and skilled mind to engage his writings.

We are aware that there may be some justification for preferring to avoid this thesis that Scotus is a progenitor of Newman. If there is a reservation, our reply is to encourage the incorporation of contemporary theories of interpretation in tandem with the absolute character of metaphysical truth, which permeates this volume. Or, better yet, mindful that significant underpinnings have been forgotten because of historical changes and changes in language usage between the death of Scotus (1308) and death of Newman (1890), almost seven hundred years, criticism of the idea of progenitor suggests that it has not been reflected upon sufficiently. The short reply is to say that for Newman to put Scotus into modern English enables both to speak to philosophical and theological labors today.

2. The intention of the presenters and their contributions is an invitation to further research. For example, the three assumptions about Scotus's and Newman's 'style,' how they conduct theology, and how the mind actually works, is open to the influence of Thomas Aquinas on the thought of Newman, a point which seems to be still in the probative stage. We know that as Newman prepared for conditional reordination, he refers to the poor state of the study of philosophy in Rome in 1846, which suggests that his theological preparation at this juncture is worthy of further study beyond our limits here. We know that in 1864, Newman appears to give a nod to the influence of Thomas Aquinas on his thought,[38] but, fifteen years earlier, in 1849, he accepts the scotistic view on the motive of the Incarnation.

3. A third area to research is the early intimations of a scotistic influence made possible by Newman's study of the Fathers of the Church, especially through the Alexandrian school, Clement and Athanasius, Butler's *Analogy* and behind Butler, some key aspects of the great scotistic tradition in England. That influence may be able to give an account of why it was a decade before his nod to Thomas in 1864 that Newman wrote about Scotus in *The Idea of a University* as one of the distinguished persons under whose shadow he once lived, and lamented the loss of those halcyon days, and identifies him as one of the boldest and most subtle of disputants. It seems to me that by 1852, when he began to write on the essence of a university, Newman had Scotus in mind as one of his primary exemplars, and, by 1858, when

---

[38] Cyril O'Regan, Classroom lectures, Spring term, 2011, University of Notre Dame.

For private consultation and not distribution without the consent of E Ondrako

he completed the occasional lectures and essays, that influence was very deeply rooted.

When one reads and re-reads Newman's *Grammar of Assent*, one cannot help but be struck by passages that have an apparent Thomistic inspiration, but upon closer analysis, are scotistic. With Newman, we invite competing views and further research by scholars with the skills and time to enter into this rewarding area of research, "to cultivate the intellect as an end which may reasonably be pursued for its own sake because the nature of that cultivation lies in fitting it to apprehend and contemplate Truth."[39] As this work unfolds it will become evident why we are advancing the thesis that Newman was not an eclectic but a systematic consistent theologian at heart and the system governing Newman's consistency was scotistic at heart.[40]

---

[39] SVAGLIC, Newman's Discourse VII, 114.

[40] In his closing remarks, Fr. H. Geisseler, the chairman of the Bl. John Henry Newman International Colloquium, which was held at the Gregorianum in Rome from November 21–23, 2010, stated categorically that Bl. Newman was not a systematic theologian without defining what he meant. Our work takes a competing view.

PART 1

FOUNDATIONS IN THE CONTOURS BETWEEN JOHN DUNS SCOTUS AND JOHN HENRY NEWMAN

For private consultation and not distribution without the consent of E Ondrako

Key Concepts

Edward Ondrako

Intuition and Certitude: A Preparatory Position to Study Contours in the Thought of Bl. Scotus and Bl. Newman

Précis

Bl. Scotus and Bl. Newman engage the problem of the unity of knowing, that is, scientific and eternal wisdom. Contours in their thought may not always seem apparent at first, but upon further reflection, become visible. The *practical* application to the unity of knowing, according to the mind of the two Oxford doctors, is to understand what Christ taught about himself.

Excursus: On Intuition and Certitude

This excursus is the first of three for each of three parts to *The Newman-Scotus Reader*, and meant to be read with a view as a complete work on intuition and certitude. These three detailed introductory emanations originate from the same source, the conviction that there are many sufficient reasons to indicate the presence in Newman's writings of considerable similarity with the thought patterns, theological and philosophical, of Scotus. The first excursus prepares the reader with ten foundational elements relating to the thought patterns of Scotus and Newman. The second excursus helps the reader to unite metaphysics and theology, each science leaning on the other to exist, in order to engage the thought of Scotus and Newman correctly in relation to secular or liberal Christianity and modern voluntarism. The third excursus prompts the reader to raise questions that are beneath the anti-metaphysical rationalism of Western secularism and voluntarism, and to turn to how scientific form may lead to real assent and eternal wisdom.

Scotus anticipated these questions and Newman developed them. Intuition and certitude are the key to the philosophical, theological, and anthropological principles that Scotus and Newman use in their quest for

For private consultation and not distribution without the consent of E Ondrako

intellectual certainty.[1] This invitation to all who study, ponder, and teach that God is love, is to contemplate with Scotus that *God always loves in an orderly manner*. The linchpin to what may appear as a complicated structure is a prescient work of a contemporary Scotist, Peter Damian Fehlner, "Mary and Theology: Scotus Revisited,"[2] which I discovered, as Newman discovered Butler's *Analogy*, to be a momentous step for contemporary theological research. Fehlner's original and personalist thought prepares the inquirer to enjoy the marrow of Scotistic and Newmanian thought in "Scotus and Newman in Dialogue."[3] Both are in *The Newman-Scotus Reader* to give practical insight how the searcher for truth starts by using all of one's personal powers, intellectual and affective, to study the divine perspective on the course of history. He suggests several arguments to answer why Scotus and Newman studied Mary as the model and guide and final support for all that they taught about God's love, the solid foundation for applying their vigilance to current thought. Properly understood, the thought of Scotus and Newman is eminently applicable to modern and post-modern parlance, such as interest in the person, relationality and beauty, self-realization and human freedom.

Although he does not stand alone in the effort to bring the thought of Scotus to the contemporary world,[4] Fehlner's ground breaking insights

---

1 Greyfriars Oxford Centre for Franciscan Studies sponsored my lecture on November 8, 2010 at the Taylor Institution. The original title was: "Intuition and Certitude: How to Embark on Studying Contours in the Thought of Bl. John Duns Scotus and Bl. John Henry Newman." Questions and answers from the audience led to rearranging the ten key concepts for the sake of clarity. The paper has been edited considerably from the original. Permission was generously granted by Brother Mark of Greyfriars Oxford to include this in *The Newman-Scotus Reader: Contexts and Comparisons*.

2 PETER DAMIAN FEHLNER, *Mary and Theology: Scotus Revisited* (Rensselaer, N.Y.: published privately, 1978, revised, 2010). It is chapter 4 in *The New Newman-Scotus Reader*. While on retreat during Easter week 2008, I read this essay for the first time and it is an invaluable guide to understand the Franciscan thesis, to how Scotus engages the hierarchy of truths, their metaphysical substratum, and, the practical application to a life of faith of what may appear to some as a dry academic exercise. In a similar way, Newman learned that as one journeys through life, one needs to read with the heart and mind, in prayer and contemplation, in quest for the truth that never disappoints.

3 See FEHLNER, "Scotus and Newman in Dialogue," chapter 7 in this volume. Excerpts were given at the inaugural Newman-Scotus Symposium 2010, Washington Theological Union, Washington, D.C. October 22–24, 2010. Henceforth, Fehlner, Dialogue.

4 For the names of several scholars committed to making the thought of Scotus available for academic research and the promotion of devotion in his spirit, see eds. MARY BETH INGHAM and OLEG BYCHKOV, *Archa Verbi: John Duns Scotus, Philosopher: Proceedings of The Quadruple Congress on John Duns Scotus* (St. Bonaventure, N.Y.: Franciscan Institute Publications, 2010). Parts one and three of three are in print at this time. See *Franciscans of the Immaculate, The Acts of the Symposium, Bl. John Duns Scotus and His Mariology, Grey College Durham, England, Sept 9–11, 2008, Mariologia Franciscana III* (New Bedford, MA: Academy of the Immaculate, 2009). Henceforth, Durham, 2009, and the name of the contributor. See Ruggero Rosini, *Mariology of John Duns Scotus*, trans. and ed. (New Bedford, MA: 2008). In general, the

For private consultation and not distribution without the consent of E Ondrako

serve as a fitting reply to the personal invitation of Charles Balič, OFM, who was perhaps the greatest Scotist of our times. In the late spring 1966, Balič thought that there were correlations between the thought of Scotus and Newman and that such a study had not been done and would be a very positive one. Fehlner engages significant scholars from the Fathers to the present, and offers several well-researched reasons why it is plausible to conclude that Scotus is the 'progenitor' of Newman.[5]

Introduction: Four objectives

The first objective is a modest attempt to assist the person who is thinking about what life is all about, to suggest why it is meaningful to discover contours in the thought of Scotus and Newman about making a judgment and giving assent, contours that converge around questions of certainty and knowledge (epistemology).

The second objective is to emphasize the faculty of making a judgment, as in Newman's illative sense, about what knowledge illumines (metaphysics) to move the conversation forward about resemblances in the thought of Scotus and Newman. For example, natural and supernatural religion for Newman illustrates the potential for apologetics to answer the problem of sin at the center of natural religion, an answer found only in supernatural revelation. The absolute primacy of Christ for Scotus means that creation exists for the sake of the Incarnation! It was forever in the mind of God to create the world to give glory to the Son and to welcome human beings to share in that glory. Freedom, will, and intellect, are shared in common with the infinite God, in a finite manner. It is the misuse of freedom, will, and intellect that results in the fall and its consequences.

The third objective is to demonstrate how "Mary and Theology: Scotus Revisited" and its sequel, "Scotus and Newman in Dialogue" converges with other philosophers and theologians, from the Fathers to the present, especially Scotists and Newmanists, to ground theological study, to reply to reservations about modern empirical method and exegesis, and to identify the consequences of the separation of doctrine from moral theology or ethics, i.e. leaving the meta out of meta-ethics. This has colossal purchase for taking care of creation and all its inhabitants, issues of health care, charity, justice and the international order for the twenty-first century.

Academy of the Immaculate has as one of its primary purposes to make available current scholarship on Scotus based on his authentic writings.

[5] That conviction was a critical hinge of the Newman-Scotus Symposium 2010. Present were professors, doctoral candidates, chairs of philosophy and theology departments, members of the Scotus critical edition team, Franciscan friars in formation, and the general public.

For private consultation and not distribution without the consent of E Ondrako

The fourth objective is to share understanding about several layers and similarities in the thought patterns of Scotus and of Newman that are not always apparent. Graduate students, upper level undergraduates, and all who think critically about life's most meaningful issues express constant interest to me about these issues. With respect for competing views, I find that Newman serendipitously puts the thought of Scotus into modern English. Newman's conviction in the *Grammar of Assent* works: what satisfies and convinces one in religious matters might satisfy and convince another. As Anglican and Catholic, he guides seekers of wisdom in the personal quest for truth to imitate the orderly love and unconditional docility of Christ.

Format: Ten defining elements

There are ten defining elements that comprise the core of this preliminary excursus. They follow a literary form, a-b-b-a, then c, and, a-b-b-a, then c. The succession of themes starts with Vatican II and the wishes for further study of Scotus by recent Popes. The inspiration of St. Francis on Scotus's Mariology and recent research by Peter Damian Fehlner on Mary as *memory of the Church*[6] demonstrates a link to *Lumen Gentium* chapter eight at Vatican II. These four elements show the way to the central scotistic insight that God merited our salvation vicariously, and not by substituting his sufferings for ours. The core of the next four elements is the Franciscan thesis. It is not a proposal that deals with what is purely speculative, but what God in fact has done for salvation and redemption. The Franciscan thesis does not contain even a hint of onto-theology, which is a split in metaphysics or split in the study of 'what is,' being. Scotus anticipated the questions raised by Kant and Newman steered clear of the result of the split, i.e. Kantian voluntarism. Next, Franciscan anthropology answers the pivotal question: is the causal capacity of the human person diminished with respect to that originally possessed by our first parents? The scotistic answer is that the human person has a causal power that has been reduced because of sin, but retains the practical potential, even with a lesser freedom, to achieve the objective end proper to being human. The final element is taken from "Mary and Theology: Scotus Revisited," ideas about the renewal of theology and philosophy. Renewal includes the asceticism of the mind, attention to *caveats* while developing skills, and, ordered love to view the divine in the course of history. It is ordered loving that leads to truth.

---

6 See 31, 33, 34, 609.

For private consultation and not distribution without the consent of E Ondrako

A concise definition of epistemology and metaphysics

The ten elements just listed use the philosophical method of epistemology and metaphysics. Epistemology is the study of the light (knowledge) that illumines all that is, being (metaphysics). The absolute center of all that is, being, is the truth of God's love, all that God has in fact done, and that God merited our salvation vicariously. This truth guides insight into the feminine in the Church and the World, and into the Franciscan thesis which reminds the audience of all that God has in fact done, while avoiding the daunting word, onto-theology and difficulties caused by splitting metaphysics. The split leads to a deep-seated challenge from Kantian thought but it has a counterpart, i.e. liberty for *interiorization*, a process of entering into the heart, while being intellectually humble. Dare to say, the sanctification of the intellect as exemplified by Scotus and Newman.

With this perspective, Franciscan anthropology and creative liberty, two contemporary concerns, take on a new urgency. The Franciscan thesis is in perfect accord with the spirit of Vatican II's evangelization of the modern world and *Nostra Aetate*, the Declaration of the Church to Non-Christian Religions. Contours in the thought of Scotus and Newman reflect familiarity with and, at times, go beyond the teaching about divine knowledge and the natural mode of man to act freely summarized by Thomas Aquinas in several of his works.[7]

> The divine knowledge does not impose necessity on contingent things, nor does His disposing by which He providentially orders the universe. ...God orders things by His wisdom and acts on them by His power. ...A tree is sometime impeded from producing fruit and an animal from begetting. ...Divine wisdom so orders things that the things so ordered occur according to the mode proper to each cause. The natural mode of man is to act freely, not constrained by any necessity, because intelligent agents relate themselves to opposites; so, then, God orders human acts, yet in such wise that human acts are not subjected to necessity, but stem from free will.

---

[7] P.D. FEHLNER, trans., *Thomas Aquinas: De rationibus fidei contra Saracenos, Graecos, et Armenos, ad cantorum Antiochenum* (New Bedford, MA, 2002), 69–70. See the many references of Thomas to his fuller works such as *Summa contra Gentiles, Summa Theologiae* I-III, and *Questiones disputate De potentia Dei*. Thomas answers ten critical questions from Muslims to a certain Cantor of Antioch in 1265. This short work gives an extraordinarily clear overview of the orderly thought of the Angelic Doctor.

For private consultation and not distribution without the consent of E Ondrako

Free will is a significant theme throughout this work and is a good example of where Newman may appear thomistic at first, and upon further reflection, scotistic.

The panorama or landscape of our subject

The intent of explaining the ten elements is to prepare one to engage with relative ease *The Newman-Scotus Reader* which includes methods of interpretation and reconstruction, the scotistic formal distinction between will and intellect, the tools of patterns and type, the mechanism of secular or liberal Christianity, modern voluntarism, and the study of scientific form that every reasonable human being has. The landscape is to understand what Scotus and Newman both teach about scientific form that leads to real assent. Moreover, the ten elements relate to the sensitive question of liberty in relation to the will and intellect raised by Pope Benedict XVI at his audience on July 7, 2010. A key to the reply of Scotus and Newman is the view of human knowledge, according to Bonaventure, which is a passing of knowledge into affection, or wisdom, and then into work, or art,[8] a realization, or *reductio*. This Franciscan view of human knowledge is wisdom that reflects the contemplative character of the intellect, one that is open to the Light that is God. That is how Scotus constructs a metaphysics which is radically personal. Human knowledge is a passing of knowledge and intellectual activity into affection or wisdom. Similarly, Newman brilliantly analyzes the complex process of apprehension and argumentation that leads to making a judgment and to giving real assent.

Element 1. Scotus, Vatican II, and recent Popes.

Scotus's thought anticipates the innovative and balanced teaching on divine revelation in *Dei Verbum*[9] at Vatican II. For Scotus, "no doctrine may contradict Scripture and all doctrine must be in perfect harmony with Scripture and the authoritative witness of the Church's [living] Tradition."[10] Moreover, in reply to any well-intentioned critique that may misrepresent Scotus, "the sources of Tradition are present in Scotus and he correctly understood their content, as to give it greater place in subsequent theological, spiritual, and missionary activity of the Church."[11] The proper relation

---

8 ST. BONAVENTURE, *Reductio Artium ad Theologiam*. See FEHLNER, Dialogue, concluding remarks.

9 Documents of Vatican II, *The Dogmatic Constitution on Divine Revelation*.

10 For a clear and persuasive scholarly presentation of this pivotal insight of Scotus with extensive references to his Prologue to the *Ordinatio*. See SETTIMIO MANELLI, "Scriptural Foundations of Scotus' Mariology," in Durham, 2009, 173–231.

11 FEHLNER, "Sources of Scotus' Mariology in Tradition," Durham, 2009, 232–294. He addresses the degree that the Mariology of Scotus has implications for Catholic theology, thought

For private consultation and not distribution without the consent of E Ondrako

between Scripture and Tradition applies in a preeminent manner to today's secularized world. The Franciscan thesis unfolds how Mary shares Christ's office as teacher and, in so doing, takes her place at the heart of the Church as *memory of the Church*. She shares Christ's office as *teacher-witness*[12] and *memory of the Church*.

In his Mariology, Scotus offers sound hope for the ecumenical movement. During the euphoria following Vatican II, Bl. Pope Paul VI expressed hope that the thought of Scotus would "provide a golden framework for serious dialogue between the Catholic Church and the Anglican Communion as well as other Christian communities of Great Britain,"[13] a hope broadened later by Pope St. John Paul II[14] to all Christian denominations, and even further by Pope Benedict XVI[15] to all people, Christian and non-Christian. At his illuminating papal audience on July 7, 2010, Pope Benedict XVI made three key points about Scotus. First, he affirmed Scotus's thought on the motive of the Incarnation. Second, he reiterated his thought not only on the role of Christ in the history of salvation but the role of Mary and the Immaculate Conception. Third, he implies a dialogue about Scotus's thought on the sensitive issue of the topic of liberty in relation with the will and with the intellect for the twenty-first century.[16] The timely invitation to study Scotus's thought by three Popes and to apply it in an authentic manner to the heart of the Church's mission remains underdeveloped even as it seems to be on the horizon of bursting forth with sound scholarship.[17]

---

and practice as a whole today in accord with the comprehensive work of ST. BONAVENTURE, *Christus Unus Omnium Magister, Christ the One Teacher of All.*

[12] The insight into Mary at the heart of the Church as the *memory of the Church* and *teacher-witness* is a development of the Franciscan thesis. For *teacher-witness*, see ch. 4, 157, 158, 163, 165 in this volume.

[13] PAUL VI, *Alma Parens*, July 14, 1966 in AAS 58 [1966] 609–614.

[14] JOHN PAUL II, Address to the Members of the Scotus Commission of the Order of Friars Minor, February 16, 2002; http://www.vatican.va/holy_father/john_paul_ii/speeches/2002/february/documents/hf_... Henceforth, Address to Scotus Commission.

[15] BENEDICT XVI, *Laetare, Colonia, urbs*, "Apostolic Letter on the Seventh Centenary of the Death of Blessed John Duns Scotus," http://jinghalls.com/holy_father/benedict_xvi/apost_letters/documents/hf_ben-xvi_apl_2... Henceforth, *Laetare.*

[16] POPE BENEDICT XVI, "On Duns Scotus: Defender of the Immaculate Conception" Papal Audience, July 7, 2010 (Zenit.org).

[17] It is not the intention of this essay to address reasons why study and scholarship of Scotus remains underdeveloped. Rather, as the critical Éditions are in progress, there is a rich field waiting to be developed with the authentic thought of Scotus and his integral connections to Bonaventure.

For private consultation and not distribution without the consent of E Ondrako

Element 2. St. Francis inspires Scotus.

"Holy Virgin Mary, there is no one like you born in the world among women, Daughter and Handmaid of the Most High Sovereign King, the heavenly Father, Mother of our Most Holy Lord Jesus Christ, Spouse of the Holy Spirit: pray for us."[18] The antiphon of St. Francis of Assisi is a key inspiration for his theologian disciples, St. Bonaventure, Bl. Scotus and St. Maximilian Kolbe. "There is no one like you born in the world among women." Scotus humbly contemplated this antiphon and other Marian writings of St. Francis.[19] He pondered Bonaventure's teaching that Mary's role is mediatrix with Christ, that she exercises her mediation in virtue of her unique relation to the Holy Spirit and is exemplar and form of our purification, recognized by Simeon who described the sword that would pierce her heart. Bonaventure expounds the mystery of Our Lady's Assumption for the Church in relation to the mystery of the Incarnation. She alone could be Virgin Mother,[20] which makes "possible our liberation from sin and incorporation into the Body of Christ which she conceived and formed."[21] In sum, Bonaventure subscribes to the insight of Henry of Avranches: Mary is our Mediatrix with Jesus, so Jesus is our Mediator with the Father.

With this foundation, one may turn to the challenging point that Scotus's Mariology builds on his univocity of the concept of being. This means that human beings have something in common with God, such as substance, will, intellect, freedom, etc., and individuality, *haecceitas*. He uses most advantageously the idea of formal distinction, such as the distinction between the Persons of the Trinity. Formal distinction applies

---

18 Antiphon in the Office of the Passion in Regis Armstrong, J. A. Wayne Hellmann, William Short, eds., *Francis of Assisi: Early Documents* (London: New City, 1999–2002), three volumes and index, vol. 1, The Writings of Francis, 141. Henceforth, Early Documents.

19 Early Documents, "The Salutation of the Blessed Virgin Mary," 163; and "The Salutation to the Virtues," 164–165. See JOHANNES SCHNEIDER, *Virgo Ecclesia Facta: The Presence of Mary in the Crucifix of San Damiano and in the Office of the Passion of St. Francis of Assisi*, trans. by the Franciscan Friars of the Immaculate, *Mariologia Franciscana* 1 (New Bedford, MA: 2004); and "Quem Amor Humanavit: Whom Love Made Man. On the Motive of the Incarnation of God According to Francis of Assisi: Pre-scotistic reflections of a Simple Man," in Durham, 2009, 25–42.

20 ST. BONAVENTURE, Sermon II: "On the Nativity of the Lord," in Z. Hayes, trans. and commentary, *What Manner of Man* (Chicago: Franciscan Herald Press, 1974 and 1989), 57–75. The Assumption makes possible the Incarnation, i.e. as New Adam and New Eve, there is a joint kingship and queenship over the redeemed. FEHLNER, "The Sense of Marian Coredemption in St. Bonaventure and Bl. John Duns Scotus," in Franciscans of the Immaculate, eds., *Mary at the Foot of the Cross* (New Bedford, MA: Academy of the Immaculate, 2001), vol. 1 of 9, 112–113. These nine volumes are filled with the fruit of research on Mary from diverse perspectives. Henceforth, *MFC* and vol, and name of author.

21 FEHLNER, *MFC*, vol. 1, 112, 113.

For private consultation and not distribution without the consent of E Ondrako

to the distinction between intellect and will. The Franciscan teaching about Mary as the maternal Mediatrix with Christ builds on St. Bonaventure's Marian thought especially in his sermons and in the sixth collation in *On the Seven Gifts of the Holy Spirit*. Scotus develops the thought of Bonaventure in his Marian mode or character of the relation between the Immaculate Conception and the 'firstness' or primacy of Christ, or absolute predestination of Christ as Head of all creation. The absolute primacy of Jesus and Mary is implicit in the theology of Scotus. That is why Franciscan theology has a Marian character and can face up to the challenges to faith, hope and charity in the twenty-first century. Challenges come from a deformation of the truths that were present in Scotus's voluntarism by promoters of the voluntarism that is the radical autonomy of the will. It comes from historians of philosophy who maintain, erroneously, that Scotus divided metaphysics into general and special metaphysics.[22] The essential difference for Scotus in avoiding this error is to understand that Mary was preserved from original sin and all sin because her will is perfectly one with the will of God.[23]

Element 3. Recognizing Scotus's Mariology.

Scotus's Mariology comes from humble reflection on the whole of Scripture and its sources in the divine Tradition of the Church explained in the light of the complete deposit of faith. His works reflect a subtle thinker in love with the One Teacher of All, Christ and His Mother Mary as Teacher-witness. His Mariology is the key to his entire philosophical and theological view that centers on the absolute primacy of Christ and Mary.[24] The Tradition begun by Scotus is an authentic development of the Tradition of the Apostles, the living Tradition of the Church.

Fehlner's research is true to the Franciscan interpretation of memory, understanding and love. He draws out the meaning of the critical reference to Newman's University Sermon fifteen and repeated by Popes John Paul II and Benedict XVI, i.e. Luke 2:19, 51: "Mary kept all these things in her

---

[22] FEHLNER, letter to the author, January 30, 2010. General metaphysics deals with principles underlying thought, or material and formal logic rather than being. Special metaphysics applies these principles to the extra-mental, first of all to the Supreme Being of God.

[23] FEHLNER, Durham, 2009, "Opening Address," 13–17. The point of view that follows is profoundly influenced by this summary statement which seeks to elaborate further the implications of Genesis 3:15 without attempting to replace Revelation with a modern theological treatise.

[24] While it is true that Scotus does not use the term absolute primacy of Mary, because of his untimely death, his immediate Franciscan disciples show the development of Scotus's thought on the primacy of Mary in perfect accord with the primacy of Christ. See SCOTUS, *Four Questions on Mary*, trans. intro and notes. Allan B. Wolter (Santa Barbara, CA: Old Mission Santa Barbara, 1988).

For private consultation and not distribution without the consent of E Ondrako

heart pondering them." This is an insight into how Mary shares Christ's office as teacher and takes her place at the heart of the Church as *memory of the Church*.[25] The apostolic hierarchy teaches as an extension of Christ and depends on Mary as memory. Understanding follows remembering and remembering leads to the love of God.

Memory, understanding and love follow a path of coming to know, to understand and to love revealed Truth as St. Francis and his theologian disciples, Bonaventure, Scotus and Maximilian Kolbe did.[26] In other words, there is no break between Francis and Bonaventure, nor Francis, Bonaventure and Scotus. Bonaventure's three modes of Franciscan theology form a totality: the symbolic, proper and contemplative. The symbolic may be viewed as the Creeds and official teachings, the proper with academic theology today, while the mystical is the contemplative, prayerful part of theological reflection. Three parts form a whole and correspond to memory, understanding, and love in coming to know and to understand and to love revealed Truth. The opposite is to deny that there is any revealed Truth, *la dictatura di relativismo*.[27] The worst denial is the cynicism that any love could be true, even divine love.

Element 4. Mary as memory of the Church.

The identification of Mary as *memory of the Church*, is the next logical step and supports the invocation of Benedict XVI "to believers and non-believers alike, of the path and method that Scotus followed in order to establish harmony between faith and reason, defining in this manner the nature of theology in order constantly to exalt action, influence, practice and love rather than pure speculation."[28] In Scotistic thought, Mary's maternal mediation serves as *memory of the Church*, founded on the mystery of the Immaculate Conception. As *memory of the Church*, Mary "provides the dynamic whereby the theological and metaphysical genius of Scotus will come to sway many spirits to peace."[29] As Spouse of the Holy Spirit, Mary is poised to help the efforts to get beyond blocks to evangelization, to find a way to explain the indivisible unity of the Church and her stainless sanctity, metaphysically speaking, of a stainless Bride of

---

25 FEHLNER, Durham, 2009, fn. 4, 238. This tightly woven footnote deserves a close reading because it gives a summary of the entire mode of theology of St. Bonaventure in "Mary and Theology: Scotus Revisited," for its via media between traditionalism and liberalism in religion. See chapter 4 in this volume.

26 Scotus has a creative and subtle interpretation of the spiritual experiences of St. Francis, an essential inspiration which builds upon on how St. Bonaventure was inspired by St. Francis.

27 The oft-quoted phrase of Pope Benedict XVI clashes, on a deeper level, with onto-theology.

28 BENEDICT XVI, *Laetare*.

29 FEHLNER, Durham, 293–294.

For private consultation and not distribution without the consent of E Ondrako

Christ, with the empirical fact of divided Christians and local churches and ecclesial communities. The reality is that there are many members who are dead or not fully incorporated, and so many not fully united, yet truly holy.

Scotus is a subtle metaphysician because all good metaphysical thought is subtle, a good metaphysician because he is "so excellent a Marian Doctor."[30] It is in the mystery of Mary in the mind of Francis and Scotus that one finds the *decuit*, fittingness, of Franciscan theology. This is the vital link to understand the rationale for the theology of contingents with the theology of necessity. They are two of the many disjunctive transcendentals for understanding the thought of Scotus. The disjunction helps to provide the rationale for the theology of the head (Christology) with that of the Body or Church (Ecclesiology).

In summary, St. Francis's theologian disciples pondered his mind and heart in a manner that raised the Poverello's experiences to responsible theological heights and insights. In God's time, these were recognized by the authority of the Church. Scotus reasoned to the possibility (*potuit*) that Mary was conceived without sin, and the weightier fittingness (*decuit*), the heart of Francis's love for the *Virgo Ecclesia Facta*, the Virgin made Church.

Element 5. God merited our salvation vicariously.

Living in the twenty-first century demonstrates an increase in demand for proof of how doctrines develop and are judged to be true vs. false developments by the Church. In this age of questioning, Newman's essay on development is prescient for questions such as the meaning of merit. One may test the idea of merit by applying Newman's seven notes. One will find that the notes express, implicitly and explicitly, the inner working of the Franciscan view that God merited our salvation vicariously by suffering that was freely accepted out of love. The teaching that God merited our redemption vicariously competes with substitution theories of redemption. Reflection on merit also contextualizes the enigmatic question of human suffering.

This Franciscan Scotistic view of God as meriting our salvation vicariously vies with sincere Protestants whose soteriology is based on substitution, that God substitutes his sufferings for the sufferings of human beings. Moreover, Scotus teaches that Christ could have redeemed human beings in any number of ways, but he chose death on the cross. He would still have loved human beings as much even if he had not died on the

---

30 FEHLNER, Durham, 14.

For private consultation and not distribution without the consent of E Ondrako

cross.[31] The mistake of substitution, from a Scotistic view, is to leave out the possibility that human beings can merit and make up what is lacking in the suffering of Christ (Col. 1:24).

This fifth element is a crucial element in the hierarchy of elements that 'God merited our salvation vicariously.' It underscores paragraph eleven of the *Decree on Ecumenism* at Vatican II which encourages Catholic theologians together with separated brethren to be open to a fraternal rivalry and to search together into the divine mysteries with love for the truth, with charity, and with humility. When comparing doctrines with one another, there is a 'hierarchy' of truths. The goal is to motivate a deeper realization and a clearer expression of the unfathomable riches of Christ. In sum, the Scotistic teaching that merit is crucial in the quest for perfection and sanctity is part of the hierarchy of truths. Merit in a time of trial, means that as we live our lives in a finite world, merit defines a person's sanctity.[32] That is why the key to understanding is that God merited our salvation vicariously.

Element 6. The Franciscan thesis: what God has done.

The Franciscan thesis is not a thesis, as every graduate student studies and hopes to formulate in his or her academic careers. It is not a proposal that deals with what is purely speculative but is integrally connected to what God in fact has done for our salvation and redemption. St. Francis of Assisi's life served as the blueprint for the Franciscan thesis that human beings are created for glory. It is no surprise to hear Bonaventure develop that insight and teach that the Incarnation is the greatest of all God's gifts. Bonaventure is separated by an abyss from Descartes, Kant and Hegel.[33] The subtlety of Scotus is his ability to reformulate these initial insights of Francis and Bonaventure to enable human beings to grasp with clarity what it means to say that even had Adam and Eve not fallen, creation would have taken place for the glory of the Son, a creation that could not take place without a mother who was full of grace because of the divine counsels. The pastoral challenge to Franciscans is to explain Scotus's

---

31 *MFC*, vol. 8, fn. 17, 130, for a reply to the view that He would have died on the cross even if Adam and Eve had not sinned, quite contrary to Scotus, related to neo-patripassionism. See FEHLNER, "Predestination of Mary and her Immaculate Conception," in Mark Miravalle, ed., *Mariology* (Goletta, CA: Queenship Publications Co., 2007), fn. 7, 217, and fn. 71, 259.

32 In the face of a world with growing skepticism, the feast of All Saints celebrates belief and hope that human beings are created by God for glory.

33 FEHLNER, "Redemption, Metaphysics, and the Immaculate Conception," in *MFC* (2005), vol.5, 205. This a comprehensive presentation of theological exemplarism and theological typology. It is important to give a background perspective on why Newman changed note one from preservation of an idea to preservation of type in his *Essay on the Development of Doctrine*, 1845.

For private consultation and not distribution without the consent of E Ondrako

teaching of a perfect redemption by a perfect Redeemer with a perfect fruit, one who was preservatively redeemed, by the merits of her Son, one who gave birth to Him without pain, whose compassion at the foot of the cross was in pain, meritorious because of and along with the merits of her Son.

The essence of the Franciscan thesis rests on the absolute primacy of Jesus and Mary. "Salvation would have been a reality of human-angelic history, even if Adam (and Eve) had not sinned, and Mary as Immaculate Mother of the Savior, would have had an active role in bringing the salvation to pass. In this view, redemption is contextualized within the context of salvation and not the reverse. The Incarnation is not primarily for the sake of the redemption, but for the greatest glory of God. Redemption is for achieving what God originally planned for his Incarnate Son, in a Marian mode."[34] Is it a surprise then to learn that Maximilian Kolbe developed a Christology, soteriology, and Mariology that was perfectly in accord with this initial insight of Francis, enhanced by Bonaventure and crowned by Scotus? From this perspective, none of the thought of the Martyr of Charity could ever be dismissed as 'mariological phantasizing.' "The Franciscan thesis, built on the primacy of Jesus and Mary, is not a hypothetical question, but one of fact: this is what God ordained."[35]

Element 7. The Franciscan thesis and ontotheology.

To repeat, the best way to understand the Franciscan thesis is that it is not a thesis on purely speculative thought, but integrally connected to what God in fact has done for our salvation and redemption! The Franciscan thesis is reflected in the work of Scotus, a metaphysician-theologian, who is consistent with the development of Anselm, the Victorines, and Bonaventure. That means that he is a Marian Doctor, inspired by Francis's Marian thought and Bonaventure's philosophy, theology and anthropology. He gives a radically definitive formulation and systematization into the universal mediation of Mary, which is a distinguishing quality of Franciscan theology. Scotus "completes the teaching of the Seraphic Doctor on the maternal mediation of Our Lady in providing a correct theological formulation of the Immaculate Conception."[36] There is not a hint of any

---

[34] FEHLNER and A. APOLLONIO, "Redemption in a Franciscan Key" in *MFC* (2008), vol. 8, 500.

[35] *MFC*, vol.1, FEHLNER, 103–118. It is rarely heard that Kolbe was a scotist. See FEHLNER, *St. Maximilian Kolbe-Pneumatologist, Mariologia Franciscana II* (New Bedford, MA: Academy of the Immaculate, 2004), fn. 45, 30. This contextualizes the difficulties several have with Kolbean thought. The phrase 'mariological phantasizing' demonstrates a difficulty, a misinterpetation of Kolbe and belongs to A. Pompei.

[36] This concise quote is from *MFC*, vol. 1, 110.

For private consultation and not distribution without the consent of E Ondrako

confusion of the concept of being, or any hint of onto-theology in the Franciscan thesis.

Similarly, Newman's *Memorandum* on the Immaculate Conception in 1854 is an accurate and a short explanation of the purpose of theological activity. There is not a hint of onto-theology in his theological method. In other words, there is no possible way of attributing Newman's thought on the development of doctrine to a Hegelian or neo-Hegelian evolutionary method. The difficulty is that Hegel rejected the classical understanding of 'being' and replaced it with 'becoming' (change). Everything is change. Another way of saying this is to put it in scotistic terms of necessity and contingency. Hegel denies necessity because, for him, everything is contingent. Scotus knew the pre-Hegelian form of this same problem as Joachimism.

The shortest answer to modern skeptics and simplest way that I know how to explain the development known as 'onto-theology' is that it creates a split in metaphysics that is potentially misleading. Think of onto-theology in the context of studying natural theology without supernatural theology. The main difficulty with onto-theology, or a particular context for studying natural theology, is the excessive reduction of knowledge to a logical construct. In explaining knowledge, Scotus takes pains to avoid any reduction to a logical construct alone.[37] He remains open to the super-natural. Newman does the same and avoids any reduction by defending the possibility of real assent as more than pious accommodation, and by explaining the nature and proper use of the illative sense.

The longer way of answering the same question about defending the possibility of faith as an assent, and not just pious affection, is to study what Scotus meant by his formulation of the univocal concept of being. In brief, Scotus explains Bonaventure's theory of divine illumination in a logical form appropriate to the finite intellect, which, obviously does not apply to the infinite intellect and will which is doing the illuminating. The knowledge which using Scotus's univocal concept of being gives to the finite intellect is prior to the logic that makes up the concept. When one thinks about all human knowledge and scientific work in this way, the conclusion of the search for knowledge is not to deny the possibility of faith, nor to reduce faith to pious feelings. Scotus contemplated, in an ingenious manner, the pure perfections (being, freedom, intellect, will, love and knowledge, etc.), and what is not evident to the senses, as more than a logical construct alone. He used the univocal concept of being to build an argument to defend the possibility of faith as an assent.

---

[37] FEHLNER, Dialogue, chapter 7 in this volume. The concept of onto-theology is a critical one and why Scotus is a complete stranger to it.

For private consultation and not distribution without the consent of E Ondrako

The illative sense, or faculty of higher judgment for Newman, is broadly the same as Scotus's thought. The illative sense is different from formal logic. That is why knowledge for both Scotus and Newman is not a logical construct alone.

All of this has a bearing on 'onto-theology,' or a potentially confusing way of organizing the logic of philosophy as distinct from science originating after the fifteenth century in Europe. A general theory of being, or general ontology, has as it key the logic of being. There are specific types of being which include natural theology. In this way of thinking, which differs from Scotus and Newman, God is the subject of natural theology who is only known by a deductive *a priori* procedure. In this context, natural theology is called onto-theology. Once again, the key to onto-theology is the manner in which logic is used in dealing with natural theology. Neither Newman nor Scotus allow their quest for knowledge to be reduced to logic alone. In the *Grammar of Assent*, formal logic differs from the illative sense. If one applies the thought about natural theology proper to Scotus, the epistemology and metaphysics of Scotus differ radically from onto-theology.

Further difficulties with onto-theological thinking developed after the fifteenth century origins in the late eighteenth century with the thought of Immanuel Kant who separates any relation between faith and reason. To counter that split, Pope St. John Paul II, in his encyclical on faith and reason, *Fides et Ratio*, begins with the simple image of two wings. "Faith and reason are two wings on which the human spirit rises to the contemplation of truth; and God has placed in the human heart a desire to know the truth—in a word, to know himself—so that, by knowing and loving God, men and women may also come to the fullness of truth about themselves."[38] To contemplate this simple image is to use logic but to soar above it. I find listeners satisfied with this relatively simple way to explain the intimidating concept of onto-theology and to avoid its trap of splitting metaphysics.

The *caveat* is to avoid the misleading split into general and special metaphysics. General metaphysics deals with principles underlying thought, or material and formal logic rather than being, while special metaphysics applies these principles to the extra-mental, first of all to the Supreme Being of God. For Scotus and Newman, being is one. To reduce being to material and formal logic, i.e. to be scientific alone, is to leave out the help of the disjunctive transcendentals as Scotus used them in relation to the Supreme Being of God. Some disjunctive transcendentals

---

[38] JOHN PAUL II, Encyclical *Fides et Ratio*, 1998.

For private consultation and not distribution without the consent of E Ondrako

are: necessity-contingency, absolute-relative, infinite-finite, cause-caused, prior-posterior, independent-dependent, one-many, same-diverse, equal-unequal.[39] Onto-theology, from this perspective, i.e. without the disjunctive transcendentals, in a closely reasoned argument, which seems to be an attempt to 'describe the indescribable' in a scientific manner alone, as if there were nothing real that is trans-experiential or trans-conceptual. This is the bear trap that Scotus anticipates, Newman avoids, and John Paul II's encyclical *Fides et Ratio* warns as potentially dangerous. Scotus's insights into the mystery of divine love and the Incarnation and Newman's insights on living with faith in a radically secularized world give witness to their avoidance of the trap.

Element 8. Scotus, Newman and Kantianism.

Recent history and debates on moral matters on a global scale demonstrate growing willfulness, voluntarism, and skepticism.[40] Beneath, one perceives the universal spread of Kantianism. The problem with Kant's transcendentalism is that the mind has to pass from principles of logic to extra-mental reality. Unless the passage is valid, no other form of natural theology is valid and a person remains a theological skeptic.[41] Contrariwise, in his quest for certitude, Newman avoided the anti-metaphysical solution of Kantianism.

I maintain that Scotus anticipated some of the problems of Kant. It may seem tortuous to study Scotus, but that is how one constructs an intelligible reply to Kantianism. Not only did Scotus anticipate some of the problems of Kant, but he anticipated some of the solutions of Newman regarding certitude. Remember Kant's onto-theology is opposed to Newman's use of the illative sense in the *Grammar of Assent*.[42] Remember

---

[39] ALLAN B. WOLTER, *The Transcendentals and Their Function in the Metaphysics of Duns Scotus* (St. Bonaventure, N.Y., The Franciscan Institute, 1946, rpt. Kessinger Publishing, 2008), 128–161.

[40] From 2001 to 2004, I had the good fortune to become acquainted with Robert P. George at Princeton's Department of Politics as he addressed issues in Contitutional Interpretation and Civil Liberties. I also attended his mentor, John Finnis's lectures on "Secularism, Law and Public Policy" in October, 2003 and "Economy or Explication? Telling the Truth about God and Man in a Pluralist Society," in October, 2004. Both scholars are natural law theoreticians and analyze causes for modern skepticism.

[41] FEHLNER, letter to the author, January 30, 2010.

[42] Modern voluntarism is a research topic of E. J. Ondrako. "Bl. Cardinal Newman and Bl. John Duns Scotus: Parallels in the Epistemology of Faith," was given at the annual Newman Conference, Notre Dame, August 14, 2009; a revised version at the Franciscan International Study Centre, Canterbury, England, January 21, 2010, and a recentering of the topic on "Bl. John Duns Scotus and his Mariology: A Golden Framework for Serious Dialogue," given at St. Joseph Seminary, Roman, Romania, March 17, 2010. Questions from the audiences provided a vital contribution to the development of the Franciscan Marian ideas and the importance of

For private consultation and not distribution without the consent of E Ondrako

that there is an affinity between the abstractive and intuitive cognition in Scotus and the notional and real in Newman, which are meant to be employed together. Abstractive cognition, abstracts from actual presence and existence. Intuitive cognition recognizes something as known as present and existing. Abstractive is to the notional as intuitive is to the real. Real assent is indispensible in the quest for truth, for certitude. This compares to the role of intuitive cognition for Scotus. It is involved in the justification of contingent propositions *vis a vis* necessary propositions, disjunctive transcendentals.[43] In other words, Scotus's theory of cognition anticipates the same quest for certitude as Newman's theory of cognition.

In addition, Scotus and Newman were not voluntarists or modernists, although they have been accused of both voluntarism and modernism. Their path and method on the nature of theology leads to strong and not to weak faith. Newman fits what Pope Benedict XVI said about Scotus that he established a harmony between faith and reason by letting himself be guided by the Magisterium.[44] Newman fits Scotus's idea of the nature of theology which accents the primacy of "love rather than speculation."[45] The profound difference between Newman and Scotus with Kant rests on his insistence "on the absolute autonomy of the transcendental 'ego' and on the radically arbitrary irrational indifference of the categorical 'imperative' of the human will in its transcendental lunge toward the infinite 'noumenon.' "[46] Conversely, Scotus risked even his career, in fidelity to the Church's teaching, especially on the Eucharist, Mary, and the authority of the Holy See. The recent Pontiffs seem to wish to incorporate Scotus into reform, renewal, and *ressourcement* [return to the sources] of the Church because he gives answers from humble contemplation of God as love.[47] The

---

a proper understanding of onto-theology. These contributions led to a further fresh approach in the version given at Oxford, November 8, 2010. The March 17 lecture is to be published in the *Franciscan International Study Centre, Canterbury, England, Ex Corde Lecture Series for 2010*.

[43] WOLTER, *The Transcendentals*, 184. Wolter concludes that the theory of the transcendentals is Scotus's metaphysics and is saturated with theological implications.

[44] BENEDICT XVI, *Laetare*.

[45] *Laetare*.

[46] FEHLNER, Durham, 2009, "Opening Address," 16, 17. This is a summary of the difficulty caused by Kant's deformation of truths of the Church's teachings which Scotus had already dealt with in an authentic and faithful way. Reflection on the metaphysical-theological substratum will lead to a satisfying and convincing answer what the difficulty of Kantianism is and why Kantianism it is an attractive force that has spread throughout the world as a profound challenge to belief and is likely to remain with us for some time. See Chapter 16: "Uncoupling Scotus from Kant with Newman's Help," and chapter 17: "Being and Becoming: Hegel's Inversion and Newman's Consistency with Scotus."

[47] *Ressourcément*, a return to the original sources of inspiration, was a slogan at Vatican II.

For private consultation and not distribution without the consent of E Ondrako

parallel to the reasons for the beatification of Newman by Pope Benedict XVI is self-evident.

Element 9. The Franciscan anthropology of Scotus.

In the academy, theological soundings, the anthropological turn, and personalism invite a solid theory of the human person. Theology, where the human person, not God is the starting point, has many premises that are being examined. I understand one purpose of the anthropological turn is to present Catholic theology in a mode that is genuinely vital vis a vis what is perceived by some as a deadening pre-conciliar scholastic version. This view is not without difficulties. In support of a solid theory of man, Richard Cross examines Scotus's contribution which presupposes the immateriality of the soul (Augustine) and phenomenology of the powers united to the body (Aristotle).[48] Keeping in mind the anthropological turn, The Newman-Scotus Reader is intended as a guide both to the premises of Scotus and Newman concerning the will, and to avoid the errors so wide spread today presenting both Scotus and Newman as nominalists and voluntarists.

For Scotus, freedom is of the very essence of willing. His emphasis on the infinite in his metaphysics is mindful of difficulties when metaphysics is not enlightened by Christian faith. William of Ockham, as a Christian theologian reduces the range of Christian philosophical intelligence to such a degree that in many minds who follow him, faith was intact but any hope of achieving, in this life, any philosophical understanding of its intelligible meaning was impossible.[49] A division between realists and nominalists developed.[50] Some refer to Scotus as the end of the *via antiqua* and Ockham the beginning of the *via moderna*.

The great value of the anthropological research of Benedetto Ippolito is his clarity in showing how Scotus is neither nominalist nor voluntarist in dealing with the crucial relation intellect-will vis-a-vis a sound Christian personalism. Ippolito frames the pivotal anthropological question as follows: "is the causal capacity of the human person diminished with respect to that originally possessed by our first parents?"[51] Scotus answers

---

[48] RICHARD CROSS, *Duns Scotus on God*. Aldershot, Hants, UK: Ashgate Publishing, Ltd., 2005.

[49] ETIENNE, GILSON, *History of Christian Philosophy in the Middle Ages*. London: Sheed and Ward, 1955, 498, 499.

[50] OWEN BENNETT, *Metaphysics of Faith and Freedom*. Rensselaer, N.Y.: Conventual Franciscan Publications, 1972, 49–53. Bennett's analysis is on nominalism is in accord with Gilson.

[51] STEPHEN DUMONT, "Theology as a Science and Duns Scotus' Distinction Between Intuitive and Abstractive Cognition" in Speculum 64, n.3 (July 1989), 579–599. This article inspired the reflections of BENEDETTO IPPOLITO, "The Anthropological Foundations of Duns Scotus' Mariology" in *Bl. John Duns Scotus and his Mariology: Acts of the Symposium, Grey College,*

For private consultation and not distribution without the consent of E Ondrako

that "the ontological change does not regard the nature of man, but his effective and existential condition."[52] Ippolito explains:

> The ontological weakening of man due to sin thus refers to man's being, and not to his essence. This means that his transcendence and his unlimited causal power are presently weakened and impoverished in their efficacy, but not suppressed. Man remains naturally inclined toward transcendence, *via* one's own causal power, even though this power is diminished in vigor.[53]

What Ippolito stresses is the importance for Scotus of the relation between intellect and will. The intellect and knowledge which is characteristic of it ultimately is given precisely in order to present to the will the goodness of the Triune Godhead as true and so to be loved for its own sake. For Scotus the primacy of the will does not exclude the integration of the intellect into the will. On the contrary in God as infinitely perfect intellect and will, though formally distinct, are really identical and hence the divine will always acts in an orderly way, such that this mode of acting: sinless, guarantees the reasonableness of contingent beings as well. This consideration leads to a second observation, more often than not overlooked in discussions of the alleged voluntarism of Scotus.

But before making the second point, it is important for the reader to understand that for Scotus, the human person has a causal power that has been reduced because of sin, but retains the practical potential, even with a lesser freedom, to achieve the objective end proper to being human. Newman explains this in the context of striving for holiness throughout his writings. He emphasizes the primacy of sanctification in the work that may be his greatest theological text, the *Lectures on Justification*.[54] Scotus puts the relation of the intellect and will and freedom of the will in the context of the will as the power to self-determine. The responsible exercise of freedom of the will in its contingency and rationality is not something arbitrary. Therefore, every will, even a culpable will, is defined in relation to sanctity and is endowed with an affection for sanctity, no matter how the person with a finite will may act unjustly. Scotus refines this notion of sanctity by two affections of the will which define the will as a pure

---

Durham-England. (Durham, 2009), 157–172. This was one of the Congresses commemorating the death of Bl. Scotus which was organized and published by the Friars of the Immaculate. It was originally to be held the following week after the Oxford Congress, but logistics impaired its realization. It may be called the fifth Congress along with St. Bonaventure University, Oxford, Cologne-Bonn, and Strasbourg-Munich Scotus Congresses.

52 IPPOLITO, (Durham, 2009), 169.

53 IPPOLITO, 170.

54 JOHN HENRY NEWMAN, *Lectures on Justification*. London: Rivingtons, 1874.

For private consultation and not distribution without the consent of E Ondrako

perfection: the *affectus justitiae* and the *affectus commodi*. The affection for justice in the will is the purest in God. Every finite will is defined in relation to what perfects its nature, the *commodum*, or affection for the advantageous. Charity is directly proportionate to the perfection of the *affectus justitiae* of the will. Scotus examines the will as a pure perfection (*perfectio simpliciter simplex*) along with intellect. The pure perfections are found in the divine nature and created persons. The will and intellect in God are perfect, or pure perfections. This is the context in which the finite human person, who cooperates with the gift of grace, because of a formal distinction between intellect and will, has the potential for drawing close to God and sharing directly the very perfection of God's intellect and will.

The second point why Ippolito stresses the importance for Scotus of the relation between intellect and will is related to freedom of the will. Critics of Scotus through the ages seem to misrepresent this critical point. Freedom of the will is not opposed to the perfect necessity of God as being *a se*. Freedom in itself consists not in doing what pleases the will as appetite, or indifference to multiple choices, but in the power to initiate action, that is to act *a se*, and thus act independently, not dependently on the action of some other. Freedom, therefore by Scotus and by Bonaventure before him is contrasted with natural action where the act is determined by something other distinct from the act, even if only formally *a parte rei*. This is why God though immutable loves himself freely and necessarily and why his freedom is never limited by the possibility of sin. At the same time divine action is never arbitrary, whether in loving the divine goodness or those contingent beings made in his image and likeness. It is always rational and orderly. Impeccability is not a limitation of freedom, but an expression of its infinity and perfect rationality, impossible without an intellect fully integrated with the will though formally distinct.

Once these pivotal points are made, then, the cloud of misrepresentations of Scotus's on the will, (or misprisonings of Scotus, which Cyril O'Regan argues in chapter 17, "Scotus the Nefarius: Uncovering Genealogical Sophistications"), can open a new look at the horizon of twenty-first century emphasis on freedom, especially freedom of the will. Here is where Scotus's univocity of the concept of being steps on center stage. It is an understatement to say that univocity of the concept of being is notoriously misunderstood in the academy. Scotus's univocity of the concept of being refines the opposition between being and nothing, exactly what Hegelian inspired thought does not, where Hegelian thought identifies being and becoming (see E. Ondrako, chapter 16, "Being and Becoming: Hegel's Inversion and Newman's Consistency with Scotus"). I have always found this easiest to understand by saying that univocity of the concept of

For private consultation and not distribution without the consent of E Ondrako

being demonstrates that a perfection in a human being, such as will and intellect, shares in something that is eminently perfect in God's will and intellect. Univocal does not mean that the Creator and creature share the same nature or experience or fit into a single category of being. Univocity is a concept that makes all other concepts and categories possible. Scotus's insight into the univocity of the concept of being is of great importance for a sound theological anthropology and has roots in Bonaventure. Fehlner[55] interprets Bonaventure's theory of divine illumination in human cognition, famously discussed in the fourth question of Bonaventure's disputation on the knowledge of Christ (*Questiones disputatae de scientia Christi*) and again in chapters three and five of his *Itinerarium mentis in Deum*, as continuous with the developments in epistemology found in Scotus's use of the univocal concept of being, pure and simple perfections, the formal distinction and common natures. Fehlner's presentation of Bonaventure and Scotus on this point has recently received indirect confirmation in Richard Cross's, *Duns Scotus's Theory of Cognition*.[56] Cross observes:

> At one point Scotus affirms the process of abstraction needs to be underwritten by some extrinsic feature: 'The quiddity of a thing is known in virtue of the agent intellect, which is a participation of the uncreated light, shining on the phantasm.'

Thus, while Scotus, like Bonaventure, affirms the natural integrity of the intellect's activities in apprehension and abstraction as well as discursive reasoning, he explicitly recognizes that simple apprehension and abstraction, while fully natural, require a participation in the uncreated light shining on the material phantasm, presumably for an adequate justification of both the stability and identity of the abstracted quiddity as well as for the mind's ability to come to a certain judgment. This, as Fehlner will argue, is precisely the point of Bonaventure's theory of illumination.[57]

---

[55] See chapter 7, "Scotus and Newman in Dialogue."

[56] RICHARD CROSS, *Duns Scotus's Theory of Cognition*. (Oxford, OUP, 2014), 68. In a note on the same page Cross writes: "I am grateful to Thomas Feeney for discussion on this issue, and for showing me that Scotus does not have a wholly naturalistic account much as I might wish that Pasnau was right: 'This marks a turning point in the history of philosophy, the first great victory for naturalism as a research strategy in the philosophy of mind' [ROBERT PASNAU, Theories of Cognition in the Later Middle Ages. (Cambridge: Cambridge University Press, 1997), 303]. At one point, Scotus contrasts the need for divine light to underwrite abstraction but not ratiocination—which, presumably, functions wholly naturalistically."

[57] I owe a debt of gratitude first to Christian W. Kappes for bringing the passage of R. Cross to the attention of J. Isaac Goff. Second, Goff was most generous in discussing this timely discovery with me in a telephone conversation, November 24, 2014. Richard Cross independently confirms Fehlner's insights into the anthropological and epistemological convergence to be found in the two great Franciscan doctors, Bonaventure and Scotus. See FEHLNER, chapter 4, "Mary and Theology: Scotus Revisited," and chapter 7, "Scotus and Newman in Dialogue," for a fuller explanation of why it is not a substantive change of position, but a

For private consultation and not distribution without the consent of E Ondrako

Being is not something becoming in order not to be nothing. Scotus came to this conclusion because he is a metaphysician-theologian who holds that the *resolutio* of metaphysics needs Revelation.[58] We understand this if we trace how Scotus's pure perfections add metaphysical insight to the biblical insight of Bonaventure. For example, Bonaventure distinguishes creatures, who are *prope Deum* (close to God) and therefore capable of God and a divine mode of living, from those that are *prope nihil* (close to nothingness) and therefore incapable of union with God.[59] Finite persons by nature cannot without grace enjoy the fullness of these perfections. These formally (conceptually) univocal pure perfections are indifferent to being instantiated in infinite or finite modes. However, they are properly and perfectly realized in God's infinite being, and in finite persons are perfected only by grace. That is how they operate in a supernatural, quasi-infinite mode. Maybe the easiest way of understanding the above is to meditate on how the divine persons of the Trinity know and love each other.

The difficulty that has to be clear before proceeding is that the same love is not true of finite persons who are free. This is because they are not impeccable and are limited in what they can will. Finite persons are rendered impeccable only by being permanently elevated to the supernatural order. But such impeccability does not deprive them of freedom because it involves necessity. Necessity, as with the divine persons, defines not the act of loving, but the ontological character of the perfect object of love, the divine goodness. So also contingency defines the ontological character of created being, not the character of willing as voluntary from the intellect as natural in its mode of acting. This is true also in the finite free person, even if without grace incapable of loving God as God loves himself, precisely because the finite will like the divine will is not merely a perfection, but a simply simple perfection or pure perfection, which when perfect is also necessary and immutable.

It ought to be clear why we stress throughout *The Newman-Scotus Reader* that Scotus emphasizes the will as a *pure perfection* which the infinite shares with the finite. Moreover, there is a substratum in *The*

---

subtler position when Scotus replaces Bonaventure's term divine illumination with univocity of the concept of being.

[58] Scotus's teaching that metaphysics needs Revelation for its *resolutio* conflicts with Thomas Aquinas who holds that philosophy at the natural level is complete in itself. Both Bonaventure and Scotus hold a philosophy purely at the natural level cannot be complete, but must find its resolution via faith in Jesus as our Savior and King. The Thomistic position is generally just the opposite.

[59] BONAVENTURE, *Breviloquium*, Part 2, ch. 6, 3. See J. ISAAC GOFF, *Caritas in Primo: A Historical Theological Study of Bonaventure's Questiones Disputatae de Mysterio SS. Trinitatis.* (New Bedford: Academy of the Immaculate, 2015), Afterword by P. D. Fehlner.

For private consultation and not distribution without the consent of E Ondrako

Newman-Scotus Reader that points, in a most compelling manner, to the relation between Scotus and Bonaventure. This critical point is too little appreciated in the academy today. Fortuitously, the gap is being filled by new scholarly work such as the dissertation of J. Isaac Goff who

> convincingly demonstrates the use Bonaventure makes of what Scotus calls univocity of being and the disjunctive transcendentals together with the formal distinction *a parte rei* and the *perfectio simpliciter simplex* as instruments to show how God is one, simple, infinite, eternal, immutable, necessary because triune, and triune and personal precisely because one, simple infinite, eternal, immutable, and necessary. All this converges synthetically on a single term: primacy of essence of all three divine Persons because the Father enjoys a primacy of person as fontal plenitude of charity, origin of the necessary divine processions and ultimately of the contingent divine creation, above all finite persons capable of formally sharing via grace the primacy of charity appropriated by the Holy Spirit.[60]

This element of the anthropology of Scotus and Newman's anthropology is a promising area of research. Given the worry that Pope Benedict XVI[61] has about an anthropological starting point that tends to be exclusive, or nearly exclusive, which I interpret as lending itself to the danger of equivocation, I think it is very important for researchers to remember that neither Scotus nor Newman has a hint of equivocation in his writings. There is a critical question of *interiorization*, or the answer of Scotus that

---

[60] GOFF, *Caritas in Primo*, Afterword. Fehlner's genial summary of Goff's dissertation is a timely complement to *The Newman Scotus-Reader*. It is fortuitous for the scholar who desires to continue serious and sustained research that both books are being published at the same time. Salient points in Fehlner's synthesis of Goff's intentions and dissertation dovetails with the ten elements in this introductory part of *The Newman-Scotus Reader* The substantive points in Element 9, "The Franciscan anthropology of Scotus," in this introduction is a very good example of how to gradually engage a correct reading of Scotus and Newman, to put to rest the vagaries or non-arguments critical of both Scotus and Newman, and to begin to understand why it is a major misrepresentation or misprisoning to think of either of them as nominalists and/or voluntarists. With that clarity, one can read *The Newman-Scotus Reader* in a new light. Then it will be very clear why Goff's dissertation puts to rest that Scotus substantially disagrees with Bonaventure. Goff demonstrates the groundwork for agreement.

[61] Pope Benedict XVI's concerns are the reason that some scholars think that his earlier creative and innovative collaboration with Karl Rahner before and during the Council did not continue. At the same time, there is little doubt about the impact both Pope Benedict's and Rahner's thought has made in the Catholic Church since Vatican II. This parting of ways is sometimes symbolized in the competing views between the authors associated with Continuum and those with Communio, both scholarly journals. Pope Benedict XVI is the quintessential catechist, while Rahner's theological soundings with his anthropological turn, as an academic enterprise, requires the examination of several premises. Both Pope Benedict and Rahner have a treasure trove for further research.

For private consultation and not distribution without the consent of E Ondrako

the ontological change, the weakening because of sin, does not regard the nature of man, but his effective and existential condition. Newman is close to Scotus here and far from the exercise of the gift of freedom as self-will in an arbitrary manner.

By entering into the heart, Scotus and Newman exemplify what it means to have causality, to have practical potential, and to possess freedom. In short, this is how they understood what it means to be intellectually humble and to sanctify one's intellect. Newman's works show that he dreaded the opposite, a proud, autonomous willfulness that veils the darkness of skepticism. I find this dread very evident and moving in his sermon, "The Parting of Friends," preached in September 1843. That is when he stepped away from active ministry for a while to sort out his questions which gave him the space to compose his masterpiece on doctrinal development with its seven criteria: preservation of type, continuity of principles, power of assimilation of ideas, early anticipations of later teaching, logical sequence, preservation of earlier teaching, and chronic vigour. In his manner of formulating the seven notes, Newman seems very close to Scotus on entering into the heart. Prior to embarking on this quest for Truth, he delivered an emotionally laden sermon. Newman said:

> 'All things come of Thee, and of Thine own have we given Thee,' (I Chron. 14: 14). If we have had the rain in its season, and the sun shining in its strength, and the fertile ground, it is of Thee. We give back to Thee what came from Thee. … How vain are all our pains, our thought, our care, unless God uses them, has inspired them! how worse than fruitless are they, unless directed to His glory, and given back to the Giver! … Oh loving friends, should you know anyone whose lot it has been, by writing or by word of mouth, in some degree to help you thus to act; if he has ever told you what you knew about yourselves, or what you did not know; has read to you your wants or feelings, … or has made you feel that there was a higher life than this daily one, and a brighter world than what you see, … or opened a way to the inquiring, … though you hear him not, … pray for him, that in all things he may know God's will, and at all times he may be ready to fulfill it.[62]

In sum, element nine addresses Scotus's anthropological thought and gives key ideas on how to call attention to considerations indispensable for appreciating why Scotus is not a voluntarist in the sense of Ockham, Kant

---

[62] JOHN HENRY NEWMAN, "The Parting of Friends," *Sermons on Subjects of the Day* (London: Longmans, Green, and Co., 1918), 397–398. 409.

For private consultation and not distribution without the consent of E Ondrako

or Hegel, considerations more often than not overlooked in most discussions of these questions. The reader searching for a fair minded scholarly presentation of the competing views, will find in Richard Cross[63] a genealogical overview of the origins of modernity that avoids misrepresentations and confusions on the level of implicit causal conditions for modern metaphysics. Cross lays out the contours of Thomas Aquinas's theory, which John Milbank appears to want to defend, and presents a narrative of why and how a close reading of Scotus and Suárez can help diagnose difficulties. I found that if Cross's approach to the study of metaphysics in this article is juxtaposed to that of Olivier Boulnois[64] one will have ample material to engage in a meaningful dialogue about modern metaphysics. Inspired by Scotus, Boulnois answers how theology determines metaphysics simply by liberating metaphysics and allowing theology to accomplish its proper ends. Theology does not dictate the contents of metaphysics, but simply requires metaphysics to be a distinct science by itself. For Scotus, "the more theology is distinguished from metaphysics, the more metaphysics is in need of it."

This excursus enables the reader to begin to see early in *The Newman-Scotus Reader* that there is a critical foundation for making the claim that there are striking similarities in the thought patterns of Scotus and Newman. Scotistic metaphysics centers on the univocity of being and the disjunctive transcendentals, together with the primacy of will and charity. Second, at the level of epistemology, we will find Newman making many points of contact with the views of Bonaventure. Conscience and the existence of God is at the heart of the 'anthropological proof.' In this vein, the similar contours of Scotus's and Newman's theological reflection dovetail with those of Newman and Bonaventure. Here the understanding of Christian philosophy which Bonaventure and Scotus were accustomed to rests on the fruit of the contemplation of Truth, of walking in the light which is Divine. Newman summarized in his chosen epitaph: *ex umbris et imaginibus in veritatem* (out of the shadows and images towards the Truth).[65]

---

[63] Richard Cross, "Duns Scotus and Suárez at the Origins of Modernity," in *Deconstructing Radical Orthodoxy: Postmodern Theology, Rhetoric and Truth*. Wayne J. Hankey and Douglas Hedley, eds. (Aldershot, Hants, UK: Ashgate Publishing Ltd., 2005, ch. 5, 65-80.

[64] Olivier Boulnois, "La nouvelle structure de la métaphysique," in *Être et représentation*. (Paris: PUF, 1999, rpt. 2008), ch 9. , 457-504, here 477-478.

[65] As *The Newman-Scotus Reader* was going to press, the President of St. Bonaventure University, Sr. Margaret Carney, brought to my attention Daniel P. Horan, *Postmodernity and Univocity: A Critical Account of Radical Orthodoxy and John Duns Scotus*. (Lanham: Fortress Press, 2014). The summary states: Horan "offers a substantial challenge to the narrative of Radical Orthodoxy's idiosyncratic take on Scotus and his role in ushering in the philosophical age of the modern." No reviews have been published at this time.

For private consultation and not distribution without the consent of E Ondrako

Element 10. "Mary and Theology: Scotus Revisited."[66]

Repetition is the mother of learning. Scotus and Newman engage the problem of the unity of knowledge, that is, scientific and eternal wisdom. They employ the philosophical method which includes epistemology to find and to study the light that illumines. What the light illumines is part of the science of metaphysics. If the light is too dim or bright, what it illumines is affected. Too much light washes out what is being illumined, i.e. the metaphysical questions. Metaphysical exemplarism is at the heart of the structure of Franciscan philosophy and theology. St. Francis is the exemplar for recognizing and contemplating the beauty and goodness of the Creator in creation. The temptation in modernity is to seek scientific proofs. Theology remains dogmatic and authoritative but offers intelligible replies to anti-dogmatic arguments. For example, there is a unity in the teaching of Scotus on the Immaculate Conception in relation to Bonaventure's three modes of theology, which are: the study of the creeds; what is proper or today is known as academic integrity; and the contemplative dimension, which is often overlooked by practitioners of pure science.

Few who are familiar with this Franciscan School and the Dominican School and other tried and tested theological Schools seem to argue with the observation that a major problem today is the breaking up of theology into unrelated parts and method by the neglect of the metaphysical. This means that the careful study of 'what is,' in the work of advancing theological knowledge is at a disadvantage. The problem is compounded by the relative independence of scientific knowledge *vis a vis* Christ the one teacher of all, and the specific characteristics of theological method set forth by Scotus and Newman. Fortunately, there are many scholars who share the conviction of Fehlner in his three *caveats* about studying Newman's thought.

First, Newman's ideas are not radically subjectivism in pious form. Second, the term 'unscientific' character in theology as practiced during a time of pilgrimage, means doing theology on one's knees. Unscientific does not mean anti-intellectual and is equally applicable to Newman and Scotus. Third, it is a misreading of Newman's epistemology to conclude that he calls into question the immutable character of revelation and dogma. Such a reading would make Newman a modernist which the Vatican clearly denied during the so called modernist crisis in the early twentieth century.

In sum, whether it is the theological activity of the Magisterium or the theological activity of faithful believers, the purpose is the same,

---

66 Chapter 4 in this volume.

For private consultation and not distribution without the consent of E Ondrako

clarification and explicitation. Nowhere is this as clear and imperative as the question of doctrines developing and pertaining to Mary. How do we know if it is a true development or a false development of doctrine? For Newman, there is a basis for enlightenment how one makes an illation between what is implicit to what is explicit about doctrine. That basis is faith. In this light, the proper understanding of the reform and renewal intended by Vatican II is continuity rather than discontinuity with the *depositum fidei*.[67]

Summary: Scotus on the primacy of Christ and the motive of the Incarnation.

God intends that all mankind shall see the salvation of God. All mankind shall understand the absolute primacy of Christ and the primacy of Mary, for without her free assent to become Mother of God, Christ could not have become incarnate of one who, according to the discovery of Scotus, was redeemed in a preservative mode and not liberative as all of the other baptized. The principle of philosophy: what is first in intention is last in execution, demonstrates how her preservative redemption took place. God planned from all eternity to share God's most perfect love by creation and had a remedy at hand. That means: prior to the creation of the world, the angels, Adam and Eve in the garden, in the event that Adam and Eve did not pass the test, a remedy was at hand. That remedy means that the Mother of God was preserved from original sin in the intention of God from all eternity. Therefore, although she was born in Adam's line, she was preserved from original sin and her Son, in time, is born after her, but his merits preserved her. That is not difficult metaphysical thought to understand for people who live their faith and reason cautiously. Scotus gave the reasons for the possibility that Mary was conceived without sin, the *potuit*. More important, he gave the reasons for the fittingness, the *decuit*, the fruit of his understanding of what St. Francis must have experienced in his love for the *Virgo Ecclesia facta*, the Virgin made Church.[68] The thought patterns of Scotus and Newman converge on this most important point. Newman gives explicit agreement to Scotus's theological synthesis of the

---

[67] BL. JOHN XXIII, "Opening Address" at Vatican II, October 11, 1962. The Holy Father made it very clear that the intention of the Council was to preserve and to teach the deposit of the Catholic faith in a manner that was more understandable to the contemporary mind.

[68] It is arguable that God gave St. Francis as a gift to the world so that the Immaculate Conception would be defined. His theologian disciples took his mind and spirit to responsible theological heights and insights which were recognized by the authority of the Church, the Magisterium, in God's time. Bl. Pope Pius IX gave the definitive teaching in the encyclical *Ineffabilis Deus*, December 8, 1854.

For private consultation and not distribution without the consent of E Ondrako

absolute primacy of Christ and its bearing on the Immaculate Conception and sacramentality of creation.

Summary: Newman and the complex process of apprehension and argumentation.

It may sound obvious to say that Newman has to be understood well, patronizing to say that he is an easy target to take out of context, and exclusivist to say that only the Newman-Scotus reading is the most accurate one. "Mary and Theology: Scotus Revisited," shows what theological activity is and that the heart of scotistic theology and Newman's theology is *faith* as a source of certainty. Theology differs from science. At the natural level it is an indistinct encounter with the teacher, while at the supernatural level, where the discipline of theology takes place, the encounter with the teacher is profoundly personal. Newman's life radiates this intensely personal quest for truth. The challenges of his times are readily accessible to the reader. The following passage from his speech upon being honored as a Cardinal captures the profile of a person who is loyal to faith and lives it.

> In the long course of years, I have made many mistakes. I have nothing of that high perfection which belongs to the writings of the Saints, viz., that error cannot be found in them; but what I trust that I may claim all through what I have written, is this, – an honest intention, an absence of private ends, a temper of obedience, a willingness to be corrected, a dread of error, a desire to serve Holy Church, and through Divine mercy, a fair measure of success.[69]

Newman's candor and loyalty to truth did not keep him from criticizing Catholics for having alienated religious minds,[70] nor the absence of devotion meaning not necessarily founded on faith. He was critical of confusing what it meant to attend Protestant or Catholic Churches and fraternizing but with the absence of any views at all of doctrine in common.[71] He called this form of privatization of religion as the great *apostosia*, an "error overspreading as a snare, the whole earth."[72] His conclusion, in the *Grammar of Assent*, is what satisfies and convinces him in religious matters may satisfy and convince another.[73] Such an approach

---

[69] JOHN HENRY NEWMAN, "BigliettoSpeech," 63.

[70] JOHN HENRY NEWMAN, "Letter to the Duke of Norfolk," *Difficulties of Anglicans II* (uniform edition, 1900), 176.

[71] BIGLIETTO, 65.

[72] BIGLIETTO, 65.

[73] *Grammar of Assent*, ch. 10.

For private consultation and not distribution without the consent of E Ondrako

in a secularized western world flies in the face of widespread cynicism by being compassionate, personalist, understanding, with a peaceful trust that truth wins because it is truth.

Conclusion to the excursus: using an anthropological 'arc' to love in an orderly way

One line from the *Spectator*,[74] immediately after Newman's death in 1890, draws out how the newspaper writer understands Newman's spiritual interests. It draws out an insight about *interiorization*." What the writer for the *Spectator* observed about Newman, may be said about Scotus.

> Never surely was there an intellect which combined a happier and more delicate insight into the concrete side of life, with a larger and more daring grasp of its abstract truths, and of that fine and intricate middle region which connects the logic of facts with the logic of understanding.[75]

However inspirational this newspaper account may be, there is much more than logic at work in the lives and writings of Newman and Scotus. There is something more than pious sentiment that lifts up the mind and heart to spiritual thought. Scotus saw it in the ontological change, the weakening of man due to sin that does not regard the nature of man, but his effective and existential situation. While the transcendence and unlimited causal power of the human person is weakened in efficacy, it is not suppressed. The human person has a reduced causal power, but practical potential and freedom, which is naturally inclined toward transcendence.[76] This Scotistic view joins the Newmanian view. Both incorporate the dynamic liberty for entering into the heart, while being intellectually humble, so as to sanctify one's intellect, *interiorization*. It seems to come down to the difference between the absolute power of willing and ordered willing. There is a difference between finite will (with a simple and complex element) and divine will, purely simple and never disordered. Said differently, *God always loves in an orderly manner.* That is why Bl. Newman joins Bl. Scotus in this approach to love and unconditional docility, i.e. the contemplative character of the intellect and primacy of the will.

---

[74] JOHN HENRY NEWMAN, *Letters and Diaries*, 32: 629–630.

[75] *LD* 32: 630.

[76] IPPOLITO, 169–172.

For private consultation and not distribution without the consent of E Ondrako

CHAPTER I

Newman's Reasonable Approach to Faith

John T. Ford [1]

Newman sought a via media—a middle ground—between "evidentialists," who considered reason supreme and so disparaged faith, and "existentialists," who wanted to create a fortress of faith impenetrable to reason. From examining the way people actually think, Newman identified three types of inference—formal, informal, natural—that lead people to make decisions. Informal inference, which is operative in the decisions of everyday life, serves as a paradigm for understanding how the human mind—particularly the illative sense—operates in religious matters; accordingly, Newman presents faith as a personal and reasonable inference.

In the tug of war between faith and reason that came to characterize much of the discussion about and between science and religion in the latter half of the 19th century—a debate that often pitted scientists against ecclesiastics and vice versa—Newman characteristically sought a *via media*: a "middle road" between the rationalistic champions of reason and the fideistic defenders of faith.

Among the champions of reason were "evidentialists" who insisted that it is basically unreasonable for anyone to assent to anything unless it can be rationally demonstrated through human reason alone; "evidentialism," when carried to its logical conclusion, considered reason supreme and allowed little, if any, room for faith. As John Macquarrie has observed:

> In the earlier phases of the Enlightenment, it was believed that reason could encompass even God, and that natural theology,

---

[1] John T. Ford, c.s.c., Professor of Theology and Religious Studies at The Catholic University of America, presented this paper at the Newman-Scotus Symposium, October 22–24, at the Washington Theological Union, Takoma Park, MD; this essay is a revision of an article with the same title that was published in Newman Studies Journal 8/1 (Spring 2011): 56–66.

For private consultation and not distribution without the consent of E Ondrako

based on reason alone, could discover all the fundamental religious truths that had been taught on the basis of the Bible.[2]

In contrast, among the defenders of faith were "existentialists" who insisted that the heart has motives, that the imagination has visions and that the mind has symbols, which can never be completely demonstrated nor entirely understood by human reason; this type of "existentialism," when carried to its confident conclusion, tried to create a fortress for faith impervious to human reason.

During the formative years of his life, Newman came into contact with advocates of both positions, yet he eventually concluded that neither of these positions was sustainable; evidentialists and existentialists might strenuously defend their respective positions in public, but each of these positions was basically a "paper tiger"—an imaginary and sometimes aggressive animal constructed in theory, but not really attainable in fact. Neither evidentialists nor existentialists could really substantiate their claims.

On the one hand, evidentialists—much to their chagrin yet unlikely to concede the fact—ultimately had to rely on faith; for example, scientific hypotheses inherently have faith-like premises that cannot be absolutely verified and so may eventually be discredited and then peremptorily discarded in favor of new and more promising explanatory paradigms.[3] On the other hand, existentialists, sometimes to their embarrassment, found that they could not stifle reasonable questions by appealing to faith alone and so were eventually forced to appeal to reason; for example, evangelicals needed some way of explaining the incongruities and inconsistencies of Scripture; however, their fideistic explanations could not always stand close scrutiny, leaving the problems that their faith-stance was meant to solve more formidable than ever.[4]

Where then can an ordinary person—not only a philosopher or theologian, not only a scientist or intellectual, but an ordinary person—find a way to balance reason and faith? Such a balance requires a strategic starting point: where should a person begin investigating the relationship of reason and faith?

---

[2] JOHN MACQUARRIE, "Newman and Kierkegaard on the Act of Faith," in *Newman and Conversion*, edited by Ian Ker (Notre Dame, IN: University of Notre Dame Press, 1997), 76; henceforth cited: Macquarrie.

[3] THOMAS S. KUHN, *The Structure of Scientific Revolutions* (Chicago: University of Chicago Press, 1970) has pointed out that scientific theories sometimes collapse in light of new discoveries; as a result, an out-dated scientific paradigm is abandoned and a new one adopted.

[4] For example, see the fundamentalist attempt of GLEASON L. ARCHER, *Reseña Crítica de una Introducción al Antiguo Testamento* (Grand Rapids, MI: Portavoz, 1987), 200–219, to reconcile the creation accounts of Genesis with modern scientific evidence.

For private consultation and not distribution without the consent of E Ondrako

Reasoning as Inferential Process

Newman was aware that many continental philosophers and theologians started their intellectual inquiry by describing the faculties of the human mind—reason, both theoretical and practical; understanding; imagination, etc.—and then asking: what is the proper function of each? In effect, many European intellectuals began their inquiry into the relationship of faith and reason with the question: how *should* we think? In contrast, Newman, in tandem with the British empirical tradition, began with a more practical question: how *do* we think? Newman's answer was both profoundly simple and simply profound: we ask questions, we consider data, we come to conclusions.[5]

First of all, sometimes this process of asking questions, considering data, coming to conclusions—which Newman called "inference"—is instantaneous; for example, I see "smoke" and immediately conclude: "fire." In fact, I may later discover that what I first thought was smoke coming from a fire was really an unusual cloud-formation—a mistake that is a salutary reminder that my spontaneous judgments are sometimes dead-wrong. Indeed, such instantaneous "natural" inferences can easily get a person in trouble: if there can be love at first sight, there can also be hate at first sight—either of which may later prove to be seriously mistaken.[6]

Second, while some human judgments are instantaneous or nearly so, sometimes the process of inference takes an inordinate amount of time—like waiting for the other shoe to drop—a person senses a problem, but needs time to formulate a precise question; a person carefully selects and mulls over data; a person ponders a variety of options before making a decision: the more important the decision, the more likely a person is to take a long time to decide. A prime example of such a prolonged inferential process was Newman's decision to become a Roman Catholic—a painstaking and painful process—that took him a half-dozen years to work through the data and come to a conclusion.[7]

Third, sometimes an inferential process is rigorously logical—when, for example, the process can be reduced to a syllogism, such as: "if a=b and b=c, then a=c."[8] The supreme advantage of logical or formal inference

---

[5] See Newman's discussion of "modes of holding propositions" in his *An Essay in Aid of a Grammar of Assent*, 3–8 (available on line at: http://www.newmanreader.org/works/grammar/index.html; subsequent references are to this on-line edition); henceforth cited: *Grammar*.

[6] See Newman's discussion of "natural inference" in his *Grammar*, 330–342.

[7] See Newman's description of his gradual disenchantment with the Church of England and his eventual acceptance of Roman Catholicism (1839–1845) in his *Apologia Pro Vita Sua*, 92–237 (available at: http://www.newmanreader.org/works/apologia65/index.html); henceforth cited: *Apologia*.

[8] See Newman's discussion of logical or "formal inference" in his *Grammar*, 259–287.

For private consultation and not distribution without the consent of E Ondrako

is that everyone arrives at exactly the same conclusion. Why? First, the data—usually quantifiable—are the same for all; second, the same process is employed by everyone; third, the conclusion is universally acceptable—at least to all those who accept the initial premises, the data and the method. This is precisely the type of process that the "evidentialists" of Newman's day—and the technologists and technocrats of our own—wanted to have: a sure-fire process of arriving at a conclusion that is completely certain and so acceptable to everyone.[9]

Such a certainty-achieving process is commonly available in the case of mathematics and formal logic; however, it is not quite so readily available in the physical sciences, where the mass of data is often overwhelmingly complex for every individual datum to be carefully examined and fitted into its appropriate place and where the methods are multiple and possibly contravening; as a result, not every possible outcome can be anticipated and so the final result cannot be predicted with complete certainty.

On the one hand, in the case of scientific experiments and techno-logical projects, sometimes some of the data can be safely disregarded as inconsequential; for example, a nuclear physicist may not need to be overly concerned about an "aberrant electron," if all of the other electrons are on target. On the other hand, what was originally deemed an inconsequential deficiency may easily turn into a monumental disaster, as has unfortunately happened in the space program on more than one occasion.[10]

Newman's crucial contention was—whether we are balancing our check-books, designing a space-shuttle, buying a new car, or deciding to become a Catholic—that the process follows the same paradigm: we start with a question, we consider the available data, and we make a decision.[11] In every inference, the critical and crucial part is the "middle term"—the data-phase, which may be instantaneous—as in the smoke-fire inference—or interminable: Newman could have postponed deciding whether to become a Roman Catholic for the rest of his life. The infer-

---

[9] Newman pointed out that we are "certain" in different ways: in his terminology, "certainty" describes the state of mind that results from formal or logical inferences, while "certitude" refers to the state of mind that results from informal or real inferences (*Grammar*, 210–258).

[10] On the one hand, it is impossible to be completely certain that a space launch will be successful; there is always an element of risk; the best that scientists can do is minimize that risk as much as possible. On the other hand, the space program has been so successful that people are surprised when launches go amiss.

[11] Even the decision not to make a decision—which at times is the best decision—follows this paradigm: I ask a question, I collect data, however, when I examine the data available, I conclude that I do not want to make a decision on the basis of the data presently available. Accordingly, I may not make a decision or I may defer a decision until I acquire more data that warrant my making a decision.

For private consultation and not distribution without the consent of E Ondrako

ential process thus may range from concise and clear-cut to complicated and confusing.

Moreover, while the "middle term"—"if b=c" in the case of a logical syllogism (if a=b, and b=c, then a=c)—can usually be stated in a neat and tidy way, in the case of practical every-day decisions, the data-phase has three inter-locking stages—which are sometimes simultaneous but which are really three different tasks or steps:

Data-collecting: what data are important?

Data-arranging: how do the data relate to each other?

Data-evaluating: what pattern emerges from the data?[12]

Although we use such a process multiple times each day, the process is so habitual, that we rarely notice what we are implicitly doing, much less stop to analyze the process.[13] Most of all, we may fail to notice how personal this process really is in practical matters.[14] Moreover, the inferential process is discretionary—like Sherlock Holmes searching for clues until they all make "elementary" sense: "elementary" both in the sense that all the "elements" fit together and in the sense that the final decision is "elementary"—simple and clear—at least to the detective or decision-maker.

Personal Inference

This personal dimension of what Newman called "informal inference" can be illustrated by that most energizing and exasperating example of American enterprises: buying a car.[15] Some years ago, I needed a new car and began by stopping at various dealerships and picking up their glossy advertisements: Chevy Cavalier, Dodge Dart, Ford Fairlane, etc. In other words, my first step was data-collecting. My choice soon narrowed to a Ford Fairlane, which was the right size (at least for me), with an attractive design (again for me), and within my budget. One might note

---

12 By way of comparison, some academic disciplines use a prosopographical approach in which statistical data are obtained and then examined in their inter-relationships within a specific historical, social, cultural or literary context: ideally, these inter-relationships will emerge from the data rather the data being fitted to pre-conceived categories.

13 See Newman's discussion of practical or "informal inference" in his *Grammar*, 288–329.

14 While Newman's Grammar was focused on an individual's mental activities, FREDERICK D. AQUINO, Communities of Informed Judgment: Newman's Illative Sense and Accounts of Rationality (Washington, DC: Catholic University of America Press, 2004), has pointed out that the dynamics involved may be extrapolated to communal decisions.

15 According to USA Today Snapshots (Thursday, 21 October 2010, 1B), most men find the process of buying a new vehicle "rewarding," while most women find it "time consuming."

For private consultation and not distribution without the consent of E Ondrako

that the data-collecting stage usually involves personal factors (my needs and preferences) as well as objective data (provided by the manufacturer's manuals).

The next step was to visit a Ford dealership. There was a Fairlane in stock—just what I wanted; however, after spending a couple hours, looking at the car inside and out, ritually kicking the tires, as well as going on a test-drive, I hesitated; and the more I hesitated, the more extras the salesman added: rust-proofing, fabric-proofing, extended warranty—and best of all, price-reduction. I still hesitated, until the salesman pleaded: "I can't give you a better deal." The salesman couldn't believe that I wasn't going to buy the car: it had everything that I wanted and the price was rock-bottom. The catch for me: the car was baby-blue—which in my opinion is a nice color for babies—but I could not see myself driving a baby blue car for the next half-dozen years or more. No sale. In effect, my personal preference had trumped all the objective arguments in favor of purchasing that particular car.

What this story indicates about "informal inference" is that when it comes to making practical decisions, there may be a single sticking point, a poison pill, a decisive deal-killer. Yet, what may be the deal-killer for one person may be the deal-maker, the selling point, the sweetener, for another person. In retrospect, I regret that I didn't ask the salesman to let me know who bought that baby-blue Fairlane, so I could find out why what was a sticking point for me, was a selling point for someone else—perhaps the color did not matter or the color might even have been the selling point—if baby blue was the purchaser's favorite color. The lesson: the very same datum that can derail an inferential process for one person can facilitate the process for another person.

In any case, in making practical inferences about matters of daily life, we go through the same process: collecting data—getting information about cars; examining data—test-driving a car; and evaluating data—when the salesman asked me: "what would it take to put you behind the wheel of this car?" I found myself answering: "a car of a different color."[16] Our personal evaluation of the data thus becomes the key factor in our decision-making.

---

[16] See Newman's remarks about "an accumulation of probabilites," as leading to faith in his Grammar, 411; in regard to the blue car, the "probabilities" did not converge for me, but they did for the person who eventually purchased the car.

For private consultation and not distribution without the consent of E Ondrako

"Three Protestants"

For Newman, the way we make practical decisions in everyday life parallels the way we make decisions in religious matters. In his *Grammar of Assent*, Newman provided the example of "three Protestants"—who bear an uncanny resemblance to the three Newman brothers:[17] "… of three Protestants, one becomes a Catholic, a second a Unitarian, and a third an unbeliever: how is this?"

Newman explained why the first Protestant—presumably himself—became a Catholic:

> The first becomes a Catholic, because he assented, as a Protestant, to the doctrine of our Lord's divinity, with a real assent and a genuine conviction, and because this certitude, taking possession of his mind, led him on to welcome the Catholic doctrines of the Real Presence and of the Theotokos, till his Protestantism fell off from him, and he submitted himself to the Church.[18]

Newman next described the religious position of the second Protestant—presumably his brother Francis:

> The second became a Unitarian, because, proceeding on the principle that Scripture was the rule of faith and that a man's private judgment was its rule of interpretation, and finding that the doctrine of the Nicene and Athanasian Creeds did not follow by logical necessity from the text of Scripture, he said to himself, "The word of God has been made of none effect by the traditions of men," and therefore nothing was left for him but to profess what he considered primitive Christianity, and to become a Humanitarian.[19]

Newman then described the intellectual journey of the third person—presumably his brother Charles—from Protestantism to Deism to Atheism:

> The third gradually subsided into infidelity, because he started with the Protestant dogma, cherished in the depths of his nature, that a priesthood was a corruption of the simplicity of the Gospel. First, then, he would protest against the sacrifice of the Mass; next he gave up baptismal regeneration, and the sacramental principle; then he asked himself whether dogmas were not a

---

[17] The three Newman brothers were: John Henry (1801–1890), Charles Robert (1802–1884) and Francis William (1805–1897).

[18] *Grammar*, 245.

[19] *Grammar*, 245–246.

For private consultation and not distribution without the consent of E Ondrako

restraint on Christian liberty as well as sacraments; then came the question, what after all was the use of teachers of religion? Why should anyone stand between him and his Maker? After a time it struck him, that this obvious question had to be answered by the Apostles, as well as by the Anglican clergy; so he came to the conclusion that the true and only revelation of God to man is that which is written on the heart. This did for a time, and he remained a Deist. But then it occurred to him, that this inward moral law was there within the breast, whether there was a God or not, and that it was a roundabout way of enforcing that law, to say that it came from God, and simply unnecessary, considering it carried with it its own sacred and sovereign authority, as our feelings instinctively testified; and when he turned to look at the physical world around him, he really did not see what scientific proof there was there of the Being of God at all, and it seemed to him as if all things would go on quite as well as at present, without that hypothesis as with it; so he dropped it, and became a *purus, putus* Atheist.[20]

Newman's comparison of the "three Protestants" seemingly presupposes a common family background: in the Newman family, all three brothers were raised in a Bible-reading middle-class Anglican home typical of the early part of the 19th century.[21]

However, even if the three brothers basically shared the same religious environment at an earlier stage in their lives, they eventually began to examine the history and doctrines of Christianity in a critical way. Such a critical examination ultimately led Newman to Roman Catholicism; however, it was neither an easy process, nor a foregone conclusion. As he later narrated the "history of my religious opinions" in his *Apologia pro vita sua* (1864), Newman passed through at least four stages of "religious opinions": first, a passing flirtation with rationalism as a teenager; next, conversion to evangelicalism at the time that he entered Oxford as an undergraduate; then, an attraction to the Liberalism of the Oriel College "Noetics";[22] finally, a growing commitment to Catholicism, first Anglican and later Roman. Had Newman stopped at the stage of his juvenile rationalism, he might have become an agnostic or atheist like his brother

---

[20] *Grammar*, 246–247.

[21] See Newman's brief description of his youth in his *Apologia*, 1.

[22] The "Oriel Noetics" were a group of dons at Oriel College (Oxford) in the early part of the 19th century, who took a rational approach to religious matters; see WILFRID WARD, *Life of Cardinal Newman* 1: 36 (available at: http://www.newmanreader.org/biography/ward/volume1/chapter2.html).

For private consultation and not distribution without the consent of E Ondrako

Charles; or had he succumbed to the allurement of Liberalism, he might have become a Humanitarian or a Unitarian like his brother Francis.

Even though the quite different religious journeys of the three Newman brothers had a common starting point, once they left the religious environment of their family, the three brothers encountered a variety of competing religious doctrines which claimed their attention and sought their allegiance.[23]   In effect, the three brothers were confronted with a seemingly endless smorgasbord of religious options that implicitly asked each of the brothers to decide: which data are important?   Each of the brothers arranged the information about Christianity in a different way; this is not to say that the data available were completely different; what each brother did was to arrange the data in a way that was for him the most personally persuasive pattern.   Like Scrabble-players with the same tiles, Charles arranged the data to spell Atheism, Francis arranged the data to spell Unitarianism, and John Henry arranged the data to spell Catholicism.   In other words, it was not a case of data that were different; rather the three brothers viewed and evaluated the same data differently.

Considering the three Newman brothers as prototypical examples of responses to the question of the relationship of reason and faith, one might say that agnostics and atheists focus entirely on reason and so demand an absolutely convincing rational demonstration for the existence of God—a type of proof that simply doesn't exist; if such a proof were available, faith would basically be the product of reason.   Similarly, Humanists and Unitarians want divine revelation to align with their own intellectual perspectives, effectively wanting a god created to their own image and likeness; such a humanly constructed god would effectively be an immanent idol, not a transcendent divinity.

In contrast, Catholics are willing to accept divine revelation, not because it is understandable in a rational way, but because revelation is a divine communication backed by the authority of God revealing.[24]   The decision to accept divine revelation is then not the result of a rational process where human reason can notionally prove the existence of revela-

---

[23] See Charles Reding's entertaining discussion with the "Irvingites and other Visitors" in Newman's *Loss and Gain*, 387–401 (available at: http://www.newmanreader.org/works/gain/index.html).

[24] See the description of faith provided by the First Vatican Council (1870): "virtutem esse supernaturalem, qua, Dei aspirante et adiuvante gratia, ab eo revelata vera esse credimus non propter intrinsecam rerum veritatem naturali rationis lumine perspectam, sed propter auctoritatem ipsius Dei revelantis, qui nec falli nec fallere potest" (Denzinger, Enchiridion Symbolorum, § 1789): "the supernatural virtue, whereby, with the aid and assistance of divine grace, we believe what has been revealed to be true, not because of the intrinsic truth of the matter as perceived by the natural light of reason, but because of the authority of the revealing God, who can neither deceive nor be deceived" (my translation).

For private consultation and not distribution without the consent of E Ondrako

tion or completely understand revelation, but a decision that is nonetheless reasonable, because the doctrinal data of revelation are seen by believers as divinely warranted. As Macquarrie has emphasized, faith "demands more than factual information"; "faith is in its very nature the acceptance of what our reason cannot reach"; and so faith entails "a recognition that truths that are spiritually discerned may not be amenable to being fully spelled out in words."[25]

For Newman, while personal inference involves an endless variety of practical matters, the process of personal inference follows the same pattern or paradigm—whether we are thinking practically, as in the case of purchasing a car, or whether we are reasoning theoretically or whether we are pondering the natural world or whether we are contemplating the supernatural: we ask questions, we examine data and we come to a conclusion.

Christian Initiation as Inferential Process

The inferential process of moving from questions about Catholicism to examining information about Catholicism to deciding to become a Roman Catholic is an integral, though somewhat implicit, part of the Rite of Christian Initiation for Adults (RCIA).[26]

The majority of participants concludes the RCIA program by entering the Roman Catholic Church—satisfied that they are making the right decision. Indeed, the very fact that the participants enrolled in the RCIA program made it antecedently probable that they would not only finish the program, but become Roman Catholics.

Occasionally, however, an RCIA participant will hesitate, perhaps saying: "all of the presentations have been very informative, making Christianity much more understandable, but I am not yet ready to become a Catholic." Sometimes RCIA teachers are taken aback when this happened; however, an RCIA participant's hesitation does not necessarily mean that the teacher has not taught the classes well or that the discussions have not answered the participants' questions. In fact, the reverse may well be true: a person may have been helped to understand exactly what initiation into Christianity means: a commitment to follow Christ; but that person may also perceive that he or she is not yet ready to make such a commitment.

---

25 MACQUARRIE, 80, 82.

26 For information on the RCIA, see: http://www.nccbuscc.org/comm/archives/rciaq&a98.shtml.

For private consultation and not distribution without the consent of E Ondrako

An RCIA teacher, of course, may instinctively ask: what could I do to convince this person? The answer is often: nothing. Like a car salesman who makes the best pitch possible, an RCIA teacher can only present the doctrines of Christianity in the most persuasive way: showing how Christian doctrines fit together both as intellectually convincing and as a practical way of leading a meaningful life and inviting RCIA-participants to experience aspects of the Christian life. In other words, while the doctrines of Christianity can be objectively taught and while people can experience various aspects of Christian community, the decision to be a Christian essentially depends on a process of personal inference about the way one wants to live one's life.

Thus, the RCIA is always an invitation; there is no way that even the most eloquent presentation can persuade an RCIA participant to become a Catholic, if that person comes to the conclusion that Christianity doesn't fit together—either intellectually or practically or both. Sometimes a person's reluctance may be motivated by a refusal to accept Christian moral teachings; sometimes a person's reluctance may stem from objections to specific Catholic doctrines; or sometimes, like the prospect of owning a baby blue car, an RCIA participant may simply feel that Christianity is not appealing at this time; perhaps this response is temporary or perhaps it will be permanent. In other words, faith must fit this person.

In a sense, every RCIA participant reacts to Christian doctrine like one or other of the three Newman brothers: one participant may see and accept the pattern of Catholicism; another may be unconvinced and choose Unitarianism, Humanitarianism, Agnosticism, or Atheism. What is the selling point for one participant may be the sticking point for another. An RCIA teacher is like a foreign language instructor who tries to teach students grammar and vocabulary. Most students learn sufficient grammar and vocabulary to be able to pass an exam; some, however, may never learn to read or speak the language. Similarly, most RCIA participants learn a great deal about Catholicism, but some may never want to live their lives as members of a Christian community.

Thus, in contrast to logical or mathematical inference, where a person who understands the terms and accepts the method is constrained to come to the conclusion—after all, who is going to deny that "if a=b, and b=c, then a=c"?—in the case of personal inferences in practical matters, one is never forced to accept a particular conclusion; a person is always fundamentally free—to buy this particular car or not, to enter the Catholic Church or not. The data as such may be very persuasive, but ultimately each individual is responsible for making a personally appropriate decision.

For private consultation and not distribution without the consent of E Ondrako

The Illative Sense

While it is quite evident that we commonly make mathematical or logical inferences in our daily lives—balancing our bank statements, calculating tax deductions, solving sudoku—we may not reflect that we make other decisions in a parallel way—by asking questions, by examining data, and by coming to conclusions—in most other areas of our lives. What we often notice, however, is that some people are better at making some types of practical judgments than others. For example, many of us might hesitate to consult a lawyer, if we knew we were that lawyer's first client; most of us might defer surgery, if we knew that this would be that surgeon's first operation; many of us would probably be reluctant to invest money with a financial advisor if we knew that we were that advisor's first customer. Why is this so?

Decisions in the real world—what Newman called exercises of "informal inference"—are highly dependent on two inter-related factors: first, the native intelligence of the decision-maker and second, that person's experience. From childhood, we recognize that each person has talents or abilities in some areas, but not in others. Perhaps the most common example is the child prodigy who goes to the piano and starts picking out melodies unexpected and untaught; we recognize that such a prodigy is gifted with an innate "musical sense." Although not ordinarily to the same degree as a musical prodigy, all of us have what Newman called an "illative sense"—a faculty of mind that aids each individual in making decisions in practical matters, a mental *organon*, which enables us to make "informal inferences"—practical decisions in every-day life-situations.[27]

Although everyone has an illative sense, we also recognize that the illative sense operates differently from person to person; some people's illative senses are more adept in some areas than in others. For example, the cook who makes a cake from scratch and adds ingredients until the dough "feels just right"; or the mosaic artist who picks exactly the right colored tessera to fit into a picture; or the detective, who examines all the clues and identifies the criminal. Such skills seem to be a combination of talent and training, of expertise and experience. Our "illative sense" helps us select, examine, and evaluate facts; our "illative sense" enables us to see a pattern in otherwise discreet and divergent data and come to our own personal conclusion about the meaning of the data—not simply in an

---

[27] See Newman's detailed discussion of the "illative sense" in his *Grammar*, 343–383. The word "illative" is derived from the past participle (illatus) of the Latin verb inferre, which is the root of "inference"; accordingly, the "illative sense" is the mental faculty that we use in making inferences and coming to decisions in actual situations.

For private consultation and not distribution without the consent of E Ondrako

abstract or theoretical way—but in way that makes the data meaningful for us.

This exercise of the illative sense can sometimes be a "eureka experience"—when a cake turns out to be a culinary delight, when a mosaic is an artistic masterpiece, or when a criminal is caught. Similarly, there is a "eureka experience" when an RCIA participant, having examined the doctrines of Christianity, is able to say not only that these doctrines are interesting to think about, or that these ceremonies are beautiful, but that Christianity is meaningful for my personal life and provide guidelines for the way that I want to live.

For Newman, faith is an example of our illative sense operating in religious matters. As part of the RCIA process, for example, my illative sense looks at the history and doctrine of Christianity to see whether there is a pattern that is meaningful—not only objectively, but also personally. In contrast, like the person who is deaf and has no appreciation for music, a person's illative sense may be deaf to religious values. Such religious deafness is all too wide-spread in the 21st century: what Newman called the "range" of the illative sense—the spectrum of data, concerns, issues that our illative sense considers—has frequently been reduced to what is philosophically subjective or technologically demonstrable—that result in a deafness to religion both in theory and in fact. For example, the so-called philosophical "turn to the subject" may condition a person to regard all religious beliefs as subjective with the result that one religion is considered as good as another; in effect, "my only criterion is how religion benefits me." Similarly, the modern technological mentality may accept only "scientifically verifiable" data and conclude that since Christianity cannot be "objectively proved," then it should be discounted or denied.

The Reasonableness of Faith

In writing his *Grammar of Assent*, Newman was not concerned with Christian anthropology or the way that grace operates in human nature. He was concerned with constructing an empirical epistemology that shows how the mind operates in general and in the area of religion in particular. As such, his *Grammar* is more concerned with describing the human dimensions of the process by which a person arrives at a conclusion—the process leading to faith—than with the product—the virtue of faith. Accordingly, Newman's *Grammar* is not specifically concerned with the role of grace either in the act of faith or in the life of faith.

For private consultation and not distribution without the consent of E Ondrako

In part, this omission was due to the audience that Newman was addressing: the evidentialists on the one hand, who considered faith irrational, and the existentialists, on the other hand, who considered faith super-rational. Simultaneously, Newman recognized that people of his age—indeed of every age—ask questions about religion, encounter all sorts of religious beliefs and practices, and come to some conclusions about religion. How is one to explain this human phenomenon?

First of all, for Newman, faith, humanly speaking, is inherent to the *persona quaerens*— "the person as seeker"—to the human penchant for asking questions about all sorts of matters, but especially about basic religious matters: Where did we come from? Why are we here? Where are we going?[28] Second, for Newman, faith is an inferential process—similar to the many personal inferences that we make in daily life; in the case of faith, we examine the data of Christianity to see whether its doctrines and practices align in a pattern that is meaningful for me and my life. Third, for Newman, faith, while never the result of a logical proof or a rational demonstration, is—like our other personal inferences—imminently reasonable as the product of an inferential process guided by a person's illative sense discerning and judging the teachings of Christianity.

Accordingly, Newman's view of faith is not only an example of nineteenth-century philosophical-theological thought, but an inviting and convincing explanation for persons seeking a reasonable approach to faith today.

---

[28] See, for example, the religious questions posed by Vatican II, *Nostra Aetate* § 1 (available at: http://www.vatican.va/archive/hist_councils/ii_vatican_council/documents/vat-ii_decl_19651028_nostra-aetate_en.html).

For private consultation and not distribution without the consent of E Ondrako

CHAPTER 2

An Overview of the Scotistic School

Edward Ondrako

Scotus's Life

This reconstruction of the life of Bl. John Duns Scotus is from several sources[1] and includes dates open to dispute, but well-grounded on those that are definitive. The definitive dates make it possible to hypothesize about those that are contested with a fair degree of accuracy. Our aim is to sketch a plausible human portrait of John Duns Scotus's life and indicate what kind of formation he must have received in his life as a Franciscan Friar.

1265–1266. John Duns was born in Scotland. His father was Ninian Duns, and his surname reflected the region of his birth.

---

[1] This outline of Scotus's life is not definitive but represents a more popularized sketch for purposes of this work. It is taken from several sources and serves as an invitation to further research. These include OLIVIER BOULNOIS, *Duns Scot: La Rigueur de la Charité* (Paris: *Les Éditions du Cerf*, 1998); THOMAS WILLIAMS, *The Cambridge Companion to Duns Scotus* (Cambridge: Cambridge University Press, 2003), 1–14; RICHARD CROSS, *Duns Scotus* (Oxford: Oxford University Press, 1999), 3–6; ALESSANDRO M. APOLLONIO, *Prologo dell'Ordinatio* (Frigento, IT: *Casa Maria Editrice*, 2006). Boulnois and Apollonio offer details not found in Williams and Cross. Williams provides a precise list of Scotus's works. Cross situates one of Scotus's prime intentions to debate the secular master Henry of Ghent (1217–1293), and several significant points about understanding Scotus, such as theologia in se (theology in itself) and theologia nostra (our theology). The latter is what we can know in this life. However, there is a major competing view to that of Cross who holds that we cannot talk of a Franciscan tradition of theology that would embrace both Bonaventure and Scotus, for he concludes that "Scotus disagrees with Bonaventure almost as much as he disagrees with the Dominican Aquinas," 5. With all respect, the reasons for the competing view will emerge as *The Newman-Scotus Reader* progresses. With English gentlemanly poise, Cross and I named the difference in views in the broader context of the differences in thought of Thomas and Scotus while I had the privilege of attending his class at Notre Dame. Our Newman-Scotus Reader will demonstrate why there is continuity between Scotus and Bonaventure. Scotus agrees with Thomas far more than is sometimes assumed in scholarly circles, and that it is one of our presuppositions. Thomas and Scotus are two of the most-important metaphysician-theologians in the history of the Church. A further competing view with Cross has to do with the relation of William of Ockham to Scotus. While Ockham learns from Scotist thought early on, there is much to be said about the view of the English Friars that Scotus is the end of the *via antiqua* and Ockham the beginning of the *via moderna*.

For private consultation and not distribution without the consent of E Ondrako

1278–1280. John Duns may have had a relative, a Fr. Elias Duns, who was the Vicar Provincial of the Franciscan Order in Scotland at this time. John frequented the friary at Haddington, and may have begun his novitiate in 1280, and thereafter would have studied in the colleges of the Order.

October, 1288. John may have begun his theological study at Oxford and William of Ware was one of his most influential teachers.

In 1274, both Thomas Aquinas and Bonaventure died. Following them, the great doctors of the University of Paris were the secular master Henry of Ghent, Godfrey of Fontaines, and the Franciscan, Peter John Olivi. In addition, the manuscripts of Simon of Faversham had an influence on Scotus's intellectual formation.

March 17, 1291. John Duns was ordained to the priesthood in Northhampton, England.

1297–1300. Some hypothesize that he was assigned to Cambridge at this time, where in 1297–98 he prepared his lectures on the *Sentences* of Peter Lombard, and in 1298–99 lectured on the Bible; his early *Lectura* probably dates from this time.

July, 1300. Scotus received faculties to hear confessions in the Franciscan Church at Oxford at the request of the English Provincial, Hugh of Hertilpole.

Summer and early Fall of 1300. He was beginning to revise his Oxford Lectures known as the *Ordinatio*, which is uncontested as the original work of Scotus, updated by views from his teaching later in Paris.

1300–1301. He was at Oxford commenting on the first three books of the *Sentences* of Peter Lombard and took part in a disputation under Philip of Bridlington. This is the probable date for completion of his theological study at Oxford; he was sent to Paris by the English Provincial where he studied under Gonsalvus of Spain and may have participated in the disputation between Gonsalvus and Meister Eckhart.

1302–03. He lectured at Paris on the first and fourth books of the *Sentences* of Peter Lombard.

June 25–28, 1303. When a dispute arose between Pope Boniface VIII and King Philip IV of France, Scotus remained loyal to the Pope and was expelled by the King along with Gonsalvus and about eighty other friars.

1303–04. During the period of exile, it is hypothesized that he edited the so-called *Lectura ─completa*, a set of lectures on book 3 of the *Sentences*. Another hypothesis is that he commented on book four of the *Sentences*.

April, 1304. King Philip permitted Scotus and the other exiled friars to return to France and Scotus to lecture.

For private consultation and not distribution without the consent of E Ondrako

November 18, 1304. The Franciscan Regent Master, Gonsalvus of Spain, appointed him Regent Master of theology for the Franciscans of Paris.

> "I assign to you John the Scot, of whose praiseworthy life, outstanding knowledge, and most subtle intelligence I have been made fully aware, partly through long experience and partly through his reputation, which has spread everywhere."[2]

Around this time Scotus disputed with the Dominican William Peter Godinus on the principle of individuation. The views of Scotus would later exercise a profound influence on the 19th century English poet, Gerard Manley Hopkins.

1305. This is the probable date for a set of Scotus's lectures in the form of a *reportatio examinata*. These were student lecture notes checked by Scotus himself, and known as the *Reportatio Parisiensis*. That he received his doctorate at this time is a well-founded hypothesis.

Advent 1306 or Lent 1307. At this time he held his public disputations known as the *Quodlibetal Questions*. These are replies to questions on any topic from those attending the disputation.

1307. In public disputations, Scotus defended the possibility and fittingness of the Immaculate Conception of the Virgin Mary.

Late 1307. He probably completed *De Primo Rerum Principio*, his proof for God's existence.

October, 1307. He was transferred to Cologne to be a lector at the Franciscan *studium*. The transfer was part of an Order policy to share the best teachers in the Order among the houses of study (*studia generalia*) in the Order.

November 8, 1308. Scotus died at Cologne. He is buried in the *Minoritenkirche*, Cologne in a simple sarcophagus with the epitaph:

> *Scotia me genuit, Anglia me suscepit, Gallia me docuit, Colonia me tenet.*

> Scotland bore me, England received me, France taught me, Cologne holds me.

July 14, 1966. To commemorate Scotus's birth, Bl. Pope Paul VI wrote the Apostolic Letter, *Alma Parens*.

March 20, 1993. Pope St. John Paul II enrolled him among the Blessed of the Church.

February 20, 2002. Pope St. John Paul II addressed the Scotus Commission.

---

2 A. G. LITTLE, 1892, 220.

For private consultation and not distribution without the consent of E Ondrako

October, 2007. The first of five Congresses was held commemorating the anniversary of Scotus's death. It was at St. Bonaventure University in New York State.

July, 2008. The second Congress was held in Oxford.

September, 2008. The third Congress on Scotus's Mariology was held at Durham, England and Duns in Scotland.

October 28, 2008. Pope Benedict XVI issued the Apostolic Letter, *Laetare, Colonia urbs.*

November, 2008. The fourth congress was held at Cologne.

March 2009. A fifth Congress was held at Strasbourg.

July 15, 2009. The idea for inaugurating a comparative study of the thought of Bl. John Duns Scotus and the soon to be Bl. John Henry Newman was born at Fatima.

July 7, 2010. Pope Benedict XVI dedicated his reflections at the general papal audience to the thought of Bl. John Duns Scotus.

October 22–24, 2010. The inaugural Newman-Scotus Symposium was held in Washington, D.C.

2011-2015. Editing the critical edition of Scotus's works continues at the University of Notre Dame.

2013-on Tobias Hoffmann at The Catholic University of America editing Scotus bibliography.

Continues at the University of Notre Dame (Reporpatio Parisiensis).

Excursus on Pope Benedict XVI's Papal Audience July 7, 2010

Pope Benedict gives a convincing affirmation that Bl. Duns Scotus joins the ranks of theologians such as St. Thomas Aquinas and St. Bonaventure. Scotus preferred voluntary exile rather than sign a document hostile to the Supreme Pontiff. He defended Mary's Immaculate Conception that the majority of theologians at the time opposed or saw as insurmountable. The subtle doctor preached the mystery of the saving passion of Christ as the expression of the loving will, of the immense love of God. He defended the Real Presence of Jesus in the Eucharist as the sacrament of unity and communion that induces us to love each other and to love God. The Holy Father added: "For Duns Scotus a free act is the result of the concourse of intellect and will, and

For private consultation and not distribution without the consent of E Ondrako

if he speaks of a "primacy" of the will, he argues this precisely because the will always follows the intellect."[3]

In brief reply, Pope Benedict is spot on with his thoughts on how sensitive the topic of freedom and its relation with the will and with the intellect is in modernity and post-modernity. However, his papal audience misses the critical point that Scotus conceives the will as the power to self-determine, to initiate, and voluntary action is essentially free. The intellect is moved by its object, truth. The will is not objectless, but love, the characteristic act of the will, is distinct and more excellent than knowledge. Love moves itself toward being which is perceived as good. This perception in the divine will and finite will perfected by grace is from within the will itself.[4] If the finite will is separated from the justice of God, and lacks being gratified by divine grace, the will is radically irrational and arbitrary.[5]

Scotus's Works

Here is a shortcut to help identify Scotus's works. After his unexpected death, his immediate students edited his works. Luke Wadding edited his *Opera Omnia* in 1639. At Paris from 1891–95, Louis Vivès edited his *Opera Omnia* known as the Vivès edition.[6] The edition of the *Opera Omnia* under the Scotistic Commission was begun in 1950 at the Vatican City: Vatican Polyglot Press and is still in progress. Our work reflects the use of the primary works that have been declared authentic and annotations about other works. In 2003, Thomas Williams[7] published a concise and comprehensive explanation of this new critical edition of Scotus's works from the Vatican. The English translation of Ruggero Rosini's, *The Mariology of Scotus*, uses the works of Scotus that are authentic,[8] especially, *Ordinatio* I, II, III, and now IV (as of 2010) up to distinction 13 in 12 volumes; and *Lectura* volumes 16–21 in print.

---

[3] http://www.vatican.va/holy_father/benedict_xvi/audiences/2010/documents/hf_ben-xvi_aud_20100707_en.html

[4] See W. HOERES, *Der Wille als reine Vollkommenheit nach Duns Scot.* (Munich, 1962).

[5] Peter Damian Fehlner alerted me to Scotus's thinking on the will and the interlinking of all of these themes especially in the work of Hoeres.

[6] Olivier Boulnois uses the Vivès edition, while the other contributors usually use the Vatican edition.

[7] WILLIAMS, Cambridge Companion, xiii–xvi, and 6–14. The references to the works of Scotus are xiii–xvi and the details that explain the major works are from 6–14.

[8] RUGGERO ROSINI, *Mariology of Blessed John Duns Scotus* (New Bedford, MA: Academy of the Immaculate, 2008), 6–7.

For private consultation and not distribution without the consent of E Ondrako

Every medieval scholar commented on the four books of the *Sentences* of Peter Lombard. Scotus's commentary is known traditionally as the *Opus Oxoniense*. That same authentic work of Scotus is now called the *Ordinatio* by the Scotistic Commission. Books one, two, three and four up to distinction 13 are available in print at the time of this publication. The Scotistic Commission also edited books one, two, and three of the *Lectura* which are available in print. *Theologiae Marianae Elementa*, edited by Carlo Balič, Sebenico, 1933, consists of extracts from codices of Scotus, published and unpublished, about Christ and Mary. The *Reportata Parisiensia* consists of the notes taken by Scotus's students during his lectures and then approved by Scotus. The *Disputatio Quodlibet* and *Collationes*, and *Questiones super libros Metaphysicorum Aristotelis* are the remaining authentic sources used in this Newman-Scotus Reader.

The Franciscan Studium at Paris and Oxford.

The course of studies for Franciscans at Paris and Oxford began shortly after the arrival of the friars to Paris c. 1217 and Oxford in 1224 and include some of the main forerunners of Scotus. George Marcil, in "The Franciscan School,"[9] gives a concise, necessarily incomplete, but engaging narrative of the Franciscan *studium* at Paris and at Oxford, and its development. That they had the very best teaching is not a matter of dispute, nor that once trained, the friars taught their own. Alexander of Hales, Haymo of Faversham, John of Rupella, and William Militona, are names associated with Paris. At Oxford, Robert Grosseteste protected the friars and lectured on theology from 1229–1235, before becoming bishop of Lincoln. It is significant that at this early date William of Ware reported that Grosseteste affirmed the doctrine of the Immaculate Conception but without any further information.[10] William had a profound influence on Scotus. Some of the Franciscan lectors were Adam Marsh, Thomas of York, Richard Rufus of Cornwall, John Pecham, Roger Marston, Philip of Bridlington, and Roger Bacon.[11] Almost within fifty years of arriving in

---

[9] GEORGE MARCIL, "Franciscan School," in *The History of Franciscan Theology*, ed. Kenan B. Osborne (St. Bonaventure, N.Y.: The Franciscan Institute, 1994), 313–316. The notes follow Marcil's outline but are supplemented by significant points to underscore the impact of the Enlightenment project and to prepare the reader to contextualize Newman's preoccupation with the thought of John Locke and his concern to avoid what is rightly called the Lockian trap.

[10] TIMOTHY FINIGAN, "Belief and Devotion to the Immaculate Conception in Medieval England," in *Mary at the Foot of the Cross* (New Bedford, MA: Academy of the Immaculate, 2005), vol. 5, 344–359. See 354.

[11] STEPHEN F. BROWN, "Reflections on Franciscan Sources for Duns Scotus' Philosophic Commentaries" in *Archa Verbi: John Duns Scotus, Philosopher, Proceedings of The Quadruple Congress on John Duns Scotus*, eds. Mary Beth Ingham and Oleg Bychkov (St. Bonaventure,

For private consultation and not distribution without the consent of E Ondrako

England, a friar, John Pecham became the Archbishop of Canterbury, a tribute to their way of life and intellectual formation.

Bonaventure died in 1274, was canonized in 1482, and made a primary Doctor of the Church in 1588. He was succeeded in the chair of theology at Paris by Gilbert of Tournai, Walter of Bruges, John Pecham, Matthew of Aquasparta, and Richard of Middleton. Marcil points out that the thirteenth century theologians kept an independent style, but generally followed the Bonaventurian lead while departing on some points. Marcil has in mind Peter Olivi and John Dun Scotus. But for the purposes of this narrative on Scotus, the *caveat* is that Scotus's style may only *appear* to be more arid, and a digression from Bonaventure. Therefore, the critical question is: is Scotus's thought a digression or a fuller explanation of what Bonaventure began? Upon close examination, Scotus does not represent a substantial change in approach to the nature of philosophy and theology. Rather, it can be argued that he gives a more rigorous analysis.

Conclusion

There are four very important points that will be developed in the chapters ahead. They center on the Franciscan thesis which originates in St. Francis himself. It is the theory about the nature of the predestination of Jesus and Mary. Jointly they are prior to anything else willed by God for existence and not conditioned on the sin of Adam and Eve, a priority that is at the root of any possibility of redemption after sin. Exemplary causality includes their mediatory influence in the world, not only after sin, but before, in the human and angelic and natural orders. The next two sections of this chapter will explain.

Four points form the foundation for the Franciscan thesis.

FIRST, familiarity with Scotus's life, works, and some of his forerunners confirms the place of Scripture, Tradition, the Fathers of the Church, especially the Alexandrine School, Augustine, Pseudo-Dionysius, John of Damascene, the Victorines, and Anselm.

SECOND, the Scotistic School is inseparable from the overall context of what is called the Franciscan School. Francis of Assisi wanted educated friars who did their theology on their knees. He was not a tenured theologian, but, in this sense, no less a theologian.

THIRD, from this vantage point, there is no split between Bonaventure and Scotus, but rather a more exact mode of defining by Scotus that

---

N.Y.: The Franciscan Institute, 2010), vol. 1, 1–12. Brown helps to put Bacon's judgment into context.

For private consultation and not distribution without the consent of E Ondrako

anticipates the future objections of Kant, and, anticipates the overall outline of chapter 8 of Lumen Gentium at Vatican II.

Fourth, the thought of William of Ockham (d.1347) is often presumed to be the next generation in continuity after Scotus's thought, but Ockham's nominalism is more closely associated with agnosticism that fails to have scholarly verifiable purchase in Catholic philosophy.

The Perdurance of the Scotist School

As a point of departure, it is a marvel to keep in mind what Newman often said: "time is our best friend and champion." In 1845, Newman asked to be received into the Roman Church once he became convinced that the Holy Spirit guides the history of the true development of doctrine and he could trace those reasons historically. The Immaculate Conception is an example. In 1307, Scotus gave the reasons why it was possible for Mary to be conceived without sin and their fittingness, but humbly deferred to the Magisterium to define the doctrine. During the first half of the 14th century, there was opposition to the arguments in favor of the Immaculate Conception from theologians at Paris and, in their private teaching, three who would become Avignon Popes.[12] The latter years of the 14th century were marked by aggressive opposition to the idea of the Immaculate Conception, but notwithstanding this there was a growth in devotion to the Immaculate Conception and celebration of the feast. In 1483 Pope Sixtus IV condemned those who said that anyone who held the doctrine of the Immaculate Conception sinned grievously.

The 15th and 16th centuries witnessed a growing consensus among theologians such that they were no longer asking whether the doctrine was true, but whether it could be defined as of faith. By the early 16th century, the doctrine was taught at the Universities of Paris, Oxford, Cambridge, Toulouse and Bologna. For example, Luther personally believed in the doctrine of the Immaculate Conception although he held the contrary doctrine was not reproved. The latter view the Sorbonne condemned as false and disrespectful to Mary. Many saints including St. John of the

---

12 Timothy Finigan, "Immaculate Conception after Scotus. Scotistic Mariology from Scotus to the Dogma of 1854: The Formation of a Mariological Tradition Based on the Immaculate Conception," in *Bl. John Duns Scotus and His Mariology* (New Bedford, MA: Academy of the Immaculate, 2008), 297–319. See 299. This is enlightening for understanding, by analogy, how the mind of John Henry Newman was working as he thought to discern between true and false development of doctrine.

For private consultation and not distribution without the consent of E Ondrako

Cross and St. Theresa of Avila promoted the doctrine. Among their rules on the choice of theological opinions, the Jesuits were bound to hold the Immaculate Conception. England had been known as Our Lady's Dowry and all vestiges of Catholic devotion were to be wiped out according to statutes under Elizabeth I. In France, Bishop Bossuet defended the doctrine. Subsequent developments involved a complex theological probing up to the solemn definition on December 8, 1854. Newman's "Memorandum on the Immaculate Conception,"[13] which was written at this time, is a deeply moving personal account of his theological conviction.

The development of the doctrine of the Immaculate Conception is an appropriate demonstration of the importance of the philosophy and theology of Scotus. Some of his students and advocates of his thought follow him faithfully. This fact underscores that there was a lively Scotistic school as an integral part of the Franciscan School and not separated from it. The 14th century students of Scotus were William of Alnwick, Anthony Andrea, Hugh of Newcastle, Francis of Meyronnes, and John of Bassolis. The 15th century Scotist William of Vorilong flourished in France. Bernardine of Siena and John of Capistran read Scotus; so also Francesco della Rovere, the future Pope Sixtus IV, read Scotus at the University of Padua, by this time the major center of Scotistic study in Europe. Less recognized are Nicholas Orbellus, and the Marian contributors, Francis Vidal y Noya, and Pelbart of Temesvar. John Foxal wrote on the Porphyry Commentary on Scotus. Stephen Brulefer, Anthony Sirectus, and Anthony Trombetta wrote on the Formalities in the mind of Scotus and their work was published by the Irish Scotist Maurice O'Fihely. In the 16th century, the Observant Franciscan, Philip Varagius and the Conventual James of Malafossa wrote theological compendiums based on the mind of Scotus, and Francis Lychetus wrote on the Oxford commentary of Scotus. Juan de Cartagena stressed Marian teachings that were inspired by Scotus. The Conventual, Cornelius Musso, brought a Scotist presence into the leadership of the Council of Trent. Newman refers to him in the appendix to his *Lectures on Justification*. The labors of the Council of Trent, replies to the Reformers, and challenges of the counter-reformation were monumental and soon compounded even more by the scientific revolution.

To understand the crucial importance of the history of scotistic theology and philosophy in the 17th century, it is imperative to take note of a reference, one that is a famous assessment, of J. Caramuel y Lobkowitz, a Spanish Cistercian of the common observance (died 1682), about the spread of Scotism in Catholic Europe around 1650: "*Scoti schola numerosior est omnibus aliis simul sumptis*." (The scotistic school of

---

13 JOHN HENRY NEWMAN, *Meditations and Devotions* (London: uniform edition).

For private consultation and not distribution without the consent of E Ondrako

theology counted more theologians than all the others put together).[14] This significant quote is the title of an article in 1956 by Felix Bak which is identical to the quote from Caramuel. Bak's research coincides with an old, but good study of the Franciscan traditions in P. de Martigné, *La scholastique et les traditions franciscaines*, Paris 1888. However, Bak was the scholar who finally located the quote about the breadth of scotistic studies in one of the works of Caramuel y Lobkowitz after Charles Balič, arguably the greatest Scotist of the twentieth century, had claimed that he thought it was a pure fiction to glorify Scotus.

The breadth of the scotistic school in the 17th century coincides with the entrance upon the stage by Descartes and John Locke who bring us to the critical meeting point between the new scientific method of Newton and pastoral awareness of the Anglican divines in the 18th century and eventually to Newman's 'worries' about Lockian thought. Neither St. Paul, nor the Fathers, nor the great scholastic theologians shared the assumptions of Protestant –Cartesian theology, especially the *fides sola* thinking to which the *Christus solus*[15] theory of atonement is attached. From the time of Locke's *The Reasonableness of Christianity* (1695), the principle of private judgment as something self-evident became the basis for the cultural assumption that religion is a private affair. Ecclesiastical jurisdiction, the authority of Sacred Scripture, and defense of religious matters in public, were assumed to be no longer worth defending. Newman questioned assumptions that were being made by pointing out that the "enlightenment" itself has its presuppositions. However well intentioned he may have been to promote tolerance, Locke dismissed traditions, reduced doctrines to secondary importance, and gave the functional authority to the individual. The title Son of God was purely metaphorical, and there one has the so-called Lockian common sense interpretation of the Gospels.

Prior to the publication in 1639 of the *Opera Omnia* by Wadding with its rich mine of commentary mostly by Irish Scotists, the Conventual Philip Faber, professor in the University of Padua published a systematic commentary on Scotus's theology; so also the Croatian Conventual Matthew Ferčhič. At the theological studium or college of the Conventuals in Naples, John di Napoli and Angelus Vulpes formed an entire generation of influential Scotists. Among them was the Conventual Barthlomeus Mastrius (1602–1673) who did for counter-reformation Scotism what the Salmanticenses did for counter-reformation Thomism: compose a master

---

14 See the work of the Conventual Felix Bak, "Scoti schola numerosior est omnibus aliis simul sumptis," in *Franciscan Studies* 16 (1956): 143–165. He makes reference to Caramuel whose brief biography is in the *Old Catholic Encyclopedia* (1910), vol 3. Caramuel is also listed in Hurter's Nomenclatura.

15 Faith alone. Christ alone.

For private consultation and not distribution without the consent of E Ondrako

textbook which became a standard reference for the next three centuries. Another important student of Vulpes, the future Cardinal Lawrence Brancati de Laurea, in addition to his monumental commentaries on theological works of Scotus, introduced study of the patristic background of Scotus theology. Vulpes himself relies on the *Breviloquium* of Bonaventure for his understanding of Scotus.[16] He seems to have been the first to compose a Mariology based on Scotus. The Conventual, Bartholomew Mastrius, and the Observants, John Mortinero in Spain (c. 1659) and Claude Frassen (c. 1668) in Paris are important for their philosophy and theology programs according to the mind of Scotus. The Conventual Sebastian Dupasquier, composed a textbook of theology according to the mind of Scotus which also had considerable influence almost to the beginning of the 20th century. The textbooks of these scholars were commonly used in the houses of study of the Franciscans throughout the world.

As Newman was creative in coining the term, the *illative sense*, Scotists, including Mastrius, did something similar. They reflected on the relation between freely bestowed efficacious grace and the exercise of freedom by a person which they called *condetermination*. As the term illative sense continues to be both misunderstood and extremely useful when understood, the term condetermination has the same challenge. The short answer is that both terms are perfectly in accord with Catholic thought although Newman has been called a modernist and the Scotists who hold condetermination have been said to be opposed to Catholic teaching. These are two significant points that will be developed in the essays in this volume. In fact, condetermination and the illative sense may provide the clues necessary to reply to the critical question asked by Pope Benedict XVI in the papal audience which he gave on the thought of Scotus, July 7, 2010: what is the relation of freedom to the will and intellect today?

With the 18th century came the application of Locke's views about inference and the precarious trail leading to skepticism, but the trail was to become more dangerous with the skeptical views of David Hume. The violence of the French Revolution and codification of the "enlightenment" as the new common law of the world by Napoleon had consequences for the continuity of the *studium* in the Order. During this period the Observant Jerome of Montefortino, inspired by an earlier work of the Conventual Cardinal Constantius Sarnano (c. 1585), prepared five volumes to study theology (1728–38) juxtaposing Scotus according to the order of questions in Thomas's *Summa Theologica* so as to stress their complementarity in defending the faith rather than their divergence. Crescence Krisper, an

---

16 See *Mary at the Foot of the Cross*, vol. 5, 260.

For private consultation and not distribution without the consent of E Ondrako

Austrian Observant, prepared several volumes on Scotus's philosophy and theology. Another important 18th century Scotist is the Conventual Joseph Ferrari, who composed three volumes on fundamental theology and apologetics *in via scoti*.

In the mid 19th century Newman was in Rome preparing for conditional re-ordination. In general, for complex reasons after the French Revolution and reign of Napoleon, the status of philosophical studies at Rome was very poor. With Pope Leo XIII's *Aeterni Patris* in 1879, that would take a turn for the better, but not without some undesirable side effects. Newman, the controversialist, knew how to engage the issues of the day, in fidelity to Scripture, Tradition and the official teachings of the Church. He knew how to shepherd souls. His was always a *via media* in the scholarly world and remains a stellar role model for contemporary critical engagement using primary sources and the potential contribution toward the development of doctrine. Newman thanked the Holy Father for *Aeterni Patris*, which inspired renewal of scholarly study of the scholastics such as that represented by the Observant, Fidelis a Fanna, who began to edit the critical edition of Bonaventure's writings (1882–1902). Wadding's edition of Scotus was redone in twenty-six volumes by Louis Vivès, 1891–95. The Observant Lodovico Colini da Castelplanio was a theologian at Vatican I and important in the Scotistic Mariological tradition.

In the 19th century, the Sistine College of the Conventuals in Rome continued to cultivate the thought of Bonaventure and Scotus but was suppressed in 1873. It was difficult to keep this tradition going, but Pacifico Rabuini (1838–1902), a graduate of the College of St. Bonaventure just before its suppression, fortunately trained future professors, some of whom taught the young Maximilian Kolbe (1894–1941) to be a Scotist, in particular Dominic Tavani (1875–1938). Kolbe was a student in Rome from (1912–1919), a period in which Scotists were viewed with suspicion. The problem seems to have been caused by some influential neo-Thomists who absorbed the teachings of Thomas that Thomas had gained from Scripture, Tradition and the Magisterium, but apparently without the appreciation of other Catholic schools of thought. Moreover, they did not demonstrate the pastoral advantages of being able to combine the best insights from the Dominican School with the Franciscan School. This is a work that remains to be developed in the 21st century.

For the sake of discussion, the 19th century saw the beginning of the movement known as *La Nouvelle Theologie* with its complex origins. About the time of Johann Adam Möhler (*Die Einheit der Kirche, The Unity of the Church*, 1835) and during the lifetime of Newman, the writings of Kant, Schleiermacher and Hegel gave rise to the Catholic reply in one form

For private consultation and not distribution without the consent of E Ondrako

among many, the Tubingen School. The problems of ultramontanism and modernism gave rise to the need for a proper return to the Fathers and scholastics in dialogue with the work of the theologians. Newman is an extraordinary model of how to find the *via media*, to avoid the extremes of rationalism and fideism, to keep unbound the hands of a 'controversialist,' as he referred to himself, i.e., one who is willing and capable of engaging the world. From the time of Newman's death in 1890 to 1959, when Bl. John XXIII invoked the Second Vatican Council, there were several stresses with theological reform and renewal. Bl. John intended that the Council was not to change the *depositum fidei*, but to update the formulations of the teachings of the Church for the modern world. It is not an accident that Vatican II was called "Newman's Council."[17] When, in 1943, Karl Rahner wrote: "handbook theology lacks nothing except life,"[18] one gets the picture.

After the Second Vatican Council, Newman's claim to Christian truth continues to serve as the role model for commitment to absolute truth. However, his is not a formula for a zero sum game because it recognizes the ray of truth that may be present in the history of other religions, and, therefore, Newman's thought always shows respect for the history of all religions. Vatican II produced documents on the Church, the Church in the modern world, ecumenism, on the relationship to non-Christian religions, and religious freedom and more, all extraordinary and waiting for virtuous, intelligent, and creative implementation.

Jurgen Mettepenningen's work is a helpful aid to a first understanding of *La Nouvelle Théologie* as a significant movement prior to Vatican II, with ramifications for the work of theology after Vatican II. Unfortunately, his overview deals mostly with the Dominican and Jesuit versions, and leaves out any mention of the Franciscan contributions in France and Germany between the time of Newman and Vatican II. The Belgian overlooks the research of those who were using the critical edition of the works of Bonaventure and the Vivès edition of the works of Scotus, which were prepared at the end of the 19th century. He and I discussed this lacuna at the Catholic Theological Society of America Meeting in Cleveland in June 2010, and he intends to do further research.

---

17 EDWARD J. ONDRAKO, *The controversy between William Ewart Gladstone and John Henry Newman in 1874–75 and its shadows and images over Vatican II* (Ann Arbor, MI: 1994).

18 JURGEN METTEPENNINGEN, *Nouvelle Théologie: New Theology, Inheritor of Modernism, Precursor of Vatican II* (New York: T and T Clark, 2010), 116. Mettepenningen gives a brief explanation of why neo-Thomists are not the same as Thomists or transcendental Thomists, 25–27. To conflate the three opens the possibility of misreprésentation of Thomas's original thought.

For private consultation and not distribution without the consent of E Ondrako

A major difficulty remains to be resolved, one centering on the fact that Scotus continues to be accused of opening the door to modernism. For example, some who promote an onto-theological rendition of Christianity, and some in the school of Radical Orthodoxy, seem to fall into this trap by blaming Scotus for the origins of the problem of modernity. Several of the entries that follow will uncover in a cautionary manner some of the presuppositions in this misreading of Scotus. Some competing views will be included for they help to promote further conversation on these critical points for understanding modernity and its radical repudiation of the Redemption. Curiously, during this period before the end of World War I, Newman was accused of being a modernist. The question was sent to Rome and the reply came back, no!

The Franciscan contributions between the time of Newman and Vatican II include the *compendia* of Parthenius Minges in Bavaria which spearheaded new interest in Scotus. This was felt at the *Antonianum* and the *Seraphicum* in Rome, in Spain, France and in the Rhineland and in North America. In the midst of this historical context, in 1849, W. Frederick Faber helped Newman to understand Scotus's teaching on the Immaculate Conception, a significant step in the developing scotistic consistency in Newman. In 1872, Gerard Manley Hopkins fell in love with Scotus's thought which influenced all of his poetry from that day on. Deodat de Basly in France and M. Oromi in Spain were influential Scotists, but it took a truce, so to speak, and the attrition of the rather violent suspicions about Scotus before a new generation of scholars who had interest in Scotus's thought was able to breathe the air he breathed. Ephrem Longpré and Charles Balič (1899–1977) stand out and pave the way for the more recent growth of Scotus scholars. The recently deceased Allan B. Wolter was one of several outstanding scholars who are laboring today with the authentic works of Scotus.

Balič is to be remembered especially for his contributions to the discussion on the Marian schema at Vatican II. The title of chapter 8 of *Lumen Gentium* reflects the teaching of Scotus: "The Role of the Blessed Virgin Mary, the Mother of God, in the Mystery of Christ and the Church." That should come as no surprise for Bonaventure, Thomas and Scotus accept the Anselmian dictum: "Our Lady could not have been made holier by the Father than she actually has been made in any other possible world, however more perfect than this one." Shortly after the Council, Balič inspired Peter Damian Fehlner to take seriously the study of possible and probable connections between the thought of Scotus and Newman. Chapters 4 and 7 in this volume are the fruit of Fehlner's labor.

For private consultation and not distribution without the consent of E Ondrako

Some of the younger Scotists who had to endure the charges of modernism against Scotus prior to the end of World War I lived to witness the crowning of Scotus's thought in chapter 8 of *Lumen Gentium* and to hear the Apostolic Letter on July 14, 1966, of Bl. Pope Paul VI, *Alma Parens*[19] commemorating the birth of Scotus. "Alongside the majestic chair of St. Thomas, among others worthy of honor, however different in size and structure, is that which on solid foundations with soaring pinnacles raises to heaven the ardent speculation of John Duns Scotus."

Along with the euphoria following Vatican II, was the dream of those who recognize the complementarity and the differences in the thought of the two great scholastic theologians. The work of these contemporary theologians is predicated on the desire to teach the truth in the authentic works of Thomas and Scotus, as they labored to illumine the mysteries known by faith, and to explain how these can be, i.e., their intelligibility. Bl. Pope Paul VI says that "one can take arms of light to repel the black cloud of atheism darkening our age."

> The spirit and ideal of St. Francis of Assisi are imbedded in and animate the work of John Duns Scotus, where in accord with the spirit of the Patriarch of Assisi knowledge is subordinated to holy living. In affirming the excellence of charity over any form of knowing, the universal primacy of Christ, masterpiece of God, glorifier of the most Blessed Trinity and Redeemer of the human family, King of the natural and supernatural order, at whose side is seated resplendently the Virgin Immaculate in all her original beauty, Scotus unfurls the sovereign concepts of the Gospel Revelation, particularly those which St. John the Evangelist and St. Paul the Apostle consider preeminent in the plan of salvation.

"To take arms of light to repel the black cloud of atheism darkening our age" is reminiscent of Newman's speech upon being named a Cardinal in 1879 where he refers to the great *apostosia*. That poignant image of light versus the black cloud was repeated by Pope St. John Paul II on March 20, 1993, in his beatification homily of Bl. John Duns Scotus. He said:

> In our times, however rich in human, technological and scientific resources, but in which so many have lost any sense of faith and lead a life that seems far from Christ and the Gospel, Bl. John Duns Scotus is present, not only with his subtle intellect and extraordinary capacity for insight into the mystery of God, but also with the persuasive force of holiness of life, which makes him for the Church and for all mankind a master of doctrine and life.

---

19 PAUL VI, *Acta Apostolicae Sedis* 58 [1966] 609–614.

For private consultation and not distribution without the consent of E Ondrako

> His doctrine, from which in the words of our venerable Predeces-
> sor Paul VI, "one can take arms of light to repel the black cloud
> of atheism darkening our age," builds up the Church on strong
> foundations, supports her in her urgent mission of the new evan-
> gelization of the peoples. In particular, for theologians, priests,
> and pastors of souls, religious, and above all for Franciscans, Bl.
> John Duns Scotus constitutes an example of fidelity to revealed
> Truth, of fruitful sacerdotal activity, of serious dialogue in the
> cause of unity....[20]

The intention of Vatican II was to renew the Church. The official time
of experimentation, as it was called, immediately after the Council, made
many large and fruitful steps, but often left sincere Catholics wondering
what was necessary for renewal, what did dialogue, working for unity,
co-responsibility for the planet and everyone on it, really mean? One finds
a sure answer about the non-contradictory nature of theological study in
the service of renewal in Pope St. John Paul II's address to the Scotus
Commission in February, 2002.

> Duns Scotus, with his splendid doctrine on the primacy of
> Christ, on the Immaculate Conception, on the primary value of
> the Revelation and of the Magisterium of the Church, on the
> authority of the Pope, on the capability of human reason to make
> the great truths of faith accessible, at least in part, and to show
> their non-contradictory nature, is even today a pillar of Catholic
> theology, an original Teacher, full of ideas and incentives for an
> ever more complete knowledge of the truth of the faith.

Furthermore, any doubt about the continuity of thought between
Bonaventure and Scotus, indeed, any significant controversy about Scotus
and the Franciscan School, is laid to rest by Pope Benedict XVI in *Laetare
Colonia Urbs*, on October 28, 2008,[21] his Apostolic letter commemorating
the death of Scotus. Pope Benedict refers to Scotus as "a teacher and guide
of the Franciscan School, and a light and example to the entire Christian
people." The ideas begun by Bl. Pope Paul VI, and carried forward by Pope
St. John Paul II, are developed in *Laetare Colonia Urbs*. He writes about
Scotus on the harmony between faith and reason, so central to Newman's
life and thought, and to the thought of his predecessor in *Fides et Ratio*:

> We, therefore, desire to remind scholars and everyone, believers
> and non-believers alike, of the path and method that Scotus

---

[20] JOHN PAUL II, *L'Osservatore Romano*, 22–23 March 1993.

[21] BENEDICT XVI, *Apostolic Letter to Joachim Cardinal Meisner on the Seventh Centenary of the Death of Bl. John Duns Scotus*, October 28, 2008.

For private consultation and not distribution without the consent of E Ondrako

followed in order to establish harmony between faith and reason, defining in this manner the nature of theology in order to constantly exalt action, influence practice, and love, rather than pure speculation; in fulfilling this task, he let himself be guided by the Magisterium of the Church and by a sound critical sense regarding growth in knowledge of the truth, and was convinced that knowledge is valuable to the extent that it is applied in praxis.

In several of the chapters in *The Newman-Scotus Reader*, Scotus's teaching on the primacy of the will, and primacy of charity, serve as the foundation for the arguments being advanced. Since Pope Benedict's three encyclicals center on charity, it makes an easy comparison of his thought with what he says about Scotus.

The primacy of the will sheds light on the fact that God is charity before all else. This charity, this love, Duns Scotus kept present when he sought to lead theology back to a single expression, i.e. to practical theology. According to his thought, since God "is formally love and formally charity,"[22] with the greatest generosity he radiates his goodness and love beyond himself.[23] And in reality, it is for love that God "chose us in him before the foundation of the world, that we should be holy and blameless before him. He predestined us in love to be his adoptive sons through Jesus Christ" (Eph 1:4–5).

Pope Benedict XVI's papal audience on the thought of Bl. John Duns Scotus, July 7, 2010, raises the question that seems to him be one of the most sensitive for our times: What is the relation of freedom to the will and intellect? *The Newman-Scotus Reader* takes up the challenge implicitly and explicitly.

In his exhortation at the beginning of the *Newman-Scotus Symposium*, Oct 22–24, 2010, at Washington Theological Union, the Minister General of the Conventual Franciscans, Marco Tasca, encourages the leaders and participants to become on-going and loyal devotees of the thought of Bl. Scotus and Bl. Newman, so that they may advance the understanding of continuity in tradition according to the mind of Pope St. John Paul II and Pope Benedict XVI. Mindful of the recent exhortation of Pope Benedict XVI to the Franciscans and Dominicans about paying attention to the intellectual component of their vocations, the Minister General of the

---

22 Benedict XVI is using the Vatican edition of SCOTUS's *Ordinatio* 1, d. 17, n. 173 (ed. Vat v, 221–222).

23 Benedict XVI is using SCOTUS's *Tractatus De Primo Principio*, c.4 (ed. M. Müller, Friburgi in Brisgoviae, 1941, 127).

For private consultation and not distribution without the consent of E Ondrako

Conventuals takes the lead and encourages the same. There is cause to celebrate the renewal of the combined ministry of laity and clergy and religious with respect for the responsibilities in each other's vocations, rather than to dwell on the current decline in the numbers of religious and clergy. Today many more young and well-prepared lay men and women are graduating who know their Catholic faith, live it with the intention of being holy, and are very highly skilled to take their places in public life. They are eager to join the clergy and religious in the arduous ministry of teaching Christ as the Way, the Truth and the Life in a secularized world in the spirit of Bl. Newman's *The Idea of a University*. Bl. Newman anticipated this change in 1859 with his bold, *On Consulting the Faithful in Matters of Doctrine*.

This is the spirit of love and hope that imbues the chapters ahead on the thought of Bl. Scotus and Bl. Newman. The intention is to encourage the work of theologians to seek to illumine their labors with the thought of two Oxford giants who sought the sanctification of the intellect in their desire to be holy. This is the formula for every age and for those who seek to be contemporary saints. When one looks back on the history of the Church, there is a discernible pattern that every major dogmatic definition gives witness to the theological contribution of a great saint.

Finally, Pope Benedict XVI's question about freedom in relation to the will and intellect has an affinity with Bl. Scotus's thought inspiring and leading to the theory of condetermination associated with the Conventual B. Mastrius. It is fully in accord with the Magisterium of the Church and gives more than a hint of the direction to search for a comprehensive answer. Both Bl. Scotus and Bl. Newman exemplify the correct answer in their lives and writings that condetermination is the point where the created spirit meets the uncreated Spirit and chooses either radical autonomy or humble contemplation and so exercises the gift of freedom!

The Scotistic Tradition, Modern Secularism, and the Redemption

The Scotistic theological tradition is a most willing partner to engage what is today, undeniably, secularism as a systematic repudiation of the Redemption. The subtitle for this section of our overview is: "Why Scotistic Thought on the Absolute Primacy of Christ Matters in Discussing Redemption." In the chapters ahead, one will find an x-ray, so to speak, of the problem of secularism as a contemporary systematic repudiation of redemption and Christ as the Redeemer. Often, this is Hegelian inspired

For private consultation and not distribution without the consent of E Ondrako

thought. Inspired by the experience of St. Francis, the Franciscan School teaches that Christ could have redeemed us in any way, but chose to suffer, not because he had to, but out of love. Thomas, Bonaventure and Scotus teach about the perfection of the redemption, but Scotus adds a key concept to what may be imprecise and misleading in Bonaventure's thought about the christo-centric character of theology. Scotus's answer is the absolute primacy of Christ. While Bonaventure did not actually hold the absolute primacy of Christ before the foundation of the world, his reasoning supports the subordination of redemption to the Incarnation and implies that Mary has a special role in the objective redemption. Scotus demonstrated why Mary could be preserved from original sin as the rest of humanity must be liberated from original sin and why to be preserved is superior to being liberated.

Therefore, it is God's holiness revealed in Christ and Mary that is the key to defining the redemption as it actually took place. He is first the Mediator because he is absolutely predestined. That is what primacy means. He is secondarily Redeemer. Since all of humanity is in solidarity with Adam and Eve for better or worse, this means that Adam and Eve had all of the gifts that they needed to remain faithful, to retain original justice. Their fall resulted in original sin. The mystery that requires extended contemplation is that even if Adam and Eve had not fallen, humanity would still need a Mediator. That Mediator was to be the new Adam along with the new Eve, the Mediatrix, who was preserved prior to the fall, which is preservation in reference to the moral headship of Christ as it is in the eternal counsels of God. Her perfect redemption is not dependent on Adam's moral headship, although she is daughter of Adam in the moral order. All of the children of Adam and Eve depend on Mary and through her on Christ, as she depends on Christ in the eternal counsels of God.

In scotistic thinking, defining redemption means that it has a basis for the most perfect redemption from sin in everyone else redeemed. Mary is that basis because Mary's justice transcends the original justice of Adam. As she is the basis for the original justice of Adam and Eve, after the fall from original justice, she is the basis for the liberation from original sin. Mary is preserved from sin by the foreseen merits of her Son and Savior and elevated to the highest holiness possible in a created person. This happens prior to any consideration of her dependence on Adam. This is what it means for her to be lowly and subordinate to her Son and Savior. He, in turn, willingly depends on her.

In the preceding historical sketch, Scotus's thinking is shown to have contributed to the definition of the Immaculate Conception in 1854, but not without heated competing views soon after his death in 1308. In

For private consultation and not distribution without the consent of E Ondrako

Sermon III on the Assumption, Bonaventure refers to Christ and Mary as sharing the *patriarchus* or headship lost by Adam and Eve. Scotus adds that all of humanity depends on Christ and Mary in the perfect economy of salvation, before and after the fall. The economy as original justice is subordinate as type to the economy based on the order of the hypostatic union. In other words, there is a justice that is proper to the grace of the hypostatic union and to the grace of the Immaculate Conception.

Since the time of Pelagius, several theories continue to be shaded by his views and they will be referred to and explained in the chapters ahead. The Protestant *solus Christus unus Mediator* is one. Patripassionism in its recent versions is another. The logic of both objections would reveal a Creator who, in creating, did so with great imperfection and has to learn as world history progresses. The answer, not only in the Franciscan School, is that the world that God creates, whatever the limitations, the Creator is all good and all sufficient. The disjunctive transcendentals, as incorporated by Scotus in his metaphysics, leaves no doubt that the Creator is all good and all sufficient. That is why the love of the Incarnate Savior cannot and does not increase by suffering. That is why Scotus refers to the most perfect redemption by the most perfect Redeemer in any possible world.

The question of the universality of redemption is more complicated and too complex to answer comprehensively in this chapter which is an overview of the Scotistic School. A glimpse into the answer will have to suffice. The universality of redemption raises the question whether one may affirm it absolutely, and then exclude the angels, who could only be redeemed preservatively. Scotist theologians at the Council of Trent contributed to the formulation of that Council's exemption of Mary from its decree on the universal transmission of original sin. This exemption provides the basis for later explaining her relation to us in view of our perfect redemption and the absolute goodness of God who creates human beings with the possibility of falling into original sin. Mary is not simply a symbol of the sinlessness of all mankind, which is a modern Pelagian based view.

Scotus's logic shows how original sin is genealogically contracted. The offspring of Adam lack an element indispensible for the infusion of sanctifying grace. That element is original justice. At her conception Mary has a higher justice, a fullness of grace that makes her daughter and Salvatrix of Adam and Eve. The Immaculate Conception defines her personhood, not just the first moment of her conception. That is how she is related to Christ and to Christians. When one adds consideration of original sin and personal sin, her holiness, in the words of Anselm, greater than which none can be conceived, makes possible the analogical character of the

For private consultation and not distribution without the consent of E Ondrako

notion of redemption, including preservative as well as liberative. Both are properly speaking forms of redemption, but preservative is the more perfect form and key to the possibility of liberative. Preservative redemption, then, is not the natural innocence of the will as Pelagians claim, but the fullness of grace and justice. If one accepts the scotistic thesis of the absolute primacy of Jesus and Mary as the motive of the Incarnation, then the analogical character of the notion of redemption is possible in the economy of salvation because that is the way it has occurred. Without accepting the scotistic thesis of the primary motive of the Incarnation, one will remain in a dilemma how Mary can be redeemed and how she can be Immaculate Coredemptrix. The objection, in sum, is that there can only be one Mediator because God is one.

A current objection to the scotistic thesis on the absolute predestination of Christ is that humanity needed the fall of Adam, or the salvation won by Christ for humanity would be less than perfect. This is evolutionary thinking, indicative of Hegelian thought. Hegel is the farthest distance conceivable from the theological metaphysics of Scotus. The obvious danger here is that of reducing the redemption to a mere historical reflection. In brief, if one reflects metaphysically from the point of view of the divine counsels of salvation, the concept of preservative liberation from sin does the opposite of reducing the full mystery of redemption and of mercy to something that is just an accident of sin and therefore not so great. Scotus and the Scotists understand what the mistake is to make the redemption the primary motive of the Incarnation. That would mean that sin is not only permitted in view of the Incarnation, but necessary to a greater glory of God. On such a hypothesis, to avoid sin would be to suggest that God's glory might be diminished. Scotus anticipated all of these future variations on this theme as irrational. Christology that is identified as adoptionist, i.e. understood as from below rather than from above in terms of pre-existence and the prior predestination of Christ, is irrational. In Scotus's terms, any suggestion that the perfection of the Incarnation is not at the virginal conception, but at the term of an evolutionary process, is irrational.

In several of the chapters in *The Newman-Scotus Reader*, it will become apparent how Newman, who flourished at a time when radical, pantheistic, and dualistic winds were blowing, gradually broke free of their power and influence. He intuited the major misconceptions of the redemption at their origins. That included the Calvinist views that he had accepted immediately after his first conversion at the age of fifteen. Unfortunately, the Calvinist point of view, which did not reject the fact of the redemption, cannot bridge the gap between thinking that there is one Mediator

For private consultation and not distribution without the consent of E Ondrako

and the cooperation or mediation of the individual, i.e. as making up what is lacking in the sufferings of Christ (Col 1:24). It is a rejection of vicarious redemption in favor of substitutionism. In this view, Christ merely suffers but does not merit or satisfy as man, a view completely alien to Scotus.

The second problem centers on the difference between making a fundamental option to be sincere, as with the faith of the anonymous Christian,[24] or as with fundamental option under grace. Neither view involves questions of satisfaction, justice and injustice, merit and satisfaction as preliminaries for making a fundamental option. Ever mindful of misreprésentations of the Incarnation, and the redemptive work culminating on Calvary, Scotus anticipates these modern developments. He rejects both approaches to the fundamental option above because both omit the Marian coefficient of redemption and entail a modern Pelagian view of redemption. *Contra* this view, the Franciscan School was the first to formulate the concept of the perfect redemption, which is the redemption as it was in fact. Scotus contributed above all to illustrating the bases for Mary's holiness as Immaculate as the key to realizing our perfect redemption as it planned in the eternal counsels of salvation.

The serious student asks for the definition of terms such as perfect redemption, the Marian coefficient of the Incarnation as in *Redemptoris Mater* by John Paul II, the relation of the papal exegesis to the quasi-infinite of Thomas (Incarnation, divine Maternity, and our salvation), evolutionary adoptionism, and what it means to be the *Panhaghia* as a condition for the divine Maternity. Moreover, how is it that foreseeing the sin of Adam, God the Father willed the redemption of the human family, but not that of the fallen angels? The scotistic answer is implicit in Scotus. "Mary was predestined as daughter of Adam to be the Mother of God, Spouse of the Holy Spirit, and firstborn daughter of the Father prior to any provision of the fall."[25]

---

[24] HANS URS VON BALTHASAR, *The Moment of Christian Witness*, trans. Richard Beckley. (San Francisco: Ignatius Press, 1994), 127–130. Balthasar has grave reservations with the term anonymous Christian and challenged Karl Rahner's take on it with a poignancy that deserves to be pondered. Balthasar uses the imaginative dialogue between the well-disposed commissar and the modern Christian professor. Anyone familiar with Stalin's orders to execute Polish commissars on sight during World War II will find Balthasar's reservations compelling. In brief, the term, anonymous Christian, as proposed by Rahner, warrants critical theological assessment as to its strengths and limits and possibilities for dialogue. Be that as it may, Balthasar was more than superficially acquainted with Scotus. The jury of Balthasar's students is still out deliberating how well this extraordinary scholar understood Scotus.

[25] This is a classic formulation of the answer from the Franciscan School. See ALESSANDRO APOLLONIO and PETER DAMIAN FEHLNER, "The Concept of Redemption in the Franciscan-Scotistic School: Salvation, Redemption, and the Primacy of Christ," in *Mary at the Foot of the Cross*-8 (New Bedford, MA: Academy of the Immaculate, 2008), 111–156. Their fidelity to the primary sources and original thought of Scotus and to the scotistic theologians is second to none today. They have the advantage of working with the texts of Bonaventure and of

For private consultation and not distribution without the consent of E Ondrako

The thumbnail historical sketch of the theological tradition of Scotus, earlier in this chapter, brings attention to the importance of the only complete manual of theology that has been composed according to the mind of Scotus since the 18th century, that of the Bavarian, Parthenius Minges, OFM, *Compendium Theologiae Dogmaticae*.[26] His work incorporates the earlier works of Angelus Vulpes (d. 1649), Bartholomeus Mastrius (d. 1673), Claudio Frassen (d. 1711), and Jerome of Montefortino (d. 1738). These Scotists call attention to distinctive features of redemption in the scotistic school. A very brief summary of further scotistic thinking follows in order to prepare to embark upon a deeper critical study of our thesis. Depending on how one defines the term systematic theologian, one can substantiate the claim that Newman was a consistent systematic theologian, if such a one values unity in the midst of apparent disunity. At heart, Newman's consistency, for several of us contributors, has key elements that are scotistic.

These earlier works form a basis for further contemporary development of scotistic thought. It is more than ninety years since the appearance of the last scotistic *compendium*. What follows reflects a hint of the developments in understanding Scotus's thought since Minges. The point of departure remains the same: the absolute predestination of Christ and the unique inclusion of Mary Immaculate in the order of the hypostatic union as His Mother. Mary did not and could not sin in Adam. Therefore, Satan cannot have a definitive victory over the plans of God for it is Mary who guarantees a correct understanding of redemption. In this context, salvation is sharing with Christ, in those jointly predestined with Him, and in the most perfect praise of God and enjoyment of the Father's love. Redemption is the resolution of the contingent obstacle to that sharing, original sin, by a sacrificial mediation which God the Father accepted in satisfaction for the offense of sin. Consequent, through the satisfactory merit of Christ, the satisfaction that was effected is the liberation of mankind from sin and its effects.

All are predestined in Christ for glory. The *happy fault* from the Easter *Exultet* is a proof that the actual redemption is most perfect only because it is consequent on the absolute predestination of Christ as the new Adam to be Head of this creation and his work of mediation. The Headship-

---

Scotus that are judged to be authentic. The theme of redemption which is assailed by the Reformers and "enlightenment" inspired religious writing is a foundation that promises even greater light when read through the lens of Scotus and Newman. They point out reasons for recognizing the provenance of most of the Bonaventurian elements of Marian soteriology, either explicit or implicit, in the scotistic synthesis. Before the end of the 14th century, the blanks were filled in by the disciples of Scotus.

26 Parthenius Minges, *Compendium Theologiae Dogmaticae* (Ratisbon, 1921), 304 ff.

For private consultation and not distribution without the consent of E Ondrako

mediation includes Mary as Mediatrix. Christ does not save Himself. His predestination is a gift of grace, par excellence. Mary, too, is redeemed to assist in the redemption of others including angels. Scotistic soteriology is the basis for the title in ch. 8 of *Lumen Gentium*: "The Blessed Virgin Mary in the Mystery of Christ and of the Church." Salvation is to praise God in himself, for his own sake, because he is the supreme good to be loved as he loves himself. If the notion of perfectly redeemed is changed to mean a most perfect finalization of the fundamental option, or most perfect liberation to be free, then Scotus and scotism is incompatible with such a view. That is because Scotus accents the active involvement of Mary which is entailed in the preservative redemption.[27]

Minges divides the scotistic treatment of redemption into redemption as our liberation from sin, and redemption as satisfaction in justice offered to God and accepted by God as such. For Scotism, redemption is contingent on the completion of the work of justice by atoning for original sin. If I am reading Karl Rahner correctly, justice, satisfaction and reparation for sin addressed to the Father, are incidental to the experience of absolute salvation. This means that vicarious satisfaction and expiation is not the core element in redemption and eliminates any need to discuss mediation and merit. Here is where it is important to note that Thomas and Scotus differ on a number of questions in soteriology, but insist upon redemption as essentially defined and realized by a work of vicarious satisfaction. That means it is satisfaction because it is reparation of an injustice to the Creator. It is vicarious because Christ as Head does for us what we could not do. This is not Protestant substitutionism.

Although both Thomas and Scotus share the same premise that our redemption is a work of vicarious satisfaction, Scotus differs from Thomas and Bonaventure on the *Cur Deus homo* thesis of Anselm. Thomas stresses how Christ and the Church form one mystical person. Scotus stresses the possibility of the cooperation of others with Christ the man as the one Mediator of God and man, especially Mary. The primary motive of the Incarnation for Scotus insists on the need of the Incarnation for a perfect redemption. In his early ministry as an Anglican priest, Newman gradually began to break from the Calvinist influence in his theology. By 1849, with the help of F.W. Faber, Newman came to understand and subscribe to the Scotistic thesis on the motive of the Incarnation.

---

[27] If we are reading Rahner correctly, he seems to eliminate the notion of perfectly redeemed and hence the difficulty with Scotus and the Scotists. To what extent Rahner's views are soundings remains to be researched. If he means that the role of Christ or of His Mother could, at best be exemplary, this seems to be a kind of extrinsic quasi-formal causality that is being debated in theological circles today.

For private consultation and not distribution without the consent of E Ondrako

Moreover, there is a co-relation between the redemptive work of Christ and the prophetic, sacerdotal, and royal roles. They are roles shared by His Mother as part of the order of the hypostatic union. Scotus continues along the line of Bonaventure's Mariology and ecclesiology, which is rooted in St. Francis of Assisi. For Scotus, the prophetic role touches theology and philosophy. In metaphysics the univocal structure of being is in full flight from non-being. Here is where Scotus may seem, on first look, to abandon the terminology of Bonaventurian illuminationism, but retains the essentials of that teaching in terms of the absolute primacy of Christ. The sacerdotal role of Christ (and Mary) is fulfilled on Calvary by his passion and her compassion. The Eucharist continues this sacrifice in an un-bloody manner. Mary's link is with Christ's ministerial priesthood and with the royal priesthood of the faithful. Hers is a sacerdotal rather than priestly dignity, meaning belief in the authority of the priesthood. In terms of the royal role, the Kingship of Christ has its coefficient in the Queenship of Mary.

Thomists and Scotists debate the infinite character of the offense given God by sin. Thomas and Bonaventure use quasi-infinite and Scotus prefers the term maximal. Maximal means that sin is clearly not on a par or quasi-par with God. Secondly, no good work by a finite human can ever be so good as to be quasi-infinite. The infinity of the Second Person is what makes the sanctity in the man. He is Priest and Victim, maximally perfect. Mary's unique sanctity is to be one with her Son as Priest and Victim.

For Scotus, the true concept of redemption entails merit, and hinges on merit. Christ's merit for us is *de condigno*, that is, most worthy. The Thomist tradition holds that Mary merits *de congruo*, or in harmony with Christ. Bonaventure and his followers hold that Mary merits *de digno*, out of her dignity. Most followers of Scotus claim that Mary merited on Calvary, *de condigno relative*. This is possible because redemption is predicated on the absolute primacy of Christ and Mary.[28] The Protestant *solus* and Pelagian *everybody* alter the true dogma. Scotus and his scotistic followers hold that for a theology to claim to be authentic, and a soteriology, without a Marian coefficient, it cannot be a true theology or genuine soteriology.

Finally, it is not radical autonomy, but what Scotus teaches about the true exercise of freedom which includes merit and humble contempla-

---

[28] MAXIMILIAN DEAN, *A Primer of the Absolute Primacy of Christ: Bl. John Duns Scotus and the Franciscan Thesis* (New Bedford, MA: Academy of the Immaculate, 2006), is a very readable explanation of why Scotus was responsible for the correct understanding and use of the terminology of the absolute primacy of Christ. It is a work accessible to the non-professional to explain what is meant by the Franciscan thesis, or the absolute joint predestination of Jesus and Mary, to be the King and Queen of the universe.

For private consultation and not distribution without the consent of E Ondrako

tion that is essential to the quest for sanctity. In Newman's *Parochial and Plain Sermons* I, which were edited in 1834, his first sermon is "Holiness Necessary for Future Blessedness." Newman wrote:

> No one is able to prepare himself, that is, make himself holy in a short time. We are the instruments of our own salvation but only the instruments. All of us have the gifts of grace pledged from our youth up. We know this well; but we do not use our privilege. Narrow indeed is the way of life, but infinite is His love and power who is with the Church, in Christ's place, to guide us along it.[29]

---

[29] JOHN HENRY NEWMAN, *Parochial and Plain Sermons* (London: uniform edition), vol. 1, 10 and 14.

For private consultation and not distribution without the consent of E Ondrako

CHAPTER 3

John Duns Scotus on Intuitive Cognition, Abstractive Cognition, Scientific Knowledge, and our Knowledge of God

Timothy B. Noone[1]

One of the many contributions of Duns Scotus to the history of philosophy is his formulation and application of the distinction between intuitive and abstractive intellectual cognition. Though our present inquiry will only take us partly towards our ultimate goal of comparing Scotus and Newman, understanding what Scotus means by 'intuitive cognition' regarding intellectual knowledge and perceiving how he relates his psychological doctrine to his accounts of our knowledge of individual objects, our scientific knowledge, ordinary claims about general historical knowledge, and theological knowledge coming to us through tradition and the Scriptures are indispensable conditions for any meaningful comparison between the two authors. Let us begin with the more ordinary and commonplace Aristotelian psychology which Scotus substantially qualified by adding his own teaching.

Standard Aristotelian-Scholastic Psychology

In Aristotelian psychology, intellectual knowledge is, generally speaking, distinguished from sense cognition through its being concerned with the universal. Mind, for Aristotle, knows the eidos or natural type of a given thing: 'dog' and not 'this dog.' True, according to the Aristotelian teaching, all knowledge, including intellectual knowledge, begins in the senses, and, in that regard, begins with individual substances and their properties. But that is because sense cognition knows things first and as individual items or qualities prior to any intellectual knowledge. The process leading up to intellectual knowledge is a complicated one, but the senses, the five external senses with which we are so familiar and the internal senses of the *sensus communis*, memory, imagination, and sense

---

[1] Newman-Scotus Symposium, Oct. 22, 2010. Washington Theological Union, Washington, D.C. Timothy B. Noone (The Catholic University of America).

97

For private consultation and not distribution without the consent of E Ondrako

judgment (or estimation), are all of them concerned with singulars in the classic Aristotelian picture. Intellectual knowledge takes its proximate starting point from an act of abstraction produced by the active part of the mind, known as the agent intellect, thereby allowing a universal intelligible form to activate the passive part of the mind, known as the possible intellect. This pre-conscious activity is what leads to an actual thought and explains why a thought is about a thing or feature of a thing in the world.

Now this is all fairly commonplace teaching among Scholastic philosophers in the thirteenth century. But one further qualification needs to be introduced into this sketch before Scotus's teaching occupies our full attention. The external senses are activated by the immediate presence and concomitant causal impact on them of their external objects. By contrast, as many of Aristotle's commentators pointed out, a faculty such as the imagination, though a sense power, makes us aware of an object in its absence. So, too, for that matter does another sense power memory, though it makes us (and the higher mammalia at least) of an object that was previously encountered in sense experience and of that past experience. Sometimes, Scholastic authors, long before Scotus, spoke of the object of the imagination (and occasionally, the memory) as being abstract or as engaged in the mode of abstract cognition because of this feature of making what was not immediately present to the senses to become an item of sense awareness. This terminology of 'abstractive cognition' needs to be kept distinct from the 'abstraction' found in the case of intellectual knowledge, for imagination is not an intellectual faculty for the Scholastic authors.

Scotus's Philosophical Psychology: Intuitive and Abstractive Cognition

Now for Scotus himself. There can be no doubt that Scotus inherited a tradition that used the Latin terminology of 'intuitive cognition' (*cognitio intuitiva*) and 'abstractive cognition' (*cognitio abstractiva*), a tradition that largely (though not exclusively) was found among Franciscan authors, especially such figures as Matthew of Aquasparta and Vital du Four.[2] Furthermore, the complaints of these late thirteenth century Franciscan psychologists regarding the delimitation of intellectual knowledge to

---

2 FR. MATTHAEI AB AQUASPARTA, *Quaestiones disputatae de fide et cognitione*, BFS I, editio secunda, cura Patrum Coll. S. Bonaventurae (Quaracchi, Florentiae: Typographia Collegii S. Bonaventurae, 1957), q. 4 , 284–286; VITAL DUFOUR, *Quaestiones de cognitione animae* in F. Delorme, "Le Cardinal Vital Du Four: Huit questions disputées sur le problème de la connaissance," in ADFHLMA 2 (1927), 163–166.

For private consultation and not distribution without the consent of E Ondrako

knowing universals characteristic of the standard Aristotelian psychology were well known to Scotus and he received their observations warmly. But, if we are to really grasp what is essential and unique in Scotus's teaching, we should begin back at the senses, just as the Aristotelian standard psychology does.

The point that I am about to make is one that has received little attention in recent literature on Scotus's theory of knowledge; in the last fifteen years, only two publications have taken note of it.[3] Scotus's theory of sense knowledge does not agree at all with the standard Aristotelian picture. The senses, for Scotus, are only improperly or concomitantly aware of the singular; they are really aware of the common features of individual things. You will notice that I said 'common' and not 'universal,' for these two terms are not, in Scotus's thinking, interchangeable. An example of what he is talking about will make matters, I hope, a little clearer. Say I perceive a blue ball. What I see, to start with one of the external senses, is blue, but not this blueness in precisely its unrepeatable uniqueness. For if that is what the saying 'the senses apprehend the singular' (*sensus apprehendit singularia*) meant, then I would immediately become aware of what made this blue different from all other blues and my sight of sense would exhaust itself by knowing just this blue. Some different sense power would be needed to perceive another blue item, let alone a white item, were the senses so intimately tied to the singular. Instead, Scotus thinks that what even the senses detect is that which is common in the singular and what communicates itself to the sense and can be found in other things as well. In other words, although the item I perceive through the senses is, to be sure, a singular, none of my senses reach it in its radical singularity; I perceive what is singular, but not precisely as singular.

Now inasmuch as the senses furnish the starting point for all of our intellectual knowledge in the present life, the singular cannot be reached in its singularity through intellectual knowledge so grounded in sense knowledge. Things cannot give what they do not have, to paraphrase Augustine, and if the senses are not themselves acquainted with the singularity of individual things, they cannot give our intellects the means of knowing singulars in their singularity either. The knowability, or better the intelligibility, of the singular, then, is one consideration behind Scotus's way of approaching intuitive, intellectual knowledge.

But there is another, and in some ways, more important consideration. We see this in the efforts of earlier authors such as Vital du Four

---

[3] See GIORGIO PINI, "Scotus on the Object of Cognitive Acts," *Franciscan Studies* 66 (2008), 281–315 and ALAIN DE LIBERA, *La querelle des universaux: De Platon à la fin du Moyen-Âge* (Paris: *Éditions du Seuil*, 1996), 337–339.

For private consultation and not distribution without the consent of E Ondrako

and Matthew of Aquasparta, who pointed out the importance of knowing something through its existence and how mere acquaintance with the relevant concepts and the formation of true judgment regarding the property of some type of thing would not be the same as knowing that there existed such an item with such a property.[4] Furthermore, Matthew and other Franciscans had pointed out the unsuitability of holding the position, seemingly held in the standard Aristotelian psychology, that the senses knew the presence and existence of a thing, but the intellect, the higher cognitive power, lacked such an ability.[5] Here then is another, perhaps the more important, reason for holding what Scotus does in reference to intuitive cognition on the part of the intellect: to allow for the intellect to know the actual presence and existence of an individual and the common features it has.

Abstractive cognition, for Scotus, is a term that refers to any mode of awareness of a thing or feature of a thing that functions equally well in the presence or absence of the item. Given such a broad description of 'abstractive cognition,' we may say that such abstractive cognition is found in the cognitive activities of internal senses such as the memory and the imagination, but also in ordinary conceptual thinking. For when we are aware intellectually through concepts, we are thinking in such a way that the presence or absence of the item about which we are thinking is irrelevant. Abstractive intellectual knowledge is the first kind of intellectual awareness in which we engage since our intellects begin by abstracting intelligible features of sensibly perceived items communicated to the intellect through the phantasm, but not actually abstracted until the agent intellect exercises its function, co-causing the production of an intelligible species in the possible intellect. Such awareness is also what most often occupies our attention in theoretical inquiry and scientific discovery.

Still Scotus thinks that, even in the present life, we enjoy a certain amount of intellectual intuitive cognition. This is the mode of intellectual cognition whereby we are aware of something in its existence and presence. In the position that he holds throughout his career—there is quite a literature on the different views Scotus held on intuitive cognition that I am here encapsulating briefly—Scotus teaches that we always have intellectual intuitive cognition of our own so-called mental acts, that is, our own acts of thinking and willing, though we do not enjoy in the present life such cognitive access directly to things outside the soul, at least in a certain

---

4 MATTHEW OF AQUASPARTA, *QDC* q. 4 (ed. Gál, 285): "Verumtamen, quia species in intellectu et etiam in imaginatione non repraesentat rem esse vel non esse, sed rem tantum simpliciter, ut imago Herculis repraesentat Herculem, non mortuum vel vivum…."

5 MATTHEW OF AQUASPARTA, *QDC* q. 4 (ed. Gál, 280).

For private consultation and not distribution without the consent of E Ondrako

respect. The importance of such immediate, non-inferential intellectual cognition of our own acts is emphasized by Scotus in his questions on the knowledge of Christ in book III of the *Sentences*, where he tells us that such direct intellectual acquaintance with our own acts, their objects and our remembering that we were the ones engaged in such acts is crucial for our judgments of prudence and efforts at moral reform:

> I make a further distinction regarding intuitive cognition since it is either occurrent intuitive cognition of an existing object, or such knowledge lingering in the soul from which the soul has intellectual memory, namely about an object previously grasped in experience; otherwise, a human being would not provide for himself or others and would fail to be prudent. Whence it is in the mode of intuitive cognition that I am aware that I am sitting, and through such cognition that a memory is formed whereby I remember that I was sitting. Otherwise, moreover, a human being would not repent of his own sins.[6]

Because Scotus, as has been mentioned, has such numerous reservations regarding the extent to which intuitive cognition is operative in the ordinary human being in the present life,[7] we must examine Christic psychology to see both abstractive and intuitive cognition functioning at their fullness. The Subtle Doctor's description of intuitive and abstractive cognition is perhaps clearer in his account of Christ's knowledge, moreover, than anywhere else in his writings. Abstractive cognition is the type of intellectual awareness that prescinds from the order of time, targeting solely the essences of the things known. As such, abstractive cognition may be concerned with either natures, whether generic or specific, or singulars in their singularity. Intuitive cognition is the type of intellectual cognition that directly concerns either natures or individuals as existing. In its most perfect form, the latter type of cognition can only be obtained in the actual presence of the thing known. As Scotus expresses the point, acquaintance with the terms of a contingent proposition, such as 'Peter is

---

[6] "Distinguo ulterius quia vel est intuitiva actualis vel derelicta ex actuali de qua habet memoriam intellectivam, scilicet, de re apprehensa prius in externa <pro: experientia>; alias nunquam homo provideret sibi nec aliis, nec esset prudens. Unde intuitive cognosco me sedere et per istam cognitionem sequitur memoria qua memoror me sedisse et alias homo non paeniteret de peccatis suis." Scotus, *Reportatio Parisiensis* III-B (Barcelona, Arxiu de la Corona de Aragó, Ripoll Ms. 53, f. 37rb).

[7] B. Ioannis Duns Scoti, *Quaestiones in libros Metaphysicorum Aristotelis* (St. Bonaventure, N.Y.: The Franciscan Institute, 1997), II q. 2–3 n. 81 (ed. cit. 225): "In intellectu, notitia visionis vel intuitiva … non est possibilis in via, quia nulla potentia reservans speciem vel formale principium cognoscendi in absentia obiecti potest sic cognoscere, quia illa idem habet principium, re praesente et non praesente."

For private consultation and not distribution without the consent of E Ondrako

sitting' cannot yield knowledge of the truth or falsity of the proposition in marked contrast to an abstractly known necessary proposition such as 'every whole is greater than its parts,' whose truth can be known through acquaintance with its terms. What this means for Christ's knowledge is that, if we set aside knowledge through the Word which precontains all things, Christ could only know the contingent truth of a proposition such as one bearing upon His own crucifixion in the presence of the actual events.[8]

The mechanics of Christ's cognition, moreover, are determined, in general, by Scotus's wish to attribute as perfect a mode of cognition to Him as would be consistent with his creaturely human nature. Such a manner of cognition involves, Scotus thinks, one parallel with, though distinct from, the one found in the natural cognition of the angels. The angels, in Scotus's view, have innate (or naturally infused) intelligible species supplied by God that allow them to know things, though their thinking involves discursive reasoning and they naturally have possible and agent intellects that function in regard to knowing individuals. Likewise Scotus holds that Christ's mind, endowed though it is with agent and possible intellects, has naturally implanted within it species that are equivalent to what the agent and possible intellects would normally produce.[9]

All of this Christological speculation about the principled limits of human psychology has the following to teach us about Scotus's approach: we may have, in principle, and Christ does have in fact either abstract awareness of either natures or individuals, that is awareness that prescinds from the order of time and existence and remains true independent of the actually existing individual things and the natures that they instantiate. Furthermore, we may have, in principle, and Christ does in fact have intuitive cognition, that is, awareness of the actual individuals that encompasses knowing their existence and presence both in terms of their natures and themselves as individuals. We see that this is quite clearly the case in remarkably succinct summary given by Scotus at the end of a key question of his *Ordinatio* in which he treats the manner in which Christ learned or progressed in his intellectual knowledge:

> So, too, when a sensible item is present to a sense power, two kinds of cognition can be caused through the power of that sensible experience: one is an abstractive cognition whereby the agent intellect abstracts the species of a quiddity (or essence) from the

---

[8] Scotus, *Lectura* III d. 14 q. 3 n. 153 (ed. Vaticana XX, pp. 354):"Et ideo nec hanc omnium in genere proprio habuit Christus; et sic non prius quam crucifigeretur vidit se crucifixum nisi in Verbo."

[9] Scotus, *Lectura* III d. 14 q. 3 n. 134–139; 143 (ed. Vaticana XX, 349.351).

For private consultation and not distribution without the consent of E Ondrako

species in the phantasm, which (i.e., the species of the quiddity) represents its object absolutely and not as it exists now and then; the other that can occur is an intuitive cognition in the intellect whereby the object cooperates with the mind inasmuch as the object exists. And from this second type of cognition a habitual intuitive cognition can linger, brought to pass in the intellectual memory; this type of cognition is not of the quiddity absolutely understood (as was the first and abstractive cognition), but rather of the thing known as existing, namely, in the manner that the thing was apprehended as existing in the past. In this way Christ is claimed to have learned many things through experience, that is through intuitive cognitions (that is to say, of those things known in terms of their existence) and through the memories left behind from those intuitive cognitions.[10]

Scientific Knowledge

Regarding scientific knowledge, Scotus's teaching is much more in line with standard Scholastic views, though his own outlook tends to be much stricter than what is seen in some writers. The notion of *scientia* or scientific knowledge needs, in the first place, a comment. In modern English, at least, we tend to think of the physical sciences such as physics, chemistry, or biology, if someone remarks that a student is studying science. Even the other inquiries that, on face value, seem to be quite different, disciplines such as anthropology, sociology, and psychology, aspire to be 'social sciences' by modeling themselves upon empirical and mathematically measurable experiments that result in positive knowledge. To the extent that we tend to think of such positive knowledge, based on empirical investigation, whenever we hear the term 'science,' we are remote from what medieval philosophers meant by science. For them, science meant an organized body of teaching and learning that concerned or bore

---

[10] "Ita etiam praesente aliquo sensibili sensui, potest virtute illius causari in intellectu duplex cognitio: una abstractiva, qua intellectus agens abstrahit speciem quidditatis ut quiditas est a specie in phantasmate, quae repraesentat obiectum absolute (non ut exsistit nunc et tunc) ; alia potest esse cognitio in intellectu intuitiva, qua obiectum cooperatur intellectui ut exsistens—et ab hac potest derelinqui habitualis cognitio intuitiva importata in memoria intellectiva, quae non sit quidditatis absolute (sicut fuit alia prima abstractiva), sed cogniti ut exsistens, scilicet quo modo in praeterito apprehendebatur. Hoc modo per experientiam dicitur Christus multa didicisse, id est per cognitiones intuitivas (hoc est illorum cognitorum quantum ad exsistentiam) et per memorias derelictas ab eis." Scotus, *Ordinatio* III d. 14 q. 3 n. 117–118 (ed. Vaticana IX 470–471).

For private consultation and not distribution without the consent of E Ondrako

upon one subject-matter and hence for them mathematics, grammar, logic, geometry, and physics were all sciences (*scientiae*).

Their model for science was largely indebted to Aristotle's *Posterior Analytics*, a rather difficult work in which Aristotle lays down his canons of epistemology. The examples of scientific knowledge are usually taken by Aristotle from geometry, astronomy, and physics, but most frequently geometry. In the case of geometry, there is a clear subject (figure) which has its constituent elements (line and point), its axioms or presuppositions connected to the subject, and the conclusions that clearly follow from the axioms when the latter are applied to specific types of figures such as triangles and circles.

Generally considered, Scotus's appropriation of this Aristotelian teaching emphasizes: 1) that the starting points of science in the most complete sense are necessary; 2) that the key feature of such knowledge is the evidence it provides to the intellect; 3) that the intellect must assent to the propositions that are evident to it, whether these proposition are self-evident or mediated by syllogistic deductions; and 4) that sciences, properly so called, are formally unified branches of knowledge produced by reasoning commencing from self-evident propositions and terminating in demonstrated conclusions.[11] Professor Steven P. Marrone has expressed the point well by saying that, according to Duns Scotus, "Science … that truly aspired to being the best knowledge of all had to worry only about attaining certitude and producing evidence upon which it could rest."[12]

Scotus himself gives us several overviews of his teaching on scientific knowledge in the strict sense, but the most pertinent one to our queries comes at a convenient spot, in the midst of his treatment of the issue of whether there can coexist in the same mind at the same time both faith and reason. Here Scotus summarizes his views as follows:

> But if we understand science properly, as it is understood in Posterior Analytics I, four conditions are needed in the following way in science: first, it must be certain knowledge, excluding any doubt or deception; the second condition is that it must be about a necessary object known; third, it must be through a cause evident to the intellect; fourth, it must be a necessary cause, evidently applying the principles to the conclusion through discursive

---

11 On the theory of *per se* known propositions in Scotus, see Peter C. Vier, *Evidence and its Function according to John Duns Scotus* (St. Bonaventure, N.Y.: The Franciscan Institute, 1951), 88.

12 Steven P. Marrone, *The Light of thy Countenance: Science and Knowledge of God in the Thirteenth Century* (Leiden/Boston/Köln, 2001), II: 439.

For private consultation and not distribution without the consent of E Ondrako

reasoning. … And understanding science in this way, it is impossible for there to be science and faith about the self-same thing.[13]

So much for knowledge in the strictest sense in terms of its formal structure. A final point to be made before leaving this topic altogether is Scotus's underlying reasons for holding that the intellect, when presented with clear evidence, must assent to the truth of self-evident propositions or the syllogistic reasoning based upon such propositions. For Scotus, intellect is, taken in its own right, a natural cause or principle as opposed to will. Will and agents endowed with will may act or not act since the activity of the will lies in the power of the voluntary agent. Natural agents and causes by contrast must act and to the utmost of their power once the proper conditions for their proper activity are realized. As a natural power, the intellect too has to act, i.e. assent, to propositions that are evident to it, to the extent that they are so.

Knowledge of God

In approaching our knowledge of God, we come to a topic that intensely concerned Duns Scotus along with most Scholastic philosophers and theologians. The theme of the knowledge of God, however, may have concerned Scotus more than most of his fellow Scholastics because he held theses that made it necessary for him to explain more clearly than his predecessors and contemporaries why natural knowledge of God would not suffice for human fulfillment and happiness since he believed that we can have knowledge of God's essence and that this was obtained, at least in part, through the notion of being gotten from creatures. Like most of his contemporaries, he divides our knowledge of God into two types, natural and supernatural; the former is found in its highest form in the philosophical science of metaphysics, a study concerned with being as being; the latter is given to us through revelation communicated through Scripture and the living tradition of the Church. The latter topic, knowledge of God through revelation, leads to a discussion of whether theology or the systematic study of the revealed data merits the term of

---

13 "Sed accipiendo scientiam proprie, prout accipitur I Posteriorum, sic requiruntur condiciones quattuor in scientia: prima, quod sit cognitio certa, excludendo omnem dubitationem et deceptionem; secunda condicio est quod sit de cognito necessario; tertia, quod sit per causam evidentem intellectui; quarta, quod sit per causam necessariam, evidentem et applicantem principia ad conclusionem per discursum syllogismum. … Et isto modo accipiendo scientiam, impossibile est de eodem esse scientiam et fidem." SCOTUS, *Lectura* III d. 24 q. unica n. 50 (ed. Vaticana XXI 144). For a parallel text outlining the four conditions, see SCOTUS, *Ordinatio* I prol. pars 4 qq. 1–2 n. 208 (ed. Vaticana I 141).

For private consultation and not distribution without the consent of E Ondrako

'science' in the sense we saw above. But in addition to his treatments of the two more formal ways in which we know God, Scotus discusses at unusual length for a medieval theologian the topics of acquired faith as opposed to infused faith and the reasonability of Christian revelation in particular. The last topics will be broached in the present lecture, but more thoroughly explored with an eye to points of comparison to Newman in the succeeding lecture.

To ensure that we have the broader picture in view, I would like to offer a sketch of Scotus's account of our formal knowledge of God, both natural and supernatural. Natural knowledge of God is acquired in the science of metaphysics. Following the mainstream thirteenth century tradition, Scotus holds that God falls under the subject of the science through the concept of infinite being. What distinguishes Scotus's position from such figures as Robert Kilwardby and Albert the Great is that he argues that the notion of being acquired from creatures applies univocally to God and creatures. The doctrine of the univocity of being is, at one and the same time, the earmark and badge of Scotism; it has been frequently reviled as the catalyst for the decline of Scholastic thought. Rightly understood, however, the doctrine seems no threat to traditional thinking, but rather the articulation of the underlying epistemic conditions for any positive knowledge of God through natural reason. For Scotus's doctrine of univocity amounts to the following modest claims: first, that the notion of being we acquire through acquaintance with creatures has a core meaning that lets us talk of God as a being, albeit the precise notion of God is 'infinite being'; second, that the core meaning regarding being extends to being's attributes and perfections so that, for example, when we say God is infinite truth, the term 'truth,' like being, has a meaning such that to say God is truth and to deny that God is truth is to state a contradiction.

Now, if we endorse Scotus's argument for God's existence, probably the most elaborate effort at proving God's existence ever produced in medieval philosophy, we seem, on the strength of Scotus's theory of univocity to be committed to saying that we can and do have knowledge of what God is, namely, infinite being, infinite unity, infinite truth, infinite goodness and all the other pure perfections, such as love, knowledge, and will in an infinite degree. To the extent, moreover, that we would identify positively what God is with His essence, we may say that Scotus's approach to our natural knowledge of God entails that we know, to some extent, the divine essence.

This may strike us, as it did some of Scotus's students, as undermining the need for supernatural or revealed knowledge of God. But Scotus invokes here his own teaching regarding knowledge through intuitive and

For private consultation and not distribution without the consent of E Ondrako

abstractive cognition. However great our knowledge of God through the concept of infinite being, such knowledge remains mediated knowledge, that is knowledge through a cognitive intermediary, and knowledge that holds good independent of the presence of the thing. Hence, even in the most refined conceptual analysis of God or the most lofty philosophical contemplation of the divine nature, we are dealing with abstractive awareness, awareness that thinks of God as an object and does not enjoy the divine presence in the manner of the beatific vision. It is not, as Scotus tells us repeatedly, knowing God as a 'this.' To know God as a 'this' would involve God's gracious self-disclosure to us, communicated to us through revelation, but only enjoyed fully in the beatific vision.

Supernatural knowledge of God comes from Scripture and the teaching of the Church, including conciliar decrees, Patristic writings, and Papal pronouncements. Such teaching was believed by many thirteenth century authors to meet the criterion for scientific knowledge laid down by Aristotle. On this point, Scotus takes the position that theology in the present state is a practical science inasmuch as it fits the broad description of a knowledge that would conform to praxis and would govern praxis. In terms of the four conditions of science, furthermore, theology taken in itself, apart from human beings, could be found in God insofar as He could know theology without engaging in discursive reasoning.[14] The blessed can know theology, too, but their knowledge will involve the quasi-discursive sequencing of what is logically prior and posterior. Our own actual theology is thus practical, but only imperfectly science insofar as its starting points are not evident to us through the terms of the propositions, but are accepted on authority through faith in the Scriptures.[15] Still, as Prof. Stephen Dumont showed some twenty years ago, Scotus wanted to allow in his Parisian prologue for the possibility that God could give us, if He wished, a species or representative proxy that would allow us to know theology in a higher way, rather analogous to the way that angels have a distinct, though abstract awareness of God through a species. Were we to

---

[14] SCOTUS, *Ordinatio* I prol. pars 4 qq. 1–2 n.208 (ed. Vaticana I 141–142): "Ultimum, videlicet causatio scientiae per discursum a causa ad scitum, includit imperfectionem et etiam potentialitatem intellectus recipientis. Ergo theologia in se non est scientia quantum ad ultimum condicionis scientiae; sed quantum ad alias tres condiciones est scientia in se et in intellectu divino."

[15] SCOTUS, *Lectura* III d. 24 q. unica n. 61 (Ed. Vaticana XXI 148): "Si autem exponit [Henricus] per alias scientias, ad quod ultimo devenerunt doctores immiscendo philosophiam sacrae Scripturae, … ut veritas Scripturarum de trinitate et unitate abstracta intelligatur, tunc dico quod conclusion non habet maiorem certitudinem quam altera praemissarum quae minus certa est … et cum praemissa primo sumpta de Scriptura non sit evidens ex terminis, sed credita, ideo nec conclusion erit demonstrative, generans scientiam, quamvis possit generare habitum alium a fide."

For private consultation and not distribution without the consent of E Ondrako

be endowed through God's will with such a starting point, theology would become a higher level of science, one close to what Scotus's predecessor, Henry of Ghent, held to be attained through a special light (the *lumen medium*) in the case of theologians.[16] Yet even in such circumstances, this rigorous knowledge of God that we could, in principle, have would remain abstract awareness of God, not intuitive.

Having covered Scotus's formal treatments of our knowledge of God and the distinction between intuitive and abstractive cognition, we have the bulk of our work before us. For it is a key feature of Scotus's treatment of our knowledge of God to relate our ordinary informal awareness of God to our everyday beliefs and judgments and to argue in this regard for the reasonableness of Christian faith and belief. This feature of Scotus's works, though unusual in reference to the common Scholastic pattern, has its origins, I think, at least in terms of inspiration, in the writings of Matthew of Aquasparta. Matthew spends considerable time in his *Quaestiones de fide* arguing that any strict modeling of inferences governing everyday life upon the model of science found in the *Posterior Analytics* is highly problematical for explaining daily reasoning and belief. Scotus's distinction between science in the strict sense, which we have today been examining, and a broader, though less demanding notion of knowledge is tailored to fit everyday inference and historical knowledge. Study of this looser notion of science or knowledge together with Scotus's treatment of faith, both acquired and infused, will occupy our attention in the next lecture.

---

16 See Stephen Dumont, "Theology as Science and Duns Scotus' Distinction between Intuitive and Abstractive Cognition," *Speculum* 64.3 (1989), 589–591. Scotus's *Quodlibet* q. 7 art. 2 (ed. Alluntis, 363).

For private consultation and not distribution without the consent of E Ondrako

CHAPTER 4

Mary and Theology: Scotus Revisited

Peter Damian Fehlner[1]

Sedes Sapientiae, ora pro nobis

This invocation may serve as the introduction and conclusion of this study: Mary is the Mother of Faith, and therefore the *Magistra theologiæ par excellence*, the model and guide and final support of all who study or teach about God. Without her love and active involvement in our lives, and a corresponding love and unconditional docility on our part, there can be no theology worthy of the name.

For some time now there has been a tendency abroad, in Catholic as well as non-Catholic circles, to minimize as much as possible, and even eliminate the place of Mary in theology, of which the latest, but by no means the only example, is the volume edited by R. Brown, *Mary in the New Testament*.[2] It is claimed that the Scriptures provide relatively little evidence of a factual kind for the life and work of Mary, far less than is available for the person of Peter, itself little enough, and certainly woefully inadequate as a viable intellectual basis for the mariological superstructure that Catholic tradition has built up over the ages and has, in substance, passed on as dogma. While pious accommodation would like to discover a scriptural basis for subsequent developments, the minimizers go on "modern scientific method" quite unable to remove all doubt.[3] We are

---

[1] Completed, Dec. 7, 1978.

[2] R. Brown, *Mary In the New Testament* (Philadelphia, 1978).

[3] *Ibid.*, chapter 2, pp. 28–31, for a general statement of method consistently followed through-out the rest of the volume. The method, to which appeal is made to justify the theological relevance of the conclusions, rests on three assumptions (among others) simply untenable: that the human dimensions of the Scriptures as literature can be understood with clarity and certainty by means of an exegesis that prescinds *formaliter* from doctrinal criteria; that the Bible can be considered in the proper sense an object of science, and that the methodology for its study, even at the literary level, can be organized strictly according to the canons of scientific scholarship; that at a distance of nearly 2,000 years methods of study prescinding from the testimony of a living tradition and the witnesses who actually observed the events narrated, can determine in any way the meaning and truth and character of the literature which narrates these events.

For private consultation and not distribution without the consent of E Ondrako

told in effect that if the old axiom, *de Maria numquam satis*, might still be valid for the devotional ends, it has no place in the scholarly theology.

It seems, however, to others (including myself) that "modern scientific method" has accomplished little else theologically except to reformulate the old axiom without the final *satis* so as to read: *de Maria numquam*. From an orthodox point of view, the results have been predictable: nothing about God either.

Whatever the immediate sources of this attitude, it is neither my direct purpose to analyze nor to refute the errors contained therein. I only mention what has far more amply been documented by others, in order to clarify the theme I am about to sketch. The old axiom, *de Maria numquam satis*, is perfectly sound and absolutely essential, not only to Mariology but to theology as a whole. For Mary is indeed a primary teacher of theology. This is no more than an aspect of her role as Mediatrix of all grace, including the grace of faith which, on our part, corresponds to that hyperdulia, a unique and total dedication engaging all our personal powers, intellectual as well as affective, in a manner beyond compare.

Maria conservabat omnia verba hæc, conferens in corde suo.[4] The reflection or pondering of Mary on the word of God is a positive influence on our own. And since Mary, in the terms of my thesis, is not simply a subordinate or incidental pedagogue, but a primary exponent of the Sacred Page, for the Church as well as for the Christian, it is the nature of theology to be Marian in character, with the tendency of sound theological thought to reflect her personal influence as teacher, the more it progresses. Our theology can be what it is, the knowledge of God, because of her unique place in God's love and her delight to be with the children of men. Far from being minimally present in the pages of Revelation, her presence pervades these sources as no other except her Son's. She is a person very much a part of the *lumen quo theologiæ*. If that presence—so transparent by nature—is not clear, then the difficulty is not with the content of Revelation, but with the reader. He does not know how to read, let alone read between the lines. Ignorance of Mary is ignorance of the nature of theology; a neglect of Mary is in effect the cultivation of theological blindness, doubt and despair. The bankruptcy of the "modern scientific method," so well described by E. Mascall,[5] has its roots here. Theology as an intellectual activity is not scientific. It is not scientific because, in the first instance, it deals with a person, Christ, not bare facts. And in the second instance, it is not scientific, because it does not deal with Christ

---

[4] *Lk* 2:19.51.

[5] E. Mascall, *Theology and the Gospel of Christ. An Essay in Reorientation.* (London, 1977).

For private consultation and not distribution without the consent of E Ondrako

impersonally, but reverentially, as did and does Mary: in a word, because it is Marian.

The alternative is not anti-intellectual, pragmatic, sentimental, or pietistic. Here again I would add: precisely because sound theological method is Marian. My aim is to show that Mary is a unique teacher of theology without whom we would understand nothing of God, because she is full of grace, the Immaculate, who, in the words of Hopkins, "lets all God's glory through, God's glory which would go through her and from her flow off, and no way but so." And did she not, like air, "make this bath of blue and slake his fire, the sun would shake, a blear and blinding ball with blackness bound, and all the thick stars round him roll flashing like flecks of coal, quartz-fret, or sparks of salt, in grimy vasty vault."[6] Further, my aim is to note that the implications for theological method can best be described with John Duns Scotus, whose name is so intimately linked with the doctrinal exposition of this primordial mystery. Paradoxically, the most metaphysical of theologians is also the one who insisted most strongly on the "unscientific" or authoritarian-dogmatic and practical character of our theology as wisdom, in contrast to science. Sound theology is metaphysical in this way, because it is Marian. Metaphysical subtlety is the tool we possess to understand the profoundly cognitive value of an exercise different in so many ways from what we are accustomed to in the "academy." That metaphysical subtlety is difficult for us, is not the fault of sound metaphysics, but the fault of a vision unaccustomed to light.[7] And if our knowledge of God—metaphysical in character—is the center and clarification of all striving to understand reality from within, i.e., as intelligible *a parte rei*, then Hopkins has caught and well expressed the link between metaphysics and Mary Immaculate when he describes Scotus as the man "who of all men most sways my spirits to peace; of reality that rarest-veined unraveller; a not rivaled insight, be rival Italy or Greece; who fired France for Mary without spot."[8]

My thesis is this: Mary is in a preeminent way our teacher of theology, directly and intimately involved in any fruitful pursuit of this activity, because she is the Immaculate Conception, therefore Mediatrix of all grace. Hence the understanding of her involvement is the key factor in determining the nature and methods of this activity. Without her engagement, this activity is sterile; and without understanding of her activity, we cannot fully grasp what it is we are doing when we practice theology.

---

6 G. M. HOPKINS, *The Blessed Virgin compared to the Air We Breathe*, in *The Poems of Gerard Manley Hopkins* (4th ed., London, 1967), p. 96.

7 ST. BONAVENTURE, *Itinerarium Mentis in Deum*, c. 5, 4.

8 HOPKINS, *op. cit.*, p. 79.

For private consultation and not distribution without the consent of E Ondrako

Formulated syllogistically the theme might go like this:

Major: Who enjoys a plenitude of perfection in any order is the source in that order of the same perfection for others.

Minor: Mary enjoys a fullness of grace in the spiritual order of knowing and loving God.

Conclusion: Mary is the source of spiritual perfection in that order for others, i.e., for believers in God.

So formulated, the argument affirms that Mary, in virtue of the Immaculate Conception, enjoys a primacy in the order of theological learning. This primacy gives her a teaching role in the lives of all others who seek to know God. There are two objections to this thesis. First, a general one: whether the teacher is Mary or anyone else, such a concept of teaching is authoritarian and pietistic, and is in direct opposition to the freedom and maturity of an adult, personal act. Second, a special one: such a concept of Mary's role as teacher either conflicts with or detracts from the unique mediation of Christ as Teacher.

In the first section to follow, I will examine concepts of learning and teaching in relation to serious misunderstandings of the nature of theology inherent in assumptions underlying these objections. A second section illustrates how a scotistic exposition of the Immaculate Conception quite easily leads us to recognize that, under Christ, Mary is a primary teacher of theology. And in the final section, I will note how the traditional characteristics of theology, as expounded by Scotus, are perfectly consistent with the assumption that Mary is a unique teacher of theology, and do enable us to identify Mary's activity therein. Indeed, as Mary is associated with Christ the King as Queen, and with Christ the Priest as Coredemptrix, so she is associated with Him as Teacher. This is the logic of the joint predestination of Christ as Savior and Mary as His Immaculate Mother.

With a theme as basic and as potentially vast as this one, it is not possible within the limits of this essay to do more than illustrate its principle features *per summa capita*. My objective is not to say the final word on this subject, but to stimulate discussion of an aspect of Mariology not only crucial to the importance of Mariology as a part of theology, but to the renewal of every aspect of theology at a time when the very nature of theology is being questioned or ignored. I have chosen to do this with a scotistic accent precisely because, at such a time, whether one considers the negative aspects of the crisis or the positive sources of solution, the central feature of theological method is its "metaphysical" character. Scotus is at once Marian and metaphysical. I do not mean to suggest that any metaphysics will do, but only one which is Marian. Nor

For private consultation and not distribution without the consent of E Ondrako

do I wish to suggest that only scotistic metaphysics is Marian and that of St. Thomas or of St. Bonaventure is not. Rather, the scotistic exposition of theological method has the merit of making a connection explicit in terms of its *fundamentum in re*. This is especially helpful today in dealing with the all-pervasive problem of hermeneutics. Finally, I by no means wish to suggest that theology is not essentially biblical and practical. Rather, sound exegesis is implicitly, and to a certain extent explicitly, metaphysical in the sense I shall give this term. A sound Christian praxis, at least implicitly, must rest on an orthodox metaphysics. The conduct of theology today has provoked a crisis of faith, because this point has so often, with irresponsible abandon, been neglected or rejected outright. Signs of this are such studies as *Mary in the New Testament* with its "modern scientific method" and the widespread neglect of hyperdulia in spiritual "praxis."

I. Magisterium Theologicum: Teaching and Learning

Our theology is possible only to the extent that our knowledge of God is in its every moment essentially and intrinsically coordinated from within and from without by the action of a divine teacher. This teaching, though essentially one, involves two teachers, whose activities, while formally distinct, are harmoniously coordinated: not as two partial causes, but as two total causes of learning interpenetrating each other in the simplicity of the spiritual act of teaching, rooted in the divine essence. This is because the essential characteristics of knowledge—certainty and infallibility—reflect quite exactly the personal characteristics of the Word and Spirit in the unity of the Godhead. This *magisterium*, consequently, is a particular aspect of that broader mediation of Word and Spirit which makes creation in general, and the spiritual creature in particular, possible. In the case of theology whose central and immediate object is God, i.e., the teacher himself, this mediation entails a visible term for each mediator, i.e., missions, whose distinct character in each instance, and whose perfect coordination with each other, constitute the primary structure or mode of teaching for others who might engage in such activity in a subordinate role. In the more recent terminology of theology, the teaching mission of the Son is entrusted with the *objectum formale quod* of theology; that of the Spirit is entrusted with the *objectum formale quo*.

This summary definition of teaching, to be used in this thesis, is taken from St. Bonaventure,[9] and in fact provides the assumptions on which

---

[9] The notes which follow in this and subsequent sections are not intended as a complete documentation of the views of Bonaventure and Scotus or others frequently cited in the text

For private consultation and not distribution without the consent of E Ondrako

Scotus conducts his analysis of theological method. A closer examination of these assumptions will make clear why the affirmation of the Immaculate Conception, along the lines of Scotus, places our Lady among the primary teachers of theology, precisely as the primary, visible term of the mission of the Spirit.

There are two radical objections to the thesis as stated. The first is this: Knowledge, in order to be personal and free, must be essentially autonomous, i.e., essentially independent of the influence and activity of any teacher. Otherwise it remains infantile and servile. Further, knowledge, in order to be knowledge or rational, must essentially prescind from any affective elements. In fact, an inherent faith and confidence in the influence of a teacher as honest and knowledgeable must, at least, implicitly entail such affective elements. In the first instance, knowledge tends to be identified with the subjective process or psychology of the act of knowing; in the second, with the logic involved in the understanding of its content. The assumptions that lie behind these two objections, so long as they are not effectively challenged, constitute a block to the acceptance of the Catholic notion of theology as involving from within and from without a *magisterium*.

Both points are aspects of the same objection to, and rejection of, the traditional Catholic view of teaching and learning as set forth especially by St. Bonaventure in his classic, *Christus unus omnium Magister*. As Bonaventure notes on many occasions, this is the source of a counterproductive violence frustrating the natural bent of the intellect to truth when so sought without the one Teacher of all. To the extent that certitude or personal assurance is attempted without Christ, knowing in fact never transcends the level of subjective bias or fiction (we might say today "myth"). And to the extent "objectivity" is attempted without reference to the eternal Word, learning never passes from the stage of hypothesis, inference, proof, to that of unconditional or infallible assent, i.e., it remains skeptical or agnostic. Together, they tend to cancel each other: pure objectivity is

---

and whose teaching is there summarized, but as a useful guide to readers who wish to pursue the theme in greater detail and depth. Generally, I have cited those commentaries providing an extensive anthology of texts as well as a full and balanced exposition. The following short works, or sections of longer works, by St. Bonaventure contain fuller explanation of the Seraphic Doctor's classic thesis on the nature of teaching-learning, or knowledge, in terms of fontal illumination, metaphysical exemplarism (with its counterpart, moral exemplarism), and the mystery of the Trinity, all centering on the divine and human understanding of the Word Incarnate. Unless other citations are given, subsequent references in this essay to the thought of Bonaventure on this theme can easily be located in these works: *Christus unus omnium Magister*; *De excellentia Magisterii Christi*; *De reductione artium in theologiam*; *Itinerarium mentis in Deum*; cc. 2, 3, 5; *Breviloquium*, Prol. 3; *Quæstiones disputatae de scientia Christi*; *Collationes in Hexæmeron*, cc. 1–3; 19; *Collationes de septem donis Spiritus Sancti*, c. 4.

For private consultation and not distribution without the consent of E. Ondrako

impersonal—personal knowing without objectivity is purely arbitrary and irrational, as Bonaventure notes in his frequent discussion of divine illumination.

Bonaventure's reply is at root a simple denial of the underlying premise: namely, that knowledge to be knowledge must be essentially solipsistic at its origin and end. Rather, at both points, it is with another: the teacher, who illumines the mind of the learner in virtue of his fullness of wisdom, thereby assuring, at its origin, the personal character of the act of knowing. By his infinite being and intelligence, the divine teacher is the source of all being and intelligibility elsewhere, thereby making possible the logical, infallible, unconditional character of knowing at its termination in a judgment of assent. This teacher is the Word of the Father. His teaching has a twofold aspect in relation to the twofold aspect of knowing qua certain and infallible: as the eternal image of the Father, the exemplar through whom all have been made, exist and are intelligible; and as the inspired Word, who with the Father in the Spirit, is the source of light by which any other knower can be certain of what is known, i.e., interiorize or personalize what is true and real as his own. For Bonaventure, knowing is not simply or primarily a passive reaction to the real, a kind of mechanical, imprinting process. It is preeminently a personal act, a *judicatio*, in which absolute assent in some degree is given to the Truth.[10] It may be unsure and erroneous in particular instances; but even these errors of science can occur, only because they include some sure and infallible (however faint) assent to the truth that is wisdom. This is because all creaturely knowing involves a relation between persons: one who learns, and one who teaches. The *judicatio*, or assent as described, occurs when an identity of understanding is reached. For Bonaventure, no teaching can be fully outside the one taught, if it is to be more than mechanical manipulation of logical processes, as with a computer. And no teaching can be taken within by the learner, except to the extent that the teacher in question merits love and respect because of his honesty and knowledge, i.e., infallibility. And no assent can simply be itself, i.e., unconditional, unless the one teacher who is all holy and omniscient is himself taken in wholly, as he takes us wholly into himself as the source of all that is real.[11]

The objection that at root such a premise is essentially fideistic—that it confuses in an inadmissible way the cognitive and affective orders—can be met with a distinction at this point: of course this is so, if the teacher

---

[10] *Itinerarium*, c. 2, 6. Cf. L. Veuthey, OFMConv., *S. Bonaventuræ philosophia Christiana* (Rome, 1943), pp. 46–146; R. Sciamannini, OFMConv., *La contuizione bonaventuriana* (Florence, 1957).

[11] Cf. *Christus unus omnium Magister*, nn. 11–14, on Christ who teaches by feeding us, especially in the mystery of the Eucharist.

For private consultation and not distribution without the consent of E Ondrako

in question is not all holy and omniscient. No, if the teacher in question is the Eternal Word who, in creating, makes what exists capable of being intelligible or motive objects of knowledge; and the inspired Word who, in illuminating, makes them capable of being understood.

For Bonaventure, then, all knowing begins personally, not simply in an arbitrary act of the learner's will, but with a judgment that in the first instance is, or should be, an act of fidelity and trust, an act establishing within the learner the first, immediate, transparent, lucid point of identification with the real as intelligible, i.e., true. Total lack of fidelity is precisely what produces incertitude at the starting point of knowledge and skepticism at its conclusion. To the extent that this general faith or fidelity (to be carefully distinguished from supernatural faith motivated solely by the authority of God and not naturally intelligible objects) is purer, more intimately related to the corresponding act of enlightenment or clarification of the teacher, the act of understanding is thereby rendered more perfect as an assent to the truth as the translucent understanding of the real. In this, Bonaventure would agree with Newman in the *Grammar of Assent* that the notional aspect of assent is only perfected to the degree it is conjoined to real assent, i.e., fully engages the person in contact with the real as such.[12] This entails not only a final, unconditional illation or judgment in respect to the intelligibility of the object known, but one bearing on the certitude with which the meaning is personally realized as true. In fact, no notional assent, as distinct from inference, is possible apart from some minimal degree of realism. Or in scotistic terms, abstract knowledge of the universal is not possible without some minimum encounter with that being or essence as singular (*cognitio intuitiva singularis*). This is the point at which the learner, as a person as well as logician, is directly engaged in thinking. For direct contact with the singular as singular is established by an act of the will. An assent that is purely notional is totally enclosed in itself, like a Kantian category, in reference to anything real, *a parte rei*.

For that kind of personal judgment: engaging the will as well as the intellect—prudence as well as logic—only one explanation suffices to be true reality. "At the beginning of all our knowing," says Newman,[13] "when light first dawns in our conscience and our first judgments about truth and justice are formed, we are obscurely aware, not only of our own activity in knowing some particular, but of a light or criterion of judgment that is

---

[12] J. H. Newman, *An Essay in Aid of a Grammar of Assent* (London 1898), pp. 75ss. For expositions of Scotus's views cf. P. Vier, OFM, *Evidence and its Function according to John Duns Scotus* (St. Bonaventure, N.Y., 1951); S. Day, OFM, *Intuitive Cognition; a Key to the Significance of the Later Scholastics* (St. Bonaventure, N.Y., 1947).

[13] A. J. Boekraad, *The Argument from Conscience to the Existence of God according to J. H. Newman* (Louvain, 1961), pp. 68 ss. for texts, with cross references to the *Grammar of Assent*.

For private consultation and not distribution without the consent of E Ondrako

the judge of the truth and justice of our judgments, before which I must render an account of my conduct. What may appear initially as a principle within me and above me is but the vague yet, nonetheless, real presence of a person greater than me. For like gratitude, accounting can only occur between persons." In this, Newman's view coincides with that teaching of Bonaventure known as fontal illumination: not a vision of God, but a direct and particular dependence on his personal activity precisely at the moment when one is becoming aware of the moral and p ersonal order of existence in becoming aware of something—anything other than self.

To the criticisms of H. Weatherby[14] that this is radically subjectiv-ism in pious form, the answer very simply is that the critic has failed to perceive two very important points. First, there is an essential difference between the teaching of the subordinate and the teaching of the primary teacher. The teaching of the first can never be an adequate criterion of truth by itself; while the teaching of the primary teacher can, for he alone is all wise and omniscient, assured and infallible. Second, the wisdom and omniscience of the primary teacher is also the source of being and intelligibility in the particular objects of one's cognitive activity. What Bonaventure calls metaphysical exemplarism, in the realm of teaching what at the objective pole provides the counterpart of fontal illumina-tion at the subjective, Newman discusses under the general heading of sacramentality of the world in relation to its Creator as the counterpart of the presence of the Creator in the activity of the illative sense. The refusal to acknowledge the obvious, viz., the existence of God signaled by his creatures and indicated obscurely in the light by which we understand them, is nothing more than a refusal to accept the nature of the intellect as ordered to the truth, ever tending to affirm truth to the extent the knower loves the truth, i.e., the primary teacher who cannot deceive. That we should doubt, that we should err, that we should experience guilt and fear the one who judges us when we judge sinfully, is not a part of the nature of intellectual activity *per se*, but a result of the effects of sin, original and personal, *in statu isto*. As Newman remarks,[15] and as we shall later note more at length in view of Mary's fullness of grace, the Christian conscience encounters the one teacher of all in this illumination, not merely as Judge, but as one who saves. For in recognizing explicitly by infused faith and loving the Name of the one Teacher, those inter-personal relations essential to knowledge and leading not to fear and servility, but to joy, peace and certitude, are perfected ever more intimately. In both orders, the natural

---

[14] H. WEATHERBY, *Cardinal Newman in His Age* (Nashville, 1973); *The Keen Delight: the Christian Poet in the Modern World* (Athens, Ga., 1975).

[15] BOEKRAAD, *loc. cit.*

For private consultation and not distribution without the consent of E Ondrako

and the supernatural, there is a marvelous balance between the subjective and objective, because both poles are anchored in the activity of the one teacher of all. One does not, strictly speaking, prove the existence of the extra-mental real by appeal to the inner light, nor prove the existence of a divine guide within by appeal to the extra-mental real. In accepting or rejecting existence in the one order, and regeneration in the other, as gifts from the giver of all good things, one accepts or rejects simultaneously that marvelous balance between the inner light and that which it illumines, between faith and the reality of the sacrament which it grasps.

It is often said that St. Thomas explains more convincingly the objective structure of our knowledge in relation to the divine light, *in thy light we see light*, with his analysis of the human mind in terms of active and passive intellect. In some ways this is true, until we note how such an approach renders more difficult an explanation of how natural and supernatural knowledge are coordinated. It is also said that Scotus rejected Bonaventure's theory of divine illumination and exemplarism. True, he dropped the terminology, but retained the Bonaventurian concept of the mind, finite as well as infinite, as a pure perfection. At the heart of the human mind stands the unique concept of being as univocal which, in the epistemology of Scotus, plays the same role as the divine light as a fontal object in Bonaventure.

This brings us to theology in particular. As a kind of knowing it is for Bonaventure, as for Newman, a particular and central instance of what it means to know. For in the instance of theology, not only is something real known, but the teacher *par excellence* is known directly. It is the particular, distinctive manner whereby the teacher exercises his *magisterium* in this instance that determines primarily the manner in which our revealed knowledge of God differs from our knowledge, both speculative and practical, of God and of things other than God, in a non-theological manner. For the purpose of this discussion two differences are all important. First, this *magisterium* is exercised in a direct and immediate fashion—not the case in those areas of cognitive activity which may be designated natural or scientific, even where these include some knowledge of God and of his *magisterium*. Second, this *magisterium*, insofar as it is exercised directly and immediately, entails a "visible" term, a direct, singular, immediately identifiable point of contact with the person of the teacher as such.[16]

---

16 ST. BONAVENTURE, *Quæstiones disputatæ de mysterioTrinitatis*, q. 1, a. 2; *Christus unus omnium Magister*, nn. 2–5. NEWMAN, *Grammar of Assent*, pp. 98 ss.

For private consultation and not distribution without the consent of E Ondrako

Both Bonaventure and Scotus define the human person as the image of God and his likeness.[17] As such, he is capable of knowing and loving God, and indeed does know and love him up to a point. But both are equally firm in the insistence that even with the initial involvement of the teacher in such activity, man is not able, i.e., it is not within his native power, to know and love God directly.[18] We can know God as the term of a process of reflection, as Bonaventure would say, either through or in the creature, but beyond this point we cannot go.[19] (Indeed, we cannot even define the point exactly without an actual, positive awareness of the other side of the point, which comes only with revelation and the light of faith.) "Theology begins," writes Bonaventure,[20] "where philosophy leaves off," viz., where the one who concludes the search for wisdom, is instead the direct and immediate starting point for the knowledge of all else. Scotus makes the same point when he observes that strictly speaking only a divine person is naturally a theologian, i.e., only such a person has it within his native power to know the divine nature directly.[21] He certainly does not mean that philosophically we are agnostics by definition, and only theologians to the extent that we become fideists. What he means is that God is not naturally evident to us. It is not in our power to make him present directly as intelligible *in se*, something possible for him to do if he so wills, precisely because we can know him indirectly as working in others as the supreme intelligibility at the source of all intelligibility. Before we can actually know him directly as intelligible *in se* (attain a knowledge whose formal object is God, not something other than God), another magisterial action must occur whose distinctive feature is best described as revelation: the making of an object of knowledge directly present to a knower, that otherwise is not within the power of the knower to make so present or evident.[22]

Correlative to this revelation is the conferral of another light of knowing, called faith, whose distinctive feature is the ability conferred

---

[17] St. BONAVENTURE, *Breviloquium*, p. 2, cc. 9–12; *Itinerarium*, cc. 3–4. SCOTUS, *II Sent.* d. 16, q. 1, in *Opera Omnia*, ed. Wadding vol. 6, pp. 760 ss.

[18] St. BONAVENTURE, *Breviloquium*, p. 4, c. 1; *Itinerarium*, c. 4. Cf. VEUTHEY, *op. cit.*, pp. 247–297. For Scotus cf. L. BERARDINI, OFMCONV., *La nozione del sopranaturale nell' antica scuola francescana* (Roma, 1943), pp. 115–121.

[19] *II Sent.*, d. 23, a. 2, q. 3; *Itinerarium*, c. 1.

[20] *Breviloquium*, p. 1, c. 1, 3.

[21] For the views of Scotus on this and other questions concerning the nature of theology cf. the prologue to his *Ordinatio*. A very useful edition, with excellent introduction, is to be found in: *Obras del Doctor Sutil Juan Duns Escoto*, vol. 1 (Madrid 1960) (Latin-Spanish text). For general expositions of Scotus's views on revelation and theology cf. J. FINKENZELLER, *Offenbarung und Theologie nach der Lehre des Johannes Duns Scotus* (Münster, 1960), A. MAGRINI, OFM, *Joannis Duns Scoti de scientia theologiæ natura* (Rome, 1952).

[22] St. BONAVENTURE, *Quæstiones disputatæ de mysterio Trinitatis*, q. 1, a. 2.

For private consultation and not distribution without the consent of E Ondrako

on its possessor to know, to assent, and to be able to understand with certainty, what is revealed as intelligible, but not evident, because as yet only present by way of revelation.[23] In this way, avers Bonaventure, the master of theology teaches not only from without, i.e., making what is known directly present as an object of that knowledge, but from within as well, i.e., making what is so knowable luminous, clear, the object of a certain assent, or personal *judicatio*, what we might in generic fashion call the interiorization of the intelligible in a personal way. Insofar as the magisterial involvement of the teacher, both from without and from within, is primarily a personal action whose characteristic is judgment, the key feature of our theology based on revelation and faith throughout: as a process and as a term, is authority: the exercise without by the teacher and acceptance within by the learner.

Revelation can also be employed (and Bonaventure so employs it) to designate other aspects of the *magisterium* of Christ which this activity has in common with that particular exercise of it customarily designated revelation in this time of pilgrimage which is the proper object of faith. Thus, the vision of God in heaven is also an act of revelation or teaching in the sense that, without this, the blessed are unable to make God present so as to see him. But when he makes himself so present, he does so as also to be evident. In the vision of God in heaven, which is the theology of the blessed, God makes himself intelligible so to speak in terms of his own intelligibility. We know, as Bonaventure says, the divine in the divine light itself, therefore with evidence.[24] In the revelation accepted by faith, we are able to know God directly, because he makes himself directly present, but not in a form proper to himself. He makes himself directly intelligible, but not evident; hence in terms of a comparison or analogy with something else known, but not himself. The analogical content of revelation as the form of divine intelligibility made directly available to us now, and centered on the manifestation of the invisible divinity in the manhood of Christ, is rightly described as a manifestation of the mystery or mysteries of faith; not because nothing is known or understood directly, but because it is understood without being evident. On the other hand it is also described as a manifestation of the sacraments or symbols of faith, because what is known is directly present so as to make possible an intelligible encounter. The light of faith illumines not simply the believer's experience, nor simply the mind of God, but something distinct from both, viz., the sacrament of faith revealed, while the light of glory bears directly on the divinity itself. The actual experience of belief is indeed an understanding of God, but in

---

23 *Christus unus omnium Magister*, 1.

24 *II Sent.*, d. 23, a. 2, q. 3; *Breviloquium*, Prol. 3, 2.

For private consultation and not distribution without the consent of E Ondrako

this sign or analogy; whereas in heaven the need for sign and sacrament will cease as a medium for expressing intelligibility. But what will not cease in heaven will be the need for a mediation that makes God present as knowable *in se*.

Evident and intelligible, then, are not convertible terms. What is non-evident is that which is not in one's power to make present as knowable, or, if made present, cannot be understood in terms of its own intelligibility, but only in a form that is not itself, and whose degree of actual expressiveness of the intelligibility of God is determined in the first place not by the knower or the form, but by God. In neither case does lack of evidence mean unintelligibility, but only inability of the knower to apprehend an object by himself without faith; or after apprehension, to understand apart from the guidance of the revealer, since without faith the terms of comparison by which enlightenment is attained are not within one's control.

Scientific knowing, on the other hand, also involves an act of revealing on the part of the divine master, an act, however, indirect in contrast to that of revelation in the strict sense; and which is clearly perceived only at the conclusion of one's activity rather than at its beginning where, in fact, it must already be active, if not directly evident, if any kind of knowledge is to be possible on our part. Bonaventure discusses this in terms of the exemplary causality characteristic of the eternal Word that is the basis for all being and, therefore, for all intelligibility in things other than God.[25] The practical conclusion is this: scientific knowledge is only relatively or indirectly autonomous vis-à-vis the revelatory activity of the Word eternal as teacher and, hence, radically open to coordination with His revelatory activity in the stricter sense as Word Incarnate. The practical conclusion is this: scientific knowledge is only relatively or indirectly autonomous vis-à-vis the revelatory activity of the Word eternal as teacher. This is why wisdom, a kind of consciousness bearing in some way, however indirect, on the teacher as teaching, is always a more perfect realization of what it means to know, than is science in any form. And, hence, our theology now based on faith, even if analogical and, therefore, incomplete in relation to the theology of the blessed in heaven, is more intellectually fulfilling than any mere science, because it entails a direct and immediate acceptance of a more perfect revelation of the Word than that occurring in and with scientific activity.

I note further, in order to correct a too facile inference, that philosophy and theology differ, not in this, that the first knows nothing of God and the second, everything; or in this, that what is known of God in the

---

25 *Collationes in Hexæmeron*, c. 1.

For private consultation and not distribution without the consent of E Ondrako

first case can be understood, while in the second it cannot. Rather, the difference, as stated above, consists in this: what is known philosophically about God is known to the degree the knower makes God evident, which he can do only indirectly. Whereas in the second case, the knower knows God only to the extent God makes himself present as knowable, either incompletely in an analogical manner, or perfectly in a proper way in the light of glory.

The position of Scotus is essentially the same, even if he ostensibly rejects the theory of illumination. Scotus does this, first, in order to avoid any confusion between the lights of faith and reason, and between revelation in the restricted sense and more generic revelatory role of creatures as objects of scientific knowledge.[26] But there is also a second consideration germane to this essay. Those attentive to the Bonaventurian texts cited so far may have noticed that the Seraphic Doctor always refers to the Word eternal as primary teacher, and to the Word Incarnate only insofar as Redeemer of a fallen world. Scotus instead identifies the universal Teacher with the Word as incarnate, precisely because creation exists only for the sake of the Incarnation; whereas, for Bonaventure, the Incarnation is only occasioned by the fall of Adam and Eve. By restating the theory of divine illumination in terms of the univocity of being, Scotus is strengthening the bases for the respective mediatory roles of Christ and Mary not only in the theological order, but in the intellectual order in general. The univocal notion of being, with its two intrinsic but really distinct modes, surely resembles faintly but authentically, the mystery of the hypostatic union, from which Mary Immaculate cannot be disjoined.

The proper object of theology according to Scotus is not our univocal notion of being, but rather the infinity of God, of whose revelation and explanation the univocal concept of being is, however, a privileged instrument, viz., an instrument of light or illumination. This latter we cannot know directly, except there precede a revelation in the strict sense. In this life, that revelation is not a vision of the divine essence as infinite, but an analogical manifestation, whose acceptance on our part as intelligible, entails a constant acceptance of the authoritative, magisterial judgments of

---

26 For a good exposition cf. W. Hoeres, *La volontà come perfezione pura in Duns Scoto*, tr. A. Bazzotto, OFMConv., and ed. A. Poppi, OFMConv. (Padua 1976), pp. ix–x; 44 ss. The Italian translation of the original German, *Der Wille als reine Vollkommenheit nach Duns Scotus* (München 1962), contains material not included by the author in the German edition. The texts of Scotus where he corrects certain fideistic exaggerations of the theory of illumination in the Augustinian school, opening the way either to ontologism or skepticism, can be found in the anthology edited by A. Wolter, OFM, *Duns Scotus. Philosophical Writings* (London 1962), pp. 96 ss. On univocity of being cf. T. Barth, OFM, *Being, Univocity, and Analogy according to Duns Scotus*, in J. K. Ryan, *John Duns Scotus 1265–1965* (*Studies in Philosophy and the History of Philosophy*, vol. 3) (Washington 1965), pp. 210–262.

For private consultation and not distribution without the consent of E Ondrako

the divine teacher determining the poles of comparison not evident to us. The univocal concept of being and of the pure perfections is but the point of insertion for the revealed analogies, not the power by which we actually come to understand these. This power is the light of faith. The uniqueness of the univocal concept of being, in contrast to other notions we form about the things of this world and its purpose, is substantially identical in the thought of Scotus with that of fontal illumination and exemplarism in Bonaventure, where, as I have noted, these form the basis of revelation in the strict sense, but are not the revelation itself.

So too, the light by which we personally accept or interiorize revelation may be taken to designate a power of understanding distinct from all others, or we may consider what that which all power to know on our part has in common in relation to the primary source of enlightenment, viz., the inspired Word. In this latter sense, faith designates fidelity, the loyalty, trust and obedience given to the teacher as such, which is the beginning of understanding on our part. It is often objected—as it is against the views of Cardinal Newman on the relation between real and notional assent on the one hand, and the involvement of the teacher *via* the illative sense on the other—that such a view involves the will intrinsically in the process of knowing. The answer is: indeed it does. But this does not lead to the alleged subjectivism, when the involvement springs from one's fidelity to a holy and truthful teacher who is Creator and thereby source of intelligibility or light in the particular known. Such a teacher is at once the ultimate, self-authenticating criterion, both of the being in that which is known, and of the discernment of that being in terms of truth and justice. The encounter with the Master or Judge in the primitive act of awareness is the beginning of knowledge and understanding formally consummated in the assent of the intellect. Such an act at the scientific level, in view of a particular object of science, is within the range of our native intellectual light, and in the consideration of which we may err. By the same token we are also capable of correcting the error, to the extent we are faithful to the Truth, i.e., to our Teacher teaching.

When we consider the light of faith in the narrower sense, viz., infused faith which is not supported by evidence, we do not dispense with these two elements. Rather, faith perfects the natural light in a double way. First, the fidelity or love of the teacher directly bears on his immediate personal presence distinctly recognizable as such, i.e., on his teaching authority. Second, the assent that consummates this initial understanding, or acceptance of the presence of the theological intelligible revealed, is an understanding of that intelligible analogically, i.e., without evidence. At the other end of the spectrum, the light of glory does not differ from faith

For private consultation and not distribution without the consent of E Ondrako

because it dispenses with fidelity, but because it is consummated in a direct understanding of God which is not analogical, but proper, i.e., evident.

There are several practical conclusions that have importance for any discussion of the unique role of Mary in the teaching of theology, and for the satisfactory resolution of the relation between doctrinal development and the immutability of revealed Truth that certitude implies. Unlike scientific learning, theology cannot in any manner whatsoever enlarge the limits of revelation or increase the range of what we can actually know directly about God, or in what form we can actually understand God directly, viz., the analogical, for the simple reason that it is not in our power to make God present or intelligible in this manner. The master or revealer may extend the range of comprehension and make the mode of understanding proper—and this he does in the case of the saints in heaven, and in the case of some contemplatives on earth *per modum actus*.[27] He does not do so in the case of what is customarily termed public revelation. This has been closed or completed in a final way by the Word Incarnate in a form that is human and analogical, and so confided to the Apostles and their successors as the unchangeable deposit of faith. In terms of the objective pole of knowledge or its content, it is simply impossible that development should occur in theology. Whoever serves Christ by teaching in reference to this pole does so in a subordinate role which is limited to the guarding of the deposit, maintaining its purity, neither adding to nor subtracting from its present contents. The gift of infallibility, wherever possessed in the Church, is a negative kind of assistance, preventing that, in the exercise of a teaching office in a subordinate way, error or change or impurity should creep into the deposit under the guise of credible authority. But it is not a positive gift enabling its possessor to know more than anyone who already believes in Chris knows implicitly about God in believing Christ; or to establish new analogies or mysteries of faith not already revealed objectively. Who knows me, in encountering me directly in faith, says our Lord to Philip (*Jn* 14:9), *eo ipso* knows the Father directly and the ocean of goodness that is the infinite being of Father and Son in the Holy Spirit. For this reason theology is by definition dogmatic, as science and philosophy are not; not because the latter are essentially independent of a teacher, but because the former, more closely dependent and therefore more perfect as knowledge, reflects the immutability of the eternal light (*Jas* 1: 17) more directly in its objective form.

Teaching that is only from without is not yet a teaching that has attained fruition. Unless it is interiorized, what is taught remains opaque,

---

27   *Collationes in Hexæmeron*, c. 3, 30.

For private consultation and not distribution without the consent of E Ondrako

unclear, and unintelligible to the learner. If accepted in such circumstances, i.e., as non-interiorized, faith is indeed experienced as a kind of compulsion; and the direct encounter with the theological real becomes an encounter that is fearsome, like the faith of devils and the damned, which is indeed faith insofar as it is an experience of authority whose truth cannot be avoided or denied, and yet cannot be willingly affirmed. Such a direct encounter with the face of Christ on the Day of Judgment is not the beatific vision, but exactly the contrary: an encounter with final damnation. The exercise of pretended authority, in fact not authority but naked force, cannot be other than an experience of abuse and enslavement by those who are its victims. The exercise of true authority, directly or indirectly, of which teaching from without, or revelation, is an instance of direct exercise, only incidentally fearsome, where those who encounter this authority or obey it, are lacking the spirit of the teacher, wholly or in part. They are not taught simultaneously from within, because they lack that saving faith by which the teaching is clarified, rendered intelligible and reasonable, i.e., "approved by the believer" as Bonaventure says and so theology in the proper sense. When the learner of theology shares the spirit of the teacher in the form of saving faith, his understanding will indeed be dogmatic in form, in view of the content of that understanding. It will be equally loving and personal in view of the identity of spirit. For Bonaventure, if the *Verbum Incarnatum* teaches from without, it is the *Verbum inspiratum* who teaches from within.[28] This presence of the Word within, in the course of the conduct of theology, is nothing more than the mission of the Holy Spirit. It is important to note, then, that the inner activity of understanding is not personal solely because it is ours, but because it is also the activity of another, rightly acting as teacher-clarifier, the other advocate or intercessor, as Christ Himself notes in John 14: 17, and again in John 16: 13–15.

This progressive clarification of what is present as intelligible, i.e., its explication, is nothing more or less than intellectual growth and, in the case of theology, doctrinal development. At the natural level, both for the individual and for the community, it can and does lead to an actual, but still limited extension of our range of comprehension. In theology, such is not the case. Rather, this explication makes clear what we already knew *in globo*. It is certainly not an illogical process when it occurs, although the possibility of error and incompletion is quite real. But when this growth is correct, this is not the result primarily of the logic of our mental processes, but of the guidance of our teacher. So too, it may reflect the circumstances

---

[28] *Quæstiones disputatæ de mysterio Trinitatis*, q. 1, a. 2.

For private consultation and not distribution without the consent of E Ondrako

of the person reflecting; yet these are not the decisive factors determining in what degree that understood from within is an understanding of that which is revealed *a parte rei*. Rather, the activity of my teacher with me, to the extent that I accept and follow his guidance, is decisive. This teaching activity in theology is a grace of a very particular kind, and it is known as witness. Without this it would be impossible to know or to understand the object of theology, since this is not normally evident to us now. Witness is but the setting of one's seal on this that God's word is true in such wise as to enable another who does not see to accept that word as true, and understand, and understanding, have life in his name. (*Jn* 3:18; 19:35; 20:31). Witness is possible only insofar as the witness is sure and knowledgeable. Where a host of witnesses is involved, each of whom himself believes, there must ultimately be one whose witness is first, who in some way has direct access to the truth as evident or observable. Witness, then, is the complement of revelation, as the light of reason is the complement of evidence at the natural level. As the use of reason gradually makes clear the intelligibility of its object, so the activity of the witness accepted in faith by the believer makes the truth of what is revealed clear, but not evident. Bonaventure insists that without the witness of a living tradition anchored in a primary witness (*originalia Sanctorum*) to guide, neither will the literal sense of Scripture (its content) nor its spiritual sense be assimilated or be capable of assimilation by the student of the Sacred Page; in such a juncture neither the *summæ* of the professors of theology, always imperfect in contrast to this living tradition, much less the treatises of the philosophers which provide only the tools of understanding, will be of use in attaining understanding.[29] For Bonaventure, the witness of the Apostles and their successors naturally enjoys a special role in this unbroken tradition. For in witnessing they also confirm and guard infallibly the one, final revelation of Christ. But to the extent any believer, clerical or lay, gives witness by an authentic faith, he is part of the living tradition that grows, at whose root and center for both and for all, according to the place assigned each in the Church by Christ, is the Spirit of Christ.

The foregoing provides a context in which the nature and purpose of the visible missions of the Son and Spirit can be defined in reference to questions of theological activity on our part. The dual pole of knowledge at the natural level, viz., its certitude and infallibility, is but a distant reflection of the distinction between Word and Spirit as persons, and the manner in which their activity is coordinated in any teaching. That his activity should be "visible" or direct, does not mean that its nature should be evident

---

[29] *Collationes in Hexæmeron*, c. 19, 8–11.

For private consultation and not distribution without the consent of E Ondrako

without faith in the first instance. Rather, the person so teaching is so present as to be recognized directly, in a distinct way, as the one teaching by those who accept that teaching. Thus, Bonaventure defines mission as nothing more than the divine procession whose term is now visibly present in creation. The visible term of each mission is consonant with the personal property of each person proceeding. The visible coordination of these two activities is governed by that of the processions within the Trinity. With this in mind, we see that the final resolution of every epistemological question is one of Trinitarian theology.[30]

The source of all knowledge and understanding of the truth is God, and in the first instance, God the Father, who, from all eternity, shares that knowledge and understanding with the Son in the Holy Spirit. The Father is the fontal plenitude of light and knowledge that is fully and always in the other Divine Persons. "No man has ever seen God." (*Jn* 1:18). Because creatures are not always with God the Father, i.e., do not have access to him directly, as do the Son and Spirit by nature, light and knowledge in creatures must be mediated, and in a very special way in the case of theological knowledge. This is precisely the role of Son and Spirit as teachers, the first as the one who reveals, the second as the one who enlightens, clarifies, give witness. The two teaching missions are not activities of a partial kind which together combine to form one complete action. Each has a completeness, a fullness in its own order. Nor do they compete as though needing coordination from without. They are ordered from within the unity of the Godhead, each to the other in a mutual circumincession, so that the teaching of the Spirit does not and cannot occur without the realization of the mission of the Son and the clarification of that Son, who, with the Father, sends the Spirit. Neither can the Son consummate His mission, unless He also teaches in the Spirit and vivifies from within those who would assent to the truth He has revealed and form "one mystical person" with Him.

The fullness of wisdom and knowledge in each, and the perfect coordination between Word and Spirit in the Trinity, are the remote bases for the possibility of any cognitive activity and consistent growth in wisdom and knowledge on the part of creatures. It is the visible character of the mediatory activity of Word and Spirit that makes possible any cognitive, theological activity on our part, one that has as its direct purpose or objective the understanding of God. To identify the visible term of each mission: the manner in which the plenitude of wisdom or fullness of divinity is found in each mission singly and coordinated with the other, is to provide a

---

30 *Breviloquium*, p. 1, c. 5, 5.

For private consultation and not distribution without the consent of E Ondrako

specific and definitive solution to the problem of how theological teaching is carried out, and how theological learning is to be achieved.

Both Bonaventure and Scotus, as does every orthodox theologian, identify the visible term of the Word's mission with the sacred humanity assumed in the Incarnation.[31] In the proper sense only that human nature formed in the womb of Mary, and no other, constitutes that term. Such a view is perfectly consonant with the personal property of the Word as image of the Father, and explains at root why revelation is at once full and definitive with the accomplishment of the Incarnation, and why the sacred humanity must enjoy a fullness of wisdom and understanding. In whatever manner the mediatory activity of the Word Incarnate is continued in the Church, that continuation is not a simple extension or addition to the Incarnation. As the term of the mission of the Son, it is complete. Thus, the activity of the *magisterium* of the Church as a continuation of the teaching mission of the Word in the Church is not a further revelation, but a confirming, guarding, unchanged transmitting of the entire, complete deposit: in a word, a vicariate.

For Bonaventure, the visible term of the mission of the Spirit likewise entails a fullness and finality without which it could hardly complement and vivify the visible term of the mission of the Son.[32] But because the Spirit is a different person proceeding from the Father and the Son, in a manner formally distinct from the procession of the Son from Father, his mediatory mission is not—(and for Bonaventure and Scotus, whatever might be said *de potentia Dei absoluta*, cannot be otherwise than *de potentia Dei ordinata*, in view of the wisdom that accompanies God's every choice)—another hypostatic union. Thus, the term of the Spirit's mission may be, and is multiple, as that of the Word is only one. Where that term is personal, the Spirit's mission perfects rather than suppresses the person of the creature. For that indeed is the character of the procession of the Spirit: to be a bond of interior unity between persons as persons: one Person in many persons who love each other in an ego-tu relation: not from without, but from within the *Nos* as Father and Son, but now including the adopted sons. At the cognitive level this is exactly the function of light and fire in general. Light is not what is known, but that by which we know, clarifying what is real, so as to enable us to identify in a personal way from within with the intelligibility of the object that is *a parte rei*. So too, fire is not what we love, but that by which we love. So knowing and loving is to interiorize the real within us, so as to be drawn within the ambit of the intelligible and loveable real as intelligible and loveable on its own terms, i.e., because

---

[31] *Ibid.*; and p. 4.

[32] *I Sent.* dd. 14–16.

For private consultation and not distribution without the consent of E Ondrako

true, in what Bonaventure calls the *judicatio*. At the level of theological knowledge this light is faith and this fire is love, which is not simply our response to Christ, but our response with the witness, or teaching, of the Spirit of Christ. If the authoritative teaching of Christ takes the form of a command because He repeats what He has received from His Father, the authority of the Spirit received from Father and Son as a bond of love takes the form of an attraction of a lover to the beloved, of the desire for truth to its fulfillment in assent.[33] Teaching for us is an extension of the witness of the Spirit; without that witness we know nothing of the Father and Son, nor do we love them.

It is this presence of the Spirit of Christ in the Church that explains how the Church continues the mission of Christ, not by revealing, but by confirming, guarding and transmitting the revelation of Christ as a sign to the nations; and how the Church and the Christian by believing, give witness, i.e., are able to transmit with understanding and clarity to the degree necessary for teaching from within, thus growing in understanding and clarity by this very service. This is what is commonly called "development of doctrine." The Church, and every structure and ministry of the Church, is vivified by the mission of the Spirit, whose coordination with that of Christ explains how in fact the functioning structure does actually secure, as we know it does, a growth of the Church and Christians, ever consistent with the unchanging will of Christ.[34] In this way the quintessentially charismatic sustains and vivifies the institutional.

Two questions pose themselves in regard to the visible term of the Spirit's mission: what is the primary term of that mission in view of its multiple terms in the life of the Church; and how can it be encountered as primary and visible?

In contradistinction to the mission of the Son, that of the Spirit is in the nature of a sign, according to Bonaventure, which clarifies, which makes known something other than itself. In theology, where the object made known is not thereby evident, the teaching value of this sign is precisely that of witness. To this end, in contradistinction to the mission of the Son, the temporal mission of the Spirit has multiple terms. While the mission of the Son occurs once, perfectly, in all its fullness, that of the Spirit occurs many times successively, and with varying degrees of perfection or fullness. According to Scotus, a series involving multiple units can neither be, nor be understood, except there be a single term whose perfection is such as to constitute it first in the series; not merely chronologically or accidentally, but essentially, and whose primacy explains the series; and whose fullness

---

[33] *I Sent.* dd. 10–13.

[34] *Breviloquium*, p. 4, c. 10, 8.

For private consultation and not distribution without the consent of E Ondrako

or perfection, its relative immutability, makes possible the intelligible and consistent growth or coming-to-be of all the components of that series or order. The infinite regress of the ancients or eternal process of Hegel is an absurdity.[35]

In view of the multiple terms pertaining to the mission of the Spirit, tradition has always indicated the Church in general, and the hierarchical *magisterium* in particular, as it centers on the office of Peter, as the privileged locus or primary term of the mission of the Spirit, the certain sign of Christ, the unshakeable witness that clarifies His presence in the world. Yet, the answer is not an entirely complete and final resolution to the problem of how theological growth occurs, both for the Church and for the single believer. Of the fact of development there can be no doubt. And although, in fact, the Church is infallible, and the single believer certain in his belief while in union with the Church, neither enjoys a perfect fullness during the process of development sufficient to account (if we consider the Church itself as the primary, visible term of the mission of the Spirit) for the finality and consistency that is proper to each assent, and whose coefficient is the immutability and irreversibility of dogma, conceptually and verbally.

On the one hand, an attempt to account for the immutability which ignores actual changes entailed by development makes both the original deposit of revelation and the accumulated dogmatic tradition as opaque and lifeless as a stone, a brute fact, to be dissected solely with the tools of dialectics and science. On the other hand, attempts to account for the actual growth in wisdom, whether this be stimulated by the activity of the hierarchy in teaching or by the laity in believing, which dispenses with the immutable and final character of revelation, leaves us with a kind of process, undefined at either end, i.e., the absurd "infinite regress."

The second question is related to what might rather improperly be termed the objectivity, but better called the infallibility and certainty of our theological understanding at any point in its progress. In normal circumstances it is easy enough to confuse the light of reason with that which it is not, my *arbitrium* or experience as such. In the absence of any evidence for what is understood in belief, the possibility is compounded. The immediate, practical solution is clear: follow the authoritative guidance of the Church. But why and how this authoritative guidance on the one hand is not identical with the *arbitrium* or judgment of him who exercises it, and how that non-identity can be discerned; and why and how the experience of true faith includes the presence of a witness who

---

35 SCOTUS, *De primo principio*, c. 1.

For private consultation and not distribution without the consent of E Ondrako

illumines, whose presence is wholly within and immediate, yet distinct and unconfused with one's experience, and which can be "visibly" discerned as such across time and space, is the mystery on which these reflections turn. Briefly, the problem posed is that of defining more exactly the difference between Christian intellectual experience and that called pantheistic, or theosophy.

To the extent that the Church, *Magisterium*, Sacramental system, are terms of the mission of the Spirit, they teach not only from without, but from within. To the extent that they are without, they are clearly not confused or confusable with one's experience and, hence, can function as signs clarifying what they make known as real though non-evident, rather than as projections of one's "faith experience." But to the extent that the Church is without, it is not entirely within; or to the extent that it is wholly within, it is not at all visible. It is of course true in practice that the sign which is the Church will not deceive because of the power of the Spirit, even if I do not have the answers to these questions. But the question raised here can be useful and it is this: how these signs can be infallible in practice in the context of a multiplicity, both temporal as well as special, not entailing perfect identity, and whose very visibility or interiority increase and decrease seemingly in inverse proportion to each other as they become objects of reflection. By themselves, as terms of the mission of the Spirit, none of these signs is the primary explanation of its effectiveness or cohesion with the others. One may of course appeal to the Church as a whole. But unless that is taken in an ideal sense: what will be actual only at the last day when the Kingdom is consummated, one cannot point to any existing entity that fills Scotus's definition of primary term.

What then is the primary term of the mission of the Spirit, whose perfection is such as to enjoy the immutability that permits growth consistent with the truth that is infallible, and whose personal intimacy is such as to guarantee assurance within, without engendering confusion of teacher with learner, or the process of knowing with the truth known? Bonaventure hints at the solution when he says that the fullness of the Spirit of Christ, now in the course of realization in the Church and believers, and only to be consummated on the day of Christ's second coming, is already full in Our Lady who has been gloriously assumed into Heaven.[36] Her presence as

---

[36] "Ecclesia vero trahit ab ipsa (Maria) originem… Unde est mons domus domini, quae habet super praedicta tria (fides, spes, caritas) aedificari, quae etiam pollebant (in sanctis) …Unde et ipsi montes domus Ecclesiae et fundamenta dicitur… In horum omnium vertice beata Virgo mons praeparatus dicitur, quia quidquid illis est promissum vel revelatum, hoc est in ea impletum; et quidquid gratiae in istos influxit, ab ipsa et per ipsam derivavit…" *Sermo 1 de Assumptione B.V.M.* (IX, 688 a–b). "Quidquid enim dignitatis et gloriae istis partialiter est collatum, sacrae Virgini integraliter est concessum." *Sermo 2 de Assumptione B.V.M.* (IX, 692 b).

For private consultation and not distribution without the consent of E Ondrako

full of grace in the midst of the Church provides just that visible, singular term for the mission of the Spirit that explains how that mission can have multiple terms, yet still be united and consistent with the will of Christ. Further, in reply to the question: - How anyone can be sure that the Pope may not err, or that the Church so fall away in practice from faith in Christ, as no longer to be visibly identifiable as the bride of Christ, spotless and without wrinkle (except as an ideal to be hoped for)?—Bonaventure replies that the promise of infallibility and indefectibility to the Church by Christ is such as to require that at no time will there be an insufficiency of believers strong enough to resist the pressures of hell such as to render the Church invisible and inefficacious as a sign.[37] And as if to answer that the first and absolutely unshakeable of these believers is Mary, Bonaventure writes in his conference on fortitude as a gift of the Holy Spirit that Mary exemplifies this gift in a preeminent and incomparable way as the Mother of God who fully shares the sorrows of her Son, who does not break at the foot of the Cross. Just as Mary is the Coredemptrix: the strong woman whose faith is irreversible, so too is the Church to the extent that Mary is at its center. Bonaventure urges all to take refuge with their Mother: first Mary, and then the Church, in all necessity, because the Mother is an efficacious Mediatrix. Only when the sinner has found his Mother, will he also find the home of his Father.[38]

With his explanation of the Immaculate Conception, Scotus simply completes and explicates the thrust of Bonaventure's Mariology. In one sense, i.e., in the order of final causality, Mary depends on her Son, as the mission of the Spirit presupposes that of the Word. But in another sense, in the order of efficient causality, the mission of the Word depends on that of the Spirit. The logic of the Incarnation demands that this be a work accomplished not invisibly, but visibly. It is clear enough that the visible character of this work, *finaliter loquendo*, is the Incarnation. What is the visible character of this work in the order of efficient causality, when it is finally brought to term? It is not the Church in the order of efficient causality, for the Church only issues from the side of Christ at the completion of His work. The answer is clear: Mary, the Mother of God, for without a temporal generation the hypostatic union (and the rest of the metaphysics it implies) is for all practical purposes beyond our ken,

---

For a longer exposition cf. P. D. FEHLNER, OFMCONV., *The Role of Charity in the Ecclesiology of St. Bonaventure* (Rome, 1965), pp. 74–95.

[37] *IV Sent.* d. 4, p. 1, dub. 2. FEHLNER, *op. cit.*, pp. 44 ss.

[38] *Collationes de septem donis Spiritus Sancti*, cc. 5–6. FEHLNER, *op. cit.*, pp. 83 ss. For a general exposition of the universal mediation of Mary according to Bonaventure, cf. L. DiFONZO, OFMCONV., *Doctrina S.Bonaventuræ de universali mediatione B.Virginis Mariæ* (Rome, 1938).

For private consultation and not distribution without the consent of E Ondrako

as invisible, opaque, impenetrable, far away, as if it had not occurred. It is Mary's activity as Mother that is the key to the Incarnation and salvation, as it is her character as Virgin to be the ultimate, immediate, unmistakable, infallible sign that illumines the final fulfillment of God's promise of a Savior. It is she who works the epiphany of God from our point of view, for the same reason that my actual understanding of Christ begins with faith rather than with revelation (i.e., my faith in revelation, and not revelation merely as it exists independently of me, for that can be known and accepted partially by merely "natural and not saving faith"). The identity of her faith before and after the Incarnation, before and after Calvary, is the utterly irreducible, primary, visible witness behind every other witness to the Incarnate Savior. All this is accomplished by the powerful working of the Holy Spirit.

How then can she do this, if she too belongs to the order of sin; if she too only enjoys the powers of nature? The answer is that she does not belong to the order of sin, but to the order of the hypostatic union; and that her ideals are not circumscribed by the limitations of her natural powers. This is what was always implied in some way by calling Mary most holy, i.e., *beyond compare*. Scotus removed the final ambiguities and resolved the principal objections and, in so doing, formulated the doctrine of the Immaculate Conception which simply states how, with a fullness of grace and beauty beyond compare, Mary both precedes and follows Christ at once, i.e., is mother and spouse. Indeed, the very method of arriving at this conclusion, i.e., of attributing to Mary in the highest degree whatever is of perfection and otherwise not inconsistent with revelation as authoritatively confirmed,[39] thus making her in this order beyond compare and the source of perfection for all other created persons, reflects the nature of theological method rooted in the possibility of knowing directly the fullness of divinity in human guise. That possibility only becomes real when Mary is exalted beyond compare in our lives by a total dedication and consecration to her as to no other human being. The principle is not an arbitrary "petitio principii," neither in our lives nor in our intellectual activity, because as the Immaculate, Mary is in fact the primary term of the mission of the Spirit, and enjoys a fullness of wisdom and grace that, in the economy of salvation, is the guarantee of certainty and inerrancy by grace, as the Spirit of God is the guarantee of the fidelity of Father and Son by nature within the Trinity.

In his pondering on how the universal mediation of Mary Immaculate might be reconciled with the uniqueness and once-for-all character of

---

39 SCOTUS, *III Sent.* d. 3, q. 1, n. 10 in *Opera Omnia*, ed. Wadding, vol. 7, p. 95.

For private consultation and not distribution without the consent of E Ondrako

Christ's atoning sacrifice, St. Maximilian Kolbe has simply extended the theology and theological method of Scotus: Mary is the primary, visible term of the mission of the Spirit in her Immaculate Conception, so as to be Mother of God.[40] That is why she is also Coredemptrix. As Coredemptrix she gives birth to the Church as its Mother, and so Mediatrix of all graces. This is why, assumed gloriously into Heaven, she is not above the Church but at its very center, whereby her constant, personal involvement with each believer, beginning with the Pope, the grace of the Spirit is deployed for the attainment of the full measure of the manhood of Christ. Without that involvement of a very real and singular person, one would be hard put to discover the invisible light of the Spirit, or avoid mistaking one or another of our own enthusiasms for the Spirit of God. As it is, the realization that this mediation includes an intellectual dimension as intimate to each member of the Church as any other of Mary's activities as Mediatrix of all grace, is the discovery of that first, indomitable and always efficacious witness to the full reality of the Incarnation.

II. I Am the Immaculate Conception

That Mary is the "visible" term of the mission of the Spirit, enjoying thereby a fullness of grace, a plenitude, which confers on her a primacy in the exercise of the mediation of the Spirit, is the cornerstone of St. Maximilian Kolbe's Mariology. It is also the proximate source of inspiration for this study, whose central theme is but a particular aspect of this mediation.

The remote basis for this insight is the teaching of Scotus concerning the Immaculate Conception seen against the backdrop of St. Bonaventure's explanation of the teaching missions of the Divine Persons. Scotus has made explicit the one point not fully clarified in the theological synthesis of teaching-learning according to St. Bonaventure. If the preceding analysis has been lengthy, it has been so, only in order to make clear the permanent value of Scotus's contribution to theological epistemology. I do not mean to imply that Scotus made all the applications I am suggesting in terms

---

[40] Cf. G. Domanski, OFMConv., *Lourdes et le Père Maximilien Kolbe. Esquisse de sa mariologie*, in *Miscellanea Francescana* 58 (1958) pp. 195–224 (reprinted as a pamphlet Rome, 1974) ; H. M. Manteau-Bonamy, OP, *Immaculate Conception and the Holy Spirit.The Marian Teachings of Father Kolbe* (Kenosha, Wis., 1977). Besides the critical Polish edition, the complete works of Bl. Maximilian are available in only one other language, Italian (3 volumes, Florence, 1975–1978). Cf. in this edition SK 1229. The most important passages touching this insight can be found in the appendices to the work of Manteau-Bonamy just cited; more extensive excerpts are found in the anthology of G. Domanski, *Mary was His Middle Name*, tr. by R. Barwig (Altadena, Calif., 1977). Cf. also E. Piancentini, OFMConv., *Dottrina mariologica del P.Massimiliano Kolbe* (Rome, 1971).

For private consultation and not distribution without the consent of E Ondrako

of theological method, but only that he established clearly the perspective from which, if faithfully maintained, the applications could and would be made. Once the unique character of Mary's sanctity as Immaculate in her Conception has been realized, then we are in a position to grasp the manner in which the mediation of the invisible and transparent-translucent Spirit of God is carried out in a decisive, visible, but still translucent way, both in Christ and in the Church, and in single believers.

On this point of the Immaculate Conception, as in the matter of the primacy of Christ, as also in the matter of fontal illumination and exemplarism, Scotus is the continuator rather than the corrector of Bonaventure, as he is more the continuator rather than the critic of the great work of St. Thomas. Dr. Gerken has already shown that the position of Scotus in the matter of the primacy of Christ is only a correction of Bonaventure at the level of an incomplete formulation of the underlying insights of his theology.[41] I would say the same in respect to the Immaculate Conception and the universal mediation of Mary. What Scotus has done is to sharpen and complete the basic principles of Bonaventure's Mariology, namely: that the fullness of grace in the course of being realized now in the communion of saints and in the body of Christ which is the Church, and which will only be completed on the last day, is already full in the person of Mary. I stress the term *fullness*. It indicates in Bonaventure, not a quantitative measure of something material, but a qualitative aspect of existence.[42] As the fullness of divinity dwells in the human nature of Christ—not making his humanity infinite, but conferring on it such perfection as to be beyond compare with any other creature and to be the source and cause of perfection in His mystical member's sanctity, wisdom and merit—so that same fullness of grace predicated of Mary implies a same primacy, paralleling the *gratia capitalis* in Christ, with one difference, that Mary is not its author as is Christ, but the one through whom, by her maternal mediation, all grace passes from Christ to us.[43] She is, therefore, the Mediatrix, not only of grace in general, but of wisdom, i.e., the understanding of God in particular, or theology.

Thus, Scotus's correction of Bonaventure's metaphysics and epistemology becomes a subtle sharpening of our perception of the exact nature of

---

[41] A. GERKEN, *Theologie des Wortes* (Düsseldorf, 163), On Scotus and his relation to Bonaventure and Thomas cf. E. BETTONI, OFM, *Duns Scotus: the Basic Principles of His Philosophy* (Washington, 1961) pp. 15 ss.; on the originality of the Scotistic synthesis, *Idem* in RYAN, *op. cit.*, pp. 28–44; and L. VEUTHEY, OFMCONV., *Les divers courants de la philosophie augustino-franciscaine au moyen âge*, in *Scholastica ratione historico-critica instauranda* (Rome, 1951) pp. 627–652.

[42] ST. BONAVENTURE, *Breviloquium*, p. 4, cc. 5–7; *Quæstiones disputatæ de mysterio Trinitatis*, especially q. 4, a. 1, for the concept of fullness and its relation to infinity.

[43] Cf. FEHLNER, *op. cit.*, pp. 58–61, for Bonaventure's view on the *gratia capitis*.

For private consultation and not distribution without the consent of E Ondrako

teaching in theology: authority as the basis of certitude; univocity as the root structure of correct analogy; and both in terms of the visible missions of Spirit and Son. Because Mary's position in the economy of salvation is a preeminent one in virtue of her fullness of grace, once that position has been made clear and explicit, then the primacy and central position of her Son, the Incarnate Word, becomes fully clear and explicit; and with that the nature of that knowledge whose direct and formal object is the divine.

The merit of Scotus in the matter of the Immaculate Conception does not rest in the fact that he was the first to affirm it, because he was not, or because he drew out all the implications of the theology involved. Rather, it is to be found in this, that he not only accurately resolved the principal objections to its affirmation as an integral part of the deposit of faith, but so formulated the doctrine as to clarify what I would term the basic principle, not only of Mariology, but of theology and of Christian living as well: *De Maria numquam satis*.[44]

In substantiation of this, I call attention to two aspects of Scotus's exposition that strike me as particularly significant. One is the negative, the question of the *debitum*; the other is positive, the question of Mary's fullness of grace.[45]

It has been stated often enough that Scotus himself either never raised the question of the *debitum peccati*, or if he raised it, took no position in the matter, i.e., on the question whether had Mary not been preserved from original sin, she would or should have contracted this. To me it seems clear enough that the point of the *debitum* controversy is that of a question whose purpose is not to demonstrate a new point, but only explicate more clearly what has already been realized as true. Thus, the point of the controversy is ultimately to demonstrate that there is no *debitum peccati* for anyone in the proper sense, but a *debitum justitiae*; and, therefore, preservative redemption is not an exception to a law, a dispensation, but something far more mysterious.[46]

---

[44] For the history of the doctrine cf. E. O'Connor, CSC, *The Dogma of the Immaculate Conception. History and Significance* (Notre Dame, Ind., 1958) pp. 51–326; *Marian Studies*, vol. 5 (1954) (Washington, 1954). For summary of Scotus's arguments cf. A. Carr, OFMConv. – G. Williams, OFMConv., *Mary's Immaculate Conception*, in J. Carol, OFM, *Mariology*, vol. 1 (Milwaukee, 1954) pp. 328–394. And for a convenient grouping of all the texts of Scotus cf. *Joannis Duns Scoti theologiæ marianæ elementa*, ed. C. Balic, OFM (*Bibliotheca Mariana Medii Aevi*, 1–2) (Sibenik 1931–1933).

[45] A more extensive and detailed probing of the mind of Scotus along these lines can be found in A. Equiluz, OFM, *Presupuestos metafisicos de la teologia de la preservacion en Juan Duns Escoto*, in *Juan Duns Escoto en el septimo centenario de su nacimiento* (Madrid, 1966) pp. 169–214.

[46] On the history of the *debitum* controversy cf. J. Carol, OFM, *A History of the Controversy over the "DebitumPeccati." A Bibliographical Consensus* (St. Bonaventure, N.Y. 1978). For Scotus on

For private consultation and not distribution without the consent of E Ondrako

We contract original sin, as Scotus remarks, not because of a "law" or obligation to sin, but because a proper debt or obligation to be just and holy from the first moment of existence is in fact not fulfilled, as intended by the Creator and Savior. Contraction of original sin results not from anything positive, such as a law, or process of generation (though this last is in fact the occasion and condition for the contraction), but from the absence of some perfection that ought to be present—namely, the righteousness of grace. It is in fact not present at conception in all the descendants of Adam, because Adam, as head of the human family, enjoying a certain primacy with the responsibility not only of being the source of natural life, but moral rectitude as well, acted irresponsibly and lost the ability to be the source of life at once morally as well as naturally good.[47] In the case of our Lady this debt or obligation to be just is fulfilled; hence she is immaculately conceived. Her preservation from contracting original sin is not the prevention of incurring a debt; it is the fulfillment of one. It is the fulfillment of one, because she comes under the absolute primacy of Christ, prior to the consideration of anyone else's relation to him. Adam's headship or primacy is, then, a relative one, including all those, but only all those, whose reason for existence is not immediately subsumed under the absolute primacy of Christ, as is Mary's.

Mary is preserved from contracting original sin in virtue of the merits of the Redeemer, not because otherwise she would need liberation from sin, but because this is how God will achieve most perfectly what he ultimately intended in creating in the first instance, the most perfect work that is the Incarnation and the fruit of that mission, the grace of the Holy Spirit. That sin should have intervened, and that when in fact that perfect work is realized it should also put right what the envy of Satan and the foolishness of Adam and Eve put wrong, accounts for the fact that Mary's sanctification, when it is realized, is realized by the grace of one who is in fact Redeemer also. It does not change the original personal relations between Christ, Mary and Adam, or that Adam's relative headship, not only to Christ, but also to Mary, or that his original justice as well as existence is predicated on the prior predestination of both Christ and Mary. Hence, the grace by which Mary is sanctified comes indeed from the one who dies to save his people from sin, but in her it has nothing to do with sin or a *debitum peccati*.

We miss in part the originality of Scotus's insight, "preservative redemption," formulated primarily to answer an objection based on the

---

the *debitum justitiae*, cf. *Ordinatio II*, d. 32, q. un., n. 7; *Reportatio Parisiensis II*, d. 33, q. un., n. 27.

47 SCOTUS, *II Sent.* d. 32, q. un., in *Opera Omnia*, ed. Wadding, vol. 6, pp. 944 ss.

For private consultation and not distribution without the consent of E Ondrako

universality of redemption and of original sin, if we regard it merely from the perspective of the universality of sin and the universality of Christ's redemptive work in this regard. This perspective by itself is neither fully clear nor fully adequate, because it fails to take note of another perspective, not only more fundamental than the fall, but more basic to the existence and unity of the human family than the relative headship of Adam. Preservative redemption is more than preservation from sin. Preservative redemption in the actual economy of salvation is what makes liberative redemption possible. Through Mary's preservation and mediation, Christ frees all others from sin. Her salvation is unique: she is saved by Christ, but independently of the headship of Christ, even if Adam had not sinned. Were this not so, the only difference between liberative and preservative redemption would be a chronological and quantitative one, in which one person at least, Mary, would enjoy the fruits of the redemption from the first moment of existence, and the rest after some later moment of existence. On such a showing there is no reason why this should constitute anything but a secondary aspect of sanctity, an exception to a general condition. In a sense Eve was formed immaculately, but such innocence hardly has the same significance as that of Mary's. Such an interpretation hardly fits the spirit of Christ-like fairness, in which the hour of entry into the vineyard has nothing to do with the relative joy therein. It has more to do with that elitism and "chronolatry" which sees time of birth, or that of the "first settlers," or that of the final "product of evolution," as the patent to paradise.

Mary's privilege quite clearly is a unique privilege touching not merely the first moment, but that moment insofar as it defines her person before all others, especially God, in a unique way. Mary possesses a fullness of grace that constitutes a primacy with Christ. She belongs to the order of the hypostatic union, as no other person can or does, because in God's mind, before all others, and before any consideration of the problem of sin, she is to be the Mother of the Word, the Mediatrix of grace, and the most glorious, attractive and beautiful work of the Savior, as the Incarnate Savior is the most beautiful work of the Father. Enjoying such a primacy of grace, she is the source of life for all others, both those who preceded her as well as those who come after, beginning with Adam. Her predestination absolutely with Christ is the reason for their existence. Neither Adam's sin, nor that of any other human being, changes this. Her descent from Adam naturally is the realization of his reason for existence, and therefore of the entire human family. Her preservation from sin by grace is the realization of the final basis of perfect fellowship in the communion of saints, the expression of the fact that the fall is not final, and that we can each and all

For private consultation and not distribution without the consent of E Ondrako

have a part in the attainment of God's glory and the consummation of his kingdom by grace.

This leads to the second, positive observation. The clarification of the Immaculate Conception is equivalently the unambiguous definition of the name given to Mary by the Angel of the Annunciation: full of grace. The Immaculate Conception is not simply one of many graces, the first chronologically. It entails a plenitude in the same sense as Bonaventure uses this word of the humanity of Christ. Who is essentially first in any order possesses a plenitude that is the source of perfection for all others in that order. The order involved here is that of salvation, the perfecting of spiritual activity, of angels as well as of men. This is true not only for Christians; it is also true for Christ in His humanity. Mary is the Mother of God's Son, not merely in a passive way, nor simply as an instrument of God in effecting the Incarnation. For Scotus, she is actively and person-ally the Mother of the Word Incarnate, and therefore "first" in respect to Him in her own order, as the Father of the Son is in his.[48] To Mary's question: how can this be? the answer of Scotus is in effect that of the Angel: by the power of the Holy Spirit. Mary is able to act decisively and in a primary way in conceiving the Son of God virginally, because she is full of grace. She is not simply more holy than others. This would not constitute a sufficient basis to do what in fact is beyond the natural power of the creature. She is incomparably most holy, enjoying a plenitude that places her in an order transcending the limits of the created and of the state of sin. In formulating his exposition of the holiness of Mary in terms of a preservation from sin from the first moment of her existence, Scotus has placed Mary as a person directly within the order of the hypostatic union, not as another divine person incarnate, but as that created person whose union with the Father and Son is so perfect by grace that no more perfect example of this can be found or conceived, unless we recall the eternal relation of Spirit to Father and Son by nature. Hence, such a union of grace is nothing other than the work of the Holy Spirit, and where this is full, there we may speak of the primary, visible term of that mission. In this sense Mary is not simply most holy in comparison with other creatures. She is not simply immaculately conceived. She is holiness itself in created form; she is the Immaculate Conception.

The objection that this in fact makes the Incarnation the effect of Mary's cooperation, rather than Mary's sanctification the fruit of her Son's

---

[48] For the history of the theology of the divine maternity in general cf. H. M. MANTEAU-BONAMY, OP, *Maternité divine et incarnation* (Paris, 1949); for the position of Scotus and the scotists in particular cf. S. RAGAZZINI, OFMCONV., *La divina maternità di Maria nel suo concetto teologico integrale* (Rome 1948).

For private consultation and not distribution without the consent of E Ondrako

work, I would reply with Scotus that both are true. Mary is indeed full of grace in virtue of the merits of her Son in the order of final causality. But in the order of efficient causality Mary by the power of the Holy Spirit is the one who makes real the Incarnation, and thereby has a part with the Holy Spirit in the accomplishment of Christ's mission. There is no reason why God cannot beforehand, in view of the merits of his Son as Incarnate, send his Spirit fully into the one who will be the most perfect fruit of his Son's work, precisely for this that the visible, human, personal cooperation required by the wisdom and logic of the Incarnation and the economy of salvation in the attainment of the Father's will might be proportionate to that end. Such is the logic of the infancy narratives summarized by St. John: *Et Verbum caro factum est et habitavit in nobis, et vidimus gloriam eius gloriam quasi Unigeniti Patris* (*Jn* 1:12), who alone has seen God and who has made God (the Father) known to us who believe. Through Mary we come to recognize the mystery of the Incarnation by her virginal maternity and maternal virginity. And in understanding the Immaculate Conception we find the light in which we understand how and why this Incarnation has come to pass, i.e., the primacy of Christ. Hers, then, becomes the first or primary witness which provides the assurance found in all other witness. That is why she is teacher as well as mother. And like all the work of the Spirit, Mary's teaching has a certain lucidity, purity, transparency: it is aimed at the clarification of another, her Son. We may indeed recognize Him without adverting to the light, as we breathe without adverting to the air. Yet what we breathe and what we see can better be appreciated to the extent that we advert to air and light. So too with the work of the Spirit which is to make the Incarnation fruitful, to glorify Jesus. It is in realizing the unique relation of Mary to the Spirit of God that we come to appreciate the Spirit as a person. As the Immaculate Mary is the visible term of the invisible Spirit, so to know her as the Immaculate is to know clearly and distinctly the Spirit as well, the person who in the Trinity is the bond of love between persons, the light that clarifies persons to each other and is the assurance to each that all are united in each other in the truth and in the bond of charity.

In summary, the absolute predestination of Mary to be the Mother of God's Son is, like the mission of the Spirit, second *in ordine intentionis* in relation to the predestination of Christ. But *in ordine executionis* the realization of Mary's fullness is first in respect to the accomplishment of the Incarnation. And what is true at the beginning of that work is true at its completion. When we consider the glorification of the Incarnate Word as the Lord of all, this is first in the order of intention and last in the order of execution. The work of Mary and the Holy Spirit precedes the

For private consultation and not distribution without the consent of E Ondrako

glorification of Christ on the Cross and in the Resurrection, as the sending of the Spirit on the Church brings to realization the fruit of the priestly work of Christ on the Cross in preparation for His final coming in glory. And to the extent that we consider this work as having a visible term, that term is primarily Mary, both before and after the establishment of the Church. All other manifestations of the Spirit are centered on this one without which the Incarnation would not have happened, without which the "hour" of Christ would neither have begun nor ended successfully, and without which the Church would remain a lifeless skeleton.

As the Abbé Feuillet remarks,[49] we shall have no difficulty in understanding how Mary could actually offer her Son on the Cross, indeed how anyone can actively participate in the sacrifice of Christ, without derogating from the unique mediation of Christ, if we keep in mind the distinction and coordination of the processions of Son and Spirit within the Trinity and the missions of the same without. In this latter case we are dealing with the visible terms of these processions. The relations of Christ and Mary, respectively as Incarnate and Immaculate, exactly reflect this distinction and coordination of the two orders of mediation. Nor need we fear that in insisting on the absolute predestination of Mary, with its implications for her unique and decisive role in the drama of salvation and the destruction of the serpent, we have placed her outside the Church. What we should fear is the downgrading of Mary, for it leads to a confusing of distinct missions, in effect a kind of modalism or unitarianism that denies the divinity of the Spirit as a distinct person, nowhere so obvious than in the heated agitation for the ordination of women.

Mary is thoroughly within the Church, not simply as another member, or the first chronologically, but as the preeminent member, because she is the one who enjoys the fullness of the Spirit in a primary way. In being what she is, the most holy, immaculate Virgin, she does indeed mediate, not as does her Son by atoning, but as Vatican II notes, by making her Son and His followers who believe in Him one in each other, i.e., transparent to each other in their mutual love for her who enjoys the fullness of the Spirit. Without citing him, both Vatican II and many theologians have in fact come to realize the import of the Immaculate Conception in a manner anticipated by St. Maximilian and fully in accord with the thrust of Scotus's theology.[50]

---

[49] A. FEUILLET, *Jésus et sa Mère* (Paris, 1974) pp. 234 ss.

[50] H. M. MANTEAU-BONAMY, OP, *La Vierge Marie et le Saint-Esprit* (2 ed., Paris, 1971). Cf also P. D. FEHLNER, OFMCONV., *Mary, Mother of the Church according to the* Constitutio de Ecclesia in *Miles Immaculatæ* 1 (1965) pp. 31–40. Likewise: *Le Saint-Esprit et Marie*, vol. 1–3, in *Bulletin de la Societe Française d'Etudes Mariales* 25–27 (1968–1970), wherein can be found ample documentation for the patristic tradition that shaped the inheritance of Bonaventure and Scotus.

For private consultation and not distribution without the consent of E Ondrako

There is no need to give credit, except to our Lady. For looked at from the perspective of the theme I am expounding, such insights and advances are primarily the work of our Lady as the *Magistra theologiæ*. For Scotus, in clarifying the sanctity of our Lady in terms of the Immaculate Conception, not only clarified the primacy of Christ, but the nature of that knowledge and understanding we have of His person: Thou art the Christ, the Son of the living God. Thus, the method of theological reflection on Scotus's part in this question clarifies as well the method of teaching on Mary's part involved in any theological effort within the Church; and whose neglect will always be the reason for efforts that end in doubt and despair concerning the will of God.

A quite striking confirmation of this can be found in a short *Memorandum*[51] of Cardinal Newman on the Immaculate Conception. The importance of Newman does not consist in the fact that he cites or is even influenced by the writings of Scotus. Indeed, that he was only casually acquainted with the "metaphysical theology" of Scotus, makes the confirmation striking. Not only does his theological epistemology in the *Grammar of Assent* and elsewhere closely parallel that of Bonaventure and Scotus,[52] but this is particularly apparent in the use the Cardinal makes of it in summarizing the theology of the Immaculate Conception in response to Protestant objections, and in pointing out the exact character of theological progress and doctrinal development.

On both counts, both in respect to his epistemology of faith in general, and in respect to his notion of theological activity in particular, Newman has been subjected to severe criticisms. Recently, Prof. Weatherby has observed that Newman's theories, especially in the *Grammar of Assent*, concerning the basis for certainty and objectivity in fact lead to the opposite.[53] Weatherby does not mean that Newman personally is a subjectivist; only that his explanations are not merely inadequate, but in fact counterproductive, if pursued logically. All that prevents this is piety and rigid obedience to authority, not the inner consistency of the theory. In the opinion of this critic, Newman has confused affective certitude (piety) with intellectual in making the use of the illative sense decisive for the attainment of assent, a position that does in fact involve a personal or prudent judgment, whose firmness and correctness becomes at once the major premise and the conclusion to be proven.

---

51 J. H. Newman, *Memorandum on the Immaculate Conception*, in *Meditations and Devotions* (London 1903) pp. 79–86.

52 This is noted particularly by H. Weatherby, *The Keen Delight*.

53 Weatherby, *Ibid.*, and also in his earlier work, *Cardinal Newman in His Age*.

For private consultation and not distribution without the consent of E Ondrako

More particularly, in respect to the methods characteristic of Newman's theological discussions, he has been accused of being "unscientific," i.e., of using pious accommodation as a substitute for logical analysis of a truly critical kind in reaching conclusions. Thus, Cardinal Journet, apropos the aforementioned *Memorandum*, remarks that while the discussion is helpful for devotional purposes, on the assumption that its content is true, the argument itself does not establish the Immaculate Conception as revealed dogma in a critical way.[54] Journet, of course, does not reject either the truth of the revealed character of the dogma, or the possibility of discovering this in the sources of revelation. Clearly, the criticism is implicitly a rejection of a methodology, Scotus's as well as Newman's, rooted in the "unscientific" character of theology as practiced during a time of pilgrimage. In Journet's mind, and in that of so many others, the "decuit" of Newman and Scotus is not the basic form of theological reflection, but merely a secondary *argumentum convenientiæ*.

Other critics of Newman are more radical.[55] They maintain that the value of Newman's epistemology, and its application in matters of development, rests not in the fact that it is correct, but in the fact that he opened to discussion in Catholic circles a problem that previously had not been faced, thereby calling into question the immutable character of revelation and dogma, hence in thrust intellectually skeptical vis-à-vis an authoritative tradition. While these critics would reject Newman's personal solution as intellectually adequate, they would approve it as a first step toward an understanding of revelation as an ongoing process. It is with this new, creative, approach to theology, so it is claimed, that the old dilemma between a "modern scientific exegesis" which cannot establish the truth of revelation beyond cavil and its alternative, an anti-intellectual fideism appealing to piety or authority or both, will be broken. It is significant, I believe, that not only Newman, but his critics should illustrate their positions with examples drawn from Mariology, and almost always in reference to the Immaculate Conception, as the question most crucial to the resolution of issues fundamental to theological method, viz., its intellectual and developmental character.

---

54 C. JOURNET, *Scripture and the Immaculate Conception*, in E. O'Connor, CSC, *op. cit.*, p. 39. At issue is not the maternity of our Lady as a basic principle of Mariology, but the metaphysical and epistemological presuppositions for our certitude concerning a point seemingly more explicit than the Immaculate Conception. It is in relation to this latter dimension that the views of Scotus and Newman reveal their full importance. It is our certainty concerning the Immaculate Conception that enables us to comprehend the divine maternity in its completeness.

55 N. LASH, *Newman on Development* (Shepherdstown, Va., 1975).

For private consultation and not distribution without the consent of E Ondrako

Newman's summary of the issue and answers involved in the question of Mary's Immaculate Conception could not be clearer or more exact as a formulation of the *status quæstionis*. He writes in the *Memorandum* first that the dogmatic definition of Mary's Immaculate Conception is not at all a new revelation. Whatever development or progress is involved, this is not a matter of discovery, of addition or subtraction from the deposit of revelation, of something not known previously, and hence not a matter of proving the truth of its contents. The dogma is truly revealed; otherwise it could not have been declared a dogma. The purpose of theological activity: whether that of the *Magisterium* or that of believers, is clarification and explication. If then by proof one means this, that there is no departure from traditional views, merely a further explication of the procedures, one is correctly identifying an aspect of doctrinal development. But if by proof in matters of development one means doing what the scientist has in his power to do in making the object of his science present as intelligible, then indeed that is exactly what true doctrinal development does not mean. That has already been done in a final, irreversible way by the revealer. This is a capital point for, on Newman's own testimony, it excludes the possibility of approaching the problem of doctrinal development in terms of some form of Hegelian evolution.

Secondly, when asked where this clarification can be found in the sources of revelation, viz., Sacred Scripture and primitive doctrine, Newman responds: in the revelation and affirmation of Mary's unique sanctity as Mother of God, and in the contrast between the first Eve and Mary in terms of their quite contrary relations to the Deceiver, the father of lies. Again, another capital point: the question of Mary is also very much a question of truth versus error at its very root.

Thirdly, when asked how we can discover what is implied in revelation, particularly in respect to what God has done freely, and how such is possible and intelligible, Newman replies that faith is the source of enlightenment, the basis of an illation from the implicit to the explicit, from the unconfirmed to the confirmed. Faith is this source of certainty, precisely because it entails the kind of *pietas* for a teacher who is omniscient, and this is at the heart of the scotistic theology as well.

It is precisely by reason of the piety of faith, that theology differs from science as a form of knowledge at once certain and infallible. The difference can be measured in terms of the closeness or distance of the one teacher of all in each case. At the natural level the teacher is encountered at a distance, indistinctly, hence as a remote, though very real Judge who inspires awe, a sense of justice and injustice as absolutes. At the supernatural level, at which our theological activity occurs, that encounter is one of immediacy,

For private consultation and not distribution without the consent of E Ondrako

directness: not of vision, but of the personal presence of Christ our God and Savior, who forgives our guilt. It is the piety or loyalty of faith that makes such a response possible, and whose obedience, respect, devotion and docility are no more than the natural correlatives of a loving attraction to the authority of the revealer *in actu exercito*. It is this piety which makes certain and true understanding of God actual in the first instance. The *argumentum pietatis* which grasps the implications and ramifications of the essential point is no mere accommodation of a certitude already reached on other grounds. It is the very heart of the theological process, as much in those points touching the "necessary" essence of God, as in those touching the "contingent" facts of creation and grace. It is this *pietas* that enables us to absorb the intelligibility of God and the wisdom of his deeds, in such wise as to understand God's point of view from within.

In this process revelation—the objective pole—does not change, for it is something final and complete for this age, made such by the will of Christ. What is subject to progress is the degree of clarity attained in the subject who believes. Once we assume, as does Newman, the complementary relationship between the mission of the Word and that of the Spirit, then the criteria distinguishing true developments from false, both in the life of the Church and that of the believer, are exactly what we would expect them to be. And the final confirmation of the correctness and freedom from error of this reflection and clarification is exactly where we should expect it: in an authoritative and infallible exercise of the teaching office of Christ. And since those who exercise this ministerial office can do so faithfully only to the extent they are clearly certain of the revealer's mind, not only those who come to understand, but those who guide by confirming and preserving the deposit of faith from error, do so under the Spirit of Truth, the one who primarily clarifies and witnesses that what is believed is true.[56]

In all this Mary stands very obviously at the center of Newman's reflections (even before his conversion in 1845) on the truth of Christ's teaching.[57] She is the primordial, visible witness who "clarifies" her Son, who manifests him to the world, who signals the beginning of his hour,

---

[56] NEWMAN, *An Essay on the Development of Christian Doctrine* (3rd ed., London, 1903). For Newman's views on infallibility cf. *A Letter Addressed to His Grace the Duke of Norfolk*, in *Certain Difficulties Felt by Anglicans in Catholic Teaching*, vol. 2 (London, 1903) pp. 320 ss. The first part of this volume deals with Newman's reply to Pusey's difficulties with Marian belief of Catholics, particularly the Immaculate Conception.

[57] NEWMAN, *The Theory of Developments in Religious Doctrine*, in *Fifteen Sermons Preached before the University of Oxford* (3rd ed., London 1900) pp. 312–351. For Newman's Mariology cf. F. FRIEDEL, S.M., *The Mariology of Cardinal Newman* (New York, 1928); and for its relation to his personal life cf. L. GOVAERT, *Kardinal Newmans Mariologie und sein persönlicher Werdegang* (Salzburg 1975).

For private consultation and not distribution without the consent of E Ondrako

who stands at the foot of the Cross, who reigns with Him gloriously in heaven; the one who, before all others and in the midst of all others, kept the whole revelation in her heart, pondering it. For Newman, even the most explicit truths of Scripture concerning Christ are impervious to understanding, if one attempts to understand them apart from the influence of Mary.[58] We can unravel the logic of doctrinal development, not by relating this solely to the laws of logic, or comparing this to the life of something it is not, but by relating it to the personal influence of Mary Immaculate on each believer in the Church and on the Church itself. The *pietas* at the heart of theological effort is Marian: first of Mary for us and then of us for Mary. To understand this is not simply to understand another point of theology; it is also the key to understanding the method itself. And the reason for this is the Immaculate. Newman wrote the *Essay on Development* in 1845. The dogma of the Immaculate Conception was declared in 1854. Two great names in theology, Scotus and Newman, widely separated in time, but both students and teachers at Oxford, both manifest a striking similarity in their understanding of theology and in their testimony to Mary Immaculate, as it were framing the beginning and the end of that process culminating in her clarification by the Church in 1854, and marking the beginning of a profounder, more explicit grasp of the mystery of the Church itself. Is this not also a sign of her wisdom in the Church, that among other things is the effective source of a more perfect unity, and an essential component in defining the goal and nature of ecumenical activity?

Whatever may be said in reply, there is no question that the place of Mary in the Church, as set forth in *Lumen Gentium*, and Mary's relation to the Spirit of Christ, is in substance what has hitherto been expounded. Superficial commentaries since the Council have stated that because Mary was not treated in a separate constitution, she was in fact being downgraded in contrast to the excessive veneration of recent centuries, especially since the definition of the dogma of Immaculate Conception, and this was in fact a repudiation of scotistic maximalism in Mariology.[59] The implications of the present essay are quite the contrary. Rather, what has emerged from the work of Vatican II, whatever the passing character of the disputes accompanying its work, or the intentions of certain participants, is a confirmation of the scotistic insight into the Immaculate Conception, just as the work of Vatican II has in fact strengthened the sense of the primacy

---

[58] NEWMAN, *The Glories of Mary for the Sake of Her Son*, in *Discourses Addressed to Mixed Congregations*, (London 1902), p. 348.

[59] For the background of the disputes concerning our Lady at Vatican II cf. R. WILTGEN, *The Rhine Flows into the Tiber* (New York 1967).

For private consultation and not distribution without the consent of E Ondrako

of Christ as it has always been understood in the Franciscan school. And it is this sense of Mary's preeminent mediation, not as an extension, but as the complement to Christ's in illumining, in clarifying, that justifies Bl. Pope Paul VI's summation of Vatican II on the mystery of the Church and Mary in the title: Mary, Mother of the Church.[60]

In the next section I shall examine the specific characteristics of theological method, as these are set forth by Scotus, for a time of pilgrimage in the light of this assumption: they are such because of the continuous influence of Mary Immaculate as a teacher of theology, and as such enable us to identify more exactly the character of that transparent activity which permits us to know her Son ever more clearly.

III. Theology and Theological Method: Mary as Teacher

In all learning, human and angelic, the psychological and logical aspects of the process of learning do not primarily determine either their soundness or their successful outcome, viz., an assent to the certain and infallible truth, simple and independent of reasoning supporting them, but rather the assumptions guiding the learner in arriving at that *iudicatio* both certain and correct. For Bonaventure and Scotus these assumptions are sound and adequate, to the extent that the right teacher is directly and personally involved in the process. In theology this teaching is that of Mary and Christ.

In describing the nature of theology during a time of pilgrimage, Scotus notes[61] three properties basic to this activity. These properties distinguish theological activity both from other modes of learning possible to us during this time and from the theological activity of the blessed. These are (1) its authoritative, dogmatic or "unscientific," (2) its metaphysical, and (3) its practical character. His analysis resting on these points is in substance nothing other than a more precise analysis of the three elements in Bonaventure's description of theology as the "credible, ut transit in intelligibile, ut boni fiamus." This description synthesizes the manner according to which the three moments essential to any spiritual

---

[60] Paul VI, in *Acta Apostolicæ Sedes* 56 (1964) pp. 1014–1018.

[61] Scotus, *Ordinatio* I, Prol. The discussion which follows is based on a study of the entire Prologue, in view of three major questions raised by Scotus: what is the nature of theology in contrast to science (a wisdom based on authority); what is its primary object (infinity of God); what is its purpose (love of God, or praxis). For a convenient anthology of texts from all this works bearing on this subject cf. Deodatus a Baliaco, OFM, *Capitalia Opera B. Joannis Duns Scoti*, 2 vol. (LeHarve 1911), vol. 2, pp. 1–162. One may compare this threefold description with that of Bonaventure: symbolic (dealing with the concrete in theology), proper (dealing with the cognitive), and mystical (dealing with the affective). Cf. *Itinerarium*, c. 1, 7.

For private consultation and not distribution without the consent of E Ondrako

act, cognitive or affective, are engaged in what is called theology.[62] These are memory, in which that to be known or loved becomes present to me as knowable and loveable; understanding, in which the object is clearly affirmed, i.e., judged to be true or good; love in which the activity in question attains its purpose, i.e., becomes fruitful. In more contemporary language the first moment might be called apprehension, the second assent, and the third application.

In the Augustinian tradition these three moments are formally distinct, because they reflect the personal distinctions of the divine persons. They are on the other hand inseparable by nature because they also reflect the real unity and simplicity of these persons. Apprehension naturally tends to clear and certain assent; and to the degree apprehension is actual, already includes it implicitly. So too understanding naturally tends to "praxis," and in some way already implies this latter incipiently. And a "praxis" that is just in respect to the truth affirmed tends to apprehend more exactly, so as to understand more profoundly, thus leading to a more perfect fruition of the good for its own sake. It is only when in spiritual activity these three moments are realized in disjunction that the activity, cognitive or affective, is experienced as unsound. Apprehension, apart from understanding and love, becomes merely servile, rote or mechanical memorization. Understanding, apart from "praxis," remains merely notional, sterile, speculative, cut off from the real, a prisoner of doubt. And "praxis" cut off from sound apprehension and understanding, tends to be arbitrary, whimsical, sentimental, a prisoner of despair and an experience of nothingness and sin.

The general import of my theme is this: such occurs to the extent that the influence of the right teacher is not engaged in the spiritual activity, cognitive or volitional, according to the nature of the power in question. By contrast, to the extent that influence becomes more direct and immediate (as is the case with theology by definition) these elements attain a harmonious balance which simultaneously preserves their formal distinction. In his analysis of theological method, Scotus has in fact specified the manner in which the joint theological *magisterium* of Christ and Mary finds an appropriate response in the cognitive activity of the disciple in each of these moments, in such wise as to account for their formal difference and harmonious interpenetration.

Authoritative

Scotus's view of theology as non-scientific is nothing more than a way of saying that its starting point is the *credible*, rather than the evident, even

---

[62] *Itinerarium*, c. 3.

For private consultation and not distribution without the consent of E Ondrako

when it deals with an object whose nature is necessary as is God's. Unfortunately, this has been taken to mean, apparently on the assumption that intelligibility and understanding are coextensive with what is now evident to the knower, that theology is anti-intellectual, pragmatic, fideistic and illogical *a priori*. By science Scotus means a body of knowledge, whose starting point or formal object is within one's power to apprehend as intelligible *in se*, i.e., evident, and in terms of which the content of that body of knowledge can be organized as intelligible. This is not the case when knowing directly concerns the essence of God or the determinations of his will in this time of pilgrimage. The misunderstanding stems from the often unspoken assumption which identifies attainment of understanding and use of logic *exclusively* with the scientific. What cannot be proven scientifically cannot be known. This is the position of the great logician, Locke, against whom in great part Newman's *Grammar of Assent* is directed. And while the modern notion of science may differ in particulars from the ancient, this same assumption is widespread and is at the root of so much current abuse of theology. It is this solipsistic view of the cognitive process in theory and/or in practice that I am challenging as radically false.

In the light of what was expounded earlier in this essay, theology, to the extent it involves memory or the apprehension of God as knowable, cannot be other than non-scientific, i.e., knowledge of God, not as the conclusion drawn from some other knowledge, e.g., metaphysical knowledge of being, but as St. Bonaventure notes, the starting point for understanding all else; is authoritative and dogmatic.[63] It presupposes a revelation, an act of teaching therefore on the part of another, by which what is non-evident to one, becomes present to one as knowable, even if still non-evident (i.e., not intelligible *in se*, but analogically). Such a teaching activity is possible only on the assumption that what is apprehended in this manner by the believer is immediately evident to at least one teacher who by that fact is the primary teacher, in this case, Christ. Hence the stress placed by Bonaventure and Scotus on the plenitude of intellectual charisms in the sacred humanity of our Lord in establishing the starting point of their theological epistemology.

Further, since this apprehension on our part is not necessary, but contingent on the free action of another, the love of the teacher for disciple is as much an essential premise of theology, as is the love of the believer for his teacher an essential component of understanding. Hence, whether our theological understanding bears on the necessary being of God or his contingent acts, neither our apprehension, nor our subsequent understand-

---

[63] Cf. *Breviloquium*, part 1, ch. 1, 3.

For private consultation and not distribution without the consent of E Ondrako

ing of the intelligibility of either are the cause of the certain and infallible character of our knowledge apart from an obedient response, called faith, to a gracious teaching initiative, called revelation, for the simple reason that these objects are not made present to us as intelligible by nature, but only by grace.

True understanding of what is apprehended can follow, precisely because an object has been made present as intelligible. It is, however, dogmatic in character and form, whatever degree of clarity or explicitness is attained, because its starting point is not evidence, but faith. Progress in understanding cannot in any way change the nature of this presence, nor its limits. Whatever can be understood must already be actually contained within the revelation apprehended. Where knowledge is scientific, efforts at research can indeed lead to the apprehension of an object and the widening of intellectual horizons. In theology this is not so. Research may aid in attaining a clearer, more exact apprehension; it cannot alone or principally bring about the apprehension itself which is a matter of faith. In this sense theology is not only non-scientific; it is non-original, uncreative as well. Christ is the one Teacher who reveals definitively and fixes definitively the range of theological apprehension. This is but a particular aspect of the sacramental economy of salvation. Indeed other names for the content of faith or dogmas are mysteries and sacraments: mysteries because still not evident; sacraments because directly present in human form, in a word, symbols or analogies. Quite logically, those who are Christ's ministers in this matter, can neither reveal, nor change the limits of the revelation entrusted to them by Christ. In handing this on, they can only repeat, confirm, guard the deposit, *salva semper substantia sacramentorum*. Neither for the Church, nor for the believer, is doctrinal progress possible as regards the range of theological apprehension. All that we can understand is already implicit in the total apprehension of a single act of faith in the Revealer revealing. In this sense, Christ is the one and only Teacher of "positive theology," because only He has seen the Father, and knows his will in every detail as well as in its entirety.

Teaching, however, that remains only from without is incomplete. So, too, apprehension of the intelligible that bears only on the real in an objective way, would remain opaque, merely mechanical, void of meaning and uninteresting, if in fact the presentation of the object were not complemented by an act of teaching from within, as it were the intelligibility of the object of knowing made translucent by the light of knowing. That teaching from within which is the complement of revelation, or teaching from without, is called witness, and may well be compared to a light, for its purpose is not to make present what is knowable, but to make

For private consultation and not distribution without the consent of E Ondrako

possible in the apprehension of the knower identity with what is known and revealed by the Teacher. The assurance provided by witness is no more than such an identity, unchanging and permanent, because such is the character of truth and justice. The witness must be prepared to die, rather than to deny the truth of what he knows. Otherwise, his witness would in fact not be witness, but mere opinion. In addition the witness must be immortal; otherwise what he avers to be true would be indistinguishable from fanatical bias. According to Bonaventure, it is the very nature of a spiritual act tending to truth and justice, as involving a teacher who is eternal, as well as a learner who is finite, that furnishes the basis for the proof of immortality and of the natural desire for the Resurrection.[64] In such a context the assumption of Mary is a plainly logical indication of the term of this desire and the manner of its attainment by faith in Christ, first exemplified in the fullest way by Mary's faith in giving witness at the

Thus Christ is the one and only visible, primary Teacher of positive theology, as *Revealer revealing*. Mary is associated with Christ as the visible, primary teacher, as *witness*. By the fullness of her witness, she teaches in a *visible* manner what the Holy Spirit, implementing the work of Christ, teaches in an *invisible* manner. This witness does for the revealed in theology, what the light of reason and fontal illumination do for the evident object in science. As it is the purpose of teaching-revelation to communicate by making present the mysteries of faith, so it is the purpose of witness-teaching to communicate by enlightening. Mary's singular witness makes possible the prudence involved in the use of the illative sense by which we pass from a consideration of revelation as plausible to an unconditional assent to revelation as true. The act of one who affirms that what God has revealed is true, is not only an act of learning; it is also an act that enlightens by assuring those who, out of love, accept that witness, that they, too, without fear of error or change, can assent to the truth of what is revealed. In this sense every believer, and the Church as a whole, is a witness to revelation. Mary's witness, however, in the visible order is such in a preeminent fashion, because prior to her, there is essentially no other witness: only the invisible Holy Spirit of whose grace she is full. In this fullness her witness authenticates the preceding prophetic witness as the final, definitive sign of complete fulfillment, and sustains that which follows as the source of understanding, viz., the birth of the Son of God as man, His death for our sins and rising for our justification. Hence her witness is related to the teaching office and mediation of Christ and His ministers, not in a subordinate, so much as a complementary manner,

---

64 For Bonaventure's teaching on this point cf. VEUTHEY, *S. Bonaventuræ philosophia christiana*, pp. 200–206.

For private consultation and not distribution without the consent of E Ondrako

much as the mission of the Holy Spirit is related to that of Christ in the fulfillment of His various offices of teacher, king and priest. Without a willing acceptance of this witness of Mary, no effort on our part aimed at apprehending the matter of theological study, let alone understanding this, can transcend the level of plausibility and probability and reach that of faith. Hence the love of Mary as teacher by those who would believe Christ is as indispensable as the love of Christ.

To conclude from this that the exercise of authoritative teaching on Mary's part must take, if true, a form exactly parallel to that of her Son, e.g., in the formation of a deposit of faith or a structured hierarchy, as does the objection[65] that so little of Mary is recorded in the New Testament and prophesied in the Old, or that there is so little testimony to her active influence in the primitive Church, is to miss the entire point of the formal differentiation between the teaching of theology as revelation and the teaching of theology as witness. The first is tangible, visible, and proximate to our grasp as the matter or content of what is known. The second is tangible, visible and immediate to us as the air or light is tangible in its transparency, i.e., as the heart of a living tradition by which the deposit is interpreted. The authority of the first is experienced as that which definitively commands and establishes an order, and then maintains it intact; the second as that which definitively persuades, attracts, and harmoniously inserts the learner within that universe, much as a child learns to think and speak by spontaneously imitating and identifying with the thought and speech of its mother.[66] It is the assurance or witness of the mother that supports the assurance and confidence of the child; and the rightness of the maternal *judicationes* that makes possible the correctness and naturalness of the child's, precisely as personal assents of the child. That is why, from its inception, human thought and speech is neither merely logical nor merely mechanical, but as metaphysical and as true at its heart as that of any adult, providing the witness is credible. Without that witness, the child will never in fact transcend the level of the savage, and neither will the adult. That the child only later should advert consciously to the nature of that influence does not render it any less real or specific or visible. Nor does it argue against the perfection of that teaching. For only in proportion as that witness is a perfect assurance concerning the intelligibility of its object can that witness be effective as teaching or sharing of understanding.

---

65 Cf. the answer of St. Bonaventure to this objection in *Collationes in Hexaemeron*, c. 13, n. 20.

66 The pedagogical theories of a modern Franciscan educator rest on an application of this point. Cf. L. Veuthey, OFMConv., *Un grand éducateur, le père Girard* (Paris, 1934); A. Maas, OFMConv., *Père Girard Educator* (New York, 1931).

For private consultation and not distribution without the consent of E Ondrako

So it is in theology, except that where the adult in many areas of learning may well go beyond the "witness" of his first teacher in natural matters, the theologian can never dispense with the primary witness of Mary in any area of theology, if he expects the credible to be anything other than an opaque, impenetrable, brute "factum" in his experience. If, then, Mary, by her Immaculate Conception, is constituted primary witness to Christ, the fullness of revelation, and therefore primary teacher of theology, it is only logical to conclude that her actual competence in matters theological is the most perfect of any witness. And that whatever in the course of the history of the Church comes to be clarified in the life of the Church is already clear in her mind. While the perfection of her knowledge during her time of pilgrimage may have grown in depth and extent as she approached the moment when she would enjoy the beatific vision, it did not grow, as ours must, in clarity. Otherwise, she would not be that first, visible witness, in whom the Spirit of Christ begins to exercise in a definitive way the purpose of His mission: to witness, to clarify, to glorify the Word Incarnate. With this hindsight we can appreciate what purpose contemplative and infused theology serves—as explained by Scotus (along with "our" acquired theology)—during a time of pilgrimage in the lives of the saints; above all Mary, and why so many theologians over the centuries have attributed such contemplative and infused theology in the highest degree to Mary, and why, antecedently, it is as plausible, indeed more plausible, to expect her to have conversed intelligently about the mystery of the Incarnation with Gabriel, to have composed the *Magnificat*, than not.[67]

In its effects, however, the exercise of Mary's intellectual mediation is cumulative and coordinative in the life of the Church and of Christians. Anyone who believes in an authentic way in Christ, the Son of the living God, becomes *eo ipso* a witness to Christ for others, i.e., a teacher who clarifies. Yet taken singly or collectively none of this witness is self-explanatory as the primary source of assurance that what is believed is so. That the belief of each should be a sign, a seal of the truth, rests on this in fact (although not always noted), that the primary witness is actively engaged as witness in the belief of each secondary witness. The effect of this is cumulative, leading to an ever clearer and more exact perception of the truth. Each subsequent insight, confirmed dogmatically by the guardians of the deposit of revelation, itself serves to further illumine what remains implicit in our belief. The silence of Scripture and primitive tradition in regard to Marian dogmas is only a relative silence and, this, in an improper sense of that word, one that appears such in contrast to the manner and

---

[67] For the text of Scotus cf. DEODATUS A BALIACO, *op. cit.*, vol. 2, pp. 82 ss.

For private consultation and not distribution without the consent of E Ondrako

degree of perfection with which the object of that witness is explicitly perceived in faith, but in itself no more vague and indistinct than air or light. In retrospect this is quite sensible, for to attempt to understand the light first (epistemological questions) before assenting to what the light illumines (metaphysical questions) is to risk being overwhelmed by the brilliance of the light. But methods of study or research or of interpretation that ignore the witness of Mary, i.e., the light, are blind and deaf and dumb. In a word, Mary is found at the heart of that living, unwritten tradition of the Church, without which the written tradition is illegible, or read distortedly in ways leading to perdition (2 *Pet* 3:16). It is Mary's preeminent place at the heart of this tradition, actively and personally teaching as witness, that explains how the witness of the Church and believers can be assured and infallible, at once living and growing and perfectly consistent with the fixed and immutable character of the original revelation. The tradition is neither vague nor imprecise; however it may strike the neutral observer, for it always reflects the assurance, infallibility, and perfect clarity of the primary witness.

Because this cumulative effect is not organic, but personal, this Marian influence is also at the root of the coordination of tradition throughout the life of the Church and of the believer. Doctrinal development is not the result of necessary, natural factors, whose uniform and antecedently predictable operation forms its explanation. Rather, this development stems from the intelligent and coordinated personal participation of free agents. But neither the circumstances of history nor of our own subordinate efforts in positive theology are the final source of that unity governing the coordination of these efforts and assuring the consistency required for the gradual clarification of revelation. What accounts for the progressive implementation of God's will during the ages of grace is Mary's personal involvement as a free agent, who guides us to do what her Son commands us to do. Her guidance is primarily responsible for the choice of time, place, pace and degree of perfection with which the meaning of those commands is realized. Her decisions impart a teleology to the actual events at once intelligent and consistent, by which we come to recognize more clearly not only who Christ is, but how we come to Him as Incarnate Word, i.e., through His Mother. In response to the common objection that this is to so maximize Mary's role as to substitute her for God, I merely remark that her activity is related to that of Father and Son, as is that of the Spirit, with whom she is so intimately and fully united as the visible term of his mission. The Spirit is decisive in a personal way, not apart from Father and Son from whom he comes, but precisely with them in being the bond of unity by which each is in the other in being in him. So the theologian who

For private consultation and not distribution without the consent of E Ondrako

is one with Mary intellectually in taking her witness within, is one with Christ and with Christ in the Father. Who sees me, who knows me as I am, says our Lord, sees and knows the Father also, whom no man has ever seen (cf. *Jn* 14:8; 1:18).

Herein is the great tragedy of that positive theology, exegesis in particular, which would claim theological validity for its results, but systematically bracket the Marian witness as foreign to its starting point; that would allow it, perhaps as a pious frill on the periphery, not as an essential and intrinsic component of the method itself. Who would, in the name of scholarly critical norms, of truth and of academic freedom, begin his study of theology by doubting the critical value of the cumulative effects of Marian witness in the Church, has already abused scholarship, truth and freedom, and has opened the door to deceit and to the deceiver. The choice, in fact, is not between Marian pietism and scientific accuracy in theology. Rather, the real choice is between a method of research shaped by the influence of Mary and one which, for whatever reason, is not. The tools of study are common to all. But they do not by themselves account for the wildly opposite results in their use. Juxtaposing, for instance, the works of A. Feuillet on our Lady in the New Testament, alongside the recent volume *Mary in the New Testament,* will easily make this plain. The first finds her on every page; the second only doubtfully present, and that only in a few places. The difference, it seems to me, is simply that Feuillet does accept the witness of Mary and the dogmas of the Church as effective guides in the use of his tools of research, while the second *ex professo* prescinds from this. I do not intend to deny anyone's freedom to opt for the second; I do regret such a choice so inimical to faith and so irresponsible in the face of the real need of souls. But what I object to most is the assertion or implication that any other choice is that of a method *per se* unscholarly and unintelligent, because not enjoying the approval of contemporary consensus in scholarship. I question likewise the prudence of those who would justify this second option as a legitimate one in the Church, particularly for those entrusted with the deposit of revelation and the feeding of Christ's flock.

To sum up: theology is dogmatic and authoritative in a double sense. Christ as Teacher-Revealer accounts for the sacramentality, or specific form which the intelligibility of the divine takes for us *in via*. Mary as teacher-witness accounts for the prudence or rectitude of the assent of faith, by which I am sure that what I believe is, in fact, unconditionally so.

For private consultation and not distribution without the consent of E Ondrako

Metaphysical

I have deliberately chosen this word as a way to focus attention on the most distinctive feature[68] of theological knowledge as an understanding of the God apprehended in revelation and loved and served in practice. It is a knowledge at once certain and infallible, in contrast with those forms of knowing admitting of a relative freedom to experiment, hypothesize, and revise in a manner precluded by the dogmatic character of theology. St. Bonaventure calls this the "proper" aspect of our theology in time of pilgrimage (study of the proper use of notions in dogmas), in contrast with the preceding aspect which he calls symbolic (study of the proper use of words in creeds and sacraments), and with the one following, which he calls mystical (study of the enjoyment of revelation in prayer).[69]

Because of the relative independence of scientific knowledge vis-à-vis the one Teacher of all, research in the sciences can be conducted without arriving immediately, or ever in some instances, at certain and infallible conclusions concerning the object of study. It is in our power to suspend judgment, i.e., definitive judgment in the form of a final, unchangeable assent, and to continue research, keeping an open mind *re* further developments, where it is in our power to deal directly with the evident intelligible; and, yet, the causal features at the basis of that intelligibility are not easy to ascertain. Unfortunately, this type of intellectual exercise is too often taken as normative for the general need of men to satisfy their restless yearning to assent to the truth as such, when in fact most men in most practical matters naturally act on the basis of firm convictions not questioned, whose certainty ultimately finds its root in the authority of another.

When this type of procedure is employed normatively in the study of revelation, especially the Scriptures, the results are bound to be disastrous as far as any real knowledge and understanding of God is concerned. Theological research is directly subordinate to the primary initiative and influence of Christ and Mary, respectively as Teacher-Revealer and teacher-witness. Hence, the correct use of these methods includes an implicit understanding of the object whose apprehension they are intended to make more exact. Their use cannot begin with a doubt about the definitive content of that revelation, or the certainty and competence of its primary witness. Simply put, what are today called positive and speculative theology, though distinct, cannot be carried on apart from

---

[68] Mascall, *op. cit.*, pp. 15 ff. According to Mascall, this feature of theology is the one most neglected today in the English speaking world. This, he says, accounts for the breaking up of theology into unrelated parts, each with its own method.

[69] *Itinerarium*, c. 1, 7. Cf. also *Christus unus omnium Magister*, 1.

For private consultation and not distribution without the consent of E Ondrako

one another, nor can this study be carried on apart from the immediate, authoritative initiative of the one Teacher of theology. Positive theology, to the extent that it is fruitful, already includes an implied understanding, a metaphysics, identical with that of the teacher's.

Conversely, speculative theology, or the metaphysical aspect of theological activity, carried on apart from the immediate and active influence of Christ and Mary, i.e., apart from revelation dogmatically apprehended and the law of Christ effectively lived in charity, does tend to become abstract, dry and unreal. This is the second reason I have chosen the word metaphysics: to uncover an ambiguity. Certainly, a concentration on questions of understanding in theology (hermeneutics), as distinct from the other moments, will entail a style similar to that of Scotus. This is inevitable, perfectly natural, and useful. It only becomes reprehensible when engaged in apart from the direct influence of Christ and Mary, i.e., when conducted in a solipsistic way, as though the process of understanding and judgment qua my act were its own justification. The natural consequence of such an assumption is the identification of understanding with the logical processes of the same, and, in the case of theology, the confusion of the divine with my reasons for affirming the divine. Such is usually the case with forms of metaphysics that are theosophic or pantheistic. Such too is the case when a solution to the so-called hermeneutical problem is attempted apart from faith in the right teacher. So too "theologies" pervaded by methods of demythologizing and adaptation to the needs of the "modern mind" are not theological, but scarcely veiled speculation for speculation's sake of the most fantastic kind. The alternative is a systematic skepticism of one kind or another. Conducted rightly, the metaphysical style will blend quite easily with styles more properly those of positive and practical theology (the symbolic and mystical-moral), since distinction of style in sound theology reflects diversity of moment without loss of unity in the grasp of truth. Each really implies and includes what is at the heart of the other, because all are anchored in the mediation of Christ and Mary. An excellent example of this is the *Breviloquium* of St. Bonaventure, the unity of whose method in terms of the one teacher of all is explained by Bonaventure in a passage cited earlier.[70]

It did not occur to the medievals to suspect a problem of development in terms of the mysteries of faith considered as the content of revelation, for the simple reason that there is no problem in fact for anyone in this sense. This is Christ's affair exclusively as Founder of the Church to reveal as much as He wishes, at the pace He wishes. The medievals, however,

---

[70] *Collationes in Hexæmeron*, c. 19, 8–11.

For private consultation and not distribution without the consent of E Ondrako

were aware of the possibility of development (and error) at the subjective pole. If this did not seem to them an insoluble problem, this is because they had a firm grasp of the nature of theology. What they did not concern themselves with was the full mechanics of this growth as it touched the entire community of faith, i.e., the Church. In this, Newman has not so much innovated as merely completed their line of thought. However much needed this explication, the basis of a resolution is always present in a sound theology where Bonaventure, Scotus and Thomas locate it: in the responsible pursuit of understanding metaphysically, something not possible except by way of an ever more intimate harmony with the primary *lumen quo*, the Spirit and Mary. This is what accounts for difference of style without loss of unity of meaning.

In view of this, we can perceive at once the source of a fatal assumption concerning style and meaning: if the style varies, the meaning must also vary. If the style is metaphorical, the meaning cannot possibly include the singular contingent and historical event as real. Since by definition our theological understanding is analogical, it is assumed that theological meaning is essentially unrelated to the historical singular in any definitive fashion. Above all, the Incarnation is a metaphor or myth. The source of this assumption is a failure to appreciate the distinction between style (and the study of style) and metaphysics, characteristic of the study of the content of revelation.

Any verbal style can be studied as a distinct object of study. This is what is done in the field of literary study; the Bible being literature can be studied in this way. So, too, conceptual style can be studied in logic. But the study of style by itself does not yield any results in respect to what is expressed by that style, except by way of appeal to principles beyond the scope of such formal studies, taken *formaliter*. It is here that the equivocations begin. For, in the name of literary studies, the traditional metaphysics of theology such as are being defended in this essay, are declared outmoded, and in the name of a new hermeneutic and consensus in positive theology, the methods of these literary studies are authenticated as a *medium theologicum formaliter loquendo*.

To speak of a literal (univocal) or metaphorical style, a concrete or abstract style, in literary or logical studies may indeed be related to or overlap with what these same terms designate when employed in a study of the content of that style, as has been the case for centuries in theology. But what is meant by analogy or allegorical, mystical, spiritual sense of revelation in theological study on the one hand, and by literal sense on the other, is not at all identical with what is meant by these same terms in literary study, just as univocity in logic does not designate fully what the same

For private consultation and not distribution without the consent of E Ondrako

term designates metaphysically for Scotus in explaining the unity which must ground analogy. The reason is this: not every mode of understanding prescinds or abstracts from that which is formally distinctive *a parte rei* of another mode. To conclude, as C. S. Lewis observes,[71] that, because some person or historical event in Scripture is described metaphorically in the literary sense, the description is only mythical in the religious sense, not designating a real person or real event, but only a way of speaking about a transcendent truth, is to betray an astounding ignorance of the nature of language in general and of theological language in particular. Similar in kind is the assumption that the literal sense, theologically speaking, must be rendered in a style that is literal or scientifically exact, or that those narrating history must employ the style of modern critical historiography, if they are to be accepted as conveying reliable testimony. In practice, this is a tacit nominalism, found in all forms of literalism, one which refuses to acknowledge even on the level of ordinary experience that there is no word or sentence or discussion that can actually express any real meaning, except in combination with others, i.e., analogically. A pure literalist would be a perfect stutterer. And, yet, in normal matters of everyday life most persons have no difficulty in arriving at coherent judgments, certain and true, bearing both on universals like justice and on singulars like this or that man, event, place. In theology based on a sound metaphysics, the question is not primarily one of style, but of those conditions under which the revealer can reveal the intelligibility of the divine.

The comment of Lewis, moreover, is not exactly new. St. Bonaventure[72] has a rather extensive treatment of rules for interpreting Scripture which he organizes around the importance of this point. The literal sense of Scripture (often designating singular persons or events) as well as the spiritual senses (often designating principles or universals) admit a multiplicity of styles from the literary point of view. The rules of interpretation must reflect the complex, rather than naïve one-to-one, correspondence between theological style and content. A principle explained in parabolic form is no less absolute and identical in meaning as its expression "metaphysically." And an event described graphically in terms of its religious significance is no less true than, and identical with, the same event described "literally" by virtue of stylistic difference. In all cases, it is what the revealer wished to express, or the witness certifies as true, and not the manner he chose to express this, that resolves the question of what is meant. And in our theology now, by definition, the expression of the most singular and contingent object, as

---

[71] C. S. LEWIS, *Miracles, a Preliminary Study* (New York, 1947), chapter 4: "Horrid Red Things." Cf. also LEWIS, *Christian Reflections* (Grand Rapids, Mich., 1967) pp. 152–166.

[72] *Breviloquium*, Prol. 6.

For private consultation and not distribution without the consent of E Ondrako

well as the most abstract principle must, in literary terms, involve some element of association with or comparison to something other than itself, if the study of revelation is to yield any understanding of what is revealed.

That which is more prominent—when the moment of understanding is the conscious focus of reflection—is the metaphysical, because metaphysics is precisely that study enabling us to discern the difference between style of expression and the real which is the content of thought. It is, further, by way of the univocal concept of being and its properties, i.e., the subject of metaphysics, that Scotus finds the opening for the insertion of theological understanding. This understanding itself, as a direct understanding of God, is not univocal, but analogical. The actual understanding of the divine on our part *in statu isto* is not that characteristic of the evident, but by way of representations, of concepts, forms, analogies, none of which can fully express what they represent, but can do so partially, if in fact God chooses to so make them represent him or his will by revealing himself in this way. The capacity of these analogies to enable us to understand the nature or the will of God rests not in what they are naturally, but in the proportion in which God has in fact made these expressive of himself or of his will. That these proportions should actually convey direct understanding of God is not then a matter of natural necessity, but of gracious revelation. *A parte rei* they are intelligible theologically "appropriately," not apodictically. But the reason these can be so appropriated and invested with an intelligibility transcending their normal limits is to be found, as Scotus finds it, in the univocal concept of being. This is why metaphysical so well describes this aspect of theological understanding.

Actual theological understanding begins, not with the study of univocal being, but with the perception in faith of this appropriateness, this *decuit*, through the witness of the Spirit from within, what Bonaventure calls the Inspired Word. On the one hand, a simple meeting with Christ in the flesh would by itself give us no direct understanding of His divinity. On the other hand, by faith we do understand the divinity of Christ, not fully or in an evident way, but as reflected in the face of Christ Jesus. Though partial, this is an understanding of what is real and what transcends the limits of our native powers to understand directly; thus, according to Scotus, metaphysical in the very exact sense of that term.[73] The logical consistency of all the articles of faith rests on the *decuit* centering on the wisdom of the Incarnation. Neither the "necessary reasons" explain-

---

73 For the texts of Scotus cf. Deodatus a Baliaco, *op. cit.*, pp. 3 ss. For the bearing of metaphysics on our understanding of "person" cf. H. Mühlen, *Sein und Person nach Johannes Duns Scotus* (Werl, 1954). On Bonaventure, cf. J. Ratzinger, *Der Wortgebrauch von Natura und die beginnende Verselbstständingung der Metaphysik bei Bonaventura*, in *Miscellanea Mediavallia*, vol. 2 (Berlin, 1963) pp. 483–498.

For private consultation and not distribution without the consent of E Ondrako

ing the divine essence, nor the "pious reasons" explaining the economy of salvation, prove anything apodictically in theology, since what they render intelligible is not evident by that fact. What they accomplish is something else. They bring into relationship two things that for us would otherwise remain quite apart: that which is present by revelation, but not evidently intelligible, and expressed analogically; and that which expresses the theoretical or possible grounds for intelligibility, as reflected in that same form naturally. It is not our judgment or reflective process that unites the *potuit* to the *fecit* by way of the *decuit*. It is rather the antecedent judgment of the teacher who reveals that establishes the juncture, and so constitutes a viable intellectual analogy, a kind of mirror that truly reflects the divine in an intelligible way. Our theological activity, except in a very improper sense, is not an evaluation of evidence, but an effort in the Spirit to perceive the harmony and proportions reflected in that mirror. This is but the method of the analogy of faith (of Vatican I), or of the hierarchy of truths (of Vatican II) traditionally regarded as the heart of theological understanding in this life.[74]

Theological understanding, as an effort to develop the analogy of faith and express the inner consistency of the content of revelation, culminates in an assent which is certain, infallible and clear. Not every part of the process is equally perfect, or equally useful in attaining the goal, or equally free from error. Certain, true and clear understanding is only attained, to the extent that the analogy of faith is illumined and clarified by the light of faith. As in the case of apprehension, so in the case of understanding in theology the proper use of this light entails the active influence of the primary teacher-witness, whose own pondering, understanding and intellectual competence in regard to that which is witnessed is the basis for our understanding and fruitful pondering of the same. The witness is indeed also a sign that makes something other than himself known and understood. To the extent that I accept this testimony and thereby this person as worthy of credence, to that extent I understand what I believe. The understanding of any sign in this sense is not an end in itself, but the understanding of what is signified. Theological understanding is but an activity of faith accepting the teaching of the perfect witness, namely the Spirit, in such wise as to understand the mysteries of faith in a certain and infallible manner. And to the extent that acceptance is "visible," it is an acceptance of the witness of Mary, pondering and clarifying the mystery of the Incarnation and Redemption (cf. *Lk* 2:19, 51).

---

[74] "Hierarchy of truths" indicates not a new approach to theological method in terms of the certainty and truth of each doctrine objectively considered, but the determination of its specific place on the "ladder."

For private consultation and not distribution without the consent of E Ondrako

"Mary kept all these things in her heart, pondering them." To the extent that Mary's witness is full and therefore includes a full understanding of the Incarnation and the mysteries of faith, acceptance of her testimony and pondering in union with her is the light or sign that illumines for us what she kept in her heart. This corresponds with the prophetic words of Isaiah that the sign of completed revelation to be given would reach as high as the heavens and as deep as hell. Mary's perfect appreciation of the *decuit* of the Incarnation makes her in every sense a teacher of Christian metaphysics. And to understand the nature of this understanding, i.e., the nature of theology, one must understand the *decuit* of Mary as a person who is Mother and teacher. Because Scotus did grasp just this point clearly, viz., her Immaculate Conception, Hopkins calls him "the rarest veined unraveller of reality." The basic, practical rule of all theological understanding, for the Church and for the individual believer, is this: the more Mary is glorified, the more revelation is *eo ipso* clearly understood. This glorification of Mary on our part is not simply our action, singly or collectively; it is an action with Mary as pondering, and this is because she is the Immaculate. *De Maria numquan satis*, if theology and metaphysics are to progress.

Practical

The radical answer to the objection that the metaphysical character of theology conflicts with the personal aspect of religious understanding is simply this: sound religious understanding at its most notional involves a judgment that is at once mine and Mary's. For St. Bonaventure, understanding is knowledge passing into affection.[75] Nothing could be more personal or more loving insofar as the love of God is bound up in the understanding of God. Whether this understanding is couched in the style commonly associated with "metaphysics," whether the theologian is consciously and explicitly aware of the nature of that relation, if his judgment is true, the relation is real. Otherwise, it would not be true.

This brings us to the third and final characteristic of theology: the manner in which this activity is coordinated with that of the will.[76] Scotus has often been taken to be a voluntarist or pragmatist because of his insistence on the primacy of the will over the intellect. Whatever the merits of his position on this question, he is by no means a pragmatist, a position

---

[75] Cf. *Collationes in Hexaemeron*, c. 5, nn. 10–12.

[76] For a summary of texts of Scotus on *praxis* cf. DEODATUS A BALIACO, *op. cit.*, pp. 132 ss. For Scotus's teaching in general on the will cf. HOERES, *op. cit.*

For private consultation and not distribution without the consent of E Ondrako

abhorrent to him as the source of irrational and sinful conduct.[77] His epistemology is not radically subjective because of the manner in which he unites and correlates intellect and will from within in the unity of the soul, and insists, like Bonaventure before him and Newman and Marcel after, on the place of fidelity at the starting point of knowledge.[78] Fidelity, gratitude, and love must be directed to someone. In the case of intellectual activity, that someone is a teacher. It suffices that for correct use of the intellect, that teacher be the right one. To the question: "how can we recognize him?" the answer is: the teacher will make himself known, as I myself am known, to the extent that he wishes. The initiative is his, not ours. In theology the teacher makes himself known directly. Christ is the one Teacher of all. How do we come to recognize Him? With the help of competent witnesses who point Him out so that we can recognize Him. In this sense, it is Mary who must take the first step. In this case, love for Mary Immaculate, our Mother, is the first step in becoming conscious of Christ through faith, and that quite obviously engages my will as well as intellect.

Fidelity in this sense is obedience to the norms laid down by the teacher as the measure of intellectual activity. Unlimited academic freedom, i.e., without restrictions except those self-imposed, for Scotus as well as for Bonaventure, is nothing more than unbridled curiosity,[79] a vice that breeds confusion and doubt in the intellect, although it may appear as an attractive brilliance and convenience. Unlimited academic freedom is simply a corollary of that notion of the will which sees it only as a power to do as one pleases, even to the point of redefining good to justify what is not justice: pleasure, or to justify injustice or sin as righteousness in God, a blasphemy. This is a vice, then, all the more tragic when it is the motive for the study of God (as it was in the case of the first Eve and in a great many modern theologians), since the limits of theology are directly set by the teacher-revealer, and the degree of clarification by the teacher-witness, for the good of all. The more perfect and intimate our obedience to Christ and Mary, viz., our humility, the more perfect and enjoyable will our understanding be and the wiser will the actual measure of intellectual activity appear for each and all ordained by God, and why it will approximate the theology of God himself. "I praise you, Father of heaven and earth," said

[77] Cf. HOERES, op. cit., pp. 131 ss. Also, M. DAMIATA, OFM, I e II tavola. L'etica di G.Duns Scoto (Florence 1973).

[78] For Newman on the realism of our understanding cf. J. BRECHTKEN, Real Erfahrung bei Newman (Bergen-Enkheim, 1973). For Marcel, cf. G. MARCEL, The Mystery of Being (Chicago, 1950), vol. 2.

[79] BONAVENTURE, Collationes in Hexæmeron, c. 1. For the texts of Scotus cf. HOERES, op. cit., pp. 364 ss.

For private consultation and not distribution without the consent of E Ondrako

our Lord, "that you have hid these things from the wise and prudent, and have revealed them to the little ones" (*Mt* 11:25).

Further, the love of Mary Immaculate for us and her teaching role as witness is precisely that aspect of faith assuring knowledge and understanding of the singular, one that is, as Scotus would say, intuitive cognition of the singular, or with Newman, real assent. In the lack of evidence for the inner intelligibility of what is apprehended, any attempt to understand the things of God in a solipsistic way must terminate in the merely notional and hypothetical. Carried on in union with Mary, every effort to understand more clearly, however metaphysical, will always be an assent tending on real because, in this case, the metaphysical style is what it is intended to be: an ascesis of the intellect, a purification that enables one to perceive more clearly, and a preparation for the ecstatic joy of contemplation. No better example of this can be found than St. Bonaventure's *Collationes in Hexaemeron*.

And, thus, in a still profounder sense, theology is bound up with the activity of the will. In the former two instances, love of the teacher is seen as a moment of cognitive activity, that which places the intellect in contact with its real starting point—the intelligible, and its concluding point—the understanding of the real. The formal character of the will, however, as distinct from the intellect, is realized in an activity called affective and which, in the case of theology, is the essential purpose of understanding. The knowledge of God is the condition for the love of God for his own sake. The desire to understand, to believe is only an aspect of another desire—to love and enjoy God as God loves and enjoys himself. The love of the teacher at this point becomes the following and service of the teacher. Just as the teaching roles of Mary and Christ complemented each other, so also service to Christ the King and Priest is complemented by consecration to and service with our Lady as Mediatrix of grace and Queen of the universe. This is how we become good, in the service of Mary and Christ. And this is why Bonaventure writes that theology "est speculationis gratia ut boni fiamus, principaliter ut boni fiamus," where to be good means to love God for his own sake, because he is so lovable. No one did this more perfectly than Mary.

There is no orthodoxy without orthopraxis: love of God and love of neighbor as Christ did, giving his life. Nor is there any orthopraxis without orthodoxy. Those who find in this a dilemma entailing a choice between pure intellectualism or pure pragmatism in selecting which comes first, have failed to see that these are more than two aspects of a purely individual experience on my part. Each aspect entails a direct relation to another person as fully true and fully just, such as to authenticate by itself uncon-

For private consultation and not distribution without the consent of E Ondrako

ditional assent to the Truth and unreserved obedience to the commands of Justice on my part, and the correctness with which the cognitive and affective aspects balance and support each other in the complete human experience.

Two questions occur at the end of this exposition. First, what grounds exist for regarding this interpretation of scotistic analysis of theology as essentially and not incidentally, Marian? It is true that in no place does Scotus state this explicitly. Nonetheless, I believe that the elaboration of the thesis has been faithful to the mind of Scotus. I know of no reason for denying the logical nexus between the Immaculate Conception, understood along the lines of St. Maximilian Kolbe's insight[80] into the relation between Mary and the Spirit as created and uncreated Immaculate Conception. Thus, the mission of the Spirit as witness is linked to that of Mary as visible term of that witness and soundly conducted so to the nature of theology. There is a passage from the *Breviloquium* of St. Bonaventure (who in so many ways provides the broad exposition of the principle assumed, but not always fully articulated, by Scotus) that does synthesize quite exactly the process of theological reflection, as we have described it under the three headings of this section, in terms of the one teacher Christ who teaches from without by revealing and from within through His Spirit by witnessing. I will cite the passage in its entirety, and then indicate where the name of Mary might be inserted.

> ...Theology as a science founded on faith and revealed by the Holy Spirit, deals with those matters which pertain to grace and glory and eternal Wisdom as well. Whence, theology employs philosophical knowledge as a support in making use of natural things, as much as needed, to construct a mirror with which to make representations of the divine. In this manner it constructs a ladder, at its lowest point touching earth and at its highest heaven. And this it does under the direction of the Hierarch, Jesus Christ... Scripture itself does not only contain themes sublime which delight the mind and by which it lifts the understanding of our minds on high. It is also itself extraordinarily beautiful, and in stupendous ways attracts our intellects. Thus, as it more and more delights us, it accustoms us to the contuition and contemplation of wonders divine.[81]

---

[80] *Scritti*, vol. 3, n. 1318.

[81] *Breviloquium*, Prol. 3, 2–3: ...theologia tamquam scientia supra fidem fundata et per Spiritum Sanctum revelata, agit et de eis quae spectant ad gratiam et gloriam et etiam ad Sapientiam aeternam. Unde ipsa, substernens sibi philosophicam cognitionem et assumens de naturis rerum, quantum sibi opus est ad fabricandum speculum, per quod fiat repraesen-

For private consultation and not distribution without the consent of E Ondrako

If in the first section we relate the formation of the mirror to the teaching activity of Christ as revealer, and the formation of the ladder to that of the Spirit sent by Christ, by which a sign or light is made to bear on the reflections in the mirror of heaven and of earth, then indeed the place for the insertion of Mary in this process has been found. The *Breviloquium* passage in question would certainly have been known to Scotus.

The final section of the citation simply indicates how naturally theology conducted under the aegis of Christ and of His Spirit in Bonaventure's passes into love of Christ and delight in His beauty. Once the beauty of the Immaculate is appreciated as the loveliest of God's children by adoption and, as a consequence, the manner in which she is Mediatrix of all grace, it is not too difficult to infer that knowledge of this passes in the same way into love and delight—exactly the position of St. Maximilian with his total consecration to Mary under this title.

Indeed, the key insight of St. Maximilian's Mariology, the correlation between the procession of the Holy Spirit and the Immaculate Conception, is no more than an explication of a basic dimension of Bonaventure's theology by way of Scotus's theology of the Immaculate Conception, which clarifies both the mediation of Mary and that of the Church. The present thesis is but a particular application, on which a great many probabilities converge.

Further, it might be asked whether there is any evidence to indicate how Mary's involvement in the elaboration of the theology of the Immaculate Conception by Scotus was decisive, as the thesis defended here implies? It was the view of St. Maximilian that such, indeed, was the case.[82] The gradual clarification of this privilege over the centuries, culminating in the dogmatic definition of 1854, not only served to clarify the primacy of Christ and the notion of His universal kingship, but to prepare the way for a more intense involvement with Mary in its final realization. Such a view, similar to that which sees in the clarification of Mary's divine motherhood the key to the clarification of the Incarnation in the fifth century, is tantamount to regarding the understanding of Mary as a light by which we are able to see Christ. Drawn out in personal terms this is equivalent to saying Mary is a teacher of theology, and that glorification of her is in fact

---

tatio divinorum, quasi scalam erigit, quae in sui infimo tangit terram, sed in suo cacumine tangit caelum; et hoc totum per illum unum hierarcham, Jesum Christum.... ipsa Scriptura non tantum habet altissimam materiam, per quam delectat et per quam in altum levat intelligentiam mentis, verum etiam ipsa est venustissima et miro quodam modo intellectum nostrum delectat, et sic magis ac magis delectando assuefacit ad divinorum spectaculorum contuitus et anagogias. In his *Commentarium in Lucam*, c. 1, Bonaventure calls Mary the ladder to heaven. Cf. Fehlner, *The Role of Charity*, p. 82.

82 M. Kolbe, *Scritti*, vol. 1, n. 486 (p. 895).

For private consultation and not distribution without the consent of E Ondrako

an integral factor in the successful conduct of theological reflection as a process of clarification. In all these instances there were undoubtedly other factors of a natural kind influencing such reflection. Yet, in no case can the outcome be attributed to these as effects to cause. In each instance the purely natural factors would seen to have indicated the probability of quite a different and possibly contrary conclusion. And in the case of Scotus, the position taken at his time was not the easiest to justify as traditional, although indeed it was a part of the deposit of revelation.

In such circumstances, a plausible case can be made historically that the will of another person, specifically Mary, was the key factor guiding the entire process to a determined end, consistent and identical with the original tradition of Christ. I note the following as a basis for discussion.

Scotus was formed in a community in which the study of theology and the cultivation of the intellect are directly and intrinsically subordinated to the spirit of prayer and devotion by the will of the founder, St. Francis.[83] There can be no question about Scotus's unconditional acceptance of this condition, particularly since he joined the community in a Province where the sense of this injunction was still quite vivid. This way of life was claimed by its founder to have been directly inspired by Christ, and was confirmed as authentic by the Lord Pope, two points certainly reflected in Scotus's practice of theology.[84] Further, this way of life entails a christocentrism whose intellectual articulation found its most exact and profound formulation in the thesis of Scotus on the primacy of Christ. This christocentrism in the life of St. Francis, however, was achieved and sustained through a devotion to Mary most holy, equally central and primary, and which in practice, in view of Newman cited earlier, would be the reality of what in theory is the dogma of the Immaculate Conception. For St. Francis devotion to our Lady, as a response to her love for him, centered on her title as Queen of the Angels and Mother of the Word Incarnate.[85] In fact, such a devotion unites, on the one hand, the passages of *Apocalypse* 12 (and with it *Gen* 3:15) with, on the other, those of the Lukan infancy narratives (with the title "full of grace"); or in terms of the liturgical poles of his spirituality, the Crib is conjoined with the exaltation (*sursumactio*) on the Cross. In such an environment where the personal influence of Christ and Mary was regarded as the primary and essential factors effecting spiritual growth (and therefore intellectual as well), it is certainly not implausible to surmise that Mary's influence on a gifted student such as Scotus might

---

[83] ST. FRANCIS OF ASSISI, *Regula Bullata*, cc. 5 and 10.

[84] Cf. W. LAMPEN, OFM, *B. Joannes Duns Scotus et Sancta Sedes* (Quaracchi, 1929).

[85] THOMAS A CELANO, O. MIN., *S. Francisci Assisiensis Vita et Miracula*, ed. P. Eduardus Alenconiensis, OFMCap. (Rome, 1906), *Legenda prima*, n. 106 (p. 111).

For private consultation and not distribution without the consent of E Ondrako

lead to the clarification of the primacy of Christ (and all that it implies for Christian thought and action) by way of a clarification of the Immaculate Conception. Thereby a key is provided as well for the elaboration of a sound theological methodology, a methodology which the late Pope Paul VI lauded as particularly useful in these latter stages of our struggle with atheism and the father of lies.[86] One may also choose to hold all this as a kind of chance coincidence. But then, at least, it is not simply the result of natural evolution or iron-clad rules of logic. What appears as chance to us is such only because it is the partial manifestation of a careful and wise guidance. Only when we know who is guiding events from the perspective of that person, and why, can we discern the pattern of development clearly and with certainty.

Conclusion

Sedes Sapientiae, ora pro nobis. Someone may observe that this is an overly long exposition of the obvious that, in practice, Mary is always doing her part, and that what we must do to renew theology is not a matter of piety, but of intellectual culture.

It is certainly true that the effectiveness of any teacher is proportionate to his assurance and intellectual competence in the matter that he teaches. No one can teach unless he knows what he is talking about and is sure that what he says is correct. But it is just the obvious that is often overlooked and neglected. And in contemporary theology, whatever the motive, Mary is quite consistently overlooked, forgotten, or rejected outright. The great merit of Scotus is to have clearly laid a basis adequate for illustrating how Christ teaches from within through His Spirit, and Mary Immaculate, in a way that issues in a practicable, theological method.

It is precisely here that the renewal of theology, so much desired by Vatican II, must begin, with the realization that the involvement of Mary is a personal one, not to be taken for granted, and hence one to be begun in prayer, not merely as a pious adjunct, but as a primary, internal determinant of the renewal in the practical order. Mary must be allowed to have a preeminent place within the life of each theologian, as Vatican II assigns her a preeminent place within the Church, as Mary herself says in the words applied to her in the liturgy: "Come to me, all ye that desire me, and be filled with my fruits… He that hearkeneth to me, shall not be confounded, and they that work by me, shall not sin. They that explain me shall have life everlasting." (*Ecclus* 24:26, 30, 31) "For in her is the

---

[86]   PAUL VI, *Alma Parens*, in *Acta Apostolicæ Sedes* 58 (1966) pp. 609–614.

For private consultation and not distribution without the consent of E Ondrako

spirit of understanding… for God loveth none but him that dwelleth with wisdom. For she is more beautiful than the sun, and above all the order of the stars…" (*Ws* 7:22, 28, 29). "From the beginning, and before the world, was I created…. And so was I established in Sion, and in the holy city likewise I rested, and my power was in Jerusalem. And I took root in an honorable people, and in the portion of my God his inheritance, and my abode is in the full assembly of saints" (*Ecclus* 24:14–16).

The alternative is not freedom and the tolerance of theological pluralism, but the horrendous, diabolical darkness of religious doubt and ignorance, which is not the absence of a teacher, but the influence of the wrong teacher. "After this cometh night, but no evil can overcome wisdom" (*Ws* 7:30). This activity of Mary is not a substitute for that of Christ, or of the hierarchy, for whatever she inspires is intended to confirm and be confirmed by the Lord Pope in the name of Christ. For her influence always clarifies her Son and His designs. "I am the mother of fair love, and of fear, and of knowledge, and of holy hope. In me is all grace of the way and of the truth, in me is all hope of life and of virtue" (*Ecclus* 24:24, 25): for those who believe this clarification are unto blessedness; for those who refuse belief, unto judgment. It is my personal view that the manner of St. Maximilian's death on the vigil of the Assumption in Auschwitz was no mere accident, but a providential sign to remind us of these very real grounds for unbounded hope and joy in the worst of circumstances.[87] "I was exalted like cedar in Libanus, and as a cypress tree on mount Sion" (*Ecclus* 24:17).

But neither is the prior love and initiative of Mary an excuse for apathy and inactivity on our part. Her mediation is not intended to replace ours, but to make possible an effective cooperation in the work of salvation on our part. And this brings us to the second part of our response to Mary's love, especially as it touches intellectual effort. This may be stated in one word: penance. Like all true devotion to Mary, that in the intellectual order achieves a kind of interior asceticism of the mind, or purification. It entails risk and sacrifice. This is particularly acute when the servant of Mary incurs the displeasure of the "Zeitgeist," of the "consensus," as he exposes and refutes the errors of those who would, in the name of "truth" and "objective, scientific method," minimize or eliminate the role of Mary in theology; of those who, in the name of "academic freedom" and doctrinal pluralism, call into question the indispensable obedience of faith to a divinely appointed *magisterium* as the only starting point for an

---

[87] On the wider significance of St. Maximilian's sanctity in the history of eastern Christianity in view of the struggle between light and darkness, cf. J. RUPP, *Héros chrétiens de l'est. Hommage au déporté Kolbe* (Paris 1972).

For private consultation and not distribution without the consent of E Ondrako

effective and fruitful realization of the truth. Intellectual devotion to Mary in one way or another involves us in her struggle and that of her Son with the prince of this world and his deceits.

Far more important is the positive side of this asceticism of the mind, which consists in putting into practice the principle: *De Maria numquam satis*, precisely by cultivating methods of theology reflecting Mary's central initiative as teacher. We shall not be effective witnesses and sharers of revelation with others, unless we ourselves practice as perfectly as possible devotion or fidelity to Mary as teacher—precisely because Immaculate—and unless we make ever more unshakeable in ourselves the unchanging witness of Mary to the truth of the Incarnation and Redemption, and understand ever more clearly in the light of her person, the truth of revelation as she understood it at the foot of the Cross and as she understands it at the right hand of glory. In relation to the three moments of theology, this calls for obedience to divinely appointed authority that proclaims the "credible," especially the voice of Peter; doctrinal reflection in harmony with the "pondering" of Mary and of the Church (the practice of the analogy of faith); and discipline in accord with the form of life commanded by the law of Christ.

There is no need to fear what in fact is an unconditional devotion or consecration to Mary Immaculate, along the lines of St. Maximilian. Such a "maximizing" may be abused by the pietistic, just as faith may at times be confused with credulity in the lives of the ignorant. That is not a reason for placing limits on our belief in God rightly understood *a parte rei*. So too, in the case of Mary we are dealing with a person whose perfection in such that we can never in this life sufficiently honor or recognize this. Specifically, there is no need to fear that such enthusiasm will become a substitute for profound, intellectual penetration of the mysteries of faith, where this is needed for personal purification or in order to share these mysteries with others. Herein is the value of a renewed study of Scotus as an example of one who was unconditionally devoted to Mary Immaculate and, because of that devotion, thoroughly competent intellectually to unravel the obscurities of the real. Subtlety in such a context in not cleverness; it is but a sharper perception of the real, and the natural coefficient of dedicated, intellectual labor. Marian theology and subtle theology are interchangeable at the point where theology must be metaphysical, as is so necessary today to deal with the questions raised concerning the nature of theology. And for the very reason of Mary's presence we need not fear that the cultivation of speculative theology will become divorced from the sources of revelation or its practical goal, or worse, as Bonaventure warns,

For private consultation and not distribution without the consent of E Ondrako

that the wine of revelation become diluted with the water of the philosophers.[88] It is the presence of Mary as teacher that secures for us a harmonious integration of all the factors involved, who notes the limits: what is too little or too much intellectual activity, and checks the exaggerations. For she is a teacher perfectly credible who knows whereof she speaks and who does not speak falsely. It is her presence and activity in the practice of theology that accounts for the resolution of those two basic objections to the concept of knowing as naturally dogmatic, because (it is claimed) knowing in general is either subjective or skeptical by definition: subjective, because any assurance rests ultimately on an act of the will; skeptical, because every first principle is itself subject to questioning and revision. It is her presence as teacher that in practice permits us to break the vicious circle and enjoy the epiphany of the Christ who is the one Teacher of all.

There are, then, really only two perspectives from which to view the divine and the course of history: that of Mary and that of the serpent. One leads to truth, the other to the death of the mind. If in our time, as in Bonaventure's, the irresponsibility of the intellectuals—theologians and philosophers (or artists as Bonaventure calls them)—in the pursuit of their own interests apart from the teaching authority of Christ has contributed greatly to a crisis of faith concerning the doctrine and law of Christ, then, more than so many other things, we need responsible intellectuals who choose to view the divine from the perspective of Mary.[89] The concluding lines of Hopkin's poem: *The Blessed Virgin compared to the Air We Breathe*, well expresses the mind of St. Maximilian and of Scotus, particularly if we include in our reading of the word sin, error, deceit, doubt, despair: "Be thou then, O thou dear Mother, my atmosphere; my happier world, wherein to wend and meet no sin; above me, round me lie fronting my froward eye with sweet and starless sky; stir in my ears, speak there of God's love, O live air, of patience, penance, prayer: world-mothering air, air wild, wound with thee, in thee is led, fold home, fast fold thy child."[90]

Editor's Note

The study to follow was composed by Fr. Peter Fehlner during the fall of 1978 for presentation at the 1979 annual meeting of the Catholic Mariological Society of America. Because of its length it was not published in *Marian Studies* for 1979, but in a private printing of 100 copies (Rens-

---

[88] *Collationes in Hexaemeron*, c. 19, 8.

[89] *Collationes in Hexaemeron*, c. 1, 9.

[90] HOPKINS, *op. cit.*, pp. 96–97.

For private consultation and not distribution without the consent of E Ondrako

selaer NY 1979), long since out of print. The study still has value, both for its insights on Our Lady, not only as a subject of theological study, but as a teacher of theology, precisely because Mediatrix of all graces. Just as she is uniquely associated with her Son and Savior Jesus: Priest and King, as Coredemptrix and Queen, so also is she intimately associated with Him as Teacher. The unfolding of this theme involves many points of contact not only between St. Bonaventure and Bl. John Duns Scotus, but also between Scotus and Bl. John Henry Newman and St. Maximilian M. Kolbe. These are points not covered in the conference on similarities in the thought patterns of Scotus and Newman, but certainly useful aids to understanding that conference better.

Except for correction of typographical errors and simplification of overly long sentences, the study is a reprint of the private printing.

Study Questions for Part 1

1. Scotus reflects the profundity of the Augustinian tradition and its interpretation through Anselm and the Victorines. He completes and crowns the synthesis of Thomas Aquinas and Bonaventure, thereby anticipating the solution of Newman. In the quest for knowledge in the midst of nineteenth century secularized Britain, Newman did not compromise or relativize knowledge of truth of Catholic teaching in regard to how or how much one knows, or can know. He preached, taught, and wrote to a secularized Britain, first as an Anglican and later as Catholic. Show why this is true. Why is it accurate to say that "there was no gulf, no darkness, nor skepticism between pulpit and pew, between parish priest with the care of souls and scholar with a thoroughgoing knowledge of history, philosophy, theology and anthropology?"

2. Newman's life exemplified the personal quest for truth. The serendipitous process he followed in putting Scotus into modern English meets the epistemological and metaphysical criteria for true and valid interpretation reached through phenomenological investigations. He sought to understand the light (illumination), and to apprehend and to assent to what the light was illuminating, or else he could be overwhelmed by the brilliance of the light. Discuss why the epistemological questions were Newman's attempt to understand the light and how the metaphysical questions helped him to apprehend and to assent to what the light illumined. Why it is that together, but not separated, they make up Newman's epistemology of faith and metaphysics of freedom? Show how Newman subtly asks his students to take an extra step to find the reward that lifts up the soul.

3. By December 1849, Newman agrees with the Franciscan thesis and approach of Scotus to revealed religion. Scotus taught that the fall was not the cause of Christ's predestination; indeed, even had neither angel nor man fallen, Christ would still have been predestined in the same way, indeed, even if no one but Christ had been created. How does Scotus lay to rest any misrepresentation of predestination? Why is the *Ordinatio* so important to answer this? Is the Franciscan thesis, as Newman discovered, exclusive to Franciscans? Is it accurate to say that the thesis holds that the Word was predestined absolutely, independently of any other consideration, (independent of humanity's possibility of falling into sin), predestined to be the Incarnate Redeemer and, with Him, the Immaculate, to be His Mother and our mother? Is the answer for the greatest possible glory of God satisfying and convinc-

ing? Was this the heart of the scotistic view which W. Frederick Faber, fellow Oratorian, helped Newman to understand about the not yet solemnly defined doctrine of the Immaculate Conception, in letters they exchanged in December, 1849?

4. If Scotus argued that the Incarnation was not occasioned by sin, but for the glory of God, as metaphysician-theologian, Scotus centers his entire philosophical and theological system on predestination, how he conceives the origin of all things outside of God. (See *Lectura II*. d. 20, q.1, n. 22). In his *Fifteen University Sermons* (1826–1843), Newman was breaking from a Calvinist predestination and developing themes that remained deep within his prayer life and study, and holding them together with the significant help of Butler's *Analogy*. Without being familiar with many of Newman's works, is it plausible that there is a golden thread in his answers, in his theory of development in 1845 (*Essay*), his theory of education in 1852–1858 (*Idea*), his theory of faith in 1864 (*Apologia*), and his theory of knowledge in 1869–1870 (*Grammar*)?

5. Newman uses both Thomas and Scotus in the sphere of epistemology, metaphysics, and ethics. In some places he is more clearly thomistic, and in others, scotistic, appearing thomistic at first; and only later, the scotistic pattern is identifiable. This is not readily apparent and requires on-going development of skills in the thought patterns of both Thomas and Scotus. For example, Newman's argument for the existence of God from conscience is that of Anselm-Scotus in phenomenological form, or set forth in terminology with its psychological antecedents. Discuss Newman's key that ideas grow, multiply and develop in many ways. The analysis of things and notions or facts and thoughts as objects of assent for Newman is essentially the position of Scotus put in modern English in the *Grammar of Assent*. Does the importance of using both intuitive and abstractive cognition together for Scotus convince and satisfy you? Why?

PART 2

CONTEXTUALIZING THE THEOLOGICAL CONSISTENCY OF NEWMAN AND SCOTUS

For private consultation and not distribution without the consent of E Ondrako

INTRODUCTION

Secular Christianity and Modern Voluntarism

Précis

L'intuition est un flamboiment de certitude qui déchire la nuit des senses.[1] Intuition is a blaze of certitude which tears the night of the senses. Intuition is at work in the familiar epitaph on the tombstone chosen by Bl. John Henry Cardinal Newman (1801–1890), *Ex umbris et imaginibus in veritatem*, out of the shadows and images to the truth. The two quotes are part of the many strands that link the Oxford Plato's thought patterns with those of Bl. John Duns Scotus (1265–1308). The quotes reflect a language of faith which develops in a community of faith as a living reality. There is certainty about how to engage the relationship between faith and reason, a certainty that cannot be silenced at will.[2] There is a common root in their thought patterns about intuition and the rapport between necessity and contingency. Necessity is something that cannot be other than it is. Contingency is something that may or may not happen. Necessity is in relation to the infinite, or uncreated, and contingency is in relation to the finite, or created. Necessity and contingency are disjunctive transcendentals in Scotus's univocity of the concept of being as a unique formulation to keep logic linked to reality. Newman's 'illative sense' is integrally connected to this thought of Scotus. Moreover, Scotus does not reject but gives an emanation of Bonaventure's theory of divine illumination.

Excursus: Scotus Unites Metaphysics and Theology

This excursus gives the grounding for being more at home with Scotus than with Kant. Scotus, more than his predecessors, unites metaphysics

---

[1] OLIVIER BOULNOIS, *Être et Représentation: Une geneologie de la metaphysique moderne a l'epoque de Duns Scot (XIII–VIV siecle)* (Paris: *Presses Universitaires de France*, 1999, rpt. 2008), 134. Henceforth, *Être*.

[2] JOSEPH RATZINGER, *Eschatology*, 2nd English ed., trans. Michael Walstein, trans. ed. Aidan Nichols (Friederich Pustet Verlag: Regensburg, 1977, rpt. The Catholic University of America Press, Washington, D.C. 2007), 257, 260. The future pope was commenting on "A Letter on Certain Questions of Eschatology" by the Congregation for the Doctrine of the Faith, 17 May 1979. He began by stressing the importance of the papal teaching office to be linked with the episcopal body, 241–242.

For private consultation and not distribution without the consent of E Ondrako

and theology, each science leaning on the other to exist. This serves as the foundation for our thesis that Scotus is a *projenitor*[3] of Newman. It appears that Scotus enjoys more of an era of the synthesis of faith and reason, a harmony in the relationship between philosophical and theological thought, while Newman's era follows the modern outgrowth of the Enlightenment, the Reformation, and the rebellion of clerics and nobles. The sad outgrowth, a part of modernity, finds a corresponding loss to the harmony between faith and reason. The growing perception in the twenty-first century is that modernity does not favor Christianity. For example, there are opponents on many sides to the Christian tradition of the existence and immortality of the soul. However, not all is gloom, if one understands and learns from Scotus and Newman how to interpret and be faithful to the Church's teachings, her perennial wisdom, and what it means to be a person. Although in a weakened existential condition, human beings are inclined toward transcendence possessing unlimited causal power, potential, and freedom.

Metaphysics and theology lean on each other to exist

The hypothesis about Scotus as projenitor of Newman involves a decisive invitation to objective and scholarly interpretation, and not merely an appeal for the barren repetition of ancient or medieval formulae. It is a hypothesis mindful that the Church and her scholars engage the methodological background of modernity, its philosophical or natural-scientific standpoint, which has resulted in the change in the manner of conceiving the relationship of faith and reason. Her theologians recognize the importance of teaching about the inner unity of the history of faith.[4] This noble quest for inner unity and certitude finds support from properly using the tools of Scotus, such as intuitive and abstractive cognition,[5] and the tools of Newman, such as real and notional apprehension and assent.[6]

The modes of rationality: historical, philosophical, theological and anthropological, demonstrate the continuity in tradition of particular themes such as intuition and certitude in living the Christian faith. The goal is a positive use of these methods, and not to reconstruct the essential theological themes. The problem of reconstruction came into prominence

---

3   The idea of *projenitor* was first put forth by Peter Damian Fehlner in "Scotus and Newman in Dialogue," which is chapter 7 in this volume.

4   RATZINGER, *Eschatology*, 256.

5   TIMOTHY B. NOONE, "John Duns Scotus on Intuitive Cognition, Abstractive Cognition, Scientific Knowledge, and our Knowledge of God," chapter 3 in this volume.

6   JOHN FORD, "Newman's Reasonable Approach to Faith," and "Newman's Personalist Argument for Belief in God," published in this volume as chapter 1 and 5.

For private consultation and not distribution without the consent of E Ondrako

shortly after the Second Vatican Council. Pope Benedict XVI helps to clarify the historical method, not to misuse it to distill "the pure quintessence of the past." The trustworthy continuum is tradition. He sees the problem of historical reconstruction on its own as unable to visualize faith in its pure state. If one desires to remove what is theological from every philosophical formulation, then philosophical reason alone may be unable to play a decisive role in the quest for truth. Scotus and Newman intuited that in the quest for truth and for understanding the development of doctrine, there are strengths and limits to using the historical method and of importing philosophy into faith.[7] In other words, the absence of the cautious eye that Scotus and Newman have towards history, philosophy, theology, and anthropology runs the risk of relativism in living the Christian faith.

Newman and Scotus contribute insight to the balance that the Holy Father desires and to the peaceful resolution of the development of doctrine and inherent tensions felt between what is inseparable, that is, interpretation and fidelity to the fundamental truths of the Catholic faith. When he was Archbishop of Munich and Freising, Pope Benedict XVI replied gently to the spiritual upheaval of our age: "Only the person who makes the truth accessible once again, who actually mediates it, remains true to it; but only the one who remains true to it interprets it correctly. An interpretation that is unfaithful ceases to be a genuine interpretation and becomes a falsification."[8]

The works of Scotus and Newman demonstrate the Holy Father's *caveat* and purpose of genuine interpretation and fidelity to fundamental truths of the Catholic faith. The works of the two great English scholars, separated by five centuries, demonstrate a progressive illumination and realization of God's most perfect love. They interpret the supreme love and goodness and mercy of God correctly regardless of sin and suffering. In his early years as a curate, Newman's experiences in pastoral care drew him toward the freedom that Scotus demonstrates. It is unreasonable to claim sin as the necessary premise for the realization of salvific love. Rather, the Franciscan answers from the recognition of love willing to suffer and to become incarnate in order to suffer. Newman was gradually discovering this truth that permeates his writings, the heart of his 'slow-paced truth' as Scotus teaches. Christ might have redeemed us in any number of ways, simply be being born, but freely chose the cross, and his love would have been as great even if he had not chosen the cross.

---

[7] RATZINGER, *Eschatology*, 250, 257.

[8] *Eschatology*, 241–242.

For private consultation and not distribution without the consent of E Ondrako

In his beatification homily, the Holy Father mentions Scotus specifically when he names Newman as "worthy to take his place in a long line of
saints and scholars from these islands." "In Bl. John Henry, that tradition
of gentle scholarship, deep human wisdom and profound love for the Lord
has born rich fruit, as a sign of the abiding presence of the Holy Spirit deep
within the heart of God's people, bringing forth abundant gifts."[9]

The short answer about being at home with Scotus more than with
Kant is that never before Scotus had the distinction between abstraction
and intuition been so firm.[10] The longer answer is that Scotus fine tunes
the metaphysics of Aristotle with his study of the disjunctive trancenden-
tals and shows that theology requires metaphysics to be pushed to its final
end in order to exhaust its possibilities. To drive metaphysics to attain its
final end is to permit access to beatitude! Short cuts do not work. If there
is an absence of a firm distinction between abstraction and intuition, there
is a danger of blurring boundaries by uncritical thinking. This blurring
of boundaries may give way to the generation of ideas that focuses on
contours of self. Besides a healthy side, this new pattern or *type* has a
seductively deceptive side, that of liberal or secular Christianity which is a
modern pattern or *type* built on an anti-holiness principle. For Scotus and
Newman, it is an irreconcilable contradiction to living the Gospel.

There is a crucial but often overlooked historical development. If one
examines the development of this new pattern or *type* in the structure of the
relation between metaphysics and theology between the time of Thomas
Aquinas and Immanuel Kant, one has to include the thought of Francisco
Suarez. For all of his contributions, the re-thinking of earlier problems
by Suarez in the late humanistic and Renaissance culture, demonstrates
that Suarez is an eclectic and closer to Thomas than Scotus. According
to Olivier Boulnois,[11] the Kantian achievement is largely guided by the
Suarezian tradition of metaphysics. This is a compelling point, beyond
the preliminary scope of this excursus. Here is where I join the chorus of
those who hold that it seems that Newman intuits something wrong in
the Kantian achievement very early in his Oxford career. His felt difficulty
motivates his life long quest and inimitable synthesis about certitude in
the *Grammar of Assent*. His views radiate from his acceptance speech upon
being named a Cardinal in 1879.

---

9 POPE BENEDICT XVI, "Beatification Homily for Bl. John Henry Newman" (www.zenit.org,
  September 19, 2010).

10 *Être*, 477.

11 *Être*, 493.

For private consultation and not distribution without the consent of E Ondrako

A close reading of Scotus unfolds a panorama of reasons why he may be a progenitor[12] of Newman and not of Kant. Newman's writings convey an intuition that metaphysics is not a laicization of theology and that theology does not govern the development of metaphysics. This is strikingly evident in his definition of the essence of a university. Newman's *Idea of a University* is replete with his understanding of the autonomy of metaphysics and indispensible interdependence with theology. The autonomy was never argued with as much conviction and clarity prior to Scotus and in a new form by Scotus, according to Boulnois. Moreover, the subtle doctor uses the short synthesis from Bonaventure's *Reductio Artium ad Theologiam*. This is often translated in a manner that may miss the true meaning of "The Reduction (or Return) of the Arts to Theology." Rather than a reduction, in the twenty-first century sense, *reductio* means being brought to a full realization. The key is that Christ is the one who guides Christian philosophy. There are revealed foundations for Christian philosophy which Bonaventure, Scotus and Newman incorporate into their writings. Nowhere is this as apparent as in Newman's masterpiece about the essence of a university and the role of theology in a liberal education. The similarities with Bonaventure's *reductio*, or *resolutio*, or full realization leap out of the pages of the vital importance of theological training in *The Idea of a University*. Bonaventure and Scotus examine the character of human knowledge which lifts the activity of the human mind towards the divine. Bonaventure describes this as a passing of human knowledge into affection or wisdom. Scotus treats this passing under intuitive and abstractive cognition, while Newman develops it under the making of a judgment, the illative sense.

In terms of logic, ontology, and natural theology recentered around a Kantian onto-theology focus,[13] there is a critical gap lest one fall into the trap of binding theology and metaphysics from accomplishing their respective tasks. Onto-theology is a peculiar separation of faith and reason which brings confusion into the argument for the existence of God from reason (Scotus) and from conscience (Newman). Said another way, the anti-holiness principle has many strands. Scotus anticipates them. Newman consciously avoids them. If one understands Scotus and Newman, they help counter the darkness of contemporary skepticism about ontology (being) and the cynicism that comes from the darkness. Theirs is the blueprint for *right reason* in true liberty of will and intellect.

---

[12] Fehlner thesis demonstrates profound metaphysical, theological, and anthropological roots.

[13] *Être*, 504.

For private consultation and not distribution without the consent of E Ondrako

Pope Benedict XVI knows the negative attitude toward the study of being (ontology) which seems to counter the "function and act centered thinking" of theological thought since the Council. He defends the study of ontology and dismisses the view that ontology is unacceptable.[14] The way that shift in emphasis plays out in the study of theology, is that ontological thought is perceived or dismissed as static, one that ought to be replaced by the historical and dynamic approach of Scripture. The Holy Father recognizes this rejection of the ontological as a counter position to the dialogical and personal, instead of incorporating the ontological and historical as a method of research. A clear sign of his worry is in his Scotus address on July 7, 2010. He invites dialogue with ontological and anthropological considerations to answer the challenges to use right reason in true liberty of will and intellect.[15] This is important to him from a Scotistic perspective: what is at stake is access to beatitude which is experienced by the blessed and accessible in glimpses by the intuition of an ordered finite intellect that desires union with the Truth.

His pastoral sensitivity to teachers and to students in the United Kingdom demonstrates the gravity of these truths about access to beatitude from a pastor who is catechizing. He invites teachers to form the human person, to equip him or her to live life to the full—which is to impart eternal wisdom to the young. He invites the young to become saints and explains that the key is very simple—true happiness is to be found in God. Only God can satisfy the deepest needs of our hearts. As you come to know God better, you find you want to reflect something of his infinite goodness in your own life. All the work you do in your Catholic schools is placed in the context of growing in friendship with God, and all that flows from that friendship.[16] The young heard and responded affirmatively. "Holy Father, we want to be saints."[17]

Three caveats when studying modern voluntarism and secular or liberal Christianity

The first *caveat* is with ways of thinking about development in metaphysics. Olivier Boulnois traces three ways from the thirteenth century

---

[14] *Eschatology*, 250. Graham Leonard resigned as Bishop of London and explained that he did so because of the loss of the ontological and increasing stress of the functional in the Anglican community. He later became a Catholic priest.

[15] BENEDICT XVI, *Papal Audience*, July 7, 2010.

[16] BENEDICT XVI, *Addresses to Educators and to the Students of UK's Catholic Schools*, September 17, 2010 (www.zenit.org).

[17] British television showed a young teenager who shouted these words with much enthusiasm in behalf of his friends to the Holy Father who received their desire and expression with a most appropriate smile of gratitude.

For private consultation and not distribution without the consent of E Ondrako

of what he calls the evolutionary structure of metaphysics to Kant. The first is that of Albert the Great and Thomas Aquinas; the second, Roger Bacon, Giles of Rome and others; and the third, Siger of Brabant, Henry of Ghent, Augustine of Ancona, Peter of Trabes, Alexander of Alexandria, and Scotus.[18] Boulnois places Scotus in the third approach.

Three approaches to studying the will in relation to the intellect by Peter Damian Fehlner differ from Boulnois. Aristotle and Thomas Aquinas are his first; Ockham, Hume and Kant, his second; and Bonaventure, Scotus and, arguably, Newman, his third. Whether one follows Boulnois or Fehlner, both recognize the problem of splitting ontology and theology. One effect is the development of liberal or secular Christianity in the thought of John Locke.

The second *caveat* is with the daunting word, onto-theology, which means, in practice, the detachment of revealed theology from philosophy. Ontology developed as the branch of metaphysics that is the study of reality, or being. Theology that is detached from revealed theology means natural theology, or theology that is using the tools of reason alone, without revelation. Onto-theology, detached from revelation, came into use as natural theology. Kant and the onto-theologians make a recognizable change to the study of truth and structural orientation of metaphysics to theology as it was perceived in the thirteenth century. He inspired further onto-theological systems, such as Hegel and Heidegger. Allan B. Wolter explains how far the onto-theology split in metaphysics is from Scotus: "the theory of transcendentals is not simply an important section of Scotus' metaphysics. It is his metaphysics. Like his metaphysics, it is saturated with theological implications."[19]

Hegel tried to correct some of Kant's thought by replacing being with becoming or change. Becoming means change, which means everything can change. Onto-theology replaces being with material or formal logic, a major contemporary problem. One has to be alert to the seductive thought of neo-Hegelian sympathizers since Vatican II. Pope Benedict XVI gently dismisses neo-Hegelian thought as misleading. An example is in dealing with the problem of suffering.[20] Without intuitive metaphysical resources, there is a strong temptation to explain the mystery of suffering and evil by anthropomorphizing God and confusing the mystery of the Trinity to

---

[18] *Être*, 457–504.

[19] ALLAN B. WOLTER, *The Transcendentals and Their Function in the Metaphysics of Duns Scotus* (The Franciscan Institute: St. Bonaventure University, St.Bonaventure, N.Y., 1946, rpt. Kessinger Publishing, 2008), 184.

[20] The ancient heresy of patripassionism and neo-patripassionism are fertile ground for neo-hegelian sympathizers. See E. ONDRAKO, "Being and Becoming: Hegel's Inversion and Newman's Consistency with Scotus," chapter 16 in this volume.

For private consultation and not distribution without the consent of E Ondrako

the extent that false comfort is given to the human person in pilgrimage. Cyril O'Regan elucidates this difficulty with Hegel: "Hegel provides the template for a suffering God within a Trinitarian horizon."[21]

Scotus answers in plain words: *God as God cannot suffer!* Suffering and becoming are not pure perfections. Becoming is not being. The pure perfections, include being, freedom, will, intellect, love and knowledge, etc., take precedence over becoming and experience. Suffering is a contingency in personal life in finite human beings, not suffering in the divine nature, which is impossible. Suffering, in the sacred humanity of Christ, changes human suffering from punishment for sin to the manifestation of the Father's love for our salvation. That is why Scotus taught that a person can never be predestined to damnation but all are predestined in Christ to share the glory of the Blessed Trinity.[22] Newman intuited this truth in his early days as an Anglican priest.

Heidegger wrote a qualifying dissertation on Scotus but seems to have fused medieval logic with neo-Kantianism and phenomenology.[23] He was a contemporary of Edith Stein in Edmund Husserl's classes. She broke away from neo-Kantianism, but Heidegger does not seem to have made the same exit. Perhaps that is why Heidegger's polemic with theology is complex. Sean McGrath refers to Heidegger's 'theological moratorium'[24] that makes it very difficult to be open to new ways of being modern while not losing what it means to be an authentic person with human dignity. This is another way of saying that Heidegger obscures the *type*, or pattern of behavior of Christianity, and its impression on its surroundings. Newman held sacred the principle: *to alter the type corrupts the type.* The silence of the saint before the infinite chasm that separates the human person from God, finite being from infinite Being, is the silence of humble contemplation, the key to understanding Scotus and Newman.

If one applies the logic of ontotheology to the extramental, there is a risk of skepticism. The onto-theology of Kant, Hegel, and Heidegger separate faith from reason, or separate truths which are authentically present in the witness of the saints and martyrs, the Fathers, Augustine, Anselm, Thomas, Bonaventure, Scotus and Newman from reality, being. That is why we subscribe to the metaphysics of faith and freedom. God and the human person share the pure perfection of being in two modes, finite

---

21 CYRIL O'REGAN, Theology and the Spaces of Apocalyptic, *The Pere Marquette Lecture in Theology, 2009* (Milwaukee, WI: Marquette University Press, 2009), fn.103.

22 SCOTUS, *III Sent.*, d. 7.

23 SEAN L. MCGRATH, *Heidegger: A Very Critical Introduction* (Grand Rapids, MI: W.B. Eerdmans, 2008), 12.

24 MCGRATH, 129.

For private consultation and not distribution without the consent of E Ondrako

and infinite, including the pure perfections of will, intellect, freedom, love and knowledge.

The third *caveat* is to define voluntarism. Voluntarism usually means the study of the primacy of the will over the intellect, but it has ancient, patristic, medieval and modern perspectives. Without distinguishing, one may conclude erroneously that the thought of Scotus on the will and intellect is a preparation for Kant's onto-theology. There is an erroneous corollary in some academic circles today: that Scotus is a modernist. Some scholars even posit that Newman is a modernist. They think that along with Scotus, Newman prepares future generations to be modernists and voluntarists. What they mean is an arbitrary use of the will. Nothing could be farther from the truth. Newman was intuitively uncomfortable with Kantian thought on the radical autonomy of the will.[25] Arguably, Ockham is the more likely precursor of Kant's arbitrary voluntarism.

Voluntarism comes from *voluntas*, the will. For the scholastics, it is any theory that gives the will prominence.[26] Voluntarism is not a mask for self-will, but in the Scotistic and Newmanian sense, a profoundly personal quest for truth. It is a most noble exercise of the will and intellect. Scotus and Newman are pilgrim scholars who support a principle of holiness rather than a reduction to an anti-holiness principle, or posture of virtue as meaningless, and vice and sin as morally neutral. They avoid reducing the human struggle for holiness by the knowledge of and free practice of virtue to overcome vice. Scotus and Newman recognize the desire for cultivating genuine virtue to overcome self-will, sin, and vice as a life long struggle. Christians believe in help from the gift of grace to reach holiness.

Cyril O'Regan offers an original analysis of the problem of "secular or liberal Christianity"[27] with its anti-holiness stance as rooted in Cartesian

---

[25] ADRIAN J. BOEKRAAD and HENRY TRISTRAM, *The Argument from Concience to the Existence of God* (Louvain: Éditions Nauwelaerts, 1961), 29–30. In a letter to W. S. Lilly, August 17, 1884, Newman said that he had never read Kant or Coleridge. In his Correspondence I, 226, Lord Acton adds that Newman only got to know Kant very late. In his earlier work, Boekraad concluded that Newman never read Kant but learned about his thinking along with Hegel from a book on the history of philosophy. See BOEKRAAD, *The Personal Conquest of Truth* (Louvain: Éditions Nauwelaerts, 1955), 60, 81. It seems to me that the argument can be made that Newman had a reasonalby significant understanding of Kant and Hegel simply by being in the presence of learned scholars at Oriel where there must have been conversation on what was happening on the continent, especially in Germany. Newman makes reference to Germany in *The Idea of a University*.

[26] Some modern thinkers use voluntarism to identify any theory that explains the universe as emanating ultimately from will itself. See *The New Catholic Encyclopedia* (Washington, D.C., 1967), vol. 14, 745f.

[27] CYRIL O'REGAN, "John Henry Newman and the Argument of Holiness," *Newman Studies Journal* 9, no. 1 (Spring 2012). "Newman and Holiness" address at the National Newman Conference, Pittsburgh, PA, August 5–7, 2010, to be published in Newman Studies Journal, 2011.

For private consultation and not distribution without the consent of E Ondrako

thought in the seventeenth century. In his early life at Oxford, Newman perceives the problem, avoids it, and chooses to spend his life in the quest for certitude. In his *Grammar of Assent* he addresses how one can believe what one cannot understand and believe what one cannot absolutely prove. O'Regan's view is that the only right reasoned answer is to choose to live the Gospel message to be perfect as the heavenly Father is perfect. His argument is drawn from a selection of Newman's writings, and serves as an x-ray of the problem of secular or liberal Christianity, at once seductive as it appears to be freeing, but clearly modernist. Modernism, in this context, means an ideology which uses naturalistic evolutionary philosophy and arbitrary historical criticism in such a manner as to attempt to change Catholic doctrine in a manner that it can never be changed. The problem of modernism was complex and seductive. Pope Pius X required clerics and seminary professors and religious superiors to take an oath against modernism.[28] O'Regan's critical thought clarifies the seductive problem of modernism, perhaps more seductive today because the oath against modernism is too often perceived as antiquated and unnecessary by those who fail to understand its salutary meaning, but should.

Scotus and Newman are infamously thought of as modernists and voluntarists, meaning rationalists with an arbitrary view of the will. Private judgment never became the ultimate authority in their decisions about faith and reason. One easy way to understand what Scotus and Newman hold about modernism and voluntarism is in their teaching about intuition and certitude in relation to the unchanging character of revelation and dogma. Newman's columns, "The Tamworth Reading Room," written as an Anglican in 1841, sum up his respect for the intrinsically excellent and noble scientific pursuits in liberal education which were in the air, including Lockian and Kantian thought. He wrote:

> …knowledge does not occupy, does not form the mind; that apprehension of the unseen is the only known principle capable of subsuming moral evil, educating the multitude, and organizing society; and that, whereas man is born for action, action flows not from the inferences, but from impressions,—not from reasonings, but from Faith.[29]

The role of faith for Newman pin points his problem with modernism and its corollary, voluntarism. His knowledge of intuition and certitude helps him to recognize the weaknesses in the increasingly secularized

---

28 J.J. HEANEY, "modernism," NCE, vol 9, 991–995.

29 JOHN HENRY NEWMAN, "Secular Knowledge without Personal Belief Tends to Unbelief," *Discussions and Arguments on Various Subjects* (London: uniform edition, 1872), 304.

For private consultation and not distribution without the consent of E Ondrako

thought of the nineteenth century. It is an end run around or rejection of the unchanging character of revelation and dogma. Scotus knew this attempt in its early thirteenth century Joachimite[30] or pre-Hegelian form. Newman knew the mechanics of the problem of modernism and voluntarism in those who espoused private judgment and scientific pursuits in the place of ethical training. The impact of Joachimite and neo-Hegelian thought is reflected in the following remark of Pope Benedict XVI to Archbishop Rowan Williams of Canterbury at Lambeth Palace.

> On the one hand, the surrounding culture is growing ever more distant from its Christian roots, despite a deep and widespread hunger for spiritual nourishment. On the other hand, the increasingly multicultural dimension of society, particularly marked in this country, brings with it the opportunity to encounter other religions. For us Christians this opens up the possibility of exploring, together with members of other religious traditions, ways of bearing witness to the transcendent dimension of the human person and the universal call to holiness.[31]

The second imperative definition is the formal distinction between the will and intellect and the power to judge which is called *ratio*. It cannot be said too often that a major contribution to the science of metaphysics is Scotus's formula that there is a formal distinction between will and intellect, *realiter unum, formaliter distinctum*, one reality with a formal distinction.[32] This real unity of will and intellect, while formally distinct, explains the split in the study of metaphysics by onto-theology, in particular, the form that it took in the thought of Kant. Splitting metaphysics into general metaphysics and special metaphysics or natural theology continues to have far reaching ramifications that differ from Scotus who identifies a unity between the will and intellect that has a formal distinction, meaning, will and intellect are one reality. The will is not the intellect and the intellect is not the will, but they compose a real unity while formally distinct. That is why one can say that the nature of the person is to think metaphysically. Joseph Cardinal Ratzinger examined significant resistance to this point in his reflections on eschatology.[33]

Christians teach a unity in the Persons of the Trinity with a real distinction between each Person, one reality, formally distinct. The Father is not

---

[30] Joachimisam is pre-hegelian movement attributed to a Calabrian Monk, Joachim of Fiore, 1130–1202.

[31] POPE BENEDICT XVI, "Discourse at Lambeth Palace," September 17, 2010 (www.zenit.org).

[32] MAURICE GRAJEWSKI, *The Formal Distinction of Duns Scotus* (Washington, D.C.: The Catholic University of America, 1944), 199.

[33] See note 4.

For private consultation and not distribution without the consent of E Ondrako

the Son and the Son is not the Holy Spirit. Theology is compenetrated by metaphysics. That is an example of how the theology of the Trinity lets itself be ballasted by metaphysics. When a person thinks metaphysically, using the power to judge, *ratio*, the person is pushing metaphysics to its proper end which is access to divine beatitude.

The third important definition is *ratio*, a personal power to judge which touches the will and intellect. This is significant when one reflects on why Newman changed his first note from preservation of an idea to preservation of *type* in the *Essay on the Development of Doctrine*. Idea for Newman was closer to *ratio* as it was understood in medieval thought, i.e. the personal power to judge. It is a critical juncture for *to alter the type corrupts the type*. Newman never let up on his critique of the anti-holiness principle seen as a new *type*. His acceptance speech in 1879 upon receiving the honor of Cardinal reveals his use of *ratio*. He begins with the intentions in his heart.

> In a long course of years I have made many mistakes. I have nothing of that high perfection which belongs to the writings of the Saints, viz., that error cannot be found in them; but what I trust that I may claim all through what I have written, is this,–an honest intention, an absence of private ends, a temper of obedience, a willingness to be corrected, a dread of error, a desire to serve Holy Church, and through Divine mercy, a fair measure of success.[34]

This is a portrait of a person who knows the meaning of humble contemplation in the quest for truth. He goes on to the heart of the quest, "For thirty, forty, fifty years I have resisted to the best of my powers the spirit of liberalism in religion."[35] That is the integral connection to the problem of the anti-dogmatic, anti-sacramental and anti-holiness stance that he resisted with all his might. His fervor is intense: "Never did Holy Church need champions against it more sorely than now, when, alas! It is an error overspreading, as a snare, the whole earth."[36] In my view, Newman implies that the error has a Kantian form with Lockian roots. His love for the Church and her future prompt him to renew the protest.

> Liberalism in religion is the doctrine that there is no positive truth in religion, but that one Creed is as good as another, and this is the teaching which is gaining substance and force daily. It is inconsistent with any recognition of any religion, as *true*. It teaches that all

---

34   JOHN HENRY NEWMAN, "Biglietto Address," 63–65.

35   Biglietto, 64.

36   Biglietto, 64.

For private consultation and not distribution without the consent of E Ondrako

are to be tolerated, for all are matters of opinion. Revealed religion is not a truth, but a sentiment and a taste; not an objective fact, not miraculous; and it is the right of each individual to make it say just what strikes his fancy.[37]

Newman carries his criticism of the Lockian view further, a gentle reminder to those living in a post Vatican II age, that the successes of the ecumenical movement are the work of prayer and engagement with doctrine under the influence of the Holy Spirit and mediation of Mary.[38]

> Devotion is not necessarily founded on faith. Men may go to Protestant Churches and to Catholic, may get good from both and belong to neither. They may fraternize together in spiritual thoughts and feelings, without having any views at all of doctrine in common, or seeing the need of them.[39]

Then Newman adds his critique of a problem that is constant, that of private judgment, which has a Lockian-Kantian form, meaning the arbitrary delineation of revealed truths as strong or weak, and a subtle, arbitrary voluntarism.

> Since, then religion is so personal a peculiarity and so private a possession, we must of necessity ignore it in the intercourse of man with man. If a man puts on a new religion every morning, what is that to you? It is as impertinent to think about a man's religion as about his sources of income or his management of his family. Religion is in no sense the bond of society.[40]

Newman includes the result of such a relativistic mindset. In the place of religion and supernatural sanctions, philosophers and politicians are bent to solve the problem of law and order without the aid of Christianity. The search is for great working principles to take the place of religion. Newman summarizes: "Religion is a private luxury, which a man may have if he will; but which of course he must pay for, and which he must not obtrude upon others, or indulge in to their annoyance."[41]

Newman concludes this section of his speech with a powerful word: this great *apostosia*. *To alter the type corrupts the type.* Preservation of *type* is

---

[37] Biglietto, 64.

[38] In September 2009, Archbishop Rowan Williams and Walter Cardinal Kasper inaugurated a joint pilgrimage from Walsingham, England to Lourdes, France. The Archbishop observed that the ecumenical movement would not advance without Mary.

[39] Biglietto, 65.

[40] Biglietto, 66.

[41] Biglietto, 66–67.

For private consultation and not distribution without the consent of E Ondrako

the note of true development of doctrine. Liberalism in religion corrupts religion.

The fourth important definition is to clarify Newman's primary goals in his *Grammar of Assent* in relation to certitude and certainty. *Ratio*, the power to judge, is at the heart of Newman's *Grammar of Assent*. In 1870, after a lifetime of preparation, he gave the world his original contribution about certitude and certainty. The *Grammar of Assent* has two goals according to Oratorian Edward Caswall. Newman told him: "the first part shows that you can believe what you cannot understand. In the second part, you can believe what you cannot absolutely prove."[42] The first time I tried to explain the two goals to my university students, they grimaced with disbelief. In retrospect, I searched for a way to make this succinct comment of Newman's intelligible. It was only when I studied the intuitive and abstractive cognition in Scotus[43] that the light illumined what I was trying to teach, that metaphysical questions pertaining to certitude ought not to scare any thinking person away. Rather the very answers that are sought in the depth of one's being have an intelligible form. For Scotus, intuitive and abstractive cognition are parallel to the real and notional apprehension and assent of Newman, but they are meant to be used together.

Newman's *Grammar of Assent* challenges the faulty reliance on the deformation of the will in modern arbitrary voluntarism. The subtle doctor's clarity between abstractive and intuitive cognition and Newman's notional and real apprehension and notional and real assent are an intelligible reply to a runaway will. Scotus and Newman exhibit their pastoral concern to help a person understand the proper role of the will and intellect in the personal quest for certitude. The human will is subject to human frailty, to sin. Grace is necessary to overcome the tendency to the arbitrary, self-serving, irrational drive of the human will even in matters of human rights and duties. In an age filled with rights talk, Newman's observation is prescient: "we have rights because we have duties."[44]

Ratio, the power to judge, is at the heart of examining rights and duties. *Ratio* is at the heart of the three *caveats*, a cautious reply to the ambiguities of the term voluntarism. Many distinctions separate ancient, patristic, and medieval voluntarism and modern theories of the will. The entry in the *New Catholic Encyclopedia*, for example, needs some clarifications. It risks

---

[42] CHARLES STEPHEN DESSAIN, *John Henry Newman* (Oxford: University Press, 1961, rpt. 1980), 148.

[43] Timothy B. Noone's two chapters, 3 and 6, in this volume make the pivotal idea of Bl. Scotus easy to follow.

[44] JOHN HENRY NEWMAN, "Letter to the Duke of Norfolk" in Difficulties of Anglicans II (London: uniform edition, 1900), 250.

For private consultation and not distribution without the consent of E Ondrako

leading to false conclusions. The *NCE* places the historical dividing line with the rationalistic humanism of Rene Descartes, *vis a vis* the harmonious interchange between reason and faith present in Augustine, Anselm of Canterbury, Scotus, and the Franciscan William of Ockham. The *NCE* fails to clarify the essential differences between Scotus and Ockham. If it is correct to make the historical distinction between Scotus as the end of the *via antiqua* and Ockham as the beginning of the *via moderna*, as the English Friars did, it has to be said. Otherwise, the *NCE* entry is helpful. The authors place Blaise Pascal's reply to Descartes, which is based on faith and reason, on the other side of the Cartesian divide. Their concern is about the consequences of Immanuel Kant's purely ideal Absolute and Kant's analysis of understanding which lacks the intuition proper to it. The main problem of modern voluntarism that the *NCE* authors find is Kant's analysis of knowledge, its lack of ontological currency,[45] but they fail to add insights from Pope St. John Paul II's encyclical, *Fides et Ratio*, on faith and reason. The Holy Father does not allude to nor clarify the helpful scotistic-thomistic divide, which leads back to the three *caveats* for Newman-Scotus research. By applying the *caveats* to ambiguities related to voluntarism, the hypothesis begins to take shape that it is a mistake to claim threads of modern voluntarism in the metaphysician-theologian Scotus. Rather, Ockham is the more likely thread bearer for he is more of a logician.

It is not a surprise that some find the *Grammar of Assent* very dry after their first reading, at least the first few chapters. The Jesuit poet Gerard Manley Hopkins, who was received into the Roman Church by Newman in 1866, read the *Grammar* shortly before discovering the thought of Scotus while doing research at the Bodleian Library in the summer of 1872. He found the *Grammar* to be very dry, but his discovery of Scotus seems to have changed his entire philosophical, theological and anthropological approach to life. About a decade later Hopkins offered to write a commentary on the *Grammar of Assent*, but Newman declined. I think it is fair to assume that his commentary would have shown the influence of Scotus on his interpretation of the *Grammar* because Hopkins loves the thought of Scotus which imbues all of his poetry.[46] I am convinced

---

45 P. Ortegat, L. J. Walker, "Voluntarism," *New Catholic Encyclopedia* (Washington, D.C., 1967), 14, 745–747.

46 W. H. Gardner and N. H. MacKenzie, eds., *The Poems of Gerard Manley Hopkins* (Oxford: Oxford University Press, 1990), fourth edition, 272. They identify the discovery of Scotus in August, 1872. See Catherine Phillips, ed., intro., and notes, *Gerard Manley Hopkins: The Major Works* (Oxford, University Press, 2002).

For private consultation and not distribution without the consent of E Ondrako

that Fehlner's two chapters in *The Newman-Scotus Reader* are the closest approximation to that unfinished commentary by Hopkins.[47]

The contra-distinction between Scotus and Newman from Kant on the will.

Scotus and Newman are far removed from secular or liberal Christianity. The univocity of the concept of being of Scotus may appear dry, but it is the key concept to support the hypothesis that Scotus is a 'precursor' of Newman and not of Kant. Fehlner explains that the univocity of the concept of being is not a rejection but a development of Bonaventure's theory of divine illumination.[48] Bonaventure gives an Augustinian inspired argument about truth. "Truth, which is absolutely immutable, can be seen only by those who are able to enter into that innermost silence of the soul, and to this, no sinner is able to come, but only one who is supremely a lover of eternity."[49] The change in Bonaventure's theory of divine illumination by Scotus is "not as a pure logical construct first, but a unique, incomparable formulation of divine illumination in logical form so that it can be the light guiding all our thought, keeping logic securely linked to reality or being."[50] Newman's illative sense shares the *dijudicatio*, or the natural making of a judgment of Bonaventure. Newman agrees with Bonaventure that assent is different from inference that leads to assent.[51]

Secular or liberal Christianity and first principles.

The problem of secular or liberal Christianity, evident in a secularized West, has, at its root, a clash between those who accept and those who reject first principles. Those who claim to keep faith but reject any Christian religion, represent a problem of the relation between will and intellect in the use or refusal to use first principles. In addressing the relation of the will to the intellect, Scotus, more than any of his predecessors, uses first principles which require metaphysical and theological reflection to keep

---

[47] FEHLNER, chapter 4 and chapter 7 in this volume. Several private conversations with Fehlner on why Newman may have declined the offer in 1883 from Hopkins to write a commentry on the *Grammar of Assent* convince me to make this point.

[48] The misreprésentation is to say that Scotus dismisses the theory of divine illumination of Bonaventure for more or less the same reasons that Thomas Aquinas dismisses the theory of divine illumination. Thomas differs from Bonaventure on illumination for reasons that need precision. See *ST* I, qq. 82, 83, 85, 86, 87.

[49] ST. BONAVENTURE, *Disputed Questions on the Knowledge of Christ*, ed. Zachary Hayes (St. Bonaventure, N.Y.: The Franciscan Institute, 2005), 143–144.

[50] FEHLNER, letter to author, July 31, 2010.

[51] FEHLNER, "Dialogue," chapter 7 in this volume. He develops this point in the final section on the *Grammar of Assent* and *Oxford University Sermons*.

For private consultation and not distribution without the consent of E Ondrako

the independence within interdependence of both sciences. *Au contraire*, Kant's onto-theology divides metaphysics, and insists on the absolute autonomy of the transcendental 'ego,' that the will is radically arbitrary. In contradistinction to the unity of metaphysical and theological reflection as with Scotus and Newman, Kant argues for the radically arbitrary indifference of the categorical imperative of the human will. Kant breaks the harmony that Scotus insists on between metaphysics and theology which need each other to exist. Metaphysics and theology need the intellect with its transcendental powers to be sciences.[52]

Kant's thinking is irrational for holding as radically arbitrary the indifference of the categorical imperative of the human will, even though he changes his mind three times on its formulation. In the vein of transcendental idealism, Kant adds that this is a transcendental lunge toward the infinite 'noumenon,' which means that the idea of God is necessary, but that it remains just a concept and not a substance.[53] Newman replies: who would be willing to give his or her life for an opinion? The glaring difficulty is the Kantian teaching that if there is a God, the emphasis is not that God is love, but, if God exists it is only a fact, a scientific answer alone. In other words, the profoundly personal relationship with God to which every Christian is called is emptied of its essence. The two Marian oriented scholars, Scotus and Newman, would come up empty from a search of the Kantian framework of the human will in relation to the essence of the will as a profoundly personal act of the perfect will of the Mother of God.

For Scotus, the primacy of the will over the intellect is an 'orderly' voluntarism because it is rational, with humility, and in faith. The voluntarism of Kant is an exercise in rationalism and is 'arbitrary.' The logical outgrowth of this Kantian view is secular or liberal Christianity. Newman uses first principles, as Scotus, to expose its false assumptions. Jan H. Walgrave summarizes these as: the dogmatic principle, the principle of faith, the principle of theology, the sacramental principle, the principle of the mystical sense of Sacred Scripture, the principle of grace, the ascetic principle, the principle of the natural conscience which identifies the intrinsic malice and the absoluteness of sin, the principle of the possibility of the sanctification of the intellect, and the principle of development.[54]

---

[52] Être, 478.

[53] PAUL GUYER, "Kant, Autonomy, and Modernity," Unpublished Lecture at the Philosophy Department of the Catholic University of America, October 15, 2010. Guyer thought that this view of the elder Kant was an alternative to onto-theology.

[54] JAN H. WALGAVE, *Newman Le développement du dogme* (Tournai, Belgique: Casterman, 1957), 142–143. See WALGRAVE, *Newman the Theologian* (New York: Sheed and Ward, 1960) Walgrave gives a brief and concise sketch of ten key principles in Newman's thinking in the section of chapter 2, La psychologie générale du développement, Article 2, Foi et développe-

For private consultation and not distribution without the consent of E Ondrako

The problem that the medievals may never have conceived would have as much currency as it did in Newman's day and the twenty-first century is the anti-holiness principle. The roots of this deformation of the Christian will are a challenge to faith but the historical, philosophical, theological and anthropological evidence converges into a cogent explanation of the reason "that only faith can guarantee the blessings that we hope for, or prove the existence of the realities that at present remain unseen" (Heb. 11:1).

Epistemology and metaphysics assist an orderly voluntarism.

Scotus's use of the science of epistemology, the science that studies knowing or how the light illumines, relates to the science of metaphysics, what the light illumines, the study of what is, being, or reality. Kant's split of metaphysics has a practical result or logical reduction to the radically autonomous will. The saints demonstrate the divide in the road towards skepticism or towards belief, an autonomous will based on the anti-meta-physical position of Kant, or a contemplative will. Fehlner observes that the universal spread of Kantianism throughout the world can be countered by a study of Scotus's systematic Mariology for it is grounded in faith, hope and charity.

From another point of view, that of Heidegger, beyond the scope of this essay, one may find persuasive the argument of Sean J. McGrath who reacts to Kantian challenges to will to live with virtue in their Heideggerian form. McGrath's view is helpful in observing that Heidegger "undid the Cartesian-Kantian turn in philosophy—a turn that replaces metaphysics with epistemology and ontology with transcendental psychology."[55] McGrath's take on Heidegger seems to be that 'transcendental empiricism' does not resolve the problem with the light that overwhelms what is illumined. I take it that the reason for McGrath's critique is that Heidegger relies too exclusively on logic,[56] as did Kant. That is the clue. There is an absence of St. Bonaventure's theory of divine illumination and apparent misunderstanding of the unique, incomparable formulation that it has in

---

ment, 136–155. Nicholas Lash takes a competing view of development. See NICHOLAS LASH, *Newman on Development* (Shepherdstown, VA, 1975). See FEHLNER, chapters 4 and 7 in this volume for an extensive analysis. In July 1983, at a Symposium at Newman College near Birmingham, England, I was present when Walgrave and Lash expressed their differing points of view in a very animated manner. That meeting was very important for it inspired me to take further steps to understand Newman and his theory of development of doctrine, a concern that has never left me. I am translating matière in the context of sanctification of the intellect, grey matter, *matière grise*.

55 SEAN J. MCGRATH, *Heidegger: A Very Critical Introduction* (Grand Rapids, MI: W. B. Eerdmans, 2008), 122.

56 MCGRATH, 63, fn. 4. See Heidegger's letter to Rickert, 24 April 1914.

For private consultation and not distribution without the consent of E Ondrako

Bl. Scotus's univocity of the concept of being which is *not* a pure logical construct first.

There is one straightforward point that cannot be overstated. If the epistemological light overwhelms metaphysics, the problem remains in determining what epistemology illumines, i.e. being, reality, what is. The problem at the heart of Kantian voluntarism is with what is illumined by classical metaphysics. Being, reality, is reduced to the science of transcendental empiricism or transcendental psychology with the absolute autonomy of the transcendental 'ego.' The human will is based on the arbitrary indifference of the categorical imperative or duty.

Whatever the refinement of Kant by Heidegger, there is a further problem. No longer does the light illumine reality but seems to overpower what is being illumined. Kant and Heidegger separate faith from reason. The separation confuses the Christian trying to live the Gospel without succumbing to skepticism. McGrath answers further that he cannot be a Heideggerian because "Heidegger's effort to think the history of the West without Christianity, and Judaism out of which it developed, or the humanism that grew out of it, weakens his entire project."[57] Scotus's metaphysical and theological distinctions anticipate this weakening. Kant and Heidegger and their onto-theological answers buckle under the weight of secular or liberal Christianity.

Newman was no stranger to the separation of faith from reason. His 'illative sense' in making prudential judgments about reality or being, the power to judge touching the will and intellect, is one of the most evident contours between Newman and Scotus. Newman uses many thomistic tools but there is a difference between the thomistic and scotistic solution to the exercise of the will in making judgments about reality, being, change and becoming. The thomistic solution seems to be less developed and more an exercise in logic than a profound personal act presupposing the will as a pure perfection. This important difference means a pure logical construct vs. a formulation in logical form, as one finds in Scotus. For the subtle Doctor, the will as a pure perfection is shared in common with God. Moreover, the incomparable discovery of Scotus is his formulation of the univocity of the concept of being, which has its greatest exemplar in Mary who is without sin because her will is perfectly one with God.[58]

---

[57] McGrath, 129.

[58] Peter D. Fehlner, *Acts of the Symposium on Scotus' Mariology, Grey College, Durham, England, September 9–11, 2008, Mariologia Franciscana III* (New Bedford, MA: Academy of the Immaculate, 2009), 16. Opening Address. Henceforth, Durham.

For private consultation and not distribution without the consent of E Ondrako

Scotus's anthropology differs from naturalistic anthropology.

Scotus's anthropology is easy to understand by contemplating the perfect will of Mary in union with God, her perfectly free and human acceptance to be the Mother of God. Benedetto Ippolito points out: her free consent is freedom fully in accord with her human essence, "freedom natural to the whole species, but is such as to render that freedom fully complete in itself and ontologically more suited to choosing the good given by God in Christ, for the Redemption of all mankind."[59] Ippolito's original contribution about Scotus's anthropology follows the thought of Pope St. John Paul II about the horizontal and vertical transcendence of the person.[60] One reasons to the primacy of will in Scotus not as individualistic and anti-intellectual, but an active and personal quest for truth. In Scotus and Newman this is the transcendence that is the natural inclination of the person.[61]

The opposite is the heteronomy of secular or liberal Christianity[62] which identifies the behavior of human beings from a naturalistic anthropology, where vices are morally neutral, religious practices (prayer, the free and intelligent choice to witness to truth, even martyrdom) are obsolete, and/or pathological, if practiced. The heteronomy of secular or liberal Christianity is characterized by insisting that only the beliefs of the day, as Newman put it, should be recognized as valid and encouraged. Christian wisdom as handed down from antiquity means little, if anything, and has to be re-read in a contemporary cultural ambient. The practical result of such a re-reading of Scotus and Newman would make it difficult for them to understand what they originally wrote.

Scotus and Newman view the human person as made for glory, the glory that shares in the unchangeable glory of the Creator. Human beings retain causal power to will, to make free decisions, even as the will is reduced in varying degrees within the person by sin. Scotus and Newman agree that it is the essence of the person for that causal power to remain free. Transcendence and causal power may be weakened but not extinguished. Sin and sinfulness may be overcome by grace. Holiness is not only practical and achievable, but a principle defendable with coherent anthropology

---

[59] BENEDETTO IPPOLITO, "The Anthropological Foundation of Duns Scotus' Mariology," in Durham, 170–171.

[60] IPPOLITO, 168, makes a reference to John Paul II, *Person and Act. The Acting Person* is the common English translation, but *Person and Act* is more accurate.

[61] IPPOLITO, 157–172.

[62] CYRIL O'REGAN, "Newman and Holiness." O'Regan gives an x-ray of the problem of secular or liberal Christianity in its many forms.

For private consultation and not distribution without the consent of E Ondrako

that challenges the inadequacies of the anthropology of secular or liberal Christianity, the rejection of the Gospel principle to strive after perfection.

Recapitulation: The autonomous will of Kant vs. Scotus's primacy of the will.

Point 1. The rationality of the will as a pure perfection.

Scotus and Newman reject any form of the autonomous will that does as it pleases without any reference to goodness itself. Scotus respects the will as a pure perfection that requires profoundly personal judgments. Newman spent his life answering the nature of profoundly personal judgments. The role of the will, in the term unique to Newman, is the 'illative sense,' the faculty of making a prudent judgment. Although the thomistic and scotistic point of view are often alike, such as in the use of the analogy of being and the analogy of faith, one can identify where Scotus and Newman differ from the thomistic solution to the will.[63] The thomistic solution[64] appears somewhat less convincing when it seems to be more of an exercise in logic. That difference between the primacy of the intellect over the will of Thomas centers on the personal character of the intellectual life. The view of Kant is that the intellectual life is imprisoned in the person's own mind. The result is that the will that is radically autonomous provides no escape from relativism and agnosticism. The Scotistic and Newmanian answers center on the rationality of the will as a pure perfection. For Scotus, all pure perfections are mutually compatible with every other pure perfection, compatible with infinity, communicable, and irreducibly simple.[65] In this context, Thomas's primacy of the intellect is incomplete. Pope Benedict XVI's Scotus audience might be just the invitation needed for scholars to reach a salutary resolution of the question of the liberty of the will in relation to the intellect.

Point 2. The causes of the deformation of 'private judgment.'

There is a further gap in the epistemology of Bonaventure, Scotus and Newman from the agnosticism of Kant's pure speculative reason and the arbitrary voluntarism of his ethics or practical reason. In the gap is the thought of Ockham and Hume. With Kant, they make up the second

---

[63] FEHLNER, "Dialogue," chapter 7 in this volume.

[64] *ST I*, qq. 85–87 and qq. 82, 83.

[65] WOLTER, 166–170. This indispensable study gives the primary sources for Scotus's metaphysical and theological thinking.

For private consultation and not distribution without the consent of E Ondrako

approach to the study of the will and intellect. Ockham blurs the synthesis of Christian wisdom with his new form of ancient nominalism. The univocity of the concept of being of Scotus clashes with Ockham's nominalism and the individualism that accompanies it. Ockham's *via moderna* sowed the seeds for a new clash between realists and nominalists, especially in universities, and it has far reaching consequences.

The harvest came in the form of one of the hallmarks of secular or liberal Christianity, the appeal to conscience in a preemptory fashion, which Newman called 'private judgment.' This deformation is not interested in objective truth, but submits to the unreflective decisions of the will, a mask, at best, of self-will. Since voluntarism, broadly used, is any theory that regards the will rather than the intellect as the fundamental principle, without distinctions, voluntarism may confuse as a mask for self-will. The personal quest for truth of Scotus and Newman is the most noble exercise of the will and intellect in freedom. The essential differences between the study of the will and intellect and why Ockham, Hume, and Kant are far from Bonaventure, Scotus, and, the hypothesis that Newman fits more closely to St. Francis of Assisi's theologian disciples, deserves contemporary purchase.

Point 3. Newman's thought on illumination is close to Bonaventure.

Our view is that research into the relationship between Newman and Scotus is viable because Scotus anticipates the problems of modernity and answers the same questions as Kant in a superior and more persuasive manner. Scotus anticipates secular or liberal Christianity and its naturalistic anthropology. Newman's anthropology reflects his replies to dimensions of modernity in his early career as university chaplain at Oxford. Newman's thought on illumination develops close to the theory of divine illumination of Bonaventure and its formulation in the univocal concept of being of Scotus. The thesis becomes comprehensible in Newman's words in discourse five of *Discourses to Mixed Congregations*, preached in 1849: "the inward light given as it is by God, [as] powerless to illumine the horizon, to mark out for us our direction, and to comfort us with the certainty that we are making for our Eternal home." With this light, Newman exposes the moral reduction, naturalism, and pseudo-versions of conscience of secular or liberal Christianity. As Anglican and as Catholic he is always vigilant to every substitution for the Christian call to holiness,

For private consultation and not distribution without the consent of E Ondrako

an example of his presence at Vatican II.[66] *Lumen Gentium* retrieved the call to holiness in the spirit of the "absent father at Vatican II."[67]

Newman wrote:

> It is a most miserable and frightful thought, that, in this country, among this people which boasts that it is so Christian and so enlightened, the sun in the heavens is so eclipsed that the mirror of conscience can catch and reflect few rays, and serves but poorly and scantily to preserve the foot from error. That inward light, given as it is by God, is powerless to illumine the horizon, to mark out for us our direction, and to comfort us with the certainty that we are making for our Eternal Home.[68]

Conclusion to the excursus: a reply to runaway autonomy of the will.

Scotus anticipates the problem today: 'the game is rigged against Christianity.' This outgrowth of a post-Lockian ethos is from distinctions that Locke made between strong and weak logic. Both terms are Lockian and refer to the relative firmness in the relation of an inference to its premises. For Locke, that there is a God is based on strong logic. That the Son of God was human and divine is based on weak logic. Newman lived with Lockian ethos, the 'rigging' in his day. The problem of the Lockian ethos is that it tends to reduce objective truth to little or nothing of much value, a trap vs. prudential judgments that lead to real assent.

Opposition abounds to Church teaching, even to the existence of the soul and immortality, and to the perfect love of God. Pope Benedict XVI welcomes study about the liberty of will in relation to intellect. Careful study of the philosophical and theological and anthropological approaches of Thomas Aquinas and Scotus will help Newman-Scotus research. The aim is to reach a consensus in continuity with tradition without reducing the question to philosophy alone or unwittingly falling into a Lockian or rationalist trap or yielding to a subtle, arbitrary voluntarism.

Scotus and Newman exemplify the axiom: Be Catholic! Be intellectual! Be holy! They reply to the question: how did the radical autonomy of

---

[66] E. J. ONDRAKO, *Freedom Within the Church: The Controversy Between William Ewart Gladstone and John Henry Newman in 1874–1875 and Its Shadows and Images over Vatican II* (Ann Arbor, MI 1974).

[67] Ondrako speculates about why several participants at Vatican II referred to the Council as "Newman's Council."

[68] JOHN HENRY NEWMAN, Discourses Addressed to Mixed Congregations (London: uniform edition, 1892), Discourse 5, 84. See The Dogmatic Constitution on the Church, Lumen Gentium, chapter 5.

For private consultation and not distribution without the consent of E Ondrako

the will, with its subtle and arbitrary voluntarism, develop? The answer is in studying freedom and how the will is defined in relation to the intellect. The anthropology of Scotus about the ontological change, the weakening of the human person due to sin, but not the loss of causal power, practical potential, and freedom are critical elements. A forthcoming intelligible answer to the question raised by Pope Benedict at his Scotus audience reaches out to the thought of Newman.

Part three of *The Newman-Scotus Reader*, the scientific form and the real assent of Newman and Scotus, will compare the symmetry between Christian wisdom and the wisdom that is the origin and goal of all science. The first approach is the structure provided by Aristotle and Thomas Aquinas. The second approach is that of Ockham, Hume and Kant. Ockham is an innovator in relation to Scotus, while Hume endorses study of one's feelings and experiences, and Kant the examination of one's reason. The third approach is that of Bonaventure and Scotus who teach the art of *interiorization* in order to keep reason, *logic*, linked to reality. Newman and Scotus research builds on the hypothesis that Newman reflects the thought of Bonaventure and Scotus.

The theory of divine illumination of Bonaventure and incomparable formulation of divine illumination in logical form by Scotus is the light guiding our thought. The univocity of the concept of being is not a pure logical construct first, but a unique formulation to keep *logic* linked to reality.[69] Newman's 'illative sense,' a faculty of judging, connects to Bonaventure and Scotus on making the judgment about the existence of God. It flees in full flight from skepticism, rationalism, and what is rigged against Christianity, from the radical and arbitrary autonomy of the will, with freedom as its ultimate end, freedom that would separate God from reality by reducing God to a concept alone, not substance. This is the dark night of the senses!

---

[69] FEHLNER, letter to author, July 31, 2010.

For private consultation and not distribution without the consent of E Ondrako

CHAPTER 5

Newman's Personalist Argument for Belief in God

John T. Ford [1]

Although Newman was initially attracted to rationalism, his teenage conversion-experience made him life-long, a person of faith. Yet, perhaps surprisingly, he had reservations, both practical and theoretical, about philosophical proofs for the existence of God: in practice, he felt that most people are unlikely to investigate such proofs or, if they did, unlikely to be convinced by them; in theory, he objected to such proofs as leading merely to a notional or theoretical assent, not to a real assent of faith. Accordingly, Newman proposed an argument for the existence of God on the basis of conscience—an argument which, theoretically considered, is defective both in its subjectivity and in supposing what needs to be proved. From an apologetical perspective, however, Newman's proof from conscience effectively challenges seekers to ask whether their conscience is truly the "voice of God" calling them not to take a philosophical position but to make a personal act of faith.

As a teenager, Newman was temporarily attracted to rationalism:

I read Paine's Tracts against the Old Testament, and found pleasure in thinking of the objections which were contained in them. Also, I read some of Hume's Essays and perhaps that on Miracles. … Also, I recollect copying out some French verses, perhaps Voltaire's, in denial of the immortality of the soul, and saying to myself something like "How dreadful, but how plausible!"[2]

---

[1] John T. Ford, c.s.c., Professor of Theology and Religious Studies at The Catholic University of America, presented this paper at the Newman-Scotus Symposium, October 22–24, at the Washington Theological Union, Takoma Park, MD.

[2] JOHN HENRY NEWMAN, *Apologia Pro Vita Sua*, edited by David J. DeLaura (New York: W. W. Norton, 1968), 15–16; hereafter cited: *Apologia*; this edition is especially useful because of its footnoted explanations and interpretive essays.

For private consultation and not distribution without the consent of E Ondrako

In fact, Newman's flirtation with rationalism was short-lived; at the age of fifteen, he experienced a conversion to evangelical Christianity.[3] Yet, unlike those evangelicals who attempted to exclude reason from their faith-life by divorcing faith and reason into separate compartments, Newman saw faith and reason as complementary—a complementarity that was subsequently described by Pope St. John Paul II: "Faith and reason are like two wings on which the human spirit rises to the contemplation of truth ... ."[4]

Since Newman, after his first conversion, was life-long, a person of faith, some may be surprised that he was dissatisfied with the customary proofs for the existence of God. For example, the Five Proofs (*Quinque Viae*) of Aquinas may well demonstrate the theoretical existence of a Prime Mover, but how personally satisfying is it to say: "I profess belief in a Prime Mover"? Similarly, on the basis of the Argument from Design, who really feels drawn to professing: "I believe in the Master Architect of the World"?[5] Likewise, how congenial is it to have faith in a "God of the Inexplicable"—postulated on an argument for the existence of a "God of the Gaps."[6] Even Pascal's wager was apparently unappealing to Newman, who caricatured the danger of reliance on probability by citing the "celebrated saying, 'O God, if there be a God, save my soul, if I have a soul' ... ."[7] For Newman, the deficiency common to these philosophical proofs for the existence of God was that they are theoretical and impersonal, they emphasize the theoretical and notional, not the personal and real.

The distinction between the notional and the real is pivotal to Newman's epistemological thought. On the one hand, real apprehension and real assent involve experience and information about concrete realities; in the present, such real objects can be experienced or pointed out; in the past, such actual experiences or real objects can usually be recalled—memorably if not exactly. On the other hand, notional apprehension and notional

[3] See Newman's description of his "first conversion" in *Apologia*, 16; for a more extended discussion of Newman's "first conversion," see WALTER E. CONN, *Conscience & Conversion in Newman. A Developmental Study of Self in John Henry Newman* (Milwaukee: Marquette University Press, 2010), 18–22.

[4] JOHN PAUL II, "Introduction," *Fides et Ratio* (15 September 1998); this encyclical, which specifically mentions Newman (§ 74), is available at: http://www.vatican.va/holy_father/john_paul_ii/encyclicals/documents/hf_jp-ii_enc_15101998_fides-et-ratio_en.html.

[5] See KEVIN MONGRAIN, "The Eyes of Faith: Newman's Critique of Arguments from Design," *Newman Studies Journal* 6/1 (Spring 2009): 68–86.

[6] See PATRICK J. FLETCHER, "Newman and Natural Theology," *Newman Studies Journal* 5/2 (Fall 2008): 26–42.

[7] *Apologia*, 28; Newman was referring to the thought of the Anglican Bishop, Joseph Butler (1692–1752); on Pascal's influence on Newman, see: BRIAN W. HUGHES, "Une Source Cachée: Blaise Pascal's Influence upon John Henry Newman," *Newman Studies Journal* 7/1 (Spring 2010): 29–44.

For private consultation and not distribution without the consent of E Ondrako

assent are abstractions—intellectual relationships and theoretical comparisons—divorced from reality. Notions—such as philosophical theories and mathematical symbols—though originating in the real world are extrapolated from it.[8] Although some people become passionate about specific notions—for example, the principles of a political party or the goals of a reform movement—notions as such leave most people neutral, disengaged, uncommitted.[9]

Notional assents are, of course, an important and indispensable part of life. Without notions or concepts or ideas, people could scarcely share their thoughts with each other; there would be no way of classifying experiences or organizing data, no way of advancing knowledge and few means for proposing solutions to problems. Notional knowledge—such as the Pythagorean proposition, Newton's law of gravity, Einstein's theory of relativity, etc.—all contribute to the human understanding of the workings of the universe. Nonetheless, notional assents have a major drawback; they are intellectually satisfying, but motivationally uninspiring and often practically ineffective: "they tend to be mere assertions without any personal hold."[10] As Cyril Barrett has pointedly observed: "Someone who gives notional assent commits himself only to accepting the truth of the assertion, even if that truth has practical consequences."[11]

In contrast, the most vitally important decisions that people make—whether about love and family or about vocation and life—are real assents. Yet real assents labor under an insurmountable handicap; they always include an element of probability; they are always subject to misinterpretation and mistake; love and life always entail real risk; real assents are always a gamble—perhaps a sure bet, but a gamble nonetheless. But this is a wager that everyone must make, if one truly and really wants to live. Yet what is the importance of real assents? If few people would be willing to sacrifice their life for the Pythagorean proposition, or Newton's law of gravity, or Einstein's theory of relativity, millions of people are willing to sacrifice their lives for love—whether it be for their

---

[8] See the philosophical adage: Nihil in intellectu nisi prius in sensu ("Nothing in the intellect unless first in the sense").

[9] See Newman's discussion of "Notional and Real Assent" (Chapter 4) in his An Essay in Aid of a Grammar of Assent, 36–97; available at: http://www.newmanreader.org/works/grammar/index.html; hereafter cited: Grammar. Although real and notional assent are distinct and different, they are complementary: without real assent, the mind indulges in speculations; without notional assent, the mind has a small circle of knowledge derived from, yet limited by, one's personal experience.

[10] Grammar, 40.

[11] CYRIL BARRETT, "Newman and Wittgenstein on the Rationality of Religious Belief," in Newman and Conversion, edited by Ian Ker (Notre Dame, IN: University of Notre Dame Press, 1997), 89–99, at 91; henceforth cited: Newman and Conversion.

For private consultation and not distribution without the consent of E Ondrako

family or friends, or for their most cherished convictions, especially their religious faith.[12]   Newman summarized this wager of life so memorably: "Many a man will live and die upon a dogma: no man will be a martyr for a conclusion."[13]

Granted this implication of Newman's distinction between the real and the notional—"When we are not personally concerned, even the highest evidence does not move us; when we are concerned, the very slightest is enough"[14]—it seems clear why he was disenchanted with the standard philosophical proofs for the existence of God. Even if, on the notional level, the "Prime Mover" can be seen as engineering the entire universe, on the real level, it is difficult to pray devoutly to the "Prime Mover." Similarly, the rationale that posits a "God of the Gaps" as an explanation for those areas where scientific explanations are absent is slowly deflated by new scientific discoveries that progressively narrow the gaps where God is needed as an explanation; as the gaps disappear, the need for God diminishes to the vanishing point. Theoretical arguments aside, Newman was extremely dubious about the practical usefulness of such arguments for the existence of God: "Tell men to gain notions of a Creator from His works, and, if they were to set about it (which nobody does) they would be jaded and wearied by the labyrinth they were tracing."[15]

Newman then was suspicious of the notional, because it can be an illusion; for example, a person can have a notion of a unicorn or other imaginary forms of reality.   Moreover, one's pre-conceived notions sometimes obstruct one's perception of reality. Such was the well-known case of the English scientists in 1799, who were invited to examine a specimen of the recently discovered duck-billed platypus and pronounced it a clever hoax: such self-deception can easily occur when the notional is preferred to the real.[16] As Newman succinctly observed:

> And so of the great fundamental truths of religion, natural and
> revealed, and as regards the mass of religious men: these truths,
> doubtless, may be proved and defended by an array of invincible

---

12 In fact, millions of people have sacrificed their lives for their religious beliefs; see, for example, Robert Royal, *The Catholic Martyrs of the Twentieth Century: A Comprehensive History* (New York: Crossroad, 2000).

13 *Grammar*, 93.

14 Newman, *The Via Media of the Anglican Church*, 1:86; available at: http://www.newman-reader.org/works/viamedia/volume1/lecture3.html.

15 *Grammar*, 94.

16 For an account of the reaction of British scientists in 1799 to the first specimen of a duck-billed platypus, see: http://www.museumofhoaxes.com/hoax/Hoaxipedia/Duckbilled_Platypus/.

For private consultation and not distribution without the consent of E Ondrako

logical arguments, but such is not commonly the method in which those same logical arguments make their way into our minds.[17]

Real Assent to the Existence of God

Newman was apparently dissatisfied with the traditional proofs for the existence of God—not because such proofs are unreliable or fallacious—but because they can only lead to notional assent—a type of assent that can be given not only to the existence of God, but also to non-existent phenomena—indeed, the possible existence of a unicorn may seem notionally more convincing than the possible existence of God. On more than one occasion, Newman indicated his dissatisfaction with logical approaches to God; indeed, his dissatisfaction seems to have been summarized on the title page of his *Grammar of Assent* with a citation from St. Ambrose: *Non in dialecticâ complacuit Deo salvum facere populum suum*—"it did not please God to save his people by logic."[18] Dialectical arguments may be notionally convincing, but obviously are not personally salvific.

For Newman, the critical question was—can a person give real—not simply notional but real—assent to God's existence? Newman's answer took the form of a personal appeal to human nature—specifically to human conscience.[19] Stated schematically, his argument ran: every person has a conscience which aids each individual in distinguishing what is good from what is evil. Second, a person's conscience is similar to the other human sense faculties insofar as these faculties are activated by external realities—for example, my sense of the beautiful is stimulated by beautiful objects in the real world; my sense of smell is repelled by nauseating odors; similarly, my conscience is activated by the recurring dilemma of needing to make real choices between what is good and what is evil. Third, just as there are real extra-mental objects that activate my sense of the beautiful or my sense of smell, in parallel fashion, there must be an external agent—God—who prompts my conscience to recognize what is good and what is evil.[20]

---

[17] *Grammar*, 336.

[18] Newman discussed this phrase of St. Ambrose at greater length in *Apologia*, 136.

[19] Newman's appeal to conscience as an argument for the existence of God parallels his appeal to the pattern of human thought in the process of coming to faith in his Grammar: in both cases, the personal dimension was all important for Newman.

[20] See Newman's argument from conscience for "Belief in One God" (Chapter 5, section 1), *Grammar*, 101–121; Newman also discussed "conscience" in the fifth section of A Letter Addressed to the Duke of Norfolk on Occasion of Mr. Gladstone's Recent Expostulation,

For private consultation and not distribution without the consent of E Ondrako

As John Macquarrie has observed, in comparison to Kierkegaard, who claimed that "it is the sense of sin that brings a human being towards the path of faith," for Newman, "it is not the negative phenomenon of sin, but the positive phenomenon of conscience that performs this office."[21] Moreover, Newman's view of conscience as "the voice of God" acting within us[22] has the double merit of both reality and universality: what respectable Victorian would have denied that he or she had a conscience? And, even though some Victorians acted in unconscionable ways, aren't these instances exceptions proving the rule: all people have a conscience—whether they use it rightly or misuse it wrongly?[23]

Similarly, many people today act in unconscionable ways—however, the premise that their misdeeds violate conscience is no longer such an obvious matter of consensus as it was in the Victorian era. For example, some point out that so-called "sociopaths" and "psychopaths" apparently do not have a conscience at all,[24] so how can one defend a God of conscience, if some people really have none? More commonly, in the twenty-first century, self-gratification has become the primary good and self-deprivation the primary evil. Accordingly, just as scientific advances have progressively foreclosed the need for a "God of the Gaps," contemporary solipsism and hedonism have seemingly obviated not only the need for conscience and but also the need for a God of conscience.

In addition, if subjectivity is a liability for Newman's argument from conscience, *a fortiori*, his supposition of a parallelism between the visible world of the senses and a postulated invisible world is gratuitous at best. Although it is self-evident that the external world really stimulates our sense faculties, it does not necessarily follow that a person's conscience is stimulated by God. At most, one might legitimately claim that conscience is activated by external realities in a way similar to the stimulation of the senses by extra-mental objects. Seeing a beautiful object stimulates a person's sense of the beautiful; smelling a pungent odor activates a person's sense of smell; similarly, a pressing need to choose between a specific good and a specific evil prompts a person's conscience to make a decision. But

---

reprinted in *Certain Difficulties Felt by Anglicans in Catholic Teaching*, 2: 246–261; available at: http://www.newmanreader.org/works/anglicans/volume2/gladstone/index.html

21 JOHN MACQUARRIE, "Newman and Kierkegaard on the Act of Faith," in *Newman and Conversion*, 75–88, at 86.

22 *Grammar*, 122; Newman also described Revelation as "the voice of God to man" (*Grammar*, 404).

23 See the Latin adage: abusus non tollit usum (abuse does not take away use).

24 For a panoramic view of psychological investigations, see John Seabrook, "Suffering Souls: The search for the roots of psychopathy," *New Yorker* (November 10, 2008): 64–73.

For private consultation and not distribution without the consent of E Ondrako

neither the beautiful nor the odiferous, neither good nor evil, necessarily mandate the real existence of God.[25]

Accordingly, notional though they be, the *Quinque Viae*, the Argument from Design, the God of the Gaps and even Pascal's Wager seem more objective and so more theoretically satisfying than Newman's recourse to conscience as a basic argument for the existence of God. Given this double difficulty of subjectivity and supposing what needs to be proved—weaknesses which were presumably recognized by Newman—why did he appeal to conscience as a real basis for personal belief in God?

Conversion as Catalyst

Arguments for the existence of God can be viewed from two different perspectives: *intellectus quaerens fidem*—"Understanding seeking faith"—or *fides quaerens intellectum*—"Faith seeking understanding." From the viewpoint of the intellect seeking reasons for faith, notional arguments, such as the *Quinque Viae*, seem the best available and, if not unequivocally demonstrative, assuredly sufficient to present honest seekers with a challenging conundrum: I am forced either to imagine an infinite series of movers or to acknowledge a "Prime Mover." Nonetheless, such arguments always remain notional—unless and until a seeker has a real religious experience.[26]

In this respect, the conversion-experience of Avery Dulles provides an insightful example. As an agnostic undergraduate at Harvard, Dulles studied a variety of classical and modern philosophers; however, it was not his academic research, but an unexpected experience during a casual break from his studies in the library that prompted his conversion, which occurred, as he later recalled, while walking along the Charles River in Boston:

> As I wandered aimlessly, something prompted me to look contemplatively at a young tree. On its frail, supple branches were young buds … . While my eye rested on them the thought came to me suddenly, with all the strength and novelty of a revelation, that these little buds in their innocence and meekness followed a rule, a law of which I as yet knew nothing. How could it be, I asked, that this delicate tree sprang up and developed and that all the

---

[25] Although the argument that the beauty of creation can only be explained by a Creator of Beauty is persuasive, it is nonetheless notional.

[26] As MACQUARRIE, *Newman and Conversion*, 75–88, has pointed out, for Kierkegaard, this experience was the experience of sin, for Newman, the experience of conscience.

For private consultation and not distribution without the consent of E Ondrako

enormous complexity of its cellular operations combined together to make it grow erectly and bring forth leaves and blossoms?[27]

Dulles responded to his own question:

The answer, the trite answer of the schools, was new to me: that its actions were ordered to an end by the only power capable of adapting means to ends—intelligence—and that the very fact that this intelligence worked toward an end implied purposiveness – in other words, a will. It was useless, then, to dismiss these phenomena by obscurantist talk about a mysterious force called "Nature." The "nature" which was responsible for these events was distinguished by the possession of intellect and will, and intellect plus will makes personality. Mind, then, not matter, was at the origin of all things.[28]

Viewed analytically, Dulles's conversion seemingly combined philosophical elements from the teleological argument of purpose and the argument from divine design; yet, such arguments previously had had no apparent effect on his life; it was a sudden and unanticipated personal experience that catalyzed what were previously notional arguments into a real conviction;[29] as he succinctly summarized the effect of his experience: "That night, for the first time in years, I prayed."[30]

From a theoretical perspective, as long as arguments for the existence of God remain at the level of *intellectus quaerens fidem*—the intellect seeking faith—they remain notional: intellectually challenging, philosophically interesting, speculatively intriguing, but assertions without "personal hold."[31] However, as the result of a conversion-experience, what

---

[27] AVERY DULLES, *A Testimonial to Grace and Reflections on a Theological Journey, Fiftieth Anniversary Edition* (Kansas City: Sheed & Ward, 1996), 36.

[28] Ibid.

[29] An unanswered, and perhaps unanswerable, question is the extent to which knowledge of philosophical arguments for the existence of God have an antecedent role in preparing for a conversion-experience. Newman provided a presumably autobiographical description of the transition from notional to real assent in his Grammar (78): "Let us consider, too, how differently young and old are affected by the words of some classic author, such as Homer or Horace. Passages, which to a boy are but rhetorical common-places, neither better nor worse than a hundred others which any clever writer might supply, which he gets by heart and thinks very fine, and imitates, as he thinks, successfully, in his own flowing versification, at length come home to him, when long years have passed, and he has had experience of life, and pierce him, as if he had never before known them, with their sad earnestness and vivid exactness."

[30] Grammar, 38; see the discussion of Newman's conversion by AVERY DULLES, "Newman: The Anatomy of a Conversion," in *Newman and Conversion*, edited by Ian Ker (Notre Dame, IN: University of Notre Dame Press, 1997), 21–36, especially the "lessons" (33–34).

[31] *Grammar*, 40.

For private consultation and not distribution without the consent of E Ondrako

was previously a notional understanding of the proofs for God's existence changes—often unexpectedly—to a real understanding that God exists. A conversion-experience is a catalyst that enables a convert to see what was previously notional in a new and real light. As a result of such a conversion-experience, a seeker previously *quaerens fidem* becomes a believer *quaerens intellectum*.

In this perspective, Newman's discontent with the conventional proofs for the existence of God is understandable; such proofs only begin and end on the notional level. Only a conversion-experience provides the lens of faith that makes such notional arguments real and personally convincing. Accordingly, Newman's argument from conscience is both simple—everyone has a conscience, however faulty or dim it may be—and apologetically successful—his implicit question: "do you have a conscience?"—effectively puts seekers on the spot, provocatively challenges them to consider the meaning of life.

If a person denies having a conscience, the conversation is effectively over. However, presuming that most people will acknowledge having a conscience, the conversation continues: "what does your conscience tell you?" If a person replies, "Do good, avoid evil," then Newman, ever the adroit apologist, puts a person on the spot again: "Is your sense of good and evil your own personal view?" "Or is your conscience the voice of a higher power?" Thus, Newman's argument for the existence of God on the basis of conscience appears most successful as an apologetical or existential question, rather than a theoretical or philosophical argument.

God's Existence: Notional or Real?

A crucial question in both evangelization and apologetics is what moves a person from a philosophical notion of God to real belief in God. This movement from notional assent to real assent is a perennial challenge—not only in religious education, but in every form of instruction. For example, foreign language teachers spend a considerable amount of time teaching students grammar and vocabulary—a largely notional type of instruction—in the hope that their students will learn to read, speak and write that language. Unfortunately, some students never progress beyond the level of word-for-word translation—a task that computers can now do reasonably well—the result is a literal translation whose meaning escapes not only the computer but sometimes the student. Fortunately, for other students, a foreign language provides entrance into a whole new world, a world that they already knew existed, but was previously inaccessible. As

For private consultation and not distribution without the consent of E Ondrako

these students develop fluency in the language, they develop an appreciation for its nuances, its poetry, and its ethos.[32]

Foreign language teachers are often puzzled and perplexed to find these two groups of students in the same class—at least at the elementary level. Although the teaching is the same, why are the results so different? Professional language teachers customarily use a variety of techniques to help students move from the notional world of grammar and vocabulary to the real world of comprehension, conversation and composition: audio/video tapes, movies, study abroad—all potential catalysts designed to aid students in developing real language proficiency. Yet very few foreign language teachers have a 100% success-rate among beginning students.

Just as there are vaccinations that don't take, there is no pedagogical method that can guarantee that a given student will or even can move from the notional world of grammar and vocabulary to the real world of reading, speaking, writing. The most a language teacher can do is to provide the encouragement, as well as an environment and pedagogical media, as catalysts that will enable students to make a personal transition from notional knowledge—grammar and vocabulary—to real use—proficiency and fluency. Parenthetically, a foreign language teacher once remarked that one sign that students are beginning to have a real apprehension of a language is when they start dreaming in that language; obviously, there is no way that any teacher can guarantee that a given student will become fluent, much less dream in a language. Similarly, a religious educator can creatively present the doctrines of Christianity, but there is no way that anyone can guarantee that religious instruction will result in real faith on the part of students.

In a parallel way, Newman realized that there was no way in which he could provide his audience with a personal conversion experience. What he could do—and in fact did in his *Apologia*—was to share the development of his own personal "religious opinions" as a personal illustration of the conversion-process, as well as encouragement to engage in a similar process.[33] In effect, he provided the basic questions, the equivalent of grammar and vocabulary, for his readers to prepare themselves, to dispose themselves, for a similar conversion-experience. In particular, Newman's

---

[32] Some languages distinguish between knowing facts and knowing people, between "objective knowledge" and "personal knowledge" (for example, wissen/kennen, savoir/connaître, saber/conocer); for some students, language learning always remains at the notional level of "facts" (vocabulary, grammar, etc.), while other students come to a personal knowledge of the language (fluency and feeling or Sprachgefühl).

[33] Newman characterized the four chapters of his *Apologia* as the "History of My Religious Opinions"; in his narrative, one can observe a series of "conversions": Evangelicalism, Noeticism, Anglo-Catholicism, and Roman Catholicism.

For private consultation and not distribution without the consent of E Ondrako

implicit question: "do you have a conscience"?—is both formidably and engagingly personal; it not only asks people whether they possess a conscience, it also asks people to reflect on the rationale undergirding their choices between good and evil: "Does the rationale for your choice between good and evil point to God"?

In some respects, this is an embarrassing question—a person who chooses or even prefers evil may be reluctant to admit it. But Newman's question, like Pascal's wager, asks a person why doing good and avoiding evil is important in the first place. For self-centered hedonists, this is not an issue. For Victorian deists, this was perhaps a matter of respectability. But to the really conscientious person, Newman's question raised the challenge of recognizing "the voice of God" within.[34] In effect, Newman resembled foreign language teachers, who use all sorts of media as catalysts to facilitate the language-learning of their students; he could not provide a conversion experience for his audience; however, he could and did provide a catalytic question that could prompt people to dispose themselves for a conversion experience. Newman's questions about conscience are comparable to the young buds on the supple branches of spring that prompted the conversion of Avery Dulles.

Conscience and Conversion

Newman's argument for the existence of God from conscience is best read in light of his first conversion experience, which he described in his *Apologia*: "the inward conversion of which I was conscious, (and of which I still am more certain than that I have hands and feet, would last into the next life, and that I was elected to eternal glory."[35] His experience had the effect "of confirming me in my mistrust of the reality of material phenomena, and making me rest in the thought of two and two only absolute and luminously self-evident beings, myself and my Creator—."[36]

On the one hand, Newman's conversion-experience made him distrustful of the material world and presumably the notional information that he derived from that world; as C. S. Dessain once commented: "The visible world, so beautiful and significant, seemed less real than that which was unseen."[37] Simultaneously, as Terrance Merrigan has pointed out, conscience, as a feeling of right and wrong, is accompanied by intense emotions, whose "presence implies an Invisible Being both exterior and

---

[34] *Grammar*, 122.

[35] *Apologia*, 16.

[36] Ibid.

[37] CHARLES STEPHEN DESSAIN, *John Henry Newman* (London: Nelson, 1966), 5; henceforth cited: Dessain, *Newman*.

For private consultation and not distribution without the consent of E Ondrako

superior to ourselves, with whom we are in immediate relation, 'One to whom we are responsible, before whom we are ashamed, whose claims we fear.' "[38]

On the other hand, his conversion-experience made Newman absolutely confident of the presence of God in his life. Newman's experience resembled an evangelical conversion in which a person acknowledges God as personal Lord and Savior.[39] In Newman's case, however, his first conversion was not a once-and-for-all event, but rather the beginning of a life-long journey in which he felt that God was guiding him in a personal way and so he had a personal mission from God. This sense of the guidance of divine Providence is exemplified by his conviction, after his recovery from a near fatal illness in Sicily in 1833, when he confidently, even condescendingly, told the servant who had cared for him: "I have a work to do in England."[40] But perhaps the most memorable indication of his confidence in divine guidance is found in his best-known poem: "Lead, Kindly Light":

> The night is dark, and I am far from home—
> Lead Thou me on!
> Keep Thou my feet; I do not ask to see
> The distant scene—one step enough for me.[41]

Newman's first conversion was still remarkably fresh in his mind four dozen years later when he wrote his *Apologia* (1864)—which was written a half-dozen years before he published his *Grammar of Assent* (1870).[42] At the time of its publication, presumably many, if not most, of the readers of Newman's *Grammar* had already read his *Apologia*. Unfortunately, such is not always the case today, when his *Apologia* is usually read by historians and litterateurs, while his *Grammar* is read by philosophers and theologians. Yet as Robert A. Colby perceptively recognized,[43] there is a comple-

---

[38] Terrance Merrigan, "The Anthropology of Conversion: Newman and the Contemporary Theology of Religions," in *Newman and Conversion*, 117–144, at 128, citing a number of passages from Newman's writings.

[39] In contrast to typical evangelical conversions, which occur instantaneously, Newman's first conversion extended over several months (*Apologia*, 16).

[40] Ibid., 40.

[41] Ibid. Commonly known by its opening lines, "Lead, Kindly Light," the poem's title is "The Pillar of the Cloud" (poem 90) in *Newman's Verses on Various Occasions*, 156–157; available at: http://www.newmanreader.org/works/verses/verse90.html.

[42] Newman dated his conversion experience to the "autumn of 1816" (*Apologia*, 16); his *Apologia* was published in 1864 and his *Grammar*, on which he had been at work for some twenty years, in 1870.

[43] Robert A. Colby, "The Structure of Newman's Apologia pro Vita Sua in Relation to His Theory of Assent," in *Apologia*, 465–480.

For private consultation and not distribution without the consent of E Ondrako

mentarity between the two works: Newman's *Grammar* was a "notional" discussion, explaining how "you can believe what you cannot understand" and how "you can believe what you cannot absolutely prove."[44] Newman's *Apologia*, in contrast, can be described as a "real" presentation—an auto-biographical account of his personal journey of faith. In other words, the works are companion-pieces: his *Apologia*, a journal of a believer *quaerens intellectum*, his *Grammar*, a guide for a seeker *quaerens fidem*.

Both books had an apologetic aim: Newman's *Apologia* was an invitation to his contemporaries—especially his former Anglican followers—not only to understand the history of his religious opinions, but also to make those religious opinions their own. Similarly, his *Grammar* was intended to show the reasonableness of faith and so invite his readers—some of whom were non-believers—to come to Christian belief.[45] Newman seems to have sensed that the customary approach to non-believers—via such traditional philosophical arguments as the *Quinque Viae*—was not only unsuccessful, but counterproductive—unsuccessful insofar as such notional arguments were usually not convincing in practice and counter-productive insofar as they only led people to a notional acceptance of a God, not a confession of faith in the God of Christianity.

For Newman, a new apologetical strategy was needed. An effective argument for the existence of God needs to lead persons from notional assent to real belief. How can such an argument be framed? On the one hand, short of a real manifestation of God in the world—and even divine manifestations are not convincing to everyone[46]—reasoning about God are inevitably going to be abstract, speculative and notional. The other option is to look for an argument for the existence of God within oneself; the one obvious locus where each person can recognize the intrapersonal "voice of God" through conscience. The obvious limitation to such an approach is that it is insurmountably subjective: what if a person claims not to have a conscience? Or more likely, what if a person claims that one's conscience is unavoidably personal, historically conditioned, and cultur-ally circumscribed? For a seeker *quaerens fidem*, Newman's argument from conscience may be too subjective to be convincing—unless and until a seeker has a conversion-experience.

---

44 This description of the respective objects of the first and second parts of Newman's *Grammar* was recorded by Edward Caswell (1814–1878) after a conversation with Newman on 3 December 1877; see DESSAIN, *Newman*, 148.

45 Parts of Newman's Grammar were developed from his correspondence with the English scientist, William Froude (1810–1879); Newman continued to discuss the points that he made in the Grammar with Froude until Froude's death; see DESSAIN, *Newman*, 151, 158.

46 A prime example is the rejection of Jesus as Son of God by many of those who saw his deeds.

For private consultation and not distribution without the consent of E Ondrako

However, from the perspective of a believer *quaerens intellectum*, the very subjectivity of Newman's argument is one of its strengths—especially in a post-modern era that emphasizes a "turn to the subject," the argument from conscience is appealingly personal.[47] As the result of a conversion-experience, a believer can recognize conscience as the inner "voice of God" which has provided not only a sense of right and wrong in regard to individual actions, but also a sense of the guidance of divine providence in life as a whole. Faithfulness to the dictates of conscience then gives a believer's life a sense of meaning and mission. In this perspective, Newman's argument for the existence of God from conscience is the strongest of arguments precisely because it is both real and personal.

Newman's Codicil on Conscience[48]

Five years after his discussion of "conscience" in his *Grammar of Assent* (1870), John Henry Newman unexpectedly but fortuitously had the opportunity to return to the topic with a supplementary treatment of conscience—an important codicil—in his *Letter to the Duke of Norfolk*.[49] Newman's "*Letter*"—which in fact was book-size—was prompted by the anti-Roman Catholic accusations of the British Prime Minister, William Ewart Gladstone, who wrote "a political expostulation" against *The Vatican Decrees*.[50] Gladstone, distressed by the teaching of the First Vatican Council in 1870 on "papal infallibility,"[51] maintained that since Roman Catholics give their allegiance to the pope, they could no longer be considered loyal

---

[47] For a discussion of the "personalist" dimension of Newman's theology, see ROBERT C. CHRISTIE, "Newman's 1826 Essay, The Miracles of Scripture, and the Role of Witness: The Beginning of his Personalist Theology," *Newman Studies Journal* 2:2 (Fall 2005): 52–59.

[48] This essay is an expansion of some remarks made by John T. Ford, c.s.c., Professor of Theology and Religious Studies at The Catholic University of America, at the concluding session of the Newman-Scotus Symposium, October 22–24, at the Washington Theological Union, Takoma Park, MD.

[49] A Letter Addressed to His Grace the Duke of Norfolk on Occasion of Mr. Gladstone's Recent Expostulation (London: B. M. Pickering, 1875), was republished in *Certain Difficulties Felt by Anglicans in Catholic Teaching*, Volume 2: 175–378; hereafter cited within the text; available at: http://www.newmanreader.org/works/anglicans/volume2/gladstone/postscript.html.

[50] The Vatican Decrees in Their Bearing on Civil Allegiance: A Political Expostulation (London: John Murray, 1874) was republished in *Newman and Gladstone: The Vatican Decrees*, with an introduction by Alvan Ryan (Notre Dame, IN: University of Notre Dame Press, 1962), 6–72. Gladstone (1809–1898) served as both Chancellor of the Exchequer (1852–55, 1859–66, 1873–74, 1880–82) and Prime Minister (December 1868 – February 1874; April 1880 – June 1885; February – July 1886; August 1892 – March 1894).

[51] In fact, the First Vatican Council (1869–1870) did not use the term "papal infallibility" but described the "infallible magisterium of the Roman Pontiff"; the Latin text of Pastor Aeternus is available in H. Denzinger, Enchiridion Symbolorum, §§ 1821–1840.

For private consultation and not distribution without the consent of E Ondrako

British citizens. Newman pointedly replied that he could "see no inconsistency in my being at once a good Catholic and a good Englishman."[52]

Newman's *Letter to Norfolk*, which was twice the length of Gladstone's *Vatican Decrees*, has three main sections, book-ended by "introductory remarks" and a "conclusion" to which Newman eventually added a lengthy "postscript" of specific responses to Gladstone. Newman began his *Letter* with a discussion of the ancient and papal churches and the historical precedents for "divided allegiance"; at the center—and in a way the centerpiece of the work—was his treatment of "conscience"[53]; the third section was a four-part treatment: Pope Pius IX's Encyclical, *Quantâ curâ*, the Syllabus of Errors (both issued in 1864), the Vatican Council and its definition of 1870.

Newman began his treatment of conscience by emphasizing that the Supreme Being "has the attributes of justice, truth, wisdom, sanctity, benevolence and mercy, as eternal characteristics in His nature, the very Law of His being, identical with Himself; and next, when He became Creator, He implanted this Law, which is Himself, in the intelligence of all His rational creatures."[54] Appealing to the authority of St. Thomas Aquinas for whom the "natural law is an impression of the Divine Light in us, a participation of the eternal law in the rational creature,"[55] Newman pointed out that not only for Catholics, but also for Anglicans, Wesleyans and many Presbyterians, conscience is understood as "the voice of God in the nature and heart of man, as distinct from the voice of Revelation"[56]:

> Conscience is the aboriginal Vicar of Christ, a prophet in its informations, a monarch in its peremptoriness, a priest in its blessings and anathemas, and, even though the eternal priesthood throughout the Church could cease to be, in it the sacerdotal principle would remain and would have a sway.[57]

Newman next pointed out that such a view of "conscience," although ecumenically acknowledged, was nonetheless widely rejected by many contemporary philosophers:

> We are told that conscience is but a twist in primitive and untutored man; that its dictate is an imagination; that the very notion of guiltiness, which that dictate enforces, is simply irratio-

---

[52] Norfolk, 177.
[53] Norfolk, 246-261.
[54] Norfolk, 246.
[55] Norfolk, 247.
[56] Norfolk, 248.
[57] Norfolk, 248–249.

For private consultation and not distribution without the consent of E Ondrako

nal, for how can there possibly be freedom of will, how can there be consequent responsibility, in that infinite eternal network of cause and effect, in which we helplessly lie? and what retribution have we to fear, when we have had no real choice to do good or evil?.[58]

Simultaneously Newman felt that the English public had lost the Christian notion of conscience:

> There too the idea, the presence of a Moral Governor is far away from the use of it, frequent and emphatic as that use of it is. When men advocate the rights of conscience, they in no sense mean the rights of the Creator, nor the duty to Him, in thought and deed, of the creature; but the right of thinking, speaking, writing, and acting, according to their judgment or their humour, without any thought of God at all. They do not even pretend to go by any moral rule, but they demand, what they think is an Englishman's prerogative, for each to be his own master in all things, and to profess what he pleases, asking no one's leave, and accounting priest or preacher, speaker or writer, unutterably impertinent, who dares to say a word against his going to perdition, if he like it, in his own way.[59]

For all practical purposes then, in the popular mind, conscience had become "the right of self-will."[60]

Papal Authority and Conscience

Next, in a digression that was both theologically insightful and rhetorically strategic, Newman discussed the relationship of conscience and papal authority. While acknowledging that various popes had spoken against "liberty of conscience"—even calling it a "deliramentum"[61]—Newman emphasized that their real target was a false understanding of conscience; accusations such as those of Gladstone to the contrary, in fact, "there is no scoffing of any Pope, in formal documents addressed to the faithful at large, at that most serious doctrine, the right and the duty of following that Divine Authority, the voice of conscience, on which in truth the Church herself is built."[62] Rather, in both theory and fact, every pope in virtue of his office must be a defender of conscience:

---

58 Norfolk, 249.

59 Norfolk, 250.

60 Norfolk, 250.

61 Norfolk, 251.

62 Norfolk, 252.

For private consultation and not distribution without the consent of E Ondrako

So indeed it is; did the Pope speak against Conscience in the true sense of the word, he would commit a suicidal act. He would be cutting the ground from under his feet. His very mission is to proclaim the moral law, and to protect and strengthen that "Light which enlighteneth every man that cometh into the world." On the law of conscience and its sacredness are founded both his authority in theory and his power in fact.[63]

Accordingly, on the one hand, the "championship of the Moral Law and of conscience is" the pope's *raison d'être* [64]; on the other hand, if the pope "trampled on the consciences of his subjects,–if he had done so all along, as Protestants say, then he could not have lasted all these many centuries till now ..."[65]

Newman then summarized four important dimensions of conscience: first, conscience is not "a fancy or an opinion," but "a dutiful obedience to what claims to be a divine voice, speaking within us ..."[66] Second, "conscience is not a judgment upon any speculative truth, any abstract doctrine, but bears immediately on conduct, on something to be done or not done."[67] Third:

> conscience being a practical dictate, a collision is possible between it and the Pope's authority only when the Pope legislates, or gives particular orders, and the like. But a Pope is not infallible in his laws, nor in his commands, nor in his acts of state, nor in his administration, nor in his public policy.[68]

Fourth, conscience "has the right of opposing the supreme, though not infallible Authority of the Pope"[69]; however, such a decision "in order to prevail against the voice of the Pope, must follow upon serious thought, prayer, and all available means of arriving at a right judgment on the matter in question."[70]

---

63 Norfolk, 252.

64 Norfolk, 253.

65 Norfolk, 254.

66 Norfolk, 255.

67 Norfolk, 256.

68 Norfolk, 256. Although theologians in the twenty-first century commonly restrict the "object" or scope of infallibility to "doctrine concerning faith and morals," in Newman's time, there were some who claimed that infallibility could extend to all papal teachings; see JOHN FORD, "Different Models of Infallibility?" in Proceedings of the Catholic Theological Society of America 35 (1980): 217–233.

69 Norfolk, 257.

70 Norfolk, 257–258.

For private consultation and not distribution without the consent of E Ondrako

In the case of conscientious objections to Church teaching, however, Newman counseled his audience: "Unless a man is able to say to himself, as in the Presence of God, that he must not, and dare not, act upon the Papal injunction, he is bound to obey it, and would commit a great sin in disobeying it."[71] Newman was quite aware of the "mean, ungenerous, selfish, vulgar spirit" of human nature that "at the very rumour of a command, places itself in opposition to the Superior who gives" such an order.[72] Nonetheless, following traditional Catholic teaching—that has been reiterated by church councils and theologians—Newman insisted "on the duty of obeying our conscience at all hazards."[73]

After sampling a catena of theological opinions, Newman summarized his treatment of conscience in the form of a memorable toast:

> I add one remark. Certainly, if I am obliged to bring religion into after-dinner toasts, (which indeed does not seem quite the thing) I shall drink—to the Pope, if you please,—still, to Conscience first, and to the Pope afterwards.[74]

Conscience in the Twenty-First Century

What Newman taught about the role and rule of conscience nearly a century and a half ago, seems more urgently needed than ever in the twenty-first century. On the one hand is the post-modern subjectivism that too often twists conscience into "the right of self-will."[75] On the other hand—in flagrant contradiction and sometimes violent opposition to freedom of conscience—is a spectrum of authoritarianisms—cultural, political, social and, unfortunately, religious—that infringe on the right of personal conscience.[76] In response to these contemporary fallacies, there is, on the one hand, an urgent need to recover Newman's awareness—basic to the Christian Tradition—that conscience is "the voice of God in the nature and heart of man,"[77] precisely because every person is created in the image and likeness of God. On the other hand, there is pressing need for not only agreeing with Newman's toast but also finding a judicious

---

71 Norfolk, 258.

72 Norfolk, 258.

73 Norfolk, 259.

74 Norfolk, 261.

75 Norfolk, 250.

76 In this regard, the teaching of the Second Vatican Council on religious freedom as an essential part of "human dignity" is particularly important; see Dignitatis Humanae, available at: http://www.vatican.va/archive/hist_councils/ii_vatican_council/documents/vat-ii_decl_19651207_dignitatis-humanae_en.html.

77 Norfolk, 248.

For private consultation and not distribution without the consent of E Ondrako

balance between reverence for conscience and respect for authority; indeed any authority which fails to respect conscience in theory and in fact is effectively committing "a suicidal act."[78]

---

[78] Norfolk, 252.

For private consultation and not distribution without the consent of E Ondrako

CHAPTER 6

Bl. Duns Scotus and Bl. Cardinal John Newman on Knowledge, Assent, and Faith

Timothy B. Noone [1]

Tenent philosophi perfectionem naturae[2]

In the prologue of the *Ordinatio* Scotus deals at length with the position of the 'philosophers.' Who are they? We do not know exactly who they are, but their arguments tell us a great deal about what their aims are. For these arguments are understood to be addressed specifically to supernatural revelation and to deny its necessity. Though they are certainly Aristotelian arguments in terms of their textual and historical point of origin, they are not simply listings of the Aristotelian *dicta*; they are ordered so as to target revealed religion as their point of opposition. In light of this observation, I think that the view recently advanced by Gérard Sondag to the effect that the controversy between the philosophers and theologians in the *Ordinatio* prologue is more typological than historical needs to be qualified. The opposition between philosophers and theologians may be, indeed, perennial in Western thought, much as Sondag suggests, but we would be incorrect to view the controversy as lacking any contemporary reference in Scotus's time, particularly in light of the recently published studies by Carlos Steele, Albert Zimmermann, and Zdzislaw Kuksewicz upon such Parisian figures as Ferrandus Hispanus and Gilles d'Orléans.[3]

---

[1] Newman-Scotus Symposium, Oct. 23, 2010. Washington Theological Union, Washington, D.C. Timothy B. Noone (The Catholic University of America).

[2] Scotus, *Ordinatio.* I prol. pars 1 q. unica n. 5 (Vat. I 4:5). For an excellent study on this theme in the text of the Ordinatio along with some poignant reflections upon its value for relating philosophical discourse to other types of wisdom, see Joseph Owens, "Tenent philosophi perfectionem naturae," in *Essays Honoring Allan B. Wolter*, ed. William A. Frank and Girard J. Etzkorn (St. Bonaventure, N.Y.: The Franciscan Institute, 1985), 221–244. Scotus, *Ordinatio.* I prol. pars 1 q. unica n. 6–9 (Vat. I 5–7).

[3] Carlos Steel, "Medieval Philosophy: An Impossible Project: Thomas Aquinas and the 'Averroistic' Ideal of Happiness," *Was ist Philosophie im Mittelalter: Akten des X. Internationalen Kongressus für mittelalterliche Philosophie der Société Internationale pour l'Étude de la Philosophie Médiévale*, 25. bis 30. August in Erfurt, herausgegeben von Jan A. Aertsen un Andreas Speer, *Miscellanea Medievalia* bd. 26 (Berlin/New York: Walter de Gruyter, 1998), 152–174; idem, "Siger of Brabant versus Thomas Aquinas on the Possibility of Knowing the Separate

For private consultation and not distribution without the consent of E Ondrako

What the text of the *Ordinatio* prologue tells us is that Scotus is keenly interested in delineating the boundaries of natural reason, while vindicating the legitimate claims for religious knowledge and revelation. Scotus's solution to the first question of the prologue, namely, whether the human person needs supernatural knowledge, is that the human person does need supernatural knowledge in the present life, endorsing the fundamental reason given by many of his contemporary theologians. There is a gulf between what we may naturally know and what we need to know in order to achieve our true end.[4] To clarify his solution, Scotus proposes a distinction between different senses of the terms 'natural' and 'supernatural.' The human possible intellect, insofar as it is a passive power, may be rightly said to be naturally inclined to every intelligible object, including God, in the sense that the intellect has a natural disposition to receive every intelligible form. To this extent, the human mind has a natural inclination to beatitude in the sense that intuiting the divine essence does no violence to it and it is not related indifferently to that essence but rather has a natural aptitude to know it. But the possible intellect is not related to the divine essence in the present life in such a way that the latter prompts it to engage in acts of intellectual cognition. Rather what naturally moves the possible intellect in the present life are the agent intellect and the phantasm. Consequently, any knowledge that would be efficiently caused by something other than the agent intellect and the phantasm would be supernatural knowledge to that extent, supernatural in its causal origin, however, not supernatural in the sense of exceeding the natural capacity of the intellect. Furthermore, any knowledge that would normally remain beyond the scope of what is discernible on the basis of the ordered activities of the agent intellect and the phantasm on the possible intellect is also supernatural knowledge since its propositional contents exceed what would naturally be available and are matters towards which our intellects would, but for the gift of faith, remain neutral.[5]

The core of the position taken here is that we simply cannot know by any natural means that the triune God is the end towards which we

Substances," Nach der Verurteilung von 1277: Philosophie und Theologie an der Universität von Paris im letzten Viertel des 13. Jahrhunderts, herausgegeben von Jan A. Aertsen, Kent Emery, Jr. und Andreas Speer (Berlin/New York: Walter de Gruyter, 2001), 211–231; ALBERT ZIMMERMANN, "Ferrandus Hispanus: ein Verteidiger des Averroes," Nach der Verurteilung von 1277, 410–416; and ZDZISLAW KUKSEWICZ, "La foi e la raison chez Gilles d'Orléans: philosophe parisien du XIIIe siècle," Geistesleben im 13. Jahrhundert, herausgegeben von Jan A. Aertsen und Andreas Speer (Berlin/New York: Walter de Gruyter, 2000), 252–261. Also for an earlier study, see ZDZISLAW KUKSEWICZ, De Siger de Brabant à Jacques de Plaisance: La théorie de l'intellect chez les Averroistes latins des XIIIe et XIVe siècles (Cracovie: Ossolineum, Éditions de l'Académie Polonaise de Sciences, 1968).

4   SCOTUS, *Ord.* I prol. pars 1 q. unica n. 62 (Vat. I 38:3–7).

5   SCOTUS, *Ord.* I prol. pars 1 q. unica n. 57–65 (Vat. I 35–40).

For private consultation and not distribution without the consent of E Ondrako

must strive and that, if we participate in the life of grace, we are destined to enjoy Him forever in the beatific vision. The emphasis Scotus places is upon the reasons for our ignorance.

One reason and the chief one is that the propositions bearing upon the articles of faith are simply neutral to our intellects so long as they operate merely from the resource provided by the natural order. True, we may form the propositions 'God became man.' or 'God is one in three persons.' without any supernatural aid; as Scotus points out, the non-believer and the believer – not to mention the heretic and the orthodox believer – must have the same propositions formed in their minds in order to communicate with each other and hence intelligently disagree. Awareness of the propositions, however, is one thing and assent to them is another. The latter is possible only through divine assistance.[6]

Furthermore, God may be known as the end of the universe and in that sense known as the end toward which we are directed as part of the universe; the theological issue is not whether or not God is our end in this generically understood or broad sense, but rather to know whether or not to He is our end in the sense of an object that we may reach or obtain, whether in this life or the next.[7] From Scotus's point of view, to know God is our end in the sense of something which we may attain and that He will accept certain deeds as worthy of eternal life requires that we know the divine will since such matters have their ultimate originating cause in the divine will. This, of course, is tantamount to saying that it is both logically and metaphysically possible for God to create human beings without ordaining them to eternal life with Him. Such a claim may be thought of us disturbing, perhaps both in the sense that it breaks the continuity between the nature of human persons and their actual destiny (or if you want *de facto* end) and in the sense that it provides little if any basis for hope for a higher destiny should our convictions be grounded exclusively in natural reason. Yet the motivation behind Scotus's reasoning is not skepticism, as is sometimes alleged, but rather a firmly planted desire to preserve the contingency of salvation history and the freedom of the divine will. To the mind of the Subtle Doctor, if we press our reasoning too far in the direction taken by earlier Scholastic authors such as St. Thomas and St. Bonaventure, we verge on making of God's decision to share eternal life with us a metaphysical requirement of the reality of creation and hence begin to eradicate, though in a different manner, the distinction between the natural and supernatural. In sum, I would suggest that, however much

---

[6] SCOTUS, *Ord.* I prol. pars 1 q. unica n. 68–71 (Vat. I 42–44; 52–54).

[7] SCOTUS, *Ord.* I prol. pars 1 q. unica n. 28 (Vat. I 16–17).

For private consultation and not distribution without the consent of E Ondrako

Scotus's reasoning may upset the serenity of our ordinary convictions, it accords well with the theological facts of the matter.

What is the status of Scotus's own arguments, or those of other theologians, against the position of the philosophers who would claim completeness for their competing conception of life led only by truths known by reason? Are they in any sense demonstrative? Are their principles discernible through natural reason? Far from it. A note added to the *Ordinatio* text by Scotus himself, according to the testimony of two of the most authoritative manuscripts, reads as follows:

> Note: no supernatural quality can be shown by natural reason to belong to the wayfarer, nor can any such thing be required for his perfection. It is not even possible for someone who has such a [supernatural quality] to know that he has it. Therefore it is impossible to use natural reason against Aristotle in such a case: if one argues from matters believed (*ex creditis*) that is no argument (*ratio*) against a philosopher since he will not grant the premise that is believed. Since the arguments made here against him have as one of their premises a matter of belief or a claimed derived from a matter of belief, these arguments are only theological persuasions, [reasoning] from matters believed to a matter of belief.[8]

No cleaner statement could be asked for regarding the status of the arguments presented **against the philosophical position. The arguments have a dialectical character (*persuasiones*) and are ultimately grounded in principles belonging to the supernatural order.**

Newmanesque Intimations: Scotus on Faith and Pedestrian Knowledge

In book III of his *Commentary on the Sentences* recently published as *Lectura* III, we find a precious treatment of the concept of faith by Scotus at distinctions 23 through 25. This text is remarkable since it is the longest *ex professo* discussion of faith in the corpus, but also because it, apparently,

---

8 'Nota, nullum supernaturale potest ratione naturali ostendi inesse viatori, nec necessario requiri ad perfectionem eius; nec etiam habens potest cognoscere illud sibi inesse. Igitur impossibile est hic contra Aristotelem uti ratione naturali: si arguatur ex creditis, non est contra philosophum, quia praemissam creditam non concedet. Unde istae rationes hic factae contra ipsum alteram praemissam habent creditam vel probatam ex credito; ideo non sunt nisi persuasiones theologicae, ex creditis ad creditum." Scotus, *Ord.* I prol. pars 1 q. unica n. 12 (Vat. I 9).

For private consultation and not distribution without the consent of E Ondrako

is the only such text available: the *Ordinatio* parallel is unavailable, the Roman editors tells us,[9] since the text reproduced in the *Ordinatio* manuscripts is simply a copying into the *Ordinatio* of the relevant section of *Lectura* III and the genuine *reportationes* of the Parisian lectures stop at III d. 17, where Scotus himself most likely had reached at the time, June 25, 1303, that Philip the Fair required all dissenters from his anti-papal policy to leave Paris. The questions for dd. 23–25 are only three in number: d. 23: whether we need to posit infused faith for items that are revealed to us; d. 24: whether someone can have both faith and science in regard to items revealed; and d. 25: whether, prior to the coming of Christ, faith was needed in the items that we now believe. It is the first two questions with which we shall be principally concerned here since it is in these that we find Scotus treating of acquired faith as pertaining to both ordinary and religious matters and as a type of knowledge (*scientia*).

The question of whether we need to posit infused faith for revealed items of belief is divided into two further issues: whether we have acquired faith and how one should understand the doctrine that there is in us infused faith. Scotus unqualifiedly asserts that we have acquired faith in revealed truths, that is, we have the habit of believing those truths through an act of will combined with an act of intellect. Basing himself upon Augustine's writings, Scotus argues that just as we trust the Church, so too we would believe the writings declared by the Church to be authoritative, much as we are disposed to believe historical claims by well-known authors:

> But then even if there not any infused faith, I would believe by acquired faith the stories of the books of the Canon on account of the authority of the Church, just as I do believe in a certain way other stories written down or related to me by famous men.[10]

What Scotus does next to bring home the point that one might believe even truths of the faith without necessarily possessing the supernatural gift of infused faith is to introduce two examples. The first is that of an unbaptized Jewish boy brought up by Christians. Such a boy might believe and firmly hold (*crederet et adhaereret*) all the same things we Christians do:

> Just as I believe by acquired faith through hearing others (such as parents whose truthfulness I trust) that many ages have passed away and that the world did not begin with myself; and I believe, thanks to the report of persons worthy of trust, that Rome, which

---

9 Ed. Vat. X, Prolegomena, p. 42*.

10 "Sed tunc, si nulla esset fides infusa, crederem tamen fide acquisita historiis librorum Canonis, propter auctoritatem Ecclesiae: sic credo quemadmodum aliis historiis a viris famosis scriptis et narratis." SCOTUS, Lectura III d. 23 q. unica n. 14 (ed. Vaticana XXI 101).

For private consultation and not distribution without the consent of E Ondrako

I have never seen, exists, so too I hold firmly the things revealed in Scripture through faith acquired through hearing these things said, thanks to my trusting the Church which approves the truthfulness of those [Scriptural] authors.[11]

The other example that Scotus mentions is that of a heretic, who initially believes all of the truths of the faith but eventually comes to doubt the Trinity; such a person continues to believe after his lapse into heresy the other articles of the faith with acquired faith since there can be no question of his believing those retained articles through infused faith inasmuch as infused faith is incompatible with any sort of heretical belief.[12]

The upshot of this for Scotus is that we do not need to posit infused faith in order to explain why we believe the articles firmly and without fear of being wrong (*ut homo firmiter credit omnibus articulis revelatis et determinetur ad alteram partem sine opposite formidine*). Acquired faith is above opinion, though below science:

> For acquired faith is above opinion (which holds to one side of a contradiction with fear of the other being true), although it is nonetheless below the level of science (which flows from the evidence of the scientific object). For I believe that 'the world did not begin with myself' not for the reason that I know it came before me (for there can be no science, according to Augustine, of things in the past), nor do I simply have an opinion that the world came before; but I firmly hold to the proposition that the world came before me through acquired faith from the hearing of others whose truthfulness I firmly believe. Nor do I doubt that the world came before me, nor do I doubt the existence of the parts of the world that I have not seen, for I do not doubt about the truthfulness of those telling me such things and claiming that such things are true. Accordingly, just as I do not have a moment's hesitation regarding their truthfulness (which functions as a kind of principle), so too I do not have any either regarding their statement (which functions as a kind of conclusion that follows).[13]

---

11 "...sicut etiam ego fide acquisita ex auditu aliorum (scilicet parentum, quorum veritati credo) credo multa tempora transivisse et mundum non incepisse mecum; et credo Romam esse, quam nunquam vidi, ex relatu fide dignorum; sic revelatis in Scriptura—per fidem acquisitam ex auditu—firmiter adhaereo, credendo Ecclesiae approbanti veritatem illorum scriptorium." Scotus, *Lectura* III d. 23 q. unica n. 15 (ed. Vaticana XXI 102).

12 Scotus, *Lectura* III d. 23 q. unica n. 16 (ed. Vaticana XXI 102).

13 "...quia fides acquisita est supra opinionem (quae adhaeret uni parti contradictionis cum formidine alterius), licet tamen sit infra scientiam (quae est ex evidentia obiecti scientialis). Credo enim 'mundum non incepisse mecum' non quia scio ipsum praecessisse me (quia

For private consultation and not distribution without the consent of E Ondrako

This first Newmanesque moment in the text of Scotus is certainly noteworthy and remarkable, but perhaps not as remarkable as a similar passage in the succeeding question. In the meanwhile, Scotus has answered that one must posit infused faith, not in order to explain how belief can be without deception, but in order to explain the greater intensity and perfection of the act of belief. The position Scotus takes is that one may know that he has the habit inclining him/her to believe something not evidently true, but cannot know that he or she has true faith in such a way as to know that the faith is true. Instead, he or she must believe that they have infused faith.[14] The question now becomes whether someone can have faith and knowledge (*scientia*) in regard to revealed truths.

As we saw yesterday, Scotus here gives his overview of science in the strictest sense. Just before he does so, however, he outlines two other forms of knowledge that may be called *scientia* in a broader, though less proper, sense:

> To the question posed I answer in a different manner that *scientia* may be understood in the soul in many ways.
>
> In one way, every knowledge (*notitia*) which is with conviction is called *scientia* and thus is consistent with faith. … But the question here in dispute does not ask about *scientia* in this sense, for not only about revealed things can there be science in this sense, by our relying upon testimony of others (and so it would consistent with the faith), but faith itself is science in this sense, just as is clear from Augustine XI On the City of God…
>
> Likewise, there can be even formal assent (*formalis assensus*) not only through credence by relying on the testimony of others, but there can also assent just as if it were to a truth known, though not for the same causes, namely, [not] from necessary evidence. And about such an assent the Philosopher speaks in VI *Ethics*, claiming that someone endowed with intellectual habits says something determinately true and assents to one part of a contradiction, just as someone assents to a demonstrated conclusion. And so the faith whereby we assent to one part of a contradiction determi-

---

praeteritorum non est scientia, secundum Augustinum), nec opinor mundum praecessisse me, sed adhaereo huic 'mundum praecessisse me' firmiter per fidem acquisitam ex auditu aliorum, quorum veracitati credo firmiter; nec dubito mundum praecessisse me, nec partes mundi esse quas non vidi, quia non dubito de veracitate narrantium mihi talia et asserentium haec vera esse. Ideo sicut non haesito de veracitate illorum (quae est quasi principium), sic nec de dicto illorum (quod est quasi conclusio sequens)." SCOTUS, *Lectura* III d. 23 q. unica n. 19 (ed. Vaticana XXI 103–104).

14 SCOTUS, *Lectura* III d. 23 q. unica n. 54–57 (ed. Vaticana XXI 118–119).

For private consultation and not distribution without the consent of E Ondrako

nately would be science, according to the Philosopher ... And in this way infused faith and science about revealed matters would compatible at the same time, for science is not understood in its proper sense in this fashion.[15]

The first of these more general ways of understanding science is clearly the same as what Scotus described in the previous question as acquired faith and is a state that can attach to either matters of religious belief or historical and everyday matters. The second of these broader meanings of science is equally clearly the knowledge obtained through infused faith. This would mean that the kind of knowledge gotten even by perfect, i.e., infused, faith may legitimately be called science because of its truth, promptitude, and certitude. The appeal Scotus makes to Aristotle's intellectual virtues in the *Nicomachean Ethics* would not be understandable in any other way.

Points for Comparison and Contrast

In approaching Cardinal Newman's writings, I am going to confine myself to the work *An Essay in Aid of a Grammar of Assent*. What I would like to draw our attention to immediately is the scope and purpose of this work. The title does not indicate any proclivity towards religious assent, though that is the type of assent that Newman ultimately wishes to consider. Rather the work as a whole wants to examine assent in general and to see what transpires in the case of religious assent as relating to a more general phenomenon. Indeed, Newman's oft-repeated example of a case of knowledge through illative sense, namely, 'Great Britain is an island' is deliberatively a non-religious example whose point is to have us realize that the assent we give to that proposition is real, though not based upon demonstrative or apodictic reasoning. Much of the first part of Newman's

---

15 "Ad quaestionem aliter respondeo, quod 'scientia' multipliciter potest accipi in anima. Uno modo, prout omnis notitia quae est cum adhaesione dicitur scientia et sic potest stare cum fide. ... Sed isto modo non quaerit quaestio de scientia, quia non tantum de credibilibus revelatis potest esse scientia hoc modo, firmiter adhaerendo testimonio alieno (et sic staret cum fide), sed etiam ipsa fides est scientia hoc modo, sicut patet per Augustinum XI De civitate ... Similiter potest esse adhuc formalis assensus non solum per credulitatem adhaerendo testimonio alieno, sed potest esse assensus sicut esset veritati scitae, licet non ex eisdem causis, scilicet ex evidentia necessaria. Et de tali assensu <K and Wadding, vol. VII, 482; evidentia MB> loquitur Philosophus VI Ethicorum quod habitibus intellectualibus dicit aliquis verum determinate et assentit uni parti, sicut assentiret aliquis conclusioni demonstratae; et ita fides qua assentimus alteri parti contradictionis determinate esset scientia ... Et isto modo fides infusa et scientia de revelatis starent simul, quia sic scientia non proprie accipitur." Scotus, *Lectura* III d. 24 q. unica n. 49 (ed. Vaticana XXI 143–144).

For private consultation and not distribution without the consent of E Ondrako

Grammar of Assent is devoted to building up a vocabulary of analysis regarding propositions and what we would label propositional attitudes that will only achieve it intended purpose in the second half where more mundane, but from Newman's viewpoint more germane, propositions are at stake that prove analogous to the case of religious assent.

Let me run, quite briefly, through the distinctions he makes. Apprehension is the first notion considered and is divided into notional and real. This follows upon his claiming that apprehension is the "imposition of a sense on the terms" used in a proposition.[16] The precise meaning of the term 'sense' here is not clear, but it is perhaps best understood as the aptitude of the terms to refer to concepts or things, i.e., to what medieval logicians would call supposition, since Newman speaks of terms standing for ideas or things in the same passage. The subject or predicate may stand for "what is abstract, general, and non-existing..."; if they do within a given proposition, the resulting apprehension is notional and corresponding assent also notional. By contrast, real propositions have terms standing for individual things and the grasp of individual things is what is involved correspondingly in real assent.[17] Real propositions and real assent have to do with things, communicated or grasped through experience in their concreteness by direct sense encounters or through images. The two modes of apprehension are compatible, both being found in the same individual minds and both arising ultimately from sense experience. But they differ considerably in their force and impact on the individual human mind.[18]

Newman's examples contrasting notional and real apprehension are quite revealing; they are based upon the same Latin sentences being understood by, in the first case, a schoolboy and a poet or a historian and, in the second case, by a schoolboy and a soldier. The first sentence 'Dum Capitolium scandet cum tacita virgine Pontifex' (when the priest climbs the Capitol accompanied by the silent virgin') is notional for the schoolboy, but real for the Vergil since he is pointing to the actual practices in which he has participated and real for a classicist whose training lets him through his imagination grasp the scene. The second sentence 'Dulce et decorum est pro patria mori' (To die for one's country is both fitting and pleasant.) is once again notional for the schoolboy, but real for the soldier who knows death on the battlefield and the honor of dying for one's country.

---

16 JOHN HENRY CARDINAL NEWMAN, *An Essay in Aid of a Grammar of Assent*, new impression (London/New York/ and Bombay: Longmans, Green, and Co., 1903), 9.

17 NEWMAN, *An Essay in Aid of a Grammar of Assent*, new impression (London/New York/ and Bombay: Longmans, Green, and Co., 1903), 9–10.

18 NEWMAN, *An Essay in Aid of a Grammar of Assent*, new impression (London/New York/ and Bombay: Longmans, Green, and Co., 1903), 34–35.

For private consultation and not distribution without the consent of E Ondrako

Assent, the central topic of the *Grammar*, is the unconditional acceptance of a proposition. One of the main points Newman makes in this regard is that, although assent presupposes apprehension and, normally, inference, the assent itself does not admit of degrees and hence is not stronger and weaker depending on the mode of inference.[19] His phenomenological analysis is often at its best when he points out the disproportionality between assent, on the hand, and inference and argument, on the other. The same holds true of his brilliant observation that real assent always involves personal commitment and judgment.[20]

Real assent, like real apprehension, is keener and involves the concrete; notional assent involves notions, not things. The two may be hard to sort out, not least because an individual may initially have a notional assent to a proposition and then, under changed circumstances, a real one.[21]

A point that is worth observing prior to starting upon our comparison and contrast with Scotus is Newman's distrust of abstraction and his apparent nominalism regarding universals. Under the influence of Hume's *Treatise*, Newman describes real apprehension as "stronger…, the more vivid and forcible."[22] Just a two pages earlier, we find the following description of general ideas:

> All things in the exterior world are unit and individual and are nothing else; but the mind not only contemplates those unit realities, as they exist, but has the gift, by an act of creation, of bringing before it abstractions and generalizations, where they have no existence, no counterpart, out of it.[23]

An Effort at Drawing some Comparison and Contrasts

If we start with simple apprehension in the Scholastic sense as our point of departure, we might think that we could readily align Scotus's terminology and teaching with Newman's by merely rendering equivalent

---

[19] Newman, *An Essay in Aid of a Grammar of Assent*, new impression (London/New York/ and Bombay: Longmans, Green, and Co., 1903), 35.38. 171–174.

[20] Newman, *An Essay in Aid of a Grammar of Assent*, new impression (London/New York/ and Bombay: Longmans, Green, and Co., 1903), 232.

[21] Newman, *An Essay in Aid of a Grammar of Assent*, new impression (London/New York/ and Bombay: Longmans, Green, and Co., 1903), 78–80.

[22] Newman, *An Essay in Aid of a Grammar of Assent*, new impression (London/New York/ and Bombay: Longmans, Green, and Co., 1903), 11. See Hume, Enquiry sect. 2 (ed. Steinberg, 9–11).

[23] Newman, *An Essay in Aid of a Grammar of Assent*, new impression (London/New York/ and Bombay: Longmans, Green, and Co., 1903), 9.

For private consultation and not distribution without the consent of E Ondrako

Newman's notional apprehension and Scotus's *cognition abstractiva* and Newman's real apprehension with *cognition intuitive*. But actually this won't work, for several reasons. First, notional apprehension involves grasping the universal largely from the mind's own inventiveness, whereas abstractive cognition has to do with legitimate eidetic insight. In Scotus's thinking, the basis for such acts of apprehension is the common nature and as we can see from the discussion of abstract knowledge in the case of Christ, there are both natures and individuating principles within the ontological constitution of a given individual. Scotus's ontological foundation, in other words, for universals is quite different from Newman's and so too are his beliefs about what would be the mode of such apprehension. Still, we may rightly say that Newman and Scotus share the understanding that in notional (or abstractive) cognition, the presence and absence of the thing cognized does not enter into the picture.

Initially the alignment of real apprehension with intuitive cognition appears more promising: both bear upon individuals and concrete facts and both seem to be irreplaceable for allowing us to know what is actually the case. A moment's reflection, however, quickly dismisses this facile identification. Intuitive cognition always has the thing as existent and present as its proximate object. Real apprehension can occur in matters historical where the proper items can never be grasped as present and existent. Furthermore, Newman's tendency to allow real apprehension in the case of images or eidetic représentation apart from direct experience of the items would never be countenanced by Scotus as intuitive cognition. Images of the imagination are représentational and for that reason do not target the thing as existent and present.

So I would suggest that it is not in their accounts of ideogenesis, their philosophical psychology, or their outlook on the ontology of universals and individuals that Newman and Scotus approach each other. Rather it is in their thinking that the concrete has a richness in it that abstract thinking cannot exhaust and in their insistence that our real assent to faith is paralleled by a type of preparatory thinking analogous to what we use in making everyday decisions and forming normal, everyday beliefs.

For private consultation and not distribution without the consent of E Ondrako

CHAPTER 7

Scotus and Newman in Dialogue

Peter Damian Fehlner

During the eight centuries of its existence the University of Oxford was never graced by theologians greater than Bl. John Duns Scotus (1265 c. – 1308) and Bl. John Henry Newman (1801–1890). But rarely have students of Scotus and of Newman suggested there might be something more than mere happenstance to link their names in the world of theology, or that their linking might have a significant bearing on the future of Catholic theology.

However infrequent suggestions of this kind, those making them cannot be dismissed easily as fanciful persons who mistake groundless hypotheses for reality. The first to hint that similar approaches to the study of theology are shared by these two saintly scholars is none other than Bl. John Henry himself. In a letter to F. W. Faber, dated December 9, 1849, Newman clearly states his position on the motive of the Incarnation to be that of Scotus. Here is the text:

> Certainly I wish to take the Scotist view on that point [the motive of the Incarnation]. It seems to me more philosophical (if one has a right so to talk) to throw the difficulty on creation—as if creation is *the* great mystery—and if the Supreme condescended to create, to partake in creation was involved. But as I understand the Scotist view it simply is, that He would have been incarnate, even had man not sinned—but when man sinned it was *for* our redemption; in *matter of fact* the end was to make satisfaction.[1]

---

[1] *The Letters and Diaries of John Henry Newman*, vol. 13, ed. C. S. DESSAIN, Edinburgh 1963, p. 335. Newman returns to this theme in the P.S. of a letter to Faber, dated 14 Dec., 1849, ibid., p. 342. The passage in question is found in sermon 2: Neglect of Divine Calls and Warnings, in *Discourses for Mixed Congregations*. Faber in a letter of 8 Dec., 1849, to Newman had noted an inconsistency in this sermon with the scotist position espoused elsewhere in this volume of sermons, when he wrote in this one: "showed what He thought of sin by resolving to become man," a formulation apparently indicating that the Incarnation was first thought of in view of the forgiveness of sin. Newman replied that, indeed, the formulation misstated his meaning, and should rather read: "resolved to suffer." In subsequent Editions, the passage states that the Son "showed what He thought of sin by dying for it." Redemption was, indeed, a de facto motive of the Incarnation, but not the primary one. Newman presupposes here the scotistic distinction between the "signs of God's will" or order of intention (in the mind of God) and order of their execution (in history). Cf. R. STRANGE, *Newman and the Gospel of Christ*, Oxford 1980, pp. 113–114. The scotistic preferences of Faber are well known. Cf. A. B. CALKINS, "Mary

For private consultation and not distribution without the consent of E Ondrako

In this same letter Newman also evidences sympathy for scotistic positions in sacramental theology. In an earlier letter to W. G. Ward, March 11, 1849, concerning the forthcoming definition of the Immaculate Conception—very much involving the theology of Scotus—he says this:

> However, returning to the question of development, it is wonderful—St. Thomas and St. Bernard flatly silenced.[2]

Further comments in this letter on various theologians of the day, including Doellinger and Perrone, who in one way or another opposed his theory of doctrinal development, show he regarded the approach of Scotus to questions bearing on the motive of the Incarnation and on the Immaculate Conception as implicitly supporting that theory. Most important, however, remains his remark about development and the Immaculate Conception. For it shows he appreciated one of the key theological principles in the development of a coherent Christology-Mariology: the relation between the order of intention in the divine counsels of salvation (metaphysical dimension) and their order of execution (historical dimension): first in intention, last in execution. Lack of consideration of the order of intention leads to a thoroughgoing evolutionary historicism; neglect of the order of execution leads to an arid rationalizing.

Given the key role the absolute primacy of Christ plays both in scotistic theology and metaphysics, we may assume, brief though these comments be, that Newman in a general way was sympathetic to many of the major themes characteristic of Scotus's metaphysics, and certainly would not subscribe to the fashion among so many Catholic theologians

---

the Coredemptrix in the Writings of Frederick William Faber (1814–1863)," in *Mary at the Foot of the Cross*, vol. 1, New Bedford MA 2001, 317–343, here pp. 319, 327, 331.

[2] *Letters and Diaries*, vol. 13, cit., p. 82. Favorable references to Scotus can also be found in Newman's *Lectures on the Doctrine of Justification*, e.g., in his discussion of the views of Cornelius Musso, the famous Scotist at the Council of Trent, in Appendix one: On the Formal Cause of Justification, numbers 3 and 14. Musso's views on the question of created and uncreated grace and the formal cause of justification seemed to Newman substantially the same as his own. Questions of grace and of the relation of natural and supernatural are very much related to positions taken on the question of the motive of the Incarnation. Lecture 9 on Righteousness the Fruit of Our Lord's Resurrection, pp. 202 ff., seems to parallel the thought of St. Bonaventure on the uncreated gift of grace and divine acceptance, a position presupposed by Scotus. Newman quotes Bonaventure in his favor in Appendix one, number 5. And in note 4 he adduces the doctrine of the plurality of forms of the Franciscan school to support his position. Cf. P. Fehlner, *The Role of Charity in the Ecclesiology of St. Bonaventure*, Rome 1965, p. 93, note 54; W. Dettloff, *Die Lehre von der Acceptatio Divina bei Johannes Duns Scotus mit besonderer Berüchsichtigung der Rechtfertigungslehre*, (Werl in Westf. 1954).

For private consultation and not distribution without the consent of E Ondrako

since Vatican II, to simply substitute the historical dimension and a new "hermeneutic" for the "pre-conciliar" metaphysical approach.[3]

Nor is it illogical that someone who had come to abandon an initial acceptance of Calvinistic predestinationism (where the only motive of the Incarnation was sin), should find in Scotus's defense of the absolute primacy of Christ and of the Immaculate Conception exactly the right stress on the goodness of God to set in perspective the overstress on sinful man in Calvin and on sinless man in Pelagius, without sacrificing the primacy of charity and of the will.[4] We may also see in this contrast the difference between the mystery of predestination in Christ, as Scotus explains it, and the predestinationism condemned by the Church, the first reflecting the will of God as goodness itself, always ordered in acting because always loving justice for its own sake (called *affectus justitiae* by Scotus), always just in this way because always loving the divine essence; and the second reflecting the divine will as tyrannical—an omnipotent version of a finite will whose defective mode of acting (called by Scotus, *affectus commodi*)—is confused with freedom, turning it into license.[5] Without mentioning names Newman's *Memorandum* on the Immaculate Conception underscores precisely this contrast.

On the publication of the *Grammar of Assent*, another perceptive student of both Newman and Scotus, the Jesuit poet Gerard Manley Hopkins (1844–1889), though at first not much impressed, later became enthused on realizing how much of what Newman explains in this classic is for a contemporary audience: in fact, if not in intent, an elaboration of themes found in Scotus, and further support for his aesthetical theory of "inscape" and "instress."[6] Newman refused Hopkins the requested permission to write a commentary on the *Grammar* illustrating these very points. Although Newman's reasons for this refusal are not entirely clear, his reply does not include a denial of the thesis Hopkins proposed to demonstrate.

---

3 Cf. M. Bordoni, Cristologia: lettura sistematica, in G. Canobbio-P. Coda (eds.), *La teologia del XX secolo. Un bilancio. 2. Prospettive sistematiche*, Roma 2003, pp. 5–22.

4 On the historical affinities of Scotism and Calvinism: Reformed scholasticism, in the university world, cf. A. Vos, *The Philosophy of John Duns Scotus*, Edinburgh 2006, pp. 540 ff.

5 Failure to make this distinction almost always accounts for the confusion of scotistic teaching on the primacy of the will and charity with what is known as voluntarism both in Islamic and in modern, western philosophy where will and intellect, goodness and truth, are divorced from each other and from being. Scotus, following Bonaventure, would say: being is perfectly one or first, one because true, true because good.

6 Cf. C. Devlin, *The Sermons and Devotional Writings of Gerard Manley Hopkins*, Oxford 1959. The commentary and notes of the editor are especially valuable in illustrating how Hopkins is a disciple of Scotus, "of reality the rarest veined unraveller," and how subscription to the views of Scotus on the Incarnation and Immaculate Conception brings with it acceptance of his views in metaphysics, epistemology and spirituality, not least Scotus's convictions concerning the person, the will and freedom, and the sacramentality of creation.

For private consultation and not distribution without the consent of E Ondrako

Refusal of Hopkins . Perhaps Newman had some doubts about Hopkins's qualifications to carry off such a study successfully; or that too close an association of the *Grammar of Assent* with the more metaphysical language of Scotus would frighten away the very people for whom it had been written; or that the *Grammar* might be interpreted as a criticism of the recent encyclical *Aeterni Patris* favoring the promotion of thomism.[7] In any case, Newman's praise of Scotus in his *Idea of a University* as the finest theological fruit of Oxford's traditional program of study seems to confirm Hopkins insight.[8]

During the course of a symposium to honor Scotus on the seventh centenary of his birth, held at the former Duns Scotus College near Detroit in late spring of 1966, I had the privilege of conversing privately with perhaps the greatest scotist of our times, Fr. Charles Balič. I took the occasion to ask his opinion concerning the possibility and value of a study dealing with correlations between the thought of Scotus and Newman. His reply was a very positive one: a study which, as far as he knew, had as yet to be undertaken, but should be.

A few years later, during the 1970's, Harold Weatherby, an Anglican Thomist, later Greek Orthodox, and now deceased, published two studies to illustrate the affinities linking the thought of Scotus, Newman and Hopkins.[9] His goal was not the promotion of Scotus and Newman.

---

[7] Cf. B. Berganzi, *Gerard Manley Hopkins*, London 1979, p. 108. A letter of Newman to Hopkins, dated Feb. 27, 1883, in *Letters and Diaries*, vol. 30, Oxford 1976, p. 191, is the basis for this information. Newman explains that any commentary at this time would be superfluous and, hence, he would not want to burden Hopkins with so onerous and fruitless a task. This is hardly a convincing reason as commentaries can serve many more important ends than apologetic or polemic. The letter of Dec. 7, 1849, cited in note 1 above, refers to criticism of his support of Scotus as contrary to an obligation to follow St. Thomas. *Aeterni Patris* contains a rather negative comment on scholastic masters whose "excessive subtlety" tends to confuse and weaken the faith, and many have interpreted and still interpret this as a veiled reference to Scotus. Leo XIII, in a letter to the Franciscan Minister General (cf. Quaracchi edition, III *Sent.*, Praefatio, for text, where the Pope cites approvingly the position of Sixtus V on the parity of Thomas and Bonaventure; and implicitly, Scotus, as a continuator of Bonaventure, in matters of systematic theology, later distanced himself from an exclusively thomistic, anti-scotistic interpretation of the comment. Additional information on the position of Leo XIII on Scotus can be found in W. Lampen, *B. Joannes Duns Scotus et Sancta Sedes*, Ad Claras Aquas 1929. For the rest, the Apostolic Letter, *Alma Parens*, of Paul VI (1966) for the seventh centenary celebration of Scotus's birth, his beatification in 1993 by St. John Paul II, and the praise of Scotus by Pope Benedict XVI in the general audience of July 7, 2010 [notwithstanding some criticism], should put to rest any fear that Scotus is responsible for modern voluntarism in the sense of absolute will to power, or that St. Thomas must be preferred to Scotus in matters theological-metaphysical.

[8] *The Idea of a University*, part 1, discourse 7:3; part 2, discourse 5, 2:2, p. 396. [Page references are to the uniform edition.]

[9] H. Weatherby, *Cardinal Newman in His Age*, (Nashville: 1973); Idem, *The Keen Delight: The Christian Poet in the Modern World*, (Athens, GA: 1975). Weatherby also includes G. Marcel among the pious subjectivists of our times and heirs of Scotus. For a sympathetic summary of Marcel's position on efficient (physical) causality and personal or voluntary causality

For private consultation and not distribution without the consent of E Ondrako

Rather, on the assumption that the theological and metaphysical positions of Scotus underlie the late medieval nominalism and voluntarism, source of so much subsequent subjectivism and idealism, those same positions in Newman have produced identical fruits: first among Anglicans and then among Catholics such as Hopkins, and, thereafter, among the modernists at the turn of the nineteenth century. Scotus via Ockham and Luther will always be the granddaddy of Kant and Hegel. Note well: Weatherby is not accusing Scotus and Newman, or even Hopkins, of formal heresy. Rather, he blames them for sowing the seeds of heresy, for leaving orthodox faith and philosophical certainty to rest solely on a blind act of obedience to authority. To Weatherby this is worse than a simple denial of some article of the Creed. Scotism, says Weatherby, is merely agnosticism (nominalism)-voluntarism thinly disguised in pious form, while Newman and Hopkins are simply the current English version of a radical tendency in the Roman Church since the late Middle Ages, viz., since Scotus.

Excursus: Table of Parallel Thought Patterns in Bonaventure, Scotus, and Newman

Frequent reference in this conference to theological-metaphysical views of St. Bonaventure as a basis for understanding those of Scotus and the many parallel patterns of thought in Scotus and Newman, obviously implies that Bonaventure and Scotus, whatever their differences, represent a single, coherent school of theological and philosophical reflection inspired by St. Francis of Assisi. The overall vision illuminating this school of thought found its first, definitive formulation in the Seraphic Doctor, particularly in such works as the *Itinerarium mentis in Deum*, the *Quaestiones Disputatae de Scientia Christi*, the *Quaestiones Disputatae de Mysterio Trinitatis*, the *Collationes de septem Donis Spiritus Sancti*, and the *Collationes in Hexaemeron*. This vision is, in fact, a presupposition for the distinctive contribution of Scotus: identification and logical reformulation of the key insights governing that synthesis in view of the absolute primacy of Christ or "joint predestination of Jesus and Mary." A full exposition of this point would have gone far beyond the limits of this study. Nonetheless, it would be worth undertaking, since the "accepted view" today claims that Bonaventure and Scotus represent, in the first instance, two quite different schools of Franciscan theology: the old school of Bonaventure representing thomism before

(influence), akin to that of Newman and Scotus, and how this differs from transcendental thomism and Kant, cf. O. BENNETT, *Metaphysics of Faith and Freedom*, (Rensselaer, NY 1972).

For private consultation and not distribution without the consent of E Ondrako

Thomas at a half-way house, and the new school of Scotus proceeding on quite different assumptions.

In the meantime, to facilitate reading of this study, this table of parallel thought patterns in Bonaventure, Scotus and Newman, notwithstanding difference of terminology, is placed here as a handy guide to the development of this theme.

St. Bonaventure	Bl. John Duns Scotus	Bl. John Henry Newman
First-Memory-Origin	First-Memory-Origin	First-Memory-Origin
Contuition (in speculo)	Intuitive cognition	Real apprehension
Discursive knowledge (per speculum)	Discursive knowledge	Inference
Abstraction	Abstractive cognition; word	Notional apprehension
Dijudicatio	Understanding	Illative sense
Illumination	Univocity of being	Unity of knowledge
Ratio essendi	Formalitates a parte rei	Perfections; Ideas; Notions
Esse: in fuga a non-esse	Ens cui non repugnat esse	Being or nothing
Liberum arbitrium (discretion-choice)	Will: essentially rational (core of personal life)	Will: power to be good (core of holiness)
Amor complacentiae	Affectus justitiae	Love of justice, purity; liberality
Amor concupiscentiae	Affectus commode	Benevolence; usefulness
Vestige (prope nihil)	Perfectio simplex	Physical
Image (prope Deum)	Perfectio simpliciter simplex	Natural; Anthropological
Similitude	Supernatural	Supernatural
God: in full flight from nothing	Ens infinitum	Infinite Being
God: necessary, independent being; Incommunicable existence of intelligible nature	God: personal being Incommunicable, etc.	God: personal Incommunicable…

Prima Pars: Essential Components

Newman Metaphysician and Scotus Phenomenologist

What is of prime interest here is not Weatherby's negative assessment of Scotus, Newman, Hopkins and the Roman Catholic Church (an assessment I obviously do not share). It is rather his perception of the similarities in their thought patterns. Although his interpretation of those similarities is a radical misrepresentation, Weatherby's observations are valuable, not only because he has spotted a deep affinity linking Scotus and Newman, but a key factor at the core of that affinity: their position on the critical question arising from "interiorization": entering into the heart.

For private consultation and not distribution without the consent of E Ondrako

Quite often, the enemy rather than the friend first spots a point crucial to some discussion and, in this case, what could be a most important discovery for the future of Christian thought and the support of faith. Newman's acceptance of Scotus's position on the motive of the Incarnation and his very correct understanding of this is no mere exercise of theological eclecticism. It is profoundly linked with the metaphysics and epistemology of Scotus. That provides the framework for a theological exposition of this thesis so central to Catholic theology and spirituality, and absolutely indispensable to a Catholic understanding of the relation between Incarnation and Redemption particularly in contrast with the Calvinist one. The goal of this study is to illustrate in Newman the very same link between Christology and metaphysics-epistemology which is found in St. Bonaventure and Scotus.

Weatherby, then, is right in saying that Scotus and Newman, unlike the majority of Thomists (except for the "transcendental" one's[10]), acknowledge the existence of a critical question. At the very least aspects of their thought, e.g., those resembling what Thomists such as C. Fabro call Hegelian "onto-theology," provide valid grounds, according to those who agree with this analysis, for ascribing to both Scotus and Newman a radical affinity with Kant and with the overall thrust of his idealism in matters epistemological and theological. But Weatherby and those sympathetic to his point of view fail to see that far from being a pious, blind orthodoxy resting on a notion of the will as absolute—a voluntarism opening the door on Kant's agnosticism—the critical insights of Scotus and Newman are sources of a powerful corrective for Kantian deviations.[11] That remedy is in fact a genuine

> process of interiorizing in which reason and willing play a central role, faith in Christ is received with profound conviction and one feels a harmonious correspondence between this real conviction and satisfying communion with God.[12]

This citation from Pope Benedict XVI, a great admirer of Newman, reflects a very ancient, traditional position on the primacy of the will and charity and its bearing on rationality and conviction during the Middle

---

10 On how transcendental thomism radically differs from Scotus as seen from the perspective of neo-patripassionism, cf. P. Fehlner, "Neo-Patripassionism from a Scotistic Viewpoint," in *Quaderni di Studi Scotisti* 3 (2006) 35–96.

11 W. Hoeres, *Kritik der transzendentalphilosophishen Erkenntnistheorie*, Stuttgart 1969, pp. 22. 62 ff.; Idem, *Der Wille als reine Vollkomenheit nach Duns Scotus*, (Munich 1962); O. Boulnois, *Être et représentation*, (Paris 1999), in particular ch. 4; F. Wiedmann, "Theorie des realen Denkens nach John Henry Newman," in *Newman Studien, vierte Folgen*, (Nürnburg 1960), pp. 144–248; J. Brechten, *Real-Erfahrung bei Newman*, (Bergen-Enkheim 1973).

12 Benedict XVI, *Catechesis on William of Saint-Thierry, General Audience, Dec. 2, 2009.*

For private consultation and not distribution without the consent of E Ondrako

Ages and since—a hallmark of the Franciscan school. It also reflects that notion of interiorizing found in chapters three and four of St. Bonaventure's *Itinerarium mentis in Deum* and in his *Christus unus omnium Magister*. In these works, recently praised by the Holy Father,[13] the Seraphic Doctor, in the footsteps of St. Augustine, but also heeding the directives of St. Francis concerning study,[14] notes the importance of this process. But more importantly he also notes how the process, deliberately detached in fact from any relation to Christ, terminates at "indifference" and "secularization" instead of sanctification of the intellect: at finding only self instead of God. Stopping short of what is its connatural term: God—it ends in what Bonaventure understands by spiritual "vanity," or what today goes under the name of autonomous or secular person. Scotus's "metaphysics" of the rational creature or created person via intellect and will as *perfectiones simpliciter simplices*,[15] and Newman's "phenomenological" discussion of conscience and of assent-inference in the *Grammar of Assent* both presuppose the position of the Seraphic Doctor on the difference between the secularized and contemplative intellect. The second belongs to the intellect by nature; the first is fruit of a deliberate option blinding the intellect to the light connatural to it, viz., rendering it skeptical or agnostic re those two luminous creatures of which Newman speaks: my Creator and myself.

Point of departure for our study of parallel thought patterns in Scotus and Newman are the remarks of Weatherby concerning the existence of such patterns. But underlying their existence is a radical similarity of approach to metaphysics, person and experience, one whose paradigm is clearest in the *Itinerarium* of St. Bonaventure, especially chapter 3 on memory, understanding and will, and in his *Quaestiones Disputatae de Mysterio Trinitatis*, especially question 8 on Primacy: within the Trinity and as Creator. That approach may be summarized in terms of a simple but profound correlation: Firstness or primacy-origin-memory, whether (1) dealing with the one and triune God in himself as independent-personal, viz., metaphysical necessity and the origin of the three divine Persons; or (2) in that creature which is uniquely the image of God or independent-personal *secundum quid*, viz., metaphysical necessity and the origin of personal life, at once rational and free as a sharing in the circumincessory life of the divine persons. It is not my intention at this point to illustrate this premise in detail, but merely to indicate that all of the following

---

[13] Benedict XVI, *Catechesis on St. Bonaventure, General Audiences March 3, 10, 17, 2010.*

[14] St. Francis, *Regula Bullata*, ch. 5 and 10; Idem, *Letter to St. Anthony*.

[15] On the scotistic concept of a *perfectio simpliciter simplex* cf. Hoeres, *Der Wille...*, cit., pp. 61 ff. The concept in Scotus depends directly on St. Anselm.

For private consultation and not distribution without the consent of E Ondrako

considerations on parallel patterns of thought in Scotus and Newman tend to converge on this premise. What is often called the phenomenology of Newman rests on the metaphysics of Scotus, and the metaphysics of Scotus easily finds expression in the English of Newman. And both are supported by the profound theological vision of St. Bonaventure.

The Will, the Critical Question and Faith

Without doubt interiorizing and the critical question are indeed inter-related. But in this approach, the critical question—far from stemming from a need to "verify" the correspondence or adequation of thought and extra-mental reality—arises out of a need in the finite mind to obey the truth, to be docile in the face of reality; first of all, the Reality which is the very goodness of God and to love that Goodness for its own sake and above all else: absolutely and not relatively, with the same *affectus justitiae*, as Scotus says, whereby God loves himself. Were the will merely an appetite of the intellect, it would not be free to choose among many contingent objects, but only be drawn to this or that good insofar as it is advantageous to it as determined by the *affectus commodi*. Freedom in choosing among contingent goods, presupposes freedom to love justice or the perfect good for its own sake, and the ability to assess the reasonableness of choosing a particular good critiqued in relation to goodness itself.[16] With this the critical question no longer is centered on the intellect, as Kant mistakenly thought, but on the will where every personal judgment is ultimately rooted, either as rational or as disordered. The autonomous will of Kant, unlike his heteronomous will or appetite, may be free. But it is also radically arbitrary and, hence, disordered, because detached from the truth of being as good in itself. In a word, the critical question is no longer primarily one of epistemology and logic or of physics, but one of a metaphysics underlying the moral-spiritual-personal obligation to recognize the Primacy of the Creator-Savior, an obligation to use one's intellect rightly and give thanks (cf. Rom 1: 21).

On this point the position of Newman coincides with that of Scotus when the English Cardinal says that our cognitive faculties are to be used correctly rather than as we please. No question of trust is involved, because they are designed to be used correctly; persons, however, are to be trusted or believed rather than used.[17] The intellect does not by nature

---

16 For Scotus's understanding of the *affectus justitiae* see *Ordinatio* II, d. 6, q. 2, 49; *Rep. Par* II., d. 6, q. 2; *Rep. Par.* III, d. 26, q. un.; *Rep. Par.* IV, d. 49, 5. For some further reflections on Scotus's treatment of will in relation to this conference cf. M. Pangallo, "La filosofia cristiana come filosofia della libertà in Duns Scoto," in *Quaderni di Studi Scotisti* 3 (2006) 21–34.

17 Newman, *An Essay in Aid of a Grammar of Assent*, p. 1, ch. 4, pp. 60–61.

For private consultation and not distribution without the consent of E Ondrako

make mistakes; but this is not its highest perfection. Its highest perfection is only attained in that knowing which accompanies perfect love of the Creator. Kantian skepticism is a consequence of not trusting persons, above all the Creator, in humbly believing and loving him rather than proudly insisting on one's autonomy. This very point is why Newman's *Grammar of Assent* is not to be read, as we shall see, in a Kantian, much less Ockhamistic frame of reference, whatever incidental phrases may suggest to the contrary.

Newman, then, would agree with Scotus[18] when he describes not the intellect, but the will as the "rational" faculty par excellence, the root of reasonableness: *ordinatissime volens*,[19] precisely because the core of rationality is not logic, but discretion, what St. Bonaventure calls *arbitrium*.[20] Discretion entails a "personal judgment" or what Bonaventure calls a *dijudicatio* as well as an abstraction.[21] Discretion is not simply a scientific analysis of some object considered abstractly, but one involving a critical assessment of particulars and of the complex process by which they come to be known by the finite mind in comparison with an Absolute point of reference, the absolute First. In scotistic terms, this critical assessment of Bonaventure: *dijudicatio*, in a creature *prope Deum* (image) and not in one *prope nihil* (vestige),[22] reflects the simple character of what Scotus calls a *perfectio simpliciter simplex* in the creature. Abstraction reflects its complexity. From this perspective, intuitive cognition and abstractive cognition complement one another. Separated, they lead either to a pantheistic ontologism or skeptical fideism because separation is another name for proud autonomy and self-sufficiency. The same thought pattern reappears in Newman under the headings assent and inference, illative sense and formal logic. The core, then, of Bonaventure's epistemology, based on divine illumination and on the consequences of its deliberate rejection, and most perfectly examined in the human nature of the God-Man,[23] finds an echo in Newman's theory of the "illative sense" and of assent as formally distinct from the conclusion of a discursive exercise.[24] That "order" or rationality of the all-perfect divine will, one with the divine being, is that

---

18 For texts cf. HOERES, *Der Wille...*, cit., pp. 86 ff., and 205 ff.; W. A. FRANK, editor of A. B. Wolter, *Duns Scotus on the Will and Morality*, (Washington: 1997), *Preface*, pp. ix–xi.

19 *Ordinatio* III, suppl., d. 32.

20 Cf. II *Sent.*, d. 25, p. 1, a. un., q. 3; *Breviloquium*, p. 2, c. 9, 8; *Itinerarium mentis in Deum*, c. 3, 4.

21 BONAVENTURE, *Itinerarium*, c. 2, 6; the *dijudicatio* is not merely another term for an abstraction, but its radically simple aspect accounting for its uniqueness as a pure perfection participating the divine Light and making created thought possible.

22 Cf. *Breviloquium*, p. 2, ch. 6, 3.

23 Cf. BONAVENTURE, *Quaestiones Disputatae de Scientia Christi*, q. 4.

24 *Grammar of Assent*, p. 1, ch. 1, pp. 5 ff.; ch. 6, p. 188.

For private consultation and not distribution without the consent of E Ondrako

of liberality, of the freedom that is generosity affirmed by St. John when he proclaims: "God is love and who abides in love abides in God and God in him" (I Jn 4: 16). The logic which is reason in the intellect—only such, to the degree it is correctly used—is sanctified by the will, when "science" of the intellect passes into "affection" of the will and becomes "wisdom."[25]

The position of Scotus on the relation of intellect and will is a development of that of Bonaventure. There is nothing so "unreasonable" as pure logic, so utterly divorced from reality and so impersonal. On the other hand there is nothing so reasonable as the freely acknowledged worth and primacy of goodness for its own sake. Thought is never so reasonable as when it is fully personalized, and this can only come about with holy use of thought on the part of the will. Conversely, the will is never so holy, just and loving as when it is orderly and reasonable, viz., humble and docile to the light of truth and fire of divine love. The integration of intellect and will, of reason and holiness, is always perfect in God. It is not in the created spirit. For the finite intellect, discursive thought is a condition for assent; just as for the will, the intellect is the spiritual power whereby the object of love is made present to the will. Nonetheless, the activity of the intellect, of itself determined by the truth of being, does not determine the will to love; the will determines itself in a personal, reasonable, orderly manner to love the good for its own sake, viz., justly, with the *affectus justitiae*. Newman's distinction between liberal and useful knowledge[26] parallels that of Scotus between love of *justice* and love of *advantage*, and suggests very strongly a radical agreement with the approach of Scotus to the primacy of the will: not an arbitrary "will culture" or voluntarism, doing what one pleases as the norm of good and evil, but the very core of rationality and goodness in doing what pleases God.

The views of both on reason as the heart of judgment and on judgment as a radically personal act of the elective power are anticipated and neatly summarized by St. Bonaventure in his *Itinerarium*:

Intra igitur ad te et vide, quoniam mens tua amat ferventissime semetipsam; nec se posset amare, nisi se nosset; nec se nosset, nisi sui meminisset, quia nihil capimus per intelligentiam, quod non sit praesens apud nostram memoriam....[27]

---

25 Cf. BONAVENTURE, *Collationes in Hexaemeron*, c. 5, 12–13.

26 NEWMAN, *The Idea of a University*, Discourse V.

27 *Itinerarium*, c. 3, 1.

For private consultation and not distribution without the consent of E Ondrako

Bonaventure draws out the implications when in the same chapter he notes the three operations of the elective power or will: counsel, judgment and desire or love.[28]

Scotus, Newman and Onto-theology

What, then, is to be made of arbitrary, irrational, disorderly, sinful choices? And of the accusation that Scotus and, after him, Newman and Hopkins, in sustaining the primacy of the will, are proponents of an ethic whose fundamental premise is personal pleasure or displeasure as a norm for distinguishing good and evil, rather than goodness itself? To answer such criticisms we must first briefly review a number of key positions of Scotus which, in the course of this study, will appear (under different names) in the writings of Newman.

The distinction *natural-voluntary* [29] refers to the primary modes of action, above all in the spiritual order of knowledge and love, first in God and then in the spiritual creature. Natural action is that mode of action according to which something not formally identical with the act determines the action to occur in one way rather than another. Voluntary action is that mode of action in the same subject, directed toward an object, but self-determined to one object rather than another: *facultas ad multa*, viz., a free and therefore personal action; and, because free, a rational action, one at the root of rational order rather than merely logical (non-contradictory) intelligibility. The two modes are formally distinct, but, at the level of infinity, are really identical, precisely because the object of each is the same divine essence. The metaphysical necessity of the object, viz., that it is impossible for it not to be, does not alter the free mode of a voluntary action, as is the case in thomist theology. Thought, as an infinitely perfect mode of action, is a condition for voluntary or free action: namely that the being which is object of the will as good, be present to the will, but not the radical cause of the voluntary action of love.

The distinction *necessary-contingent* [30] refers not to the mode of action of the will, but to the metaphysical character of will's object as being. The necessary object of the will is the divine being qua goodness; and when it

---

[28] *Itinerarium*, c. 3, 4.

[29] *Rep. Par.* I, d. 10, q. 3; cf. Hoeres, *Der Wille…*, cit., pp. 75 ff. The background for this can easily be found in St. Bonaventure, *Quaestiones Disputatae de mysterio Ss. Trinitatis*, q. 7, a. 1 & 2.

[30] *Rep. Par.* I, d. 10, q. 2; q. 3; *Quaestiones Quodlibetales*, q. 16, n. 8 & 9. The scotistic analysis reflects exactly that of St. Bonaventure, *Questiones Disputatae de Mysterio Trinitatis*, q. 7, a. 1, where metaphysical necessity of divine being is really identical with absolute independence of divine being qua personal and free. Such necessity is carefully distinguished both from violence and from natural necessity or determination to one course of action via a power not formally intrinsic to that acting.

For private consultation and not distribution without the consent of E Ondrako

is present to a most perfect will, it is necessarily loved freely. Neither the metaphysical necessity of divine being as goodness itself, nor the infinite perfection of the divine will, changes the formal mode of action of the will from free to that natural determination from without—typical of the intellect. But precisely because the perfect will, as a *perfectio simpliciter simplex*, is really identical, like all the powers and attributes of the divine essence with that essence, the object of the divine will can never be, as it is for Kant and Hegel, the will itself, or the ego itself apart from the goodness of being, but only the divine goodness.[31] This is why the divine will is all-holy and the rational, not arbitrary norm for all ethical conduct of those creatures made in the image and likeness of God. The contingent object of the will is what God loves in loving himself. It only comes to be, because God, in loving himself, chooses also to love this rather than that creature.[32] The created will, however, while radically ordered to being qua being as good, in fact enjoys a limited power to act freely, one entailing multiple acts of love and, more importantly, the possibility of a voluntary action culpably divorced in fact from its essential condition: knowledge of the difference between good and evil. It may in fact choose to make the finite self and its pleasure the norm of voluntary action. This is another way of saying that the finite will, not fully sanctified, can and does sin.[33]

With this the *perfectio simpliciter simplex* and the *distinctio formalis a parte rei*, so crucial to Scotus's theology and metaphysics, become important for the analysis of the divine essence and of the human soul.[34] Pure perfections are those characteristic of spiritual being, and, of themselves, considered univocally, do not entail limitation; and hence, fully realized, are infinite and really identical, although still formally distinct or non-identical as perfections. By essence these perfections, e.g., intellect and will as modes of action of a spiritual subject, are only infinite, and so really identical, in God. They are so in a certain order: the intellect in the will. This is why the will enjoys a certain primacy: not because it can act absolutely apart from the truth about goodness, but because its mode

---

31 Cf. HOERES, *Der Wille*...cit. pp. 86–91. This capital point cannot be stressed enough. Scotus does not disjoin, as do modern philosophies, will and being, freedom and nature, the voluntary from the intellectual. Where he differs from Thomas is in assigning a primacy to being as good, rather than to being as true, to the voluntary rather than to the intellectual and natural in his analysis of being as all perfect, as infinite. The voluntarism and nominalism of Ockham is something as much a rupture with Scotus as with Thomas.

32 *Ordinatio* III, d. 28, q. un.; cf. HOERES, *Der Wille*..., cit., pp. 86 ff.

33 Cf. HOERES, *Der Wille*..., cit., pp. 122 ff. In recent literature on the ethics of Scotus and natural law, little consideration has been given to key points of Hoeres exposition on will and being and the relation of natural law to the person of Christ along the lines traced by St. Bonaventure.

34 Cf. HOERES, *Der Wille*..., cit., pp. 15–72.

For private consultation and not distribution without the consent of E Ondrako

of action is the key to that real identity found in the plenitude of being or divine infinity. In created persons this integration of formally distinct perfections is something not attainable by nature, but only by grace or the supernatural; but when attained it involves the same sanctity and impeccability as in God without loss of freedom as the essential characteristic of voluntary action. But the presence of such perfections in rational creatures provides the objective grounds *a parte rei* for their elevation to the order of grace and to sharing the circumincessory life of the divine Persons.

Scotus and Newman on the Definition of Free Will: Integration of Discretion and Choice

The teaching of Scotus here concerning the inherent rationality of the will qua *perfectio simpliciter simplex*, is substantially the same as that of St. Bonaventure when the latter states that free will is at once a power of reason and of will: *liberum arbitrium est facultas rationis et voluntatis qua bonum eligitur.*[35] Reason (intellect) and choice (will) are two formally distinct perfections of a single, simple nature, the soul. They are reducible to the substance of the soul, not a faculty in the Aristotelian sense of accident of the soul, really and not merely formally distinct from it. The more perfectly these two powers are integrated, yet remaining formally distinct in the unity of the substance, the more perfect the discretion of free will: *liberum arbitrium*, or, with Scotus, the rationality of the will and the goodness of its choice. We see here that when Scotus speaks of the rationality of the will, he does not intend a reason other than that found in the intellect, but that its perfection as reason is only attained to the degree it is integrated into the affective life of the will. Bonaventure makes it very clear in the course of his discussion of freedom in distinctions 24, 25 and 26 of *II Sent.*, that freedom as he defines it is not a third power over and above intellect and will, but rather the integration of intellect and will, reason and choice insofar as they are "reduced to the simple substance of the soul" and thus the immediate perfection of the person.

It is this point which establishes the great difference between the thomist analysis of the will as either appetite of the intellect in itself radically irrational and natural, and the scotist analysis of the will as a *perfectio simpliciter simplex* radically rational and voluntary. In the Franciscan context this approach is reflected in a tendency to view saving faith not simply as intellectual assent, nor simply as personal trust, but as the integration of the two, just as freedom at level of metaphysics is

---

[35] *II Sent.*, d. 25, p. 1, a. un., q. 3. The content of distinctions 24, 25, and 26 is most helpful in discovering the presuppositions of Scotus in Augustine and in the Franciscan school for his teaching on the will and its relation to being and to the other powers of a person.

For private consultation and not distribution without the consent of E Ondrako

the integration of discretion (rationality) and choice. Just as metaphysical necessity of the object loved by the will is, according to Bonaventure, no obstacle to that love being a free choice,[36] so the authority which motivates saving or infused faith is no obstacle to the free, personal choice involved in believing divine Revelation. For Bonaventure, as for Scotus after him, the metaphysical necessity of the perfect good loved by the perfect will is to be carefully distinguished from that necessity proper to a natural action of a creature as distinct from a voluntary one and still more from compulsion or violence.

For Scotus,[37] then, it is not the object of the intellect and above all of the will which distinguishes nature and grace as in thomist theology, but the relative perfection of the mode of thinking and loving the same divine goodness: not according to a love ever conditioned primarily by the *affectus commodi* or personal advantage, but by the mode whereby God loves his own goodness for its own sake and all else in loving that good. This is why, for Scotus, grace and charity are really identical and, why, in the final analysis, he insists on the primacy of charity and of the will over the intellect and the freedom of God *ad intra*. With St. Thomas the divine will is only free in regard to contingent being outside it, and the divine intellect enjoys a primacy over the will. In view of this we can appreciate why Scotus and, after him, Newman, among many others, insists on the need to sanctify the intellect and conscience. Thus Newman remarks:

> It is the mind that reasons, and controls its own reasonings, not any technical apparatus of words and propositions. This power of judging and concluding, when in its perfection, I call the Illative sense.[38]

Without a holy mind, that judgment, as a personal action and commitment, will ever be culpably skewed, not truly in accord with what it is in itself as a *perfectio simpliciter simplex*. The appearance of the terms "judging" and "perfection" in the same sentence provide an immediate link with both Bonaventure's theory of divine illumination and Scotus metaphysics based on univocity of being and the disjunctive transcendentals. Newman's *notional* apprehension set in this context suggests not

---

36 Cf. BONAVENTURE, *De Mysterio Ss. Trinitatis*, q. 7, a. 1.

37 SCOTUS, *Ordinatio*, prologus, p. 1, q. un.; p. 3, q. 3; *Ox.* IV, d. 10, q. 8; *Rep. Par.* IV, d. 10, q. 9. A very useful summary (with many texts) of Scotus's views on natural-supernatural can be found in JOSEF FINKENZELLER, *Offenbarung und Theologie nach der Lehre des Johannes Duns Skotus*, Münster 1960, pp. 19–25. Also helpful in grasping the position of Scotus on this point and its relation to his teaching on the will and merit is W. DETTLOFF, *Die Lehre von der Acceptatio Divina bei Johannes Duns Scotus mit besonderer Berücksictigung der Rechtfertigungslehre*, (Werl 1954).

38 *Grammar of Assent*, ch. 9, p. 348.

For private consultation and not distribution without the consent of E Ondrako

Ockham's nominalism, but the realism of Scotus's formalities *a parte rei*. Further, the term "mind" used in Bonaventure's sense of "mind" in the *Itinerarium*, indicates a common premise with the metaphysics of person cultivated in the Franciscan school. Thus, unity of knowledge so central to Newman's pedagogical theory rests on univocity of being, linking the reality of creation to the Primacy of the Creator through the primacy of the Incarnation. We can also appreciate, consequent on this, why what Newman calls liberal knowledge, with theology and metaphysics at its center, is so important a consideration in assessing parallel thought patterns in Scotus and Newman. With this in mind we can go on to examine what is meant by interiorizing in Bonaventure and Newman, so much praised by Pope Benedict XVI.

Interiorizing and Anthropological Theology: Natural Faith in Newman[39]

Interiorizing is precisely how the created person is brought to face this choice: either to be intellectually humble, to sanctify one's intellect, or to be proud, self-centered, ultimately enclosed within oneself in the darkness of doubt. It is another way of speaking about and stressing the importance of the subjective or personal in knowing vis-à-vis the objective, what Newman calls the predicate of any proposition. Without this personal dimension, knowledge, in the sense of a pure perfection, is not possible. In addition to the complexity of discursive knowledge in the human subject: concepts, propositions, arguments, there is also a simple, unconditional element encased in these acts, characteristic of what Scotus calls a pure perfection and explaining what Bonaventure means when he says that the image of God, unlike the vestige, is not *prope nihil*, but *prope Deum*.[40] For a creature "near God" is precisely such because it possesses a pure perfection formally *a parte rei* in the Creator and in the rational creature. But in God that perfection is infinitely and simply without the complexity which in the rational creature accounts not only for limitations on what in itself has no limitations, but accounts for the possibility of sin, of a deliberate deviation from the natural thrust of the will as such to love

---

[39] As will be noted later in discussing passages from the *Idea of a University* and *Grammar of Assent*, Newman's use of the term "natural" to qualify theology as anthropological does not anticipate Rahner and transcendental thomism, but rather the usage of Rosmini reflecting the influence of Bonaventure and Scotus, where man, as image of God rather than as a vestige of God, is the starting point for a demonstration of God's existence. But image of God in this approach is understood at the metaphysical level, not psychological, as in various versions of transcendentalism. The validity of this distinction of levels is defended precisely on the basis of the rational creature possessing a *perfectio simpliciter simplex* in the scotist sense.

[40] *Breviloquium*, p. 2, ch. 6, 3.

For private consultation and not distribution without the consent of E Ondrako

justice as such (*affectus justitiae*) in order to prefer advantage to self (*affectus commodi*). Bonaventure and Newman both relate this pure perfection in a created spirit to a *personal* judgment: *dijudicatio* for Bonaventure,[41] assent for Newman.[42] Without this judgment or critique (in Greek) of mental objectification or formation of a mental word, without this unconditional assent as a personal act distinct from inference, it is impossible to show how human knowing is anything but a more sophisticated process not essentially or radically different from that of the brute at the level of sensation. All this accords well with what Bonaventure says concerning the relative metaphysical necessity characteristic of a created person, an independence *secundum quid*.[43]

On the one hand, <u>human thought is not possible</u> *pro statu isto* <u>without sensation and abstraction</u> (apprehension: real and notional) <u>and without inference</u> (science); on the other hand, thought is not thought unless it is simple and personal and certain (not subject to change or variation). The preface to the 1871 edition of Newman's *Oxford University Sermons* read in this context suggests many points of contact with the epistemology of St. Bonaventure and Scotus, not least the convergence of faith and reason on the personal character of assent as homage to the authority of the Truth of truths and recognition of the Light of lights. Infused faith and natural reason are certainly distinct for Newman in the traditional Catholic sense; yet both have this in common that they presuppose a personal assent whose core is not searching for, but finding *Reality* definitively. That finding in the form of assent, whether natural or supernatural, may be described as "faith."[44] In both cases it involves a "convergence of probabilities" and exercise of the "illative sense," or what Bonaventure calls[45] the *naturale judicatorium*: a kind of trust or faith in the light of reason. This light is a sharing in the divine Light enlightening the created mind so as to perceive the truth of things reflecting the divine creative art (exemplarism). This illumination and this exemplarity are prior to and presupposed by inspired, supernatural faith whose motive is the personal authority of God revealing as such. On this basis Bonaventure explains the unity and distinction of reason and supernatural faith. At the heart of this natural assent is a natural "faith," a profound reverence for and docility to the Truth, without

---

41 *Itinerarium*, ch. 2, nn. 6. 9.

42 *Grammar of Assent*, passim; *Oxford University Sermons*, (London 1871), preface, 12: "Faith is properly assent, and an assent without doubt, or a certitude."; 14, 34.

43 Cf. *de Mysterio Trinitatis*, q. 7, a. 1.

44 Cf. *Grammar*, part 1, ch. 5, where Newman discusses this point in more detail; for Scotus cf. L. Walter, *Das Glaubensverständnis bei Johannes Duns Scotus*, Paderborn 1968.

45 St. Bonaventure, II *Sent.*, d. 24, p. 1, a. 2, q. 4.

For private consultation and not distribution without the consent of E Ondrako

which the intellect is culpably abused. This natural faith is the point where intellect and will are integrated in the unity of the soul's life. Without such integration the life of the soul remains "disunited," locked within itself, a prey to the doubt and despair of "absolute autonomy," what Pope Benedict XVI calls the "dictatorship of relativism"[46] consequent on the failure to resolve the "critical question" in a humble acceptance of the voice of God in conscience rather than a silencing of that voice.[47]

Here are some pertinent passages from the preface to the *Oxford University Sermons* illustrating this point:

> Faith is properly assent, and an assent without doubt, or a certitude. "Faith is an acceptance of things as real." [xi: 9] "Faith simply accepts testimony." [x: 8] "Faith is not identical with its grounds and its object." [xiii: 4] "Faith starts with probabilities, yet it ends in peremptory statements; it believes an informant amid doubt, yet accepts his information without doubt." [xiv: 34][48]

Clearly, for Newman, the possibility of supernatural faith presupposes the method of verisimilitude or convergence of probabilities on a personal act of assent in the natural order:

> Since, in accepting a conclusion there is a virtual recognition of its premises, an act of Faith may be said (improperly) to include in it the reasoning process which is its antecedent, and to be in a certain aspect an exercise of Reason; and thus is coordinate, and in contrast, with the three (improper) senses of the word "Reason"

---

46 BENEDICT XVI, *Homily for the election of the Roman Pontiff*, 8 April, 2005.

47 A longer exposition of St. Bonaventure's views would take us far beyond the limits of this conference. Underlying his approach to faith and reason is a presupposition concerning the presence both of interior light and external authority in every act of knowing and understanding. This unity of objective and subjective in terms of authority and interior illumination centering on being, is explained in his *Quaestiones Disputatae de scientia Christi*, q. 4, his fullest exposition of the theory of divine illumination in relation to the human knowledge of Jesus, and the beatific and infused knowledge which it entails. Recognition of the objective or authoritative factor may be described as a personal submission to authority at the natural level, for short "natural faith" or reason as Newman describes this in discussing the authority of conscience. At a higher level of supernatural Revelation this faith is precisely a recognition of personal authority rather than of merely natural objectivity, and, hence, faith in a more perfect sense. Short of the beatific vision, infused contemplation is the most perfect exercise both of interior assent and personal homage to divine authority or Light. These observations are clearly evident in Bonaventure's short sermon or essay entitled *Christus unus omnium Magister*, where he discusses symbolic, proper and contemplative theology, and in his *de Mysterio Ss. Trinitatis*, q. 1, where he clearly supposes that both the unity and triune character of the one God are mysteries partly involving the use of reason or natural faith and infused faith in supernatural Revelation. Scotus's distinction between and explanation of natural and infused faith presupposes the position of Bonaventure.

48 *Oxford University Sermons*, preface 12.

For private consultation and not distribution without the consent of E Ondrako

above enumerated, viz., explicit, evidential, and secular Reason. [cf. xi: 8, 9] Faith, viewed in contrast with Reason in these three senses, is implicit in its acts, adopts the method of verisimilitudes, and starts from religious first principles.[49]

Newman concludes: "Faith [is] kept from abuse: by holiness and use of reason."[50] This is true, whether the faith is that of natural assent or of the supernatural, infused gift. Faith, as Newman uses it in the *Oxford University Sermons*, denotes not only that supernatural gift of infused faith without which salvation is not possible, but that aspect of assent which represents the simple, personal dimension of knowledge: humble docility, fidelity, love of the authority of truth without which certain understanding is never reached. Natural faith provides what reason cannot: engagement with and acceptance of reality as such. For the truth of being is beyond reason's ability to prove, to verify or negate by way of mental activity or argumentation. In more personal terms faith is the encounter of two luminous beings: one created and docile to the Truth, the other Truth itself. In the natural order this engagement consists in receptivity, admiration and adoration of the Truth that is not oneself by the proper use of one's faculties; in the supernatural order this engagement effected by infused faith consists in an encounter with Christ and a humble submission to His word or teaching.[51] That this is the correct interpretation of Newman is confirmed by the following passages from sermon two of the *Oxford University Sermons* dealing with natural and revealed religion, specifically the role of conscience and the knowledge of God in natural religion.

> And thus the presentiment of a future life, and of a judgment to be passed on present conduct, with rewards and punishments annexed, forms an article, more or less distinct, in the creed of natural religion. Moreover, since the inward law of Conscience brings with it no proof of its truth, and commands attention to it on its own authority, all obedience to it is of the nature of Faith, and habitual obedience implies the direct exercise of a clear and vigorous faith in the truth of its suggestions, triumphing over opposition both from within and without; quieting the murmurs

---

[49] *OUS*, 13–14.

[50] *OUS*, 15. On this and other points concerning faith cf. similar remarks of Pope Benedict XVI in: *Introduction to Christianity* (San Francisco 1990) 24–25; 39–48; 57; *Mary: the Church at its Source* (San Francisco 1995) 49.

[51] The views of Newman are clearly reflected in many passages from the writings of Pope Benedict XVI: cf. D. LEMIEUX, *She is Our Response. The Virgin Mary and the Church's Encounter with Modernity in the Mariology of Joseph Ratzinger*, New Bedford MA, 2011, in particular where he deals extensively with faith, conscience and moral law: in part 1, chaps. 2 and 3, and throughout part 2.

For private consultation and not distribution without the consent of E Ondrako

of Reason, perplexed with the disorder of the present scheme of things, and subduing the appetites, clamorous for good which promises an immediate and keen satisfaction.... While conscience is thus ever the sanction of Natural Religion, it is, when improved, the rule of morals also. But here is a difference: it is, as such, essentially religious; but in morals it is not necessarily a guide, only in proportion as it happens to be refined and strengthened in individuals... Natural Religion teaches, it is true, the infinite power and majesty, the wisdom and goodness, the presence, the moral governance, and in one sense, the unity of the Deity; but it gives little or no information respecting what may be called His Personality...[52]

His thought is still more clearly expressed in the *Grammar of Assent*:

Accordingly, instead of saying that the truths of Revelation depend on those of Natural Religion, it is more pertinent to say that belief in revealed truths depends on belief in natural. Belief is a state of mind; belief generates belief; states of mind correspond to each other; the habits of thought and the reasonings which lead us on to a higher state of belief than our present, are the very same we already possess in connection with the lower state.[53]

Natural and Supernatural: Scotus and Newman Correlated

This analysis of faith, natural and supernatural, reflects, in fact, that of Scotus and no doubt accounts, in part, for many other similarities between Scotus and Newman to be noted in the course of this conference, not least the relation between natural and supernatural based on the absolute primacy of Christ and univocity of being, together with being qua being and not simply the being of material things as object of the intellect.[54]

St. Thomas and his disciples, however, distinguish the natural and supernatural primarily in terms of different formal objects of the intellect.[55] From their standpoint the natural order is a closed circle, complete in itself with its own natural end. The order of grace before the fall of Adam was simply a superstructure resting upon it, making possible a higher end for angels and men, but in no way initially related to the merits of the Incarnate Word. The initial grace of Adam was the grace of God,

---

52 "The Influence of Natural and Revealed Religion Respectively," Sermon 2 in *Oxford University Sermons*, 8.9.10.14.

53 *Grammar of Assent*, part 2, ch. 10, pp. 413–414.

54 Cf. Walter, *Das Glaubenverständnis...*, cit.

55 St. Thomas, *Summa Theologica* I, q. 12, a. 4.

For private consultation and not distribution without the consent of E Ondrako

not of Christ. The latter only enters the picture after the fall of our first parents. The analogical concept of being and indeed the psychology of the soul based on the primacy of the intellect very much facilitates such an explanation of the purpose of the Incarnation and of revealed theology as a science in the Aristotelian sense subordinated to the knowledge of God.

Bl. John Duns Scotus proposes[56] a very different approach to the distinction of natural and supernatural. Scotus holds that objects of intellect and will are related to these powers in only three possible ways: as connatural or proper objects of these powers; or as objects doing violence to these powers, or as "neutral": viz., irrelevant to them. A supernatural object of these faculties would fall into the last category of irrelevant. Grace is distinguished from nature in the spiritual order precisely as that by which the inability of the created spirit to attain the full range of intellect and will, on the basis of its natural powers, is surpassed with the support of supernatural grace. Like the univocal concept of being and its application to pure perfections, this approach to the supernatural reflects the implications of the Incarnation as such as the de facto reason for creation and then redemption. Hence, it stresses the degrees of grace conceded to the creature so as to be able to fully participate in the glory of the Incarnate Word qua Incarnate. In the present order of creation, all grace, and not merely that after the fall of Adam, is the grace of Christ; for, in fact, the natural or created order was only brought into existence for the higher order of grace centering on the Incarnation and divine Maternity. The Creator might have created the universe without in fact willing the Incarnation; but the objective intelligibility of a created order does reflect the prior possibility of an Incarnation.

In such a perspective, shared by Newman,[57] one postulating a certain unity of knowledge and of love as the condition for revelation and elevation to the supernatural order in order to love God and neighbor as Christ loves His Father and us, it is only connatural that the formal, adequate object of the *human* intellect be *ens qua ens* and not merely the being of material creatures, and that this object be discerned intellectually via the univocal concept of being with the disjunctive transcendental. So, too, it is only connatural that the formal object of the human will be not some end perfective of human nature, but, rather, the love of goodness or justice simply for its own sake. But the noblest object of both intellect and will as such is God. For this reason it is also only to be expected that the psychology of Scotus should differ from that of Thomas and that the thomist and scotist approaches to the critical question should also differ.

---

56 Scotus, *Ordinatio*, Prologus, p. 1, q. un.

57 Cf. *Idea of a University*, part 1, discourse 3, 4; part 1, discourse 5, 1.

For private consultation and not distribution without the consent of E Ondrako

As we shall see, this difference is crucial in explaining the relation of natural and infused faith not only in Scotus, but also in Newman. Failure to recognize this leads to accusations against both: either fideists or Pelagians. Both from the standpoint of the Savior and from that of the believer who is saved, it is a personal or voluntary action which primarily differentiates the order of nature and of grace. This is why for both Scotus and Newman psychology confirms what theology and metaphysics teach: the primacy of the will and charity. That personal action of the person saved by grace has its immediate support in the psychological order in what both Scotus and Newman tend to call natural faith: openness to contemplation of the Truth which is Christ foreshadowed in the univocal notion of being, and obedience to the authority of conscience which is the authority of God. This stress on the primacy of contemplation of the Truth, the heart of metaphyics, rather than on the construction of scientific hypotheses (called "mental fictions" by St. Bonaventure), is what radically differentiates the epistemology of Scotus and Newman from that of Kant and modern transcendental philosophy.[58]

Here is how Fr. Devlin, a very perceptive student of Hopkins, describes the psychology of Scotus who so much influenced Hopkins:

> I would compare the mind, as St. Thomas represents it, to a limpid and motionless pool in which both the nature of the surrounding objects and movements of the heavens can be clearly discerned; everything is reflected in a two-dimensional surface, and yet there is no mistaking the differences of depth and distance, there is no confusion between earth and heaven. One might add that the quiet pool of Aquinas has replaced the rushing torrent of St. Augustine, who indicated and emphasized but at the same time obscured what he had represented by attempting to reach and touch it—on the principle of the Psalmist, *mirabilis elationes maris*.... Scotus arrives later on the scene, accepts the pool and all it represents with an impatient gesture, but implies that it is not sufficient.... He complains that the pool fails to represent two things of vital importance without which it could not long exist. These two things are the secret entrance and secret exit by which there is a continual influx and a continual drawing-off of the water, without which it could not long remain fresh and sweet and limpid. Thus, while accepting the principle of the pool, he reintroduces the principle of the river. But of course he disturbs the surface of the pool...

---

58 Cf. HOERES, *Kritik...*, cit., pp. 62 ff.

For private consultation and not distribution without the consent of E Ondrako

The pool is the rational mind, and Scotus complains that if it is regarded as a closed circle, sufficient unto itself, it does not adequately represent the human soul. The human soul is not co-extensive with reason and understanding as a distinct faculty; it is a mistake to regard the other powers of the soul simply as functions or adjuncts to understanding. There is a power of the soul which is below understanding but which has better evidence of the soul's origin; and there is a power of the soul which is above understanding and which is more in touch with the soul's destiny. The secret entrance to the pool is the point where the unconscious begins to influence the conscious mind. The secret exit is the point where the soul finds that its intellectual powers extended to their fullest have still failed to satisfy it, and that it must bring a higher faculty into play. In this way he returns to, and hopes to reinstate, St. Augustine's hierarchy of memory, understanding and will. He sees these powers as the one soul operating on different levels of consciousness.[59]

Natural faith, then, accounts for the real difference between assent and inference or reasoning [Newman]. It accounts for the difference between the relatively simple and complex in a finite "pure perfection" [Scotus], and between the fontal and motive objects of the human intellect [Bonaventure]. Natural faith, while truly an act of the will or obedience, is not fideistic, since supported by evidence; yet, not dependent on it, the leap of faith in the use of the illative sense is perfectly rational and the crown of rationality. Infused faith, a leap from assent supported by evidence, to assent without that support, therefore a living "by faith alone," accounts for the real difference between ordinary knowledge centered about an assent (natural faith) to the real within our power and salutary or saving knowledge whereby we take Christ as our Savior, not either on the basis of evidence we can examine nor in accord with experience we have had, but solely on the Authority of God as exercised by his ministers. Without the gift of the Spirit, no one can exercise this kind of faith in the mercy of Jesus as Savior. All this can be summarized thus: the learner is not merely a logician, but also a person; and it is as a person that he controls, as Newman says,[60] the entire activity of the intellect: the notional and real, assent and inference, informal and formal reasoning. Where that control reflects fidelity to the truth—there, certainty is attained; where the

---

59 C. Devlin, *The Psychology of Duns Scotus*, Oxford 1950, pp. 3–4.

60 *Grammar of Assent*, part 2, ch. 9, p. 348.

For private consultation and not distribution without the consent of E Ondrako

contrary is the case, agnosticism is the only alternative.[61] For Newman the most striking example of natural faith is that linked with obedience to conscience.

Those who maintain that the subject of knowledge as distinct from its object cannot be divorced from the subjective or personal activity of the knower (and Kant was by no means the first to perceive this point: Bonaventure long before him saw this clearly), logically admit the existence of a critical question in some form. Such a question arises out of the need to explain why or how a personal act is an indispensable element of knowing, yet, as an act of the will it neither compromises the reliable extra-mental in any way: objective-rational-certain character of this judgment nor the logical, scientific worth of the [necessary] process involved in attaining it.

Resolution of this question for Scotus and for Newman involves a constant effort to integrate rather than separate, not only the simple and complex in the activity of the finite intellect, but also an integrated psychology as well as metaphysics of the human mind. The intellect, the highest form of natural action in the language of the Franciscan school, cannot be explained in isolation from the will and voluntary actions, just as, vice-versa, the voluntary cannot be explained independently of the intellectual. Not only in Bonaventure, e.g., in the *Itinerarium*,[62] does this activity of the created mind originate in the memory, pass through the intellect and culminate in the will, but also, with refinements, we note the same pattern in Scotus.[63] For the Franciscan masters, the powers of the one soul are not rooted in two *really* distinct faculties as in Aristotle. They are rather *formally* distinct *a parte rei*, yet really identical in being rooted in the same soul. For St. Bonaventure (and implicitly for his disciples), this constitutes an objective, formal reflection of the mystery of the Trinity, even at the natural level.[64] Once this is grasped, one can easily see how the *memory* in Bonaventure, place of contact between the *motive* object [the finite object, occasion and cause of conscious activity of the intellect] and *fontal* object [the light by which one comes to understand and "speak" an interior word] of the *intellect*; and in Scotus, locus of *intuitive* cognition and origin of *abstractive* cognition in the intellect [alone in the finite intellect making possible understanding] guarantees a neat balance between mental activity and extra-mental influence of the real or being on thought, thus supplying

---

61 For a longer exposition of this point, cf. P. Fehlner, *Mary and Theology. Scotus Revisited*, (Rensselaer, NY: 1978), pp. 8–10. Cf. reprint in ch. 4 of this volume.

62 *Itinerarium*, ch. 3.

63 *Ordinatio* I, d. 2, p 2, q. 4.

64 T. Szabó, *De SS. Trinitate in creaturis refulgente*, Rome 1955; O. González, *Misterio trinitataria y existencia humana*, Madrid 1966, in particular part 2, section 1.

For private consultation and not distribution without the consent of E Ondrako

the foundation for the integration of the personal-voluntary activity and necessary-certain character of genuine thought.[65]

Careful study of the texts from the *Grammar of Assent* adduced in part 3 of this conference will reveal a similar context for the discussion of notional and real apprehension-assent precisely in relation to the mystery of the One and Triune God. Accusations that Newman is a nominalist for the most part fail to take account of the fact that the notional and real, like the intuitive and abstractive can de facto be treated independently of one another, as was commonly the case with a large majority in the days of Newman. But what Newman, in effect, sets out to show is that they ought to be integrated, and can be integrated on what turns out to be a basis very similar to that of Scotus. This makes it possible to differentiate assent from inference, the natural logic of contemplative wisdom from the formal logic of complex science, and so integrate infused faith within the natural context God designed for it, particularly conscience.

A full presentation of this theme would take us far beyond the limits of this conference. Here I wish only to make two points. First, the critical question is a valid one; failure to acknowledge this, as Bonaventure pointed out centuries ago,[66] leaves us unable to account for the most basic requirement of intellectual knowing in the creature: its absolute or certain character and its "fidelity" or personal character. Rejection of special divine illumination over and above the general concursus with all creatures leaves only a choice between Kantian agnosticism and voluntarism [ethical or practical reason] or Averroistic determinism [one intellect], neither of which accords with Christian philosophy. Though Scotus changes the formulation, he makes the same essential point in differentiating the rational creature from the vestige in terms of a pure perfection [*perfectio simpliciter simplex*], rather than in terms of a theory of act, and, potentiality, a position which like that of Bonaventure, postulates a personal element in the cognitive activity.

Second, recognition of this personal element raises a question concerning the objective or rational character of thought, and why some aspect of faith or fidelity is associated with assent or *dijudicatio*, in the sense that Newman describes natural faith as acceptance of reality,[67] particularly in the case of assenting to the authority of conscience: known, yet not capable of proof.[68] In discussing the illative sense as a translation

---

[65] Cf. C. DEVLIN, The *Psychology of Duns Scotus*, (Oxford 1950), for a very insightful presentation of just this point.

[66] *Quaestiones Disputatae de scientia Christi*, q. 4.

[67] *Oxford University Sermons*, sermon 11, 9.

[68] "The Influence of Natural and Revealed Religion Respectively," cit., 9.

For private consultation and not distribution without the consent of E Ondrako

of what Aristotle means by *phronesis*, Newman uses exactly this term of Bonaventure: judgment.[69] This is exactly what Bonaventure means in recognizing divine illumination of the intellect in the natural order; not intellectual fideism, yet not intellectual autonomy either. This said, it also becomes apparent how <u>divine faith, though supernatural, is not irrational,</u> and on what grounds rests the unity of knowledge as wisdom, so dear to Bonaventure, Scotus and Newman.

Integration of Knowledge and Love or Wisdom: scientia in quantum transit in affectum[70]

To questions arising out of the need to integrate knowledge and love, two basic approaches to a resolution, mutually contrary, are offered. One is secular (that of Kant which presumes the process of knowing is not essentially different from any other physical process, ultimately a mere instrument of an absolute will divorced from truth). The other conceives the intellect as radically orientated to sacred knowledge of God. It may be observed in those versions of a Christian philosophy, such as the Franciscan, where knowledge is not a physical process structured in terms of act and potency, but primarily person-orientated as indispensable disposition to the act of loving the good for its own sake, rather than for advantage; and, so, a radically simple and divine-like judgment or critical act guiding a critical choice.

The answer, then, to the question just posed, for better or worse, radically depends on how the will is defined in relation to the intellect and vice versa. For our purposes there are three major approaches. The first is associated with the names of St. Thomas and Aristotle: <u>the will is an intellectual appetite,</u> the necessary desire to know the truth, <u>free,</u> therefore, not in itself, but <u>only in regard to those goods which are contingent</u>. A second approach, associated with the names of Ockham, Hume and Kant, defines the <u>will as absolutely free to do whatever it pleases,</u> radically indifferent to any prior intellectual assessment of good and evil and above any such determination if it pleases. Curiously, both these approaches, despite their differences or perhaps because of them, identify rationality or reason primarily with the intellect; the first, in order to exalt the primacy of the intellect over the will; the second, to exalt the radically arbitrary character of voluntary action in order to be essentially free.

Scotus disagrees with both approaches because, above all, he situates rationality, though entailing intellectual activity, primarily in the will as a

---

[69] *Grammar of Assent*, p. 2, ch. 9, pp. 353 ff.

[70] Cf. Bonaventure, *Collationes in Hexaemeron*, c. 5, 12–13.

For private consultation and not distribution without the consent of E Ondrako

perfectio simpliciter simplex.[71] He does this for the same reason Bonaventure does: because a rational act is primarily an act of discernment, one making possible a personal, voluntary act which is ordered. Thought otherwise ceases to be personal, a kind of personal responsibility for the honor of Truth; and, hence, reason is not simply to be reduced to logic, specifically to the third act of the mind, divorced of its essential personal character. This is exactly what underlies Newman's "illative sense" and the distinction of assent from inference. Hence, though not wanting in logic, reasoning also transcends logic as a personal action, and a personal action is the very heart of perfect *being*, a truth reflected in the definition of person preferred by Scotus: *existentia incommunicabilis naturae intellectualis.*[72] For Scotus, the intellect as a natural rather than voluntary power is not distinguished from the will in terms of an object, but in terms of a mode of action concerning the same object: being. The formal character of intellect as a natural power is to be determined by that object as truth, whereas the formal character of the will is to determine itself in relation to the same object as good. By itself the intellect could not be discerning or critical; by itself the will would be merely arbitrary. In fact, though *formally* distinct according to a certain order of priority in the will because such priority fully expresses the divine aseity, they are *really* identical at the level of divine infinity, an identity only imperfectly realized by a rational creature apart from the order of grace, none the less present in some way. The indispensable condition for orderly or rational willing, intelligibility or objectivity, is always present to the divine will; hence, the divine will cannot sin, and always discerns in a most orderly fashion.[73] And the indispensable condition for reasonableness in the divine intelligence, perfect freedom to discern or judge, perfect liberality or generosity,[74] is always present to the divine intellect. The divine Persons never abuse the intellect, as do finite persons, because there can be in God no "love of advantage" or selfishness. This is exactly the position of Newman in the *Grammar of Assent.*[75] We do not trust our cognitive faculties; we only use them properly. The critical question, then, is not an intellectual one in the first instance, but metaphysical-moral, because correct use is primarily a question of personal discernment.[76] That this is the view of Scotus is

---

[71] Cf. HOERES, *Der Wille…*, cit., pp. 86 ff.; FRANK, Preface…, cit., pp. ix–xi.

[72] Cf. H. MÜHLEN, *Sein und Person nach Johannes Duns Scotus*, (Werl 1954).

[73] *Ordinatio* III, suppl. d. 32.

[74] Cf. BONAVENTURE, *De Mysterio Ss. Trinitatis*, q. 7, a. 2.

[75] Cf. NEWMAN, *Grammar of Assent*, p. 1, ch. 1, pp. 5 ff.; ch. 6, p. 188.

[76] Cf. A.B. WOLTER, *Duns Scotus on the Will and Morality*, translation edition by W.A. Frank. (Washington, D.C.: CUA Press, 1997), *Preface*, cit., pp. ix–xvi. This is perhaps one of the best assessments of Scotus on freedom and how the scotist position relates to questions of

For private consultation and not distribution without the consent of E Ondrako

clear when he says that we cannot understand the will by comparing it to a natural action, any more than we can understand a person by comparing him to a non-personal entity, because the mode of action of the will and mode of being of the person are *sui generis*.[77]

A third approach, then, associated with the names of St. Bonaventure, Duns Scotus and, in my opinion, with that of Newman as well,[78] considers the appetitive and indifferent features of the voluntary act as characteristic of the finite will qua elective, and not of the will as such, or as pure perfection in the finite will, seen in the natural tendency of the will to goodness as such, but not perfectly attainable via the formal act of the will.[79] In this view the voluntary act is defined as the power to initiate an action rather than as a power (natural) to be initiated from without itself. Will power is essentially free, whether the act is necessary (as in God) or contingent (as in the creature). It is essentially free because as a pure perfection it is first of all the *affectus justitiae*, or power to love the good for its own sake, or rationally, and not as an advantage to the lover: the *affectus commodi* or appetitive power—in the finite will, one opening on the possibility of doing solely what the lover pleases apart from whether it is good in itself rather than good for me.[80] Conversely, the Franciscan school has always seen what seems to be an unsolvable problem in the thomist position: where the will is not permitted to be indifferent to some good or evil by the intellect, it appears to be moved by an agency outside itself. This is not a voluntary, but a merely natural or physical action. Where the will in thomist theory is left indifferent toward some contingent good by the intellect, there it appears to act merely in an arbitrary fashion, i.e., voluntaristically, irrationally, without order. Or by contrast, the appetite: *affectus commodi*, without subordination to a will defined by the *affectus justitiae*, essentially free, does not rise above the level of instinct.

St. Bernard writes[81] that the only reason for loving where love is perfect, where love in Scotus's terms is an exercise of the *affectus justitiae*, is love itself: a voluntary act essentially free. It is goodness in itself, not good as the pleasure of a lover, which attracts, but does not determine the will to act. For that is the very nature of an act of love, to be self-determining

---

cosmology and ethics. Frank shows clearly how Scotus, though evidently not in agreement with the essentialism of the Aristotelian position, is not the progenitor of the nominalist-voluntarist anarchical point of view so widespread today, particularly in its Kantian form.

[77] *Quaestiones super libros metaphysicorum Aristotelis*, IX, q. 15, 3.

[78] *Oxford University Sermons*, sermon 4, 4, p. 57, where love in us of "justice and purity" corresponds to the *affectus justitiae*, and love of "benevolence" to the affectus commodi in Scotus.

[79] Cf. Hoeres, *Der Wille…*, cit., pp. 113 ff.

[80] *Ordinatio* II, d. 6, q. 2, 49; cf. Hoeres, Der Wille…, cit, pp. 149 ff.

[81] St. Bernard, Sermo 83, 4–6, in *Opera Omnia*, Editio Cisterciensis, vol. 2 [1958], pp. 300–302.

For private consultation and not distribution without the consent of E Ondrako

rather than determined by something not itself. In God freedom is perfect and so coincides, as Bonaventure teaches,[82] with metaphysical necessity or personal independence. Where that is so as in God, the will is ever ordered, therefore rational, therefore never without relation to the truth about being as good presented by the intellect, never acting arbitrarily and making its pleasure the norm of virtue. This is because the divine intellect and the divine will are really one, even if they are formally distinct *a parte rei*. The finite will is only potentially ordered at the formal level of choice and must become such by an integration of the truth into itself via sanctification. The disordered, arbitrary, irrational will is but another name for the autonomous proud will of the creature; whereas the ordered, rational, divine will is but a way of speaking of the kindly will, ever generous, ever just, ever virtuous, never self-seeking.[83]

It is a grievous misrepresentation of Scotus to describe his definition of the will qua essentially free to be the equivalent of divorcing the will as such from the guidance of truth as known. Scotus is simply polishing the position of Bonaventure who maintains that perfect necessity of being in God: independent existence, *aseitas*, personal being, and the essentially free character of the perfect will are identical in God. "Non omnis necessitas competit divino esse nec etiam Trinitati beatae, sed immutabilitatis et independentiae."[84] By necessity of immutability and independence, he means "personal independence" or "incommunicable existence," the apex of aseity, not "natural necessity" so typical of *natural* action when contrasted with the *voluntary*. Such personal, independent existence: *simpliciter* in God or *secundum quid* in creatures, Scotus defines as *existentia incommunicabilis naturae intellectualis*. In Newman the same concepts occur in an analysis of causality as voluntary and physical: the first in intellectual agents endowed with personal freedom; the second in non-personal agents, with the second dependent on the operation of the first—above all, the Creator.

This independence as the formal perfection of the will is really identical with the essential immutability and necessity of divine being. This is the nature of the will as a pure perfection formally distinct *a parte rei* from the intellect, but in God really identical, impossible to separate. It is this real, but not formal identity of intellect and will where both pure perfections

---

82 *De mysterio Ss. Trinitatis*, q. 7, a. 1 & 2.

83 On the teaching of Scotus cf. HOERES, *Der Wille* …, cit., p. 75 ff.; B. IPPOLITO, "The Anthropological Foundations of Duns Scotus' Mariology," in *Bl. John Duns Scotus and His Mariology*, New Bedford MA 2009, pp. 157–172. On the will and the possibility of finite being according to Scotus cf. H.-J. WERNER, *Die Ermöglichung des endlichen Seins nach Johannes Duns Scotus*, (Bern: 1974).

84 *Quaestiones disputatae de mysterio Ss. Trinitatis*, q 7, a. 1 & 2.

For private consultation and not distribution without the consent of E Ondrako

are infinitely such, which explains why the voluntary act as free does not admit of sin, viz., of doing as one pleases independently of goodness or justice as the object of that act: being as truly good made present to the will by the intellect. Both the object of the will: goodness as such, and its radically free character: together and not apart, account for the voluntary act as distinct from the natural act of understanding.[85] The divine will, then, is impeccable by nature, unable to be attracted except by what is goodness itself because, by nature, is an *affectio justitiae*, not an appetitive power.

As attracted freely, the act of love may be defined as a *dilectio boni* or "acceptance" or "choice" of the good, because this is the nature of a voluntary rather than natural act. Thus, the well-known axiom describing freedom as "the acceptance or preference of one good rather than another": *acceptatio unius boni prae alio*,[86] set in the context of the will as a pure perfection, means first of all, for the created person as well as for God, the absolute acceptance of divine goodness before all other goods and their relative ordering in reference to that absolute. This is the *affectus justitiae* which in man defines the natural tendency of the will as a pure perfection to goodness. Behind the phrase coined by Scotus: *affectus justitiae*, stands a mysterious reality: the real identity of charity and justice (or rightness), though remaining formally distinct. Apart from grace, however, that thrust cannot be fully realized by choice or self-determination: the formal act of the created will as voluntary, because this act is limited or qualified in each act of choosing by the *affectus commodi*, a need to perfect oneself. In one who is not impeccable as is God, justice can be exercised uncharitably, and charity unjustly.

If we consider the mode of action of the will: voluntary or free rather than natural, self-determining rather than determined to an object from without, then we shall describe interior freedom as a kind of indetermination, a power or faculty to determine oneself to do many different things rather than be determined by nature to one or more things: "facultas ad plura, etiam opposita." If we consider the object of the will as a good which attracts, then we shall describe the will as a kind of acceptance or preference for that which is more attractive. If we consider each in isolation from the other, then we shall either define the will in itself as radically

---

85 Cf. Scotus, *Lectura Oxoniensis* II, d. 25, q. un, n. 69–70 (Editio Vaticana, vol. 19, 253–255).

86 Cf. St. Bonaventure, *De Mysterio Ss. Trinitatis*, q. 7, a. 2: "Est tertio voluntas concomitans et acceptans; et haec est in Deo respectu sui et respectu creati; approbat enim et acceptat voluntas divina omne bonum, sive creatum sive increatum, sive contingens sive necessarium." The association of "approval" with "acceptance" is precisely what is meant by the intrinsic "rationality" or "reasonableness" of the perfect, divine will, precisely because the divine intellect is really identical with that will.

For private consultation and not distribution without the consent of E Ondrako

arbitrary rather than rational, or as moved by goodness from without by a necessity of nature rather than independence. But if we follow the key insight of bothBonaventure and Scotus concerning the relation of intellect and will within perfect personal-divine being, we shall speak of approval and acceptance of the good by the will, acting freely, yet necessarily. With that we shall grasp why the will for Scotus is radically reasonable, not arbitrary; and why the will can be essentially free, not only in respect to contingent objects, but also in respect to the love of the necessary good: necessary not by virtue of any kind of necessity, but only that personal necessity of immutability and independence. We will also grasp why for Newman, assent, the core act of the intellect, is not identical with a logical conclusion, but entails a personal approval of the Truth. Neither is fully realizable, except in the divine nature, where intellect and will are really identical in a certain order: knowledge of the Truth so as to love that Truth as good for its own sake, and not merely as fulfillment of the intellect qua natural faculty.

And with this we can see why Scotus and Newman approach the critical question: its definition and solution, on the same basis: the primacy of the will and the person. At the same time, we can see why those who do not define the difference of intellect and will in terms of their formally diverse modes of acting: natural and voluntary, are logically committed to restricting freedom to only contingent objects of the will, and the critical problem: its nature and existence, to merely a question of logic.[87]

If we adopt the position of St. Thomas (primacy of intellect), no critical question arises, since the operations of the finite intellect naturally arrive at certain and objective knowledge. But precisely in this approach, explana-

---

[87] Both molinists and thomists define the will in relation to the primacy of the intellect and so limit freedom of the will, both in the divine as well as created will, as limited to contingent goods alone. But they do not agree on what element of the voluntary is to be stressed as central. The molinists stress "indetermination" or autonomy and, hence, define the will as "facultas, quae, positis omnibus ad agendum praerequisitis, potest agere vel non agere." For this school, the molinists, this definition is the basis of one's self position. For the thomists (and with them the scotists) hold that this leaves the will in itself radically arbitrary and unreasonable, and both go on to stress the "attractive" value of the object and guidance of the intellect in the form of "right reason." Thus, the will is described as "facultas quae operatur sub lumine judicii indifferentis." To this the molinists (and scotists) object that there remains nothing of the power to move oneself rather than be moved by something other than self, in this case an intellectual judgment or appetite (in the case of indifferent judgment preceding voluntary act). For Scotus the solution of the dilemma is found in the analysis of perfect intellect and will, formally distinct *a parte rei*, but really identical. For a brief, but good explanation of the molinist and thomistic approaches in relation to the problem of efficacious grace and free will, cf. S. González, *De gratia Christi*, in *Sacrae Theologiae Summa*, (Madrid 1953), vol. 3, 665–666; 676 and 679. The author, however, in his judgment on scotistic theories of "condetermination," does not understand the relation of necessity and freedom according to St. Bonaventure and Scotus.

For private consultation and not distribution without the consent of E Ondrako

tions of the personal character of intellectual life become problematic. If we adopt that of Kant in which a critical question inevitably arises with the imprisonment of the person within his own mind, there is no escape from the relativism and agnosticism consequent on the absolute primacy of the arbitrary, tyrannical will. Finally, the approach characteristic of the Franciscan school permits us to acknowledge in some sense the presence of a critical question linked to the personal features of intellectual life, but it also provides a resolution of the questions raised in a concept of the intellect as essentially contemplative, therefore linked to the will as a power to move oneself to act, identical with necessary being.

If the notion of will in Scotus and Newman is confused with that of Ockham as a power essentially free, therefore radically irrational and above reason as the basis of order, and so with that of Kant [*affectus justitiae* misinterpreted as "autonomous will" or "doing as one pleases without reference to goodness as such, and *affectus commodi* as "heteronomous will" or radical selfishness by definition], then the epistemology of Bonaventure-Scotus and of Newman will be indistinguishable from the agnosticism of Kant's pure, speculative reason and the arbitrary voluntarism of his ethics or practical reason. For Scotus and Newman base their resolution of the critical question on a personal act ultimately originating in the will. On the other hand, without that *dijudicatio* and use of the illative sense, each a personal act presupposing the rationality of the will as pure perfection, the thomistic solution remains incomplete and unconvincing, a mere exercise in logic. If Newman, like Scotus, is not a voluntarist in the Ockhamistic sense, then neither is he a nominalist, despite the appearance of some passages in the *Grammar of Assent*.[88]

Franciscan Epistemology, Newman and Kant

These distinctions Weatherby failed to consider in assuming that the critical question only arises from the erroneous premises of Kant, where all knowledge: scientific and logical in character, is primarily a product of thinking rather than a contemplation of reality for its own sake. This leads, of course, to skepticism about the reality of the noumena behind the phenomena or mode in which the real appears in the conscious or thinking subject: not so much whether they are, but what they are. For the Kantians the problem of agnosticism is especially acute in relation to the human ego (the transcendental ego) and to the divinity, and can only be resolved by invoking the postulates of the practical reason in relation to duty or conscience. Curiously, these two transcendental noumena show

[88] Cf. FRANK, *Preface*..., cit., p. x ff.

For private consultation and not distribution without the consent of E Ondrako

a certain correspondence with the two luminous beings of Newman: God and the soul (or ego), the latter however in a very different epistemological context, one redolent of St. Bonaventure and his theory of divine illumination. In any case the critical question is inseparable from the question of how we know ourselves and God. What Bonaventure discusses under the heading of *dijudicatio*, Newman discusses under the heading of speculative *phronesis* or illative sense[89]: both rational, not arbitrary, yet independent of proof as Newman remarks about the authority of conscience.[90] Apprehension may accompany and proof precede assent, but in the created mind these are conditions for, not causes of certain assent to truth. This often unspoken, unrecognized presence of God in the created mind is, in the Franciscan school, postulated not on the basis of act and potentiality (as in St. Thomas), but on that of a pure perfection in the finite realm. It guides the cultivation of the intellect from its onset to its completion. The same seems to be true in Newman.

Bound up with Bonaventure's solution is the theory of divine illumination of the finite intellect. But since the theory of divine illumination is so often presented as only a hair's breath away from fideism (the flip side of agnosticism, the pious voluntarism or fideism of which Weatherby accuses Scotus and Newman), even though Bonaventure clearly and convincingly distinguishes it from illuminationism,[91] we will do better to first consider interiorizing or "entering into oneself" as this is set forth in the Seraphic Doctor's *Itinerarium mentis in Deum*. For the character of introspection or coming to know oneself is very much conditioned by its place within the mind's journey to God.

It is just on this point that we encounter perhaps the greatest difference between two radically contrary concepts of self-knowledge and their relation to knowledge of God, or what Newman calls the two great luminous beings at the center of his thought. With Descartes and Kant one might say: *cogito, ergo sum*. Introspection is the very heart of thought; there it begins and there it ends. For Kant, what Bonaventure calls a journey of the mind, and Newman a development, is in the profoundest sense an evolution of self or self-divinization. With Bonaventure one might say: *sum, ergo cogito*. Introspection is a part of thought, a step on the journey, but it is neither its center, nor its beginning and end. The journey can only begin and end with a forgetfulness of self and a remembrance of

---

89 *Grammar of Assent*, part 2, ch. 9, pp. 353 ff.

90 "The Influence of Natural and Revealed Religion Respectively," cit., discussed *infra* in last section of this conference. This aspect of conscience in Newman may be compared to synderesis in Bonaventure and Scotus.

91 *De scientia Christi*, q. 4.

For private consultation and not distribution without the consent of E Ondrako

the Divine, the essentially *First*. Introspection or entry into self is only a means to consciously recognize the unique nearness of the created image of God: man, to his Creator and to the still more perfect way of knowing God as he is above oneself: in his Name. Thus, one comes to be ready to pass from this imperfect, discursive way of knowing, to knowing God as he knows himself. For Bonaventure this passing or *transitus* from earth to heaven alone completes the journey—a passing which requires grace as well as nature, love as well as thought.[92]

With this in mind we may briefly consider a second key difference between Kant and Bonaventure in assessing the critical question. The *transitus* concluding the journey is preceded by six steps or, better, three steps, each with two modes of knowing God, to be followed in order if the passage is to be successful.[93] The three steps, according to Bonaventure, are provided by the Creator, whereas the Kantian mind evolves in steps self-produced. For Bonaventure—and we shall see that Newman employs almost the same terms when dealing with the critical question in his *Grammar*[94]— the powers of the mind to know are to be used, and, if used correctly, will always enable the thinker to know what is, extra-mentally, not a fiction of his own mind. For Kant, this is not the case. Correct use for him does involve a problem, ultimately insoluble, of being able to trust, without further proof, one's mental faculties to provide certain knowledge of the extra-mental. For Bonaventure the critical problem in the first instance does not concern doubt whether the human intellect is naturally capable of attaining sure knowledge of the extra-mental, including God, discursively and without any second intention reflecting on the problem of certitude. Newman quite agrees.[95] This is because the created mind, though not infinite, is still a mind, and all minds are radically contemplative by nature. For Kant, just the contrary is the case: the human mind is not only radically secular by nature; it is *in statu naturae institutae* agnostic. Only the intra-mental is absolutely certain, i.e., self-awareness. Here is an interesting passage of Newman easily capable of a Bonaventurian reading:

> Certitude is a mental state: certainty is a quality of propositions. Those propositions I call certain, which are such that I am certain of them. Certitude is not a passive impression made upon the mind from without, by argumentative compulsion, but in all concrete questions (nay, even in abstract, for though reasoning

92 *Itinerarium*, ch. 7.

93 Cf. *Itinerarium*, ch. 1, for Bonaventure's explanation of the terminology.

94 Cf. *Grammar*, third section of this conference.

95 *GA*.

For private consultation and not distribution without the consent of E Ondrako

is abstract, the mind which judges of it is concrete) it is an active recognition of propositions as true, such as it is the duty of each individual himself to exercise at the bidding of reason, and, when reason forbids, to withhold. And reason never bids us be certain except on an absolute proof; and such proof can never be furnished to us by the logic of words, for as certitude is of the mind, so is the act of inference which leads to it. Everyone who reasons, is his own centre; and no expedient for attaining a common measure of minds can reverse this truth; - but then the question follows, is there any *criterion* of the accuracy of an inference, such as may be our warrant that certitude is rightly elicited in favour of the proposition inferred, since our warrant cannot, as I have said, be scientific? I have already said that the sole and final judgment on the validity of an inference in concrete matter is committed to the personal action of the ratiocinative faculty, the perfection or virtue of which I have called the Illative Sense, a use of the word "sense" parallel to our use of it in "good sense," "common sense," a "sense of beauty," etc.[96]

Finally, a third set of considerations will permit us to see how Bonaventure supplies a very traditional context for appreciating the contributions both of Scotus and of Newman to the resolution of this question. The final *transitus* in the mind's journey to God is reached, according to Bonaventure, after passing through three steps, each progressively higher in its knowledge of God than the earlier, and each entailing two modes of knowing, characteristic of discursive knowledge. The first step has as its starting point creatures of God as such, or vestiges; the second has as starting point for the knowledge of God those creatures known as images; and lastly, the third has as starting point the very name of God. This structure evidently reflects Bonaventure's catalogue of proofs for God's existence in the disputed questions on the Trinity in what we would call cosmological, anthropological and ontological arguments, the last recalling the famous proof of Anselm. *A parte rei* the last is the most basic; from the point of view of effectiveness, the first must precede and the second must then be acknowledged, before one can appreciate the third. None of these steps, however, reaches, or can reach what is known as the beatific vision: an immediate, direct, intuitive knowledge of God, although the last reaches a point where the knowledge of God is no longer

---

[96] *GA*, p. 2, ch. 9, 344–345.

For private consultation and not distribution without the consent of E Ondrako

the conclusion of a complex demonstration, but the starting point (in revealed theology) of a knowledge of things through God.[97]

For the purposes of our discussion, the two modes of knowing at each step of the journey: knowledge of God *per speculum* and *in speculo*, are crucial. By the first, Bonaventure means that knowledge of God obtained via a syllogism. By the second, he means knowledge of God which comes simultaneously with the knowledge of something else in which the knowledge of God is attained as one attains the knowledge of oneself in knowing or looking into a mirror. In looking at the mirror one cannot know the mirror, unless he also knows himself. Both vestiges and images of God may be considered as mirrors reflecting their Maker. In looking at either, one knows both the mirror and the reflection in it. This, Bonaventure calls contuited knowledge or contuition.[98] It is still a form of discursive knowledge, not to be confused with intuition and used as a reason for accusing Bonaventure of ontologism. Hence, it is not an immediate knowledge of God as is the beatific vision; but neither is it a demonstration of God's existence from effect to cause. The first type of procedure corresponds to the third act of the mind; the second, which Bonaventure calls contuition, is less familiar to us. Yet, when we are dealing with those two luminous beings which Newman places at the center of all knowing: the subject knowing and object known, both personal and both incapable of being immediately known in a time of pilgrimage, it is crucial to human knowing qua pure perfection (Scotus), as we will see in a moment critical in the second step. Without contuition, mere inference, viz., knowledge of God through the vestige, image and similitude, tends to overemphasize the merely abstract at the expense of the person; without the support of logic the contuitive or intuitive cognition of Scotus tends to remain obscure. Integrated, they provide the basis for avoiding the skepticism of Locke, Hume and Kant, a basis fully recognized in the doctrine of the absolute primacy of Christ to which Scotus and Newman both subscribed.

It is from the mystery of contuition that the theory of divine illumination in part arises as well as the distinction between fontal and motive object of the created intellect in the natural order. If Bonaventure chooses to accent the divine presence and role indispensable to the finite intellect, in order to be truly such, Scotus, in dispensing with the terminology, retains the substance of the doctrine with his theory of univocal being and concept of the finite intellect as a pure perfection. The human mind

---

[97] *Breviloquium*, p. 1, ch. 1.

[98] Cf. L. Prunieres, "Contuition," in *Lexique Saint Bonaventure*, Paris 1969, pp. 41–46, in particular his assessment of R. Sciammanini whose views in part seem to coincide with those of the transcendental thomists.

For private consultation and not distribution without the consent of E Ondrako

would not be truly finite without a certain complexit; but it would not be a pure perfection without a certain simplicity at its core, a simplicity nonetheless knowable even if not objectifiable. The scotistic epistemology tries rather to integrate the two dimensions in order to provide that unity and light without which nothing else can be known. Univocal being, like Bonaventure's fontal object, is not so much a source of knowledge about things as it is that which makes any activity of the human mind intellectual in the proper sense. Nowhere does the radical identity of views of these two Franciscan Masters become so clear than in comparing how Anselm's argument appears in chapter 5 of Bonaventure's *Itinerarium* and in the *De primo omnium rerum principio* of Scotus. The concept of being of Bonaventure is univocal without the name; and the essential primacy of divine being in Scotus's proof is nothing if not an analysis of question 8 of the disputed questions on the Trinity of Bonaventure and his commentary on memory in chapter 3 of the *Itinerarium*, explicitly related to divine illumination.[99] We may add as well that the disjunctive transcendentals so crucial to this argument, as A. Wolter notes,[100] are taken from question 1, article 1 of the disputed questions on the Trinity of Bonaventure, as are many other concepts crucial to Scotus, such as infinity, necessity, freedom of will, etc. In any case scotistic epistemology would only represent a radical break with that of Bonaventure (as so many claim today), were it also to adopt the thomist analogical concept of being as basis for explaining the agent intellect as a participation in the divine light. That is exactly what Scotus does not do.

Where does the critical question enter in? It appears at the end of chapter 3 and beginning of chapter 4 of the *Itinerarium*. Toward the end of chapter 2 (paragraphs 6 and 9), when discussing contuition of God in the vestige both in relation to sense and to intellectual cognition, the Seraphic Doctor introduces the term *dijudicatio*, the act of a human mind which distinguishes human knowing from that of the brutes. In a sense, the latter do sensibly know particular facts, goods, beautiful objects, but they cannot know being, good, beautiful, truth essentially, because they cannot account for why this object is a being, a good, etc. This judgment is a comparative assessment of an object sensed as a mirror in which is discerned the presence of being, goodness, etc. Closely related to this is the Bonaventurian concept of synderesis, the natural thrust of the will to

---

99 Boulnois, *Être et représentation*, cit., ch. 4, pp. 157–221, brings out two points: memory as starting point of process; and concluding in relation to Word-image, a revision of Bonaventure in *Itinerarium*.

100 Cf. A. Wolter, *The Transcendentals and Their Function in the Metaphysics of Duns Scotus*, St. Bonaventure, NY, 1946, pp. 132 ff.

For private consultation and not distribution without the consent of E Ondrako

love the good and hate evil, a thrust spontaneously activated in the natural use of the faculties in the first step. But that first step, if it is to arrive at the third, must also become a deliberate, freely taken personal judgment "approving" that *judicatio* in considering the presence of God reflected in the mind itself.

Newman shares this point of departure of Bonaventure just noted.

> One of the first acts of the human mind is to take hold of and appropriate what meets the senses, and herein lies a chief distinction between a man's and a brute's use of them. Brutes gaze on sights, they are arrested by sounds; and what they see and what they hear are mainly sights and sounds only. The intellect of man, on the contrary, energizes as well as his eye or ear, and perceives in sights and sounds something beyond them. It seizes and unites what the sense present to it; it grasps and forms what need not have been seen or heard except in its constituent parts…[101]

That there should appear in the light of this text to be correlations between what Bonaventure means by *dijudicatio* and what Newman means by the illative sense—between the ways in which each deals with conscience and the critical choice between intellectual pride and humility, and between the key role which univocity of being plays in the unity of knowledge for both Scotus and Newman—will come as no surprise.

Whence arises the need of this entering into self and personal assent to confirm, approve: a kind of "natural faith" or fidelity to truth that God is, and is a rewarder to those who serve him (cf. Heb 11: 6)? Bonaventure says that in the absence of this *resolutio plena* the need of certitude can rest only on the natural *motive* object of the mind (*objectum movens* apart from the *objectum fontanum* enlightening the intellect), and/or to the mind's operation itself, the position championed by Kant. The first is subject to change, the second alone is a fiction.[102] Without recognition of the divine light as fontal object of every created mind, or, with Scotus, an acceptance of that incomparable concept: univocal being, an apprehension which is also a simple assent, a judgment which is not judged—it is impossible to escape a culpable skepticism. To fully "naturalize" intellectual and voluntary activity in the created person would be to annihilate such activity. By definition such activity is divine-like, a kind of "relative supernatural," whether explained as pure perfection with Scotus or as divine

---

[101] *Idea of a University*, part 1, discourse 4, 3; this convergence is confirmed by a text from the *Grammar of Assent*, ch. 4, pp. 62–64, which is in the third part of this chapter, fn. 231. There Newman comes close to calling the illative sense a form of *dijudicatio*.

[102] *De Scientia Christi*, q. 4.

For private consultation and not distribution without the consent of E Ondrako

illumination with Bonaventure. This unique finite existence *prope Deum* is the very mystery of a finite person, what Bonaventure calls "intrinsically necessary being, *secundum quid*."[103] Bonaventure's famous *Summa* of spiritual theology, *De Triplici Via*, explains precisely how this tragic error of secularizing interiorization, fruit of intellectual pride, is to be avoided or corrected through intellectual humility, in order to attain the surpassing knowledge of the love of Christ (cf. Eph 3: 19).

Newman Metaphysicus in via Bonaventurae et Scoti

Hence, the need arises to enter into oneself in order to rise above oneself. Yet, tragically, without the help of grace, *pro statu naturae lapsae,* the vast majority concludes this interiorizing with an assessment of themselves as autonomous agents.[104] From this stems the inability to see the argument of Anselm in the hands of Bonaventure and Scotus other than a primitive version of Hegelian "onto-theology," or the glorification of logic as key to theology. From this stems that distrust of the faculties of intellect and will unless proven trustworthy. Skepticism is the fruit of a deliberate indulgence of a "will to power."

By "onto-theology" is meant the organization of philosophy as distinct from science around a general theory of being, or general ontology, common in Europe after the fifteenth century. On the basis of this general ontology, the key to which is the logic of being, the study of the specific types of being is organized, including what is called natural theology. Natural theology in such a context is known as "onto-theology," precisely because the existence of its subject, God, is only known via a deductive *a priori* procedure: the logic of univocal being in general founds the extra-mental character of theology in particular. Neither in Scotus nor in Newman is such the case. Newman, like Rosmini, does not define natural or anthropological theology on the basis of the canons of general ontology, but in contrast with the "physical theology" of Paley. In Scotus, the univocal concept of being is not in the first instance a logical construct with solely gnoseological value, but a unique, incomparable formulation of divine illumination in the logical form appropriate to the finite intellect. The knowledge which this concept gives of being in general is not consequent on, but prior to the logic characteristic of this concept, and so the foundation for the realism of

---

[103] *De mysterio Ss. Trinitatis*, q. 7, a. 1.

[104] *Itinerarium*, ch. 4, 1: "Sed non solum per nos transeundo, verum etiam in nobis contingit contemplari primum principium; et hoc maius est quam praecedens: ideo hic modus considerandi quartum obtinet contemplationis gradum. Mirum autem videtur… quod Deus sit ita propinquus mentibus nostris, quod tam paucorum est in se ipsis primum principium speculari."

For private consultation and not distribution without the consent of E Ondrako

all human knowledge and scientific endeavor, above all when dealing with what is not evident to the senses. This relation is exactly that which we find between the illative sense of Newman and formal logic, whether weak or strong reason in Locke's sense. More than to Kant (who in many ways depends on Locke), the metaphysics of Scotus and *Grammar of Assent* of Newman provide the radical basis for any defense of the very possibility of faith as an assent rather than a merely pious affection.

In this analysis Scotus clearly appears as a disciple of Bonaventure. One concluding comparison of Bonaventure and Scotus will help us to see the continuity between the two. Bonaventure's fullest and profoundest exposition of the theory of divine illumination is found in question 4 of his disputed questions on the knowledge of Christ. There, in a brilliant analysis of the most perfect human intellect ever, he shows exactly how the simple and complex involved in a pure perfection are perfectly coordinated, and in view of that which should be coordinated in all men. That this should be the case is perfectly consistent with the mystery of the hypostatic union, and opens up new avenues of reflection on the human experience of Jesus. But it also points to the absolute primacy of Christ defended by Scotus. If all of creation, and, in a very special way, Adam and Eve, were designed precisely in view of the Incarnation and divine Maternity, then are we not correct in viewing the univocal concept of being and its disjunctive transcendentals: divine and natural, as a kind of foreshadowing of the hypostatic union: the human and divine natures substantially united in the person of the Word? Here is the key to that unity of knowledge so stressed by Scotus and later by Newman, and which explains the characteristic approach of each to the distinction of nature and supernatural, not in terms of object of intellect and will, but in terms of the dynamic influence on those faculties, to the extent of enabling the created mind and will to attain their objects qua intellect and will, not in a finite, but in a divine, personal mode. For this to be possible, as Scotus notes, the object of the intellect as a pure perfection cannot be restricted to material beings structured in terms of act-potentiality, but *ens qua ens*, without which it would not be possible to provide any continuity between metaphysics and revealed theology.[105] This appears to be the position of Newman in his *Idea of a University* implied in his insistence on the unity of liberal as distinct from useful knowledge.[106]

Setting Scotus's innovations in this context enables us at once to appreciate how they tighten the loose ends in the presentation of the Seraphic

---

[105] Cf. L. HONNEFELDER, *Ens in quantum ens. Der Begriff des Seienden als solchen als Gegenstand der Metaphysik nach der Lehre des Johannes Duns Scotus*, (Münster 1979).
[106] *Idea of a University*, part 1, discourse 3, 4.

For private consultation and not distribution without the consent of E Ondrako

Doctor, particularly the relation between the simple and quasi-divine element in knowledge and its finite case, a point central to the distinction of Newman between assent and inference and his understanding of the relation between natural and revealed religion.[107]   But it also enables us to see exactly how the so called cosmological proofs in Scotus are linked to the "ontological" proof, via the anthropological or argument from conscience; and in what way, the ontological proof of Scotus differs *toto coelo* from the approach of Kant and how the critique of Kantian errors in no wise invalidates Scotus's proofs. The same is true of Newman, once we admit his affinity with Scotus, even if his distinction between notional and real apprehension has appeared to some as Kantian in flavor.

The difference between Scotus-Newman on the one hand, and Kant and his followers on the other, does not consist in the fact that the first would accept the validity of an "onto-theology" and the other would reject this. Neither Scotus nor Newman accepts as theirs what transcendentalist theologians, including the thomistic, mean by "onto-theology," where ontology is a form of universal logic permitting the deduction of the extra-mental or ontic character of perfect being.[108] For Scotus and Newman, as for Bonaventure before them, a place in metaphysics is reserved for experience, above all the experience of the authority and of the love of God. Our metaphysics, as Scotus says, is related in origin and in finality to the praxis of love: love of Christ. If in scotistic discussions an abstruse, precise, dry language seems to predominate, there is present just beneath the surface a profound sense of the phenomenological at the level of thought and affection. Even if Scotus abandons the language of divine illumination, he reformulates the insights of Bonaventure in terms of the *perfectiones simpliciter simplices* of intellect and will, formally distinct, yet really in-existent [identical], with their roots in the memory, intellect, heart, soul, and person. Newman completes the analysis in locating that experience of authority in conscience, thus integrating the role of light on the intellect and will.[109] Without the reality of divine illumination [whatever name it is given], there is no way of avoiding the views of Kant concerning a metaphysics based on being, or of really distinguishing the spiritual creature: *prope Deum*, from the merely material: *prope nihil*.[110] Without this antecedent, there is no way of finding a speculative or intellectual basis

---

107   "The Influence of Natural and Revealed Religion," cit.; *Grammar of Assent*, part 2, ch. 6–8; 10.

108   Cf. O. BOULNOIS, *Être et représentation*, (Paris 1999), ch. 4, pp. 151 ff.

109   "The Influence of Natural and Revealed Religion Respectively," cit., 9: authority postulates not proof, but faith or assent, and faith entails a personal act of obedience. See text supra, pp. 6–7.

110   ST. BONAVENTURE, *Breviloquium*, p. 2, ch. 6, 3.

For private consultation and not distribution without the consent of E Ondrako

for religion, for supernatural faith and grace. This is exactly the position of Luther. And it eventually collapses into the position of Pelagius, who identifies grace and nature. This, too, is an unspoken premise of Rahner.

This brings us to recognize the personal character of what St. Bonaventure calls the *dijudicatio* accompanying the process of abstraction and discursive thought, clearly apparent in what Newman calls assent as distinct from inference and in the exercise of the illative sense. Where the personal character of this act reflects the goodness of divine being, there is nothing arbitrary or irrational about it—indeed, just the opposite; for, as Scotus notes, the divine will cannot be irrational or disordered. This is the point where the real—not formal, identity of intellect and will as pure perfections—is evident, even in these perfections as finite; and where the rejection of this obeisance to the Truth or divine Light [a kind of natural faith] constitutes a radical abuse of these powers of the soul and a preference for darkness.

Metaphysics without the experiential personal aspect of "intuitive" cognition is "onto-theology": unrelated to anything but logic.[111] On the other hand, an anti-metaphysical and anti-dogmatic phenomenology is nothing but a cloak for skepticism. But phenomenology need not be an aspect of the anti-dogmatic principle and cloak of skepticism; it may just as well cloak a realistic metaphysics. The difference bears always on the acceptance or rejection of the radically contemplative-mystical character of all thought. Precisely because "our theology"[112] is ordered toward the mystical where the speculative is revealed as contemplative and contemplative because within love of the Real; therefore, "our theology" bears always a metaphysical and phenomenological aspect: abstractive (objective representation) and intuitive (experiential) cognition in scotistic terms; notional and real in Newman's terminology.[113]

The inherent phenomenological character of Scotus's metaphysics has been sufficiently illustrated in the studies of Hoeres on the will and

---

111 A. APOLLONIO, "Il contributo di Hugo Cavellus, OFM (†1626) alla teoria dell'intellezione dei singoli materiali," in *Quaderni di Studi Scotisti*, n. 6 (2009), 155–156.

112 Cf. SCOTUS, *Ordinatio*; NEWMAN, *Oxford University Sermons*, passim.

113 S. DUMONT, "Theology as a Science and Duns Scotus' Distinction between Intuitive and Abstractive Cognition," in *Speculum* 64 (1989) 579–599. Dumont suggests that contrary to the position sustained in the prologue of the *Ordinatio*, Scotus elsewhere maintained the possibility of "our theology" during a time of pilgrimage being also strictly scientific. In the *Ordinatio*, Scotus is speaking of "our theology" *pro statu naturae lapsae* after the fall, based on the gift of faith where this is not possible, since it does not enjoy any proper concept of the divine essence. Perhaps the suggestions of Dumont pertain to considerations similar to those of Bonaventure for theology *pro statu naturae institutae* before the fall, when, not faith, but infused knowledge, a *gratia gratis data*, provided the basis for the theology of Adam and Eve, scientific in character. Cf. *Breviloquium*, p. 2, ch. 11, 6.

For private consultation and not distribution without the consent of E Ondrako

those of Boulnois on being and representation in Scotus.[114] What I wish
to illustrate, if only so briefly, is the inherent metaphysical character of
Newman's theological achievement. It is often asserted that Newman
eschewed metaphysics, including its scholastic form. This is evidently a
very generic assertion, once we take note of the very different meanings
which the term "metaphysics" can bear. For instance, if one understands
by metaphysics a detailed treatise in logical form on what is meant by
"being" and on the questions or theses associated with such a study, it is
obvious that Newman was not a professor of metaphysics or personally
very interested in becoming one. Clearly, the style of such a treatise is
very different from the style of Newman's greatest writings, but so is such a
treatise from those of a Bonaventure and, as Hopkins so clearly perceived,
from that of Scotus as well, when he described the Subtle Doctor as the
person "who most moved his spirit to peace, of reality the rarest veined
unraveller, a not rivaled insight, be rival Italy or Greece, who fired France
for Mary without spot."[115]

Most people fail to grasp that, for Scotus, genuine metaphysics is not
primarily another science, but wisdom, even if "our metaphysics" is always
embedded in a scientific or "physical" context which it transcends as the
term "metaphysics": surpassing physics or science. It is the beginning of
wisdom without which no science worthy of the name is possible nor can
it realize those ends for which the Creator designed it. It is the use of our
minds to contemplate the mystery of being in an enigma, even before we
come to contemplate distinctly the Reality of that infinite being who is the
One God who made heaven and earth. All this has been designed so we
may love this One Being who-is-who-he-is, and further tells us that this
Being, whose Name is I AM, is charity.

There is, then, for Newman a certain asymmetry between knowledge
as such and instances of knowledge, such as human knowledge in logical,
discursive or scientific form. At this level Scotus also notes (*Lectura*, d.
22) a certain asymmetry which leads him to reject what in modern times
is the teaching of Locke: "nihil potest nominari a nobis magis proprie
quam intelligatur": nothing not in the realm of logic can be known by us.
What Newman calls the "surplussage" of assent over inference and other
complex processes accompanying assent is a reflection of this asymmetry.
The certain, immutable character of assent cannot be explained in terms
of those processes preceding (apprehension), accompanying (inference),
and normally required for it in the natural order. It is the same asymmetry

---

[114] Cf. HOERES, *Der Wille…*, cit.; BOULNOIS, *Être et représentation…*, cit.

[115] G. M. HOPKINS, *Duns Scotus' Oxford*. Note relation between reality and actuality, and how
this sense of actual precedes that of act contrasted with potency.

For private consultation and not distribution without the consent of E Ondrako

met in univocal concept of being (Scotus) and in fontal object-pivotal object (Bonaventure). Though only in a shadowy way for Scotus and Bonaventure as for Newman the fact of the asymmetry arises from the presence of God, and, hence, need of holiness to reach full contemplation in love. For all three the beginning of philosophy is already in some way the conclusion at which we aim to arrive and the process of demonstration required to know God naturally is suspended, as it were, between starting and concluding points radically the same. This process ends exactly where revealed theology begins.[116] Further, this asymmetry explains why intellectual certainty is anchored exactly where St. Bonaventure tells us it is: with the source of that fontal illumination and exemplarity without which knowledge is impossible; with that incomparable concept of being as univocal in Scotus; with that simplicity and absolute character of assent as distinct from inference. Science in its complexity is by itself subject to change; wisdom is eternal or it is not wisdom, the origin and goal of all science.

In this sense Newman shows himself a great metaphysician who clearly does have an appreciation of scholastic theology and metaphysics, although he never formally studied scholasticism as a young man. But he shows himself also a great metaphysician, one who can see beyond the merely physical and appreciate metaphysical asymmetry, basis of that surplusage of evidence perceived by the illative sense, that is, a great Christian mystic, even at the level of metaphysics as distinct from theology and mystical contemplation. This is at root what he means by the great dogmatic principle: respect for and acceptance of the authority of Truth at whatever level and mode this is made known to us: reason, faith, vision of God.[117] In discussing certitude in the *Grammar of Assent*, we meet this profound metaphysical insight so redolent of the tradition of Anselm, Bonaventure and Scotus:

> I am what I am or I am nothing. I cannot think, reflect, or judge about my being, without starting from the very point which I am at concluding [God].[118]

---

[116] Cf. St. Bonaventure, *Breviloquium*, p. 1, ch. 1, 4.

[117] Cf. Biglietto Address. Supporting the dogmatic principle are the views of Newman on knowledge as an end in itself, or liberal before it is useful: The Idea of a University, part 1, discourse 5. Newman understands liberal here, in the medieval sense, whereas the moderns often intend liberal as a form of pragmatism opposed to the dogmatic principle. This is what Newman anathematizes in the Biglietto Address: liberalism in doctrine or indifferentism in religion.

[118] *Grammar of Assent*, p. 347.

For private consultation and not distribution without the consent of E Ondrako

Newman's definition of being here: I am precisely what I am to the degree I am not nothing, reflects Bonaventure when he says that any being is that to the degree it is in flight with nothing: *ens est in fuga a non-esse*,[119] and reflects Scotus when he says reality or an entity is what being does not reject: ...*ens, hoc est cui non repugnat esse*.[120]

This must be kept in mind in order to grasp correctly what Newman means in the *Apologia* when he tells us that he believes in the Church because he believes in God and believes in God because he believes in himself.[121] Understood here is: as made in the image and likeness of God, viz., the two luminously self-evident beings, himself and his Creator.[122] Implied here, as we shall see in more detail in parts two and three of this conference, is Bonaventure's concept of divine primacy, further developed by Scotus, and its bearing on divine illumination and the mind as a *perfectio simpliciter simplex* and the response to that illumination in personal form. Not to accept this point: radically bound up with the metaphysics of univocity of being and theology of absolute primacy, threatens us with universal skepticism.[123]

Effectively, this observation implies a reflection, in a sense shadowy yet real, of the dogmatic definition of the hypostatic union: the really distinct divine and human natures in the substantial unity of one divine Person, in the univocal notion of being with its really distinct infinite and finite modes (the disjunctive transcendentals). Simo Knuuttila, in a review of *The Philosophy of Duns Scotus* by A. Vos, remarks how this study is "very theological, since Vos argues that Scotus' philosophy is essentially based on the Christian doctrine of creation."[124] This philosophy, in particular its metaphysics, is for Vos the infrastructure of his theology, and has as its matrix "synchronic contingency." Translated into older scholastic terminology, a metaphysics based on the Christian doctrine of creation in a theology proclaiming the absolute primacy of Christ as reason for both creation and redemption will logically reflect that mystery in the structuring of its focal point, the univocal concept of being with its disjunctive modes.

Such a concept of philosophy as inherently Christian and contemplative-mystical is very much akin to the adage of Tertullian: *anima natu-*

---

[119] Cf. *Itinerarium*, ch. 5, 3.

[120] Cf. *Ordinatio* IV, d. 8, q. 1.

[121] *Apologia pro vita sua*, pp. 198–199 [Page references are to the 1865 edition.].

[122] *Apologia*, p. 4.

[123] DEVLIN, *The Psychology of Duns Scotus*, cit., pp. 11 ff.

[124] S. KNUUTTILA, "Review of The Philosophy of Duns Scotus," in *Ars Disputandi*, 7 (2007), paragraph 2.

For private consultation and not distribution without the consent of E Ondrako

raliter christiana, to which a Bernard or Bonaventure might add: <u>*anima naturaliter Christiana et contemplativa*</u>.[125] And of course it means agreeing with Bonaventure that philosophy, viz., love of wisdom, attempted apart from Christ, is doomed to incompletion. Obviously the acceptance or rejection of this point will have considerable bearing on how one goes about integrating *love of learning and desire for God*, as does Newman in his *Idea of a University*, or simply denying that there exists a link between these.

The Metaphysical-Dogmatic Thread during the Course of Newman's Life

Before illustrating how Newman fits in this tradition with examples from his great writings, principally the *Grammar of Assent*, but not exclusively, I want to examine the basis for the preceding reflection in the life and writing of Newman, as it were, in a personal experience of development of doctrine along a scotistic path. The order of presentation here follows that which Newman himself indicates in his *Apologia pro vita sua* to illustrate the development of his intellectual and religious convictions in fidelity to the truth.

This is what Pope Benedict XVI calls the continuity or stability indispensable to any genuine unfolding of a mind, whether that be of the individual Christian or of the Church itself.[126] I think this is an important preliminary in order to avoid the impression of reading into the writings of Newman what one would like to find there. It seems to me that such a procedure also involves an example of what Newman calls in the *Grammar of Assent* a convergence of probabilities bringing us to recognize what others have already suggested, but left undocumented. In the light of this we can see why <u>the "metaphysics" of the *Grammar of Assent* is not only a metaphysics in phenomenological form</u> underlying the journey <u>of faith recounted in the *Apologia*, but also is one supporting the theory of doctrinal development</u> and, so, an important instrument of dogmatic theology, as Newman indicates in the *Grammar*, with examples bearing on the mystery of the Blessed Trinity. In a letter to Ward already cited in the introduction to this conference, Newman clearly sees the doctrine of the absolute primacy of Jesus and Mary Immaculate as a concrete instance of his theory of development so important to account for the correlations

---

[125] Cf. *The Triple Way*, translated and edited by P. Fehlner, New Bedford 2011, Appendix I for references to St. Bernard's *Jesu dulcis Memoria*, St. Anselm, *Proslogion*, St. Bonaventure, *De Scientia Christi*, and Scotus on primacy of charity and *De primo omnium rerum principio*.

[126] Benedict XVI, *Address to Roman Curia*, Dec. 22, 2005.

For private consultation and not distribution without the consent of E Ondrako

between order of intention or eternity, and order of execution or history in "our theology."

Two Luminously Self-evident Beings

A first, perhaps most important point, is what Newman tells us about the heart of his conversion when he was about fifteen years of age, how he rested

> in the thought of two and two only absolute and luminously self-evident beings, myself and my Creator.[127]

He does not mean here what in Catholic circles has come to be associated with "ontologism" or an immediate vision of the divine essence dispensing with the need of any proof of God's existence. Were I to suggest a Catholic term to indicate what is involved, it would be that of St. Bonaventure: *contuition*, and discussed by Scotus under the heading of direct "intellectual intuitive cognition" or sense of the presence of God, however shadowy. By this the Seraphic Doctor means the contemporaneous knowledge of God not by way of a demonstration from effect to cause, viz., through another [above all discursive thought about God *per speculum*], but in those effects as in a mirror: *in speculo*, and not by way of a clear, objective representation, but in a vague, shadowy, enigmatic fashion, much as Newman suggests in the epitaph for his tomb: *ex umbris et imaginibus in veritatem*.

That said, W. Barry's comment on this is correct:

> In other words, personality became the primal truth in his philosophy; not matter, law, reason, or the experience of the senses. Henceforth, Newman was a Christian mystic, and such he remained.[128]

This comment is amply confirmed in the motto chosen by Newman for his coat of arms as Cardinal: *Cor ad cor loquitur*. These are two solitudes in the sense that Scotus calls the person metaphysically considered a *solitudo*, an *existentia incommunicabilis naturae intellectualis*. Person so defined is not isolated, not autonomous, but at once unique and relational, capable of loving communion with another, precisely because the intellectual nature of a person is capable of knowing the divine Persons, each an incommuni-

---

127 NEWMAN, *Apologia pro vita sua*, p. 4.

128 W. BARRY, *Newman, John Henry*, (1801–1890), in *The Catholic Encyclopedia*, New York 1911, vol. X, p. 795. Newman's own testimony to this can be found in the first section of the *Apologia*, especially pp. 26–27.

For private consultation and not distribution without the consent of E Ondrako

cable existence, yet perfectly and totally within each other. Newman fully realized this communion in the Catholic Church.

What is implied here will become more explicit in the texts cited in the second and third parts of this conference. Knowledge and holiness are means to wisdom, the union of these two "absolute and luminously self-evident beings." Wisdom, says St. Bonaventure, is knowledge as it passes into affection; and understanding is knowledge as it passes into the choice whereby wisdom is joined to affection.[129]

In this sense an old adage mentioned by Newman in the *Apologia* is very apt: *numquam minus solus quam solus*, provided one is alone with Jesus.[130] The motto chosen for his coat of arms more than sufficiently shows how a single thread, an unchanging *ratio* or idea (as Bonaventure understands this or as Scotus a *formalitas a parte rei*), to which he was ever faithful: the *ratio* underlying the way, the truth and the life, which guided his life from beginning to end. Coincidentally, the proximate source of the motto was St. Francis de Sales whose spirituality was very much shaped by the study of Scotus at the University of Padua, particularly by the thesis on the absolute primacy of Christ and the primacy of charity, so closely related to the theology of the heart and the person.[131] Padua, during the most of the 15th, 16th, 17th and 18th centuries (up to the eve of the French revolution), was a major center for the teaching of Scotus (in a certain sense inheriting the position of Paris before the great western schism and hundred years war). Even after the Reformation triumphed in England, Padua remained a favored place of study not only for English Catholics, but for Anglicans as well.

Commentators generally note the Calvinist background of this conversion and the rather negative baggage that Newman would gradually shed: an odious predestinationism, a suspicion of the reality of matter, an indifference to the mystery of the Church and its crucial importance, all of which might distort, and to a degree did distort the meaning of this central truth and the sense of the dogmatic principle it entailed. This predestinationism gives rise to an intellectual and affective narrowness indifferent to community and genuine freedom. Very often human nature reacts to this puritanism by way of stress on a contrary extreme, and this reaction

---

[129] Bonaventure, *Collationes in Hexaemeron*, c. 5, 12–13.

[130] *Apologia*, p. 16.

[131] Details of the Saint's life and study at the University of Padua can be found in F. Russo, *Filippo Gesualdi da Castrovillari, Ministro Generale dei Minori Conventuali e Vescovo di Cerenzia-Cariati (1550–1618)*, (Roma 1972). Fr. Filippo Gesualdi, a saintly friar whose cause for beatification is still pending, was professor of philosophy and theology in via Scoti at the University of Padua and director of a devotional confraternity while St. Francis de Sales was a student at that University and member of this confraternity.

For private consultation and not distribution without the consent of E Ondrako

in Newman's life found expression in the company of the "noetics," a 19th century version of Ockham so akin to the fashionable Kantianism of that time, with its stress on *academic excellence* (love of learning) rather than *mystical contemplation* (desire for God). The reconciliation of these two is a central concern of Newman's *The Idea of a University*. There, as we shall see, he proposes an approach to the conciliation of these two apparently incompatible goals similar to that of Scotus. Indeed, twice in the course of these lectures Newman praises Scotus as one of the greatest luminaries ever of his beloved Oxford University.[132]

But just as reflection on these "two luminous beings": the heart of God and his own heart, shows how his youthful Calvinism is only incidental to his love of the Light, so it does the same for whatever momentary inclinations toward an Ockhamistic or Kantian position: "liberal Christianity," might have been present during that period when he came under Whateley's influence. The two luminous beings are precisely those which Kant claimed (under the heading of *noumena*) to be just the opposite of luminous: unknowable, whereas only the *phenomena* conditioned by the mind are lightsome. If Newman's thought is congenial to the tradition of Scotus and uncongenial to that of Kant (and all the transcendentalists thereafter, including the thomistic, e.g., Rahner and Lonergan), it also shows why "onto-theology" in the Kantian sense cannot find its paternity in Scotus. Logic in Scotus and Newman is the instrument supporting a genuine contemplation of truth, not the soul of understanding. Newman makes this point crystal clear in his distinction between assent and inference and the role of personal judgment [illative sense] as well as formal logic in the act of assent, whether this be at the natural or supernatural level of human thought.

That said, the thought central to Newman's conversion remains in essence profoundly true and reflects a point central to the spirituality of Bl. John Duns Scotus as a reformulation of that expounded by St. Bonaventure. The metaphysics of Scotus revolves about the univocal concept of being and his dogmatics about the absolute primacy of Christ and its analogical (hierarchical) interpretation of the sacramentality of creation for the sake of Jesus and Mary. Scotus's metaphysics is the instrument of his dogmatic exposition of the absolute primacy of Jesus. From the scotistic tradition on the primacy of the will and charity which the old Calvinism so violently and perversely altered from a profound recognition of the gift of freedom into an arbitrary and inhuman predestinationism, a sense of that central thought so important to Newman was kept.

---

132 *Idea of a University*, part 2, Discourse 5: A Form of Infidelity of the Day, p. 396.

For private consultation and not distribution without the consent of E Ondrako

Newman came to understand the meaning of this thought more fully after he accepted and lived the maternal mediation of Mary Immaculate rooted in the correct understanding of this mystery of being. This is quite evident in his well-known *Memorandum* on the Immaculate Conception, where he points out that the doctrine of original sin, so central to Calvinism that it leads to a rejection of Mary, only makes sense, not when we consider Mary in relation to sin, but sin and above all original sin in relation to the Immaculate Conception, a mystery far easier to grasp than that of sin. Is this not, practically speaking, the thesis of Scotus: even if Adam had not sinned, the Word would have become incarnate?[133] But even before this we see traces of this sympathy in the *Lectures on the Doctrine of Justification* (1836) where he deals with uncreated grace, created grace and divine acceptance in a manner, if not identical with the position of Scotus, certainly tending in that direction. Significantly, he refers to the famous 16th century Conventual Scotist at the Council of Trent, Cornelius Musso, who played a prominent role during and after that Council.[134] By 1840, we see the first explicit references to the absolute primacy in his *Select Treatises of Athanasius* and *The Arians of the Fourth Century*.[135]

Butler's Analogy

A second consideration crucial to our discussions in this symposium is Newman's discovery of Bishop Joseph Butler's *Analogy*, first read by him in 1823. By this time he was already under the influence of Whateley and the noetics of Oriel from whom Newman tells us he first came to an appreciation of the Church and of the sacramental order: divinely, not politically instituted. He was beginning to shed his Calvinism and certain aspects of "low-church" evangelicalism and individualism. With his parochial work he came to see that the key feature of Calvinism: its "odious" predestinationism, did not work, viz., was inhuman, depersonalizing and unworthy of a good God. Under the influence of Whateley, Hawkins and others, he came to appreciate the importance of the Church together with that of the single person and why erastianism was such a danger for the Church as he knew it in England. On the other hand he began to find himself stressing academic excellence, scholarship, scientific precision as more important

---

[133] Cf. letter to Faber, 7 Dec., 1849, cit.

[134] *Lectures on the Doctrine of Justification*, Appendix one. Newman also refers to Musso under his title of Bishop of Bitonto.

[135] Cf. R. Strange, *Newman and the Gospel of Christ*, Oxford 1981, pp. 111 ff. [For a kindred approach, see Robert Pattison, *The Great Dissent: John Henry Newman and the Liberal Heresy* (Oxford: Oxford University Press, 1991), 149. n. 9.]

For private consultation and not distribution without the consent of E Ondrako

than sanctity and wisdom, typical of the influence of Ockham and of his nominalism in the history of modern European, and, in particular, British philosophy and theology.

Newman's sympathies, even though they always retained a certain care for logical exactitude and a love for learning, are not closely related to the essential concerns of the noetics, much less of Kant and the modern German intellectual fashions. This is perfectly evident from two observations he leaves us in the *Apologia*:

> I understood ... that the exterior world, physical and historical, was but the manifestation to our senses of realities greater than itself. Nature was a parable, Scripture was an allegory; pagan literature, philosophy, and mythology, properly understood, were but a preparation for the Gospel. The Greek poets and sages were in a sense prophets.[136]

There had been a "dispensation" of the Gentiles as well as of the Jews. Both had outwardly come to naught; yet, from and through each, the evangelical doctrine had been made manifest. Thus, room was granted for anticipation of deeper disclosures of truths still under the veil of the letter [cf. Eph 3: 1 ff]. Holy Church, he continues,

> will remain after all but a symbol of those heavenly facts which will fill eternity. Her mysteries are but the expression in human language of truths to which the human mind is unequal.[137]

It is not too difficult to appreciate the similarity between the basic thrust of Newman's spirit: not an attempt to escape from the inward to the extra-mental *à la* Descartes and Kant, but a movement from the outward signs of the divine to the inward, and the thrust of St. Bonaventure's thought in his *Itinerarium* and in his reflections of the hierarchies in his *Collationes in Hexaemeron*, cc. 20–23, so deeply influenced by the Alexandrians [through Augustine] and Pseudo-Dionysius. That reflection of the Seraphic Doctor anticipates the implications of this "sacramentality" or analogical character of creation in the context of the absolute primacy of Christ, on an analogy which finds its fulcrum in "our metaphysics" in the univocal rather than analogical concept of being. What Bonaventure means by divine illumination and the natural "*judicatorium*," is redefined

---

136 *Apologia*, p. 24.

137 *Apologia*, 27. Compare this with similar thought patterns of St. BONAVENTURE, *Itinerarium*, ch. 2, where the Seraphic Doctor deals with knowledge of God *in vestigio*, particularly in the Sacraments. In the Apologia, p. 18, Newman tells us that he had never studied Berkeley. It is far more plausible to see in the views of Bonaventure a form of that Christian philosophy which, in fact, always supplied the interpretation which Newman put on this and other similar statements suggesting the "unreality" of matter.

For private consultation and not distribution without the consent of E Ondrako

by Scotus in terms of that unique, incomparable concept known as univocal being, without which no other concept is luminous. This, it seems to me, is what ultimately the two self-evident luminous beings of Newman are all about metaphysically.

Thus, his enthusiastic acceptance of Butler and its expression in the collection of sermons with the title, *Parochial and Plain Sermons,* comes as no surprise. We can understand without difficulty why, on his discovering Scotus's thesis on the absolute primacy, he would find himself in agreement, even though he had not read the works of Scotus. Butler is famous, not only for his preference for "natural theology" (the anthropological argument of Bonaventure) rather than the "physical theology" of W. Paley, but for his teaching on the sacramentality of creation as taught by the Alexandrians, Clement and Athanasius, a doctrine which most certainly shaped Newman's philosophical view of the world and a patristic anticipation of the views of Scotus on the relation of the natural and supernatural orders based on the absolute primacy of Christ.[138]

By natural theology Butler meant the proof for God's existence drawn not so much from the visible world outside us, but from what Newman would call "conscience," what in Augustine and Bonaventure is the proof from the created image of God rather than vestige.[139]   Without this proof, the so called teleological or cosmological arguments, particularly as expounded by Paley, tend to be simply conclusions of empirical science and so subject to all the criticisms of Locke and Kant. More importantly, the proof of Anselm, generally rejected by the proponents of the priority of "physical theology," tends to be indistinguishable from "onto-theology." When Scotus is read as a continuation of Bonaventure, we see immediately why the metaphysics of theology is not an ontology in the sense of Kant, even if Scotus realistically deals with the critical question in dealing with the importance of "intuitive" cognition, and why his natural theology is neither "onto-theology" nor "physical theology."[140]   Closely related to these questions, both in Newman as well as in Scotus, is what Newman in the

---

138   Cf. A. KERRIGAN, "The Predestination of Mary according to St. Cyril of Alexandria," in *Alma Socia Christi*, vol. 3 (Roma 1952), pp. 34–58. On the key influence of the Alexandrian school, above all Athanasius and Cyril, on the development and final formation of Newman's theological mindset, cf. B. J. KING, *Newman and the Alexandrian Fathers: Shaping Doctrine in Nineteenth-Century England*, (Oxford: Oxford University Press, 2009).

139   ST. BONAVENTURE, *Itinerarium*, ch. 4; *De Triplici Via*; *Quaestiones Disputatae de mysterio Ss. Trinitatis*, q. 1, a. 1.

140   Cf. *Idea of a University*, part 1, discourse 3, 6.

For private consultation and not distribution without the consent of E Ondrako

Grammar of Assent calls "natural faith," an aspect of personal assent in metaphysics which brings with it a solution to the critical question.[141]

Key to the natural theology of Scotus read in the Augustinian, Anselmian, Bonaventurian tradition is the reformulation of the theory of divine illumination in terms of univocity of being and the concept of image as distinct from vestige of God in terms of *perfectiones simpliciter simplices*, and, therefore, not structured in terms of act and potentiality. Only the created "image" of the Creator shares such pure perfections. They confer on them a relatively supernatural character vis-à-vis the mere vestige of God, exactly what Bonaventure means by divine illumination in the natural order. In a sense this makes them, as Bonaventure says in the *Breviloquiun*, near God (*prope Deum*), rather than near nothing (*prope nihil*). Such creatures enjoy, like God, a mysterious, personal dignity, which, when perfected in the order of grace, entails the integration of intellect and will as in God, the subordination of physical to voluntary causality on which Newman so much insists. This is without doubt a major reason why Bonaventure, Scotus and Newman all see the value of the cosmological proofs of divine existence as resting on the anthropological (the proof from conscience) and ontological.[142]

What is still more interesting is how the analogical knowledge we have of God is explained in relation to what Newman calls the sacramentality of creation; what is so often discussed in Bonaventure under the heading of hierarchies and hierarchization, centering both on the choirs of angels and on the sacred order basic to the Church, both reflecting the supercelestial hierarchy which is the Trinity of divine Persons. Without a doubt we find here a key to Newman's coordination of person and community, more particularly, Church. Without a doubt it is not Hegel, but Butler who provides the hint leading to the theory of development of doctrine entailing both the idea: read *ratio* (Bonaventure) or *formalitas* (Scotus) in the Franciscan tradition. That idea remains stable, first in the midst of variations progressively leading to the completion of public revelation in the fullness of time, and then the fuller manifestation of the content of public revelation once completed, that is, in its inward understanding, both on the part of individual persons and of the community under the guidance of the Magisterium. In such a context we can easily situate

---

141 On the argument from conscience, cf. A. Boekraad, The *Argument from Conscience to the Existence of God according to J. H. Newman*, (Louvain: 1961). Newman treats the argument especially in his "The Influence of Natural and Revealed Religion," cit., and the *Grammar of Assent*, part 1, ch. 5.

142 For Bonaventure, cf. his analysis in *De mysterio Ss. Trinitatis*, q. 1, a. 1; for the position of Scotus see the texts in Wolter, *The Transcendentals...*, cit., pp. 128 ff.; for Newman, *The Idea of a University*, and the *Grammar*.

For private consultation and not distribution without the consent of E Ondrako

what is meant by *sensus fidelium* and under what conditions it serves as a criterion of belief.

Most interesting of all is the fact that much of Newman's reflection in the *Grammar of Assent* has its proximate source in Butler, and, so, in a sense, in Scotus. It is in the *Grammar of Assent* that we find the genuine phenomenology and metaphysics-epistemology underlying the *Apologia*, or his theory of faith, so central to a metaphysical theology. As we have already seen, Newman, like Scotus,[143] relates, but carefully distinguishes natural and supernatural faith. The first is not at all fideistic. The personal-mystical character of Newman's personality reflects the influence of the Alexandrians, an influence also present in Scotus's Christology.[144]

The Person and the Church

A third consideration revolves about Newman's involvement in the Oxford Movement, his theory of the *via media* and his *Tracts for the Times*, culminating in his resignation from his positions in Oxford and in the Anglican Church, and leading to the *Development of Doctrine* and entry into the Catholic Church. In a sense the discovery of Butler (and behind Butler some aspects of the great scotistic tradition in England which had never disappeared despite the Calvinist-erastian Reformation) enabled Newman to find the heart of a *via media* between scientism and pietistic fideism. But his attempt after 1830 to apply this discovery within the Anglican fold in order to secure genuine renewal of Christian faith in England, led him at first to think of the Anglican tradition as a *via media* between the dogmatic corruptions of Protestantism and the disciplinary aberrations of the Roman Church. Four works: *The Prophetic Office*, *The Lectures on Justification*, *The University Sermons* and *The Tracts for the Times*, each despite its special worth, failed in its major purpose: to demonstrate in theory and practice the viability of said theory. Instead, with the crisis over *Tract* 90, Newman came to see that what was profoundly true in each could only be fully realized within the Church of Rome, with an acknowledgment of the papal primacy of jurisdiction and the maternal mediation of Mary in the Church. Whereas the *via media* or appeal to "antiquity" Newman came to see as a characteristic device of heretics to disguise their errors as "fidelity" to tradition, his essay on doctrinal development showed the Roman Church simply to be the one, true Church instituted by Christ, simply the same in the midst of legitimate variations, not a middle way between extremes (*à la* Hegel).

---

[143] Cf. Walter, *Das Glaubensverständnis…*, cit.
[144] Cf. Kerrigan, *The Predestination of Mary*, cit.

For private consultation and not distribution without the consent of E Ondrako

Weatherby points to this theory of development as a sure sign of Hegelian influence on Newman and the reason why Anglican or Orthodox traditionalism is preferable to Roman Catholic modernism. How well grounded is Weatherby's interpretation? It is shared by many, some sympathetic to Weatherby's version of traditionalism which admits of no development at all, and some (Lash) sympathetic to the modernism later condemned by Pius X.[145]   Both groups point to Newman's later sympathetic observations on Darwin's theories and apparent nominalism in the *Grammar of Assent* as indicative of a radically Kantian-Hegelian inspiration in the *Development of Doctrine*.

This, however, is hardly conclusive. It might only have been the fruit of an interest in science and a search for a conciliatory approach to one particular question concerning the relation of faith and science. It does not seem that Newman ever called into question the received teaching on the creation of the world and formation of Adam and Eve. More importantly, Lecture 4, part 2 of the *Idea of a University*, entitled *A Form of Infidelity of the Day* in effect is a prevision of the essential error of modernism: that it is impossible naturally to arrive at any certainty of God's existence, and a firm repudiation of it.[146] It would, then, in my opinion, be quite mistaken to posit Hegelian evolutionism as inspiration for the notion of development expounded in the *Development of Doctrine*. Finally, Newman's criteria for distinguishing authentic and inauthentic variations in doctrine over the course of history should be pondered in relation to the reflections of Bossuet in his study of doctrinal variations in Protestantism. In Newman's day, Anglican divines were much engaged in showing how no such corruptions had contaminated Anglicanism as they had contaminated Catholicism. What Newman came to realize was that without an admission of the fact of doctrinal development, it was impossible to avoid one or another of two extremes which we know as traditionalism (fideism, pietism, integralism, etc.) and modernism (in its various forms such as "semi-rationalism" or semi-Hegelianism; various forms of Kantian transcendentalism, including the thomistic, etc.).

But I think there is another consideration to be introduced here, one indicating a certain relation between the premises of Newman's theory and the implications for fundamental theology (or theological hermeneutics) of Scotus's teaching in the prologue to the *Ordinatio*. Newman himself tells

---

145 Cf. E. T. O'DWYER, *Cardinal Newman and the Encyclical Pascendi Dominici Gregis*, (London 1908), and the letter of Pope St. Pius X approving this essay: *Epistula , qua Pius PP X approbat opusculum Episcopi Limericiensis circa scripta Card. Newman, die 10a Martii, 1908*. Cf. WEATHERBY, *Cardinal Newman in His Age*, cit., and Idem, *The Keen Delight*, cit.; N. LASH, *Newman on Development*, Shepherdstown, VA 1975.

146 *Idea of a University*, part 2, discourse 5: A Form of Infidelity of the Day.

For private consultation and not distribution without the consent of E Ondrako

us that the major influence in the writing of the *Development of Doctrine* was Bishop Butler. We have already observed that the approach of Butler in theology is not unrelated to the pre-reformation scotistic tradition in England. The approach of Butler contrasts with that of Whateley, with whom Newman had broken, precisely because of his rationalism, a rationalism reflecting the nominalist [and, therefore, radically "agnostic"] tradition of Ockham. Had Whateley been the major influence on the genesis of Newman's theory of doctrinal development, this would have been a good indication of his openness to the evolutionary modernism which Weatherby and so many others ascribe to him. In fact, this is simply not the case. If anything, there was an indirect influence of Scotus, an influence in Newman clearly anti-modernistic.

This is most easily seen in Newman's concept of an idea. It corresponds in Bonaventure to what is called *ratio*, and in Scotus to the *formalitas a parte rei*. If there is anything the exact opposite of the Kantian and Hegelian notion of evolution, it is this extra-mental, immutable foundation of all change and variation in formulation without change in content, one which secures a realistic point of departure for all our reasoning and the possibility of arriving at a clear grasp of the Truth. Exactly the opposite is the case with the Kantian concept of development where change of formulation leads to a change of content, as a lower species evolves into a higher. Newman's theory is equally important, it seems to me, in appreciating the doctrinal development bearing on the Franciscan thesis concerning the absolute primacy of Christ, and in the metaphysical realm the univocal concept of being which underlies the analogy or sacramentality of creation, not only in Bonaventure, but in Butler as well. Perhaps a more likely patristic basis for the theory of doctrinal development than Hegelian evolution is to be discovered in the early Christian theory of recapitulation and recirculation, a theory well known to be intimately related to the patristic bases for the absolute primacy of Christ.

Many contemporary writers,[147] in part grounding their views on Newman's theory of development, insist that the primarily dogmatic-metaphysical exposition of theology must be replaced by a method primarily biblical-historical. Hence, the metaphysical, immutable character of the traditional, scholastic manual, must be replaced by a hermeneutic sensitive to historical development. The shift in Catholic circles during the 20th century from entitling the doctrinal treatise on the mystery of Christ: *De Verbo Incarnato*, to entitling it: *Christology*, arises from this. The first title stresses the study of the Incarnation primarily for its own sake, prior to

---

[147] Cf. Bordoni, *Cristologia: lettura sistematica,* cit., for an overview of these theologians.

For private consultation and not distribution without the consent of E Ondrako

any consideration of redemption. The second stresses an exposition of the Incarnation primarily in relation to our ransom from sin and the changing circumstances in which the fruits of this ransom are realized. Stress is shifted, therefore, from a prior study of the eternal, divine counsels of salvation (the order of intention) as basis for an understanding of their realization in history to the order of execution (historical event), radically evolutionary and requiring an ever renewed and nuanced hermeneutic as basis for a theological explanation of the "Event-Christ" here and now.

But neither Scotus nor Newman make such a dichotomy between the metaphysical and historical in theology, particularly in expounding the mystery of the Word made flesh. This is clear enough in the case of Scotus from his thesis on the absolute primacy and the middle position he takes between the neo-augustians and neo-aristotelians in epistemology, and his insistence on the need to harmonize the simple and complex in the human understanding in terms of a *perfectio simpliciter simplex*.[148] The same is true of Newman in view of the reading I have given "idea": not the Kantian *fictio mentis*, but the scotistic *formalitas a parte rei*. Development of thought (or the historical character of thought) cannot be grasped correctly apart from a prior acknowledgment of the fixed "idea" in development, or concretely in the priority of the order of intention (signs of the divine will *ad extra*) over order of execution (history). History is meaningless apart from its metaphysical presuppositions and, in the case of theology, the absolute primacy of the Incarnation.[149] That this is the case with Newman will be confirmed when we examine in the next part his acceptance of the "Franciscan thesis" without reservations as basis for a correct understanding of the "Christ-event." Later in part 3 of this conference we will note the importance of these points in correctly interpreting Newman's use of notional and real apprehension-assent in relation to Scotus's abstractive-intuitive cognition.

With this we may assume that a more careful study of *The University Sermons* will bring to light many other approximations to Scotus's views on faith, reason and theology, particularly as these are sketched in the Prologue to the *Ordinatio*.[150] We also see here how the abjuration of the last vestiges of Calvinism by Newman led him to accept with ease precisely those three

---

[148] Cf. C. DEVLIN, *The Psychology of Duns Scotus*, cit., pp. 3 ff.

[149] Cf. J. RATZINGER, *Jesus of Nazareth*, New York 2007. The metaphysical presuppositions of historical study, above all of the Gospels, are continually stressed by the Holy Father in his rejoinder to the skepticism about Jesus engendered by use of historical-critical method apart from these presuppositions.

[150] *Ordinatio*, parts 1–5. If one of the common influences shared by Scotus and Newman is that of the Alexandrian school, the reflections offered here find further support. Cf. KING, *Newman and the Alexandrian Fathers…*, cit.

For private consultation and not distribution without the consent of E Ondrako

points of scotistic teaching most violently opposed by Calvinism: the Eucharist, the Immaculate Conception and the primacy of the Pope.

Love of Learning and Desire for God

My final considerations in this first part of my conference revolve about the presence of Scotus in _The Idea of a University._ Little or no attention in studies on this classic has been paid to the fact that, three times in it, Newman makes mention of Bl. John Duns Scotus.[151] No doubt one reason for mentioning Scotus in a series of lectures linked to the newly founded Catholic University of Ireland is his celtic provenance, thought by many since the time of Wadding to mean Ireland, but now commonly admitted to be Duns in southeastern Scotland. Like the northeast of England, Northumberland and Lindisfarne, southeastern Scotland, so close to Lindisfarne, was also evangelized by Irish monks from Iona. Duns is an Irish name meaning castle, and the remains of one is found in Duns, Scotland, whence the name of the town and his family. But in two of these references, Newman refers with high praise to Scotus as the greatest theological luminary Oxford ever knew and a prime example of what he, Newman, had in mind as a theory of Catholic higher or university education, especially in theology. A theory of education presupposes a theory of knowledge or explanation of the love for learning and its relation to the affective or moral power, the will focused on the desire for God.

Many students of Newman's lectures in _The Idea of a University_ have noted what seems to be a certain tension in Newman's efforts to integrate love of learning with desire for God, or how to include theology as an integral part of university formation without compromising the sound development of the sciences with religious evangelization and moralistic dogmatizing.[152] What these scholars mean can be easily discerned by comparing the first version of lecture 5 in the first part with that which appeared in subsequent editions. In the first edition Newman seemed to concede a part of what so many Irish Bishops expected a Catholic university to be: a tool to ensure that the graduates would not lose their faith in seeking to be qualified for various secular pursuits. In effect, the university was being equated with what is proper and distinctive of a seminary or internal monastic school. Newman never questioned the propriety or necessity of the Tridentine seminary.[153]

---

[151] _Idea of a University_, part 1, discourse 7, 3; part 2, discourse 5, 2; discourse 9, 3.

[152] Cf. the edition of _The Idea of a University_ prepared by C. F. Harrold (New York 1947): the preface and introduction by Harrold.

[153] _Idea_, part 1, discourse 8.

For private consultation and not distribution without the consent of E Ondrako

But it is obvious from editions of this work after 1858 that he did not equate the goal of the university with that of the seminary, nor explain the necessary presence of theology in a university curriculum as did so many of the Irish bishops. For him the immediate goal of university education was neither that of scientific research (expansion of knowledge, goal of the academies of yesteryear) nor apologetics or religious perfection (defense of the faith; growth in holiness: practical theology), but that of "academic excellence," balanced speculation, the habit of discerning prudently in view of the goal of life, and, therefore, the formation of an intellectually mature person as the prerequisite for both defense of the faith and growth in faith or holiness of life. Newman, of course, admitted the practical side of knowledge, both professionally and religiously, and devotes several lectures in this work to this subject. What he insisted upon, however, was the ideal of knowledge also as an end in itself, and that it was this which distinguished university study as such. And what he insisted on here presupposed the unity of all knowledge with theology as its queen.[154] That unity is exactly what in the metaphysical theology of Scotus is secured by the univocal notion of being or, in Bonaventure, by what he calls the fontal object of the human mind, that without which it would not be a *perfectio simpliciter simplex*, formally identical in God and in the created person, even if infinite in the first, and finite, complex in the second.

Is this position the equivalent of saying Catholic universities are only such because mostly Catholics happen to teach or study there; otherwise they are essentially the same as secular universities, e.g., the newly founded University of London where theology was excluded from the curriculum, indeed where empirical science *à la* Kant defined knowledge as such? In some ways the question resembles that over the Catholic character of Catholic philosophy. What I want to suggest here is that the position of Newman concerning the goal of the university as knowledge for its own sake, or academic excellence, ease in exercising discretion (the illative sense) represents a *tertium quid,* very similar to the views of the so called "morally neutral human act" in relation to the will as a *perfectio simpliciter simplex*, and that this discussion bears directly on what occurs when a man begins to enter into himself and reflect critically on what it means to be a person, as St. Bonaventure outlines this in chapters 3 and 4 of his *Itinerarium*. This, the Seraphic Doctor uses as point of departure for his classic on spiritual theology, *De triplici via*, a point of departure identified in that work as goading of conscience. This also happens to be Newman's

---

154 *Idea*, part 1, discourse 3.

For private consultation and not distribution without the consent of E Ondrako

major point of departure for discussing the heart of natural theology, the proof of God's existence from conscience.

In such a context, Newman, like the major representatives of the Franciscan tradition in theology, St. Bonaventure and Bl. John Duns Scotus, regards the love of learning without the stains of secular erudition, of the intellect radically agnostic, as fruit of that desire for God imbedded in our hearts, our memory, yet only realized fully with the help of divine revelation and grace in the love of God.

These considerations conclude the first part of this conference. I think they are more than sufficient to show, both on the testimony of competent scholars and on the evidence of Newman's life, that there exists an *a priori* basis for asserting a scotistic bias in the more important works of Newman, and for not regarding such an interpretation as fanciful or forced.

Secunda Pars: Examples of Scotistic Affinities in Newman

In this second part of my three part conference, I want to offer a variety of examples from the writings of Newman which, notwithstanding a somewhat different terminology, clearly coincide with what Scotus often affirms. Neither time nor space permits me to quote extensively from Scotus. Examples in the works of Scotus of what I have in mind can be found quickly in the secondary literature cited in the footnotes.

Here I want to concentrate on the text of Newman and indicate why I think the examples selected from Newman do indicate how Scotus and Newman are two luminaries moving along the same trajectory in theology, both worthy one day of being declared doctors of the Church. These examples are taken from five of Newman's writings, all composed after his conversion, viz., after his personal growth in faith had come to full term, even though many of the ideas found in them occur in works written before that event. In illustration of the latter I have drawn mainly on the *Oxford University Sermons*. The order of their presentation in this second part is as follows: selections from various *Sermons*, his *Select Treatises of Athanasius* and the *The Arians of the Fourth Century* on the motive of the Incarnation; the *Memorandum on the Immaculate Conception*; *The Idea of a University, Defined and Illustrated*; *Apologia pro vita sua*. *An Essay in Aid of a Grammar of Assent* and selections from the *Oxford University Sermons*, which Newman links with the *Grammar*, will be treated in the third and final section. We might say that in this second part attention is concentrated on the Christo-centric Christology-soteriology with the metaphysics which this entails; whereas, in the third, attention will be

For private consultation and not distribution without the consent of E Ondrako

focused on the epistemological issues in view of which Scotus-Newman are either accepted or rejected today.

While the examples offered for reflection are by no means an exhaustive listing of all possibilities,[155] they do provide illustrations of affinities between Newman and Scotus in four key areas: dogmatic in the sermons and *Memorandum*, metaphysical in the *Idea*, apologetic in the *Apologia*, and epistemological in the *Grammar* and in the *Oxford University Sermons*. The affinities are not so much revealed via identity of linguistic formulations or citations of Scotus by Newman (which do not exist) as through recognition in key discussions of Newman, the presence of fundamental themes of Scotus.   While a careful examination of Newman's sermons would yield many examples reflecting Scotus's Christology, the fact that he tells us he subscribes to the scotistic thesis on the primary motive of the Incarnation is sufficient documentation for the purposes of this presentation, whose goal is to show how this fact also includes an acceptance of the Mariology and spirituality of Scotus, based on the primacy of the will and charity.

Writings Dealing with the Motive of the Incarnation

R. Strange claims[156] that before 1840 every explicit treatment of the motive of the Incarnation by Newman seems to link this motive solely to the problem of sin. Subsequently, most probably as a consequence of his study of St. Athanasius, he came to adopt expressly the position of Scotus on this subject, one he understood quite accurately as his letter to Faber already cited shows.   Not everyone then or now agrees with Newman's interpretation of Athanasius.   Nonetheless, studies have shown that St. Cyril of Alexandria, a disciple of St. Athanasius, explicitly reads the latter "scotistically" not only in relation to the Incarnation, but the predestination of Mary—in such a context, the basis in the mind of God for the Immaculate Conception.[157] What must be noted also is that none of the texts of Newman cited in favor of an earlier thomism necessarily excludes the scotistic position, as Strange himself notes.   What Strange does not take into consideration was the apparent influence of scotism in the composition of the *Lectures on the Doctrine of Justification* as indicated above in note 2.

---

155 In particular, little attention has been paid to the *Lectures on the Doctrine of Justification* and the *Development of Doctrine*.

156 Strange, *Newman and the Gospel of Christ*, cit., pp. 111 ff.; cf. King, *Newman and the Alexandrian Fathers…*, cit.

157 F. Risi, *Sul motivo dell'Incarnazione del Verbo*, Brescia-Roma 1897–1898; C. Urritibéhéty, *Christus Alpha et Omega, seu de Christi Regno*, (Lille 1910); Kerrigan, "The Predestination of Mary," cit.

For private consultation and not distribution without the consent of E Ondrako

Here are some texts from Newman illustrating scotistic Christology with its metaphysical presuppositions to be his own.

Commenting on a statement of St. Athanasius seemingly serving to justify the thomistic thesis, Newman remarks:

> However, there are theologians of great name, who consider that the decree of the Incarnation was independent of Adam's fall; and certainly by allowing that it was not absolutely necessary for divine forgiveness of sin, and that it was the actual and immediate means of the soul's renewal and sanctification… Athanasius goes far towards countenancing that belief.[158]

In making the very same point as Scotus does concerning the absolute necessity of the Incarnation not for forgiveness of sin, but only for the revelation of the perfect love of God apart from any need of forgiveness, Newman underscores a point in fact found in innumerable Fathers and certainly in both St. Paul and St. John. He makes this even clearer in his *Discourses to Mixed Congregations*. For example, in *The Mystery of Divine Condescension* he writes:

> He [the Son] revealed to our first father in his state of innocence a higher mercy, which in the fullness of time was to be accomplished in his behalf.[159]

In Scotus and Newman this soteriological position is linked not only to the thesis on the absolute predestination of Christ, but to theories on justification and divine acceptance. As regards this last point Newman acknowledges the similarities of his views with scotism in his *Lectures on the Doctrine of Justification*.[160]

In another sermon from the same collection, *The Infinitude of the Divine Attributes*, where he seeks to illustrate the unlimited nature of God's attributes, he calls attention first to the Incarnation and Redemption.

> We know well, and firmly hold, that our Lord Jesus Christ, the Son of God, died on the cross in satisfaction for our sins… But he need not have died, for the Almighty God might have saved us all, might have saved the whole world, without His dying. He might have pardoned and brought to heaven every individual child of

---

[158] *Select Treatises of Athanasius*, II, 187–188.

[159] *Discourses to Mixed Congregations*, p. 298. Compare this with similar views of Sts. Bonaventure and Thomas on the revelation to Adam and Eve of the mystery of the Incarnation and divine Maternity before original sin: cf. P. Fehlner, "Redemption, Metaphysics and the Immaculate Conception," in *Mary at the Foot of the Cross* V, (New Bedford, MA: 2005), pp. 186–262, here 232–234.

[160] See note 2 above for references.

For private consultation and not distribution without the consent of E Ondrako

Adam without the incarnation and death of His Son… His word had been enough; with Him to say is to do.[161]

This reflects the view of Athanasius,[162] that His coming to make satisfaction was not necessary, but to take a ransom was expedient and fitting for us. Newman also notes in this paragraph that <u>the Incarnation was necessary for a true satisfaction</u> from sin, but satisfaction here, just as in Scotus, <u>should not be confused with pardon.</u> The necessity of the Incarnation in relation to Redemption is that of supplying the generosity true satisfaction demands. The possibility of such generosity is implicit in the willing of the Incarnation prior to any consideration of sin. Newman clearly holds that man could have been pardoned without satisfaction being made. But even if the satisfaction in a true sense was made, such language for Newman, as for Scotus, was itself inadequate as "rigorously speaking, one being can never, by his own suffering, simply discharge the debt of another's sin."[163] For Newman the notion of expedience will not support a relationship of essential necessity between the Incarnation and Redemption. Hence, he concludes that <u>Christ came</u> because from the first He "had had it in mind to come upon earth <u>among innocent creatures,</u>"[164] <u>to fill them with grace and prepare them for heaven</u> for which they were destined. At that time man had been innocent, but, before the plan could be fulfilled, he had sinned. Thus, Christ came,

> not in that brightness in which [He] went forth to create the morning stars and to fill the sons of God with melody, but in deformity and in shame, in sighs and tears, with blood upon [His] cheek, and with [His] limbs laid bare and rent.[165]

In the order of historical execution Christ came to redeem as well as to sanctify, but according to the order of divine intention, <u>Christ was to have come in any case,</u> because He was the reason for which the entire creation was made in the first place. As does Scotus, so Newman clearly distinguishes sanctification and redemption, and orientates our sanctification to the glory, not merely of the Eternal Word, but the Incarnate Word through a great sacrifice of praise and thanks. Further, he places the Incarnation first in the order of divine intention and subordinates creation as such—and not merely creation as redeemed—to the Incarnation, at the same time explaining how this is true even though the Incarnation in

---

161 *Discourses to Mixed Congregations*, p. 305.

162 *The Arians of the Fourth Century*, II, p. 68.

163 *Discourses to Mixed Congregations*, pp. 306–307.

164 *Discourses to Mixed Congregations*, pp. 321–322.

165 *Discourses to Mixed Congregations*, p. 322.

For private consultation and not distribution without the consent of E Ondrako

the order of execution comes after the fall. By treating this in a sermon on the infinity of the divine attributes, Newman clearly links his adoption of scotistic views on the motive of the Incarnation to the metaphysical and epistemological dimensions of Scotus's theology.

From this it is clear that Newman's interest in Scotus was hardly an eclectic one. Even before his conversion to the Catholic Church the systematic character of Scotus's theology is already beginning to appear in that of Newman. And Newman's patristic roots seem to be also those of Scotus. The following examination of the *Memorandum on the Immaculate Conception* confirms this.

Memorandum on the Immaculate Conception

This very brief, but important document clearly illustrates the scotistic sympathies of <u>Newman</u> in the context of a theme basic and distinctive to Scotus's Mariology in relation to his Christology, viz., the Immaculate Conception in relation to the absolute primacy of Christ. In this work Newman clearly states that the <u>Immaculate Conception is not in view of original sin</u>, just as in the texts about the motive of the Incarnation he says that it is not primarily in view of sin, but rather the entire creation is for the sake of the Incarnation. This, rather than the approach of Sts. Anselm and Thomas, is what determines the character of his soteriology. Hence, original sin is to be understood and explained in relation to the logically prior mystery of the Immaculate Conception and preservative redemption in the divine counsels of salvation. This is simply the Marian mode of Scotus's position: the Incarnation is not for the sake of either redemption or creation; but creation and redemption are for the sake of the Incarnation and divine Maternity. We cannot too much underscore the importance of this brief note as a clear, unequivocal acceptance on Newman's part, not only of scotistic Christology, but also of the metaphysics of univocal being characteristic of it, one providing the Christian basis for Newman's theory of knowledge both in *The Idea of a University* and in the *Grammar of Assent*.[166]

From the first section of the *Memorandum* points four and five might be described as a beautiful English rendition of the reasoning of Scotus on the Immaculate Conception, both on the "perfect fruit of a perfect redemption" and that by which Mary differs from us: not nature, but a superabundance of grace from her very beginning or Immaculate Concep-

---

[166] Cf. B. Ullathorne, *The Immaculate Conception*, New York 1904 (2nd ed.), pp. 64–80, for additional aspects of scotistic Mariology with which Newman may have been acquainted. Ullathorne and Newman were good friends; the study of Ullathorne was first published (1854) during the same time as the Memorandum of Newman was penned.

For private consultation and not distribution without the consent of E Ondrako

tion. Both points in the final analysis imply the absolute primacy of Jesus and the scotistic approach to the impeccability of Jesus in His human nature and that of Mary in hers.[167] This superabundance of grace from the very beginning of her existence: implicitly defining her person or incommunicable existence in her every moment, radically defines the difference between the truest and a merely true sense of redemption: between preservative and liberative redemption.

4. We do not say she did not owe her salvation to the death of her Son. Just the contrary, we say that she, of all mere children of Adam, is in the truest sense the fruit and the purchase of His Passion. He has done for her more than anyone else. To others He gives grace and regeneration at a *point* in their earthly existence, to her from the very *beginning*.

5. We do not make her nature different from others, though, as St. Austin says, we do not like to name her in the same breath *with* mention of sin; yet, certainly, she would have been a frail being, like Eve, *without* the grace of God. A more abundant gift of grace made her what she was from the first. It was not her *nature* which secured her perseverance, but the excess of grace which hindered Nature from acting as Nature ever will act. There is no difference in *kind* between her and us, though an inconceivable difference of *degree.* She and we are both simply saved by the grace of Christ.

The absolute primacy of Jesus is clearly reflected in the concluding section where Newman shows how the Catholic concept of the Immaculate Conception subordinates sin to grace and so doing implies that in the order of intention—creation first, and then, redemption—are willed by God for the sake of the Incarnation, willed first before both.

Many, many doctrines are far harder than the Immaculate Conception. The doctrine of Original Sin is infinitely harder. Mary just has not this difficulty. It is no difficulty to believe that a soul is united to the body without Original Sin; the great mystery is that any, that millions on millions, are born with it. Our teaching about Mary has just one difficulty less than our teaching about the state of mankind in general.[168]

---

[167] *Meditations and Devotions*, p. 79. For texts of Scotus on this point cf. R. ROSINI, *Mariology of Blessed John Duns Scotus*, (New Bedford: 2008), pp. 88 ff.

[168] *Meditations and Devotions*, p. 85. Cf. A. APOLLONIO, "Mary's So-called Debitum Peccati Originalis," in *Blessed John Duns Scotus and His Mariology*, (New Bedford: 2009), pp. 321–348.

For private consultation and not distribution without the consent of E Ondrako

I include the passage from Newman's 1832 sermon on *The Reverence due to the Virgin Mary* for the feast of the Annunciation (celebrating the Incarnation and divine Motherhood, but in the Lenten season with its focus on the Redemption and Coredemption), which Newman appended to the *Memorandum* on its publication to show the continuity of his reflection, in particular on the All-holiness of the Mother of God as implying the Immaculate Conception, exactly the way in which Scotus read tradition and concluding with a thought similar to the famous one of St. Francis.[169] It would seem that a scotistic influence in some way had touched Newman long before 1840 and the studies on St. Athanasius.

> Who can estimate the holiness and perfection of her, who was chosen to be the Mother of Christ? If to him that hath, more is given, and holiness and Divine favour go together (and this we are expressly told), what must have been the transcendent purity of her, whom the Creator Spirit condescended to overshadow with His miraculous presence? What must have been her gifts, who was chosen to be the only near earthly relative of the Son of God, the only one whom He was bound by nature to revere and look up to; the one appointed to train and educate Him, to instruct Him day by day, as He grew in wisdom and in stature? This contemplation runs to a higher subject, did we dare follow it; for what, think you, was the sanctified state of that human nature, of which God formed His sinless Son; knowing as we do, "that which is born of the flesh is flesh," and that "none can bring a clean thing out of an unclean"? [I Jn 3: 6; Job 14: 4]
> … for nothing is so calculated to impress on our minds that Christ is really partaker of our nature, and in all respects man, save sin only, as to associate Him with the thought of her, by whose ministration He became our brother.[170]

Does this last sentence suggest the influence of Mary in first guiding him along scotistic lines? One may at the very least say that the passage from Newman's reflection on Mary's All-holiness in this sermon, to an identification of its center in the Immaculate Conception, follows the same pattern of development of this doctrine which occurred in the history of the Church and in which Scotus played so important a role.[171]

---

[169] St. Bonaventure, *Legenda maior*, ch. 9, 3.

[170] The Reverence due to the Virgin Mary, in *Parochial and Plain Sermons*, vol. 2, pp. 131–132; 136.

[171] Cf. P. D. Fehlner, "The Predestination of the Virgin Mother and Her Immaculate Conception" in *Mariology. A Guide for Priests, Deacons, Seminarians, and Consecrated Persons*, Goleto CA 2007, pp. 249–262.

For private consultation and not distribution without the consent of E Ondrako

Although it is not expressly affirmed here, the scotistic approach of Newman to the Immaculate Conception implies important relations with the questions touching theology and metaphysics, apologetics, epistemology and natural faith, faith and freedom. Some of these points are insinuated in the last of the *Oxford University Sermons*.[172] One of these particularly relevant to the theme of this conference is the priority given by both Newman as well as Scotus to the importance of the *decuit* in demonstrating the divine *fiat* in predestining Mary to be immaculately conceived. This is but an application of the place of the illative sense or personal judgment in theology, an indication of how the minds of these two Oxford greats ran along similar lines.[173]

A final comment worth making here concerns another point of theology on which Newman expressly tells us he accepts the viewpoints of Scotus, one closely associated with questions touching the Incarnation and mystery of Mary. This concerns his teaching on the uncreated gift of the Holy Spirit in relation to the problem of justification and created grace. In both the original edition of his *Lectures on the Doctrine of Justification* before his conversion, and in the revised edition after that conversion, he says his views are supported by the teaching of major scotistic theologians at the Council of Trent, such as Cornelius Musso, and, therefore by implication, reconcilable with the teaching of Trent on the sole formal cause of justification as created grace.[174] I am convinced he is correct in this, and that the reconciliation rests ultimately on a theory of personal or voluntary causality such as Bonaventure and Scotus defend, and Newman as well in the *Grammar of Assent*. This type of causality is not to be confused with formal causality or quasi-formal causality suggested by some modern thomists to account for the dynamic priority of the uncreated grace in the work of sanctification. This point, together with that on the primary motive of the Incarnation and that on the Immaculate Conception, suggests that the scotistic flavor noticed in so many other distinctive positions of Newman is not mistaken.

---

172 "The Theory of Development in Religious Doctrine," sermon 15 in *Oxford University Sermons*. Cf. P. D. FEHLNER, Redemption, Metaphysics and the Immaculate Conception, in *Mary at the Foot of the Cross* V, (New Bedford: 2005), pp. 186–262; E. ONDRAKO, "Mary and the Church in Newman with an Eye to Coredemption," in *Mary at the Foot of the Cross* IX, (New Bedford: 2010), pp. 391–455.

173 Cf. PETER DAMIAN FEHLNER, "Mary and Theology: Scotus Revisited," ch. 4 in this volume.

174 Cf. *Lectures on the Doctrine of Justification*, Lecture 9 and Appendix 1: On the Formal Cause of Justification, nos. 3 & 14.

For private consultation and not distribution without the consent of E Ondrako

The Idea of a University

In modern times, preoccupation with the logical aspects of the univocal concept of being as an alternative to the Augustinian-Bonaventurian theory of divine illumination and metaphysical exemplarism, so as to provide coherent metaphysical and epistemological grounds for avoiding the dual pitfalls of [authoritarian] fideism and [agnostic] rationalism, largely accounts for lack of consideration given the more important theological background leading to this discussion, one not so much an alternative as a "reformulation." That theological background centers on the so-called Franciscan thesis, viz., the absolute primacy of Christ, of which the metaphysical shadow is the scotistic teaching on univocity of being and the radical sacramentality of creation vis-à-vis the Christian order of salvation. Closely linked to this theme are questions touching the formal object of the intellect and unity of knowledge, the place of theology in a university curriculum and its content: the relation of science and wisdom, the character of the power to know, like that of the power to will, as a *perfectio simpliciter simplex*; and how love of learning or intellectual excellence and desire for God are to be reconciled.

For Scotus, the proper object of the human intellect is not simply the essence of material beings, but being as such via the univocal concept of being and its disjunctive transcendental. Evidently, a concept of creation in view of a prior willing of the Incarnation, only finds a place in our understanding if in fact it is conceived as a "pure perfection" with an opening on the supernatural order of grace centered on the Incarnation as the good willed simply for its own sake. It is this which provides the foundation for a certain unity of knowledge in Scotus, also at the heart of Newman's reflections on the difference between liberal and useful knowledge, basis of the features of a university formation as distinct from that of a practical school, and reason for the inclusion of theological study as the queen of the sciences rather than mathematized-empirical science, central feature of the "modern" university.

Most of these metaphysical points are reflected in Newman's great work on Christian pedagogy at the university level. Carefully pondered, they disclose a striking similarity with positions distinctive of Scotus's metaphysics. This should be no surprise. No great work dealing with the basics of pedagogy can ignore its metaphysical or "meta-pedagogical" ground. This is clear enough in the most famous medieval treatise of this kind: *De reductione artium ad Theologiam* by St. Bonaventure and its link to the *Breviloquium* and *Itinerarium mentis in Deum*.

For private consultation and not distribution without the consent of E Ondrako

Considerations of time and space do not permit an exhaustive treatment of these points in the *Idea of a University*. I have selected four themes basic to Newman's explanation of the role of a university in the intellectual formation of the human mind, which I think illustrate the point just made. These are the unity of knowledge presupposed by all its various parts; the place of theology within this frame of reference; the principle of causality and the will; and knowledge: an end in itself and the relation between liberal and useful knowledge, science and wisdom.

(1.) In the introductory discourse of this work Newman clearly defines their theme: the nature and goal of university education and the position he intends to take in expounding this theme and in explaining how such a project as the proposed Catholic University of Ireland fits into this vision. In simplest terms the structure of a university is to impart Liberal Knowledge, a knowledge which by definition is universal: *de omni scibili*, and which must be carefully distinguished from Useful Knowledge, whether this be for secular or religious ends. Useful knowledge deals only with that which is useful or practical for some end beyond itself; liberal knowledge is an end in itself, deals with that which is good for its own sake. This distinction also is found in the Prologue to the *Ordinatio* of Scotus where he deals with the difference between speculative and practical knowledge. In the intellectual order it parallels the difference between the *affectio justitiae* and *affectio commodi* of Scotus in the affective order of the will, and explains how it is possible for science to become wisdom, or, as St. Bonaventure says, for knowledge to pass into affection and reach the divine mode of knowing.[175]

In taking this stand, Newman clearly intends to identify his position with what he understands the university to have been at its inception in the Middle Ages. Then, the fine tuning of academic excellence (the degree of *Magister artium*) was the indispensable prerequisite for specialization, whether this be medicine (the physical order in the service of man), or law (the social-anthropological order) or theology (the economy of salvation). In this way liberal knowledge was differentiated from useful on a sound basis without pragmatically substituting for true knowledge (as for instance in the radical reorganization of the university program of the then newly established University of London). On this basis universities are to be distinguished from academies whose goal is not the imparting but the expansion of knowledge in any field, religious included, and from schools whose goal is training in practice of any kind, such as theological seminaries for the training of priests, religious houses of formation, technical schools,

---

175 Hoeres, *Der Wille*, cit.; St. Bonaventure, *Collationes in Hexaemeron*, 5, 12–13.

For private consultation and not distribution without the consent of E Ondrako

etc. With these latter and their necessity, Newman has no quarrel. Rather, he insists that their particular goals presuppose a recognition of the importance of Liberal Knowledge as an end in itself and the only secure basis for attaining their own ends, and that the university on the one hand, and, on the other, the academy, a technical school—the seminary, the house of religious or spiritual formation not be confused with a university, nor that the University be expected to supply those needs which only a professional school can supply. This is a truism often forgotten today in many parts of the Church where for instance theological study at a university is thought to supply for that which can only be imparted in a seminary or monastery.

With the revolutionary reconstitution of the medieval universities, first in Germany during the 18th century and then generally throughout Europe and North America during the 19th century, on an exclusively pragmatic or utilitarian basis so as to provide the intellectual specialization necessary to justify and carry out the activities and projects which empirico-mathematical science makes possible, Newman very clearly does have a quarrel. Such a concept of knowledge as primarily useful rather than liberal deliberately omits as pointless the study of theology and of the liberal arts, because these are not useful in effecting secular progress. This concept reflects a Kantian epistemological bias, a good indication Newman does have a quarrel with Kant as well. At the time of delivery of these conferences, the two points of view were represented in England respectively by the renewal of the original medieval concept of a university curriculum at Oxford between 1800–1850 (a concept indispensable for understanding the pedagogical theory implicit in the teaching of Scotus), and by the revolutionary innovations in that curriculum being implemented for the first time in the English speaking world in the newly founded University of London (defended primarily in the pages of the *Edinburgh Review*). In this new university program the study of the liberal arts and above all of theology was deliberately omitted from the curriculum—for Newman, a tragic decision!

Of course, it was the Oxford model which Newman had in mind for the Catholic University of Ireland. With this came the need to show to a nation no longer familiar with the Catholic roots of this model, why this model is radically Catholic in the best sense. Like so many Catholics in the aftermath of the French revolution, the Irish were inclined to confuse a Catholic university with a training school for growth in virtue or exercise of ministry, a form of pragmatism Newman rightly thought would eventually be counterproductive. From this arose Newman's need to constantly stress the unique character of Liberal Knowledge (or the study of the liberal arts including philosophy and theology) when contrasted with secular or

For private consultation and not distribution without the consent of E Ondrako

religious use of such knowledge. Implied in this is a simple fact, denied by most modern pragmatists, whether secular (like the utilitarianism of Locke and Kant) or religious (like all forms of fideism), that Liberal Knowledge, or what Newman sometimes calls a philosophical temper of mind, does yield us a knowledge of reality which is not possible otherwise, and without which the single components of human knowledge tend to usurp roles for which they are not capable and tend to an abuse of the gift of intellect. In scotistic terms, even if *pro statu isto* it be no substitute for science, metaphysics yields us the very best kind of realistic knowledge: contemplation of the Truth or Light that is God, even if at the natural level it occurs in a dark, enigmatic manner and to attain perfection requires grace and holiness of life. This knowledge, not limited to sense objects as Locke would have it, is then no mere mental fiction, corresponding to nothing extra-mental as Kant affirms, and only authentic to the degree it provides a useful service as the epistemological justification for the empirico-mathematical scientific method, or for spiritual-ethical experience.

It might be well to note here that while Newman has in mind Francis Bacon, and in the sequel to *The Idea of a University*, which is the *Grammar of Assent*, Locke and Hume, as patrons of the utilitarian approach to learning, he is also implicitly refuting Kant. This is important in assessing the exact relation between Scotus and Kant. If the position of Newman coincides in fact with that of Scotus, we are in a good position to affirm that following Scotus will not lead to acceptance, but rejection of the views of Kant.

And indeed, we can grasp a further scotistic presence in two points fundamental to Newman's discussion of the nature and purpose of university education: it is universal: dealing with all that is knowable qua knowable: with *ens qua ens*, and not specialized; and it is liberal, not useful, an end in itself which justifies its imparting and mastery for its own sake, before it is used for any other end. Before we can appreciate these two qualities, we must briefly state what Newman understands by knowledge in the proper or formal sense of the term. He admits that this is not an easy task to accomplish briefly in English, because the term knowledge is so often used to denote, not knowledge itself without limit: *de omni scibili*, but secondary or tertiary instances of human knowing which, without the essential, are not knowledge, properly speaking, in the sense that knowledge is a pure, simply simple perfection. Behind this view of knowledge qua knowledge hovers the shadow of the absolute predestination of Christ; for the design of the intellect as a pure perfection, ultimately opening on *ens qua ens* without limit, *de omni scibili*, is precisely in view of the Incarnate

For private consultation and not distribution without the consent of E Ondrako

Word as Light of the world. This suggests further that the mystery of the hypostatic union and *ens qua ens* or being conceived initially as univocal are related, the latter being a kind of enigmatic reflection of the former, since the whole of creation was planned by the Creator in view of the glory of his Incarnate Son.

Newman, in this way, clearly and sharply differentiates human and brute "knowledge," the latter being merely a matter of the senses; whereas the former is an intellectual matter, whether we are dealing with notional or with real assents, in both cases directly centering on truth for its own sake and not merely on what is useful, workable, or least of all merely a mental fiction. Hence, knowledge as such is to be distinguished also from erudition, what might today be called encyclopedic knowledge of fact (what Newman calls the subject matter or factual content of knowledge, but not knowledge itself). Here we may note a certain scotistic touch: that knowledge being intellectual deals directly with being as such, not merely in the form of an abstract concept, but also in some way as a singular individual existent, Newman's two luminous beings, myself and my Creator-Savior. In the final analysis this is what explains why human sensation qualitatively differs from its counterparts in the animal kingdom.

In a positive manner Newman defines Liberal Knowledge in terms of its simplicity and complexity: its unity and universality and ultimately in view of the Creator's involvement in it though infinitely separate from it, an involvement centering about the Incarnation willed for its own sake, knowledge of which ultimately leads us to recognize *ens qua ens* concretely and fully.

> I lay it down that all knowledge forms one whole, because its subject-matter is one [in scotistic terms *ens qua ens*]; for the universe in its length and breadth is so intimately knit together, that we cannot separate off portion from portion, and operation from operation, except by a mental abstraction; and then again, as to its Creator, though He of course in His own Being is infinitely separate from it, and Theology has its departments towards which human knowledge has no relations, yet He has so implicated Himself with it, and taken it into His very bosom, by His presence in it, His providence over it, His impressions on it, and His influences through it, that we cannot truly or fully contemplate it without in some main aspects contemplating Him.[176]

---

176 *Idea of a University*, part 1, discourse 3, 4, pp. 54 ff. What Newman is treating here is the question underlying Scotus's development of the univocal concept of being as incomparable with other concepts, but to which other concepts qua concepts must be compared, the

For private consultation and not distribution without the consent of E Ondrako

If this passage accents the unity and, therefore, simplicity of knowledge qua assent to which faith is related, on the other hand the multiplication of sciences and their interrelations reflect the finite mode of human knowledge and ultimately give rise to the problem of certainty and the distinction of assent and inference. Newman continues:

> Next, sciences are the results of that mental abstraction, which I have spoken of, being the logical record of this or that aspect of the whole subject-matter of knowledge. As they all belong to one and the same circle of objects, they are one and all connected together; as they are but aspects of things, they are severally incomplete in their relation to the things themselves, though complete in their own idea and for their own respective purposes; on both accounts they at once need and subserve each other. And further, the comprehension of the bearings of one science on another, and the use of each to each, and the location and limitation and adjustment and due appreciation of them all, one with another, this belongs, I conceive, to a sort of science distinct from all of them [our metaphysics as Scotus conceives it, not epistemology], and in some sense a science of sciences, which is my own conception of what is meant by Philosophy, in the true sense of the word [love of wisdom], and of a philosophical habit of mind, and which in these Discourses I shall call by that name.[177]

Precisely because of this radical simplicity of the intellect as in scotistic terms: a *perfectio simpliciter simplex*, and because of its complexity as a finite process, Newman, like Scotus, insists that the human mind cannot deduce from metaphysics, not even from "our theology" as based on faith or on reason, truths proper to other "sciences." Hence, it is a tragic error to omit any science, above all theology and anthropology, from the university curriculum. Only when our theological knowledge is fully perfected can we attain a fully adequate philosophical habit of mind, capable of what St. Bonaventure calls a *resolutio plena* of all we have learned to unity. In theory at least, the perfect university formation is that of the Catholic university.

> I say, then, that the systematic omission of any one science from the catalogue prejudices the accuracy and completeness of our knowledge altogether, and that, in proportion to its importance. Not even Theology itself, though it comes from heaven, though

---

disjunctive transcendental, the divine essence as infinite, the obediential potency for the hypostatic union and sacramentality of the universe.

[177] *Idea.*

For private consultation and not distribution without the consent of E Ondrako

its truths were given once for all at the first, though they are more certain on account of the Giver than those of mathematics, not even Theology, so far as it is relative to us, or is the Science of Religion, do I exclude from the law to which every mental exercise is subject, viz., from that imperfection, which ever must attend the abstract, when it would determine the concrete.[178]

This is a perfect description of the position of Scotus in present day English. Without this philosophical habit of mind, the created intellect, so much involved in the definition of man as the image of God after the example of the Word, could not be accomplished.

As Scotus says,[179] it is this unity of knowledge which postulates the univocal concept of being as fundamental to the analogy. Without univocity the complexity and analogical character of human science cannot be reconciled with the radical simplicity of all knowing, for Newman centered on what he calls assent. The simplicity ultimately focuses on the question of God, i.e., knowledge of God or theology, or in medieval, especially Franciscan terms, the problem of the *resolutio plena* of all knowledge to its origin without which neither the universality nor unity of philosophy nor Liberal Knowledge is possible. Where this simplicity, which in the finite human intellect appears under the guise of the "pivotal" univocal concept of being, goes unacknowledged, the skepticism of Kant is unavoidable. Knowledge can only dissolve into chance or be identified falsely with one of its instances, such as empirical science.

The scotistic character of Newman's concept of "liberal knowledge" as the formal perfection of thought is confirmed as soon as it is compared with this observation of Marino Gentile on the relation of the two great approaches to metaphysics: that of Thomas and that of Scotus: the *via Thomae* and the *via Scoti* at the University of Padua during its heyday, the 15th through the 17th centuries. Gentile claims that the apparent opposition of the two chairs in Padua [before the French Revolution], is at a deeper level a kind of complementarity: that the undeniable advantages brought to human and Christian thought by the achievement of Aristotle and St. Thomas are perfected and, in a sense, rescued from the potent attack of Kant by the metaphysical synthesis of Scotus. I include here a translation of Gentile summarizing his insights.

---

[178] *Idea*.

[179] Cf. BOULNOIS, *Être et représentation*, cit., ch. 5. It is noteworthy that Boulnois first treats of memory, word, image and then univocity just as Bonaventure and Newman: from the real to the notional, to certitude and finally to ordered love.

For private consultation and not distribution without the consent of E Ondrako

In the face of the solid, compact unity of knowledge guaranteed thomism by the concept of analogy, the doctrine of univocity could not and still cannot but initially appear as a factor of disintegration. Yet this very concept of analogy would lose its fundamental meaning, if it were not shown to rest on the need to find a unitary meaning in the search for a principle, namely a need of Aristotelian speculation at its core, from the moment the theme of philosophy is individuated, both by Aristotle and Scotus, as being qua being. Even someone persuaded that the more fitting satisfaction of that basic need is offered by the division of being into a plurality of categories, can hardly not notice the duty of resolving [*resolutio plena*] that principle, everywhere and always, to a unity which does not nullify via distinction into categories the very theme of philosophy. There is hardly need to accept the strict definitions of the various schools to realize, now as well as in the past, that were it not possible to accept some unitary understanding of being, the very care to respect the singularity of forms in which it is expressed could not be realized. This occurs precisely because of a reductive equalization, such as is to be feared by whoever *in via Thomae* underscores the plurality of meanings of being... With still greater trepidation I suggest the same analysis on a point more contentious and burning and ask whether the polemics over individuality, attracting to scotism sympathies far beyond the old scholasticism, does not fit into this vision of the two ways as complementary. When Duns Scotus refutes the thomistic thesis about matter as the origin of individuation, attention should absolutely be orientated in the opposite direction and focused, therefore, on the other two poles in which the distinction between matter and form is articulated: potency and act. Even if this does not often happen, it nonetheless is not rash, as it so often seems, to procede in this direction. Thereby one unexpectedly discovers how Scotus opens precisely at that point where Aristotle eventually came to recognize the most authentic expression of being: actuality. This discovery may perhaps displease those who would prefer to find the most authentic modernity of Scotus: "this iron metaphysical theologian," in some relation to matter. To the contrary, if there is a sector where he more easily attains what is known as "haecceitas," the "thisness," it is in what not by chance Aristotle calls the "*tode ti*" or "this here," the most direct and

For private consultation and not distribution without the consent of E Ondrako

immediate mode of the actuality of being, or as it has so fittingly said, "the ultimate reality of the form."[180]

It seems to me that in great part Newman de facto is presenting the essence of Scotus's achievement in its pedagogical implications for the idea of a university.

(2.) Now let us examine the second major theme of this work, the key place of theology in this view of Liberal Knowledge. Liberal Knowledge (or liberal arts) no longer spontaneously suggests theology as a key part of the whole. Rather, at best it suggests what goes under the name of fine arts, philosophy included, which precedes the study of theology, as in a seminary or graduate school. Often enough, it assumes the exclusion of what Newman and the entire preceding tradition took for granted: that theology and its chief instrument, metaphysics, if not the whole of Liberal Knowledge, were surely crucial parts of it, without which no genuine philosophic temper of mind would be possible and no adequate unity of knowledge (or in Bonaventurian terms, no *plena resolutio*) could be achieved. Indeed, instead of mental equilibrium and exercise of the illative sense, just the opposite would occur along with its attendant skepticism. Hence, at the center of Newman's presentation, in the first two discourses after the introduction and especially in discourse 5 of part 1, we find theology: what it is and what place it has in a university education and how this is related to other forms of theological study.

What does Newman mean by the theology which is part of a university curriculum?

> Now what is Theology? First, I tell you what it is not. And here in the first place (though of course I speak on the subject as a Catholic), observe that, strictly speaking, I am not assuming that Catholicism is true, while I make myself the champion of Theology. Catholicism has not formally entered into my argument hitherto, nor shall I just now assume any principle peculiar to it, for reasons which will appear in the sequel, though of course I shall use Catholic language. Neither, secondly, will I fall into the fashion of the day, of identifying Natural Theology with Physical Theology; which said Physical Theology is a most jejune study, considered as a science, and really is no science at all, for it is ordinarily nothing more than a series of pious or polemical remarks upon the physical world viewed religiously, whereas the work "Natural" properly comprehends man and society, and all that is

---

[180] Quoted by D. CORTESE, ed., *L'orazione della Immacolata [of Sixtus IV]*, (Padua: 1985), pp. 30–31, note 34.

For private consultation and not distribution without the consent of E Ondrako

involved therein, as the great Protestant writer, Dr. Butler, shows us. Nor, in the third place, do I mean by Theology polemics of any kind; for instance, what are called "the Evidences of Religion," or "the Christian Evidences;" for, though these constitute a science supplemental to Theology and are necessary in their place, they are not Theology itself, unless an army is synonymous with the body politic... Lastly, I do not understand by Theology, acquaintance with the Scriptures; for, though no person of religious feelings can read Scripture but he will find those feelings aroused, and gain much knowledge of history into the bargain, yet historical reading and religious feeling are not a science. I mean none of these things by Theology, I simply mean the Science of God, or the truths we know about God put into a system...

For instance, I mean, for this is the main point, that, as in the human frame there is a living principle, acting upon it and through it by means of volition, so behind the veil of the visible universe, there is an invisible, intelligent Being, acting on and through it, as and when He will. Further, I mean that this invisible Agent is in no sense a soul of the world, after the analogy of human nature, but, on the contrary, is absolutely distinct from the world, as being its Creator, Upholder, Governor, and Sovereign Lord. Here we are at once brought into the circle of doctrines which the idea of God embodies. I mean then by the Supreme Being, one who is simply self-dependent, and the only Being who is such; moreover, that He is without beginning or Eternal, and the only Eternal; that in consequence He has lived a whole eternity by Himself; and hence that He is all-sufficient for His own blessedness, and all-blessed, and ever-blessed. Further, I mean a Being, who, having these prerogatives, has the Supreme Good, or rather is the Supreme Good, or has all the attributes of Good in infinite intenseness; all wisdom, all truth, all justice, all love, all holiness, all beautifulness; who is omnipotent, omniscient, omnipresent; ineffably one, absolutely perfect; and such, that what we do not know and cannot even imagine of Him, is far more wonderful than what we do and can. I mean one who is sovereign over His own will and actions, though always according to the eternal Rule of right and wrong, which is Himself. I mean, moreover, that He create all things out of nothing, and preserves them every moment, and could destroy them as easily as He made them; and that in consequence, He is separated from them by an abyss, and is incommunicable in all His attributes. And further, He

For private consultation and not distribution without the consent of E Ondrako

has stamped upon all things, in the hour of their creation, their respective natures, and has given them their work and mission and their length of days, greater or less, in their appointed place. I mean, too, that He is ever present with His works, one by one, and confronts everything He has made by His particular and most loving Providence, and manifests Himself to each according to its needs, and has on rational beings imprinted the moral law, and given them power to obey it, imposing on them the duty of worship and service, searching and scanning them through and through with His omniscient eye, and putting before them a present trial and judgment to come.

Such is what Theology teaches about God, a doctrine, as the very idea of its subject-matter presupposes, so mysterious as in its fullness to lie beyond any system, and in particular aspects to be simply external to nature, and to seem in parts even to be irreconcilable with itself, the imagination being unable to embrace what the reason determines. It teaches of a Being infinite, yet personal; all-blessed, yet ever operative; absolutely separate from the creature, yet in every part of creation at every moment; above all things, yet under everything. It teaches of a Being who, though the highest, yet in the work of creation, conservation, government, retribution, makes Himself, as it were, the minister and servant of all; who though inhabiting eternity, allows Himself to take an interest and have a sympathy, in the matters of space and time.[181]

The first point to note is this: Newman, like Scotus, admits various forms of "our theology," each of which more or less approaches or reflects theology itself, that which is proper to and identical with the omniscience of divine speculation. Newman, in the course of his exposition, identifies three forms of "our theology," forms which can also be discovered in Scotus. Newman first refers to revealed theology based on supernatural or infused faith, a form of theology Scotus calls "our theology" par excellence, and then to natural theology and to physical theology, the latter two sharply distinguished from each other. By natural, here Newman intends not a synonym for physical, but rather for anthropological or human as image of

---

181 *Idea of a University*, part 1, discourse 3, 7, pp. 60 ff. The weakness which Newman notes in the physical theology of Paley is an extreme case of the inherent weakness of the five ways as seen by the Franciscan school, Scotus included, when they are cultivated separately from the anthropological arguments of St. Augustine and the argument of St. Anselm nuance by Scotus.

For private consultation and not distribution without the consent of E Ondrako

the Word Incarnate,[182] with accent on that factor which distinguishes man from the merely physical: personhood, rooted in an intelligent nature, whose central character is free will.[183] Once again we meet a theme closely involving the absolute primacy of Christ in a scotistic sense and related to the theory of being qua being as univocal.

Because Newman sharply points out the radical inadequacies of Paley's exposition of physical theology with its almost total reliance on scientific methodologies and the principles of physical cause and effect in the world of material being, some have mistakenly concluded Newman rejects the five ways of St. Thomas in the *Summa* or those of St. Bonaventure in chapters 1 and 2 of the *Itinerarium* as invalid. In no way does he do this as the following text makes perfectly clear.

> Now first consider that reason teaches you there must be a God; else how was this all-wonderful Universe made? It could not make itself; man could not make it, he is but a part of it; each man has a beginning, there must have been a first man, and who made him? To the thought of God, then, we are forced from the very nature of the case; we must admit the Idea of an Almighty Creator, and that Creator must have been from everlasting…[184]

This, Newman continues a bit further on in the same sermon, is how we think when we

> contemplate the Almighty, as the conscience portrays Him, and as reason concludes about Him, and as creation witnesses of Him.[185]

Newman does not question the validity of notional assents encased in the scientific proofs for divine existence and divine attributes in favor of real assents entailing the anthropological arguments based on personal encounter with the divine Judge (and after Baptism, Savior) in conscience. In a long treatment of natural belief in God in the *Grammar of Assent*, he makes clear that the notion and reality assented to through natural belief

---

[182] As Rosmini, and not the transcendental Thomists, understands "anthropological" or "natural theology" centered on human-personal rather than on physical-impersonal nature. For instance, the title of one of A. Rosmini's most important books, *Antropologia soprana-turale*, uses the term with the same metaphysical overtones found in Newman's usage. Fr. William Lockhart, one of the earliest English disciples of Rosmini and a translator of many of his works into English, was also a disciple of Newman. It is possible that through Lockhart, Newman became acquainted with Rosminian ideas and terms. Cf. T. Kennedy, "Lockhart, William," in *The Catholic Encyclopedia*, New York 1910, vol. 9, pp 321–322.

[183] Cf. Cortese, *L'orazione della Immacolata*, cit., p. 30–31, note 34.

[184] "The Mystery of Divine Condescension," in *Discourses to Mixed Congregations*, sermon 14.

[185] *DMC*.

For private consultation and not distribution without the consent of E Ondrako

in God are represented by one and the same proposition, and in this same proposition, serve as distinct interpretations of it.[186]

In de facto agreement with such Franciscan greats as Bonaventure and Scotus, Newman notes the limitations of the so-called cosmological or physical proofs. For they become *primarily* notional and scientific in character divorced from what St. Bonaventure calls the argument from created image rather than vestige of God and from the argument of St. Anselm. Bonaventure, in chapter 5 of the *Itinerarium*, and Scotus in *De primo omnium rerum principio*, both note how the very name of God which is personal being: I am who am, is the most basic foundation for the demonstration of divine existence. We may here compare St. Bonaventure's two methods of constructing a proof for divine existence at ever more sublime levels as the basis of theological knowledge: (1) *through* and *in* the vestige; (2) *through* and *in* the image; and (3) *through* and *in* the similitude or Name of God, with the type of reflection preceding respectively notional and real assent in Newman and abstractive and intuitive cognition in Scotus. So doing, we will easily grasp what Newman calls the physical, natural and metaphysical levels of the proofs for God's existence. We will also see how Newman's reflections on the knowledge of God's existence and attributes from conscience easily find their place in this perspective. What must be recognized is that each of these starting points is the starting point of an argument from the real, as we experience it, to the consciousness of God's existence, even if the argumentation differs in each case, yet finds a certain point of unity in what Bonaventure calls knowledge of God *in speculo* rather than *per speculum*.[187]

The central problem of the proofs of divine existence from the physical world (not to be confused with scientific proofs) is a very simple one: how do we come to apprehend, without seeing God face to face, a realistic, personal concept of what we mean by the word God, of what it is we are seeking to find or prove; one leading not merely to conclude God exists, but to assent to that truth, and not merely in an objective, but in a personal way, a kind of natural faith or obeisance to the Truth? Or still

---

[186] *Grammar of Assent*, part 1, ch. 5.

[187] The circular argumentation so characteristic of Bonaventure as contrasted with the more linear style of St. Thomas in his *Summa Theologica* and in so much modern theological literature represents the difference between a mode of study stressing the synthetic vision as key to unity versus logical, scientific analysis. If we assume, as I do, that Scotus is a development and crowning of the Bonaventurian synthesis, then the metaphysics of univocal being is a key to the defense of the circular method, just as in Newman the defense of the priority of liberal knowledge over scientific analysis, the insistence on the distinction between assent and inference serve the same point. On the importance of circular argumentation, especially in the Bible, cf. the recent study of M. Douglas, *Thinking in Circles: an essay on ring composition*, (New Haven, CT: 2007).

For private consultation and not distribution without the consent of E Ondrako

better with Newman how do we come to discover that personal approach to knowledge of God as well as knowledge of self, viz., the knowledge of the two luminous beings which is the goal of all study, if our argumentation remains only at the level of physical causality?[188]

(3.) Connected with Newman's comments on conscience and our knowledge of God as personal are his remarks on how we become aware of the principle of causality: via precisely a knowledge of our own exercise of voluntary or personal causality, ultimately via a reflection of the perfect causal power of the omnipotent Creator, who, by an act of his will, made all things out of nothing. Physical causality in the material world, both for bringing new things into existence and for the operation and development of the world, is contingent on the reality of the volitional. Any exclusion of the study of the anthropological and still more of the theological must inevitably lead to a confusion of empirical science with the divine and to an unbalancing of the human mind, to a claim by the creature to be autonomous and secular, arbitrary and tyrannical, yet at the same time to be unable to exercise personal judgment, or what Newman calls the "illative sense." Here is a text illustrative of this point and its connection with the primary place theology occupies in a university curriculum organized on the basis of a unity of knowledge, a unity resting on the univocal concept of being:

> Let us see, then, how this supercilious treatment of so momentous a science, for momentous it must be, if there be a God, runs in a somewhat parallel case. The great philosopher of antiquity, when he would enumerate the causes of things that take place in the world, after making mention of those which he considered to be physical and material, adds, "and the mind and everything which is by means of man." [Ethic. Nicom., iii, 3]... It is incredible that in the investigation of physical results he could ignore so influential a being as man, or forget that, not only brute force and elemental movement, but knowledge also is power. And this so much the more, inasmuch as moral and spiritual agents belong to another, not to say higher, order than physical, so that the omission supposed would not have been merely an oversight in matters of detail, but a philosophical error, and a fault in division.... However, we live in an age of the world when the career of science and literature is little affected by what was done, or would have been done, by this venerable authority...

---

[188] WOLTER, *The Transcendentals...*, cit., mentions similar criticisms of the physical arguments by Scotus.

For private consultation and not distribution without the consent of E Ondrako

We will suppose that a difficulty just now besets the enunciation and discussion of all matters of science, in consequence of the extreme sensitiveness of large classes of the community, clergy and laymen, on the subjects of necessity, responsibility, the standard of morals, and the nature of virtue. Parties run so high, that the only way of avoiding constant quarrelling in defense of this or that side of the question is, in the judgment of the persons I am supposing, to shut up the subject of anthropology [used in sense of Rosmini] altogether.... Henceforth man is to be as if he were not, in the general course of Education; the moral and mental sciences are to be simply left as a matter of private judgment, which each individual may carry out as he will. I can just fancy such a prohibition abstractly possible; but one thing I cannot fancy possible, viz., that the parties in question, after this sweeping act of exclusion, should forthwith send out proposals on the basis of such exclusion for publishing an Encyclopedia, or erecting a National University....

I say, let us imagine a project for organizing a system of scientific teaching, in which the agency of man in the material world cannot allowedly be recognized, and may allowedly be denied. Physical and mechanical causes are exclusively to be treated of; volition is a forbidden subject... at length a professor is found,... who takes on him to deny psychology *in toto*, to pronounce the influence of the mind in the world a superstition, and to account for every effect which is found in the world by the operation of physical causes. Hitherto intelligence and volition were accounted real powers; the muscles act, and their action cannot be represented by any scientific expression; a stone flies out of the hand and the propulsive force of the muscle resides in the will; but there has been a revolution, or at least a new theory in philosophy [Kant?], and our Professor... limits its action to the region of speculation, and denies that it can be a motive principle, or can exercise a special interference, in the material world. He ascribes every work, every external act of man, to the innate force or soul of the physical universe. He observes that spiritual agents are so mysterious and unintelligible, so uncertain in their laws, so vague in their operation, so sheltered from experience, that a wise man will have nothing to say to them.... Human exploits, human devices, human deeds, human productions, all that comes under the scholastic terms of "genius" and "art," and the metaphysical ideas of "duty," "right," and "heroism," it is his office to contem-

For private consultation and not distribution without the consent of E Ondrako

plate all these merely in their place in the eternal system of cause and effect....[189]

Newman goes on to point out the exact link between the exclusion of anthropology and theology: what it is not and what it is.

I am not supposing that the principles of Theology and Psychology are the same, or arguing from the works of man to the works of God, which Paley has done, which Hume protested against. I am not busying myself to prove the existence and attributes of God, by means of the Argument from design. I am not proving anything at all about the Supreme Being. On the contrary, I am assuming His existence, and I do but say this: - that, man existing, no University Professor, who had suppressed in physical lectures the idea of volition, who did not take volition for granted, could escape a radically false view of the things which he discussed; not indeed that his own definitions, principles and laws would be wrong, or his abstract statements, but his considering his own study to be the key of everything that takes place on the face of the earth, and his passing over anthropology, this would be his error. I say, it would not be his science which was untrue, but his so-called knowledge which was unreal. He would be deciding on facts by means of theories... such a Professor... was betraying a want of philosophical depth, and an ignorance of what University Teaching ought to be. He was no longer a teacher of liberal knowledge, but a narrow-minded bigot.... Granting, indeed, that a man's arm is moved by simply physical cause, then of course we may dispute about the various external influences which, when it changes its position, sway it to and fro, like a scarecrow in a garden; but to assert that the motive cause *is* physical, this is an assumption in a case, when our question is about a matter of fact, not about the logical consequences of an assumed premise. And, in like manner, if a people prays, and the wind changes, the rain ceases, the sun shines, and the harvest is safely housed, when no one expected it, our Professor may, if he will, consult the barometer, discourse about the atmosphere, and throw what has happened into an equation, ingenious, even if it be not true; but should he proceed to rest the phenomenon, in matter of fact, simply upon a physical cause, to the exclusion of a divine, and to say that the given case actually belongs to his science because other like cases do, I must tell him, *Ne sutor ultra crepitam*: he is making

---

[189] *Idea*, part 1, discourse 3, 5, pp. 53 ff.

For private consultation and not distribution without the consent of E Ondrako

his particular craft usurp and occupy the universe…. If a creature is ever setting in motion an endless series of physical causes and effects, much more is the Creator; and as our excluding volition from our range of ideas is a denial of the soul, so our ignoring Divine Agency is a virtual denial of God. Moreover, supposing man can will and act of himself in spite of physics, to shut up this great truth, though one, is to put our whole encyclopedia of knowledge out of joint; and supposing God can will and act of Himself in the world which He has made, and we deny or slur it over, then we are throwing the circle of universal science into a like, or a far worse confusion.

Worse incomparably, <u>for the idea of God, if there be a god,</u> <u>is infinitely higher than the idea of man, if there be a man.</u> If to blot out man's agency is to deface the book of knowledge, on the supposition of that agency existing, what must it be, supposing it exists, to blot out the agency of God? I have hitherto been engaged in showing that <u>all the sciences</u> come to us as one, that they all <u>relate to one and the same integral subject-matter, that each separately is more or less an abstraction, wholly true as an hypothesis, but not wholly trustworthy in the concrete</u>…[190]

The association here of God as first with infinity and of cause with volitional activity suggests the approach of Scotus to a proof for divine existence. It is also evident here, and also in the *Grammar of Assent*, that Newman would agree with Scotus in rejecting the Aristotelian principle: *Omne quod movetur ab alio movetur.*[191] The will, finite as well as divine, moves itself. Once this is clear, it is also clear that the will is not primarily an intellectual appetite, but a power of self-activation in love of the good for its own sake, and in this consists freedom even when, in the case of God, love of himself is a necessary love. The voluntary is not contrasted with necessary being, but with the natural mode of acting which is to be moved by another as the intellect by what it contemplates. Acceptance of this position entails also a primacy of the will in the spiritual order, and indeed Newman does hold such a position: not that of Ockham's

---

[190] *Idea*, part 1, discourse 3, 6, pp. 57 ff.

[191] Cf. R. Effler, *John Duns Scotus and the Principle "omne quod movetur ab alio movetur,"* (St. Bonaventure, NY: 1962). The denial of the universality of this principle by Scotus permits him to affirm in the order of cause and effect, the priority of the will, and, so, support his views on the primacy of the will and charity. In his discussion of causality, Newman implicitly takes the same position.

For private consultation and not distribution without the consent of E Ondrako

arbitrary, absolute will, but of Scotus's perfect divine will, always ordered and rational in acting, never absolute.[192]

We need not fear, as does Weatherby, that such a primacy of the will and charity will bring in its wake anti-intellectual tyranny of the irrational. The will of God is the source of all order and rationality (to be distinguished from pure intelligibility or objectivity), for being all Holy and Truth itself he cannot act tyrannically or cruelly. The divine intellect and will are really one, although formally distinct. Assent to the Truth for its own sake brings with it a presentation of that truth as good to be loved for its own sake by the divine Will and all else in loving that supreme good which is God himself. The exemplarism characteristic of the Franciscan school, Scotus included, imbedded in what Newman calls the "sacramentality" of creation and natural religion, and the formal distinction *a parte rei* which is its soul, appear in this text of Newman touching on what he means by divine idea as normative. Here is a good example from the work we are discussing.

> There is a physical beauty and a moral: there is a beauty of person, and there is a beauty in our moral being, which is natural virtue; and in like manner there is a beauty, there is a perfection, of the intellect. There is an ideal perfection [viz., the formality for Scotus] in these various subject matters, towards which individual instances are seen to rise, and which are the standards for all instances whatever.[193]

Something must be added at this point, even if briefly, concerning the differences between science and natural theology, between the formal reasoning or objectivity characteristic of science and that of natural theology, so linked to the illative sense, and between natural theology and revealed theology, together with the role of holiness entailed in the process of proceeding from the outermost reaches of natural theology to those of contemplating the divine goodness face to face in the beatific vision: happiness being impossible of attainment without holiness, almost a verbatim reflection of a conviction of St. Bonaventure.[194]

---

192 *Oxford University Sermons*, sermon 4: The Usurpations of Reason, p. 57. Newman takes the same position in his discussion of the principle of causality, as we shall see in the third part of this conference. Our understanding of "physical causality" where the principle of Aristotle and St. Thomas has validity presupposes our experience and grasp of voluntary causality, where the will, on moving itself, is the ultimate reason for the existence of what it causes or moves. Cf. *Grammar of Assent*, part 1, ch. 4, n. 4, 5 (belief in causation).

193 *Idea of a University*, part 1, discourse 5, 9, p. 122.

194 Bonaventure, *Coll. in Hex.*, c. 19, nn. 19 ff.

For private consultation and not distribution without the consent of E Ondrako

For Newman, empirical science is not the whole of Liberal Knowledge, nor its most important part. Its method of reasoning accents the objective and to that degree leaves out of consideration the personal and volitional. To that extent, it cannot pretend to treat qua science the most important aspects of the physical world (as distinct from the anthropological and root of the anthropological in the theological), viz., cause and effect, as well as intelligent design which we can only begin to grasp when we consider the will and its mode of operation as a *perfectio simpliciter simplex*. The omission of philosophical anthropology and its basis in natural theology in the modern university program accounts in Newman's view for the denial of these basic truths and a skewed interpretation of the valid fruits of scientific study.[195]   Characteristic of the reasoning process entailed in the study of natural theology is the "illative sense" and the description of real assent as entailing a kind of "natural faith." This natural faith bears not on the motive of assent (as with supernatural or infused faith), but on a certain respectful conviction concerning the mysterious content of natural theology—which can include matters which are also part of Christian revelation. In this context Newman can say in the *Apologia*: I believe in God because I believe in myself.[196] This lies implicit in the great argument of Scotus centering about the revelation of the divine Name to Moses: I am who am, at once a matter of natural and infused faith. To both these forms of faith the univocity of being with the disjunctive transcendentals is key. So it is also key to what Newman calls the "sacramentality" of creation: to the hypostatic union, Incarnation and salvation as theological mysteries and reasonable truths involving at once the finite-created and infinite-uncreated in the marvelous work of recapitulation and recirculation of creation.

The proof of God's existence from conscience, characteristic of and central to Newman's concept of natural theology, is not its only theme. Also important is the recognition of the attributes of God, of their infinity (and by implication their real identity and formal distinction), of the personal character of God and the impossibility of understanding the unity and trinity of God simply in mathematical terms.[197] The study of natural theology inclines the student to recognize both the credibility of God and his desirability. This is why convictions or assents to the truths they study take on some aspects of what is called faith, and why sound natural theology is the primary instrument for the elaboration of dogmas (propositions) in revealed theology, without which it is not possible to

---

195 *Idea of a University*, part 1, discourses 3 and 4.

196 *Apologia pro vita sua*, p. 198.

197 Cf. *Grammar of Assent*, part 1, ch. 5.

For private consultation and not distribution without the consent of E Ondrako

avoid one or another pitfall: fideism or rationalism—both forms of infidelity. We may say that if natural theology begins with an examination of the argument from conscience for the existence of God and for a grasp of the divine attributes, it ends with a reflection on the relation between this line of argumentation, the Name of God as Anselm, Bonaventure and Scotus explain this: point of arrival for philosophy and point of departure for theology, and the credibility of the teaching of the Church as a proclamation of revealed theology bearing on the saving will of God. Natural theology as a part of Liberal Knowledge is speculative in the sense of systematic (as it is also for Scotus); revealed theology *pro statu isto* is practical (as "our theology" is for Scotus), with the divine theology of God and of the saints speculative in the sense of contemplative.

Newman's reflections on natural theology and the argument from conscience are not difficult to relate to key points of Anselm's famous argument and the *coloratio* of Scotus, such as the uniqueness and incomparability of our notion of being, the absolute primacy of God implicit in it and including existence, the distinction of essential and accidental series and implicitly the concept of voluntary causality and need of revelation to know the divine essence directly and immediately, as point of departure for knowing all else.

(4.) This brings us to our fourth major theme, treated *ex professo* in discourse 5 of part 1 of the *Idea of a University*: the pursuit of Liberal Knowledge as an end in itself. Critics of Newman have argued since the time these lectures were first delivered that such a concept leads precisely to the secularization of Catholic education. Newman denied this, and illustrated how his idea or concept of university education provided a sound basis for the subsequent cultivation of the Catholic principles in the exercise of vocational duties.

> I am asked what is the end of University Education, and of the Liberal or Philosophical Knowledge which I conceive it to impart: I answer, that what I have already said has been sufficient to show that it has a very tangible, real, and sufficient end, though the end cannot be divided from that knowledge itself. Knowledge is capable of being its own end. Such is the constitution of the human mind, that any kind of knowledge, if it be really such, is its own reward. And if this is true of all knowledge, it is true also of that special Philosophy, which I have made to consist in a comprehensive view of truth in all its branches, of the relations of science to science, of their mutual bearings, and their respective values…. Knowledge is, not merely a means to something

For private consultation and not distribution without the consent of E Ondrako

beyond it, or the preliminary of certain arts into which it naturally resolves, but an end sufficient to rest in… I am but saying what whole volumes have been written to illustrate, viz., by a "selection from the records of Philosophy, Literature, and Art, in all ages and countries, of a body of examples, to show how the most unpropitious circumstances have been unable to conquer an ardent desire [=love of learning] for the acquisition of knowledge."

Knowledge, indeed, when thus exalted into a scientific form, is also power; not only is it excellent in itself, but whatever such excellence may be, it is something more, it has a result beyond itself. Doubtless; but that is a further consideration, with which I am not concerned. I only say that, prior to its being a power, it is a good; that it is, not only an instrument, but an end. I know well it may resolve itself into an art, and terminate in a mechanical process, and in tangible fruit; but it also may fall back upon that Reason which informs it, and resolve itself into Philosophy. In one case it is called Useful Knowledge, in the other Liberal.

It may be objected then, that, when we profess to seek Knowledge for some end or other beyond itself, whatever it be, we speak intelligibly; but that, whatever men may have said, however obstinately the idea may have kept its ground from age to age, still it is simply unmeaning to say that we seek Knowledge for its own sake, and for nothing else; for that it ever leads to something beyond itself, which therefore is its end, and the cause why it is desirable; - moreover, that this end is twofold, either of this world or of the next; that all knowledge is cultivated either for secular objects or for eternal; that if it is directed to secular objects, it is called Useful Knowledge, if to eternal, Religious or Christian Knowledge; - in consequence, that if, as I have allowed, this Liberal Knowledge does not benefit the body or estate, it ought to benefit the soul; but if the fact be really so, that it is neither a physical or a secular good on the one hand, nor a moral good on the other, it cannot be a good at all, and is not worth the trouble which is necessary for its acquisition.[198]

What Newman says here of knowledge in the finite intellect as first an "end," in itself indifferent to the use to which it is put, corresponds exactly with what Scotus says of the finite will as an "end" in itself, viz., that it can and often does engage in human acts which are morally neutral. For both Newman and Scotus such is a postulate of finite intellect and will as pure

---

[198] *Idea of a University*, part 1, discourse 5, 2, p. 102 ff.

For private consultation and not distribution without the consent of E Ondrako

perfections. Unless a distinction is made between wisdom and science, between assent and inference, between natural faith and logic as regards the intellect and between the *affectus justitiae* and *affectus commodi* as regards the will, it is difficult to explain the difference between human and animal sensation. But precisely because finite, such human or personal acts must be open to actions bearing directly on the supreme good, that is to say, to the practice of supernatural virtue and a sanctity which is the immediate disposition for blessedness. Both Newman and Scotus accord with the position of Bonaventure in collation 19 of the *Collationes in Hexaemeron*.

> And then I may be reminded that the professors of this Liberal or Philosophical Knowledge have themselves, in every age, recognized this exposition of the matter, and have submitted to the issue in which it terminates; for they have ever been attempting to make men virtuous; or, if not, at least have assumed that refinement of mind was virtue, and that they themselves were the virtuous portion of mankind. This they have professed on the one hand; and on the other, they have utterly failed in their professions, so as to ever make themselves a proverb among men...[199]
>
> Better, far better, to make no professions, you will say, than to cheat others with what we are not, and to scandalize them with what we are. The sensualist, or the man of the world, at any rate, is not the victim of fine words, but pursues a reality and gains it. The Philosophy of Utility, you will say... has at least done its work; and I grant it, - it aimed low, but it has fulfilled its aim. If that man of great intellect [F. Bacon] who has been its Prophet in the conduct of life played false to his own professions, he was not bound by his philosophy to be true to his friend or faithful to his trust. Moral virtue was not the line in which he undertook to instruct men; and though, as the poet calls him, he were the "meanest" of mankind, he was so in what may be called his private capacity and without any prejudice to the theory of induction [=impersonal and depersonalizing knowledge].... And in spite of the tendencies of his philosophy, which are, as we see at this day, to depreciate, or to trample on Theology, he has himself, in his writings, gone out of his way, as if with a prophetic misgiving of those tendencies, to insist on it as the instrument of that benefi-cent Father, who, when He came on earth in visible form, took on

---

[199] *Idea of a University*, part 1, discourse 5, 7, p. 115.

For private consultation and not distribution without the consent of E Ondrako

Him first and most prominently the office of assuaging the bodily wounds of human nature.[200]

Out of this conflict comes Kant's epistemology where scientific knowledge is essentially impersonal and so objective; whereas religious and ethical knowledge are postulates of an absolute, practical will, viz., purely useful knowledge for which the criterion ultimately is the intramental experience of the knower. This is agnostic modernism, for which the dogmatic principle or dependence of the finite intellect on divine Authority admirably refutes.

Useful Knowledge then, I grant, has done its work; and Liberal Knowledge as certainly has not done its work, - that is, supposing, as the objectors assume, its direct end, like Religious Knowledge, is to make men better; but this I will not for an instant allow, and unless I allow it, those objectors have said nothing to the purpose. I admit, rather I maintain, what they have been urging, for I consider Knowledge to have its end in itself. For all its friends, or its enemies, may say, I insist on it, that it is as real a mistake to burden it with virtue or religion as with the mechanical arts. Its direct business is not to steel the soul against temptation or to console it in affliction, any more than to set the loom in motion, or to direct the steam carriage; be it ever so much the means or the condition of both material and moral advancement, still, taken by and in itself, it as little mends our hearts as it improves our temporal circumstances. And if its eulogists claim for it such a power, they commit the very same kind of encroachment on a province not their own as the political economist who should maintain that his science educated him for casuistry or diplomacy. Knowledge is one thing, virtue is another [primacy of charity]; good sense is not conscience, refinement is not humility, nor is largeness or justness of view faith. Philosophy, however enlightened, however profound, gives no command over the passions, no influential motives, no vivifying principles. Liberal education makes not the Christian, not the Catholic, but the gentleman. It is well to be a gentleman, it is well to have a cultivated intellect, a delicate taste, a candid, equitable, dispassionate mind, a noble and courteous bearing in the conduct of life; - these are the connatural qualities of a large knowledge; they are the objects of a University; I am advocating, I shall illustrate and insist upon them; but still, I repeat, they are no guarantee for sanctity or even

---

[200] *Idea*, part 1, discourse 5, 8, p. 117 ff.

For private consultation and not distribution without the consent of E Ondrako

for conscientiousness, they may attach to the man of the world, to the profligate, to the heartless, - pleasant, alas, and attractive as he shows when decked out in them. Taken by themselves, they do but seem to be what they are not; they look like virtue at a distance, but they are detected by close observers, and on the long run; and hence it is that they are popularly accused of pretense and hypocrisy, not I repeat, from their own fault, but because their professors and their admirers persist in taking them for what they are not, and are officious and arrogating for them a praise to which they have no claim....[201]

Both Newman and Scotus, then, are one in underscoring the fatal dangers of knowledge and study in terms of mere utility; so also are they one in pointing out the fatal limits of liberal knowledge when it is not perfected by infused faith. But such perfection normally requires an atmosphere of supernatural prayer and devotion.

Surely we are not driven to theories of this kind, in order to vindicate the value and dignity of Liberal Knowledge. Surely the real grounds on which its pretensions rest are not so very subtle or abstruse, so very strange or improbable. Surely it is very intelligible to say... that Liberal Education, viewed in itself, is simply the cultivation of the intellect, as such, and its object is nothing more or less than intellectual excellence... Your cities are beautiful, your palaces, your public buildings, your territorial mansions, your churches; and their beauty leads to nothing beyond itself. There is a physical beauty and a moral: there is a beauty of person, there is a beauty of our moral being, which is natural virtue; and in like manner there is a beauty, there is a perfection, of the intellect.[202]

As suggested in the first conference, the reasonableness of Newman's position can easily be appreciated in the context of scotistic metaphysics of the dignity of the person and its relation to what Scotus, following Anselm, calls a *perfectio simpliciter simplex*. In many ways this concept in the metaphysics of Scotus plays the same role as that of image of God in Bonaventure, and indeed, just as the concept of univocal being may be said to be a recycling of Bonaventure's theory of illumination and exemplarism to fit Scotus's teaching on the absolute primacy, so the simply simple perfection is a recycling of Bonaventure's notion of image as that

---

[201] *Idea*, part 1, discourse 5, 9, pp. 120 ff. A similar position is taken by St. Bonaventure, *Collationes in Hexaemeron*, c. 7.

[202] *Idea*, part 1, discourse 5, 9, p. 121.

For private consultation and not distribution without the consent of E Ondrako

whereby an elevation to the supernatural order of grace becomes possible in the plan of God.

Careful reflection on discourse 5 in part 1 of the *Idea of the University* shows that what Newman means by knowledge as an end in itself is exactly what Scotus means when he calls intellect and will, knowledge and love *perfectiones simpliciter simplices*: capable of infinity, yet limited in us; formally simple and so formally in God, yet complex and finite when found in rational creatures or images of God. Precisely in the presence of these perfections do we find the reason rational creatures only, among the rest of creatures, exercise personal or voluntary causality, can act as intellectual agents and be the reason for the presence of intelligent design in what they make, as God is in the whole world. But the scholar who restricts his horizon merely to the scientific and objective, will fail to grasp what is perfectly obvious in a universe created by God: a plan. This is why metaphysics is an incomparable science or wisdom, and includes knowledge of being and of separable or spiritual substances: finite and infinite, true causes of what exists, because voluntary rather than mere physical causes.

Only in God do we come to grasp how knowledge and love are perfectly integrated when found in an infinite intensity (Newman's language here is nearly identical with that of Scotus). But at the natural level (within creation a kind of "relative" supernatural vis-à-vis the merely physical vestige of the Creator) the simplicity so characteristic of the central act of the mind: assent to the Truth, or contemplation of the Truth, is at the center of an extreme complexity. From this in the finite intellect there arises a certain tension between the simplicity of knowledge as a pure perfection and its finite status in man, a tension in Scotus reflected and felt in the asymmetry of the univocal concept of being: a true concept, yet incomparable with any other, and in Newman reflected and felt in the passage from conditional inference to unconditional assent via the exercise of the illative sense. In both cases we encounter the personal character inseparable from intellectual activity if it is not to be an abuse of this gift. Bonaventure pinpoints this in linking *dijudicatio* with abstraction. Scotus does the same in linking intuitive and abstractive cognition, and Newman in linking notional and real apprehension. Here we do well to recall once again how often discussions of metaphysical and epistemological questions both in Newman and Scotus revolve about how we come to know persons, human and divine. The development of the metaphysics of univocal being in Scotus, closely linked to what Newman calls the unity of all knowledge has its roots in questions bearing on genuine knowledge of persons, each

For private consultation and not distribution without the consent of E Ondrako

in himself incomparable because incommunicable existence, yet by the same token in communion.

While the perfection and beauty of Liberal Knowledge points to beatific contemplation of the good, such knowledge is utterly incapable by itself of attaining holiness and blessedness. How often the scholar is utterly lacking in holiness, though he need not be. Liberal Knowledge as such in creatures is not a means to virtue. Love of the Good and grace make virtue and holiness a reality. As Liberal Knowledge comes in fact to include an ever profounder grasp of theology, so the scholar comes to an ever more powerful perception of the presence of God in conscience. Where it does not, there the beauty of Liberal Knowledge: the love of learning, tends more and more to be confused with Useful Knowledge and the desire of God mortified for the sake of the pragmatic and personal advantage: *affectus commodi* in the place of the *affectus justitiae*.

There has been much discussion about whether Scotus is more a fideist (limiting reason excessively) or rationalist (limiting faith excessively) in the prologue to his *Ordinatio*.[203] When we examine how Newman's teaching on knowledge as an end in itself is the ground on which his thought avoids the twin extremes of an agnostic rationalism and authoritarian fideism (neither modernist nor integralist),[204] so we see that Scotus is neither a rationalist who pushes the range of reason beyond its limit (as he says in the introduction to his *De primo omnium rerum principio*), nor a fideist who, to accent the importance of faith, exaggerates the critical function of reason: weak rather than strong inference as Newman describes this tendency of modern theologians since Ockham. Both insist on the importance of personal judgment in relation to the simple act of assent; a simple act because knowledge is an end in itself, a *perfectio simpliciter simplex,* which cannot be a means to an end, just a person cannot be a means to an end. In the created person, that end may be realized with varying degrees of perfection, indeed in ways which are mutually exclusive: pride and humility of intellect. The first excludes the mystery of faith, natural and inspired, and, so, cannot attain sanctity and wisdom; the second, by including this, arrives precisely at holiness and blessedness. What is true of knowledge is even more so of love. That the complexity of discursive thought characteristic of the human mind is a means to an end in no way negates the former affirmation; rather it is a means to realize that *resolutio plena* when knowledge no longer is separate from holiness and

---

203 Cf. Walter, *Das Glaubensverständnis…*, cit.

204 Cf. *The Idea of a University*, part 2, Discourse 5: A Form of Infidelity of the Day; the "Biglietto Address": "Liberalism in religion is the doctrine that there is no positive truth in religion, but that one creed is as good as another."

For private consultation and not distribution without the consent of E Ondrako

contemplation, but is a part of it as in the blessed Trinity and the saints as its disposition. St. Bonaventure in his *Itinerarium* and in his *Triple Way* outlines this. In question 7, article 1 of his *Quaestiones Disputatae de mysterio Ss. Trinitatis* he explains what stands behind the terminology both of Scotus and Newman on knowledge and love as root of the dignity of the person: divine and human, as the incommunicable existence of an intellectual nature. There he speaks of perfect necessity of being as the heart of freedom and, therefore, of that independence: absolute in God and relative (*secundum quid*) in the creature, which is the primary characteristic of personhood, yet not isolation.

St. Bonaventure has left us some interesting observations on the degrees of perfection involved in forming the intellect in relation to its sanctification. In this context he calls the intellectual act itself science, an act governed by logic. He calls it wisdom insofar as it passes into affection, or love of goodness known for its own sake as the end of ends, and art insofar as it passes through the will into some external work. He calls science understanding as it passes into the choice by which knowledge is integrated into the affective or voluntary power of the soul, and prudence insofar as it passes into choice by which art is joined to an effect.[205] The fontal light of Bonaventure, as distinct from the conceptual light, explains the asymmetrical character of all these various types of human knowledge, where mere logic or science would leave us unsure of the real in the final analysis. In the metaphysics of Scotus, the univocal concept of being, while avoiding the charge of potential fideism as an incomparable concept, plays a similar role, particularly in forming a concept of person: finite as well as infinite, the two great luminous beings of Newman. If there were not some mysterious surplusage of evidence to explain the difference between the absolute character of assent and conditional character of inference, we, like Kant, should remain in the noumenal dark about persons. In part, the discussion of univocity in Newman arose out of the questions surrounding our ability to know the singular, nothing being so singular as each person or incommunicable existence; yet nothing so much orientated to unity or communion; yet nothing so certain as the fact we do know persons: not merely created, but divine, the "two luminous beings of Newman," myself and my Creator.

By way of conclusion a comparison of Newman's concept of liberal knowledge as first secular, even when, and perhaps, above all, when it includes theology, and before it is holy or virtuous, with Scotus's view of human acts as first morally neutral before they are moral, shows how

---

205 St. Bonaventure, *Collationes in Hexaemeron*, c. 5, 12–13.

For private consultation and not distribution without the consent of E Ondrako

profoundly accurate Newman is in his analysis of university education as distinct from that of the academy or specialized school of useful knowledge, including the ethical and spiritual. <u>Secularity is not the same as secularism</u>. <u>Secularism is</u>, in the words of Bonaventure, <u>an option to make finite autonomy the heart of happiness</u>, when in fact this is the onset of deviltry. <u>Secularity</u>, on the other hand, is the <u>connatural antecedent of a personal choice of holiness as the way to happiness</u>. The love of knowledge and personal autonomy emerges first in the life of a person as point of departure for a conscious, deliberate desire for God and sacrifice in his service. In terms used by Newman, <u>a liberal intellectual formation is the soundest foundation for the dogmatic principle of faith</u>, thus pointing to a broader and broader cultivation of a life of faith independent of political support. Secularism (modernism) emerges from a refusal to make this principle. With this we may say that failure in theology to recognize the point of Scotus and his choice to follow Christ, rigid traditionalism follows on a rejection of liberal intellectual formation in Newman, touching the relation between secularity and freedom in a created person, and leads to a split between what should be united and integrated: knowledge of the "already" alone (traditionalists) and of "not yet" alone (modernists), rather than renewal in continuity with tradition (Benedict XVI). The real critical question first concerns not the impossibility of being sure about "extramental being," or of metaphysical knowledge, or about definitive assents, but about this choice: to be humble and seek to be holy, or to be proud and seek to make absolute freedom the norm of reason, to do as one pleases. All other forms of the critical question so called are consequent upon this decision and remain without solution so long as this pride or autonomy perdures. With this we can see how Scotus and Newman provide an indispensable basis for grasping the profound insights of *Gaudium et spes* on the Church and the modern world, avoiding at once, modernism and traditionalism (integralism).

Apologia pro vita sua

I found one passage in the Apologia which strikes me as a possible version of St. Anselm's famous proof for the existence of God, a proof appearing in the *Jesu Dulcis Memoria* of St. Bernard, in the *Itinerarium* of St. Bonaventure, chapter 5 (and in his *Quaestiones Disputatae de Mysterio Ss. Trinitatis*, q. 1, a. 1) and in the famous *coloratio Anselmi* of Scotus in his *De primo omnium rerum principio*. This proof in Scotus (not its corrupted form in Descartes) should not be described as the beginning of "onto-theology," nor as a larval form of "ontologism," but rather the

For private consultation and not distribution without the consent of E Ondrako

conclusion of a long tradition which has been synthesized by Bonaventure in the *Itinerarium* in terms of vestige, image and similitude.

Here is the text:

> And thus again I was led on to examine more attentively what I doubt not was in my thoughts long before, viz., the concatenation of argument by which the mind ascends from its first to its final religious idea; and I came to the conclusion that there was no true medium, in true philosophy, between Atheism and Catholicity, and that a perfectly consistent mind, under the circumstances in which it finds itself here below, must embrace either one or the other. And I hold this still: I am a Catholic by virtue of my believing in God; and if I am asked why I believe in a God, I answer that it is because I believe in myself, for I feel it impossible to believe in my own existence (and of that fact I am quite sure) without believing also in the existence of Him, who lives as a Personal, All-seeing, All-judging Being in my conscience. Now, I dare say, I have not expressed myself with philosophical correctness, because I have not given myself to the study of what others have said on the subject; but I think I have a strong true meaning in what I say which will stand examination.[206]

First, a brief analysis of the text: We may leave aside the observations on the logical need to choose either Atheism or Catholicity, if one is to be thoroughly consistent, except to say that this is also a corollary of Scotus's reformulation of Anselm's argument for divine existence. We should rather concentrate our attention on the meaning of existence and its personal interpretation in Scotus. Thus my being Catholic, viz., existing as a person in a very precise way, depends on my believing in the personal existence of an infinite (All-seeing, All-judging Being encountered in my conscience), which I hold as certain, because I believe in myself: not simply as autonomous, but as image of God.[207] This I could not recognize unless I recognized from the beginning what personal dignity entails: being (univocal)

---

[206] *Apologia pro vita sua*, pp. 198–199.

[207] Cf. Boulnois, *Être et représentation*, cit., pp. 128 ff.. Boulnois notes how thinking is verbal, precisely because intellectual thought is ordered to communication and love between persons (as in the Trinity); hence, notional apprehension and assent are ordered to real, impossible without words bearing on the singular and personal. To the degree that "I"—as a kind of word, become more like the Incarnate Word, that is—sanctify my thought, which I cannot do unless I grow in virtue, to that degree I neither know nor believe in myself. Hence, according to Scotus there exists between memory and will, and specifically that spontaneous tendency or desire of the will for the good as such (synderesis), which passes through knowledge. All this is a development of similar positions of Bonaventure in Trinitarian theology. The abstract or notional reflects the procession of the Word from Father in God.

For private consultation and not distribution without the consent of E Ondrako

or the light by which I know and the disjunctive transcendentals. All this I begin to clarify with an examination of the extra-mental, then the intra-mental and then the supra-mental and supra-extra-mental.

At this point I come to recognize that my initial mode of reflection: discursive, must be expressly subordinated to the supra-mental, rather than that the latter should appear merely as an inference. In the words of Scotus, this is as far as I can progress naturally without the grace of revelation. But with that grace, as Bonaventure so neatly states, I can continue from the point where philosophy leaves off: at this affirmation of the absolute Primacy of the divine, and continue in reverse: from the contemplation of the One and Triune God to the knowledge of creatures.[208] The final sentence about philosophical correctness is in fact an acknowledgement by Newman that (1) he is not a professional philosopher, but (2) he has genuine philosophical insight which will stand examination. The examination which confirms this is precisely that of the similarities between Newman and Scotus (behind whom is Bonaventure). This is especially the case when we compare the argument for God's existence based on his Name as One or Primacy, a presentation which implicitly uses a univocal concept of being: *in plena fuga a non esse*, easily converted into the definition of being as univocal: *ens cui non repugnant esse*, with the key features of Scotus's version of Anselm: univocity of being and essential Primacy in the Name revealed to Moses: *Ego sum qui sum*.

So viewed we see clearly that this brief reflection on believing in God, because I believe in myself as image of God, is not a repetition of the anthropological argument of Bonaventure or the argument from conscience, but that to which, short of the beatific vision, physical and natural theology leads: the contemplation of perfect being with both reason and faith. If this is true in Newman, it is also true in Scotus. We are dealing here not with the arid metaphysics of Kant or with a kind of exaggerated psychological introspection which Bonaventure claims is a fixation on self, but with the fruit of an authentic entry into self, viz., the recognition of an idea of being *in plena fuga a non esse*: in full flight from non being. This is Bonaventure in chapter 5 of the *Itinerarium*; scotistically translated it reads thus: *ens est cui non repugnat esse*. For Newman this being—according to St. Anselm Archbishop of Canterbury, so perfect it cannot not exist, yet so good only God can grasp it—is the reason *a parte rei* (rather than in terms of that chain of argumentation whereby I ascend from my first to final religious idea) I believe in myself.

---

[208] Bonaventure, *Breviloquium*, p. 1, ch. 1.

For private consultation and not distribution without the consent of E Ondrako

This concatenation in the life of Newman has striking parallels with that described by Bonaventure in his *Itinerarium*: from the physical vestige to natural image to metaphysical similitude, where we discover the absolute point of reference, *a parte rei*, for the concatenation and its initiation. Here we see that our recognition distinctly of a personal God is not an extrapolation of our knowledge of self, but rather a confession that we cannot understand ourselves until we know ourselves as made in the image of God, an understanding impossible if we are not able and, in some way, do not recognize God as first and incomparable. For Newman this recognition comes via a voluntary action in conformity with or not in conformity with conscience. It is this which differentiates the epistemology of both Bonaventure and Newman from the corrosive equivocations of the Cartesian *cogito ergo sum*. It is also that which enables us to understand the precise correlation between Scotus's *coloratio Anselmi* and Newman's reflection on the relation between finite and infinite being in terms of personal existence. The demonstration of the infinite divinity by Scotus is a demonstration precisely of this First being, personal or voluntary cause of all else and basis of what we recognize in Newman's concatenation as the essential, not accidental, series of Scotus.

Evidently this chain argument (poly-syllogism) is an exercise in apologetics. Apologetics is neither metaphysics nor dogmatic theology, but presupposes both and is the point where both meet in the life of any believer or potential believer in Christ, i.e., of everyone and anyone. It is essentially an explanation of those thought processes whereby I recognize in a personal way that belief in Jesus is credible and indeed obligatory. In a word, it is practical epistemology. It is this which Newman deals with in his *Grammar of Assent*, more exactly with that passing of the mind from apprehension and inference to assent and belief, from the merely logical, objective and discursive, to the simple holding of truth for its own sake, absolutely without any fear of doubt. This of course requires a recognition of the difference between science and wisdom and why science, however important, is alone not an end in itself, but only to the degree it passes into wisdom and contemplation. Scotus, in his exposition of Anselm's proof, may seem highly impersonal, yet his concept of being is radically personal: *existentia incommunicabilis naturae intellectualis*. Newman's highly personal exposition of the final and most basic proof for divine existence is radically metaphysical. Or, in more patristic terms, he is pointing out the link between Augustine's *noverim me, noverim te*, heart of the anthropological argument, and the argument of Anselm, not grounded on sensible existents as on that which is characteristic of such: the contingency of their finite being, experienced first in themselves rather than in material objects.

For private consultation and not distribution without the consent of E Ondrako

So structured, the perception of contingency is a metaphysical insight into the disjunctive transcendentals in relation to univocity of being: the other implicit part of the disjunction, being necessary being.[209] And when this point is reached, it is possible with the help of Revelation and Faith to begin an "unraveling of reality," not with the finite and contingent and concluding with the infinite, but with the infinite in order to understand the created and their creation in order to glorify the Incarnate Word.

Tertia Pars: The *Grammar of Assent* and *Oxford University Sermons*

The *Grammar of Assent*

The preceding selections of Newman texts from his Catholic writings are sufficient to indicate that resemblances between Newman's line of reflection in the *Grammar of Assent* and that of Scotus are not merely the fruit of superficial text selection, but are deeply rooted in his thought. So striking are the resemblances that one might say, had Scotus composed a similar work on this theme, it would have looked a great deal like Newman's.

I think this series of fairly evident resemblances between Scotus and Newman can easily be appreciated once the purpose and plan of the *Grammar of Assent* are set in the metaphysical and apologetic context already considered. Newman's objective in the *Grammar* is to show to a large number of educated persons infected by the false assumption that mathematized empirical science, a particular instance of "useful" rather than "liberal" knowledge, is not the heart of knowing, but merely a particular instance, and hardly the primary instance; and that faith is not an irrational act, even if it is not a conclusion of a logical inference.

Underlying Newman's exposition of this thesis is his distinction between assent on the one hand and apprehension and inference on the other. Although the terminology is different, both Bonaventure, with his distinction between *dijudicatio* and *abstraction*, and Scotus, with his distinction between *intuitive* and *abstractive* cognition, anticipate Newman in this. Scotus, for example, plainly says he does not agree with this proposition: "nihil potest nominari a nobis magis proprie quam intelligatur."[210] This proposition could have been signed by Locke and it is one of those

---

[209] DEVLIN, *The Psychology of Duns Scotus*, cit., pp. 11–15.
[210] *Lectura*, I, d. 22, 2.

For private consultation and not distribution without the consent of E Ondrako

propositions with which Newman contends in the *Grammar*. As is clear from the rest of his discussion of white and whiteness in *Lectura* d. 22 and in *Ordinatio* d. 22, intuitive and abstractive cognition (apprehension for Newman) are not symmetrical, and it is this fact which permits us to recognize how assent to the real, although not preceded by abstractive or notional scientific apprehension of the idea of whiteness, is possible, precisely because, in itself, assent is independent of scientific inference, however much that may accompany assent as its condition in us.[211]

Far from being impossible, then, because it is not the fruit of a logical inference based on sense experience, an act of faith is a perfectly personal and rational act admitting of a supernatural as well as natural dimension at the very heart of metaphysics. The skepticism so commonly leading to the assumption that infused faith as understood by the Catholic Church is *a priori* impossible, in Newman's mind as set forth in the *Grammar*, derives from the voluntarism associated with Hume and the nominalism associated with Locke. This voluntarism-nominalism is distinctive of most of modern thought in the western world, particularly in England. For Newman, an act of faith is above all a kind of assent, in varying ways associated with the act of the mind preceding assent, viz., apprehension of the object to be believed, but not identical with it, and in varying ways associated with an act of the mind accompanying it, viz., inference, but not identical with it.

According to Hume, the real is merely a matter of chance, of the merely arbitrary, without any relation to reason, and reason or logic incapable of any relation to reality because chance is simply unintelligible. Since by definition faith is independent of reason, it has nothing to do with the mind despite the claims of the Church. Faith, for Hume, is a purely arbitrary act of the will involving religious emotions. At the level of apprehension, what Hume calls reason, and Newman, notional apprehension, corresponds to the scholastic *distinctio rationis rationcinantis*, a mental fiction in the words of St. Bonaventure. Newman goes on, however, to relate notional apprehension to the real so as to show that notional apprehension need not be merely a mental construct; and that as Newman proceeds to describe what actually occurs, particularly the natural processes preceding the formation of concepts, we see how the apparent divorce of the abstract and intuitive, evident at the inception of the essay, is not a normal condition, but only the fruit of an arbitrary decision ultimately not in accord with conscience. In fact, the normal condition of notional and real is not *separation* (as it is in all forms of modern skepticism, particularly those inspired by extreme

---

211 Cf. Vos, *The Philosophy of Duns Scotus*, cit., pp. 169–172.

For private consultation and not distribution without the consent of E Ondrako

voluntarism), but *integration* very much bound up with issues surrounding the "illative sense." Newman's treatment of causality (a form of notional assent) in relation to personal experience, is, at the metaphysical level, perhaps one of the most significant points for Scotus as well. At this level Scotus also relates the abstractive and intuitive in relation to "metaphysical" experience of being.

Newman also deals with the nominalism of Locke as a basis for denying the radical possibility of faith in treating the relation of assent and inference. Locke held that faith as an assent is impossible because it is impossible to infer logically the existence or essence of the spiritual or non-sensible. Here, too, with his distinctions of formal, informal and natural logic, together with the use of the illative sense, Newman approaches the position of Scotus on the relation of faith and reason and how infused or supernatural faith presupposes natural faith, a characteristic feature of "metaphysical experience," or the experience of the authority of conscience to be obeyed, even by those without supernatural faith. The failure to obey is the critical issue ultimately moving the thinker in a very "unnatural" or arbitrary state of universal doubt.

Faith, then, is a form of mental assent. Although as an act of the mind it is radically simple, its expression in propositional form, consisting of subject and predicate, is complex, without ceasing to be simple as a personal judgment. It is this complexity of *intentio secunda* propositions which postulates attention to the critical problem: how do we account for the de facto experience of certainty and certitude? The complexity of human, intellectual activity can be observed further in the various phenomena which accompany or precede human assents, such as apprehension and inference (argumentation), without which, notwithstanding the simplicity and independence of an act of assent, that act does not in fact take place. This is the very question expressly raised by Bonaventure in his *De scientia Christi*, q. 4; and it is implicit in Scotus's explanation for the need of a proof such as that in his *De primo omnium rerum principio*, where he seeks to stretch reason unaided by infused faith to its limits, i.e., to test the limits of natural, unconditional faith in the light, to find the point where philosophy ends and revealed theology begins.

The problem as it appears today was correctly diagnosed by Newman in relation first, not to Kant, but to Locke (for the logical aspects) and to Hume (for the personal, volitional and causal aspects). Hume denied the principle of cause and effect and the radical rationality of the will; therefore, all is a product of chance, making dogmatic faith, as the Catholic Church understands this, impossible. How can one believe what by definition cannot be understood? Locke on the other hand did not deny the possibil-

For private consultation and not distribution without the consent of E Ondrako

ity of science in any sense, but denied that our certain knowledge of reality extended beyond the objects of our senses or what could be demonstrated from sense knowledge. Belief in the spiritual and supernatural is impossible because it cannot be thus demonstrated. Out of this arises the need to show how assent can bear not only on the sensible and the formally logical, but on those "two luminous beings" which cannot be objects of the senses nor solely captured by logic. Newman's objective is to explain how assent is primarily a personal act utilizing discursive knowledge, yet able to go beyond it with certainty; and how notional and real assent complement each other, or as the Franciscan school would have it: wisdom and science complement each other.

This means that, in some confused and not immediately clear fashion, our knowledge of what we mean by God is given us simultaneously with our knowledge of finite being, and not simply as a consequence or inference drawn from a prior knowledge of sensible being. In this case the proofs for God's existence are not so much discovery of someone hitherto not accessible to us, but the clear distinction of the finite and infinite, created and uncreated, in scotistic terms the recognition of the disjunctive transcendental. It further entails not only an acknowledgement of the distinction, but of the difference between the Creator and creature, of the incomparable character of the former and the personal character of God and of the image of God, the two luminous beings of Newman. That personal character requires recognition of the priority of personal or voluntary cause over physical, one neatly indicated by Scotus in his distinction between essential and accidental series, between the primacy of the Creator over the creation and the relative primacy enjoyed by the personal creature. In this progression we may note how the cultivation of science or learning progresses toward wisdom, and begins gradually to disclose the personal character of assent and the role of what Newman calls the "illative sense," a kind of "natural faith" in both of our theologians, one opening on the possibility of a supernatural faith in relation to a supernatural revelation.[212] This is where both the *De primo principio* and the *Grammar of Assent* conclude: the possibility, metaphysical and psychological, of faith as a genuine assent to truth, at once involving holiness and "approval" of reason; in both its forms (natural and infused) though differently, the gate therefore to wisdom.

From a scotistic perspective, knowledge as a *perfectio simpliciter simplex* is radically simple and therefore radically infinite; hence with the will, a divine attribute *formaliter* proper to the Creator, not to the creature. But

---

[212] Cf. SCOTUS, *Ordinatio*, prologue, part 1.

For private consultation and not distribution without the consent of E Ondrako

it is also found in some creatures *formaliter*; hence in a finite or limited or complex mode, not suppressing, but coloring the radical simplicity of any act of knowing of such a creature, an act which Newman discusses under the heading of assent. This point of contact between Scotus and Newman on the theme of the *Grammar* seems to me quite clearly and beyond question to be a key point—one reinforced by the very traditional account of the difference between creatures which are only vestiges of the Creator and those which are images, the latter being in Augustine's terminology *capax Dei,* and in Bonaventure's *prope Deum* rather than *prope nihil.* The presence or absence of such radically simple perfections in a creature makes the difference between image and mere vestige, and constitutes not the divine order of grace itself, but the proximate basis for the possibility of a creature's elevation to such an order. In the light of this we can better appreciate the insistence of Newman on the simplicity and absolute, personal character of assent in the act of knowing or judgment about truth. That act set in a scotistic context is univocal in concept, admitting of an infinite and of a finite mode. From the summaries which follow, the concept of that act in Newman is implicitly univocal. The interminable discussions surrounding questions of divine illumination, the critical doubt of Kant and the tendency of all knowing to converge on contemplation are convincingly resolved in terms of this univocity.

But it is just as clear from the outset of the *Grammar* that knowledge in a creature, in this case man, is complex and limited. Whereas assent is a personal and independent act, radically simple and ever to be distinguished from the conclusion of a reasoning or argumentative process typical of the discursive character of human knowing and of our conscious experience, an act of assent does not occur without being accompanied by apprehension of concepts, their organization in propositions consisting of subject and predicate, and preceded by forms of inference, formal and informal. Evidently, Newman is dealing with the three acts of the human intellect entailed in attaining assent to the truth, as we shall see, with many points of contact with similar presentations in Bonaventure and Scotus.[213]

Here is how Newman sets out the *status quaestionis* at the beginning of the *Grammar* itself:

> The internal act of holding propositions is for the most part analogous to the external act of enunciating them; as there are three ways of holding them, each corresponding to each. These

---

[213] Cf. BONAVENTURE, *Itinerarium*, ch. 3 (on memory); for Scotus cf. BOULNOIS, *Être et représentation*, cit., ch. 4 (on memory, knowledge of ego (subject) and of the word (object); cf. also DEVLIN, *The Psychology of Duns Scotus*, cit., pp. 4–9, for a clear summary of the scotistic psychology and how it differs from the Aristotelian-thomistic.

For private consultation and not distribution without the consent of E Ondrako

three mental acts are Doubt, Inference and Assent. A question is the expression of a doubt; a conclusion is the expression of an act of inference; and an assertion is the expression of an act of assent (or holding as true)… Moreover, propositions, while they are the material of these three enunciations, are also the objects of the three corresponding mental acts… Mental acts of whatever kind presuppose their objects.

And in fact, these three modes of entertaining propositions, - doubting them, inferring them, assenting to them, are so distinct in their action, that, when they are severally carried out into the intellectual habits of an individual, they become the principles and notes of three distinct states or characters of mind. For instance, in the case of Revealed Religion, according as one or other of these is paramount within him, a man is a skeptic as regards it; or a philosopher, thinking it more or less probable considered as a conclusion of reason; or he has an unhesitating faith in it, and is recognized as a believer. If he simply disbelieves, or dissents, then he is assenting to the contradictory of the thesis, viz., to the proposition that there is no Revelation.

Many minds of course there are, which are not under the predominant influence of any one of the three (unreflective, uncritical, impulse, unsettled, etc.)…Nay, further, in all minds there is a certain co-existence of these distinct acts; that is, of two of them, for we can at once infer and assent, though we cannot at once either assent or infer and also doubt. Indeed, in a multitude of cases we infer truths or apparent truths, before, and while, and after we assent to them.

Lastly, it cannot be denied that <u>these three acts are all natural to the mind</u>; I mean, that, in exercising them, we are not violating the laws of our nature, as if they were in themselves an extravagance or weakness, but are acting according to it, according to its legitimate constitution… (errors of individual belong to individual)… <u>We do but fulfill our nature in doubting, inferring, and assenting</u>; and our duty is, not to abstain from the exercise of any function of our nature, but to do what is in itself right rightly.[214]

---

[214] *Grammar*, part 1, ch. 1, pp. 5 ff. The notion and fact of "surplussage" assumes an asymmetry rather than symmetry between assent and discursive reason, one justified by the distinction of Bonaventure between fontal and motive objects of the finite intellect, or by the distinction of Scotus between metaphysical and scientific understanding of reality. For Newman, assent reflects the influence of apprehension and demonstration, but is not conditioned by it. As judgment it is a simple act. Cf. chaps. 8 and 9. This position of Newman represents a clear rejection of Locke (and so of Kant) in regard both to the question of certain knowledge and

For private consultation and not distribution without the consent of E Ondrako

Assent or holding of the truth, and central act of the mind, the subject matter of this treatise, is an act of the mind, therefore a radically simple action. But in a created mind, specifically the human, where the characteristic of such actions is discursive, precisely because finite, the expression of this act both mentally and externally (in the order of communication) is complex, in the form of a proposition consisting of subject and predicate. Propositions, Newman tells us, not only furnish the matter of assent, but are its objects; and in the natural order, without propositional form, no assent is possible, even in relation to those truths directly concerning persons, whether divine or created, who cannot, strictly speaking, be "objectified," as Scotus so clearly notes as well. Newman's description fits exactly what Scotus means by the human intellect: a *perfectio simpliciter simplex*. The essential, central act of the intellect is radically simple, but in the finite order is always given expression in a complex manner, without ceasing to be radically simple. Hence, every expression of knowledge in human form is a particular instance of knowing, valuable, but not the equivalent of knowledge as such. The great flaw of modern epistemology, to which Kant has given classic form, is to regard one particular instance of this expression, and not Knowledge itself as its most important. This instance is empirical, mathematized science which postulates not an integration of the abstract and intuitive, but supposes a radical disjunction between the two.

That this is Newman's position is perfectly clear throughout this treatise. Assent is not the only kind of proposition found in human, intellectual activity. There are at least two others which play a significant role in our quest for knowledge: the question and the conclusion which correspond to two other mental acts: that of doubt (bearing on apprehension or the first act of the mind) and that of inference (bearing on the third act of the mind or comparison of propositions). Assent in a finite person, though accompanied by acts of apprehension in response to a question and preceded or succeeded by acts of inference in response to need of verification, viz., is conditioned by apprehension and inference, is radically independent and absolute, viz., simple, a pure perfection. This fact is the key to his entire explanation of how we come via the "illative sense" to make assents involving a "surplusage" which transcends both the limits of apprehension and of inference (formal logic). He will later insist that

---

the realism of notional as well as real assents, and to the radical need to sanctify rather than secularize the activities of the mind. See also p. 7, point 3, where Newman summarizes the objective of the *Grammar*.

For private consultation and not distribution without the consent of E Ondrako

"assent is intrinsically distinct from inference,"[215] the point where human knowledge touches the divine, as it does for St. Bonaventure.

Newman then notes a paradox which supports his position as well as that of the Franciscan school, and differentiates it from that of Locke and Hume (and Kant):

> An act of assent, it seems, is the most perfect and highest of its kind, when it is exercised on propositions, which are apprehended as experiences and images,[216] that is, which stand for things; and on the other hand, an act of inference is the most perfect and highest of its kind, when it is exercised on propositions which are apprehended as notions, that is, which are creations of the mind. An act of inference indeed may be made with either of these modes of apprehension; so may an act of assent; but when inferences are exercised on things, they tend to be conjectures or presentiments, without logical force; and when assents are exercised on notions, they tend to be mere assertions without any personal hold on them on the part of those who make them. If this be so, the paradox is true, that when Inference is clearest, Assent may be least forcible, and when Assent is most intense, Inference may be least distinct; - for, though acts of assent require previous acts of inference, they require them, not as adequate causes, but as *sine quod non* conditions; and, while the apprehension strengthens Assent, Inference often weakens the apprehension.[217]

Both Locke and Hume, each in his own way, refuse to acknowledge this point, and hence either limit the range of reason to the sensible (Locke, and later Kant) or (with Hume and later Kant) refuse to ascribe to the notional any role in human, intellectual life, other than that of formal logic, viz., to give form to the content of experience or intelligibility in the form of mathematized science. With this modern idealism, rationalism and scientism deny the very possibility of belief or faith as an intellectual act. Whereas Newman insists on just the contrary, because every assent, even notional, precisely because assents—by virtue of their relation to the illative sense, already involve a personal act or conviction, which, while not

---

[215] *Grammar*, ch. 6, p. 166.

[216] "Images" and the power to construct these, the "imagination," are not to be taken in the strict technical sense in which they are used by Aristotle, St. Thomas and Scotus, but in a broader sense to denote the striving of the mind to understand the formally distinct not only as a unity, but also as existing, even if, as Newman notes, this effort, without the help of logic and of the notional, paradoxically falls short of its goal, in Bonaventurian terms, the begetting of an interior word.

[217] *Grammar*, ch. 4, p. 41.

For private consultation and not distribution without the consent of E Ondrako

supernatural, infused, saving faith—nonetheless enjoy some basic features of that faith and, hence, may be called acts of natural faith or belief.

This brings us to consider the charge which has been brought against Newman, practically from the first appearance of the *Grammar of Assent*, that he is a nominalist and that the interpretation of this work just given is, therefore, without foundation. Here is the text, at the very beginning of the *Grammar*, which seems, as it were, to set the tone for the entire work:

> Now what do the terms of a proposition, the subject and predicate, stand for? Sometimes they stand for certain ideas existing in our own minds, and for nothing outside of them; sometimes for things external to us, brought home to us through the experiences and information we have of them. All things in the exterior world are unit and individual and are nothing else; but the mind not only contemplates those unit realities, as they exist, but has the gift, by an act of creation, of bringing before it abstractions and generalizations, where they have no existence, no counterpart, out of it.[218]

There is no doubt that in this text he appears to suppose that which, in scholastic tradition, are called universals or abstractions, are purely creations of the human mind, not corresponding to anything extra-mental; and that while the mind can contemplate exterior realities, in so doing, it does not know the essence or nature of what exists. This is in essence what is known as nominalism and appears to have great affinities with Kantian theory. Commentators like Weatherby hold that this view pervades the *Grammar*, making it impossible to correct; others like Lash hold that this position of Newman is the only correct one and should not be corrected.

But before we conclude that Newman is a nominalist or Kantian on the basis only of these initial comments on the distinction between notional and real apprehension, a number of other points need to be taken into consideration. Newman in the *Grammar of Assent* is not writing a treatise on epistemology (extra-mental validity of knowledge) or psychology (ideogenesis), but a practical work to help those who would believe in Christ, but are hesitant because they think faith impossible as an assent to truth, this under the explicit influence, not of Kant, but of Locke and Hume. The title: *Grammar*, should remind us of this. Nowhere else in his writings do we find any adoption: expressly or implicitly, of nominalism. Hence, it might be possible to interpret this text in its overall context as a description of how propositions appear to those under the influence of the views of Hume (in matters of apprehension, viz., that there is nothing

218 *Grammar*, ch. 1, p. 9.

For private consultation and not distribution without the consent of E Ondrako

outside the mind to apprehend), or of Locke (who maintained that faith was impossible because all understanding is a matter of inference or reasoning based on formal logic), therefore rendering faith impossible as a rational act.

Newman's repeated assertion that notional and real apprehension-assent are almost always mixed in the same individual and in the same proposition, is an indication that this may well be the case. Abstract universals or notional apprehensions, then, however much they may appear in isolation as pure mental fictions, in practice are something more than this by virtue of their link with real apprehensions. Conversely, real apprehensions, however they appear in isolation, in fact do tell us something about the real existence by virtue of their connection with notional apprehension. Notional assents are broad but superficial; real are deep, but narrow. Viewed apart, they seem to favor the views of Kant; viewed in unison, they appear to favor the position of Scotus on abstractive-intuitive cognition. As will be seen below in dealing with the principle of causality and with the understanding of the Trinity, this is precisely the case. Notional propositions do correspond to something in reality. What we understand by unity in the Godhead is not mere individuality or unit as this is understood in mathmatizied empirical science. Newman, in this practical treatise, is taking assumptions about propositions characteristic of modern scientism and showing how they do not in fact coincide with normal experience. The notional cannot be restricted merely to mental constructs or scientific hypotheses; nor can the real be understood apart from the notional. In this way notional and real are reintegrated along the lines of Scotus's view of abstractive-intuitive cognition where clearly the extra-mental real (common nature and existence) as well mental activity exerts a causal influence on the process of knowing.

This is not as forced an interpretation as it might seem at first glance. St. Bonaventure tells us[219] that without divine illumination the thing known would appear indeed as a unit, nothing else, constantly changing, without the minimum of changelessness to make certainty about what is known possible; and the concept formed of that object would be no more than a mental fiction. Without univocity of being, says Scotus,[220] we would be doomed to universal skepticism. And if Bonaventure and Scotus are in fact arguing with those to whom claims of necessary deductions or inferences, and not faith, are the only kind of knowledge needed by man, Newman is arguing with those like Locke and Hume who claim that logic does not permit the possibility of faith. And whether we attend to

---

[219] *Quaestiones Disputatae de scientia Christi*, q 4.

[220] Devlin, *The Psychology of Duns Scotus*, cit., p. 11.

For private consultation and not distribution without the consent of E Ondrako

Bonaventure-Scotus with a more metaphysical analysis, or to Newman with his more phenemological approach, the conclusion is the same: the possibility of faith, natural and infused is the only sound epistemology. We may say that Bonaventure and Scotus both underscored the consequences of abandoning the divine and personal character of knowledge: nominalism and skepticism or the divorce of abstract and intuitive. Newman, instead, points out the way out of that morass with the reintegration of notional and real. Like Scotus, Newman begins by an analysis of assent in general in order to show that, far from being arbitrary and irrational, saving faith builds on a natural foundation, what stands at the heart of scotistic metaphysics: univocal being reflecting obscurely the Incarnation.

Now let us see how Newman understands the role of apprehension and inference in relation to human assent, radically simple, yet complex and limited in relation to the infinite potential of knowledge. Here is a brief, yet comprehensive statement of his position.

> By apprehension of a proposition, I mean... the interpretation given to the terms of which it is composed. When we infer, we consider a proposition in relation to other propositions; when we assent to it, we consider it for its own sake and in its intrinsic sense. That sense must be in some degree known to us; else we do but assert the proposition, we in no wise assent to it. Assent I have described to be a mental assertion; in its very nature then it is of the mind, and not of the lips.... This is plain; and the only question is, what measure of apprehension is sufficient.
>
> And the answer to this question is equally plain: - it is the predicate of the proposition which must be apprehended. In a proposition one term is predicated of another; the subject is referred to the predicate, and the predicate gives us information about the subject; - therefore to apprehend the proposition is to have that information, and to assent to it is to acquiesce in it as true. Therefore I apprehend a proposition, when I apprehend its predicate. The subject itself need not be apprehended *per se* in order to be a genuine assent: for it is the very thing which the predicate has to elucidate, and therefore by its formal place in the proposition, so far as it is the subject, it is something unknown; but the predicate cannot make it known, unless it is known itself...[221]

The goal of this complex process known as discursive or scientific thought is to know and assent to the truth about some subject. This

---

[221] Ibid., ch. 2, pp. 13 ff.

For private consultation and not distribution without the consent of E Ondrako

involves both apprehension of the predicate and inference, the ability to compare and contrast propositions about the same subject, both before and after assent; and, so, give to this knowledge, a certain unity without which understanding of the subject remains incomplete, fragmentary, unreflective, what the medieval called resolution or reduction of the multiple to unity, the work of the philosophic mind. Both apprehension and inference are necessary in order to rest in the truth; yet, for the reasons already noted, assent or holding the truth absolutely (or it is not held at all) is not to be confused either with apprehension or inference as it so often is in modern thought, nor to be made dependent on it. How it is possible to coordinate these two points in a Christian epistemology of faith is treated by Newman at great length; but here I wish only to point out the distinction Newman makes between notional and real apprehension and the manner in which each qualifies assent, yet leaves it essentially the same in both instances. It is a mistake to think that Newman assigns extra-mental value only to real assent. Here are some illustrative quotes:

> …there can be no assent to a proposition, without some sort of apprehension of its terms; …there are two modes of apprehension, notional and real;… while assent may be given to a proposition on either apprehension of it, still its acts are elicited more heartily and forcibly, when they are made upon real apprehension which has things for its objects, than when they are made in favour of notions and with a notional apprehension… Apprehension then is simply an intelligent acceptance of the idea, or of the fact which a proposition enunciates.
>
> Now apprehension… has two subject-matters; - according as language expresses things external to us, or our own thoughts, so is apprehension real or notional. It is notional in the grammarian, it is real in the experimentalist.[222]

Newman goes on to compare and contrast these two modes of apprehension more in detail. The more we follow his descriptions, the more we are reminded of the distinction Scotus makes between abstractive and intuitive cognition. The resemblance becomes stronger as we consider his concluding remarks in this chapter on the excellence and imperfection of each, and their complementarity.

> Here then we have two modes of thought, both using the same words, both having one origin, yet with nothing in common in their results. The informations of sense and sensation are

---

[222] Ibid., ch. 3, p. 20.

For private consultation and not distribution without the consent of E Ondrako

the initial basis of both of them; but in the one we take hold of objects from within them, and in the other we view them from outside of them; we perpetuate them as images in the one case, we transform them into notions in the other. And natural to us as are both processes in their first elements and in their growth, however divergent and independent in their direction, they cannot really be inconsistent with each other; yet no one from the sight of a horse or a dog would be able to anticipate its zoological definition, nor from knowledge of its definition to draw such a picture as would direct the eye to the living specimen.

Each use of propositions has its own excellence and serviceableness, and each has its own imperfection. To apprehend notionally is to have breath of mind, but to be shallow; to apprehend really is to be deep, but to be narrow minded. The latter is the conservative principle of knowledge, and the former is the principle of its advancement. Without the apprehension of notions, we should forever pace round one small circle of knowledge; without a firm hold upon things, we shall waste ourselves in vague speculations. However, real apprehension has the precedence, as being the scope and end and the test of notional; and the fuller is the mind's hold upon things or what it considers such, the more fertile is it in its aspects of them, and the more practical its definitions.

Of course, as these two are not inconsistent with each other, they may coexist in the same mind. Indeed there is no one who does not to a certain extent exercise both the one and the other. Viewed in relation to Assent, which has led to my speaking of them, they do not in any way affect the nature of Assent itself, which is in all cases absolute and unconditional; but they give it an external character corresponding respectively to their own: so much so, that at first sight it might seem as if Assent admitted of degrees, on account of the vividness in these different apprehensions.[223]

Newman, in view of his stress on the phenomenological, relates the vividness of real assent to facts which are sensed, capable of imaginative reconstruction, rightly so because from a chronological point of view *nil in intellectu nisi prius in sensibus*. But what is in the intellect, is there by way of abstraction or formation of notions—rather dull, in contrast with the vividness of real apprehension via the sense experience. But would he have denied Scotus's position on real apprehension or direct intuitive cognition

---

[223] Ibid., pp. 34 ff.

For private consultation and not distribution without the consent of E Ondrako

of the singular at the intellectual level? It seems to me he would not have denied this, particularly in view of his teaching on real apprehension of those two luminous beings: myself and my Creator-Judge-Savior at the level of conscience, and of the tragic reduction of university formation merely to the mastery of physical science and not what he calls the anthropological and theological.

This last consideration occasions a reflection on the meaning of subject in a proposition: a fact or notion to be illumined, in the first instance the extra-mental, but not as an end in itself. In the fullest sense, for Newman as for Scotus, existence is above all subjective or personal existence; and the study of the extra-mental of this world is a means to introduce questions about myself and my God, whose resolution in the form of assents is the goal of all knowing. Newman is quite insistent that this knowledge of my own person and that of my Creator and Judge, however inadequate this might be in propositional form, even the most perfect, is not merely notional, and very clearly involves the use of the illative sense where the mind passes from apprehension and inference to assent.

Perhaps this is the closest Newman comes to that aspect of human knowing often underscored by the Fathers and very much present in the great Franciscan Masters, including Scotus,[224] viz., that the notional or abstractive cognition and the entire process of "objectification" is not merely a reflection of the limitations of finite cognition, but a reflection of a key aspect of divine knowing, where the Father is the *terminus a quo* (represented by the appropriated role of memory) and the Word is the *terminus ad quem* (represented by the appropriated role of intellect or object), so making possible communication and communion of love in the Holy Spirit. The difference between the infinite and finite forms of knowing consists precisely in this, that the Father begets the Word *quia cognoscit*, whereas man forms a concept or object *ut cognoscat*. But this does not change the fact that the human notion, though produced in order to know, reflects and is adequated with the real, precisely because that is the very nature of this process, not only in the Trinity, but in the creature. Modern subjectivism, as in Descartes and Kant, simply ignores this key point.

Before going on to examine this point and its personal character (and whether or not this is implicit in Scotus), we need to examine some examples of notional and real assent important for our discussion: presumption and belief in particular, so as to appreciate Newman's assessment both of the metaphysical and natural bases of supernatural faith, a

---

[224] Cf. BOULNOIS, *Être et représentation*, cit., pp. 128 ff.

For private consultation and not distribution without the consent of E Ondrako

position very similar to that of Scotus; and the contextualization of the univocal concept of being (notional in form) in relation to the absolute primacy of Christ, as this is reflected in the sacramental character of creation and certain anticipations of true religion in the age of nature and of the law (not the Kantian notion of Rahner).

Under the heading of professions, viz., "assents so feeble and superficial, as to be little more than assertions," Newman observes how

> ... the Angels have been considered by divines [in particular thomists] to have each of them a species to himself; and we may fancy them so absolutely *sui similis* as to be like nothing else, so that it would be as untrue to speak of a thousand Angels as of a thousand Hannibals or Ciceros. It will be said, indeed, that all beings but One at least will come under the notion of creatures, and are dependent upon that One; but that is true of the brain, smile, and height of Napoleon, which no one would call three creatures. But if all this be so, much more does it apply to our speculations concerning the Supreme Being, whom it may be unmeaning, not only to number with other beings, but to subject to number in regard to His own intrinsic characteristics. That is, to apply arithmetical notions [*à la* Kant] to Him may be as unphilosophical as it is profane. Though He is at once Father, Son, and Holy Ghost, the word "Trinity" belongs to those notions of Him which are forced on us by the necessity of our finite conceptions, the real and immutable distinction which exists between Person and Person implying no infringement of His real and numerical Unity. And if it be asked how, if we cannot properly speak of Him as Three, we can speak of Him as One, I reply that He is not One in the way in which created things are severally units; for one, as applied to ourselves, is used in contrast to two or three and a whole series of numbers; but of the Supreme Being it is safer to use the word "monad" than unity, for He has not even such relation to His creatures as to allow, philosophically speaking, of our contrasting Him with them.[225]

In this extraordinarily perceptive, philosophical analysis of the problems surrounding our knowledge of person in relation to that of being, whether finite or infinite, Newman clearly differentiates his views from those of Kant (only that is knowable which is knowable in a mathematic-scientific way, or which does not go beyond the logical form of knowledge of the sensible) and those of Rahner (our only knowledge

---

[225] *Grammar*, ch. 4, pp. 51–52.

For private consultation and not distribution without the consent of E Ondrako

of person and divinity is that based on psychological introspection of the subject and thrust to infinite). Further, in insisting on the non-mutual relation between Creator and creature, he neatly underscores how notional apprehension of what we mean by God, implies the possibility of real apprehension as well (as he clearly affirms in dealing with the proof of divine existence from conscience). This is exactly the position of Scotus on the relation between intuitive and abstractive knowledge at the intellectual level: that of attaining (apprehending via union with) what is known, and that of being related to the known via a conceptual representation measured by the object known.[226]

Finally, Newman, like Scotus, insists on the impossibility of capturing the person in a notional or abstract concept or category; yet, with Scotus, he recognizes that in some way we cannot know or relate persons to one another without making use of concepts or notions more properly designed to know the non-personal.[227]

Another notional assent, particularly important for any comparative study of Newman and Scotus and their relation to Kantianism, is that of presumption. By presumption Newman means

> … an assent to first principles; and by first principles I mean the propositions with which we start in reasoning on any given subject matter. They are in consequence very numerous, and vary in great measure with the persons who reason, according to their judgment and power of assent, being received by some minds, not by others, and only a few of them received universally. They are all of them notions, not images, because they express what is abstract, not what is individual and from direct experience.[228]

Newman then goes on to deal with what is commonly called today the "objective" or "extra-mental" validity of first principles, or the problem of trusting our powers of reasoning and memory and of the first principles formulated in consequence of the use of those powers. He notes:

> Sometimes our trust in our powers of reasoning and memory, that is, our implicit assent to their telling truly, is treated as a first principle; but we cannot properly be said to have any trust in them as faculties. At most we trust in particular acts of memory and reasoning…

---

[226] Cf. Boulnois, Être et représentation, cit., pp. 149–150, perhaps one of clearest and convincing explanations of Scotus theory of human knowing.

[227] Cf. Grammar, ch. 4, p. 41 (cited above, p. 59). On the approach of Scotus, cf. H. Mühlen, Sein und Person nach Joannes Duns Scotus, (Werl: 1954), pp. 68 ff.

[228] Grammar, p. 60.

For private consultation and not distribution without the consent of E Ondrako

However, if I must speak my mind, I have another ground for reluctance to speak of our trusting memory or reasoning, except indeed by a figure of speech. It seems to me unphilosophical to speak of trusting ourselves. We are what we are, and we use, not trust our faculties. To debate about trusting in a case like this, is parallel to the confusion implied in wishing I had had a choice if I would be created or no, or speculating what I should be like, if I were born of other parents. "Proximus sum egomet mihi." Our consciousness of self is prior to all questions of trust or assent. We act according to our nature, by means of ourselves, when we remember or reason. We are as little able to accept or reject our mental constitution, as our being. We have not the option; we can but misuse or mar its functions. We do not confront or bargain with ourselves; and therefore I cannot call the trustworthiness of the faculties of memory and reasoning one of our first principles.[229]

In the foregoing paragraph Newman disposes of one of the errors of Kant leading to a mis-formulation of the critical question: the need to prove our faculties trustworthy, and does so with a reference similar to that of Scotus to memory and reason as two aspects of the cognitive faculty. He then deals with the problem of the extra-mental and suggests an analysis very similar to that of St. Bonaventure, e.g., in the *Itinerarium*, chapter 2, and, so, implicitly to the metaphysics of the univocity of being.

Next, as to the proposition, that there are things existing external to ourselves, this I do not consider a first principle; and one of universal reception. It is founded on an instinct; I so call it, because the brute creation possesses it. This instinct is directed towards individual phenomena, one by one, and has nothing of the character of a generalization; and, since it exists in brutes, the gift of reason is not a condition of its existence, and it may justly be considered an instinct in man also. What the human mind does is what brutes cannot do, viz., to draw from our ever-recurring experiences of its testimony in particulars a general proposition, and, because this instinct or intuition acts whenever the phenomena of sense present themselves, to lay down in broad terms, by an inductive process, the great aphorism, that there is an external world, and that all the phenomena of sense proceed from it. This general proposition, to which we go on to assent,

---

[229] *GA*, pp. 60–61.

For private consultation and not distribution without the consent of E Ondrako

goes (*extensive*, though not *intensive*) far beyond our experience, illimitable as that experience may be, and represents a notion.[230]

There next follow three illustrations of these considerations in how we come to arrive at our idea of God and his attributes, of first principles such as "there is a right and a wrong" and "a true and a false," as well as the belief in causation. While clearly distinguishing between notional and real assents—so sharply according to some as to suggest a Kantian bias, they also reveal the intimate interaction between both modes of assent in the effort of a human mind to assent to the truth, i.e., a scotistic bias. This latter reveals and correctly interprets the true convictions of Newman concerning the "extra-mental" reality of God, or the moral order and of causality. Let us look more closely at each of these points.

> I have spoken, and I think rightly spoken, of instinct as a force which spontaneously impels us, not only to bodily movements, but to mental acts [natural *judictorium* and synderesis in Bonaventure]. It is instinct which leads the quasi-intelligent principle (whatever it is) in brutes to perceive in the phenomena of sense a something distinct from and beyond those phenomena [reality of thing, without recognition of essence]. It is instinct which impels the child [endowed with intellect] to recognize in the smiles or the frowns of a countenance which meets to his eyes, not only a being external to himself, but one whose looks elicit in him confidence or fear. And as he instinctively interprets these physical phenomena, as tokens of things beyond themselves [the metaphysical], so from sensations attendant upon certain classes of his thoughts and actions [spiritual affect] he gains a perception of an external being, who reads his mind, to whom he is responsible, who praises and blames, who promises and threatens…. As then we have our initial knowledge of the universe through sense, so do we in the first instance begin to learn about its Lord and God from conscience; and, as from particular acts of that instinct, which makes experiences, mere images (as they ultimately are) upon the retina, the means of our perceiving something real beyond them, we go on to draw the general conclusion that there is a vast external world, so from recurring instances in which conscience acts, forcing upon us importunately the mandate of a Superior, we have fresh and fresh evidence of the existence of a Sovereign Ruler, from whom those particular dictates which we

---

[230] *GA*, pp. 61–62. The role of a general proposition makes possible *dijudicatio*: *Itinerarium*, ch. 2, 6., as Bonaventure explains this in discussing the memory in ch. 3 of the same work.

For private consultation and not distribution without the consent of E Ondrako

experience proceed [abstractive and intuitive knowledge]; so that, with limitations which cannot here be made without digressing from my main subject, we may, <u>by means of that induction from particular experiences of conscience, have as good a warrant for concluding the Ubiquitous Presence of One Supreme Master, as we have, from parallel experience of sense, for assenting to the fact of a multiform and vast world, material and mental.</u>[231]

Let us attempt a summary translation of this profound passage in the language of Scotus. That instinct or force within us impelling us not only to physical but to mental action, corresponds to what Bonaventure and Scotus call the "*naturale judicatorium*" and "*synderesis*" or natural will. This mental action initially leads to intuitive cognition of an extra-mental reality, a something beyond these phenomena whose source is without, viz., the essence of this something but, which, without the power of abstractive and critical cognition via objectification, cannot be known. What is true of intuitive cognition at the sense level and its completion via abstractive thought, is still truer of perception of spiritual phenomena, in particular those of conscience, <u>a kind of intuition of myself in relation to my Creator and Judge,</u> to be complemented via abstractive cognition of the same. In both cases, the argumentation or discursive thought exemplifies an argument *quia* rather than *propter quid*.

Then, in the next paragraph, Newman goes on to formulate the complementarity of notional and real assents in our natural theology centered on considerations of anthropology and religion, viz., perceptions of the metaphysical, rather than of the physical.

> However, this assent is notional, because we generalize a consistent, methodical form of Divine Unity and Personality with Its attributes, from particular experiences of the religious instinct, which are themselves, only *intensive*, not *extensive*, and in the imagination, not intellectually, notices of Its Presence; though at the same time that assent may become real of course, as may the assent to the external world, viz., when we apply our general knowledge to a particular instance of that knowledge…[232]

Newman applies the same analysis to first principles of the moral order: notional assents, yet not for that reason, fictions of the mind with no relation to the objective existence of the Moral Law and moral order.

---

[231] *Grammar*, ch. 4, pp. 62–63.
[232] *GA*, p. 63.

For private consultation and not distribution without the consent of E Ondrako

And so again, as regards the first principles expressed in such propositions as "There is a right and a wrong," "a true and a false," "a just and an unjust," "a beautiful and a deformed;" they are abstractions to which we give notional assent in consequence of our particular experiences of qualities in the concrete, to which we give real assent. As we form our notion of whiteness from the actual sight of snow, milk, a lily, or a cloud, so, after experiencing the sentiment of approbation which arises in us on the sight of certain acts one by one, we go on to assign to that sentiment a cause, and to those acts a quality, and we give to this notional cause or quality the name of virtue, which is an abstraction not a thing...[233]

These so-called first principles, I say, are really conclusions or abstractions from particular experiences; and an assent to their existence is not an assent to things or to their images, but to notions, real assent being confined to the propositions directly embodying those experiences.[234] Such notions indeed are an evidence of the reality of the special sentiments in particular instances, without which they would not have been formed; but in themselves they are abstractions from facts, not elementary truths prior to reasoning.[235]

But then Newman goes on to add once again that these abstractions are not pure, mental fictions à la Kant, but are indeed expressions by way of mental objects as Scotus holds, linked to real order via intuitive knowledge or mental instinct.

I am not of course dreaming of denying the objective existence of the Moral Law, nor our instinctive recognition of the immutable

---

[233] When Newman defines virtue as a "quality," he reveals a certain preference for the definition of Augustine rather than that of Thomas as a "habit." Cf. Augustine, *De libero arbitrio*, 2, 18, 50; 2, 19; *Retractationes*, 6. This approach to virtue and beauty as well, and to the notion of whiteness in terms of quality, connaturally coincides with what Scotus calls formalities, distinct or not formally identical *a parte rei*. Formalities for Newman as for Scotus are not in the first instance mental fictions, but neither is their reality identical with that which is the object of real assent. Newman, read as a Thomist, seems at times to lean toward nominalism; but read in the light of Scotus, these notions appear as what Scotus means by a *formalitas* or *perfectio a parte rei* distinct among themselves, not virtually but formally *a parte rei*.

[234] From this arise two problems: how conclusions or inferences—without which in the natural order we cannot conduct our intellectual lives—become assent, even if only notional, and how such assent is linked to reality or being. Divine illumination, univocity of being, the illative sense are all, despite differences of formulation and angle of vision, substantially identical approaches to the same question.

[235] *Grammar*, ch. 4, p. 64. But God himself is neither an abstraction nor a fact; and neither, in a sense, is the created person qua person. Here Newman's views on the two luminary beings, himself and his Creator, are identical with those of Scotus.

For private consultation and not distribution without the consent of E Ondrako

difference in the moral quality of acts, as elicited in us by one instance of them. Even one act of cruelty, ingratitude, generosity, or justice reveals to us at once *intensive* [intuitive cognition as premise of univocal concept of being, good, virtue, etc.] the immutable distinction between those qualities and their contraries; that is, in that particular instance and *pro hac vice*. From such experience—an experience which is ever recurring—we proceed to generalize; and thus the abstract proposition "There is a right and a wrong," as representing an act of inference [our formation of an idea of God *in via* involves inference as well; see above], is received by the mind with a notional, not a real assent. However, in proportion as we obey the particular dictates which are its tokens, so are we led on more and more to view it in the association of those particulars, which are real, and virtually to change our notion of it into the image of that objective fact, which in each particular case it undeniably is.[236]

Now let us examine briefly the third principle illustrated by Newman, that of causality playing so prominent a role in the formation of our natural theology and ethics, and which he treats under two forms, more or less the equivalent of what Scotus presents under the headings of essential and accidental series elucidating what is meant by voluntary, personal causality and by essential primacy in the order of efficiency (not to be equated with physical), exemplarity and finality. Indeed, the texts I am citing here begin with an assertion identical with Scotus's denial of the axiom: *omne motum ab alio movetur*. They are also a clear indication that Newman's concept of the will coincides with that of Scotus, as a *perfectio simpliciter simplex*, whose essential character is that of self-activation, the core meaning of free or voluntary action. In a word, Newman, like Scotus, disagrees with the principle: *omne motum ab alio movetur*, precisely because the voluntary or spiritual cause (*agens intellectuale*) enjoys priority over the natural cause, and the natural cause is impossible without the voluntary.

Another of these presumptions is the belief in causation. It is to me a perplexity that grave authors seem to enumerate as an intuitive [scotistic term] truth, that everything must have a cause. If this were so, the voice of nature would tell false; for why in that case stop short at One, who is Himself without cause? [A cause without cause is one who acts primarily in a free or voluntary fashion, whether the term of that act is necessary or contingent being.] The assent which we give to the proposition, as a first

236 *GA*, p. 65.

For private consultation and not distribution without the consent of E Ondrako

principle, that nothing happens without a cause, is derived, in the first instance, from what we know of ourselves; and we argue analogically from what is within us to what is external to us. [As above, arguing in this way from what is within is not passage logically from possibility to fact, but from spiritual activity to an understanding of physical activity, which does not perfectly duplicate the more perfect spiritual act.] One of the first experiences of an infant is that of his willing and doing [i.e., of self-moving: Scotus, and hence of this truth: *non omne motum ab alio movetur*]; and, as time goes on, one of the first temptations of the boy is to bring home to himself the fact of his sovereign arbitrary power, though it be at the price of waywardness [exactly the position of Scotus], mischievousness, and disobedience. And when his parents, as antagonists of this willfulness, begin to restrain him, and to bring his mind and conduct into shape, then he has a second series of experiences of cause and effect, and that upon a principle or rule. Thus the notion of causation is one of the first lessons he learns from experience, that experience limiting it to agents possessed of intelligence and will. It is the notion of power combined with a purpose and an end. Physical phenomena, as such [when divorced from creative will of an intelligent and free God] are without sense; and experience teaches us nothing about physical phenomena as causes [science divorced from metaphysics]. Accordingly, wherever the world is young, the movements and changes of physical nature have been and are spontaneously ascribed by its people to the presence and will of hidden agents, who haunt every part of it, the woods, the mountains and the streams, the air and the stars, for good or for evil; - just as children again, by beating the ground after falling, imply that what has bruised them has intelligence; - nor is there anything illogical in such a belief. It rests on the argument from analogy.

As time goes on, and society is formed, and the idea of science is mastered, a different aspect of the physical universe presents itself to the mind. Since causation implies a sequence of acts in our own case, and our doing is always posterior, never contemporaneous or prior, to our willing, therefore, when we witness invariable antecedents and consequents, we call the former the cause of the latter, though intelligence is absent, from the analogy of external appearances. At length we go on to confuse causation with order; and, because we happen to have made a successful analysis of some complicated assemblage of phenomena, which

For private consultation and not distribution without the consent of E Ondrako

experience has brought before us in the visible scene of things, and have reduced them to a tolerable dependence on each other, we call the ultimate points of this analysis, and the hypothetical facts in which the whole mass of phenomena is gathered up, by the name of causes, whereas they are really only the formula under which those phenomena are conveniently represented... And in like manner, that all the particles of matter throughout the universe are attracted to each other with a force varying inversely with the square of their respective distances, is a profound idea, harmonizing the physical works of the Creator; but even could it be proved to be a universal fact, and also to be the actual cause of the movements of all bodies in the universe, still it would not be an experience, any more than is the mythological doctrine of the presence of innumerable spirits in those same physical phenomena.

Of these two senses of the word "cause," viz., that which brings a thing to be, and that on which a thing under given circumstances follows, the former is that of which our experience is the earlier and more intimate, being suggested to us by our consciousness of willing and doing. The latter of the two requires a discrimination and exactness of thought for its apprehension, which implies special mental training; else, how do we learn to call food the cause of refreshment, but day never the cause of night, though night follows day more surely than refreshment follows food? Starting, then, from experience [intuitive thought], I consider cause to be an effective will; and by the doctrine of causation, I mean the notion, or first principle, that all things come of effective will; and the reception or presumption of this notion is a notional assent.[237]

From all this it is clear how a further discussion of the universe as a creation of God and the order which we can find in nature would coincide with the teaching of Scotus on the perfectly ordered will of God as source of all forms of intelligible order in creation, and ultimately how we are able to differentiate the necessary order of divine processions from causality implying dependence in its term.

Newman also takes up a discussion of causality in the second sense [accidental order according to Scotus] in reference to the possibility of miracles and what is called natural law.

---

237 *GA*, pp. 66 ff.

For private consultation and not distribution without the consent of E Ondrako

As to causation in the second sense (viz., an ordinary succession of antecedents and consequents, or what is called the Order of Nature), when so explained, it falls under the doctrine of general laws, and of this I proceed to make mention, as another first principle or notion, derived by us from experience, and accepted with what I have called a presumption. By natural law I mean the fact that things happen uniformly according to certain circumstances, and not without them and at random; that is, that they happen in an order; and, as all things in the universe are unity and individual, order implies a certain repetition, whether of things or like things, or of their affections and relations. Thus we have experience, for instance, of the regularity of our physical functions, such as the beating of the pulse and the heaving of the breath; of the recurring sensations of hunger and thirst; of the alternation of waking and sleeping, and the succession of youth and age. In like manner we have experience of the great recurring phenomena of the heavens and earth, of day and night, of summer and winter... Also by scientific analysis, we are led to the conclusion that phenomena, which seem very different from each other, admit of being grouped together as modes of the operation of one hypothetical law, acting under varied circumstances. For instance, the motion of a stone falling freely, of a projective, of a planet, may be generalized as one and the same property, in each of them, of the particles of matter; and this generalization loses its character of hypothesis, and becomes a probability, in proportion as we have reason for thinking on other grounds that the particles of all matter really move and act towards each other in one certain way in relation to space and time, and not in half a dozen ways; that is, that nature acts by uniform laws. And, thus, we advance to the general notion or first principle of the sovereignty of law throughout the universe.

There are philosophers who go farther, and teach, not only a general, but an invariable, and inviolable, and necessary uniformity in the action and laws of nature, holding that everything is the result of some law or laws, and that exceptions are impossible; but I do not see on what ground of experience or reason they can take up this position. Our experience rather is adverse to such a doctrine, for what concrete fact or phenomenon exactly repeats itself? Some abstract conception of it, more perfect than the recurrent phenomenon itself, is necessary, before we are able to say that it has happened even twice, and the variations which

For private consultation and not distribution without the consent of E Ondrako

accompany the repetition are of the nature of exceptions…. It seems safer, then, to hold that the order of nature is not necessary, but general in its manifestations.

But it may be urged, if a thing happens once, it must happen always, for what is to hinder it? Nay, on the contrary, why, because one particle of matter has a certain property, should all particles have the same? Why, because particles have instanced the property a thousand times, should the thousand and first instance it also? It is *prima facie* unaccountable that an accident should happen twice, not to speak of it happening always. If we expect a thing to happen twice, it is because we think it is not an accident, but has a cause. What has brought about a thing once, may bring it about twice. *What* is to hinder its happening? rather, *What* is to make it happen? Here we are thrown back from the question of Order to that of Causation. A law is not a cause, but a fact; but when we come to the question of cause, then, as I have said, we have no experience but that of Will. If, then, I must answer the question, What is to alter the order of Nature? I reply, That which willed it; – That which willed it, can unwill it; and the invariableness of law depends on the unchangeableness of that Will.

And here I am led to observe that, as a cause implies a will, so order implies a purpose. Did we ever see flint celts, in their various receptacles all over Europe, scored always with certain special and characteristic marks, even though those marks had no assignable meaning or final cause whatever, we should take that very repetition, which indeed is the principle of order, to be a proof of intelligence? The agency, then, which has kept up and keeps up the general laws of nature, energizing at once in Sirius and on the earth, and on the earth in its primary period as well as in the nineteenth century, must be Mind, and nothing else, and Mind at least as wide and as enduring in its living action, as the immeasurable ages and spaces of the universe on which that agency has left its traces.[238]

With both Hume and Kant put down, we can understand why Newman insists so much on a formation in the liberal arts and theology rather than a pragmatic scientific formation, and why he warns about its inadequacies for instruction of the people in religion, and insists "on this marked distinction between Beliefs on the one hand, and Notional assents and Inferences on the other."

---

[238] *GA*, pp. 68 ff.

For private consultation and not distribution without the consent of E Ondrako

With this we also come to a consideration of the central purpose of this essay:

> We are now able to determine what a dogma of faith is, and what it is to believe it. A dogma is a proposition; it stands for a notion or a thing; and to believe it is to give the assent of the mind to it, as it stands for the one or for the other. To give a real assent to it is an act of religion; to give a notional, is a theological act. It is discerned, rested in, and appropriated as a reality by the religious imagination; it is held as a truth, by the theological intellect.[239]

We can easily observe here a gloss on how Bonaventure relates what he calls symbolic and proper (academic) theology, a position presupposed for grasping Scotus's concept of faith and theology. Newman continues:

> Not as if there were in fact, or could be, any line of demarcation or party-wall between these two modes of assent, the religious and theological. As intellect is common to all men as well as imagination, every religious man is to a certain extent a theologian, and no theology can start or thrive without the initiative and abiding presence of religion. As in matters of this world, sense, sensation, instinct, intuition, supply us with facts, and the intellect uses them; so, as regards our relations with the Supreme Being, we get our facts from the witness, first of nature, then of revelation, and our doctrines, in which they issue, through the exercise of abstraction and inference.[240]

He goes on, then, to discuss belief, and specifically in a way very similar to that, which according to Scotus, explains the link and difference between natural and supernatural (infused) faith, viz., in relation to the way in which natural faith serves as the basis or provides the content of supernatural faith.

> Now first, my subject is assent, and not inference. I am not proposing to set forth the arguments which issue in the belief of these doctrines, but to investigate what it is to believe in them, what the mind does, what it contemplates, when it makes an act of faith. It is true that the same elementary facts which create an object for an assent, also furnish matter for an inference: and in showing what we believe, I shall unavoidably be in a measure showing why we believe; but this is the very reason that makes it necessary for me at the outset to insist on the real distinction

---

[239] *GA*, ch. 5, p. 98.
[240] *GA*, pp. 98–99.

For private consultation and not distribution without the consent of E Ondrako

between these two concurring and coincident courses of thought, and to premise by way of caution, lest I should be misunderstood, that I am not considering the question that there is a God, but rather what God is [in the sense in which Bonaventure insists that before one can consider demonstrating God's existence, one must have some idea of who God is].

And secondly, I mean by belief, not precisely faith, because faith in its theological sense, includes a belief, not only in the thing believed, but also in the ground of believing; that is, not only belief in certain doctrines, but belief in them expressly because God has revealed them; but here I am engaged only with what is called the material object of faith, - with the thing believed, not with the formal...[241]

Supernatural faith, as Scotus notes, presupposes at least the possibility of examining its content as "natural truth," as subject to metaphysical-apologetic investigation.[242] This is exactly what Newman is doing. And it is in this context that his discussion of the illative sense seems like a modern commentary on the Bonaventurian and scotistic concept of the *naturale judicatorium* so intimately related to the doctrine of divine illumination in Bonaventure and the univocity of being in Scotus. When we reach the range of reason which is the threshold of revealed theology: the "metaphysical" recognition that God is infinite and incomparable, absolutely one, yet that Oneness is incomprehensible to the mere mathematician and logician. For this, another sense is needed, one directly perfected by the theological virtue of faith and the corresponding gifts of the Holy Spirit: understanding and knowledge of the saints. This sense, although not supernatural in the strict sense, enables us to contemplate, admire, simply

---

241 *GA*, pp. 99–100. Supernatural faith is a kind of assent and so shares a key quality of all assent of whatever kind, generically faith: contemplation and adoration of truth and a personal judgment putting one's seal on this. Such an approach to natural and supernatural order of knowing is very similar to that of Scotus.

242 Cf. L. WALTER, *Das Glaubensverständnis bei Johannes Duns Scotus*, (Paderborn: 1968). We cannot repeat too often the importance of the similarities and differences between natural and infused faith according to both Scotus and Newman. The similarities account both for the personal character of knowledge (and basis of its sanctification) at both the level of nature and of grace, and for the manner in which the latter perfects the former. The differences, however, account for the manner in which the intellectual dijudicatio of Bonaventure, apprehension of the univocal concept of being in Scotus and speculative phronesis or illative sense in Newman, crown intellectual assent as an act within the power of nature unaided by grace and supported by reasoning, and an assent formally taken without that support solely in dependence on divine authority. Neither is fideistic; but, taken together, all forms of rationalism and modernism are excluded.

For private consultation and not distribution without the consent of E Ondrako

love the truth for its own sake and, in some real sense, is metaphysical or supernatural.[243] It is what is at the heart of the illative sense.

The limits of this conference permit me only to summarize the argument of Newman in the second part of the *Grammar* dealing with certainty-certitude, inference and the illative sense in relation to reaching certain assents in matters of faith, both natural and supernatural. But even such a summary will reflect the scotistic colors of the earlier section, and indicate many other points of resemblance worthy of further study.

The first part of the *Grammar* treats of assent to propositions in relation to their apprehension: real or notional. The second part deals with assent in relation to inference, the part more difficult for many persons to follow and that which has often opened Newman to charges of being either a fideist or a nominalist (Weatherby; Lash). By way of transition, he devotes a chapter to a consideration of simple and complex assents, viz., those not involving any conscious, deliberate reflection on an assent as certain and those involving such a reflection.

The first type of assent is related to real apprehension of the proposition assented to unconditionally, viz., as though certain (material or interpretive certitude). Certitude in this case is simply the natural assumption of any assent: unless the proposition is simply true—not open to doubt or mere opinion—certain assent is not possible. Newman regards this as very important, because it is a spontaneous witness to how our nature is constituted, however mysterious this might be from the standpoint of what he later calls "formal logic": the priority of the intuitive over the abstractive, to borrow the terminology of Scotus.

The second type of assent is related to notional apprehension and is possible only in relation to propositions which are notional rather than factual. In a particular way, it is related to inference which is so often occasioned by the need to resolve particular doubts about the unconditional and, therefore, immutable character of assents which so often do change, for one reason or another. Such doubts occasion the need to reflect and such reflection, both before and after assent, involves the use of inference, leading not to assent, but conclusions, of themselves admitting of weak or strong affirmation, but always conditional, and, so, possibly in error. From this arises the possibility of what today is called agnosticism: that while propositions may well be in themselves certain and true, it is impossible for us subjectively to attain certitude concerning their truth, because it is impossible ever to have such "strong" reasons as to affirm

---

[243] This is the very position of Scotus, as Hoeres convincingly shows: *Kritik der transzendentalphilosophischen Erkenntnistheorie*, cit., pp. 62 ff.

For private consultation and not distribution without the consent of E Ondrako

any proposition other than a conclusion, by nature only probable. Here is Newman's formulation of the problematic:

> It is the characteristic of certitude that its object is a truth, a truth as such, a proposition as true. There are right and wrong convictions, and certitude is a right conviction; if it is not right with a consciousness of being right, it is not certitude. Now truth cannot change; what is once truth is always truth; and the human mind is made for truth, and so rests in truth, as it cannot rest in falsehood. When then it once becomes possessed of a truth, what is to dispossess it? but this is to be certain; therefore once certitude, always certitude. If certitude in any matter be the termination of all doubt or fear about its truth, and an unconditional conscious adherence to it, it carries with it an inward assurance, strong though implicit, that it shall never fail. Indefectibility almost enters into its very idea, enters into it at least so far as this, that its failure, if of frequent occurrence, would prove that certitude was after all and in fact an impossible act, and that what looked like it was a mere extravagance of the intellect. Truth would still be truth, but the knowledge of it would be beyond us and unattainable. It is of great importance then to show, that, as a general rule, certitude does not fail; that failures of what was taken for certitude are the exception; that the intellect, which is made for truth, can attain truth, and, having attained it, can keep it, can recognize it, and preserve the recognition.
>
> This is on the whole reasonable; yet are the stipulations, thus obviously necessary for an act or state of certitude, ever fulfilled?[244]

With this question Newman points out the heart of the critical question, which he will then resolve positively via his analysis of various forms of inference leading to a recognition of the illative sense. This latter suggests many resemblances with the formulation and resolution of the critical problem by St. Bonaventure, and his analysis of inference with that of Scotus in terms of univocal being and the disjunctive transcendentals. Here is a representative text of Newman:

> Starting from intuition, of course we all believe, without any doubt, that we exist… and we are sure beyond all hazard of a mistake, that our own self is not the only being existing.[245]

---

[244] *Grammar*, ch. 7, pp. 221–222.

[245] *GA*, ch. 6, p. 177.

For private consultation and not distribution without the consent of E Ondrako

Newman also shares the reserves voiced by Bonaventure about confusing assent with the service which inference is designed to provide in forming assents and of subordinating the radically simple to the complex. "Assent is intrinsically distinct from inference."[246] What Newman calls the "illative sense," Bonaventure calls the "*naturale judicatorium*" (centering about conscience), whereby we make that initial and final "*dijudicatio*" assuring the realism of all our thought.

> We must take the constitution of the human mind as we find it [*perfectio simpliciter simplex*], and not as we may judge it ought to be; - thus I am led on to another remark, which is at first sight disadvantageous to Certitude. Introspection of our intellectual operations is not the best of means for preserving us from intellectual hesitations. To meddle with the springs of thought and action is really to weaken them; and, as to that argumentation which is the preliminary to Certitude, it may indeed be unavoidable, but, as in the case of other serviceable allies, it is not so easy to discard it, after it has done its work, as it was in the first instance to obtain its assistance. Questioning, when encouraged on any subject-matter, readily becomes a habit, and leads the mind to substitute exercises of inference for assent [complex for simple], whether simple or complex. Reasons for assenting suggest reasons for not assenting, and what were realities to our imagination, while our assent was simple, may become little more than notions, when we have attained to certitude. Objections and difficulties tell upon the mind; it may lose its elasticity, and be unable to throw them off. And thus, even as regards things which it may be absurd to doubt, we may, in consequence of some past suggestion of the possibility of error, or of some chance association to their disadvantage, be teazed from time to time and hampered by involuntary questionings, as if we were not certain, when we are...
>
> As even Saints may suffer from imaginations in which they have no part, so the shreds and tatters of former controversies, and the litter of argumentative habit, may beset and obstruct the intellect, - questions which have been solved without their solutions, chains of reasoning with missing links, difficulties which have their roots in the nature of things, and which are necessarily left behind in a philosophical inquiry because they cannot be removed, and which call for the exercise of good sense and for

---

[246] *GA*, ch. 6, p. 166.

For private consultation and not distribution without the consent of E Ondrako

strength of will to put them down with a high hand, as irrational or preposterous. Whence comes evil? why are we created without our consent? how can the Supreme Being have no beginning?... .

Again, when, in confidence of our own certitude, and with a view to philosophical fairness, we have attempted successfully to throw ourselves out of our habits of belief into a simply dispassionate frame of mind, then vague antecedent probabilities, or what seem to us as such, - merely what is strange or marvelous in certain truths, merely the fact that things happen in one way and not in another, when they must happen in some way, - may disturb us, as suggesting to us, "Is it possible? who would have thought it! what a coincidence!" Thus we may wonder at the Divine Mercy of the Incarnation, till we grow startled at it, and ask why the earth has so special a theological history, or why we are Christians and others not, or how God can exert a particular governance...[247]

These relatively long passages help us appreciate what we might otherwise overlook in reading the *Grammar*, because we are habituated to think spontaneously of formal logic as the most perfect and ultimately definitive factor in arriving at certitude, the stronger and more rigorous the argumentation leading to a conclusion. This is exactly the assumption of Locke, and, after him, Kantian philosophy, whereas the position of Newman is exactly the contrary. The more formal the logic, the more it can be implemented with symbols as in mathematical logic and in the construction of a computer, and the less relation it has to reality and truth. It is merely an instrument which leaves us in the dark, so long as it is not subordinated to informal and natural logic and ultimately placed under the control of the illative sense. In taking this position Newman bases himself, not on a theory, but on a very simple fact: assent and inference are not the same, whether assent is real or notional. In scotistic terms this is because the mind is a simply simple perfection, even if the human mind is complex, and so discursive, even if notional and real assents must complement one another and tend to be integrated in a unified vision of truth, a *plena resolutio*.

In saying this, Newman has no intention of disparaging formal logic, but merely of indicating its limitations: asymmetry, in relation to other modes of reasoning, those which are simpler and at once the context in which formal reason is to serve its purpose: supporting, not replacing these. The first of these Newman calls informal logic, the ability of a mind

---

[247] *GA*, ch. 7, 3, pp. 216–219.

For private consultation and not distribution without the consent of E Ondrako

trained in some matter to quickly pass from inference to assent without reviewing a complex assortment of notional propositions. He calls this the ability to recognize a "convergence of probabilities," as it reveals the truth of some proposition and its meaning.

The second is what he calls natural inference, a kind of unconscious reasoning which shows itself as a simple act, rather than as a process, particularly as an exercise of the "illative sense" (*phronesis*). This accords nicely with Scotus's concept of the intellect as a *perfectio simpliciter simplex*, where the simple, underlying even in the created intellect the most complex, conscious operations, must in the final analysis preside over all the various complex operations, or the cognitive power will either show itself in a state of continual paralysis, dysfunctional, unable to arrive at a simple, definitive act of certain judgment (dijudicatio), or will in fact not be the cognitive power of a person, but only of a brute.

> I commenced my remarks upon Inference by saying that reasoning ordinarily shows itself as a simple act, not as a process, as if there were no medium interposed between antecedent and consequent, and the transition from one to the other were of the nature of an instinct, - that is, the process is altogether unconscious and implicit [as with the assent to univocal being]. It is necessary, then, to take some notice of this natural and material Inference, as an existing phenomenon of mind; and that the more, because I shall thereby be illustrating and supporting what I have been saying of the characteristics of inferential processes as carried on in concrete matter, and especially of their being the action of the mind itself, that is, by its ratiocinative or illative faculty, not a mere operation as in the rules of arithmetic.[248]

Note should be made of his insistence on natural inference, and, therefore, on the illative sense and what Bonaventure calls the divine light illumining the *naturale judicatorium*. We are not dealing with a hypothesis nor with a complex argument in propounding the Anselmian proof for God's existence (nor that of Newman from conscience) so closely linked with the "illative sense." We are simply noting a fact of the mental order; one, however, not a product of our minds, but a given of that order; one true and functional, even if we choose to take it for granted. But if we do and should ask questions about certitude and about how to integrate real and notional assent in relation to such questions, then we are naturally brought to recognize those two luminous beings, nowhere more, according

---

[248] *GA*, ch. 8, 3, p. 330.

For private consultation and not distribution without the consent of E Ondrako

to both Bonaventure and Newman, than in conscience and the yearnings of the human heart for a Savior.

Newman, in his introduction to the illative sense: its sanction, nature, and range, neatly takes note of the critical question as formulated by such modern thinkers as Locke and Kant, and distances himself from this formulation, precisely because it attempts to do away with a concrete fact: natural, simple reasoning, by way of antecedent inference, instead of using inference to explain what cannot be fitted into the rigid categories of formal logic, viz., those two luminous beings, my ego and my Creator and Judge.

> My object in the foregoing pages has been, not to form a theory which may account for those phenomena of the intellect of which they treat, viz., those which characterize inference and assent, but to ascertain what is the matter of fact as regards them, that is, when it is that assent is given to propositions which are inferred, and under what circumstances. I have never had the thought of an attempt which in me would be ambitious and which has failed in the hands of others, - if that attempt may fairly be called unsuccessful, which, though made by the acutest minds, has not succeeded in convincing opponents. Especially have I found myself unequal to antecedent reasonings in the instance of a matter of fact. There are those, who arguing *a priori*, maintain, that, since experience leads by syllogism only to probabilities, certitude is ever a mistake. [Locke and Kant]. There are others, who, while they deny conclusion, grant the *a priori* principle assumed in the argument, and in consequence are obliged, in order to vindicate the certainty of our knowledge, to have recourse to the hypothesis of intuitions, intellectual forms, and the like, which belong to us by nature, and may be considered to elevate our experience into something more than it is in itself. [fideism; traditionalism; illuminationism] Earnestly maintaining, as I would, with this latter school of philosophers, the certainty of knowledge, I think it enough to appeal to the common voice of mankind in proof of it. That is to be accounted a normal operation of our nature, which men in general do actually instance. That is a law of our minds, which is exemplified in action on a large scale, whether *a priori* it ought to be a law or no. Our hoping is a proof that hope, as such, is not an extravagance; and our possession of certitude is a proof that it is not a weakness or an absurdity to be certain. How it comes about that we can be certain is not my business to determine; for me it is sufficient that certitude is felt. This is what

For private consultation and not distribution without the consent of E Ondrako

the schoolmen, I believe, call treating a subject *in facto esse* and not *in fieri*. Had I attempted the latter, I should have been falling into metaphysics; but my aim is of a practical character, such as that of Butler in his *Analogy*, with this difference, that he treats probability, doubt, expedience, and duty, whereas in these pages, without excluding, far from it, the question of duty, I would confine myself to the truth of things, and to the mind's certitude of that truth.[249]

Newman, in the next paragraph, goes on to point out how certitude de facto involves a personal act of the mind, a judgment, transcending and, hence, prior to the logic of words and supplying for the limitations of the scientific.

> Certitude is a mental state: certainty is a quality of propositions. Those propositions I call certain, which are such that I am certain of them. Certitude is not a passive impression made upon the mind from without, by argumentative compulsion, but in all concrete questions (nay, even in abstract, for though the reasoning is abstract, the mind which judges of it is concrete) it is an active recognition of propositions as true, such as it is the duty of each individual himself to exercise at the bidding of reason, and, when reason forbids, to withhold. And reason never bids us be certain except on an absolute proof; and such a proof can never be furnished to us by the logic of words, for as certitude is of the mind, so is the act of inference which leads to it. Everyone who reasons, is his own centre; and no expedient for attaining a common measure of minds can reverse this truth; - but then the question follows, is there any *criterion* of the accuracy of an inference, in favour of the proposition inferred, since our warrant cannot, as I have said, be scientific? I have already said that the sole and final judgment on the validity of an inference in concrete matter is committed to the personal action of the ratiocinative faculty, the perfection or virtue of which I have called the Illative Sense, a use of the word "sense" parallel to our use of it in "good sense," "common sense," a "sense of beauty," etc.; - and I own I do not see any way to go farther than this in answer to the question.[250]

The position of Newman sketched here is remarkably similar to Scotus's *coloratio* of Anselm and Bonaventure, suggesting in Newman the

---

249 *GA*, ch. 9, pp. 343–344.
250 *GA*, pp. 344–345.

For private consultation and not distribution without the consent of E Ondrako

same mutual relations between intellect and will in God propounded by Scotus, and what the latter means by relating the rationality of the world to the will of God. This is perfectly clear in what Newman says about the sanction of the illative sense for the absolute truth of what we know of being.

> And as we use the (so called) elements without first criticizing what we have no command over, so is it much more unmeaning in us to criticize or find fault with our own nature, which is nothing else than we ourselves, instead of using it according to the use of which it ordinarily admits. Our being, with its faculties, mind and body, is a fact not admitting of question, all things being of necessity referred to it, not it to other things.
>
> If I may not assume that I exist, and in a particular way, that is, with a particular mental constitution, I have nothing to speculate about, and had better let speculation alone. Such as I am is my all; this is my essential stand-point, and must be taken for granted; otherwise, thought is but an idle amusement, not worth the trouble....
>
> I am what I am or I am nothing. I cannot think, reflect, or judge about my being, without starting from the very point which I aim at concluding...[251]

Newman goes on to point out the radical difference between beast and man. The first has no mind and is not capable of progress; the second does. His progress is made possible precisely because of this illative sense which controls and directs from the onset all the inferences and assents which are the complex means for realizing this simple perfection. Thus, when he comes to discuss the nature of the illative sense he writes:

> It is the mind that reasons, and that controls its own reasonings, not any technical apparatus of words and propositions. This power of judging and concluding, when in its perfection, I call the Illative Sense...[252]

This corresponds more or less to what St. Bonaventure calls fontal illumination and knowing in the divine art. It explains how it is possible for the human mind to aspire to know being qua being and treat *de omni scibili*, in the same manner as does the univocal concept of being for Scotus. The very realism of Newman's treatment illustrates the realism of scotistic

---

[251] *GA*, pp. 346–347. Cf. ST. BONAVENTURE, *Breviloquium*, p. 1, ch. 1, 3; BOULNOIS, *Être et représentation*, cit., ch. 4; IPPOLITO, *Anthropological Foundations*, cit.

[252] *GA*, ch. 9, p. 348.

For private consultation and not distribution without the consent of E Ondrako

metaphysics, because its starting point is the same: the person who thinks and in thinking encounters his Creator-Judge, the two luminous beings of Newman. With Scotus, Newman extends the *phronesis* of Aristotle from the *pragma* to the speculative, once again indicating how his mind runs naturally along the lines of Scotus. Here is how Newman, in concluding his discussion of the sanction of the illative sense, applies all this to our knowledge of God, as it were, illustrating how the soul is naturally contemplative and Christian:

> Of course I do not stop here. As the structure of the universe speaks to us of Him who made it, so the laws of the mind are the expression, not of mere constituted order, but of His will. I should be bound by them even were they not His laws; but since one of their very functions is to tell me of Him, they throw a reflex light upon themselves, and, for resignation to my destiny, I substitute a cheerful concurrence in an overruling Providence... It is He who teaches us all knowledge; and the way by which we acquire it is His way. He varies that way according to the subject-matter; but whether He has set before us in our particular pursuit the way of observation or of experiment, of speculation or of research, of demonstration or of probability, whether we are inquiring into the system of the universe, or into the elements of matter and of life, or into the history of human society and past times, if we take the way proper to our subject-matter, we have His blessing upon us, and shall find, beside abundant matter for mere opinion, the materials in due measure of proof and assent.
>
> And especially, by this disposition of things, shall we learn, as regards religious and ethical inquiries, how little we can effect, however much we exert ourselves, without that Blessing; for, as if on set purpose, He has made this path of thought rugged and circuitous above other investigations, that the very discipline afflicted on our minds in finding Him, may mould them into due devotion to Him when He is found. "Verily Thou art a hidden God, the God of Israel, the Saviour," is the very law of His dealings with us. Certainly we need a clue into the labyrinth which is to lead us to Him; and who among us can hope to seize upon the true starting-points of thought for that enterprise, and upon all of them, who is to understand their right direction, to follow them out to their just limits, and duly to estimate, adjust, and combine the various reasonings in which they issue, so as safely to arrive at what it is worth any labour to secure, without a special illumination [Bonaventure] from Himself? Such are the

For private consultation and not distribution without the consent of E Ondrako

dealings of Wisdom with the elect soul. "She will bring upon him fear, and dread, and trial; and She will torture him with the tribulation of Her discipline, till She try him by Her laws, and trust his soul. Then She will strengthen him, and make Her way straight to him, and give him joy."[253]

May we not suggest that this beautiful meditation on the relation between the illative sense, natural faith and saving faith parallels exactly the reflections of Scotus on the relations between natural faith and infused faith, and how the latter finds its natural substratum precisely in the illative sense?

By way of brief summary: a careful glance at the table of contents of the *Grammar*, in the light of the foregoing, will quickly reveal the central insight of Newman linking him to Scotus. Assent, the second act of the mind, or judgment, heart of knowledge of the truth, is indeed a complex proposition and, as such, linked both to the first act of the human mind: apprehension; and the third: inference or demonstration. But this assent or judgment is also a simple act because, for Newman as for Scotus, knowledge as such is a pure perfection, a personal act, intrinsically independent of its conditions in a finite intellect. It is here that we see so clearly the correlations between intuitive cognition of Scotus and the illative sense of Newman and the indications that the metaphysics subsumed by the phenomenological interpretations of Newman is precisely that of Scotus: the univocity of being and the disjunctive transcendentals, anticipated in the theory of divine illumination and knowledge of Christ by St. Bonaventure.

The *Oxford University Sermons* and the *Grammar of Assent* in a Scotistic Framework

The *Oxford University Sermons*, a collection of sermons delivered over a period of 13 years, dealing with the relations of faith and reason and the development of doctrine, are rightly studied in connection with the *Essay on the Development of Doctrine*, a work whose conclusion was the conversion of Newman to the Catholic Church. In the Preface, however, to the definitive 1871 edition, Newman calls our attention rather to the *Grammar of Assent*, as the source for a fuller and more accurate exposition of the themes expounded in these sermons. We might say that not only are the two works mutually illustrative, but in more than a few places,

---

253 *GA*, ch. 9, pp. 351–352. Cf. St. Bonaventure, *Breviloquium*, p. 7, ch. 7, 7–9, conclusion, with long citation from St. Anselm. Cf. also his *Collationes in Hexaemeron*, c. 19.

For private consultation and not distribution without the consent of E Ondrako

the sermons help very much to confirm the scotistic orientation of the *Grammar*.

For instance sermon IV: *The Usurpations of Reason*, Newman clearly indicates along scotistic lines the order between the two *perfectiones simpliciter simplices*: intellect and will and how the intellect does not reach the highest degree of perfection except to the degree it is integrated with holiness of the will. Where that integration is achieved, there we discover not only why the intellect attains that certainty for which it was ordained; but the will attains that rationality or reasonableness, orderly choice ever characteristic of the divine will and source of all rationality in the created beings, whose existence and intelligibility are conditioned precisely by that divine will.[254] Thus, he writes:

> No one can deny to the intellect its own excellence, nor deprive it of its due honours; the question is merely this, whether it not be limited in its turn, as regards its range, so as not without intrusion to exercise itself as an independent authority in the fields of morals and religion… What would he actually see in the actual history of Revelation, but the triumph of the moral powers of man over the intellectual, of holiness over ability, for more than of mind over brute force?[255]

Where the primacy of charity in terms of this order of holiness is rejected, there, the usurpations of "secular reason," which end in skepticism, have their beginning. Further on we will see how that rejection is in fact a refusal to adore and contemplate the God whose authority is first met in conscience. It is to this "metaphysical" wisdom, even in natural theology, that the preference given liberal over useful knowledge in university training points; but it is only through virtue and grace that this holiness is attained.

Another example is easily identified in sermon VI: *Justice as a Principle of Divine Governance*, where he contrasts justice, the key to divine governance according to Christian theology, with benevolence, viz., catering to what is fulfilling for the creature.

> Now first, it is surely not true that benevolence is the only, or the chief, principle of our moral nature… it may be confidently asserted, that the instincts of justice and purity are natural to us in the same sense in which benevolence is natural.[256]

---

[254] On the rationality of the divine will in itself and source of all rationality outside it according to Scotus, cf. HOERES, *Der Wille…*, cit., pp. 86 ff.; and of the finite will, pp. 113 ff.

[255] *Oxford University Sermons*, sermon 4, 4, p. 57.

[256] *Oxford University Sermons*, sermon 6, 10, pp. 105 ff.

For private consultation and not distribution without the consent of E Ondrako

The sense of these terms here corresponds exactly to what Scotus means by *affectus justitiae* and *affectus commodi*, and clearly differentiates the positions of both Newman and of Scotus on the will as a *perfectio simpliciter simplex* essentially free from that of St. Thomas who conceives the will as an appetitive power, only incidentally free.

Here, however, I want to concentrate our attention on sermon II: *The Influence of Natural and Revealed Religion Respectively*. In this 1830 sermon where Newman deals with questions of faith and reason, in a context shaped by the relationship "natural-supernatural" or natural and revealed religion, we encounter positions which not only remind us of similar discussions in the Prologue to Scotus's *Ordinatio*, but which could also aid in attaining a better grasp of the implications of Scotus's views on the need of revealed as well as natural, religious knowledge, on the character of "our theology" *pro statu isto*, and on the relation of a metaphysics of univocal being to a vision of creation for the sake of the Incarnation.

Newman introduces his theme with a brief reference to the purpose of the Incarnation (neither affirming nor denying the absolute primacy of Christ) as our reconciliation with God and the purchase of eternal life through the suffering and death of Christ. He lists a number of graces attendant on this work and then defines the theme of this sermon:

> It is proposed… to treat of a subject with the latter of these two great Christian blessings [the former being the gathering of the scattered sheep into the Church]—viz., to attempt to determine the relation in which this revealed system of doctrine and precept bears to that of Natural Religion, and to compare the two together in point of practical efficacy.[257]

Clearly, Newman assumes that without the Incarnation and Redemption the greatest of blessings would not be accessible to us, as St. Paul teaches. On the other hand this Revealed Religion does not occur in a vacuum, but perfects the natural order which was made precisely to support the supernatural. But to understand this mutual relation Newman notes, and it is also a position of Scotus dealing with natural-supernatural:

> Now, in investigating the connection between Natural and Revealed Religion, it is necessary to explain in what sense religious doctrines of any kind can with propriety be called natural. For from abuse of the term "Natural Religion," many persons will not allow its use at all.[258]

---

[257] "The Influence of Natural and Revealed Religion Respectively," in *Oxford University Sermons*, sermon 2.

[258] *OUS* 2, p. 17.

For private consultation and not distribution without the consent of E Ondrako

Here he points out two extremes: Pelagianism and Calvinism. Then he goes on to describe his own position which, in fact, corresponds exactly to the approach of Scotus.

> When, then, religion of some sort is said to be *natural*, it is not here meant that any religious system has been actually traced out by unaided Reason. We know of no such system, because we know of no time or country in which human Reason *was* unaided. Scripture informs us that revelations were granted to the first fathers of our race, concerning the nature of God and man's duties to Him; and scarcely a people can be named, among whom there are not traditions, not only of the existence of powers exterior to this visible world, but also of their actual interference with the course of nature, followed up by religious communications to mankind from them. The Creator has never left Himself without such witness as might anticipate the conclusions of Reason, and support a wavering conscience and perplexed faith. No people (to speak in general terms) has been denied a revelation from God, though but a portion of the world has enjoyed an authenticated revelation.
>
> Admitting this fully, let us speak of *the fact*; of the actual state of religious belief of pious men in a heathen world, as attested by their writings still extant; and let us call this creed Natural Religion.[259]

Newman now goes on to show, as he did later in the *Idea of a University*, how natural theology, which is the sanction for natural religion, has its center in the conscience, or that aspect of conscience for which the scholastics more properly reserved the term *synderesis*.

> It is obvious that Conscience is the essential principle and sanction of Religion in the mind. Conscience implies a relation between the soul and a something exterior, and that, moreover, superior to itself; a relation to an excellence it does not possess, and to a tribunal over which it has no power. And since the more closely this inward monitor is respected and followed, the clearer, the more exalted, and the more varied its dictates become, and the standard of excellence is ever outstripping, while it guides, our obedience, a moral conviction is thus at length obtained of the inapproachable nature as well as the supreme authority of that, whatever it is, which is the object of the mind's contemplation.

---

[259] *OUS*, pp. 17–18.

For private consultation and not distribution without the consent of E Ondrako

Here, then, at once, we have the elements of a religious system; for what is <u>Religion</u> but <u>the system of relations existing between us and a Supreme Power, cl</u>aiming our habitual obedience: "the blessed and only Potentate, who only hath immortality, dwelling in light unapproachable, whom no man hath seen or can see"?[260]

<u>Conscience,</u> here, as the essential sanction of Religion, is more what is meant, according to Bonaventure and Scotus, by *synderesis.* As such it implies what elsewhere Newman means by two luminous beings: the soul and its Creator, the first enlightened by the second, because superior to the soul. To the degree the soul seeks holiness rather than mere intellectual excellence as its primary goal in life, to that degree the more perfect conscience becomes as a guide to such holiness, and to a recognition of the transcendent character of that goodness which is not its own possession, viz., justice or what Scotus calls the *affectio justitiae* over which, unlike the *affectio commodi,* it has no power. It is this pursuit of holiness, rather than mere knowledge, which leads the soul to recognize the unapproachable character of this object, which is object of the mind's contemplation, even in the natural order. Contemplation, even at this level, is a matter of unconditional assent, not proof, and is the very heart of metaphysics as distinct from science. Newman has here touched exactly on what Bonaventure means by divine illumination as the heart of knowledge as a perfection of the rational creature or image of God. This final comment of Newman shows why such intuitive cognition or contuition is not a form of ontologism. Whether or not this might provide a basis for a truly scientific theology—via some kind of infused knowledge such as Bonaventure postulates for the *status naturae institutae*—has been discussed above.

Newman continues by pointing out how conscience implies a difference in the nature of actions and how one particular action: that of loving and adoring the Creator, takes precedence over all others, thus leading to a presentiment of a future life and judgment to be passed on present conduct.

Further Conscience implies a difference in the nature of actions, the power of acting in this way or that as we please, and an obligation of acting in one particular way in preference to all others; and since the more our moral nature is improved, the greater inward power of improvement it seems to possess, a view is laid open to us both of the capabilities and prospects of man, and the awful importance of that work which the law of his being lays upon him. And this presentiment of a future life, and of a judgment

---

[260] *OUS*, pp. 18–19.

For private consultation and not distribution without the consent of E Ondrako

to be passed on present conduct, with rewards and punishments annexed, forms an article, more or less distinct, in the creed of Natural Religion.[261]

This last point might well indicate a part of what is meant in Hebrews 11: 6, where it is said: "Who comes to God he must believe that God exists and is a rewarder to those who seek him." Natural faith is the substratum of saving faith, and in the present economy of salvation they never exist separately, as Newman states in this sermon. Further, his concept of obligation here corresponds exactly with that of Scotus resting on a concept of the voluntary action as essentially free, even when it is necessary. Obligation in the creature is the sign that the will is a *perfectio simpliciter simplex*, opening on the infinite even if, in the creature, its mode of operation is always qualified by the *affectio commodi*. Obligation *per se* is not restrictive, but foundational for freedom in relation to contingent goods; just as the free, but necessary and impeccable love of the divine goodness by God, is the basis of his love of contingent goods. Necessary action is contrasted with contingent, not voluntary; whereas, voluntary action is contrasted with natural.

Newman now goes on to show how even at the natural element certain aspects of faith and authority are involved in the exercise of the rational faculties, but without in any way implying fideism or confusion of such natural faith with saving or infused faith.

> Moreover, since the inward law of Conscience brings with it no proof of its truth, and commands attention to it on its own authority, all obedience to it is of the nature of Faith; and habitual obedience implies the direct exercise of a clear and vigorous faith in the truth of its suggestions, triumphing over opposition both from within and without; quieting murmurs of Reason, perplexed with the disorders of the present scheme of things, and subduing the appetites, clamorous for good which promises an immediate and keen gratification.[262]

The radical link here asserted between conscience and faith and the obedience postulated by the Authority of conscience, perhaps suggested by the "sincere faith and pure conscience" of St. Paul, is fundamental to Newman's understanding both of the distinction and correlation of natural and supernatural, one in the final analysis paralleling that of Scotus. Let us examine the components of this explanation, one by one.

---

[261] *OUS*, p. 19.
[262] *OUS*, pp. 19–20.

For private consultation and not distribution without the consent of E Ondrako

First, if there is present in my conscience an Authority to which I owe obedience of faith (fidelity), that Authority must be really distinct from me and above me and all other creatures; otherwise, the unconditional obedience owed it would be incompatible with my dignity as a person. Further, this personal character of the obedience of faith or fidelity is typical of the difference between assent in general and mere inference appearing so clearly in the personal character of the illative sense, or of what St. Bonaventure calls *dijudicatio*. Intellectual life would be impossible to a creature, unless there were present this *obeisance* to the authority of Truth (postulating divine illumination according to Bonaventure). It is this light bound up with the Authority of truth which explains the difference between assent and inference.

By faith, here, Newman means what he elsewhere calls, e.g., in the *Grammar of Assent*, natural faith, of which the human mind is capable apart from infused or supernatural faith. As a component of the finite intellect it does represent that point where natural and supernatural in the intellectual order meet, natural faith being the radical foundation for the possibility of supernatural faith, and supernatural faith lifting the finite mind beyond what St. Paul calls the "range of reason." Faith is here used analogically. Natural and infused faith both involve an obedience of faith, an act of the will, a kind of personal, unconditional fidelity to the Authority of truth. In the case of natural faith this is preceded by, but not conditioned by reasoning; whereas, supernatural faith, *formaliter loquendo*, is followed by reasoning. The difference in the relation between obedient and loving contemplation of the truth in each case is that between the two axioms: *intellectus quaerens fidem* and *fides quaerens intellectum*. Without the first, supernatural faith would be purely irrational, like the *fides sola* of Luther where the will is radically arbitrary; without the second, the created mind would never attain direct access to the God, viz., the Authority met in conscience enigmatically (I Cor 13), who dwells in Light inaccessible. Here we see how the misrepresentation of the transcendental character of faith, as radically divorced from the intellectual, is corrected by Newman by introducing, as does Scotus, the concept of natural faith as an act intrinsic to any finite intellect to be a *perfectio simpliciter simplex* and basis for a possible elevation to the supernatural or saving order— this, reflecting a famous Pauline text so often cited by Scotists: "All things are yours, you are Christ's and Christ is God's" (I Cor 3: 23).

That conscience does not permit us to put its commands to the test via a proof, does not mean that we act blindly or surrender the use of our natural judgment as we do in the case of supernatural faith. It means, rather, that the kind of test or proof proper to the study of the physical

For private consultation and not distribution without the consent of E Ondrako

world is not appropriate to the study of first principles which ultimately involve the presence of divine authority in conscience. The so called proof for God's existence is unique, radically different from the methodology of physical science. This is the very point at the heart of St. Anselm's famous proof, without recognition of which none of the other proofs will convince. There is no such thing as an autonomous, created mind which can function without humble, adoring contemplation of the truth for its own sake. In the volitional order, this means obedient acceptance of divine justice, or the *affectio justitiae* over which we have no control, rather than of the *affectio commodi* which, indeed, we can manipulate in view of immediate, keen gratification. Here we note Newman's clear rejection of what Weatherby claims is the heart of his epistemology: the "keen delight."

This is exactly the position of Scotus. Natural and supernatural are not, in the first instance, distinguished in terms of natural and supernatural object of the created intellect, but in terms of the power whereby the created mind is able to know partially or more fully the one connatural object of the mind. This, in turn, presupposes the univocal concept of being, the disjunctive transcendental and ultimately the absolute primacy of Christ, so as to found the analogical or sacramental character of creation as the instrument of divine Authority revealing both from without and from within, step by step, the great mysteries of being and salvation.[263]

Newman then introduces a distinction, found also in Bonaventure:

While Conscience is thus ever the sanction of Natural Religion, it is when improved, the rule of morals also. But here is a difference: it is, as such, essentially religious; but in Morals it is not necessarily a guide, only in proportion as it happens to be refined and strengthened in individuals…. Still unformed and incomplete as is this law by nature, it is quite certain that obedience to it is attended by a continually growing expertness in the science of Morals.[264]

Yet, without grace or the supernatural, Natural Religion is severely limited in the content and correctness of the doctrine it teaches. In a word, natural faith is not saving faith, much less the beatific vision. It is a term useful to point out what is unique in man in contrast to the beast and what is the point of contact with and integration of natural and supernatural.

---

263 Cf. St. Bonaventure, Quaestiones Disputatate de Scientia Christi; Idem, *Christus unus omnium Magister*; Duns Scotus, *Ordinatio*, prologue.

264 "The Influence of Natural…," cit., p. 20. Compare St. Bonaventure, *Itinerarium*, ch. 4, and *De Triplici Via*, on repairing the sting of conscience.

For private consultation and not distribution without the consent of E Ondrako

Natural Religion teaches, it is true, the infinite power and majesty, the wisdom and goodness, the presence, the moral governance, and in one sense, the unity of the Deity; but it gives little or no information respecting what may be called his *personality*. It follows that, though Heathen Philosophy knew so much of the moral system of the world, as to see the duties and prospects of man in the same direction in which Revelation places them, this knowledge did not preclude a belief in fatalism, which might, of course, consist in unchangeable moral laws, as well as physical. And though Philosophy acknowledged an intelligent, wise and beneficent Principle of Nature, still this too was, in fact, only equivalent to the belief in a pervading Soul of the Universe, which consulted its own good, and directed its own movements, by instincts similar to those by which the animal world is guided; but which, strictly speaking, was not an object of worship, inasmuch as each intelligent being was, in a certain sense, himself a portion of it. Much less would a conviction of the Infinitude and Eternity of the Divine Nature lead to any just idea of His *Personality*, since there can be no circumscribing lineaments nor configuration of the Immensurable, no external condition or fortune to that Being who is all in all. Lastly, though Conscience seemed to point in a certain direction as a witness for the real moral locality (so to speak) of the unseen God, yet, as it cannot prove its own authority, it afforded no argument for a Governor and Judge, distinct from the moral system itself, to those who disputed its informations.[265]

With this we can easily anticipate his treatment of the need for holiness and a supernatural revelation not only in order to go beyond the "range of reason," but to correct the aberrations of an intellect darkened by original sin and prone to pantheism, specifically centered on the mystery of the Incarnation. We may add that here all these attributes of the divine Being are precisely those which can be conveniently grouped according to the threefold outline of Scotus's proof for God's existence in *De primo omnium principio* centered on that mysterious name of God: I am who am: the first, the infinite, the good (efficient, exemplary, final cause understood primarily as personal rather than physical).

We may conclude this brief commentary on the multiple meanings of faith and reason in Newman with a brief quotation from sermon 15: *The Theory of Developments in Religious Doctrine*: "But Mary kept all these things, and pondered them in her heart." Luke 2:19. The sermon was

---

265 "The Influence of Natural…," cit., pp. 22–23.

For private consultation and not distribution without the consent of E Ondrako

preached February 2, 1843, a little more than two years before his entrance into the Catholic Church and the completion of his great classic on the *Development of Doctrine*.

> Little is told us in Scripture concerning the Blessed Virgin, but there is one grace of which the Evangelists make her the pattern, in a few simple sentences—of Faith. Zacharias questioned the Angel's message, but "Mary said, Behold the handmaid of the Lord; be it done unto me according to thy word." Accordingly Elizabeth, speaking with an apparent allusion to the contrast thus exhibited between her own highly-favoured husband, righteous Zacharias, and the still more highly-favoured Mary, said, on receiving her salutation, "Blessed art thou among women, and blessed is the fruit of thy womb; Blessed is she that believed, for there shall be a performance of those things which were told her from the Lord."
>
> But Mary's faith did not end in a mere acquiescence in Divine providences and revelations; as the text informs us, she "pondered" them. When the shepherds came and told of the vison which they had seen at the time of the Nativity, and how one of them announced that the Infant in her arms was "the Saviour which is Christ the Lord," while others did but wonder, "Mary kept all these things, and pondered them in her heart." Again, when her Son and Saviour had come to the age of twelve years, and had left her awhile for His Father's service, in the Temple, amid the Doctors, both hearing them and asking them questions, and had on her addressing Him, vouchsafed to justify His conduct, we are told, "His Mother kept all these sayings in her heart." And accordingly, at the marriage-feast in Cana, her faith anticipated His first miracle, and she said to the servants, "Whatsoever He saith unto you, do it."
>
> Thus, St. Mary is our pattern of Faith, both in the reception and in the study of Divine Truth. She does not think it enough to accept, she dwells on it; not enough to possess, she uses it; not enough to assent, she develops it; not enough to submit the Reason, she reasons on it; not indeed reasoning first, and believing afterward, with Zacharias, yet first believing without reasoning, next from love and reverence after believing. And thus she symbolizes to us, not only the faith of the unlearned, but of doctors of the Church also, who have to investigate, and weigh and define, as well as to profess the Gospel, to draw the line between truth and heresy, to anticipate or remedy the various aberrations

For private consultation and not distribution without the consent of E Ondrako

of wrong reason; to combat pride and recklessness with their own arms; and thus to triumph over the sophist and innovator.

If, then, on a day dedicated to such high contemplations as the Feast which we are now celebrating, it is allowable to occupy our thoughts with a subject not of a devotional or practical nature, it will be some relief of the omission to select one in which St. Mary at least will be our example, - the use of Reason in investigating the doctrines of Faith; a subject, indeed, far fitter for a volume than for the most extended notice which can here be given it, but which cannot be passed over in absolute silence, in any attempt at determining the relation of Faith to Reason.[266]

There is much, much here which might further illustrate the theme of these conferences, e.g., Newman's deft association of natural faith with Zachary and the old axiom: *intellectus quaerens fidem*, and infused faith with Mary and the other old axiom: *fides quaerens intellectum*, in a manner alluding to the views of St. Bonaventure. Here, however, I wish to stress one point only: Newman's linking of the Virgin Mary both with his theory of doctrinal development, soon to influence preparations for the solemn dogmatic definition of the Immaculate Conception, and with the positions taken by him in the *Grammar of Assent*. Inspiration for the *Development of Doctrine* is not Hegel and that for the *Grammar of Assent* is not Kant, but is for both Our Lady. Not only Scotus, but Newman may be described as *Doctor Marianus*.

Conclusion

The foregoing is more than sufficient to indicate in Newman's writings the presence of considerable similarity with the thought patterns, theological and philosophical, of Bl. John Duns Scotus; and, indeed, still more might be adduced which for time and space limitations could not be treated except by way of brief references. The more obvious of these similarities are the following:

- the absolute primacy of Christ, its bearing on the mystery of the Immaculate Conception and sacramentality of creation;

- the concept of univocal being and in particular of a *perfectio simpliciter simplex*, rather than the thomistic act/potency analysis to explain the correlation of simple and complex in the human intellect and will;

---

266 *Oxford University Sermons*, sermon 15.

For private consultation and not distribution without the consent of E Ondrako

- the relation of such a perfection to the definition of person and relevance to the so-called critical question;

- the correlation between notional-real apprehension in Newman and abstractive-intuitive cognition in Scotus;

- the nexus between inference-assent and the illative sense in Newman and mental activity, and the *naturale judicatorium* in the Franciscan masters;

- the primacy of the will, its relation to the intellect and its relation to the principle of causality;

- the relation between the proof for God's existence from conscience, the *Itinerarium* of St. Bonaventure and the *De primo rerum principio* of Scotus;

- the correlation between the primacy of the will and rationality and order in both Newman and Scotus;

- holiness as link between science and wisdom, the latter being the ultimate goal of all intellectual activity;

- the positions of Newman and Scotus as a happy medium between secular modernism and rigid fideism.

A certain concentration of attention has been indulged around issues involved in discussion of the critical question and the relation of Scotus and Newman to Kant, not because these are the only points of convergence, but because this is the area central to interest in Scotus and Newman at the moment, both by critics (Weatherby) and supporters (Lash) who maintain the first anticipates Kant and the latter reflects him in their approach to metaphysics and ethics.

I believe that we are justified in affirming not merely a remarkable series of resemblances between two great Oxford theologians, but a "convergence of probabilities" indicating genuine unity of approach to and substantially identical convictions concerning the nature of theology and how to conduct it. I think it can be said further that the more "metaphysical" style of Scotus uncovers the implicit notional foundations of Newman's thought; while the more "phenomenological" style of Newman assists us enormously in grasping the realism and profound spirituality lying behind the superficially dry and abstract presentation of the subtle Doctor, in realizing that Scotus is not the grand-daddy of Kant, but the progenitor of Newman, and that the tortuous discipline entailed in mastering Scotus will enable us to appreciate even more the joys of wisdom Newman so beautifully describes.

For private consultation and not distribution without the consent of E Ondrako

Concluding Remarks

My presentation of striking similarities in the thought patterns of Bl. John Duns Scotus and Bl. John Henry Newman rests especially on Newman's explicit agreement with the thesis central to Scotus's theological synthesis: the absolute primacy of Christ (and with it the Immaculate Conception), the sacramentality of creation attendant upon this primacy, and the priority assigned charity in the order of being. Acceptance of the "Franciscan thesis" normally involves implicit acceptance of scotistic metaphysics that centered about the univocity of being and the disjunctive transcendentals, together with the primacy of the will and charity. From the many citations of Newman I have included in my presentation (and I am sure the careful scholar might find many more), I am convinced that this, indeed, is the case.

Recognition of this point provides a sound, indeed very clear basis for appreciation of a second approach to these similarities, that at the level of epistemology, one which in Newman also includes many points of contact with the views of St. Bonaventure, especially those linked with the theory of divine illumination and metaphysical exemplarism, and with his exposition of the unfolding of the created mind, for instance in his *Itinerarium mentis in Deum*, his *De reductione artium in theologiam*, and in his *Christus unus omnium Magister*, and at greater length in his *Quaestiones disputatae de scientia Christi*. In particular the distinct features of the *Itinerarium* are reflected in Newman's epitaph: *ex umbris et imaginibus in Veritatem.*

It is often said today that Scotus repudiated the theory of divine illumination and metaphysical exemplarism. The similar contours of Scotus's and Newman's theological reflection and, at the same time, those of Newman with Bonaventure (in particular those concerning conscience and the existence of God as heart of the "anthropological proof"), seem to me to be a strong reason for questioning the soundness of this view. If, indeed, Scotus abandoned the formularies of Bonaventure in order to give greater stress to the personal dimension of human thought, but above all to cross a *t* and dot an *i* to bring out the inner thrust of Bonaventure's thought toward the primary motive of the Incarnation, he did not thereby reject the core of the doctrine of divine illumination. It reappears: in Newman as well as in Scotus, in the study of intellect and will as *perfectiones simpliciter simplices* of knowledge and affection, as goods in themselves. Indeed, without the doctrine, if not the terminology, of divine illumination, neither the epistemology nor the Christological metaphysics of Scotus, together with his characteristic analysis of the relation "natural-supernatural" (or in Newman natural and revealed religion, or natural and

For private consultation and not distribution without the consent of E Ondrako

infused faith), can be easily explained. I have no doubt that on this basis, both Bonaventure and Scotus would have found the Newman's motto: *cor ad cor loquitur*, expressive of both the starting and ending points of Christian philosophy.

With this observation I think one other point, only alluded to in the presentation, should be touched upon more expressly because, in so many ways it not only supports and, in a sense, explains why the presentation is reasonable, but also summarizes it. This point concerns the revealed foundations for "Christian philosophy" in all three of the great figures I have discussed.

In the Franciscan school: not only in Bonaventure, but also in Scotus, Christian philosophy is that precisely because it is guided by Christ, and through the light of faith, and later of glory, is brought to its full realization or *reductio* or *resolutio* as St. Bonaventure is accustomed to say. Both for Bonaventure and Scotus, knowledge is not in the first instance a product of mental activity, the objectification as moderns would have it, of sense impressions, but the fruit of contemplation of the Truth, of walking in the Light which is Divine. In a word, the very character of finite knowledge, in scotistic terms a *perfectio simpliciter simplex*, is such as to involve an activity greater than, and lifting the activity of a creature in varying degrees to the level of the divine. Thus, human knowledge: *scientia*, from the onset of human intellectual activity to its consummation may be described by Bonaventure as a passing of knowledge into affection, or wisdom, and into work, or art—at its heart, radically simple before it is preceded and accompanied (in the terminology of Newman) by a complex process of apprehension and argumentation, to ultimately be expressed in the form of a judgment (assent).

But it may also be described with Bonaventure as a passage into that choice whereby knowledge is in fact linked by choice to the love of God and neighbor, and made effective. Then it may be called with Bonaventure understanding and prudence. As wisdom, human knowledge reflects the contemplative character of the intellect attuned to the Light that is God. Failure to acknowledge this in theory as well as in practice is to be in the darkness. As prudence, the personal character of intellectual activity whereby the complex processes so characteristic of human knowing come to reflect the simplicity and clarity of the contemplative, is underscored. Science or knowledge in itself is thereby not confused with this or that particular instance of knowledge in the development of human, intellectual life. It is this latter personal dimension which is stressed by Scotus in his treatment of intuitive and abstractive cognition, and also by Newman in his discussion of the illative sense.

For private consultation and not distribution without the consent of E Ondrako

And it is this latter personal dimension which is given place in the scotistic view of being as univocal; not, however, by sacrificing the radically simple character of intuitive knowledge made possible in logical form by the concept of being. It is this juncture between the contemplative and complex at the very heart of metaphysics which is codified in discussing knowledge as a *perfectio simpliciter simplex*. All this, Scotus, and after him, Newman, centers on the mystery of the Incarnation, not only in the economy of salvation, but in the natural order designed by the Creator to be substratum on which the economy of salvation would rest. Underlying this in both is a metaphysics, however apparently abstruse, radically personal in orientation. This is particularly the case with Scotus where the univocity of being is clearly related to a notion of existence radically personal: *existential incommunicabilis naturae intellectualis*. The fuller elaboration of this relation is found in the scotistic metaphysics of person used to explain both divine personhood and the possibility of the hypostatic union and indwelling of the Blessed Trinity in the mystical members of Christ.

Here we must remark on another point seldom considered today: Bonaventure anticipates scotistic christocentrism in his most speculative exposition and defense of the theory of divine illumination in question 4 of his *Quaestiones disputatae de scientia Christi*. There, he is at pains to explain the perfection of the most perfect human intellect at every level, above all of certainty or epistemology. He does this precisely in terms of the theory of divine illumination which he expressly defends against charges of being fideistic. For him the essence of knowledge, in a creature as well as in God, is the contemplative dimension. To contemplate is to admire the Truth of the eternal Word from the very start of the complex unfolding of the finite intellect. To do this is to walk in the Light which is that Truth. This is above all the case with that human mind which is the mind of a Divine Person, the very Truth and very Light of the world. *Erat lux vera quae illuminat omnem hominem venientem in hoc mundum* (Jn 1: 9). One cannot dismiss the theory of divine illumination as merely a construct to explain the process of theologizing, or as merely an adaptation of platonic or neo-platonic speculation to reflection on Christian revelation. Rather, it is a very valid attempt to illustrate a point absolutely central and basic to the teaching of Christ about himself as the one Teacher of all. It seems to me that this is a dimension of the Franciscan thesis about absolute primacy, profoundly expounded and lacking only the name: absolute primacy of the Word Incarnate.

There is also a Marian dimension involved. It may easily be recognized in the teaching of St. Bonaventure on the mediation of Mary in the intel-

For private consultation and not distribution without the consent of E Ondrako

lectual order. Here I would rather note the revealed basis, in particular the biblical bases of this teaching as it appears in the liturgy even today, for instance in the texts of the votive Mass in honor of Mary as *Sedes Sapientiae* (*Collectio Missarum*, n. 24).

The contemplative aspect of knowing there centers on the text of St. Luke, repeated twice in chapter two of his Gospel (a Gospel inspired by the preaching of St. Paul): Mary kept all these things in her heart, pondering them (cf. Lk 2: 19. 51). The things she kept in her heart: the mysteries of the Incarnation and our salvation and her role therein, are radically simple. The pondering is complex, what Newman calls the *conditio sine qua non* of human knowledge as it unfolds or develops, but not its cause which is the beauty of the Truth shining in the mind, never so perfectly as in the Mother of God. Newman himself makes use of this very point in sermon 15 of his *Oxford University Sermons*: "The Theory of Developments in Religious Doctrine."

This knowledge, however, insofar as it is personal: viz., entailing personal judgment, assent, determination to walk in the light, is expressed in Our Lord's comment on Mary, the sister of Martha: Mary has chosen the better part and it shall not be taken from her (cf. Lk 10: 42), a comment which applies even more to Mary the Mother of Him who spoke thus. We might call this the prudential character of all knowledge.

Finally, the complexity of human knowledge and of its development is not merely referred to the needs of the finite mind in order to attain that full resolution which is the perfection of Christian philosophy, but is explained by both Scotus and Bonaventure as a pale reflection of the eternal generation of the Word by the Father. <u>Objectification is not merely a subjective process,</u> <u>but one which reflects interiorly what is the condition of divine knowing</u>. The concept or interior word is begotten, not in the first instance in God in order to know, but because the Father knows. And while the human idea is first formed in order to know, it too also is the term of this knowing, a simple term which rightly is called in Christian philosophy a "concept" because related to a divine begetting. It is this consideration, so widely forgotten today even by Catholics, which ultimately explains why there is no critical problem in terms of an abyss between the intra and extra mental, but only in terms of the personal refusal to choose the better part. It is this choice which Newman insists must be uppermost in every mind, the choice which makes sanctity and blessedness realizable, a choice adumbrated in the natural order, but fully realized in the salvific.

For private consultation and not distribution without the consent of E Ondrako

In conclusion, I wish to read a text of St. Bruno of Asti († 1123) which anticipates the position of St. Bonaventure and the Franciscan school on the role of Mary in Christian education:

> Mother most wise, alone most worthy of such a Son! She kept all these words in her heart, preserving them for us and commending them to our remembrance, so that afterwards, through teaching them, recounting them, proclaiming them, they might be recorded, preached throughout the world, and announced to all the nations. (*Commentarium in Lucam*, p. I, c. 2 (PL 165: 355).

For private consultation and not distribution without the consent of E Ondrako

Study Questions for Part Two

1. Is Newman's pastoral sensitivity to the primacy of a well-formed conscience in the Letter to the Duke of Norfolk (1874) a significant part of a golden thread in his life? Why? Does this thread extend to understanding conscience in connection with the decisions made with the help of intuitive cognition that has been informed by the abstractive cognition of Scotus? In other words, does the true liberating effect on scientific research of real apprehension and real assent when forming one's conscience with the assistance of notional apprehension and notional assent as an integral part of a whole, convince and satisfy? Can you see why there is a beautiful linkage here between Newman and Scotus in the quest for truth? Why do they help to rethink ultimate questions?

2. Edward Caswall noted what Newman told him about his two goals for the *Grammar of Assent*: "the first part shows that you can believe what you cannot understand. In the second part, you can believe what you cannot absolutely prove" (C.S.Dessain, Newman, 1980, 148.) The challenge of secular or liberal Christianity is to make Newman's two goals intelligible and persuasive. Is Scotus's intuitive and abstractive cognition, with an understanding of the meaning of the univocity of the concept of being and the pure perfections of being, will, intellect, and freedom, comparable to Caswall's note? Is Scotus's formal distinction *a parte rei* in the context of Caswall's synthesis? If the light which illumines is epistemology, and the light that illumines is metaphysics, why is theirs an epistemology of faith and metaphysics of faith and freedom? Can you believe what you cannot understand, and believe what you cannot absolutely prove, by explaining intuition and certitude according to Scotus? Can you make the linkage with Newman's notional and real apprehension, and notional and real assent, and why this is absolutely critical to a person's right to be certain?

3. Scotus believes what he has proven as a metaphysician. "Communicating the rays of your goodness most liberally, you are boundless good to whom as the most loveable thing of all every single being in its own way comes back to you as to its ultimate end" (*De Primo Principio Rerum*, 4, 84). If one studies Scotus's search for the truth in Revelation, that is, Christ as the way, truth and life, the 'univocal concept of being' is the key. Univocity of the concept of being is a guiding light that does not overwhelm what is being illumined. Is it clear why the univocity of the concept of being is not a pure logical construct? Is it clear why

the faulty interpretation of univocity paved the way for some to name him the culprit for the anti-metaphysical dimension of modernity? Is it clear why Scotus has given the world what it is secretly looking for in the depths of the well-ordered conscience, the light that comes from God and keeps logic securely linked to reality or being?

4. In similar fashion, Newman formulated the "illative sense" and its relation to the inner voice of God in every person, in logical and intelligible form, while keeping logic within the limits of its nature, thus securely linked to reality or being. In Newman's *Essay on Development*, he wrote about change in a way that was very different from his early contemporary, Hegel. What does Newman mean when he says: to live is to change and to be perfect is to have changed often? What does Newman mean when he says: "One aspect of Revelation must not be allowed to exclude or to obscure another; and Christianity is dogmatical, devotional, and practical all at once?" (*Essay on the Development of Doctrine*, 36). How might Newman answer the question: Is there any difference between the ancients rejecting Christ and the moderns doing the same?

5. The notion of grace, the human will and freedom that perfects it, requires a very careful answer from the beginning of the Franciscan school and its subsequent faithful developments in accord with Church teaching. How does the molinist or banesian Thomist school differ from the Mastrian Franciscan school on the critical point of *condetermination*? Does Newman reject the Lockian argument of strong and weak because both terms refer to the relative firmness in the relation of an inference to its premises? Is the key the correct understanding of human freedom, and how it is perfected? What is the Kantian understanding of freedom? The Thomists hold that the will is not essentially free, but only marginally, in relation to contingent objects. The Franciscan school defines the will, freedom and necessity, or independent being, in the manner that the human will should be elevated by grace to the point where the human person, by condetermination, necessarily wills the absolute good that does not deprive the human person of freedom, but perfects it. How might this be part of the answer to Pope Benedict XVI and his question from his July 7, 2010 Papal Audience on Scotus?

PART 3

THE IMPLICATIONS FOR THE CHURCH AND MODERN WORLD

For private consultation and not distribution without the consent of E Ondrako

INTRODUCTION

Scientific Form and Real Assent

Edward Ondrako

Précis

The third part of *The Newman-Scotus Reader* raises questions that are beneath the rationalism and arbitrary voluntarism of western secularism: What is the relation of scientific form to intellectual certainty? Does every speculative proof of God's existence mean that it is merely a proof from onto-theology, a proof with no relation to reality? Is the study of reality reduced to pure logical constructs alone? The short answer is an emphatic no! There is much more from the wisdom of Scotus and Newman! They know the reasons that the ancients rejected Christ and the problem of the moderns doing the same. They answer with an underlying scientific form in all of their works based on epistemological, metaphysical and experiential traits. They give a strong religious voice in the scientific discourse and related religious dialogue. Newman explicitly agrees with Scotus's theological synthesis on the primacy of Christ and living the truth in charity.

Excursus: Seven Themes about the Light

The third excursus revisits seven themes related to the three approaches in the history of philosophy: first, that of Aristotle and Aquinas; second, that of Ockham, Hume and Kant; and third, that of Bonaventure and Scotus. Newman, arguably, fits into the third approach.[1] The perennial questions remain: what are the origin, nature and goal of wisdom? Does it matter if the firmness of an inference in relation to its premises is weak or strong? Scotus and Newman answer with deep roots in wisdom, a constant

---

1 PETER DAMIAN FEHLNER, "Scotus and Newman in Dialogue," Proceedings of the Newman-Scotus Symposium held at Washington Theological Union, Washington, D.C., October 22–24, 2010. They are chapters 4 and 7 in this volume. Bonaventure's theory of illumination and metaphysical exemplarism helps one to find a significant substratum to Fehlner's view. Henceforth, Fehlner, "Dialogue."

For private consultation and not distribution without the consent of E Ondrako

search for wisdom that avoids the rationalist trap, and the skill to use the wisdom of the scientific method in relation to eternal wisdom.

Finding the 'light that lights.'

I know of no one who seriously contests that Scotus and Newman knew scientific form and exercised scientific form in a most compelling manner. There are no shortcuts to attain wisdom, no individualism, or anti-intellectualism in their thought. Their thought is about the primacy of the will and making correct applications to issues of justice and charity. With collective wisdom, one hopes that debacles such as recent wars may not break out. With collective wisdom, many affronts to the dignity of persons and to the sacramentality of the world in the twenty-first century, especially health and education issues for all, may be creatively and effectively engaged.

Scotus and generations of his disciples are as critical of developing spiritualities and theologies that are individualistic and anti-intellectual because they corrode wisdom and healthy secularity. In this spirit, Pope St. John Paul II, in *Tertio Millennio Adveniente*, and Pope Benedict XVI, in his *Christmas Address to the Roman Curia*, 2005, address one of the most complex problems facing the Catholic community and its relationship to the world today, the interpretation of Vatican Council II. The Council is the work of the Holy Spirit who inspires finite humans. The same Holy Spirit is at work in all persons in a way known to God. That critical point affirmed, it remains that individualistic and anti-intellectual interpretations such as 'the norm that norms,' corrupts Catholic responses to the challenges of modernity and post-modernity.

I know of no one who witnessed the events that were developing at Vatican II who questions the fact that many interpretations of Vatican II have spun out with a centrifugal force with the oft-repeated comments of persons on all sides that there is a failure to speak and to listen to one another in accord with the rules of civility and nobility. The more I read the papal addresses, listen to the views of contemporaries, analyze the modern spirituality in modern theology, be the views philosophical, theological or anthropological, the more convinced I am that a disciplined and proper study of the works of Scotus and Newman will help illumine the path with the proper light. Specifically, the primacy of the will and charity for Scotus and the explicit agreement of Newman with this Franciscan thesis counter individualism and anti-intellectualism.

On life's pilgrim journey, if it is too dark or too bright, one may stumble and fall into the abyss of rationalism or fideism. It seems that both abysses are home to many who did not use the right caution to find

For private consultation and not distribution without the consent of E Ondrako

the light. They may be traditionalists, or modernists, neo-conservatives or post-modernists, individualistic intellectualists or arbitrary voluntarists. Scotus and Newman employ epistemological similarities with just the right amount of light. Moreover, Scotus, the uncontested metaphysician-theologian and Newman, the modest metaphysician-theologian, have no difficulty in applying the metaphysical exemplarism of Bonaventure.[2] Scotus does this in a singularly luminous manner with his univocity of the concept of being. All three exemplify the metaphysics of faith and freedom. They avoid the rationalist snare by not separating ethics or morality from doctrine. They keep the meta in meta-ethics and meta-physics by using a torch that lights well.

From inference to real assent: the road to interiorization.

The view of inference leading to real assent has a premise that every search for knowledge has wisdom as an implicit goal of all science. Scotus and Newman are exemplars of scientific form in search of eternal wisdom. Scotus flourished during the new discoveries of science at Oxford in the thirteenth and Newman during the more developed scientific form at Oxford in the nineteenth century. Discoveries during these centuries impact the twentieth and twenty-first century wisdom of the scientific revolution. Familiarity with certain forms of late scholasticism demonstrate the threads that prepare the way for the rise of Kantian rationalism, which is the dominant philosophical influence shaping western secularism today. A cursory glance at the policy making and mindset of American Government and Universities gives ample evidence of a Rawlsian and Dworkian[3] form of thinking that is at once Kantian and Hegelian, and can trace itself to a pre-Hegelian (Joachimite) form in the thirteenth century, one that Bonaventure and Scotus knew very well.

In the face of these extensive challenges from modernity and post-modernity, Scotus and Newman teach the searcher for wisdom how to use inference to arrive at real assent. Whether the inference is weak or strong is a Lockian division which, ultimately, in religious matters has little purchase for making a real assent. The difference between notional and real assent is the prize brilliantly unraveled in Newman's *Grammar of Assent*. 'Creative liberty,' in the human person, if not misunderstood in an equivocal manner, can be a very rich contribution of Franciscan anthro-

---

2 FEHLNER, Dialogue.

3 John Finnis, from Oxford and Notre Dame, and Robert P. George from Princeton, are examples of scholars in political philosopy who are well aquainted with the mask that the term neutral can be for atheism when it is used in the context of secularism instead of healthy secularity. They lecture and write on the influence of the thought of the legal theorists John Rawls and Richard Dworkin.

For private consultation and not distribution without the consent of E Ondrako

pological thought to the quest for scientific form that leads to eternal wisdom. The difficulty with 'creative liberty' is that it may not take into consideration, sufficiently, the lesser freedom in achieving the objective end proper to human beings, and miss the higher meaning of charity. The practical potential of 'creative liberty' has to take into consideration the ontological weakening of human beings, their lesser freedom. Scotus has a very healthy regard for human happiness, the *affectio commodi*, without forgetting charity for the other is the higher goal, the *affectio justitiae*. It is love for God above all and one's neighbor as oneself.

In 1989, Stephen Dumont's notable study of Scotus's thought on intuitive and abstractive cognition leads to an ascetic and compelling formulation of the way Scotus answers the consequences of the fall of Adam and Eve. "The ontological change does not regard the nature of man, but his effective and existential condition."[4] With reference to Dumont, Benedetto Ippolito elaborates on this pivotal insight of Scotus. He supports the Scotistic view that the primacy of the will is not individualistic or anti-intellectual. Human beings are weakened by an ontological change but the essence of the person is not weakened. The human person retains a real causal power, practical potential, and freedom that predisposes to transcendence. The reduced causal power affects the potential that persons possess. The reduction implies a lesser freedom in reaching the ends that rational beings have and capacity to reach these ends with one's own will.[5] In this lies the possible danger of ambiguous language to conceal the truth or avoiding transparency in committing oneself which is to equivocate the meaning of creative liberty.

Bonaventure, Scotus, and Newman avoid any danger of equivocation with the concept of creative liberty. The indispensible element is *interiorization*, intellectual humility that leads to the sanctification of one's intellect. The danger is that rational beings become the end in itself, not because they have reason, but because they have freedom.[6] Kant's rationalist approach puts it this way: "it is not happiness that is the ultimate end of human beings. Rather, freedom is the ultimate end. Happiness is the highest natural end of the human person, but freedom is an even higher

---

[4] STEPHEN DUMONT, "Theology as a Science and Duns Scotus' Distinction between Intuitive and Abstractive Cognition," *Speculum* 64.3 (1989), 579–599. SCOTUS, *Quodlibet* q. 7 art. 2 (ed. Alluntis, 363). BENEDETTO IPPOLITO, "The Anthropological Foundations of Duns Scotus Mariology," Acts of the Symposium on Scotus' Mariology, Grey College, Durham, England, September 9–11, 2008, *Mariologia Franciscana* III (New Bedford, MA: Academy of the Immaculate, 2009), 169–170. Dumont leaves out the connections of Scotus with Bonaventure.

[5] IPPOLITO, 170.

[6] IMMANUEL KANT, *Naturrecht Feyerabend*, 27:1321-2, trans. Paul Guyer, "Kant, Autonomy, and Modernity" Lecture at the Philosophy Department, Catholic University of America, October, 15, 2010. Henceforth, Guyer lecture.

For private consultation and not distribution without the consent of E Ondrako

rational end."[7] *Interiorization* based on intellectual humility for Bonaventure, Scotus and Newman is far from Lockian or Kantian rationalist freedom. Kant's rationalism has a subtle, arbitrary voluntarism that is a universal challenge to living by faith, with hope and in love.

'Setting the table' for scientific form and wisdom.

I favor the image of setting the table as one would for a banquet because it has the pieces that are not the ordinary daily fare. The opulent table setting for Scotus is the disjunctive transcendentals, which is his metaphysics. Newman may have lamented that he was never trained formally in the scholastic metaphysical method, but he knew how to set the table with metaphysical, theological and anthropological finery. The quest for eternal wisdom for Scotus and Newman depends on scientific form and how inference leads to certain, immutable, or, real assent. The difficulty is that not all of the late scholastics set the table with the same finery as Scotus. Newman knew the rules for setting the table but something had drastically changed from the time of Scotus to the form of Kantian rationalism that had become the new way for setting the table in the nineteenth century. A significant step was a Lockian *episteme* (John Locke 1632–1704) and the skepticism of David Hume (1711–1776) that contributed to an enervation of Christianity. Locke's broad *episteme* revolves around the principle that individual interpretation takes precedence over any ecclesiastical tradition, teaching or authority. This is the principle of 'private judgment.' His narrow *episteme* rests on high or low probability in regard to the Church's teachings about what matters for nothing can be known with objective certitude. High probability suggests assent, while low probability suggests that it is sufficient to be tentative with one's religious convictions. His strong and weak arguments do not deceive the discerning reader. This Lockian *episteme* becomes an operative principle in Kant's three critiques. In chapter ten of the *Grammar of Assent*, Newman deals with these critiques in the context of natural religion and explains why revelation has to enter the picture in the quest for eternal wisdom.

If wisdom is the quest for every reasonable human being, why make distinctions between what is the origin and goal of all science and eternal wisdom? That is a modern question made complex because of the entitlement given to scientific evidence. Cyril O'Regan observes that since the Enlightenment, "the game is rigged."[8] There is a growing perception in

---

[7] Guyer lecture.

[8] Cyril O'Regan is professor of theology at the University of Notre Dame. During his 2010 course on The Theology of Pope Benedict XVI, he gave this pithy and evocative observation and gave

For private consultation and not distribution without the consent of E Ondrako

persons who live with the deepest religious conviction, rooted in eternal wisdom, that there is a mindset or 'rigging' against Christianity. The perception is that public policy in the west seems to view everything as morally neutral, which is nothing less than arbitrary voluntarism. Anything is tolerated except to live by the conviction that there is an eternal wisdom. Eternal wisdom is integrally related to but not the same wisdom that is the origin and goal of all science. Scotus and Newman integrate both scientific and eternal wisdom.

Scotus anticipated the problem of rigging, the separating of scientific form from eternal wisdom. Scotus took the long view and prepared for it with his take of the disjunctive transcendentals and luminous univocity of the concept of being and its role in abstract and intuitive cognition. Newman lived with a nascent rigging in the Oriel common room and British society. He gradually deepened his understanding of the meaning and the value of inference, notional apprehension and notional assent, but his sights were always set on the scientific form that leads to certitude, to real apprehension, and real assent. That gradual transformation is clear within a period of about five years as narrated in the *Apologia*. Newman describes the relationship with Dr. Whately from 1822 and acts toward him as a gentle and encouraging instructor. By 1827, Newman summarized what was happening to him spiritually. "The Truth is I was beginning to prefer intellectual excellence to moral; I was drifting in the direction of the Liberalism of the day. I was rudely awakened from my dream at the end of 1827 by two great blows—illness and bereavement."[9] His youngest sister, Mary, died and at the beginning of 1829 came the formal break between Dr. Whately and Newman.

In his relationship with Dr. Whately, Newman's initial admiration turns to concern about Whately's individualism. It is the same problem that the disciples of Scotus reject, i.e. individualism contrary to belonging to a community of believers united in charity. Dr. Whately's individualism has more of the character of the modern spirituality of Ockham, but not of Scotus. There is no simple formula for the origins of modernity, however much some would like to posit one. A red flag identifies the trajectory from Ockham's form of nominalism to Gabriel Biel, who was a teacher of Martin Luther. A further step in the same trajectory is with the eclecticism of Francisco Suarez along with other historical factors that influence Kant. Kant is the one who takes the meta out of meta-ethics and meta-physics.

Newman's similarity with Scotus is that he fled from what he perceived in himself as larval individualism. He was not comfortable with the indi-

---

copious reasons for his view.

9 JOHN HENRY NEWMAN, *Apologia pro vita sua* (David D. Delaura, ed., 1968), 22–25.

For private consultation and not distribution without the consent of E Ondrako

vidualism of Dr. Whately, nor the anti-intellectualism of the Anglican Bishops. In 1839, when he was asked by the Bishops to withdraw Tract 90, his reply reveals his dual worry, his charity and his sense of responsibility to truth:

> This I refused to do: I would not do so for the sake of those who were unsettled or in danger of unsettlement. I would not do so for my own sake; for how could I acquiesce in a mere Protestant interpretation of the Articles? How could I range myself among the professors of theology, of which it put my teeth on edge even to hear the sound?[10]

Newman adds that the Bishops wanted him to keep silent and not to defend Tract 90. He agreed that if they would not condemn it and allow the Tract to continue to be sold, he would keep silent and not defend it. In other words, Newman's compromise was not to withdraw Tract 90, as the Bishops wanted him to do, and he would not defend it. The Bishops made him agree to stop the series of Tracts, which he did. Newman had to publish his own condemnation of the Tract to the Bishop of Oxford, which he did, in order to save the Tract. Newman wrote that the Bishop of Oxford was ever most kind to him and he imputed nothing whatever to him.[11] Such is ecclesiastical politics.

There is a concise message from both scholars who labored in England. Be Catholic! Be intellectual! Be holy! They demonstrate the quest for eternal wisdom by using scientific form. That is what ignites the blaze of certitude that tears the night of the senses. It is not an *incendium individualitatis*, but an *incendium amoris in caritate*.

Caveats about the approaches to the history of philosophy.

Parts one and two of *The Newman-Scotus Reader* support the wholesome presupposition and claim that one may find Newman more at home with the approach of Bonaventure and Scotus than with Aristotle and Thomas. The thought of Ockham, Hume and Kant does not convince Newman, but, there is a pairing of intellectual traditions that does, i.e. Thomas and Scotus.

Caveat about Newman's style.

In unraveling the real, what is, or being, Newman's approach in the *Grammar of Assent* is neither Thomistic nor Bonaventurian, but an original style that stands on its own, one with identifiable phenomenological

---

10 *Apologia* (Delaura, 1968), 79.

11 Apologia, 79.

For private consultation and not distribution without the consent of E Ondrako

components. It is philosophical realism, but there is more.[12] Compare the intellectual impact of Aristotle on the ancient and medieval world, the *via antiqua*, to the impact of Immanuel Kant on the modern and post-modern world, the *via moderna*. Scotus makes accessible a deeper study of the mystery of reality than the metaphysics of Aristotle. Newman's is a deeper study of the mystery of reality than Kant. As Scotus was familiar with the empirical tradition at Oxford from its origins, Newman knew the modern empirical tradition at Oxford, particularly its Kantian form. The connection between the intuitive cognition of Scotus and the way of understanding conscience for Newman is in Scotus's argument for the existence of God from reason and Newman's argument for the existence of God from conscience.

Caveat about the weak state of Catholic philosophy.

Newman's argument for the existence of God is all the more remark-able for he saw the weak state of Catholic philosophical studies in Europe. An encounter on November 21, 1846 says it all. A Jesuit told Newman that Aristotle and Thomas were out of favor in Italy. Newman asked: what philosophy is being taught? "None. Odds and ends—whatever seems to them best. They have no philosophy. Facts are the great thing, and nothing else. Exegesis, but no doctrine."[13] This weak response of Christian philoso-phers enables the new-rational-mathematical method of Descartes to find its way into the seminaries and unwittingly opened the door to an alterna-tive to Christian faith which was anti-theistic and anti-metaphysical.

Newman was not the only one to recognize the difficulties. In September 1863, the Congress of German Catholic Scholars at Munich, led by Ignaz von Döllinger tried to address academic issues that might rectify the gaps, but their good will failed to edit out a disparaging of scholastic theology, resulting in the disfavor of the Pope Pius IX. He wrote: *Tuas Libenter*, the Munich Brief. In reply, Newman sees himself as a controversialist, one who engages the problems and challenges of his day, intending to avoid extremes, and encouraging the importance of fostering the Catholic mind to take initiative. He interprets the Munich Brief to be "tying the hands of a controversialist."[14] Newman's balanced understand-ing of 'creative liberty' is evident in the following quote.

---

[12] Lawrence Richardson, *Newman's Approach to Knowledge* (Herefordshire: Gracewing, 2007), 19. See fn. 2–4 for several references.

[13] John Henry Newman, *Letters and Diaries*, 23: 213.

[14] John Henry Newman, *Apologia Pro Vita Sua*, (London: uniform edition, 1905), 263.

For private consultation and not distribution without the consent of E Ondrako

A [theologian] would not dare [to address open questions], if he knew an authority, which was supreme and final, was watching every word he said, and made signs of assent and dissent to each sentence, as he uttered it. Then indeed he would be fighting, as the Persian soldiers, under the lash."[15]

Caveat about the Syllabus of Errors.

History lectures tend to give short shrift to the complicated *Syllabus of Errors* from Pius IX, in 1864. They overlook the importance of proposition thirteen, where the scholastics were vindicated by Pius IX when he condemned the view that "the method and principles according to which the ancient scholastic doctors cultivated theology are not in accordance with the needs of our age and with the advance of the sciences." This seems to be a reply to the Kantian thought in the air. Newman knew it and the deleterious effect of Kant's rejection of metaphysics and reduction that all one knows is noumena, facts. If there is a God, he is a fact, no different from others. Catholic teaching on divine illumination, as Bonaventure develops after Augustine, and its unique formulation by Scotus foreshadows the mystery of Christ, the Word Incarnate as Light of the World. Kantian noumena are far removed and Kantian thought may lead to skepticism. What makes divine illumination appeal to Newman and to the scientific mind is Scotus's unique formulation of the univocity of the concept of being, not as a pure logical construct first, but a unique formulation to keep logic linked to reality. This is behind Newman's formulation of the illative sense.

Contra skepticism, Newman understood the typological method of the Fathers in the quest for certitude. He learned from Ireneus what is innermost to the Franciscan theological method.

> I am what I am, or I am nothing. I cannot think, reflect, or judge about my being, without starting from the very point which I am at concluding. My ideas are all assumptions, and I am ever moving in a circle. …I cannot make myself anything else, and to change me is to destroy me. If I do not use myself, I have no other self to use.[16]

On August 4, 1879, Pope Leo XIII wrote *Aeterni Patris*, with the goal of renewing philosophical thought in the Church with Thomism as the basis. The intention was not to leave out Bonaventurianism. In time

---

15 *Apologia*, 267–268. This is another insight into his mind that antedates the authentic spirit of Vatican II.

16 *GA*, 347.

For private consultation and not distribution without the consent of E Ondrako

that renewal took the form of neo-Thomism, including a later hybrid, transcendental Thomism. Newman wrote to the Holy Father:

> All good Catholics must feel it a first necessity that the intellectual exercises, without which the church cannot fulfill her supernatural mission duly, should be founded upon broad as well as true principles, that the mental creations of her theologians, of her controversialists and pastors, should be grafted on the Catholic tradition of philosophy, and should not start from a novel and simply original tradition, but should be substantially one with the teaching of St. Athanasius, St. Anselm and St. Thomas, as those great Doctors in turn are one with each other.[17]

Caveat about the pairing of Thomas and the Franciscan traditions.

Franciscans after *Aeterni Patris* asked about the official pairing of Thomas with Bonaventure, by Popes Sixtus V in 1587 in *Triumphantis Hierusalem*. Does it remain? The answer to the pairing was affirmative. The commonalities and competing views in both philosophical and theological traditions need careful study. This pairing means that revelation is not culturally and historically conditioned. Revealed truth in one age does not cease to be true in another. Moreover, the pairing affirms the work of the metaphysician-theologians, Thomas and Scotus. The subtle doctor does not break with Bonaventure, but follows with continuity that is a rigorous analysis of metaphysics and experience centered in charity.[18] There is a beauty to the pairing of the two traditions, which are built firmly on the metaphysical-theological sciences. They support the teaching that revealed truth in one age does not cease to be true in another.

Testing three approaches to the history of philosophy.

Contours in the thought of Scotus to Newman become recognizable from three approaches to the history of philosophy. The first is that of Aristotle and Aquinas. The second is that of Ockham, Hume and Kant. The third is that of Bonaventure, Scotus and, arguably, Newman. There is considerable similarity in the thought patterns of Thomas and Scotus, especially, the relation of charity that leads to holiness.[19] A major difference is their thinking on the relation of the will to the intellect.[20]

---

[17] *LD* 23: 212. 14 December 1879.

[18] OLIVIER BOULNOIS, *La Rigueur de la Charité* (Paris: Éditions du Cerf, 1998).

[19] FEHLNER, Dialogue. The monumental study of the Cartesian roots of modern atheism by Cornelio Fabro makes no mention of the thought of Scotus. CORNELIO FABRO, *God in Exile: Modern Atheism*, ed. and trans. Arthur Gibson (Toronto: Newman Press, 1968).

[20] ST. THOMAS, *Summa Theologica*, I, qq. 82–83.

For private consultation and not distribution without the consent of E Ondrako

Complementarity in their approaches especially to charity is more than antiquarian interest.[21]

To understand the three approaches to the history of philosophy, one starts with an x-ray of their works, and not just a photograph. What is their view beneath the surface? Our thesis focuses on distinctions in the third from the second approaches. The second approach has a huge impact on Newman's formulation of the great *apostosia* of the late nineteenth century. His *University Sermons* and *Grammar of Assent* are replies to the Lockian *episteme* using Thomas and Scotus, in the sphere of epistemology, metaphysics, and ethics. It is not readily apparent where Newman appears more clearly thomistic and where, scotistic. At times he appears thomistic at first, and only later, the scotistic pattern is identifiable. For example, his *Idea of a University* reveals his mind and heart about the essence of a university, while his *Grammar of Assent* reveals the science behind his convictions. In chapter 10 of the *Grammar*, Newman deals with natural and supernatural religion to illustrate the potential of the illative sense, or faculty of judging, in apologetics. A teacher of religion presents evidence, shares experiences, and awakens the illative sense in another person. The illative sense aids in making a judgment which means that in religious experience, each person can only speak for himself. However, there is a supernatural element, that Christianity is a "*Revelatio revelata*."

> It is a definite message from God to man distinctly conveyed by His chosen instruments, and to be received as such a message; and therefore to be positively acknowledged, embraced, and maintained as true, on the ground of it being divine, not as true on intrinsic grounds, not as probably true, or partially true, but as absolutely certain knowledge, certain in a sense in which nothing else can be certain, because it comes from Him who neither can deceive nor be deceived.[22]

Natural religion contains our sense of human need and the infinite goodness of God that prepares us for revealed religion. For Newman, antecedent probability is the truth which the mind anticipates.[23] Compare Newman on revealed religion in chapter ten of the *Grammar* with the

---

21 Several students at Notre Dame have discussed how their serious study of Thomas and Scotus has been a labor of love that taught them to clarify some of the misunderstandings they had from perceptions and assumptions from their own earlier studies. In sum, they have given me the impression that they understand and love the truth better even as they continue humbly on a trajectory to find the substratum in the works of two great metaphysician-theologians.

22 JOHN HENRY NEWMAN, *An Essay in Aid of a Grammar of Assent* (London: uniform edition, 1913), ch. 10, 387.

23 *GA*, 423. Ch. 10, section 2 to 10 is on revealed religion, 409–492.

For private consultation and not distribution without the consent of E Ondrako

Prologue to the *Ordinatio* of Scotus (no. 95–123), where Scotus shows the origin, nature, authority, and mode of interpretation of Scripture. What is necessary for salvation is contained in Scripture at least implicitly and the human mind discovers truth by a progressive illumination with the help of the Holy Spirit.

Newman's conclusion follows the example of the Lord and his Apostles in Sacred Scripture in contemplating Christianity as the completion and supplement of natural religion and of previous revelations. It becomes apparent that the solution for the problem of sin, which is at the center of natural religion, is found only in supernatural revelation. It is the Gospel story of love that is willing to suffer, not love that has to suffer. The Incarnation is not for the sake of the redemption, but creation or the natural order is for the sake of the Incarnation, and the Incarnation is to give glory to the Son.[24]

Another substantial agreement in the *Grammar of Assent* with Scotus is to approach it from Newman's recognition that natural faith needs to be open to the mystery of light and love, as Scotus's univocity of the concept of being engages the mystery of light and of love. Natural faith is a distinctive feature of metaphysics, which, if engaged properly, leads to the intuition of the supernatural in one's conscience. Intuition is connected to the abstract as the real is connected to the notional and both are meant to be employed together. Newman's argument for the existence of God from conscience, which he repeats in section one of chapter ten of the *Grammar*,[25] is that of Anselm-Scotus in phenomenological form, or set forth in terminology with its psychological antecedents. Ideas grow, multiply, and develop in countless ways.

For reasons as these, one can postulate that Newman is more scotistic rather than thomistic in the explanation of the natural and supernatural. Newman would agree with Scotus that the supernatural is in relation to the potential and power of the person to attain the fullness of being. The medievals referred to this potential of the person as the power to attain the infinite. The power to know and to love in this context is connatural, that is, belonging or inherent by nature, and the human person is able to assimilate it. Newman's third note in his *Essay on the Development of Christian Doctrine* is "Its Power of Assimilation," and he applies it as "The Assimilating Power of Sacramental Grace."

---

[24] This is the first point of three points in the papal audience of Pope Benedict XVI on Scotus on July 7, 2010, that gives recognition to the thought of Scotus on the motive of the Incarnation.

[25] *GA*, on conscience, 389–395. Ch. 10, section one is on natural religion, 389–408.

For private consultation and not distribution without the consent of E Ondrako

There is in truth a certain virtue or grace in the Gospel which
changes the quality of doctrines, opinions, usages, actions, and
personal characters when incorporated with it, and makes them
right and acceptable to its Divine Author, whereas before they
were either infected with evil, or at best shadows of the truth.[26]

The genius of Newman is to explain why these principles, such as
the dogmatic and sacramental, give impetus to Christian thought without
being aware of their action until a gradual realization later. The sacramental principle contributes to the integration into the body of Christian
doctrine of ideas about what the divine counsels, prior to the Incarnation,
allow, in regard to cults and rites that gradually become transformed into
Christian doctrine.

Jan H. Walgrave summarizes the scientific form that leads to real
assent.

We see true dogmatic theology growing steadily according as it
surrenders itself to loving contemplation of supernatural realities.
It draws life from the principles it carries deep within it, perhaps
without awareness of them. It advances along a way which logic
is unable to analyze completely or control entirely. Here again,
the last word is spoken by the illative sense of the believer, the
personal judgment of the Church, in whose possession is the gift
of faith, and which lives by its principles.[27]

The 'stakes' in the approach of Ockham, Hume and Kant.

Pope Benedict's audience on Scotus, July 7, 2010, gives more than
a hint of what is at stake. It is nothing less than the undermining of the
harmony between faith and reason which Newman devoted his life to
harmonize. Without commenting on liberty and its relationship to the will
and the intellect, he seems to be developing an understanding about the
more subtle difficult challenging distinctions between Thomas and Scotus.
Scotus's distinction between the theology of necessity and the theology
of contingency means distinguishing between the immanent Trinity, the
Trinity in itself, and the economic Trinity, the work of salvation. Franciscan insights relate to Thomas's pneumatological reflections, his three
quasi-infinites, the mystery of Christ, Mary and the Church.[28]

---

26 John Henry Newman, *An Essay on the Development of Christian Doctrine* (London: uniform edition, 1909), 368–382.

27 Jan Hendrik Walgrave, *Newman the Theologian* (New York: Sheed and Ward, 1960), 130.

28 St. Thomas, *Summa Theologica*, I, q. 25, a. 4.

For private consultation and not distribution without the consent of E Ondrako

Studying Thomas and Scotus are easier with our three approaches. The first, Aristotle and Thomas, and third, Bonaventure, Scotus, and Newman differ substantially from the second, Ockham, Hume and Kant. As we set the table for dialogue on liberty in relation to will and intellect in reply to Pope Benedict XVI, the approaches contextualize. When the Holy Father says: "Duns Scotus developed a point to which modernity is very sensitive, the topic of liberty and its relation with the will and intellect,"[29] he is in the approach of Ockham, Hume and Kant, the rationalist trap, which in the west today means that 'private judgment' prevails. The conflation of the three approaches runs the further risk of positing a simplistic cause for the problems of modernity.

William of Ockham (d. 1349) is in the second approach with the anti-metaphysical approach of Hume and Kant because Ockham is an innovator who blurs the synthesis of Christian wisdom. The breakdown of the Christian approach to truth from philosophy, or a gap between the vital relationships of faith to reason, enabled a new method to fill the gap, that is, the empirical or scientific method. With it came the boundless confidence of secular or liberal Christianity in the seventeenth century. The empirical method itself has to be tested. The twenty-first century is steeped in its anti-dogmatic excesses.

Ockham introduced a new form of nominalism.[30] *Nomen*, name, is a doctrine that can be found in antiquity, but with many forms of doctrines and movements prior to his beginning what was called the *via moderna*. Nominalism holds that only individual things exist in distinction to Plato's realism which holds that there is similarity of individuals by something that they share in common, a common property or nature. During high scholasticism, nominalism all but disappeared. Scotus's theory of the univocity of the concept of being, clashes with nominalism and its individualism. Finite persons may intuit that they share something in common with the infinite God: being, freedom, will and intellect. Ockham rejected Scotus's formal distinction between will and intellect because Ockham's nominalism is against the idea that common natures could be accepted in individual things.

What is at stake requires careful distinctions. There is a major problem at the root of Ockham's thought which leads to a progression to Hume and Kant. The problem pertains to human knowledge as intelligible. Ockham changes the range of Christian philosophical intelligence to almost zero. Ockham differs from Thomas Aquinas and Scotus who agree that human knowledge, the intelligible, always precedes intellection. There is

---

[29] Benedict XVI, *Papal Audience*, July 7, 2010.
[30] G. Kung, "Nominalism" *New Catholic Encyclopedia*, vol. 10, 483–486.

For private consultation and not distribution without the consent of E Ondrako

something given to the intellect that it may know. Intellectual knowledge is an expression of what really is. It does not fabricate its own content.[31]

That is why and how the idea developed among the English friars that Scotus is the end of the *via antiqua* and Ockham is the beginning of the *via moderna*. They are distinct. Thomas and Scotus hold that what "really is transcendentally—indeed is infinitely intelligible, and is known by our intellect to be so, even though our limited range of understanding is unable to go beyond a certain point in making this intelligibility explicitly clear."[32] The finite mind pales before the free decrees of the infinite and omnipotent God even as the finite mind shares something in common with the infinite mind and power of God.

Ockham continues to think as a Christian theologian, but his changes relate the human desire to know to the Christian truths that he accepts in an unfortunate reductive manner. That means that the Christian can understand almost nothing of what he or she believes. The *via moderna* inaugurated by Ockham became popular in universities and gave rise to the struggle between "realists" and "nominalists." What is at stake is that, in time, the struggle broke the synthesis of faith and reason to a non-speculative approach to Christian truth coupled with a philosophical approach divorced from faith. Ockham's criticism is open to criticism for its failure "to recognize that the universal structures and common aspects of reality dealt with in human understanding are, at the level of creaturely participation, a reflection of the infinite and ineffable life of the divine intelligence."[33]

Owen Bennett summed up the problem of Ockham as having all of the trappings of 'faith humiliating understanding' rather than 'faith seeking understanding.' Moreover, Gilson observed that Ockham's so called modernity lacked critical depth with the practical effect of retaining faith but giving up the possibility of reaching a positive philosophical understanding of life's intelligible meaning.[34] Ockham's nominalism compounds the version of nominalism taught a century later by Gabriel Biel (1410–1495), a teacher of Martin Luther.

Francisco Suarez (1548–1617) made many contributions to theology but his eclecticism in metaphysics leaves something to be desired. He combines Thomas Aquinas and Scotus with a significant amount of Ockham's thought in relation to counter-reformation thought. Unlike

---

[31] OWEN BENNETT, *Metaphysics of Faith and Freedom* (Rensselaer, N.Y.: 1972), 49.

[32] BENNETT, 49–50.

[33] BENNETT, 50.

[34] E. GILSON, *The History of Christian Philosophy in the Middle Ages* (1955), 498–499. See BENNETT, 49–52.

For private consultation and not distribution without the consent of E Ondrako

Scotus, Suarez, who writes a beautiful treatise on Mary, does not present a Marian metaphysics which has the scotistic concept of the perfect will, radically ordered and not disordered as self-will. This is a pivotal point. Mary is the perfect example of the perfect will. Scotus's idea of the perfect will is far removed from the fearful willfulness of much of what comes to be known as modern philosophy.[35] Rather, Newman names Mary the pattern of faith in University Sermon 15.

Suarez is a bridge in philosophy, but, within a century, the empiricism of John Locke (1632–1704), with his common sense reflection on human experience, takes firm root and remains to this day an abiding mindset of modern living.[36] His noble goal was to identify how violence happens and to eliminate it. His hypothesis is that violence is caused by persons of religion who have conflicting truth claims. The difficulty with Locke's noble goal to reduce violence is his hypothesis. Locke, unwittingly, blurs many important distinctions between conflicting truth claims of Christianity and the desire for tolerance. By doing so, he reduces truth claims to a degree of probability. The shortest answer is that Locke fails to acknowledge that Christian truth claims, properly understood, prohibit violence. Locke's method, for example, gives the existence of God a high degree of probability while the hypostatic union in Christ has a low degree of probability. A cursory reflection on issues of competing views in the Western world supports the observation that almost everyone in the West seems to be Lockian in thought, a subject for further critical study. There seems to be something in human nature that looks for strong arguments, dismisses weak arguments, and goes with the strong.

Within a short time, the empiricism of Locke paved the way for Hume's world that is one of a radical skeptic. Being, substance, and cause are virtually meaningless which is far from Scotus's anthropology. Moreover, Hume is anti-metaphysical, and reductive in his anthropology. To be reductive means that things are reduced to what is sensible, i.e. mind to memory and imagination. What is most misleading is that God has nothing to do with holiness. Philosophy is reduced to empirical psychology. This makes Hume the luminary of all empiricists in philosophy.[37]

Keeping the meta in meta-ethics and meta-physics.

One sure guide to avoid derailment on the journey to wisdom is to relate scientific wisdom to eternal wisdom. The light is Sacred Scripture.

---

[35] P. D. FEHLNER, Durham, Opening Address, 2008, 16.

[36] JOHN LOCKE, *The Essay concerning Human Understanding* (1690), and *The Reasonableness of Christianity*, and *The Essay on Tolerance* (1695).

[37] E. A. SILLEM, "David Hume" in *NCE*, vol. 7, 232–234.

For private consultation and not distribution without the consent of E Ondrako

Scotus's unique formulation of divine illumination in logical form can be a light guiding all our thought and Newman's illative sense in relation to formal logic, weak or strong, is the easy way to avoid the Lockian trap. The amplification of Locke on an epistemological level is in much of Kantian thought. The sincere reasoning of neo-scholastics, who claim to be looking for strong reasons and not weak reasons to back up their views, fall into a subtle rationalist trap.

What may appear innocuous, can be a slippery slope. A Catholic who has to advise the President of the United States or any foreign leader on ethical matters about the morality of a pre-emptive military strike, for example, has to engage seriously competing views. Advising on what claims to be Catholic is a formidable responsibility in any age but especially in one with sophisticated weapons beyond imagination. The debate in Catholic circles at the time of the pre-emptive strike by the United States against the government of Iraq under Saddam Hussein, surfaced Catholics who argued the validity of the pre-emptive strike while others opposed it as unethical or immoral. It is beyond the purpose of this essay to enter the debate, but, to use a neo-scholastic method to justify the position in favor of the pre-emptive strike raises grave questions. If they base their decision on a preference for strong reason, they set themselves on the edge of a precipice. In their desire for strong reason, they unwittingly divide principles of morality from principles of doctrine. Catholics sometimes state this Lockian view another way which gives a false sense of security in one's moral position. They think that by preferring the strong reason of Thomism to the weak of Kant, they stand on solid ground instead of being at the edge of a precipice. What they do not see is that both terms, strong and weak logic, are Lockian, and refer to the relative firmness of an inference to its premises, the Lockian trap.

Newman's *Grammar of Assent* is definitive proof that he was not prey to such a rationalist entrapment. In the opening pages of his reply to Gladstone's *Vatican Decrees*, in 1874, Newman demonstrates this conclusively. In reply to Gladstone, Newman wrote:

> I own to a deep feeling, that Catholics may in good measure thank themselves, and no one else, for having alienated so religious a mind. There are those among us, as it must be confessed, who for years past have conducted themselves as if no responsibility attached to wild words and overbearing deeds; who have stated truths in the most paradoxical form, and stretched principles till they were close upon snapping; and who at length, having

For private consultation and not distribution without the consent of E Ondrako

done their best to set the house on fire, leave to others the task of putting out the flame.[38]

Newman's reply in the *Letter to the Duke of Norfolk* is a practical application of his thinking in the *Grammar of Assent* about the relative firmness of an inference in relation to its premises, an application of the illative sense to formal logic, weak or strong, according to Locke. What Newman is showing, implicitly and explicitly, is that he thinks in a manner as Bonaventure and Scotus. Their contributions are meaningful, in particular, to the idea of *interiorization* that trumps the idea of strong or weak logic. For the Franciscans, the central concept of interiorization is supported by the theory of divine illumination and univocity of the concept of being, to argue why Christ is the one teacher of all. In other words, by avoiding the distinctions between weak and strong formal logic in a Lockian appearance, and its Kantian shape in Kant's epistemology, Newman instinctively avoids falling into the rationalist snare. Another way to say this is that Newman does not take the meta out of meta-ethics nor meta out of metaphysics as Kant does. Nor is he seduced by any form of individualism or anti-intellectualism, even by those who claimed to be living modern spirituality, meaning certain parts of the imitation of Christ which was developing during the fourteenth century on. Individualism and anti-intellectualism water down a genuine sense of solidarity.

Conclusion to the excursus: an outcome of the anti-metaphysical mindset

In part three of *The Newman Scotus Reader* it will become even more obvious why the second approach in our division of approaches to the history of philosophy, which is that of Ockham, Hume and Kant, demonstrates the complex development of an anti-metaphysical mindset in favor of the empirical and scientific which dominates Western thinking in the twenty-first century. The second approach for studying the relation of the will to the intellect originates with Ockham's nominalism, Hume's empiricism and ends with Kant, but includes the vast Kantian influences. Hegel shares some key assumptions with Kant, i.e., the turn to the subject as non-negotiable and to steer far from the supernatural, mystery and miracle in speaking about Christianity. However, the Kantian impact is stronger today even though Hegel captures the imagination, but not the intellect. Kant fits in this line as the one who most deforms the will with his insistence on its absolute autonomy.

---

[38] JOHN HENRY NEWMAN, "Letter to the Duke of Norfolk," *Certain Difficulties Felt by Anglicans in Catholic Teaching Considered* (London: uniform edition, 1907), 176–177.

For private consultation and not distribution without the consent of E Ondrako

The truths that are validly present in Kant are already present in Scotus the metaphysician-theologian.[39] Newman was familiar with some of the works of Kant[40] but he was ill at ease with the developing climate in religion as one can see in a sermon from volume one of *Parochial and Plain Sermons*, "the religion of the day," and the *University Sermons*, and *Discourses to Mixed Congregations*. The difficulty, in a word, is that Kant snips faith and reason.[41] Newman is no stranger to the problems of secular or liberal Christianity which he encountered in the Oriel Common Room. His self-description as a controversialist who dealt with the problems of the day gives an accurate picture. His columns in *The Times* called "The Tamworth Reading Room" c. 1841, deal with secular knowledge, the need for moral improvement and the temptation to disbelief.

Several of the contributions in part three follow upon the views in parts one and two of *The Newman-Scotus Reader*. Some underscore implicitly and others, explicitly, that Scotus answers the critical question far better than Kant. Scotus was a realist as Newman. A way to stay focused on reality is to remember the simple fact that human beings are made up of both saints and sinners and that saints can fall from virtue and become vicious, while the vicious can turn toward virtue. The unprecedented cruelty in the twentieth century and possibility of greater cruelty is an ominous reality. Contrary to the thinking of secular or liberal Christianity, the viciousness which human beings are capable of inflicting on others is not morally neutral, but cynical. Pope Benedict XVI stated candidly "why criminals like Hitler and Stalin, who act out of deep personal conviction, remain guilty. The guilt lies in the neglect of my own being that has dulled me to the voice of truth and made me deaf to what it says within me."[42] The answers lie in the following appeals to practical judgments made with sound meta-ethics, anthropology, and education. Scotus and Newman situate these in the personal quest for holiness.

In his lifetime, Newman saw a diminishing of the role of dogma, tradition, and the sacraments as reducing the vitality of Christian moral living. In their place came the substitution of the beliefs of the moment without the critical thinking from the synthesis of faith and reason, another description of secular or liberal Christianity. Sin and vice is considered

---

39 FEHLNER, Durham, Opening Address, 2008, 16–17.

40 ADRIAN J. BOEKRAAD and HENRY TRISTRAM, *The Argument for the Existence of God from Conscience according to John Henry Newman* (Louvain: 1961), 29–30. BOEKRAAD, *The Personal Conquest of Truth* (Louvain: 1955), 81. There is a debate about how acquainted Newman was with Kantian thought, but my view is that it is more than less.

41 OLIVIER BOULNOIS, *Être et représentation* (Paris: Presses Universitaires de France, 1999, rpt, 2008), chapter nine.

42 BENEDICT XVI, *Values in a Time of Upheaval* (New York: Crossroad, 2006), 90–97, here 97.

For private consultation and not distribution without the consent of E Ondrako

morally neutral. The saints no longer set the standard for Christian behavior. That plays out with the attitude that God has nothing to do with striving for holiness, and finds its expression in those who consider all religious conviction solely a matter of opinion. Newman's *Biglietto Speech* did not miss a beat with the same problem in 1879 as the collective addresses of Pope Benedict XVI to the United Kingdom to beatify Bl. Newman demonstrate.

For private consultation and not distribution without the consent of E Ondrako

CHAPTER 8

The Base and the Summit: the Nobility of the Will according to Duns Scotus

Olivier Boulnois

Translated by Agnès Deferluc

Base and summit: the nobility of the will according to Scotus *Being and représentation* – self, the knowledge and the will.[1]

If intelligence, leaning to the memory, characterizes man in his essence, it is not enough to describe what is most essential in this essence. What makes preeminently of man a self, is indeed, rather the will. It is there that the famous "voluntarism" of Scotus is so criticized for its moral consequences. But, beyond historiographical clichés, it is necessary to prove that this position is not simply the result of a moral decision. The point is to look for the non-moral foundations of the scotistic moral, non psychological bases of his psychology. This structure has a metaphysical meaning, because the point is to decide the nobility of an archetypal being, *man*.

In order to think about this nobility, Scotus starts indeed from a metaphysical principle which is one of eminence. Exactly as memory and intelligence, will is a transcendental perfection of being.[2] One can then attribute it to spiritual beings, God, the angel and man. Exactly as all of the transcendentals, the objects of metaphysics,[3] it [the will] applies in a common, univocal manner, to God and to the creature, according to a principle of eminence: "It is necessary not to place any imperfection in

---

[1] OLIVIER BOULNOIS, *Être et representation*. Paris: Presses Universitaires De France, 1999, rep. 2008, 203–216.

[2] W. HOERES (1962), p.25 sq.

[3] "Potentia sic sumpta ad considerationes metaphysici pertinet" (In *Met.*, IX, q. 2, § [2]; V, 7, 530).

For private consultation and not distribution without the consent of E Ondrako

a nature, unless its necessity should appear in this nature."[4] Every perfection which is not contradictory with the definition of a nature must be attributed to it. The principle of contradiction is the only criterion of the hierarchy of the beings: it indicates in advance their degree of perfection. One can see in that an ontological generalization of "Anselm's rule," usually applied to God: "The noblest part of every logical contradiction must be attributed to God."[5] According to this logical operator, it is necessary to attribute preeminently all the perfections to the noblest natures, including the will to man. The ontological argument is extended to all the scale of perfections, of which the will is part.

Why attribute to man the will instead of any other property? Which criterion defines its nobility? - According to the Franciscan tradition, as we saw, the modes of action are divided essentially between nature and will. Since intellect and will are the two essential forms of activity, and since act is said in a univocal manner of all the actual beings, one can attribute them, as univocal perfections, to all the beings which are endowed with it. It is true that intellect is a perfection, which allows distinguishing phantasm from concept,[6] but the essential difference passes between nature and will. And *intellect is on the side of nature*; will is then a higher perfection than intellect. Contrary to Thomas Aquinas or Meister Eckhart, the noble soul is distinguished by its will more than by its intellect. Thus, will is the highest perfection of every active being for it has supreme *nobility*: "Among all the active causes, it is the highest."[7] In Olivi's words, its transcendence is absolute and infinite.[8]

---

[4] *Ord*, I, 3, 368 (III, 224) : "Nulla imperfectio ponenda est in aliqua natura nisi necessitas appareat in natura tali."

[5] BONAVENTURE, *Collationes in decem praeceptis* III, 27 (519, tr. fr., p.93); OLIVI, *Quaestiones de incarnatione et redemptione, Quaestiones de virtutibus*, q. 1, p. 12. The pattern of Scotist generalization is Aristotelian principle of plenitude: "Illud enim est ponendum in natura, quod melius est, si sit possibile, ex secundo de Gen[eratione et corruptione, 336 b 27–28]. Natura enim semper desiderat quod melius est." In Anselm's Monologion, chap.4, the principle applies mainly to God : "Si quis intendat rerum naturas, velit nolit sentit non eas omnes contineri una dignitatis paritate, sed quasdam earum distingui graduum imparitate. [...] Cum igitur naturarum aliae aliis negari non possint meliores, nihilominus persuadet ratio aliquam in eis sic supereminere, ut non habeat se superiorem." - This Scotist principle plays a part of course in the theory of the predestination of Christ and Immaculate Conception.

[6] *Ord*. I, 3, 349, adnotatio Duns Scoti (III, 210).

[7] *Op. Ox.* II, d. 37, q. 2§ [4] (XIII, 370): "Si aliqua est totalis causa respectu sui effectus, hoc maxime concedendum est de voluntate, quia ipsa est suprema inter omnes causas activas."

[8] "Transcendit omne creatum" (*Quaestiones in II Sententiarum*, éd. Simoncioli, p. 187). Cf. E. STADTER, p. 290. See this hyperbolical text: "Sentimus cor nostrum quasi in infinitum excedere omnem alium modum existendi. Unde si sui daretur optio in quod minus vellet redigi, scilicet, in unum animal, aut in purum nihil tantum : unusquisque vellet esse nihil, ac si intimo sensu clamet quod omne esse comparatum ad suum est quasi purum nihil." (*Sent*. II, q. 57 : II, 334). Cf. p. 335: "Defectum usus liberi arbitrii, qualis est in stultis, si deberet esse perpetuus, ita horreremus sicut annihilationem." Will is infinitely beyond any other mode of existence,

For private consultation and not distribution without the consent of E Ondrako

Will is not only the eminence of the being in general, but the excellence of life. As Olivi already noticed, will is the form of the being where it dwells; as such, it implies actuality, activity, and vitality.[9] Scotus refers to this analysis: as not moved from outside (what Aristotelians, whom he rejects, seem to consider), but will is active by itself. "The act of will is life."[10] Will is the incandescence of life, which it bears to its highest degree of actuality. "It is absurd that *the noblest form*, such as the intellective soul, does not possess the active powers [corresponding to] its accidental perfection."[11] Life by excellence constitutes will in act.

There is a paradox: thought by its excellence proves to be will—and not intellect. Scotus is here in the Franciscan line, opposed to the Aristotelian definition of freedom as intellectual species of a larger kind, the natural desire.[12] According to Aristotle, only reason is the power of the opposites and only reason can allow total indifference in the choice of means to reach our natural end, happiness. To Thomas Aquinas, human beatitude is only the rational form of a desire of nature. The Franciscan line, on the contrary, is explicitly linked to Bernard of Clairvaux and William of Saint-Thierry. Walter of Bruges reminds one of Bernard of Clairvaux's expression: "Where there is will, there is freedom."[13] The freedom of will (St. Bernard) is opposed to the freedom of intellect (Aristotle). But precisely, the will is not convertible to the intellect: where there is reason, there freedom is not necessary, because reason or intellect can be compelled to assent by a syllogistic demonstration. Reason does not confer freedom to the will. It has only an ostensible function, i.e. putting forward the terms between which the will must choose.[14] To this school, reason only funds a generic *freedom*

---

and prefers stopping being rather than stooping to this inferior forms ; it is of another order, beyond which there is nothing left but nothingness.

9 Cf. OLIVI, *Quaestiones in II Sent.* q. 54, ad 1 (II, 274): "Multas habent conditiones nobiles [...] scilicet summam vitalitatem, seu vivacitas vel vitae actualitatis"; cf. E. Stadter, op.cit., p. 294.

10 *Quodl.* XVI, § [18] 49 (608): "Sicut loquitur Philosophus XII Metaphysicae [L, 7, 1072 b 25–30]: 'Intellectus actus est vita'; et pari ratione, actus voluntatis est vita." Scotus places among eminently vital acts, in addition to intellect (according to Aristotle's Metaphysics), will.

11 "Absurdum est quod nobilissima forma, cuiusmodi est anima intellectiva, non habeat potentias activas suae goes aperfectionis accidentalis." (*Op. Ox.* II, d. 25, q. 1, § [13]; XIII, 208 b).

12 THOMAS AQUINAS, *ST*, II–II, q. 17, a. 1, ad 2: freedom is located in will, but has its cause in reason.

13 De gratia et librio arbitrio, chap. 1, § 2. About this tradition, see J.-M. DÉCHANET (1945), and the conclusion, p. 373: "We are in presence of a true theology of love-intellection." The expression is in William of Saint-Thierry in the *Mirror of Faith*, chap. 10, § 97 (168). The editor says the source is Bernard, Gregory the Great, and even PLOTINUS, *Enneads*, VI, 7, 35, 24–25.

14 Gauthier de Bruges, *Quaestiones disputatae*, éd. E. Longpré, Louvain, 1928, q. 5 : "Quaeritur unde voluntas habeat quod sit libera," arg. II, 1 : "Ubi voluntas, ibi libertas ; sed non ubi ratio, semper ibi libertas, quia ratio vel intellectus demonstratione syllogistica cogi potest ; ergo voluntas a se, non a ratione, est libera." Resp. Ad II. 1 : "Primum in contrarium concede sic :

For private consultation and not distribution without the consent of E Ondrako

of indifference (libertas indifferentiae) in front of the possibles, but it is will, having the ability to choose a term rather than another one, which specifies it and allows *perfect freedom (libertas perfecta)*.[15] Olivi stretches to deny any rationality to the intellect, in a violent but remarkable expression: without will, men would be "intellectual beasts."[16]

Scotus adopts this thesis without any restriction: "Intellect (…) falls under [the genre/kind of] nature." By itself, "intellect (…) is irrational." - But unlike Olivi who would defend the nobility of will excluding the one of intellect, Scotus unifies the two aspects and poses the reverse conclusion: if man without will is only a natural being, it is because his rationality comes from will. *Man is not free because he is rational; he is rational because he is free.*[17] Devaluing intellect is not rejecting reason. Reason describes very well the essence of the spirit, if only it is brought back to its ontological origin, the will. The will itself is the intellect preeminently. *Amor, sive voluntas, ipse intellectus est.*

As Aristotle would notice, "rational" means indeed capacity for contraries. But only the will can want the contraries simultaneously.[18] In the very moment when it wants A, it can want still at the same time the contrary of A, by virtue of its fundamental freedom.[19] Rationality lies

---

quod ratio, ut est potentia, non dat libertatem voluntati effective nec formaliter, sed tantum ostensive, quia proponit sibi duo vel plura, de quibus unum est praeoptandum."

15 GAUTHIER DE BRUGES, *Questiones disputatae*, q. 5, II, ad 14 (53): [voluntas] "habet libertatem indifferentiae a ratione, ut est nomen essentiae, sed libertatem praeferendi unum alii a seipsa volunte"; commented by E. Stadter (314). Four centuries before Descartes, the opposition between freedom of perfection and freedom of indifference is several times taken up : "Omnis autem ratio et secundum ipsam rationalis potentia habet indifferentiam ad opposita, quae est libertas aliqua, quia non est ad unum per aliquem sui actum vel differentiam arctata, sed non est libertas perfecta, quia non potest alterum oppositorum praeoptare" (p. 51); "Ad libertatem tria concurrunt, scilicet quod duo vel plures diversa proponantur, et quod in eligente indifferentia quaedam ad illa habeatur, et quod unum altero vel aliis praeoptetur. Primum habet voluntas a ratione ut est essentia, quae est in eo quod ratio habet indifferentiam ad utrumlibet horum ; tertium habet a seipsa, scilicet voluntate, scilicet unius illorum praeoptationem, et quia in hoc consummatur libertas, ideo proprie et quasi formaliter a se, vel per illud quod habet in se, est libera. Sed ratio, et potentia, ostendi sibi libertatis materiam, sed ratio, ut essentia, dat sibi quamdam quasi generis indifferentiam"(p. 52, my emphasis).

16 *Sent.* II, q. 57 (II, 338) "simus quaedam bestiae intellectuales seu intellectum habentes." Cf. The text quotd by V. DOUCET (1935), 179, n. 9 : "Liberum arbitrium, quantum ad hoc quod dicit facultatem liberam et dominium habentem super totam animam, essentialiter est voluntas rationalis […] libertas essentialiter est voluntas, et libere consentire est actus eius immediatus et totalis, ad quem nihil facit intellectus nisi per accidens."

17 See A.B. WOLTER (1990), 145–173, and J. CARRERAS Y ARTAU (1923).

18 "Tota ratio potentiae ad opposita formaliter est in voluntate (In Met. IX, q.15, § [9] 47; IV, 690). "Potentia igitur rationalis perfecta, cuiusmodi est voluntas" (*Op. Ox.* II; d.25, q. un. § [25] ; XIII, 224 b).

19 *Op. Ox.* II, d. 39, q. 2 § [2] (XIII, 411–412) ; In Met. IX, q. 15, § [6], 36 : "Intellectus cadit sub natura. Est enim ex se determinatus ad intelligendum, et non habet in potestate sua intelligere et non intelligere" (IV, 684). This theory implies a remarkable theory of modality, according to

For private consultation and not distribution without the consent of E Ondrako

then in will. However, such a capacity can flow back from the summit of the soul to its crown, the intellect. For every other power depends on it. "The will is the mover in the entire kingdom of the soul, and everything obeys it:"[20] when intellect directs itself to the opposites, it is because will orders it and not by itself: it cannot think the contraries at the same time. The controversy about the dignity of man is not then something made up at the Renaissance: in the Franciscan line inherited from Saint Bernard, in the thirteenth century, well before Pico della Mirandola, the highest nobility consists in the will.[21] But with Scotus, this theory is not limited to taking up a theological anthropology. Will is not only a higher authority, it is the summit from which is inscribed the Aristotelian definition of man in his base—rationality. The Subtle Doctor does not oppose any more intellect and will as two faculties in the same rank which would fight for primacy, but he sees in the will the root of intellectuality. *The essential point of what is human* (that is to say rational) *in man, is freedom. Man as a man is mainly will.*

How does the will stand out against the background of nature, will against necessity? Here again, Scotus rejects Aristotelian determinism. The act of will is not determined by a natural principle and comes from its pure spontaneity; will is in itself undetermined, the experience of freedom proves it: "The one who wants experiences that he is able not to want,"[22]—he is not determined to act or not to act. The determination to act comes from the position of the act itself. Will is not moved by a natural desire, but by its rational status: the *affectus justitiae*, its intrinsical rectitude, leads it to the good. It is autodetermined rationally to be determined by what reason presents to it as just and right. Thus, freedom is the autoposition of the will in act; as God, it is a mover not moved.[23]

Why does the will want this rather than that? According to Aristotelians, it is because the intellect presented to it such an object under the aspect of good. To Scotus, this answer is wrong, and the question is not legitimate. If the will was moved by the evidence of a nature, it would not be free. If it was moved by a prior volition, it would be necessary to go back endlessly in the order of the causes. Consequently, will wants

---

which, at the very moment when the will wants A, it can still want non-A ; cf. S. KNUUTILA (1981), 441–450.

[20] *Op. Ox.* II, d. 42, q. 4, § [2] (XIII, 449 a) : "Voluntas est motor in toto regno animae, et omnia oboediunt sibi," quoting Anselm, De conceptu virginali, chap. 5 (146).

[21] See O. BOULNOIS (1993b).

[22] In *Met.* IX, q. 15 § [5], 30 (IV, 682–683).

[23] R. EFFLER (1962).

For private consultation and not distribution without the consent of E Ondrako

freely because it is will: there is no reason beyond itself.[24] The ultimate answer is the *fact* of freedom. If there are two modes of action, natural and voluntary, there is no explanation to the fact that this principle acts freely, except the fact that is it what it is.[25] Will is a *factum rationis*. The *reason* why will wants this act, is the *fact* that it is precisely this free will. The will is a principle without principle, rationality without reason; in virtue of its transcendence, it does not obey the principle of reason, but it commands it (by starting a new series of causes and effects). "The will wants" and of this fact, there is no reason.[26] It is a contingent, immediate, indemonstrable but obvious clause. The will is without the why, it wants because it wants.[27] From nature, one will never be able to deduct will: this one erupts as an absolute start in its order.

Can one say that the will is the exclusive cause of volition? Scotus seems to have taken a very marked doctrinal turn.[28] During his first teaching experience in Oxford, he maintained that the will is only a partial principal cause of volition, to which must be joined a secondary partial cause: the intellection of the object.[29] He would admit another cause than the will alone.[30] From the fine point of the will, the *principal* cause, freedom flows back on/to the foundation, on the whole intellect, the *secondary* cause.[31] Next, during his teaching in Paris, according to the witness of William of Alnwick, he advocated, following completely the entire Franciscan

---

[24] "Nulla est causa, nisi quia est voluntas." (In *Met.* IX, q. 15, § [5], 29 ; IV, 682). Will is not the rational form that causality takes in one term of the series of causes (man) : it is at the origin of a new series of causes. It is, as the first mover, an absolute beginning.

[25] In *Met.* IX, q. 15, § [4].24 (IV, 680) : "Nec est dare aliquam causam quare sic elicit nisi quia est talis causa" ; Quodl. 16, § [16] 46 (606). Cf GAUTHIER DE BRUGES, *Quaestiones Disputatae*, q. 5, contra 13 (199 b).

[26] In *Met.* IX, q. 15, § [5].29 : "Quare voluntas illud volet ? Nulla erit alia causa, nisi quia est voluntas.» (IV, 682).

[27] (Note by the translator) Allusion to Angelus Silesius (XVIIth century): "The rose is without why, it blooms because it blooms / It pays no attention to itself, asks not whether it is seen.

[28] K. Balič (1953), rectified by S. Dumont (1999), to be published.

[29] *Lect.* II, d. 25, § 69 (XIX, 253) : "Teneo viam mediam, quod tam voluntas quam obiectum concurrunt ad causandum actum volendi."

[30] *Additiones magnae*, ed. K. BALIČ (1927), 268. According to S. DUMONT (1999), the critical edition is wrong when it indicates : "Verba 'aliter dixit Oxoniae' non significant 'aliter quam Parisiis' sed 'aliter quam Henricus,' id est non significant retractationem vel modificationem alicuius doctrinae anterioris, sed simpliciter agnoscunt doctrinam Duns Scoti—Oxoniae traditam—diversam esse ab opinionem Henrici Gandavensis" (19, 39*). Scotus's position evolved a lot, it differs in Paris from what it was in Oxford. The motif may be linked to the status of beatific enjoyment, cf. Op. Ox. II, d. 26, q. 1, § [5] (XIII, 237–238).

[31] Scotus asserts explicitly that he plays the same causal dividing against Olivi. (In II *Sent.*, q. 58; II, 419) , in the realm of intellect and in the one of will ; these two faculties do not work but by a double causality, the one of the power and the one of the object. See Ord. I, 3, 417 : "Haec tamen ratio concluderet simili modo, ut videtur, contra actionem voluntatis" (III, 253; tr. fr. 155).

For private consultation and not distribution without the consent of E Ondrako

tradition, that "nothing else than will is the total cause of volition."[32] This teaching may be found again in the text of the Opus Oxoniense.[33] Will is not any more a simple principle of volition; it is its exclusive cause. Scotus finally sees in the intellection of the object the mere *sine qua non* condition of volition. He radicalizes the principle of the autosufficiency of the will until suppressing the collaboration of the object and of the intellect with the autodetermination of the will.

In virtue of the univocity of the will, one can attribute it preeminently to God. This concept allows one to think about the articulation of the essence and the persons in God.[34] In a first act, the divine essence knows itself by staying identical to itself: it is the act of *nature* by which God the Father begets the Word. Then the divine essence wishes itself in the Father and the Son: it produces by an act of *will* the subsisting love which the Spirit is. Nature and will, the two first principles of being in general, are also the ones of the Trinitarian emanations.

It is then by the mode of the will that God delights in himself in an infinite beatitude. Scotus is thus opposed to the Aristotelian definition of the divine act, *noesis tês noeseôs*, thought of the thought.[35] It is true that God knows himself and reaches himself in an infinite intuition. But against what Aristotle asserts, it is not in that that his true happiness consists. God reaches the sovereign beatitude by the infinite delight of the love of self. He delights by the mode of the will and not by the mode of nature, freely and to the extreme. Without doubt, there are not in God various degrees of perfection, and the act of will is not more perfect in him than that of the intellect; but it is an act more *proper* to divine beatitude than the act of nature which constitutes the foundation of his essence. Thus, the will is the fine point of divine action, voluntary emanation, the extreme flowering of the divine being. If God is love by nature, the will expresses it by the most appropriate appropriation. Unlike paternity which has to do

---

32 *Rep. Par.* II, d. 25, § [20] (XXIII, 127): " Nihil creatum aliud a voluntate est causa totalis actus volendi in voluntate." - This Franciscan position is attested in Thomas Rundell, maître régent in theology at Oxford around 1288–1289, author of a question : "Utrum obiectum voluntatis aliquid imprimat in voluntatem ?" He would already answer : "In eius potestate est consentire et acceptare et detinere obiectum in tali actu." [...] " Potentia naturalis potest moveri ab alio violenter et inquietari ut in pluribus, set voluntas nunquam ab extra violenter movetur" (A.G. Little, F. Pelster (1934), 342). But Olieu or William of la Mare are more famous in-between. According to S. Dumont (1999), Scotus's editor, C. Balič is wrong when supposing that the evolution took place in Oxford, whereas it happened in Paris.

33 *Op. Ox.* II, d. 25, § [22] (XIII, 221 b), "Nihil aliud a voluntate est causa totalis volitionis in voluntate."

34 *Ord.*, I, 10, 8 (IV, 331); see I, 2, 300–301 (II, 305–306) and here, chapt. 4, § 1.

35 *Ord.*, I, 2, 90 (II, 181) : "Primum (…) per intellegere est honorabile," what Aristotle evokes, *Metaphysics,* Λ, 9, 1074 b 17–21.

For private consultation and not distribution without the consent of E Ondrako

with origin and is linked to the foundation of the deity in God, the will is the accomplishment of it, the most proper act and the highest summit.

God's beatitude is the model for all beatitude, the one that the blessed imitate, in proportion to their finished capacity.[36] It is true that God is the beatifying object of the two powers, intellect and will, because each of them participate in the same beatitude. But in the essential order which links the powers of the soul, "it is necessary to stop at a unique principle."[37] Thus only one of the two powers reaches its object with the maximum of perfection, and beatitude consists in a unique operation. Beatitude, by itself, does not consist only in the vision of God, the intuitive act of the intellect, but in a more principal act, the one of the will. Since our end, beatitude, is the *optimum simpliciter* (the absolutely best thing taken) or the *summum bonum* (the sovereign good), and since the sovereign good must be loved sovereignly, we unite to it by an act of *willing*.[38] The act of will is more blessed than the one of the intellect because it unites it to the thing itself, whereas the intellect unites to the object only in so far as the object is intentionally within it. Love applies to the thing itself, whereas intellect can hold on to a représentation.

Since beatitude is an act of will, it is a free act. Neither the presence of charity, nor the evidence of the divine essence prevents the act unifying us to God from being autonomous. Scotus is opposed here to Thomas Aquinas and Henry of Ghent, for whom the human spirit is inclined toward God by a natural necessity.[39] It is true that in front of God, the will is only able to love him. But it takes the initiative, according to a beautiful oxymoron, with a "spontaneous necessity"[40] and not with a necessity in nature, with a free necessity and not with an external violence, with what Walter of Bruges would call a freedom of perfection and not with a freedom of indifference. This freedom joins the one of God himself, who wills himself necessarily but freely. In his highest perfection (the beatifying act), the finished will acquires the characteristics of the infinite will of God: as his, it becomes immutable, impeccable and perpetual.[41] By raising

---

36 *Rep. Par.* IV, d. 49, q. 1, § [4] (XXIV, 615–616).

37 *Rep. Par.* IV, d. 49, q. 2, § [2, 5–7] (XXIV, 620, 622–624).

38 *Rep. Par.* IV, d. 49, q. 3, § [7] (XXIV, 624) : the two powers are beatified, but only the will is beatified preeminently.

39 THOMAS, *ST.* I–II, q. 10, a. 2 ; HENRY OF GHENT, *Quodl.* XII, q. 5 (487 B).

40 Necessity de facto and not by nature : *Collatio* XV, 16 ; *Ord.* I, 1, 138 (II, 93) – against THOMAS AQUINAS, *ST*, I, q. 82, a. 2; HENRY DE GAND, *Quodl.* XII, q. 5 (487 B).

41 "Concedo quod licet intellectus naturali necessitate videat obiectum praesens proportionatum, tamen voluntas non naturali necessitate fruitur illo obiecto viso." (*Op. Ox.* IV, d. 49, q. 6, § [9] ; XXI, 187); cf. R. Prentice (1970).

For private consultation and not distribution without the consent of E Ondrako

itself to the limits of its power, the will changes status: it passes from indifference to stability, from contingence to necessity.

Even in beatitude, the will remains free before all presence, although it is God's presence. Consequently, the difference between the two degrees or two modes of presence, intuition and abstraction, does not affect the functioning of the blessed will. Should God be seen or unseen, should we be here-below or hereafter, our love for him remains the same, as the happiness which comes from him. The ideal of the earthly beatitude is not the prerogative of the rheno-flamand mysticism, of Meister Eckhart or Marguerite Porète. Even if the earthly beatitude does not have the same degree as the one of the blessed, it is by nature the same beatitude that man owes here-below or hereafter.

One could then speak of a "volitional intuition."[42] In a remarkable passage, Scotus indicates that the distinction between intuition and abstraction "is more manifest for the act of knowing, but [that] maybe one can postulate it for the act of desiring."[43] The will is the pivot on which presence and absence, intuition and abstraction articulate. In beatitude, will passes from the mere state of desire and lack to the intuitive understanding and to the pleasure of its object. But precisely unlike intellect, the intuition of the will remains free while being necessary. It receives its object only from another instance, intentionality, the one of charity. And charity is identical to the most extreme emanation of the divinity, the Holy Spirit.[44] Charity is uncreated, because only the divine love can open man's will to the love of God. Love is the intentional structure of the opening to God. Scotus even defends that the true intentionality comes from the will, the one of the intellect being only said in a derived way, because it is directed by the will.[45] It is necessary then to think again about the intentional design of the will, and the will from the point of view of the love of God.

From the spiritual nature of the free will, a metaphysical principle is working here, that of Augustine: "in spiritual beings, the base is in the peak."[46] The primacy of the will obeys an identical structure, which is repeated in every area where it appears. For every property in general, that

---

[42] G. GURVITCH (1948), 54. Though he invents a very relevant concept, the author does not give any judicious references to advocate it.

[43] *Quodl.* XIII, § [8] 27 (455) : " Et est distinctio manifestior in actu cognoscendi, potest tamen poni forte in actu appetendi."

[44] According to the doctrine advocated by PETER LOMBARD, *Sent*, I, d. 17 (I, 141–152).

[45] *Op. Ox.* II, d. 39, q. 1, § [2] (W, 6, 1011) : "Magis proprie sumitur pro illo scilicet quod tendir in aliud, et non dicitur in illud, sed ducit in se illud."

[46] AUGUSTINE, *Commentaries on Psalms*, Ps. 29, 2, 10 (PL 36, 222 ; CCL 38, 181–182), text taken by BONAVENTURE, *In Hexameron* XXII, 4 (V, 438).

For private consultation and not distribution without the consent of E Ondrako

which is the most obvious for us brings us back to a reality less visible but the highest: the base and the summit involve themselves reciprocally. It acts in a concentration which goes from a figure to its peak: here, from a transcendental in general (the fact of actuality) to the eminent will. As the peak in a conical projection, the subject is *produced* by a rule of concentration which links the appearance of the phenomenon back to a phenomenon par excellence, the will. It is produced in the double meaning of the word: manifested, and constructed by the very structure of this manifestation. This scheme is achieved several times: 1) the *transcendental* perfections of being in general lead to the *transcendence* of the will, by a remarkable extension of the ontological argument to every real perfection. 2) The general experience of *life in act* is lead to the actuality of what is life *par excellence*, to the act of the will. 3) All of the human faculties converge to the summit of human rationality: the will. The intellectual nature, *at its heart*, is rational only because it depends on a *first* principle, freedom. Thus, what is most essential in the human person is not nature, which he shares in *common* with other living beings, nor even intellect, but will, which is his *inherent property*. 4) The divine *essence* withdraws itself as an object owing to the will, the principle of its most extreme emanation. One goes from the nature—*the heart* of the deity—to the *summit* of its specific-being. 5) Human beatitude imitates as far as possible the divine beatitude, and is accomplished in the incandescence of the will. The *indifference* capable of contraries becomes in its *crown* a dazzling in front of the obviousness of the divine goodness; the highest form of liberty becomes the necessity of the love of God.

This implied structure, checked five times, which grounds the primacy of liberty, produces a *first* principle from the *universal*, the protological from the catholic. I will call it *kathoulou-protologique*.[47] What was universal becomes manifested in what is first—and at the same time is masked by it. Now this structure is that of metaphysics, which Scotus says explicitly, because according to him, the will is a transcendental, so an object of metaphysics. But Scotus reuses the structure of Aristotelian metaphysics but only with a criticism and a shifting: the primacy of intellectuality becomes that of the will.

One can build one's opposition to Aristotle term to term, by starting from the end, that is to say from the noetic model of beatitude: 1) For Aristotle, the act, *par excellence*, of divine beatitude is the *thought* of thought; for Scotus it is the *will* of the will: self-willing, which owes, at the same time, as a subject and as an object, subsisting Love. 2) For Aristotle,

---

47 Following thus R. BRAGUE (1988), p. 110, 194, 271, 391, 513–515.

For private consultation and not distribution without the consent of E Ondrako

the happiest act of the soul is the *intellection* of what is the most perfect; for Scotus, it is the finished act to *love* infinite being. 3) For Aristotle, the highest life of man is the speculative life; for Scotus, the highest form of existence lies in volition, which is why he thinks that theology is a practical science, rather than speculative. 4) For Aristotle, the being which is the highest point itself is preeminently (divine) Intellect; for Scotus, God is the highest point in Himself insofar as he attains himself by the will. - The principle of this restructuring is the thesis according to which the divine operation *par excellence* is love—the infinite beatitude of the will in itself in God. The status of the finished beatitude and the noetic in general results from it by a hermeneutical circle: the subject is produced as will from a metaphysical structure, but the center of this structure is displaced by the theological model of Christian beatitude.[48]

Did Scotus only put on the Aristotelian structure of metaphysics by replacing one term by another one? Will one even say that he draws an extended and strengthened onto-theology, since it now includes, in addition to intellect, will? - In a way, yes. But the rule of organization in not the same any more. The organizing scheme in Aristotle was the *primacy of presence*: the intellect predominates because it is the place that presence preeminently determines. And the Scotist scheme is the *liberty* towards presence: whatever the evidence of an intuitive presence may be, whatever the perfection of the seen or abstract object may be, the will remains free in front of it. Whether its object may be presented or represented to it, by intuition or abstraction, it is given to it by charity. Charity is indifferent to the difference between the modes of presentation. If Scotus describes a strengthened metaphysics, in the last place, he defines it from the outside for the sake of theological exigencies. More precisely, it is because the theology of charity has, in advance, surpassed the metaphysics of presence that this one is completed in the metaphysics of the will.

---

[48] Scotus does not seem to be conscious of this metaphysical structure nor its shifting. But he often underlines the importance of the theological model of the beatitude. To Scotus : 1) Aristotle does not pose the problem of the primacy of the intellect or of the will. 2) If he speaks more of intellect, it is because it is more obvious to us. 3) The fact that he does not speak of the primacy of the will does not prove anything against that : an authority does not prove anything in absentia. 4) The Christian theology ("Sancti et doctores nostri") explored the question beyond this silence of the Philosopher—in the direction of the enigmatical primacy of the will (*Rep. Par.* IV, d. 49, q. 2, § [12]; XXIV, 625–626). The historian cannot but aknowledge that the controversy about intellect/will is medieval and not Aristotelian. (1). The arguments 2 and 3 help to get round Aristotle's authority. I analyse here only argument 4.

For private consultation and not distribution without the consent of E Ondrako

The Scotist Doctrine of the Incarnation and the Anglican Tradition: Newman in Frame and Context

Geoffrey Rowell

In *The Victorian World Picture*, his fascinating and wide-ranging survey of how the Victorians reflected on and came to terms with the rapidly changing world in which they lived, David Newsome notes that "the doctrine of Incarnation…came very soon to be the dominant tone of Anglican theology, lasting for some three decades into the twentieth century."[1] In *Lux Mundi*, the celebrated collection of essays published in 1889, it was the unifying theme. The essayists wrote with "the emphatic conviction of the centrality of the doctrine of the Incarnation, which, when properly understood, was the most elevating and exhilarating revelation of God's purposes for man. God, by becoming man in the person of His Son, had ennobled his own creation, had—as it were—consecrated the works of man."[2] Although Duns Scotus cannot be said to be amongst earlier theologians who have had a major influence on Anglicanism, there is perhaps one important exception—his teaching that the Incarnation was implicit in God's intentionality in creation and was not contingent upon the Fall. Yet, rather than Scotus himself, it is the roots of this theological perspective in the Greek Fathers that were more important for Anglicans than Scotus's own exposition.

It is also the case that in nineteenth-century German theology, which only had a limited influence on developments in England, there was a similar incarnational stress with the Incarnation seen as the centre of history and so the fulfillment of God's realization of the purpose of history from the beginning. Thus Gottfried Thomasius (1802–1875) wrote that "the appearance of Christ in the world is the great fact that was in view from the beginning in God's revelation to humanity. It is the centre of the whole salvation-history, implanted in the midst of time; it is the conclusion of the old, the creative beginning of something new, propagated by all

---

[1] DAVID NEWSOME, *The Victorian World Picture: Perceptions and Introspections in an Age of Change* (London: John Murray, 1997), 229.

[2] Ibid., 228.

For private consultation and not distribution without the consent of E Ondrako

that is earlier and conditioning and determining all that is subsequent."[3] Likewise Isaak Dorner (1809–1884) wrote of Christ as the one in whom "creation is first perfected, the world is given as an objective one capable of absolute value through absolute receptivity to God, but in such a way that in this culmination there is also established the beginning of the personal union of the world with God, the leading of humanity back to God by the incarnation of the Logos."[4] For Dorner "the incarnation of God is also a cosmic and metaphysical fact, as much as and even more than the creation of men and rational beings generally. It has a corresponding cosmic significance, just as love is one in heaven, and on earth, and united by it all pure spirits must desire to form one community with God. Therefore holy scripture says that even the angels long to look into this mystery of the person of Christ, and that Christ has become the bond of unity even between men, and the higher world of spirits." God makes, Dorner says in a powerful phrase 'a Bethlehem of the universe.'[5]

The Orthodox theologian, Georges Florovsky, in an essay, "*Cur Deus Homo? The Motive of the Incarnation*,"[6] explores this patristic background, commenting that "the very fact of the Incarnation was usually interpreted in early Christian theology in the perspective of Redemption." That having been said Florovsky goes on to say that "it would be unfair to claim that the Fathers regarded this redeeming purpose as *the only reason* for the Incarnation, so that the Incarnation *would not have taken place at all had not man sinned*. In this form the question was never asked by the Fathers. The question about the *ultimate motive* of the Incarnation was never discussed in the Patristic Age."[7]

Professor Andrew Louth[8] takes the view that most of the Fathers say that the reason for the Incarnation is God's *philanthropia*, and the question then is whether God's *philanthropia* is manifest in man's deification or simply in man's redemption from sin. Louth judges that, especially in the Greek Fathers, it is both—"God intended man for deification; the effect of the Fall is simply to make the route to that goal more circuitous." He points out that in the opening chapters of the *De Incarnatione*, Athanasius

[3] Claude Welch, ed., *God and Incarnation in Mid-Nineteenth Century German Theology* (New York: Oxford University Press, 1965), 31. This is from Thomasius's *Dogmatik*, 2 (2nd ed. 1857), "The Person of the Mediator."

[4] Ibid., 116–117 citing Dorner, *A System of Christian Doctrine* (Edinburgh: ET, 1880–1882).

[5] Ibid., 145. On the Virgin Birth, Dorner notes that "within humanity God first creates the adequate place for his self-revelation and impartation in that one in whom the pure central receptivity of human nature was established by God's creative activity." (144).

[6] Georges Florovsky, *Collected Works of Georges Florovsky*, III, "Creation and Redemption" (Belmont, MA: Nordland Publishing Co., 1976), 163–170.

[7] Ibid., 164.

[8] Personal communication with the author.

For private consultation and not distribution without the consent of E Ondrako

speaks first of the creation of the world, "so that it may be duly perceived that the renewal of creation has been the work of the self-same Word that made it at the beginning."[9] In the creation of humanity, "God has not only made us out of nothing; but He gave us freely by the Grace of the Word, a life in correspondence with God."[10] Although it would be possible to see the Fall as the cause of the Incarnation, it would also be possible to see a broader purpose. Louth suggests that "one way of putting it is to say that there are two arcs of the divine economy: one moves from creation to deification, the other from fall to redemption. The Greek Fathers keep both of these in mind: the greater arc is that from creation to deification, the lesser arc is that from fall to redemption, the Incarnation is involved in both."[11]

In his essay Florovsky points to Maximus the Confessor as the one significant writer from the patristic period who most clearly links Incarnation and the original purpose of God in creation, a position which Hans Urs von Balthasar also notes in his *Cosmic Liturgy*, seeing the resemblance to Scotus but underlining Maximus's distance from the scholastic debate.[12] Florovsky cites Maximus:

> This is the blessed end, on account of which everything was created. This is the Divine purpose, which was thought of before the beginning of Creation, and which we call an intended fulfill-ment. All creation exists on account of this fulfillment, and yet the fulfillment itself exists because of nothing that was created.... This is the mystery circumscribing all ages, the awesome plan of God, super-infinite and infinitely pre-existing the ages. The Messenger, who is in essence himself the Word of God, became man on account of this fulfillment.[13]

Florovsky emphasizes that Maximus "stated plainly that the Incarna-tion should be regarded as *an absolute and primary purpose of God in the act of Creation*," noting also that the Russian theologian, Sergii Bulgakov, centuries later, had argued "strongly in favour of the opinion that the Incarnation should be regarded as an absolute decree of God, prior to the catastrophe of the Fall."[14]

---

9 Athanasius, *De Incarnatione*, 1.4.

10 Ibid., 5.

11 Personal communication with the author.

12 Hans Urs von Balthasar, *Liturgie Cosmique; Maxime le Confessuer* (Paris: Aubier, 1947), 204–205.

13 Migne, *Patrologia Graeca*, 90, 621 A–B, cited, Florovsky, 166.

14 Florovsky, 167.

For private consultation and not distribution without the consent of E Ondrako

One of the most significant expositions of this theological position is to be found in the long essay, 'The Gospel of Creation,' which Brooke Foss Westcott appended to his commentary on *The Epistles of St John* (1883), and which Florovsky clearly drew on significantly for his own essay. Westcott's essay will be considered in some detail later. But we should note at this point the comment of Michael Ramsey in his 1959 Hale Lectures published as *From Gore to Temple*:

> Westcott exerted a great influence during the eleven years of his episcopate which ended with his death in 1901. In those years he impressed upon the practical consciousness of .... the Church the social corollaries of the doctrine of the Incarnation. His presentation of that doctrine is summed up in the words *Christus Consummator*.[15]

One nineteenth-century figure who *was* influenced by Duns Scotus was the Jesuit poet-priest, Gerard Manley Hopkins (1844–1889). Brought up an Anglican, influenced by the Oxford Movement, Hopkins was received by Newman into the Roman Catholic Church in 1866. In 1872 he came across a copy of Scotus on the *Sentences*[16] in the seminary library, and this discovery of Scotus had an immediate impact on him. His biographer, Robert Bernard Martin, comments on its significance for Hopkins:

> One of the teachings that set Scotus apart from the main current of Schoolmen was his view that the Incarnation would have occurred even had there been no Fall or subsequent Redemption, since it was necessary somehow to make God available to the human senses. This in turn postulated that the material world was a symbol of God, not divorced from Him, a view to which Hopkins wholeheartedly subscribed emotionally, even if he needed the authority of Scotus to feel easy with it. Once he had come on Scotus, for Hopkins, Aesthetic and religious experience became one in the sacramental apprehension of beauty. His sacramentalism, moulded by Scotus and the Spiritual Exercises, has him warrant for the use of the senses. Both personally and theologically there were many reasons for Hopkins to identify with Scotus.[17]

---

[15] A. M. RAMSEY, *From Gore to Temple: The Development of Anglican Theology between* Lux Mundi *and the Second World War, 1889–1939* (London: Longmans, 1960), 1.

[16] *Scriptum Oxoniense super Sententiis.*

[17] R. B. MARTIN, *Gerard Manley Hopkins, A Very Private Life* (London: Harper-Collins, 1991), 207. For a fuller exploration of the influence of Scotus on Hopkins see JOHN PICK, *Gerard Manley Hopkins: Priest and Poet* (London: Oxford University Press, 1966), 156–159. Pick notes that Scotus's epistemology which "does not abstract the form from its concrete embodiment;

For private consultation and not distribution without the consent of E Ondrako

Hopkins wrote that his life was "determined by the Incarnation, down to the utmost details of the day." It was Scotus's understanding of the Incarnation which Hopkins found integral to his own theory of the 'Great Sacrifice.' As Hilary Fraser comments: "Christ's descent into creation was for Hopkins not primarily as a reparation for sin, but an act of love, and as such all created nature was dependent upon it—the world was created for the purpose of revealing Christ's adoration of the Father."[18] In a different vein Hans Urs von Balthasar writes that "in the unique, the irreducible, there shines forth for Hopkins the glory of God, the majesty of his oneness, to whose ultimate, creative artistry the incomprehensibility of worldly images bears witness."[19]

In the twentieth century the Christian poet, novelist and lay theologian, Charles Williams (1886–1945) is a significant witness to the continuing vitality of this perspective in Anglican theology, as, too, is William Temple (1881–1944), Archbishop of York from 1929–1942, and briefly Archbishop of Canterbury from 1942 until his unexpected death in 1944. Austin Farrer in his summary of the Christian faith, *Saving Belief: a Discussion of Essentials*, asks the speculative question as to what would have happened if humanity had remained in friendship with the will of God? "Would Christ have come? Surely he would still have come...Christ would still have come to transform human hope and to bring men into a more privileged association with their Creator than they could otherwise enjoy. For it is by the descent of God into man that the life of God takes on a form with which we have direct sympathy and personal union."[20] Brian Hebblethwaite notes that Farrer clearly sides with the Franciscans against the Dominicans [i.e., Scotus against Thomas Aquinas], commenting that Richard Swinburne was hesitant about arguments which allow us "to say what God would have done in certain unrealized circumstances," but concedes that the "Incarnation would manifest divine solidarity with God's creatures; it would demonstrate the dignity of human nature; it would reveal the nature and extent of God's love for his personal creatures;

---

rather by one act of mind and senses it apprehends the inner in the outer, the splendour of the individuated form shining upon proportioned parts of matter." This not only was congenial to Hopkins's poetic theory but, Pick suggests, was similar to Newman's maintenance of the primacy of real over notional knowledge in *The Grammar of Assent*, a book which fascinated Hopkins so much that he wanted to edit it with a commentary.

18 HILARY FRASER, *Beauty and Belief: Aesthetics and Religion in Victorian Literature* (Cambridge: Cambridge University Press, 1986), 91.

19 HANS URS VON BALTHASAR, *The Glory of the Lord: A Theological Aesthetics* (Edinburgh: T&T Clark, 1986), vol. 3, 357.

20 AUSTIN FARRER, *Saving Belief : A Discussion of Essentials* (London: Hodder & Stoughton, 1964), 111-112.

For private consultation and not distribution without the consent of E Ondrako

it would exemplify an ideal human life; and it would provide uniquely authoritative teaching."[21]

The earliest of Newman's sermons on the Incarnation is a sermon at St Clement's, Oxford, preached on December 26th, 1824.[22] Placid Murray notes that though it was a Christmas sermon—it was preached on the text from Isaiah 9:6–7—it had an Easter message, "i.e. that the Mediatorial Kingdom of Christ began at his Resurrection. By distinguishing the mediatorial from the eternal kingdom, he is able to insist on the temporary, remedial nature of the former—'a kingdom within a kingdom.' "[23] In the Incarnation "the Creator became the creature—the Lord of all became the servant of all—and 'as at this time was born of a pure Virgin.' " To "this wonderful event…are to be traced all the hopes we have of future happiness and every present comfort of religion."[24] Murray places this sermon together with the significant series of sermons that Newman preached on 'The Offices of Christ' four years later in 1828, and notes that "all through his life Newman considered the mediation of Christ to be the central doctrine of Christian revelation. In his own case it was firmly based on his boyhood faith, matured in adult life, in the divinity of the Mediator." In these early sermons there is a characteristically evangelical stress on the work of the Mediator, the Atonement preached in a certain way, but this was a way of preaching that he outgrew. As Murray notes, the "change was not merely literary or homiletic…it was much more a change of theology. It was a change from a theology of manifestation to a theology of mystery"—and this is particularly reflected in *Tract* 73 "On the introduction of Rationalistic Principles into Religion."[25]

In the second of his *Oxford University Sermons*, "The Influence of natural and revealed religion respectively," preached on Easter Tuesday, 1830, Newman declares in the opening sentence that "the main purpose of our Saviour's Incarnation, as far as we are permitted to know it, was that of reconciling us to God, and purchasing for us eternal life by His sufferings and death." He concluded that same sermon with the affirmation that "it is the Incarnation of the Son of God rather than any doctrine drawn from a partial view of Scripture (however true and momentous it may be) which

---

[21] BRIAN HEBBLETHWAITE, *Philosophical Theology and Christian Doctrine* (Oxford: Blackwell Publishing, 2005), 70–71, citing RICHARD SWINBURNE, *The Christian God* (Oxford: The Clarendon Press, 1994).

[22] PLACID MURRAY, ed., "Sermons on the Liturgy and Sacraments and on Christ the Mediator" in *John Henry Newman Sermons 1824–1843*, (Oxford: The Clarendon Press, 1991), vol. 1, 322–328.

[23] Ibid., 322, n.1.

[24] Ibid.

[25] Ibid., .xviii.

For private consultation and not distribution without the consent of E Ondrako

is the article of a standing or a falling Church."[26] In the sermon Newman argues that the 'method of personation,' whereby the revelation of Divine truth is concentrated and conveyed to us in and through a person, who embodies principles that would otherwise remain abstractions: "The God of Philosophy was infinitely great, but an abstraction; the God of paganism was intelligible, but degraded by human conceptions. Science and nature could produce no joint-work; it was left for an express Revelation to propose the Object in which they should both be reconciled, and to satisfy the desires of both in a real and manifested incarnation of the Deity."[27] Newman returned to this theme in the last of his University Sermons, 'The Theory of Developments in Religious Doctrine,' by noting that "when we pray, we pray, not to an assemblage of notions, or to a creed, but to One Individual Being, and when we speak of Him we speak of a Person, not of a Law or a Manifestation."[28]

In his study of Newman's Christology, *Newman and the Gospel of Christ*,[29] Roderick Strange writes that "Newman's presentation of Christ's death on the cross as the atoning sacrifice…echoed the Fathers' teaching on the atonement. But it gathers added significance in the light of a further question to which he gave considerable attention." This is the question of "whether the purpose of the incarnation had been principally the expiation of sin, a view which attributed paramount importance to the cross, or whether that expiation was part of a larger economy, by which creation was brought to fulfillment. The first opinion has generally been classified as Thomist; the second as Scotist."[30] Strange notes that in time Newman came to affirm explicitly his preference for Scotism.[31] Although earlier sermons of Newman reflect a Thomist understanding, by the early 1840s Newman had been led to adopt the Scotist position. This was not, however, a consequence of his reading Scotus himself, but rather it reaches further back into his reading of the Greek Fathers, and especially Athanasius. He called Athanasius "the foremost teacher of the divine Sonship, being the most modest as well as the most authoritative of teachers."[32] As Strange notes, Newman "was influenced by Athanasius's argument which classed the incarnation as 'expedient for mankind' and not a matter of

---

26 J. D. EARNEST and G. TRACEY, eds., *John Henry Newman, Fifteen Sermons Preached before the University of Oxford* (Oxford: Oxford University Press, 2006), 24, 36.

27 Ibid., 29, see on the method of personation, 32.

28 Ibid., 222.

29 RODERICK STRANGE, *Newman and the Gospel of Christ* (Oxford: Oxford University Press, 1981).

30 Ibid., 110–111.

31 Ibid., 111.

32 J. H. NEWMAN, *Select Trearises of St. Athanasius in controversy with the Arians* (London: Longmans, Green & Co., 1897), vol. 2, 56–57.

For private consultation and not distribution without the consent of E Ondrako

'what simply is possible with God.' " He further comments that it was the general teaching of the Fathers in accordance with Athanasius "that our Lord would not have been incarnate had man not sinned," citing Athanasius's comment that "our cause was the occasion of His descent, and our transgression called forth the Word's love of man. Of His incarnation we became the ground."[33] But Newman also notes that 'there are theologians of great name, who consider that the decree of the Incarnation was independent of Adam's fall...and certainly by allowing that it was not absolutely necessary for the divine forgiveness of sin, and that it was the actual and immediate means of the soul's renewal and sanctification... Athanasius goes far towards countenancing that belief.[34]

Much later, in 1883, Brooke Foss Westcott, then Regius Professor of Divinity at Cambridge, and subsequently to succeed his friend and fellow Cambridge professor and biblical scholar, Joseph Barber Lightfoot, as Bishop of Durham, published his commentary on the Greek text of the Johannine Epistles.[35] The two appended essays are on 'The Gospel of Creation'[36] and on 'The Relation of Christianity to Art.'[37] It is the first of these that has bearing on our theme. Westcott prints as an introductory text, implicitly justifying the appending of this essay on 'The Gospel of Creation' to a commentary on the Johannine Epistles, the opening of the First Epistle of John: 'ο 'ην 'απ 'αρχης...περι του Λογου της ζωης – "what was from the beginning...concerning the word of life."[38] The opening words of the essay stress that any attempt "to speak of such a mystery as the Gospel of Creation, that is of the promise of the Incarnation which was included in the Creation of man" must necessarily require "watchful and reverent care lest we should strive to go beyond the limits which bound the proper field of our powers."[39] There is the inevitable weakness of human language and the recognition that "in such speculation we are entering on holy ground."[40] What the Gospel of Creation expounds is that "the

---

[33] Ibid., 111–112 , citing Athanasius *On the Incarnation*, 4.2-3 quoted in Newman's notes on ATHANASIUS, 2, 188.

[34] Ibid., 112, citing Newman's note on ATHANASIUS, 2, 187–188. Strange also notes the work of J. GALOT, *La Rédemption, Mystère de l'Alliance* (Bruges, 1965) which noted the growing consensus that insisted on the unity of creation and incarnation, and also notes an article by J. F. BONNEFOY, "La Place du Christ dans le plan divin de la Création" in *Mélanges de Science Religieuse* 4 (1947) 247–84 and 5 (1948) 39–62, which gives an overview of the Scotist doctrine.

[35] B. F. WESTCOTT, *The Epistles of St John: the Greek Text with Notes and Essays* (London: Macmillan & Co, 1883).

[36] Ibid., 371–315.

[37] Ibid., 317–360.

[38] I John 1, 1.

[39] WESTCOTT, *Epistles of St John*, 273.

[40] Ibid., 273.

For private consultation and not distribution without the consent of E Ondrako

true Protoevangelium is to be found in the revelation of Creation, or in other words that the Incarnation was independent of the Fall."[41] What the Gospel of Creation sets forth was that 'man's self-will by which he fell was not the occasion of the supreme manifestation of the love of God in "the taking of the manhood into God."[42] "That was the end of Creation from the beginning. The Fall, and here lies the greatest mystery of divine love, did not frustrate this end which it might seem to have made unattainable consistently with that truth and justice which define omnipotence."[43] Scripture, Westcott suggests, points us to regarding "the circumstances of the Incarnation as separable from the idea of the Incarnation"—that "was due to the primal and absolute purpose of love foreshadowed in Creation, apart from sin which was contingent."[44]

It is true, Westcott continues, that the subject "belongs properly to the later ages of the Church"—and in particular to the debates of the eleventh and twelfth centuries—though he believes that "the thought of an Incarnation independent of the Fall harmonizes with the general tenor of Greek Theology."[45] The circumstances of the early Church meant that Christian teachers concentrated their efforts on "bringing out the truth of the redemption of a Church from fallen humanity" rather than embarking on a "theoretical investigation of the relation of man and humanity to God."[46] Westcott noted that "from the beginning of the thirteenth century the question whether Christ would have been incarnate if Adam had not sinned" became one of the recognized questions of the schools. In the period of the Reformation it was debated by representatives of the chief parties of Christendom; and now again in quite recent times, after falling out of sight, the subject has been, and is likely to be, keenly discussed.'[47] Thus, for Westcott, this is not an abstruse scholastic question, but a live theological issue with significant ramifications.

Westcott then embarks on a survey of the controversy, noting that, although some of the medieval scholastic arguments may "appear to us frivolous and pointless," it is worth making the effort to engage with them. "Conclusions which rest upon arbitrary assumptions as to the symmetries of things witness in an imperfect fashion to a deep sense of a divine order

---

41 Ibid., 274.

42 Words from the Athanasian Creed, one of the three creeds prescribed in the worship of the Anglican Book of Common Prayer, and which replaced the Apostles's Creed at Morning Prayer on festivals such as Christmas and Trinity Sunday.

43 *Epistles of St John*, 274.

44 Ibid., 275.

45 Ibid., 275.

46 Ibid., 275.

47 Ibid., 276.

For private consultation and not distribution without the consent of E Ondrako

in creation; and we do injustice to those who draw them if we allow even the greatest errors of expression and form to blind us to the nobility of the conception which they embody most inadequately."[48] What is at stake is a whole—and important—theological perspective.

Westcott turns first to Rupert of Deutz (c.1075–1129/30), whose work "demonstrates the interaction between the older monastic theology and the nascent scholastic way of thinking."[49] He notes that Rupert's main argument for the "absolute divine purpose of the incarnation" was based on an erroneous reading of Hebrews 2:10, using the passive *consummari* instead of the active *consummare*.[50] Rupert notes[51] that if sin had not intervened God "would not have become a mortal man" (for mortality was a consequence of the Fall); "the question is whether God would have become man as the Head and King of all as He is now, and whether this was in some sense necessary for the human race," concluding, that "it is marvelous and worthy of devout gratitude (*adoratione*) that sin coming in the way did not make of none effect (*evacuarit*) that purpose of great love in which God had purposed that the Word of God should take delight with the sons of man, by having a form limited according to human nature in the midst of angels and men." On account of sin, "not only did He not shrink from our nature *which he had purposed to assume*, but for sake descended even unto death."[52] Westcott notes that in a subsequent work, *De Glorificatione Trinitatis*, Rupert affirms that "before God made anything from the beginning, and when He was making this or that, this was His purpose that the Word of God (*verbum Deus*), should become flesh and dwell among men with great love and great humility, which are true delights."[53] For Rupert, the Incarnation is essentially independent of Sin and the Fall, yet "the Fall did in fact redound to the glory of Christ. The humiliation of love which it called out was followed by a more exceeding glory (Phil. 2:9)."[54] "The circumstances of the Incarnation have actually made the issue of it more glorious for Christ."[55]

Westcott proceeds to set out the arguments on both sides in relation to creation, Incarnation and the Fall, given by Alexander of Hales and

---

48 Ibid., 275–6.

49 'Rupert of Deutz,' F. L. CROSS and E. A. LIVINGSTONE, *Oxford Dictionary of the Christian Church*, 3rd ed. (Oxford: Oxford University Press, 1997), 3rd ed. *ODCC*.

50 "It was fitting that he, for whom all and though whom all things exist, in bringing many children to glory, should make the pioneer of their salvation perfect through sufferings."

51 In his Commentary on Hebrews dated according to Westcott to 1126.

52 Ibid., 277–278. Italics mine.

53 Ibid., 278, citing *De glorif. Trin.* 3.§§ 20. f. . (Migne, PL 169, 71 ff).

54 Ibid., 278, 279.

55 Ibid., 280.

For private consultation and not distribution without the consent of E Ondrako

Albert the Great, both of whom note the *felix culpa* phrase in the solemn blessing of the Easter candle, which implies the Incarnation is directly consequent on the Fall, Albert concluding that he believes that "the Son of God would have been made man even if sin had never been," an opinion which he believes "to accord better with the piety of faith," noting that the language of the Easter Hymn is "very inexact."[56] Westcott notes the important discussion of Thomas Aquinas in his Commentary on the Sentences (c. 1255), in which he concludes that "although God might have been incarnate if sin had not existed, yet it is said more fittingly that if man had not sinned God would not have been incarnate, since in the Holy Scriptures the ground (*ratio*) of the Incarnation is everywhere set down as springing from the sin of the first man (*ex peccato…assignetur*)."[57] After a discussion of Bonaventure, who, despite sympathy with the contrary arguments, finally comes down on the Thomist side,[58] Westcott has a brief consideration of Duns Scotus, to whom he is clearly not attracted seeing him as "simply the dialectician, without grace, without sympathy, inexhaustible in ingenuity, and unhesitating in decision. He is the master without the softening experience of the ecclesiastic," and so "in affirming the Incarnation was independent of the Fall, he dwells mainly on the conceivable order of thoughts in the divine counsel, a form of argument which was only lightly touched on before."[59] Two quotations sum up the Scotist position:

> The incarnation of Christ was not foreseen as a contingent event (*occasionaliter praevisa*) but was seen by God directly (*immediate*) as an end from eternity: so Christ, in His human Nature, since He is nearer to the end than other things was predestined before them.[60]

> If the Fall was the cause of the Incarnation of Christ, it would follow that the greatest work of God was contingent only (*occasionatum tantum*), because the glory of all things will not be so great (*intensive*) as that of Christ, and it seems to be very irrational to suppose that God would have left undone (*dimisset*) so great a work because of Adam's right action, that is, if he had not sinned.[61]

---

56 Ibid., 286.

57 Ibid., 287–288.

58 Ibid., 288–292. Westcott cites Bonaventure's conclusion that he does not wish "to confine the goodness of God, but to commend the excess of His love towards fallen man, that our affections may be roused to love Him while we mark the extremity of His exceeding love."

59 Ibid., 292.

60 DUNS SCOTUS, *Opus Oxoniense*, 3.d..9, cited Ibid., 292.

61 DUNS SCOTUS, *Opus Parisiense*, 3. d. 7 q. 4, cited Ibid., 292–293.

For private consultation and not distribution without the consent of E Ondrako

The last medieval theologian Westcott discusses is Wessel (c.1419–1489), a Dutchman educated by the Brethren of the Common Life and influenced by Plato and St Augustine. His writings were later edited by Luther, and his practical system of meditation is held to be a remote influence on the *Spiritual Exercises* of Ignatius Loyola.[62] Influenced by the much earlier writings of Rupert of Deutz, it was probably Wessel's grounding of his theology on Scripture that was attractive to Westcott, who notes Wessel's re-translation of "I am that I am" (Exodus iii, 14) as "I will be the man I will be" (*ero homo qui ero*).[63] He quotes with approval Wessel's teaching:

> God destined and regarded (*intendit*) the Lamb as first and the first-fruits of all creation. He destined that Lamb should become man. He destined the Lamb as King of a blessed state. It was fitting (*congruebat*) that the Man-Lamb being King should have men as citizens of His kingdom.[64]

The Reformation did not see the end of this particular theological debate. Giacomo Nachianti (Jacobus Naclantus), Bishop of Chioggia, defended the 'Scotist' doctrine at the Council of Trent.[65] In the Lutheran Church the doctrine that "the Son of God would have been Incarnate if sin had not entered the world" was supported by Andreas Osiander.[66] Westcott notes that Osiander interprets the Nicene Creed's affirmation that Christ came down "from heaven for us men and for our salvation," as "for us men" referring to humanity being created for Him and in His image, and "for our salvation" as having fallen through sin.[67] On the other hand, Calvin held the 'Scotist' doctrine to be a wandering speculation.[68]

So, Westcott concludes, although "the belief that the Incarnation was in essence independent of the Fall has been held by men of the most different schools, in different ways and on different grounds. All however in the main agree in this, that they find in the belief a crowning promise of the unity of the Divine order; a fulfillment, a consummation, of the original purpose of creation; a more complete and harmonious view of the relation of finite being to God than can be gained otherwise."[69] Man

---

62 'Wessel' (also known as 'Gansfort'), entry in *ODCC*.

63 WESTCOTT, 295.

64 Ibid, 297.

65 Ibid., 299–300.

66 Ibid., 300–302. Osiander's niece, Margaret, became the wife of Archbishop Thomas Cranmer.

67 Ibid., 302.

68 Ibid., 303, citing J. CALVIN, *Institutes* 2, 12, 4–7.

69 Ibid., 304.

For private consultation and not distribution without the consent of E Ondrako

is said to be made "in the image of God," and Christ is that archetypal image—"the predestined humanity of the Son of God" is "the archetype of humanity," and therefore "the essential constitution of man suggests at least the belief that the Incarnation, by which we understand in this case the taking of sinless and perfect humanity into God was part of the Divine counsel in creation."[70]

A contemporary of Westcott's, John Richardson Illingworth (1848–1915), who contributed an essay on "The Incarnation and Development" to *Lux Mundi* (1889), sets the *Christus consummator* emphasis on the Incarnation as the fulfillment of human destiny in the evolutionary context of the age. He criticizes Reformation and post-Reformation thought for narrowing the religion of the Incarnation into the religion of the atonement, with a consequent sharp division between sacred and secular, and a 'subjectivising of religion,' contrasting this with the cosmic perspective of the patristic period. "They realized that redemption was a means to an end, and that end the reconsecration of the universe."[71] As Michael Ramsey comments, evolution provided an opportunity "for the recovery of the cosmical aspect of the Incarnation as held by many of the Fathers" who saw the Incarnation as "the final act of the divine word who has ordered creation and [has] been life and light to mankind."[72] Ramsey noted that "with a naïve optimism about progress in relation to the Incarnation" Illingworth could go so far as to claim that "secular civilization is…in the Christian view, nothing less than the providential correlative and counterpart of the Incarnation." It was an optimism which subsequent years made impossible, demanding once again the centrality of the Cross.[73] Writing of the incarnationalism which was so characteristic of Anglican theology, and noting particularly Charles Gore's Bampton Lectures of 1891, *The Incarnation of the Son of God*, Ramsey notes that "the Incarnation was the centre of a theological scheme concerning nature and man, in which Christ is both the climax of nature and history and the supernatural restorer of mankind. It is significant that no small use is made of the current concept of evolution, and that the thesis is congruous in part at least of the view of the world familiar in idealistic philosophy."[74]

Michael Ramsey saw the main theological line of succession from Illingworth and Gore as running to William Temple and Lionel

---

70 Ibid., 307–308.

71 GEOFFREY ROWELL, "Historical Retrospect : Lux Mundi 1889," in Robert Morgan , ed., *Anglican Essays in Commemoration of LUX MUNDI* (Bristol: Classical Press, 1989), 212.

72 A. M. RAMSEY, 2.

73 Ibid., 4–5.

74 Ibid., 18.

For private consultation and not distribution without the consent of E Ondrako

Thornton[75] in his *Christus Veritas* (1924) saw the Incarnation, as Michael Ramsey notes, "as the climax of the series: matter, life, mind, spirit, and as the key to the understanding of the world in terms of value." "Whereas Gore in the last resort saw the Incarnation as sense."[76] In *Christus Veritas* Temple set himself "to vindicate in idealism's own terms the rationality of an Incarnation and a particular revelation," though Ramsey queried whether Temple's theology remained coloured by Hegelian ideas more "than were really compatible with a Christian view of God's relation to the world" as when Temple declared that although "God eternally is what we see in Christ...temporally the Incarnation, the taking of Manhood into God, was a real *enrichment* of the Divine life."[77] Lionel Thornton's *The Incarnate Word* (1928) used A. N. Whitehead's philosophy to see "the Incarnation [as] the climax of the progressive incorporation of the eternal order with the organic series." In respect of his manhood, Christ "stands in the succession of history in the form of concrete human individuality, organically united to the human race, and so to the whole organism of creation," yet "the human organism of the Incarnate Lord is taken up to the level of deity, with its own principle of unity."[78] Other Anglican theologians, like the modernist, Bethune-Baker, could equate Incarnation and immanence, seeing God incarnate within the whole unfolding history of the universe.[79] When William Temple wrote in 1937 the preface to the report of the Church of England Doctrine Commission, *Doctrine in the Church of England*, as the war-clouds were gathering again over Europe, and communist and fascist dictatorships were perpetrating hideous evils, he acknowledged that the optimism of Anglican incarnationalism could easily mute the needful prophetic note. "A theology of the Incarnation tends to be a Christocentric metaphysic. A theology of Redemption... tends rather to sound the prophetic note; it is more ready to admit that much in this evil world is irrational and strictly unintelligible; and it looks to the coming of the Kingdom as a necessary preliminary to the comprehensions of much that now is."[80] Temple went far in treating the Incarnation as the key to the unity and rationality of a world whose every feature—evil and suffering included—must make the righting of a world gone astray.

---

[75] Ibid., 26.

[76] Ibid., 24.

[77] Ibid., 148–149, citing both *Christus Veritas* and Temple's *Gifford Lectures, Nature, Man and God* (1934).

[78] Ibid., 25.

[79] Ibid., Ramsey quotes from BETHUNE-BAKER, *The Way of Modernism*.

[80] Ibid., 159.

For private consultation and not distribution without the consent of E Ondrako

A later significant Anglican exponent of the 'Scotist' doctrine of the Incarnation was the lay poet and theological writer, Charles Williams (1886–1945). Williams, a member of the Oxford trio of friends known as 'The Inklings'—C. S. Lewis and J. R. R. Tolkien being the other two in the group[81]—wrote in his *Descent of the Dove: a short history of the Holy Spirit in the Church*,[82] of how "the thought of St. Thomas has been subtly modified by the sensations aroused by Scotus. As, for example, in the effect on our view of matter encouraged by the Scotist opinion that the Incarnation would have happened had there been no Fall."[83] Thus Williams wrote in a review of *Fathers and Heretics* by G. L. Prestige, that "the world exists for the Incarnation rather than the Incarnation for the world,"[84] a theme, as Mary McDermott Shideler notes, was expanded in *The Forgiveness of Sins*.

> The beginning of all this specific creation was the Will of God to incarnate. God himself is pure spirit; that is, in so far as any definite human word can apply to him, he is pure spirit. He had created matter, and he had determined to unite himself with matter. The means of that union was the Incarnation; that is, it was determined that the Word was to be flesh and to be man.[85]

The phrase in the *Quicunque vult* ('the Athanasian Creed') about the Incarnation being not about "the conversion of the Godhead into flesh, but by the taking of the manhood into God" was one that resonated with Williams—he called it 'this great humanist ode' and underlay his understanding of the Incarnation, as it did his understanding of poetry.[86] As one commentator on Williams puts it: "should we think of the Incarnation as a contraction of deity, a 'conversion of the Godhead into flesh'? Or was it, as the creed specifies, an intensification of humanity, a 'taking of the manhood into God.' "[87] 'Being united with matter was the Creator's intention all along. It is why he created at all. To say that matter is good because it was so created is true, then, as far as it goes, but there is a

---

81 See Humphrey Carpenter, *The Inklings: C.S.Lewis, J.R.R.Tolkien, Charles Williams and their Friends*, London, George Allen & Unwin, 1978.

82 Longmans, Green & Co., London, 1939; New ed., Faber & Faber, 1950.

83 *The Descent of the Dove*, 1950 ed., 122.

84 *Time and Tide*, 21.46, November 16, 1940, q. Mary McDermott Shideler, *The Theology of Romantic Love: a study in the writings of Charles Williams* (New York: Harper & Brothers, 1962), 66.

85 Shideler, p. 67 q. Williams, *The Forgiveness of Sins, in He Came Down from Heaven and The Forgiveness of Sins*, new ed. (London: Faber & Faber, 1950), 119.

86 See A .M. Hadfield, *An Introduction to Charles Williams* (London: Robert Hale, 1959), 95ff.

87 Charles Hefling, ed., *Charles Williams: essential writings in Spirituality and Theology* (Boston: Cowley Publications, 1993), 10.

For private consultation and not distribution without the consent of E Ondrako

reason why it has been so created. That reason is the Incarnation.'[88] In an essay on Williams's book, *He Came Down from Heaven*,[89] Brian Horne notes both that Williams chose like many of the Greek Fathers to focus his interpretation of the salvific work of Christ, not on the Cross, but on the Word made flesh, yet, that being so, does not allow, 'even for the purposes of organizational convenience...the separation of the categories of Incarnation and Atonement in his theological system.[90]

In an article published in *Theology* in 1940 on 'Natural Goodness,' Williams writes of "an opinion permissible to the faithful" which he is told "is related to the great name of Duns Scotus."

> It is, briefly, that the Incarnation is the point of creation, and the divine 'reason' for it. It pleased God in His self-willed activity to be incarnate....Even now, in spite of the Athanasian Creed, the single existence of the Incarnate Word is too often almost Gnostically contemplated as an inhabitation of the flesh by the Word....He determined creation; He determined not only to be incarnate, but to be incarnate by means of a mother. He proposed to Himself to be born into a world.
>
> This decree upon Himself was the decree that brought mankind into being. It was His will to make creatures of such a kind that they should share in that particular joy of His existence in flesh.[91]

Like Hopkins before him, the Incarnation –and the particularity of the Incarnation, the Word being made flesh—was central for Williams. What Hilary Fraser wrote about Hopkins could be equally true of Williams.

> Christ's descent into creation was...not primarily as a reparation for sin, but an act of love, and as such all created nature was dependent upon it—the world was created for the purpose of revealing Christ's adoration of the Father.[92]

The frame and context of Newman's 'Scotist' understanding of the Incarnation, drawn as it was from the Greek Fathers—and particularly Athanasius—rather than from Scotus belongs in a sweep of Anglican reflection on Incarnation and creation, and a theology of *Christus Consum-*

---

88 Ibid., 8–9.

89 CHARLES WILLIAMS, *He Came Down from Heaven* (London: Faber & Faber, 1950).

90 BRIAN HORNE, "He Came Down from Heaven : the Christology of Charles Williams," in Stephen Holmes and Murray Rae, eds., *The Person of Christ* (London: T&T Clark, 2006), 109–110.

91 CHARLES WILLIAMS, *The Image of the City and other Essays* (Oxford, Oxford University Press, 1958), 76. See the introduction by Anne Ridler.

92 HILARY FRASER, *Beauty and Belief: Aesthetics and Religion in Victorian Literature*, (Cambridge, Cambridge University Press, 1986), 91.

For private consultation and not distribution without the consent of E Ondrako

mator, which has its biblical roots in the cosmic Christology of Ephesians and Colossians. It is interesting that a recent work of Catholic theology, Jack Mahoney's *Christianity in Evolution: an Exploration*,[93] has a significant chapter on 'Incarnation with the Fall.' In wrestling with a theology which takes evolution seriously, Mahoney notes that "the offer of an evolutionary interpretation of the incarnation creates a new relevance" for the Scotist approach to the Incarnation. Mahoney in commending the Scotist understanding does not only look back to Hopkins, but also to Illingworth.[94] The arc that runs from creation to deification is indeed a significant theme, and yet the love and grace that is disclosed there is redemptive because by it God comes down, as Lady Julian of Norwich said, "to the very lowest part of our need."[95] It is this that is the frame and context of Newman's understanding of the Incarnation.

Geoffrey Rowell
Retired Bishop of Gibraltar in Europe
Emeritus Fellow, Keble College, Oxford

---

[93] JACK MAHONEY, *Christianity in Evolution: an Exploration*, (Washington, D.C.: Georgetown University Press, 2011).

[94] Ibid., 11–12, 74–75.

[95] *The Revelations of Divine Love of Julian of Norwich*, trans. James Walsh, SJ. (Wheathampstead: Antony Clarke Books, 1973), Ch. 6, 55.

For private consultation and not distribution without the consent of E Ondrako

CHAPTER 10

Cor ad cor loquitur:
Re-fashioning the imagination around love

Mary Beth Ingham

It is a very great honor for me to be invited to address you all on this important occasion. I must confess from the outset that my knowledge of John Henry Newman is limited; however my familiarity with that other great Oxford master, John Duns Scotus, is happily more extensive. My remarks this evening intend to flesh out some of the ways that the thought of this Great Franciscan, known as the Subtle Doctor, finds an echo in the 19th century vision of Cardinal Newman. Both men offer a rich resource for Catholics today, and through them, for the world. The resource, as I hope to explicate, involves the renewed discovery of the rationality of love, and the centrality of Newman's own motto: *cor ad cor loquitur*.

In his recent article published in *America* magazine, "Refashioning Catholic Imagination," Robert Imbelli notes the significance of Newman's re-centering of the Catholic imagination for a secular age. He identifies four learnings: learning to see the whole, learning Christ, learning holy living and learning to praise. All these learnings form, in Imbelli's opinion a particular vision that is, at heart, a re-fashioning of the current way of understanding.

And, all these learnings point, I would hold, to the centrality of love, and rational love, at the heart of the renewed Catholic vision, so prized by Benedict, both in his homily last month in Birmingham, and in his recent encyclical *Caritas in Veritate*. Newman's refashioning reveals remarkable parallels with the thought of Scotus, as many of the sessions have shown. What I should like to do this evening is to trace out some of the elements that belong to Scotus's own re-fashioning for his own time. Over against a dominant Aristotelian and intellectualist model, he explored a re-fashioning of human rationality within the context of love, understood as the fullest perfection of the human person. In his own re-framing of the dominant rational paradigm of his day, Scotist thought promotes the same type of re-fashioning that Benedict's and Newman's vision advocates. With their focus on persons and human dignity, on the centrality of love, on the beauty of creation and the abundance of divine love, both Newman and Scotus might help ground a re-newed Oxford movement.

447

For private consultation and not distribution without the consent of E Ondrako

I shall reflect, first, upon a core element of Scotus's thought and, indeed, a core aspect of the Franciscan Intellectual tradition, one that effectively re-frames the medieval intellectual paradigm. Quite simply, this points to the rationality of love and freedom. This shift of rationality from the intellect to the will (our power of choosing) which we discover in Scotus, results in what is, quite simply, a "sea change" for our understanding of our human vocation, one that places him right at the center of a dialogue with Newman. This shift is so important that it requires a sustained reflection, in order to reveal other important elements for the re-newed Catholic imagination. These include the re-discovery of the *via pulchritudinis*, or Franciscan way of beauty and a life of respect and sustainability for the goods of the earth.

Most contemporary studies of Scotus emphasize his affirmation of human freedom that results from his emphasis on the human will, our power to choose. My argument holds that Scotus's Franciscan identity makes all the difference in his teaching on human freedom. It is not freedom that he cares about but love. This means that, for Scotus, the primacy of the will is really the primacy of charity, the primacy of ordered loving as central to human moral perfection, and as a way of knowing.

A moral vision centered on love

Central to Franciscan spirituality are two key elements: the order of love (*ordo amoris*) and ongoing conversion (*conversio*). Both appear regularly in Francis's *Admonitions* and are part of the ongoing spiritual *praxis* of members of the Franciscan family.[1] For the Franciscan Intellectual tradition, rationality can only make sense in terms of the moral primacy of ordered loving and in terms of the metaphysical possibility of conversion. Among the Masters of the Order, John Duns Scotus is the most famous proponent of this Franciscan re-framing of the rational. Scotus holds, surprisingly enough, that the intellect is a *natural*, but not a *rational* faculty, since the intellect cannot restrain itself in the act of knowing. Indeed, like the eye in the presence of sufficient light and color, the intellect cannot *not* see what is before it. The will, conversely, is alone rational since it can restrain itself. This is the key to the Franciscan re-framing of the rational.

As the recent encyclical *Caritas in Veritate* makes clear, the re-framing of the rational and a re-claiming of the centrality of love cannot take place

---

[1] See Robert J. Karris, OFM, *The Admonitions of St. Francis: Sources and Meanings* (St. Bonaventure: 1999). On their role in Franciscan life, see also Pierre Brunette, OFM, *Essai d'analyse symbolique des admonitions de François d'Assise* (Montreal : 1989).

For private consultation and not distribution without the consent of E Ondrako

independently of a spiritual tradition. The Scotist re-framing depends upon three distinct elements, each one with a spiritual origin: rational freedom understood as the possibility of ongoing conversion; moral judgment understood as an act of discernment; and the rehabilitation of beauty as an authentic moral concept. The foundations for this view involve a prior discussion of a re-framed rationality–centered on the rational will.

Benedictine theologian Anselm of Canterbury, writing in the 12th century, had described rational beings in the following way: each rational being is endowed with a two-fold attraction to the good: the affection for happiness or possession and the affection for justice or rectitude. These are the two metaphysical desires of our rational heart. The affection for happiness is a self-oriented and healthy love. It is not selfishness, but is self-directed in its concerns. The affection belongs to rational beings as part of their natural constitution. It is a type of instinct for goodness, and is drawn naturally to love something that the person perceives as good. Like the dog's love for a bone, the affection for happiness is directed toward objects that satisfy its natural desires.

The affection for justice, by contrast, is an affection for intrinsic goodness that considers the world of value insofar as it exists as valuable in itself, and not necessarily relative to the person who loves or admires it. This affection is, according to Anselm and Scotus, the higher rational disposition that regulates and restrains natural inclinations toward possession and self-related good.

A simple example illustrates how these two affections might function. Let's say I have the opportunity to tell the truth to a friend. Now, I happen to fear that this revelation will seriously jeopardize our friendship. Indeed, it might destroy it. From the perspective of the affection for happiness, I might be inclined to lie to protect what I value in a self-centered type of way. But from the perspective of the affection for justice, I realize that in this particular case, regardless of the consequences to me personally, the truth needs to be told. So, the rational and free act would be to tell the truth, and live with whatever the consequences might be.

Taken together, (and they must be taken in tandem) the two affections constitute free and moral action: neither one alone is capable of explaining moral choice. Indeed, alone each one would function according to a model of "stimulus-response" and is more proper to animals. Both Anselm and Scotus agree that without the two together, there would be nothing to distinguish the human from animal behavior.

What Scotus takes up and (significantly) transforms from Anselm results in his own position on rational freedom and, more importantly, on

For private consultation and not distribution without the consent of E Ondrako

the rationality of love. Let us consider this insight more carefully. According to Scotus, human rationality expresses itself in a two-fold manner:

First, we are rational because we act "with reason."[2] Thanks to our innate affection for justice, we possess a higher (and free) disposition inclined to follow the dictates of right reasoning as well as the first principle of *praxis: God is to be loved.* This disposition is never necessitated, and this leads to the second manner of its rationality.

Second, we are more properly (and more profoundly) rational in terms of our internal psychological constitution, and in terms of the way the two affections interact. The affection for justice oversees and governs the affection for happiness, in every moral action. Thanks to this ever-present interaction, rational beings possess a natural capacity for self-restraint, an innate constitution for self-control. This capacity must be developed and once perfected, expresses itself as the excellence of self-mastery. The artist, the dancer, the musician all spend years developing the expertise proper to their art. Each human person has the vocation to such excellence: we are called to develop the expertise proper to our human dignity.

The interaction between these two affections reveals three separate ways of relating to the world around us: in the presence of an object, we can choose to will it (velle), to reject it (nolle), or to abstain from choosing at all (non velle). This third act of *non velle* is the key to moral rationality, for Scotus. It is an important reflexive act. For in it we discern how our capacity for perfected self-mastery is built into our own moral constitution, as part of our way of being in the world. We will return to this point about reflexive moral action a bit later on.

When Scotus takes these two affections and integrates them into his Franciscan vision of human dignity, he expands upon Anselm's traditional teaching. With his Benedictine predecessor, Scotus affirms that both affections must be present for an act to be free. But, Scotus adds, because of this requirement, the two affections **must** belong to the will as intrinsic and innate abilities to love the good. What's more, the affection for justice holds the key to our vocation to self-transcendence. It is because I am able to make some choices in light of intrinsic goodness or other's wellbeing, that I have a vocation to be more than myself. I am called to the highest love of all: love for the good alone.

To understand the significance of this insight for a reframed understanding of our human vocation, we must remember that Anselm held

---

[2] "Sed proprie voluntas addit super appetitum, quia est appetites cum ratione liber..." *Ordinatio* III, 17, Codex A in *Duns Scotus on the Will and Morality,* edited by ALLAN B. WOLTER, Washington D.C.: Catholic University of America 1986, 180–181. See also Allan B. Wolter's "Duns Scotus on the Will as Rational Potency," *The Philosophical Theology of John Duns Scotus,* edited by Marilyn McCord Adams, Ithaca, NY: Cornell University 1990, pp. 163–180.

For private consultation and not distribution without the consent of E Ondrako

that the affection for justice, our higher affection, was lost as a result of original sin and could only be restored by grace. Scotus argues, by contrast, that the affection for justice was not lost as a result of sin. Rather, its ability to direct the affection for happiness was weakened, but it was still present in the human will, and still essential for human freedom.

Why is this Franciscan shift important for today? First, of course, it points to the enormous optimism about the human person, an optimism repeated by Newman and, importantly, in *Gaudium et Spes*, as it considers the human person and the goodness of human desires, in every age and every culture. We see through Scotus's analysis how much confidence he, like Newman, has in human desires, how much confidence he has in the human capacity to love rationally. This capacity is our gift from God. We are constituted for the love of friendship; for self-transcendence in love.

Scotus's Franciscan vision of love finds its source within the human heart, here understood as the center of all rational/human inclinations. But we must remember: this source is constituted by the act of divine creativity and mirrors the ordered structure of the natural world around us. For Scotus, the first commandment, *Love God above all*, is both a primary and self-evident first principle and, more importantly, the first principle of *praxis*, true for both divine and human rational choice.[3]

In Scotus's first principle of *praxis* we discover the way in which human moral living both imitates divine life and, more importantly, moves continually toward the integration of the two Anselmian affections. In God, love for the highest good is identical to love for the self. *Love God above all* captures the identity of these two affections in God, certainly, but in each human person virtually. For this reason, Scotus does not pit moral living against authentic human happiness[4] (as if our natural perfection need dispose of our deepest satisfaction and delight), nor does he fall prey to a moral subjectivism based upon love as a personal experience of preference.

This reframing of rationality grounds, quite literally, a paradigm shift. It moves from knowing to loving as centerpoint of human rational dignity. And, like any good paradigm shift, it will now introduce a re-organization of all elements of the vision. Said differently, the Franciscan vision is grounded upon our intrinsic constitution toward right loving and freedom as evidence of our rational being. We are **innately** gifted with everything we need to love God above all things, in concrete circumstances of our

---

3 "Deus est diligendus… est veritas practica praesedens omnem determinationem voluntatis divinae." *Ordinatio* IV, d. 46, q. 1, n. 3 (ed. Vivès 20: 400).

4 I develop this more fully in "Duns Scotus, Morality and Happiness: A Reply to Thomas Williams." *American Catholic Philosophical Quarterly*, 74, 2, 2000, 173–195.

For private consultation and not distribution without the consent of E Ondrako

lives. Even the consequences of original sin have not deprived us of our capacity to love rightly. Here we perceive the basis for the Christological re-framing that is also a part of Scotus's Franciscan vision.

What's more, this internal constitution offers us an internal goal: inner harmony of affective and rational desires. In every action, my goal is to be like the juggler or tightrope walker: balance and harmonic integration. This is the key to peace of mind and heart. Here we see Franciscan optimism and Christian humanism at their best!

An ethics of beauty and moral artistry

If we have understood this central insight of the rationality of love, then we see clearly the first two implications of Scotus's vision: the primacy of moral beauty and moral artistry. Following Augustine, Scotus describes the moral act as a beautiful whole, with all elements in harmony with one another. In the morally good act we recognize the integration of proportion and harmony. Although he uses beauty as a moral category, it is important to note that Scotus does not defend a subjective theory of human preference.[5] Classical theories of beauty, whether Platonic, Neoplatonic or Stoic, were highly structured in their affirmation of the objectivity of the beautiful. Musical harmony, itself grounded on mathematics and mathematical relationships, offered a rich exemplar for the sort of scientific recognition of beauty that medieval thinkers accepted.

For Scotus, the experience of harmony in music expresses the highest form of human rational judgment. How is this possible? How is the will, even the rational will, able to recognize beauty? Scotus calls the will a *vis collativa*, a power that, like the intellect, is able to assemble pieces of information and to place them alongside one another. The will, like the intellect, can bring items together and perceive their relationship. Scotus actually attributes a type of moral "judgment" to the will—the ability to recognize a quality we might call moral *resonance*.

---

[5] Few scholars have focused on this aspect of Scotus's work. Francis Kovach explains the relationship of virtue to the soul in terms of moral beauty: "Considered relatively, moral beauty has the character of ornament, because it is something extrinsic and added to the human act in such a way as to beautify that act and, through the act, the human soul itself. The human act is, however, not the sole proximate subject of moral beauty to Scotus. For he speaks of the moral beauty both of the human act and of the moral virtue. It is this virtue from which the soul receives its moral beauty with relative permanence; and in turn, it is this relatively permanent moral beauty for which God mainly loves the soul." "Divine and Human Beauty in Duns Scotus' Philosophy and Theology" in Scholastic Challenges to Some Mediaeval and Modern Ideas, 1987, pp. 102–3. This article originally appeared in *Deus et Homo ad Mentem I. Duns Scoti*. Rome: 1972, 445–459.

For private consultation and not distribution without the consent of E Ondrako

There are important classical and Stoic antecedents to this type of insight, insights linking moral goodness directly to beauty and illustrating moral judgment in terms of the recognition of harmony. Indeed, the Stoic identification of moral goodness with beauty reveals an intrinsic connection between ethics and the rational recognition of *to kalon*, the beautiful or good, translated into Latin by the medievals as *honestum*. In Cicero's *De Officiis*, for example, moral rectitude is presented as a species of beauty.[6] Cicero notes that just as beauty is inseparable from health, so too *decorum* (beauty or propriety) is inseparable from rectitude.[7] Later in the *De Officiis*, Cicero develops the analogy of moral hearing and harmonic attention as a type of consciousness examen.[8]

Such moral recognition in the will can be likened to spiritual discernment, where the morally mature person possesses a well-trained moral sense, a type of "moral ear" capable of picking up dissonance in a given situation. The moral agent, like the well trained musician or piano tuner, can immediately detect harmony or dissonance within a situation. Here we might find the Scotist equivalent to Newman's *illative sense*. Here we are in the presence of the convergence of evidence, leading to the immediate act of assent. Here is that keen and energetic act of real assent, with the concrete certainty. Here is the practical expertness that exemplifies the act of judgment, rather than a rule-based inferential reasoning process.

Such a model for practical and moral judgment enables us to look upon the human person as *moral performing artist*. We are able to assess the moral situation from the perspective of its potential for rational beauty, and to regard moral training as an apprenticeship in beauty—with rehearsal and practice as part of the development of character. Indeed, this aestheticized frame leads us to regard mistakes and errors as part of the life of ongoing conversion and development.

---

6 "Such is its [rectitude] essential nature, that it is inseparable from moral goodness (honesto); for what is proper is morally right and what is morally right is proper. The nature of the difference between morality and propriety can be more easily felt than expressed. For whatever propriety may be, it is manifested only when there is pre-existing moral rectitude." M. T. CICERO, *De Officiis* I, ch. 27 (Loeb 1956), n. 94, p. 97.

7 "For there is a certain element of propriety perceptible in every act of moral rectitude (virtute); and this can be separated from virtue theoretically better than it can be practically. As comeliness and beauty of person are inseparable from the notion of health, so this propriety of which we are speaking, while in fact completely blended with virtue, is mentally and theoretically distinguishable from it." CICERO, *De Officiis* I, ch. 27, n. 95, pp. 97–99.

8 "However slightly out of tune a harp or flute may be, the fault is still detected by a connoisseur; so we must be on the watch lest haply something in our life be out of tune…"; and again "As therefore, a musical ear detects even the slightest falsity of tone in a harp, so we, if we wish to be keen and careful observers of moral faults, shall often draw important conclusions from trifles." CICERO, *De Officiis*, I, ch. 40–41, n. 145–6, p. 149.

For private consultation and not distribution without the consent of E Ondrako

In this re-framed model we recognize the seeds for a program of moral pedagogy that identifies goodness with beauty and lends foundation to the universal call to holiness, an important theme of Vatican II as well as an important aspect to Newman's sermons. Moral education might be re-imagined to involve the development of *a taste for the beautiful*, not a mere attraction to the agreeable, but rather a deep appreciation of beauty as a total environment: in nature, in persons, in generosity and kindnesses.

Scotus offers us here a fruitful and dynamic way to consider the human person as *moral performing artist*, the moral situation in its potential for rational beauty (a work of art), and moral living as an apprenticeship in beauty. Far from a moral fundamentalism or rule-based legalism, Scotus's emphasis on the convergence of moral precepts (the first principle and its relationship to the Decalogue, for example) and concrete evidence reflects his commitment to the primacy of individual conscience and its judgments, another point of contact with Newman.

An ethics of right loving and right use

This vision of rational love and the focus on moral artistry that we find in Scotist thought suggest a final and perhaps, surprising, benefit to be gained from this re-framed notion of rationality. An expanded notion of the rational points beyond the practical dimension of right loving to the deeper dimension of right use as the true moral goal for the renewed way of thinking which both Newman and Scotus promote. Ordered or right loving is central to the Augustinian legacy of Franciscan moral theology. This perfection of rational loving is possible, thanks once again to the dynamic interaction of Anselm's two affections as human freedom reaches out to a world of beauty and goodness. "Right loving" does not merely mean loving the right thing. Rather, it means loving the right thing in the right way: loving persons as they deserve, loving everything that exists as it deserves.

Scotus's position on moral freedom as self-mastery, again grounded on the dynamic and rational interaction of the two affections in the will, can now be read in light of the Franciscan value of poverty, understood not as deprivation but as *usus pauper*, the restrained use of goods and possessions. Here, certainly, we find an aspect of critical importance for today's global and economic realities. A moral perspective that can link rational freedom to a notion of restrained use can easily frame discussions on global distributive justice, the environment and human stewardship, not as *consequences*, *applications* or even *extensions* of one's moral vision, but as

For private consultation and not distribution without the consent of E Ondrako

indispensable presuppositions of the highest human moral perfection. On this point, Scotus's Franciscan vision offers the most resonance with the call of the recent encyclical.[9]

The human and rational capacity for reflexive self-restraint and therefore for restrained use of the goods of the earth supports and grounds not just an ethics of love and beauty, but an ethics of environmental stewardship. The natural order, in all its manifestations, is not only the gift of divine creative love; it is also the domain for our protection and care.

Scotus's Franciscan re-fashioning now comes more clearly into view: a moral vision of love based upon human rational affections; a moral pedagogy of ongoing conversion; an image of moral artistry based upon the will's power to note the convergence of elements, in order to detect the harmony present. Here is a vision of moral discernment where the moral ear is continually attuned; a morality of right love, self-restraint and responsible use. Here is the Franciscan vision in its most contemporary relevance for our world today. Here is what we also see in the thought of John Henry Cardinal Newman.

In Scotus we discover a Franciscan vision of artistry, a *via pulchritudinis*, whose moral journey of development involves a pedagogy of beauty. We develop an awareness of the beauty of the world and a consciousness of our own ability to bring forth beauty in concrete terms–wherever things are not always as we would like them to be. The challenge for such a moral artist is to widen the moral frame beyond the narrowly circumscribed "moral dilemma," so popular today. The task of the moral artisan is to consider all aspects and all relationships that combine to enhance moral beauty, all under the direction of the primary principle of praxis, *Deus diligendus est*.

Here at last, is an ethics for this third millennium: an ethics of beauty, self-mastery and restrained use. The two revised Anselmian affections

---

9 "More than forty years after *Populorum Progressio*, its basic theme, namely progress, remains an open question, made all the more acute and urgent by the current economic and financial crisis. If some areas of the globe, with a history of poverty, have experienced remarkable changes in terms of their economic growth and their share in world production, other zones are still living in a situation of deprivation comparable to that which existed at the time of Paul VI, and in some cases one can even speak of a deterioration. It is significant that some of the causes of this situation were identified in *Populorum Progressio*, such as the high tariffs imposed by economically developed countries, which still make it difficult for the products of poor countries to gain a foothold in the markets of rich countries. Other causes, however, mentioned only in passing in the Encyclical, have since emerged with greater clarity. A case in point would be the evaluation of the process of decolonization, then at its height. Paul VI hoped to see the journey towards autonomy unfold freely and in peace. More than forty years later, we must acknowledge how difficult this journey has been, both because of new forms of colonialism and continued dependence on old and new foreign powers, and because of grave irresponsibility within the very countries that have achieved independence." *Caritas in Veritate*, n. 33.

For private consultation and not distribution without the consent of E Ondrako

provide Scotus with a point of departure for a re-imagined vision of human perfection and fulfillment. His is a vision based upon rational love as the fullest perfection of the person. In their on-the-spot rational interaction, these two affections open the door for an experience of conversion, the decisive moment where a person can stop one type of activity and turn toward another. This moment of readiness might also be termed a moment of *spiritual indifference*. At this moment, the moral decision involves the deepest attention to spiritual listening: *cor ad cor loquitur*, where heart most truly speaks to heart.

Such a vision, in Scotus as well as Newman, distills the hope and the optimism at the core of the Christian vision, along with its insistence upon right and selfless loving as the fullest expression of human dignity and perfection. Both in the order of moral living and in the order of divine communion, the way of beauty offers the bridge between human life and divine life. True moral living takes its place as part of a lifelong journey of spiritual artistic development, a pilgrimage to beauty—in the world and in the human heart.

Moral instruction thus is re-imagined as a *paideia*, whose purpose is the formation of artisans capable of bringing forth beauty in the contingent order, expressing their freedom and creativity in imitation of God. The artistic *paideia* could indeed be the basis for conceiving the domain of moral living neither as a realm of unyielding absolute legal principles nor as a field of fluid personal preference. Moral living could once again be understood in the broad and inclusive spiritual frame of ongoing conversion, the dynamic context that promotes the integration of what is best in rational human loving and spiritual aspirations. And this re-framing could open up a space for intercultural and interreligious dialogue on the deepest values of our life and future.

Mary Beth Ingham, CSJ
Loyola Marymount University, Los Angeles

For private consultation and not distribution without the consent of E Ondrako

CHAPTER 11

Newman, Scotus, and Catholic Higher Educaton: A Worthwhile Conversation[1]

Patricia Hutchison

When I received the invitation to participate in the Newman-Scotus Symposium held at Washington Theological Union in October 2010, my first reaction was to decline. I am neither a theologian nor a philosopher. My ministry for the past forty years has been in the field of education and educational administration at the elementary, secondary, and post-secondary level. As a Franciscan, I have read secondary sources related to the philosophy of John Duns Scotus and incorporated his insights into presentations on the Franciscan intellectual tradition and into a doctoral course on Ethics in Educational Administration. My knowledge of John Henry Newman was limited to a cursory understanding of the influence of *The Idea of a University* on Catholic higher education, respect for the spiritual and intellectual journey which led Newman from the Anglican to the Roman Catholic Church, and a vague memory of having read decades ago a biography entitled *Lead, Kindly Light.* Preparation for the Newman-Scotus Symposium prompted me to revisit writings on Scotus and to expand my rather limited knowledge of Newman. Moreover, participation in the Symposium ignited a desire to explore how the insights of these great thinkers from the early fourteenth and nineteenth centuries might impact Catholic university education and the lives of twenty-first century students.

This paper takes up a question which I posed in Summary Statements at the Symposium: *So what?* First, *what* might further exploration about Newman and Scotus reveal about their potential to influence Catholic higher education and the formation of young adults? Second, *what* insight might Newman and Scotus offer to faculty, campus ministers, and other student life personnel in Catholic colleges and universities? Third, *what* connections exist among Francis and Clare of Assisi, John Duns Scotus, Francis de Sales, John Henry Newman, and Gerard Manley Hopkins and why should they matter to Catholic higher education? To examine these questions in depth would require the equivalent of more than one doctoral

---

[1] This article expands on "Summary Statements" made at the Newman-Scotus Symposium, October 22–24, 2010, Washington Theological Union, Washington, DC.

For private consultation and not distribution without the consent of E Ondrako

dissertation, a task beyond the scope of this paper. Rather than attempting an in-depth analysis of these questions, in the following paragraphs I offer brief introductory comments on ten areas with the hope that the dialogue begun at the 2010 Newman-Scotus Symposium may continue.

Higher Education, Undergraduate Students, and the Journey of Faith

In Fall 2010, the Higher Education Research Institute (HERI) at the University of California at Los Angeles (UCLA) published the results of a seven-year study examining the impact of college on students' spiritual development.[2] Using survey data, personal interviews, and focus groups, researchers examined the experience of approximately 15,000 students from a representative sample of more than 130 United States colleges and universities. Although the researchers differentiated "spirituality" and "religiousness," they found that the majority of college students valued both and desired to explore spiritual and religious questions as part of their college experience. Eighty percent of students described an interest in spirituality and affirmed their belief in the sacredness of life. More than 75% of students asserted their belief in God and desire for connection with God, or a Higher Power. In addition, the researchers discovered connections between students' spiritual development and their intellectual/academic growth, personal/emotional maturation, and openness to persons of other races and cultures. In other words, students who had the freedom and encouragement to explore spiritual and religious questions during their college years seemed to advance in academic, emotional, and interpersonal areas as well. At the same time, the study identified a gap in the support students expected and what they actually experienced in college with respect to the spiritual and religious quest. Colleges and universities often separate the academic and the spiritual, the head and the heart, knowledge and love. The authors of the study decried such fragmentation and called for renewed attention to the spiritual and religious, as well as the intellectual. They also identified several practices which positively impact spiritual development, including: contemplation, participation in service, exploration of life's "big questions," engagement with persons different from themselves, and meaningful interaction with faculty and other adult mentors within the academic community

---

2 ASTIN, ALEXANDER W., HELEN S. ASTIN, and JENNIFER A. LINDHOLM, *Cultivating the Spirit: How College Can Enhance Students' Inner Live.* (San Francisco: Jossey-Bass, 2011). Information on the study may also be found at http://spirituality.ucla.edu/.

For private consultation and not distribution without the consent of E Ondrako

Although the UCLA study is significant in terms of its size and scope, the researchers emphasized that their findings are not unique; other educators have also established the importance of the mind-spirit connection. For example, Sharon Daloz Parks[3] asserts that "every institution of higher education serves in at least some measure as a community of imagination in which every professor is potentially a spiritual guide and every syllabus a confession of faith." Parker Palmer and Arthur Zajonc[4] advocate for practices which integrate "intellect, senses, imagination, intuition, will, spirit, and soul." John C. Haughey[5] addresses what he considers the "poverty" of many institutions of higher education: "an almost universal inattentiveness to the spirituality latent in the act of coming to know."

As I reflected upon the various presentations at the Symposium against the backdrop of higher education, I found myself wondering what advice Newman and Scotus might offer to those who attempt to support the spiritual quest or faith journey of today's undergraduates. Both Newman and Scotus promoted the integration of head and heart, intellect and will. While acknowledging the importance of knowing, both insisted on the place of loving/desiring. What might such integration suggest about the content and the process of the undergraduate experience?

The inferential process of Newman offers a helpful pedagogical model. This approach might begin with questions: posing questions, inviting students to raise their own questions, and encouraging students to consider what questions are worth pursuing. Next, there would be a collecting of data relative to the questions posed; not simply a gathering of intellectual data, but also a consideration of the impact of data on persons and social situations. Finally, students would be invited to identify patterns emerging from the data gathered and to determine the truth, whether the truth of a scientific quest or a psychological analysis or the ultimate Truth of God. Commenting on Newman's conversion, Walter Conn[6] asserts that "Truth here, as in most complex human realities, lies in ambiguity…Though intellectual and spiritual, [Newman's] struggle was anything but abstract and rarified. It was deeply embedded in the affective and imaginative dimensions of a very complicated individual, and it was carried out in a highly complex social and political world." So too, is the challenge and

---

3 SHARON DALOZ PARKS, *Big Questions, Worthy Dreams: Mentoring Young Adults in their Search for Meaning, Purpose and Faith* (San Francisco: Jossey-Bass, 2000), 159.

4 PARKER J. PALMER and ARTHUR ZAJONC, *The Heart of Higher Education* (San Francisco: Jossey-Bass, 2010), 20.

5 JOHN C. HAUGHEY, *Where is Knowing Going: The Horizons of the Knowing Subject* (Washington, DC: Georgetown University Press, 2009), xi.

6 WALTER CONN, *Conscience and Conversion in Newman: A Developmental Study of Self in John Henry Newman* (Milwaukee: Marquette University Press, 2010), 85.

For private consultation and not distribution without the consent of E Ondrako

complexity faced by today's young people in harmonizing faith and reason in the quest for truth.

The Importance of Companions on the Journey

The UCLA study on Spirituality and the College Student identified interaction with faculty and other members of the academic community as one of the factors contributing to the spiritual growth of students.[7] Sharon Daloz Parks stresses the importance of mentors: "Mentors care about your soul. Whatever the immediate challenge or subject matter, good mentors know that all knowledge has a moral dimension and learning that matters is ultimately a spiritual, transforming activity…"[8] Conn[9] notes the importance of mentors and friends to Newman's own psychosocial and spiritual development. Newman's devotion to the students at Oriel College is well-documented. Newman both advocated for the importance of relationships and modeled such interaction through personal contact and extensive correspondence. Unfortunately, not much is known about the details of Scotus's life. However, the content of his writings which emphasize the dignity of the human person, the primacy of love and generosity, and the centrality of beauty would certainly suggest the importance of human relationships.[10]

Having spent much of my academic career in elementary schools where it is not unusual that every faculty member knows every child and can greet parents by name and where children and adolescents often form deep attachments to their teachers, I was surprised to learn that many of my first year college advisees did not know the names of their professors. Nor could they identify by name more than a handful of the students in their classes. Moreover, in working with faculty members from various academic divisions I sometimes hear concerns about the lack of a sense of community among students who share the same major and meet several times each week in three, four, or even five classes. In the book *Altogether Gift: A Trinitarian Spirituality*, Michael Downey speaks of the importance of names and the act of naming in relation to human persons

---

[7] ASTIN, ASTIN, and LINDHOLM, *Cultivating the Spirit*, 150.

[8] PARKS, *Big Questions, Worthy Dreams*, 128.

[9] CONN, *Conscience and Conversion in Newman*, 48.

[10] For further examination of these concepts see especially MARY BETH INGHAM, CSJ, *Scotus for Dunces: An Introduction to the Subtle Doctor* (St. Bonaventure, NY: The Franciscan Institute, 2003) and *Rejoicing in the Works of the Lord: Beauty in the Franciscan Tradition* (St. Bonaventure, NY: The Franciscan Institute, 2009).

For private consultation and not distribution without the consent of E Ondrako

and to God's self-revelation.[11] Newman certainly addressed by name the persons with whom he corresponded in more than 20,000 extant letters. Pictures of friends and family adorned the walls of his room, testifying to the importance of individual persons in his life. Scotus's concept of *haecceitas* describes the uniqueness of each individual, that aspect of the human person which "can only be known by direct acquaintance, not from any consideration of common nature."[12] What might these insights offer with respect to the importance of knowing students by name and creating communities of care on college and university campuses, both within the classroom and in all aspects of student life? Such actions would certainly respond to the invitation Parks poses to educators when she recommends reflection on really "seeing" students, and challenges educators to reflect on their own experience of "being noticed": "Who recognized you?... Who saw you?"[13]

The Notional and the Real: Service and the Power of the Personal Encounter

Since the founding of Harvard in 1637, the mission of American higher education has been associated with the civic mission and the American democratic ideal.[14] It would be difficult today to locate an institution of higher education which does not promote volunteerism and service-learning. However, this was not always the case. In the 1980s colleges were accused of failing to challenge what many perceived as an attitude of self-centeredness and lack of connection with social issues among young adults. Many accused institutions of higher education of drifting away from their civic mission. To counteract this image, several college presidents founded Campus Contact in 1985.[15] Today the organization includes more than 1100 colleges and universities serving over six million students. The UCLA study on Spirituality and the College Student identified service-learning as "a powerful means of enhancing students' spiritual questing, ethic of caring, and ecumenical worldview."[16] Yet, many have raised questions about the appropriate place of service-learning within

---

11 MICHAEL DOWNEY, *Altogether Gift: A Trinitarian Spirituality* (Maryknoll, NY: Orbis Books, 2000).

12 INGHAM, *Scotus for Dunces*, 52.

13 PARKS, *Big Questions*, 128.

14 ERNEST L. BOYER, "Creating the New American College," *Chronicle of Higher Education*, March 4, 1994, A 48.

15 Campus Compact, A Season of Service (Providence, RI: Brown University, 2002).

16 ASTIN, ASTIN, and LINDHOLM, *Cultivating the Spirit*, 146.

For private consultation and not distribution without the consent of E Ondrako

Catholic colleges and universities. For example, Melanie Morey and Jesuit Father John Piderit challenge Catholic institutions to ensure that service-learning is "distinguishable" by a special focus on serving the needs of the marginalized and by reflection in light of Catholic social teaching and the call to discipleship.[17]

Unpacking Newman's distinction between the notional and the real and Scotus's insistence on the need for personal awareness to *really* "know" may offer interesting and beneficial insights for deeper, more "distin-guishable" reflection on service. Both Newman and Scotus affirmed the necessity of experience and the need to move from head to heart. What questions might their thinking suggest? For example, Conn distinguishes three dimensions of conscience as understood by Newman: conscience as *desire*, conscience as *discernment*, and conscience as *demand* for decision to act.[18] These three dimensions might structure reflection on service with questions such as: What feelings, affections, and *desires* stirred within me as I engaged in this service? Did I notice any *desires* related to the service itself or connected with the people with whom I engaged? As I participated in this service and interacted with the people, how was my heart moved? Do I *discern* a structural injustice to be challenged? Do I recognize something within myself in need of conversion? Does my experience *demand* that I respond more completely to a human or societal need? Do I sense within a *demand* that I actually devote my life to this situation or these people? There are numerous examples of young adults whose lives have been forever changed by a significant service experience. Deep reflection on service and especially on personal encounters are significant in faith development.[19] According to Parks, "Faith develops at the boundary with otherness, when one becomes vulnerable to the consciousness of another, and thus vulnerable to reimagining self, other, world, and 'God.' "[20]

---

[17] MELANIE MOREY and JOHN PIDERIT, *Catholic Higher Education: A Culture in Crisis* (New York: Oxford University Press, 2006).

[18] See CONN, *Conscience and Conversion*, 113–122.

[19] For additional insights into the potential of service-learning to engage students in the faith journey, see MICHAEL BLASTIC, "The Franciscan Difference: What Makes a College/University Franciscan?" *The AFCU Journal: A Franciscan Perspective on Higher Education* 4 (2007): 19–27 and DANIEL HORAN, "Profit or Prophet? A Franciscan Challenge to Millennials in Higher Education," *The AFCU Journal: A Franciscan Perspective on Higher Education* 8 (2011): 59–73.

[20] PARKS, *Big Questions*, 141.

For private consultation and not distribution without the consent of E Ondrako

The Incarnation and the Call to Love

Both Newman and Scotus answered the age-old question "Would Jesus have come if Adam had not sinned?" with a resounding "Yes!" This assertion does not deny the suffering and death of Jesus as redemptive and sanctifying acts, but it does change the focus of the conversation. "God so loved the world" that God desired to share the human condition. God wanted to be part of the chaos and messiness of life as we know it. What kind of a God would share love and life like this? Furthermore, what kind of a God would create human beings "in his own image and likeness"? These questions never cease to spark a sense of wonder, awe, and gratitude in others. In addition, such questions often promote generosity and a desire to give oneself in service to others. "If the world is beautiful, if the human person is so beautiful that God could think of nothing better than to become one of us, then our human response to divine graciousness can only be that of exultation and shouts of joy and praise."[21] Furthermore, when we recognize that God delights in our attempts to "do good," we (and our students) begin to grasp our call to bring forth Beauty wherever we are, with whomever we minister, regardless of the challenges presented. How might such an understanding of the Incarnation and the dignity of each person foster the desire to live and love in a manner worthy of the call to be fully and totally human?

Contemplation and Conversion: From Awareness to Reflection to Transformation

In the book *Le Petit Prince* by Antoine de Saint-Exupéry,[22] the Fox reveals to the Little Prince an important and very simple secret: "On ne voit bien qu'avec le couer. L'essentiel est invisible pour les yeux." "It is only with the heart that one can see rightly; what is essential is invisible to the eyes." Often during the Newman-Scotus Symposium, I recalled this quote from a beloved children's book. I believe the quote captures the meaning of Newman's motto, "Cor ad Cor Loquitor," "Heart speaking to Heart." Similarly, to comprehend Scotus's recognition of beauty as a moral category and his reframing of rationality in terms of love requires contemplation, a "turning over in one's heart." It is this kind of heart vision that is also essential for the full maturation of today's college student. Having

---

21 INGHAM, *Rejoicing in the Works of the Lord*, 31.

22 ANTOINE DE SAINT-EXUPÉRY, *Le Petit Prince* (New York: Harcourt, Brace & World, 1943), 71.

For private consultation and not distribution without the consent of E Ondrako

identified the importance of contemplation, Astin, Astin, and Lindholm[23] offer several examples of institutions which are intentionally introducing meditation and contemplative practices into the curriculum. The significance of contemplation is also stressed by Palmer and Parks whose writings have been previously cited.

In his Symposium paper on "Newman's Personalist Argument for Belief in God," Father John Ford recounted the experience of Avery Dulles who, as an avowedly agnostic college student, was moved to belief in God and prayer through contemplating the force of "Nature" which transformed a young bud into a flowering tree. This movement from awareness to reflection to transformation recalls Bonaventure's *Itinerarium*. One could offer many other examples of the movement from awareness to reflection to transformation. Consider Clare of Assisi's advice to Agnes of Prague to "gaze, consider, and contemplate" Christ, and Francis of Assisi's transformation before the cross in the dilapidated church of San Damiano. Of Francis's experience Michael Hubaut writes:

> This, of course was not the first time that Francis had looked at a crucifix…But that day, Francis was enlightened by the Holy Spirit to see the face of Christ crucified, a living face of simple but majestic beauty. It struck him that God has a face and He looked at our world through human eyes, that he spoke to us in human words."[24]

In light of the growing support for contemplative pedagogies in higher education, it seems appropriate to explore all that the Catholic tradition, embraced by both Scotus and Newman, has to offer to a generation which, although often "plugged in and tuned out," nonetheless has a deep desire for heart to heart connection.

Conscience Formation and Ethical Living

The ethical development of college students is an essential learning outcome of undergraduate education. A recent survey of 302 employers in organizations with more than 25 employees conducted by Hart Research Associates on behalf of the Association of American Colleges and Universities revealed that 75% of employers believe that colleges should place *more* emphasis than they do today on helping young adults to connect their

---

[23] Astin, Astin, and Lindholm, *Cultivating the Spirit*, 148–157.

[24] Michael Hubaut, "Christ our Joy: Learning to Pray with Francis and Clare," *Greyfriars Review* 9 Supplement (1995): 17–18.

For private consultation and not distribution without the consent of E Ondrako

choices and actions to ethical decisions.[25] Accrediting agencies require that colleges and universities provide evidence of how they address ethics in the general education program (that part of the program required of all students regardless of major). The 2010 National Survey of Student Engagement[26] administered annually in hundreds of institutions of higher education found that students ranked the degree to which their colleges have helped them to develop ethically at 2.8 on a scale of 0 to 4, suggesting that there is room for improvement. Additionally, an increasing number of graduate professional programs now require an ethics course. In light of the current emphasis on ethics and ethical decision-making at both the undergraduate and graduate level, it is certainly timely to consider what Newman's view of conscience and Scotus's ethical vision, centered on love, might contribute to the content of ethics courses.[27]

Newman, Scotus, and Curricular Integration

The occasion of Newman's beatification has rekindled interest in Newman's ideas regarding higher education and the formation of undergraduate students. Prior to completing his term as President and CEO of the Association of Catholic Colleges and Universities (ACCU) in August 2010, Dr. Richard Yanikoski prepared a resource packet on Newman and his impact on higher education. In the introduction to that resource, Dr. Yanikoski states that "Newman's influence on Catholic higher education in the United States has not yet been thoroughly studied."[28] Since this guide first appeared on the ACCU website, several additional documents have been added, contributing to continued reflection on Newman's influence.

---

25 Hart Research Associates, *Raising the Bar: Employers' Views on Colleges Learning in the Wake of the Economic Downturn* (Washington, DC: Hart Research Associates, 2010). http://www.aacu.org/leap/documents/2009_EmployerSurvey.pdf

26 The 2010 National Survey of Student Engagement was completed by more than 362,000 undergraduate students in 564 institutions. Information is available at http://nsse.iub.edu/

27 For examples of applying Scotus's ethical vision in undergraduate education, see F. EDWARD COUGHLIN, "Can Ethics Be Taught? Harvard's Question, Scotus' Ethics, and Twenty-first Century College Students," *The AFCU Journal: A Franciscan Perspective on Higher Education* 6 (2009): 12–23; F. EDWARD COUGHLIN, "Serving Generously and Loving Rightly: Insights for a Value-Centered Life from the Franciscan Tradition," *The AFCU Journal: The Franciscan Perspective on Higher Education* 7 (2010): 28–43. Under the heading "Focus on conversion," Rev. James Bacik offers insights which relate, at least indirectly, Newman's ideas to ethical living: JAMES J. BACIK, "Habits of Mind and Spirit: What Campus Ministers Can Learn from Blessed John Henry Newman," *America* (September 13–20, 2010): 23–26.

28 Dr. Yanikoski's guide, as well as several other documents related to Newman's influence on Catholic higher education are available at the website of the *Association of Catholic Colleges and Universities* http://www.accunet.org/i4a/pages/index.cfm?pageID=3653

For private consultation and not distribution without the consent of E Ondrako

As Yanikoski asserted, "most U.S. Catholic colleges and universities still embody key principles of Newman's 'Idea of a University.' " Dr. Yanikoski illustrates this assertion by identifying six such principles: a core liberal arts curriculum anchored in philosophy and theology; integration of liberal arts and sciences with the professions, creating a "circle of Knowledge"; integration of campus ministry, residence life and student affairs programs with academic offerings to foster intellectual, spiritual, emotional, social, and moral development; education and inclusion of the laity in all areas of the university; publication of Catholic scholarship, catechetical resources, and research; and college access for students who might otherwise be excluded from higher education. These six principles could provide a helpful starting point for discussions among faculty, staff, and administrators. Such conversations could lead to heightened awareness of Newman, deeper commitment to the mission of Catholic higher education, and identification of concrete ways that institutions can integrate academic and student life programs to support the holistic development of students.

Another recent publication of the ACCU, *A United Endeavor*,[29] although mentioning Newman directly only a few times, embodies his thinking and could also spark fruitful discussion. This publication describes a recent project which reviewed the essential elements and best practices in general education for Catholic colleges and universities. In the spirit of Newman, the document stresses curricular integration and suggests strongly that "campus ministry and student life need to be brought into collaboration with general education, in order to make institutional mission come alive on campus."[30]

If Newman's influence on Catholic higher education has not yet been "*thoroughly* studied," studies of the connection of Scotus and Catholic higher education are practically non-existent. In the keynote address delivered at the second biennial symposium of the Association of Franciscan Colleges and Universities at St. Bonaventure University in June 2006, Sr. Mary Beth Ingham initiated a conversation worth continuing by suggesting that we might "fruitfully understand Franciscan education as a personal invitation to enter into an 'ever-widening circle of meaning.' "[31] In developing her thesis, Sr. Mary Beth's focus was on Franciscan thinkers like

---

[29] *Association of Catholic Colleges and Universities, A United Endeavor* (Washington, DC: ACCU, 2009). Available as a PDF version at http://www.accunet.org/i4a/pages/index.cfm?pageid=3617

[30] *A United Endeavor*, 9.

[31] MARY BETH INGHAM, "Responding from the Tradition: Franciscan Universities in the Third Millennium," *The AFCU Journal: A Franciscan Perspective on Higher Education* 4 (2006): 7.

For private consultation and not distribution without the consent of E Ondrako

Scotus, but her sentiments certainly echo those of Newman. The questions with which Ingham concluded her presentation are worth repeating:

> As we stand at the dawn of a new millennium, are there not ways to promote a fuller spiritual-intellectual vision of the human person and of the deepest human aspirations? Can we not help re-define the expression "Catholic university" as not only an open circle, but as a dynamic, opening circle?...This points toward a discussion, not simply about the content of coursework in an established curriculum, or even about strengthening current ties among academic disciplines. It is the discussion about the possibility of an integrative educational experience informed by a teleological perspective and framed by self-transcending and self-transforming activities, in the classroom and beyond. It is an opening circle: a conversation for all levels of the institution.[32]

I believe that this is a conversation that would interest both Newman and Scotus!

The foregoing remarks pertain to the influence of Scotus and Newman on Catholic higher education. It is important to note that several scholars continue to explore the relevance of Newman to higher education, both Catholic and secular. One can locate several recent scholarly peer-reviewed journal articles which might engage educators in lively discussions about the nature and purpose of the undergraduate experience and the value of a liberal arts core curriculum. I will offer only one example here because of its relevance to a recent debate about the presence of religion in a revision of the core curriculum at Harvard. In an article in the *British Journal of Educational Studies*, Alasdair MacIntyre[33] identifies three key arguments often raised to dispute the contemporary relevance of Newman's views on university education. The arguments he enumerates include: Newman's belief in the unity of knowledge/understanding which implies the need for the study of many disciplines, their connections with one another, and the limitations of each; Newman's belief in the central and unifying place of theology within the curriculum; and Newman's belief in the intrinsic value of interdisciplinary education against a view which claimed the primacy of the social utility of education. After explaining each argument, MacIntyre offers counter-arguments which establish not only the relevance of Newman's thought for twenty-first century undergraduate education, but also the significance of such education in light of contemporary social,

---

32 INGHAM, 17–18.

33. ALASDAIR MACINTYRE, "The Very Idea of a University: Newman, Aristotle, and Us," *British Journal of Educational Studies* 57 (December, 2009): 347–362.

For private consultation and not distribution without the consent of E Ondrako

political, and economic realities. This article would provoke stimulating conversation. The section on the place of theology in the undergraduate curriculum would also be very timely in light of the recent debate over Harvard's proposal to include in its undergraduate core curriculum a requirement of at least one course in a category called Faith and Reason. This recommendation, eventually abandoned, sparked a lively debate about the pursuit of truth. MacIntyre's arguments in support of theology might have reversed the outcome of the debate. I believe that Newman (and Scotus) would have agreed with *Newsweek's* religion editor, Lisa Miller, who closed her analysis of the Harvard situation by asserting (with an interesting play on words): "To dismiss the importance of the study of faith—especially now—out of academic narrow-mindedness is less than helpful. It's unreasonable."[34]

Catholic Studies and the Catholic Imagination

The concluding plenary presentation of the 2008 Symposium of the Association of Franciscan Colleges and Universities featured four professors who shared the manner in which they integrate the Franciscan tradition into their respective disciplines: History, Mathematics, English, and the Humanities. The presentation was energizing. The content included excellent pedagogical ideas with concrete examples and attested to the positive impact of their teaching on students. However, what most intrigued the audience was the fact that the four professors do not serve on the faculty of a Franciscan university, but rather at the State University of New York at Geneseo. It was clear from the questions raised by the audience that many of the participants in the symposium, all members of Franciscan universities, sometimes struggled to understand how to integrate the Franciscan tradition in a manner appropriate to their discipline. It was also clear that some members of the audience were skeptical about the relevance of such integration. It was equally clear that the quartet from SUNY considered what they were doing a perfectly natural outgrowth of solid scholarship as evidenced by the following comments:

> "The Franciscan perspective has guided how I look at the universe in my whole teaching career at a state university."

> "The faculty trusts that what we do is scholarly and compatible with the mission of a state university."

---

[34] LISA MILLER, "Harvard's Crisis of Faith: Can a secular university embrace religion without sacrificing its soul?" *Newsweek* (February 11, 2010).

For private consultation and not distribution without the consent of E Ondrako

"The [Franciscan] tradition is treated with great intellectual honesty and is part of the rhythm of life."

"We have a Catholic, Franciscan perspective and we believe that this, like other perspectives, is academically honest—unless we resort to proselytizing, which we don't!"[35]

The obvious message that the professors conveyed was that appropriate integration of any tradition flowed from solid academic scholarship and that historical figures and traditions which had made a significant contribution to the advancement of knowledge deserve a place within the curriculum. I could not help but recall this message as I heard the various presenters at the Newman-Scotus Symposium connect such great figures as Francis of Assisi, Bonaventure of Bagnoregio, John Duns Scotus, Francis de Sales, John Henry Newman, and Gerard Manley Hopkins. For centuries these men have influenced philosophy, theology, art, literature, poetry, environmental studies, and education, to name but a few areas. Yet how consistently do their names appear on syllabi within the typical undergraduate curriculum? How many graduates of Catholic colleges and universities could discuss the contributions of even a few of these men? In my own university, I was reminded by an undergraduate student of the importance of sharing the great legacy which is ours in Catholic higher education. I had been invited to speak about Clare of Assisi in an upper level Gender Studies class. After the presentation a young woman raised her hand and asked politely, but rather indignantly, "Why am I only now, as a junior, hearing this story if this is really a Franciscan university?" Our young adults deserve to hear the stories of the women and men who are such an integral part of the rich Catholic tradition.

Sacred Spaces: The Impact of Sacred Space

For the past three years, in the University in which I serve, we have invited faculty, staff, and administrators to participate in a full or half day of reflection to contemplate the ministry that we share in Franciscan Catholic higher education. Each year between 150 and 200 employees have accepted the invitation and registered for one of a dozen days scattered throughout the academic year. This past year, we spent the morning reflecting on two of our core University values, Reverence and

---

[35] For an interview with the professors, see PATRICIA SMITH and PATRICIA HUTCHISON, "Living the Franciscan Tradition through the Writings of Saint Francis: An Interview with William R. Cook, Gary W. Towsley, Ronald B. Herzman, and Weston L. Kennison," *The AFCU Journal: A Franciscan Perspective on Higher Education* 6 (2009): 36–41.

For private consultation and not distribution without the consent of E Ondrako

Integrity. During the afternoon session we invited graduates, two each day, to share with us their experience of these values during their time as undergraduate or graduate students. In essence, we invited them to tell us how we were (or were not) living the values we professed. It was a very enriching and humbling experience. Each of the graduates, in his or her own unique style, shared a similar message: how their lives (and especially their hearts) were touched by the "uniquely personal" manner in which they were loved, supported, and challenged; and also how the University became for them "sacred space."

Much has been written about the sacredness of space and the impact of place on personal development. Gerard Manley Hopkins recognized the sacred in his description of "Duns Scotus' Oxford" when he wrote:

Yet ah! this air I gather and I release
He lived on; these weeds and waters, these walls are what
He haunted who of all men most sways my spirits to peace...

A further exploration of the sacredness of place and the formative role of the space that John Duns Scotus, John Henry Newman, and Gerard Manley Hopkins shared could be an interesting prelude to a consideration of how "place," in particular one's alma mater, has the potential to impact and shape the intellectual, spiritual, emotional, ethical, and social development of young adults.

A Call for Further Research on Newman, Scotus, and their Influence on Higher Education

After reading Dr. Yanikoski's assertion that Newman's influence on contemporary Catholic higher education has not yet been fully explored, I decided to investigate doctoral dissertations over the last ten years. A search on the Pro Quest Dissertation database surfaced only six doctoral dissertations related to Newman's influence on higher education. Three of the six were associated with Catholic higher education. Furthermore, there were no dissertations linking Scotus in any way with higher education. A search revealed approximately thirty scholarly peer-reviewed articles on Newman and higher education and none connecting Scotus with higher education. Perhaps the beatification of John Henry Newman will ignite interest in further research. Perhaps Franciscan institutions could promote scholarship on the relevance of Scotus for higher education.

For private consultation and not distribution without the consent of E Ondrako

Conclusion

The motto of the institution in which I minister, Neumann (another John—saint and fourth bishop of Philadelphia) University, is *Veritas - Caritas, Live the Truth in Love*. The University seal includes, among other symbols, the Chi-Rho, the Gospel Book, and a Crown, all resting upon a Globe. The Chi-Rho represents Jesus Christ, the unity of all truth and Truth itself. The Gospel reminds us of the call to live and share the fullness of Christ's message. The Crown symbolizes Mary, Queen and Mother, and a model of the virtues embodied in our mission. The Globe encourages us to share knowledge in service of others throughout "all the world." I believe that this motto and the symbols on our seal offer a fitting reminder of the challenges of Blesseds John Duns Scotus and John Henry Newman for Catholic higher education in the twenty-first century. In their spirits, may we all "Live the Truth in Love"!

For private consultation and not distribution without the consent of E Ondrako

Holiness in John Henry Newman's Theory of Doctrinal Development: The Harmony of the Intellect and Affective Spirit

Robert C. Christie

The work of John Henry Newman forms the foundation for Aidan Nichols's study, *From Newman to Congar, the Idea of Doctrinal Development from the Victorians to the Second Vatican Council.* Today I will comment on the necessary link of holiness with doctrinal development evident in the life and writing of Newman. Louis Bouyer has written regarding Newman's spirituality that it is difficult for anyone who has never experienced it to form even a remote idea of what a religious training, founded wholly and solely on a study of the Bible, really is. For a thoughtful and imaginative child it results in a kind of supernatural humanism quite unique in its character ... . The presence of God, everywhere active, all-powerful, reigns over all things, animate and inanimate ... . Let us make no mistake about it, we have here the underlying *stratum* of Newman's spiritual nature, the lasting soil from which its fairest blossoms, its choicest fruits were to spring."[1]

Notably, Newman had this religious experience in the context of home and very loving interpersonal relationships. His parents provided nourishment for his young soul, which set the pattern for each of his major spiritual conversions, as human relationships mediated his relationship with God which was, as Bouyer notes, a divine *presence*, an interpersonal relationship. Between 1816 and 1845, his close personal relationships with Walter Mayers, Richard Whately and Edward Hawkins, his parishioners at St. Clement's Church, Hurrell Froude, and finally Charles Russell all produced major intellectual and religious changes in Newman.

Newman himself espoused a necessary connection between holiness as an affective interpersonal relationship with God and the development of doctrine as its intellectual expression. To explore this connection, I will reference six documents Newman wrote between 1826 and 1845. In an 1826 sermon, Newman stated that the function of one of Christianity's

---

1 JOHN HENRY NEWMAN, *Parochial and Plain Sermons.* "Holiness Necessary for Future Blessedness." (San Francisco: Ignatius Press, 1997), 11.

For private consultation and not distribution without the consent of E Ondrako

primary dogmas, the Incarnation, is to effect our holiness, which consists in attaining the presence of God and the fullness of joy in that presence. Also, it is the presence of the Holy Ghost within us that promotes this relationship. The very first note of holiness, then, lies in its context: the gratuitous, interpersonal encounter with God. Furthermore, "holiness is the result of many patient, repeated efforts after obedience, gradually modifying and changing the heart."[2] Here we find three other notes of holiness: "it is a gradual process which is both affective and moral. Its key traits are self-denial, humility, and pleasure in obedience."[3] In sum, holiness is an inward character developed from doing good works under grace which changes the heart.

Newman's first major book, *The Arians of the Fourth Century*, was completed in 1832, just about a year before he helped found the Oxford Movement for church reform. Here Newman correlated doctrinal orthodoxy and holiness, stating "When the spirit and morals are debased, doctrinal error springs up."[4] Understanding revelation, or the gracious encounter with God, requires holiness. Thus, growth in holiness is necessary for growth in knowledge of God. Likewise, decline in holiness produces error. In an 1835 sermon, he wrote that attaining sound doctrine and right practice is by means of Christocentric, rather than egocentric, contemplation.[5] However, during the height of the Oxford Movement of the 1830's, Newman himself exhibited a self-centered willfulness, as his intellectual development outpaced his spiritual development. It was during this time that, as Aidan Nichols notes, Newman first advanced the concept of development in his *Prophetical Office* of 1837 as a major criterion by which to attack the Roman Church and its corrupt changes in dogma,[6] since he was convinced that development ceased with the end of the patristic era.

In the fall of 1839, however, a major change occurred when a former pupil called his attention to an ecclesiastical image derived from Augustine: "*securus judicat orbis terrarum*, which Newman translated as, "The universal church is in its judgments secure of truth."[7] This was a severe jolt to Newman with permanent consequences. With this image, he

---

[2] Ibid. 5–6.

[3] Ibid. 10.

[4] John Henry Newman, *The Arians of the Fourth Century* (London: Longmans & Green. 1833), 20.

[5] *Parochial and Plain Sermons.* "Self-Contemplation," 336.

[6] AIDAN NICHOLS, *From Newman to Congar: The Idea of Doctrinal Development from the Victorians to the Second Vatican Council.* (Edinburgh: T & T Clark, 1990), 35.

[7] JOHN HENRY NEWMAN, *Essays Critical and Historical* (London: Longmans, Green, & Co., 1895), vol. 2, 101.

recounts that "(T)he theory of the *Via Media* was absolutely pulverized."[8] However, this reminiscence was written in 1865, more than twenty-five years after the fact. In 1839 he was far from reaching this conclusion, which required spiritual and not merely intellectual development. Three documents he wrote between 1842 and 1845 help us to understand that journey and the connection between holiness and doctrine in his theory of development.

The first two have a curious link. In December, 1842, Newman delivered a sermon which is a reflection on the Church's holiness, and it was the very last he wrote before his Oxford University Sermon on the Theory of Developments two months later. Thus, it can be suggested that these two themes, holiness and ecclesiology, were on his mind along with the issue of doctrinal development.

Here Newman notes the scriptural revelation of a gracious relationship: "I will pour my spirit upon thy seed ... and they shall say ... 'I am the Lord's.' " Another repeated note is that the heavenly kingdom is an inward change resulting from moral influence. The heavenly kingdom is moreover a Church, a kingdom of truth and righteousness, and not of this world.

Most important, however, is that one of the major means by which the church gains and keeps power is by sanctity.[9] Unselfish holiness and faith are examples of the "remarkable law of ethics" from which the Gospel kingdom draws its power. "The Church conquers—not by force, but by persuasion." Others "are overcome by the beauty of holiness, and they yield freely," in accord with what the Psalmist has written, "Thy people shall be *willing* in the day of Thy power."[10]

Newman continued some of these themes in his sermon on the theory of developments exactly two months later which investigated "the connection between Faith and Dogmatic Confession ... and to show the office of the Reason in reference to it."[11] Citing Mary as the pattern for the method of investigation, Newman claims that belief must precede reasoning upon the sacred mysteries. This act of trust implies a divine Other, and Newman's analysis of dogma and revelation bears this out: "Theological dogmas are propositions expressive of the judgments which

8   John Henry Newman, *Apologia pro vita sua*, ed. Ian Ker (New York: Penguin Books, 1994), 110, 111.

9   John Henry Newman, "Sanctity, The Token of the Christian Empire," in *Sermons Bearing on Subjects of the Day* (Westminster: Christian Classics, 1968), 243.

10   Ibid. 245, 253.

11   John Henry Newman, *Fifteen Sermons Preached Before the University of Oxford between 1826 and 1845* (Notre Dame: University of Notre Dame Press, 1997), 319.

For private consultation and not distribution without the consent of E Ondrako

the mind forms, or the impressions which it receives, of Revealed Truth."[12] The impressions amount to a "master vision, which unconsciously supplies the mind with spiritual life and peace."[13]

Dogma, then, begins with an aesthetic perception and ends in intellectual reflection upon, and explication of, that vision. But the key is the content of that vision: "the true inward impression of Him, made on the recipient of the revelation."[14] According to Newman, before it is an impression, revelation consists of supernatural facts, actions, beings, and principles. The impression, therefore, is one of a personal encounter, and this relationship is thus the ground of dogma. But the nature of the impression, or of God, presents the problem for development of dogma. "As God is one," Newman writes, "so the impression which he gives us of Himself is one; it is not a thing of parts; it is not a system … . It is the vision of an object."[15]

It is the mystery of the Trinity alone which we know, Newman says, and thus, like Mary, we must begin by believing it in order to understand it. This knowledge of God through revelation, then, is that of a personal being who acts graciously on our behalf. Such knowledge is in essence a gift which requires trust. "All is dreary till we believe what our hearts tell us," Newman writes. Reason must follow where faith leads.

At the close of the sermon, in characterizing revelation as "echoes from our Home," Newman reiterates our opening theme that for him, heaven is something like that time and place wherein Newman himself first experienced love. At home he was led through human love to an understanding of divine love.

But Newman passed through another major stage of development in his own personal holiness journey between this sermon in early 1843 and his essay on the Development of Christian Doctrine almost three years later. He referenced that change in the closing pages of the University Sermon when he linked obedience in faith to submission of the will to God. Newman acknowledged this intellectually but he struggled greatly regarding the will. He has written that intellectually he knew by 1843 that Rome was in fact the true Church, but due to a moral problem of will, he could not yet submit himself to her.

During this period, Catholic devotional literature had come Newman's way as part of the process begun by the Irish cleric Charles Russell, about whom Newman wrote, "He had, perhaps, more to do with my conversion

---

[12] Ibid. 320.

[13] Ibid. 322.

[14] Ibid. 328.

[15] Ibid. 330.

For private consultation and not distribution without the consent of E Ondrako

than anyone else."[16] Through an interpersonal relationship with Russell, Newman's erroneous presuppositions about Roman Catholicism began to change, and he gradually opened to the spirituality of the Roman Church. Just two months after the University Sermon Newman began has first Ignatian retreat at Littlemore, and his diary entries during the Exercises confirm his battle with self-will and egocentrism:

> [M]y motive in all my exertions during the last 10 years has been the pleasure of energizing intellectually ... . How little I have used my gifts in God's service; that I have used them for myself. Hence that Self-love in one shape or another, e.g. vanity, desire of the good opinion of friends, etc, have been my motive; and that possibly it is *the* sovereign sin in my heart ... . [T]aking the ecclesiastical movement of the last ten years as a whole, it has not in any sense been performed (on my part) with a pure intention towards God.[17]

Sprinkled throughout his diary are repeated prayers for the will to submit to God, his personal theme for the next two years. We now reach the Essay on Development, and in the Introduction, Newman references a major insight from one of his primary personal influences, Joseph Butler that "certain relations imply correlative duties, and certain objects demand certain acts and feelings."[18] Thus, Trinitarian relations, at the core of the previous University Sermon, are the ground of human ethics, which establishes clearly that dogma is grounded in the interpersonal relationship of the human and the divine. Newman builds upon Butler's insight in regard to the principle of faith which, while it is an act of the intellect, is ethical in origin. This fact is grounded in Newman's epistemological analysis that affections precede acts of the intellect and as such imply an Object, which established what Newman calls the social principle in Christianity, or the principle of friendship.

Fusing Christian principles with epistemological dynamics, Newman holds that it is grace which makes possible the assent of faith in the Incarnation. These principles function to produce the sanctification of both mind and body, and they conclude in dogma, supernatural truths expressed in language.

Notably, Newman identifies faith as supreme among the principles of Christianity, referencing Aquinas that knowledge of God is through

---

16 *Apologia*, 178.

17 John Henry Newman, *Autobiographical Writings*. ed. Henry Tristram (New York: Sheed and Ward. 1957), 223–226.

18 John Henry Newman, *An Essay on the Development of Christian Doctrine* (Westminster: Christian Classics. 1968), 47.

For private consultation and not distribution without the consent of E Ondrako

faith which is above reason. "The Light of faith makes things seen that are believed."[19] What ends in dogma must necessarily begin in faith.

Newman then takes the argument of the Essay beyond that of the University Sermon when he endorses the principles of authority and infallibility. Following Augustine, Newman notes that "True religion cannot in any manner be rightly embraced ... without some weighty and imperative Authority."[20] He also references Bellarmine: "The Pope with General Council cannot err ... in framing decrees of faith or general precepts of morality."[21] Infallibility for Newman is "the power of deciding whether this, that, and a third, and any number of theological or ethical statements are true."[22]

Furthermore, dogma is a product of theology, which is "the continuous tradition and habit in the Church of a scientific analysis of all revealed truth."[23] Newman writes that "The first step in theology is investigation," patterned on Mary, as he pointed out in the University Sermon, with a "temper" of "loving inquisitiveness." Mary is the example of "a questioning in matters revealed to us compatible with the fullest and most absolute faith."[24] Thus, theology begins in faith.

Finally, Newman makes two important references toward the end of the Essay to the Jesuits and the Spiritual Exercises. He asserts that the Jesuits revived the principle of obedience "through the absolute surrender of judgment and will."[25] Also, the Exercises are an "authoritative exponent of inward communion of church members with God and Christ." The Exercises "set before the soul the beauty of holiness."[26] Thus, this major work on the development of doctrine was grounded clearly in the development of holiness.

I suggest that Newman's progression in holiness between 1843 and 1845 was the key to his conversion and ultimate surrender of will to God through the Roman Church. That this change grounded in faith had a major affect on his theology is substantiated by his own words, applicable not only to himself but to theologians in general. Commenting on Aquinas's prioritization of faith over reason, he states: "It is evident what a

---

19 Ibid. 332.
20 Ibid. 331.
21 Ibid. 87.
22 Ibid. 79.
23 Ibid. 336.
24 Ibid. 337.
25 Ibid. 399.
26 Ibid. 429.

For private consultation and not distribution without the consent of E Ondrako

special influence such doctrine as this exerts upon the theological method of those who hold it."[27]

In conclusion, then, faith mediated through his early home life of interpersonal loving relationships led Newman through a series of personal developments on the path of holiness, and this development grounded his intellectual grasp of the developmental nature of doctrine, a parallel development which, according to Newman, is essential for a truthful grasp of revelation.

In fact, he writes that one note of the heretical spirit is its contempt for the very principle of sanctity and all which that implies regarding the importance of the supremacy of faith over reason, of the surrender of self-will to God's will, and the resultant knowledge and joy of interpersonal relationship with God which is expressed in dogma, including that of authority and infallibility, as the intellectual fruit of personal holiness.

Robert Christie
DeVry University

---

[27] Ibid. 336.

CHAPTER 13

The Story of a Miracle

Deacon Jack Sullivan

My Early Life and Carol

For the greater part of my life as I reflect on it, I was a serious sinner, equal to St. Paul's self appraisal! I attribute this condition to a high degree of self centeredness and self will. I believe this self oriented attitude stemmed from a lack of spiritual development, excessive anxiety, and self destructive decision making resulting from an extremely secular environment and upbringing. I realized subsequently through Carol's influence, my future wife, that self preference lies at the root of all sinfulness and wrong doing! Conversely, an attitude of total self giving prompted by the Holy Spirit serves as the foundation for real happiness and peace. It serves as the measure of holiness simply because it replicates the self sacrificial actions of Christ Himself, as He leads us to the Father. I needed the spiritual strength and freedom of conscience to see reality and to give of myself for the sake of God and of others. Deep down I wanted to improve, to be more purposeful, to be happier, but I didn't know how! That is until I met my future wife, Carol. What initially attracted me to her were not only her good looks, but her sense of goodness and caring for others, especially for me. I'd never met anyone like her! Without question, I understand now that God in his loving providence was preparing and guiding me right from the beginning of our lives together for goals and fulfillment of dreams I never thought possible. We all have instincts for self preservation given to us by the Creator. But I had to realize that a happy man moderates these self-centered inclinations. He comes to understand that the more he gives of himself, the more he will be replenished! Thus, our spiritual maturity is measured by the degree we grow from attitudes of self-preference to those inclining us to greater self-giving, most often resulting from the influences of those close to us. They lead us to a greater understanding of our true priorities and to a greater appreciation of God's intense love for us and for gifts far exceeding those which the world can bestow.

Through Carol's example, I soon became a Church-goer. One Sunday morning, while sitting at the breakfast table in my bathrobe wolfing down

For private consultation and not distribution without the consent of E Ondrako

a bowl of Cherrios, Carol walked in all dressed up with my two year old son, Brian. After asking why they were all dressed up, she replied, "Brian and I are going to Mass, aren't you coming?" Feeling very embarrassed, I immediately got dressed and joined them! We haven't missed Sunday Mass since that eventful morning! Soon I became a Eucharistic minister, then visitor to the sick, and a permanent member of our RCIA group. A few years later, to my utter amazement I even entertained the desire to become a permanent deacon for the Archdiocese of Boston. I seemed to be inclined to dismiss it as farfetched based on my lack of spiritual and personal credentials. But the desire persisted. After looking into the prospect in greater depth and realizing that God somehow might be preparing me for some greater service, I applied for admission to the diaconate formation program. Carol would have to accompany me to most of the classes over a four year period. This was a commitment she couldn't make because she was working full time and we had two children in college and one in high school. They needed her full attention. So I had to scrub the idea of becoming a deacon because I had to agree with her assessment of these priorities. Still I couldn't shake the idea of being ordained a deacon. While I understood the diaconate formation was impossible, still I felt driven by an overwhelming desire to study all phases of theology, the Bible, books on spirituality, and the lives of the Saints for four to five hours every night and for over two years. I never felt a compulsion so strong and soon began to realize that perhaps God in His loving providence was planning something very special for me, but what it was I didn't know! Apparently Carol saw the intensity of my approach to my studies and, on the night before the deadline for refilling my application, she changed her mind. What an example of self sacrifice! She would agree to attend evening classes twice a week for four years when I knew she'd rather be at home and doing other things, simply because it was so important to me! Without realizing it, perhaps she was co-operating with God's providence with much that was still to come!

Obstacles and Challenges

Right from the beginning, my journey into diaconate formation was littered with obstacles and seemingly insurmountable challenges which, I subsequently learned, also characterized the life of John Henry Newman. Obstacles and challenges that would serve to strengthen my resolve, purify my intentions, and serve as the conduit for grace to guide me to greater service. I later learned that Bl. John Henry Newman experienced similar

For private consultation and not distribution without the consent of E Ondrako

patterns of conversion and transformation when challenged by insurmountable obstacles, which seemed to be replicated in the difficulties I experienced later in my process of healing. For example, in the invitation to speak before the 2009 Newman Conference in Pittsburgh sponsored by the National Institute for Newman Studies, Fr. Drew Morgan, C.O. and director, stated: "Your personal testament of the events that have led to Newman's designation as Blessed would be an important addition to this celebration and would offer unparalleled insight into Newman's life and spirit." I learned later that his growth and development, indeed his most important insights resulted from his persevering amidst episodes of pain, afflictions, and frustrations for following what he believed to be God's loving providential will, that "kindly light of truth." So too, if I would seek his intercession, then I would also have to experience the same measure of pain, afflictions, and frustrations which so marked his life!

Finally, when asked for some meaning for all of this, I can certainly identify with Bl. John Henry Cardinal Newman and the beautiful insights expressed in St. Paul's 2 Cor. 12: 9–10: "I willing boast of my weakness, that the power of Christ may rest upon me. Therefore, I am content with weakness, with mistreatment, with distress, with persecutions and difficulties for the sake of Christ; for when I am powerless, it is then that I am strong."

It is an honor to be asked to tell 'the world' what happened to me. I gave the following title to my account: "Please Cardinal Newman – Help Me to Walk!"

My dear friends, we cannot grow and mature in our faith unless we first practice it amidst anguish and sorrows! For none of us living in this world can escape the prospect of trials, sorrows, and afflictions, for they are indeed an essential part of our life's experiences. But if we persevere in faith amidst our sorrows and afflictions, always trusting in God's loving providence for us, then some greater good will always result, some higher purpose will always be achieved.

We see this mystery of redemptive suffering most vividly portrayed in the life of Christ. His life was marked by a life of betrayal, suffering, and death. The true image of the man who brought us forgiveness and redemption was not the God-Man who worked wonders and miracles, but the Man of Sorrows, the Man of the Cross! Indeed, the fulfillment of Christ's messianic mission could only come from the perspective of the Cross. And His Cross truly represents the fulfillment of His intense love for us, surely a fitting emblem of our faith!

For private consultation and not distribution without the consent of E Ondrako

The Mystery of Redemptive Suffering

We also see this mystery of redemptive suffering, faithfully born in the Motherhood of our Church. And our holy and enduring Church lives on and is constantly renewed, in a very special way, by those called by God as servants, to inspire and revitalize Her. One such a person, called for this purpose was Bl. John Henry Cardinal Newman. He seized upon every opportunity to exercise and perfect his faith, always trusting in God's loving providence, especially during times of persistent trials and sorrows.

So many people in Newman's time, indeed, so many of us today would prefer to enter into religious glory, without any cost or pain, without trials or sorrow, and without self denial or self sacrifice! With this in mind, Cardinal Newman once wrote, "True religion has two sides to it, a beautiful side and a severe side. And we all will surely stray from the narrow path that leads to life, if we indulge ourselves in what is beautiful, while casting aside what is severe." Commenting further on this issue, Cardinal Newman once wrote, "Religion is not meant to make an earthly person feel good, or secure in his station in life. On the contrary, true religion is to touch our hearts and souls, to incline us to seek to do the will of God. And it promises to transform us into Christ's own image, but most often at the expense of worldly suffering and poverty."

In Sermon 16 of Newman's "Parochial and Plain Sermons," he assures us that our compassionate Father will always act in our best interest, and for our greater good, especially when our hearts are immersed in sorrows. He says, "The spirits of the just are made perfect though suffering, and are encouraged to follow Christ." With this in mind, Newman wrote his celebrated poem, "Lead me on, kindly light of Truth, amidst the encircling gloom…I ask not to see the distant scene, one step is enough for me." And so Cardinal Newman surrendered his will, to follow that kindly light of truth, but frequently at great cost to himself.

So often our trials and sorrow, indeed as seen as the severe side of religion, which so distress us in their present moment, do, ultimately, have lasting significance for some greater good, or the realization of some higher purpose, surely the beautiful side of religion! In fact, we can't enjoy the beautiful side without first persevering through what is severe! And in our perseverance, we begin to discuss God's Spirit guiding us, prompting us, to follow "His kindly light of truth," along the narrow path He has chosen for each of us.

And so it was with me on June 6, 2000, when I began a rather wondrous and mysterious journey, from pain and suffering to the unfathomable reaches of the communion of saints in heaven—by means of a

For private consultation and not distribution without the consent of E Ondrako

simple prayer! I awoke that morning in excruciating and debilitating pain in both legs. Rushed to a local hospital, the physician in the ER ordered a CAT scan of my back. It revealed a serious succession of lumbar disc and vertebrae deformities protruding inward and literally squeezing the life out of my spinal canal, blocking my spinal cord and femoral nerves, causing severe stenosis in both legs. The doctor advised that I should seek immediate treatment from one of the spinal specialists in Boston, as it appeared likely that all of my lower functions would soon shut down, resulting in permanent paralysis.

The problem was that it would take months to make appropriate appointments with spinal specialists, to schedule surgery, and additional time required for recuperation. And as time went on, I became increasingly gripped by tension and anxiety, because I was also scheduled to begin my third year of studies in the diaconate formation program in Boston on September 5, 2000. You see, I had just completed the second year of a four year formation program, leading to my ordination as a permanent deacon. I loved this beautiful program, and had my heart set on being ordained!

In mid July of 2000, I met with the chief of spinal surgery at one of the major hospitals in Boston. After reviewing the films he stated: "Without question, yours is the worst back I've seen in 17 years of performing spinal surgery!" He warned me that I should forget my plans for diaconate formation because I needed immediate surgery; otherwise, I would likely end up paralyzed! In a myelogram he pointed out that the vertebrae and discs were totally blocking the spinal canal, causing significant bulges above and below the affected area. Because of the very high risk of paralysis, he scheduled my surgery at the same time my classes were to begin!

I returned home after this tragic news, totally distraught and turned on the TV to the EWTN channel for some consolation. The program featured Fr. John McCloskey interviewing an English Newman scholar, Fr. Ian Ker. They spoke of Newman's uniquely difficult life, the crisis in his vocation, as well as the ongoing efforts at his beatification. At the end of the program the viewing audience was asked to report details of any divine favors received after praying to Cardinal Newman, by posting the address of the Birmingham Oratory on the screen. In view of this request, I prayed to Newman with all my heart," Please Cardinal Newman, help me to walk so that I can return to classes and be ordained." I didn't pray for complete healing, as that would be too much to ask—merely to grant me that favor, which at that time was so urgent! that somehow I might return to my classes! Then I went to bed. To my utter amazement, I woke up the following morning virtually pain free! I could walk normally with strength

For private consultation and not distribution without the consent of E Ondrako

in both legs, whereas the day before I was all hunched over in complete agony! Although pain free, still, I was scheduled for surgery in three weeks!

Because of these obviously inconsistent medical realities, I was then directed to Dr. Robert Banco, renowned as one of the foremost spinal surgeons in the U.S. He first examined me, noting my ability to walk upright without pain and with strength in my legs. Then he viewed the MRI and myelogram, noting my physical condition hadn't changed, but I was completely pain free. He was totally mystified, admitting that something totally remarkable was happening! As a result, he stated that he personally wouldn't recommend such delicate surgery without any symptoms such as pain or disfigurement. He suggested that I cancel the surgery and return to my classes and promised he would stay with my case, for "this situation can't possibly last very long!" In fact, it lasted for nine months! Then the pain unexplainably returned in full fury, immediately after my last class in April of 2001! But my prayer to Cardinal Newman was answered! Remarkably, I had just completed my third year!

But now I was faced with the physical rigours of my summer pastoral internship program, three nights a week for the next four months, at one of the largest hospitals in Boston. During these months it was a total agony every time I had to walk, and I had to walk extensively, while visiting patients! So I continued to pray to "My intercessor and faithful friend," whom I knew was still with me, supporting and guiding me throughout these difficult months.

Although Dr. Banco was booked through October, remarkably, he scheduled my surgery for August 9, 2001! The surgery, however, was more difficult than anticipated, as he unfortunately encountered serious complications. My dura mater or protective lining housing the spinal fluids, surrounding the spinal cord was very badly torn. Apparently it had been that way for several months. For days after the surgery I was still suffering incredible pain with no relief in sight. If I were lucky, my recovery would now take, at a minimum, four to six months, definitely preventing me from returning to my classes, scheduled to begin in three weeks! I was completely devastated when it became obvious that now my ordination was no longer possible! Five days after my surgery, I was told I couldn't return to classes, so I felt compelled to get out of my hospital bed, and attempt to walk! But the pain was so agonizing that it took me ten minutes merely to slide to the edge of my bed for support. I was completely helpless and the situation now seemed hopeless! It was again this severe moment that led me to prayer! "Please Cardinal Newman, help me to walk, so I can return to classes and be ordained." By this prayer, heart was certainly speaking to heart!

For private consultation and not distribution without the consent of E Ondrako

The Miracle

Suddenly I felt a tremendous sensation of intense heat all over, and a strong tingling feeling throughout my body, both of which lasted for a long time! I also felt an indescribable sense of joy and peace, as though in the presence of God and a strong sense of confidence and determination that finally, I could walk! When this beautiful occurrence subsided, I realized I was standing upright, and I immediately exclaimed to the nurse, "I have no more pain," whereas minutes before, I was bent over in complete agony! During these precious moments, I was totally captivated, totally transfixed by God's loving presence! I had utterly no will power of my own! Then I realized that now I could walk, when I couldn't for months! I could walk upright! I could walk with strength in my back and legs!

You see my healing became remarkably and unexplainably accelerated in one mysterious moment, rather than four to six months! Totally invigorated, I sprinted out of my room and then up and down all the corridors on my floor and was discharged that day! And to everyone's astonishment, returned to classes on time!

Dr. Banco, in a recent film interview stated:"The spine is usually the size of a quarter, but in Jack's case it was compressed to the circumference of a pea. He should have been paralyzed long before! And after the surgery, it would normally take months for the compressed nerves in his spinal cord to decompress to its normal size, but with excruciating pain and severe headaches. He had none! Recovery from spinal surgery ranges from weeks to months depending on its severity. Jack's condition was the worst I've seen and surgically the most difficult! But, in Jack's case there was no period of recovery whatsoever! You see, his condition was as if he never had a spinal problem or even surgery, for that matter! There is absolutely no medical or scientific explanation for what happened to Jack. It was truly a miracle! In all my years before Jack's surgery or since, I've never seen anything like it!"

One year later, on September 14, 2002, the Feast of the Triumph of the Cross, I was ordained a deacon at the Cathedral of the Holy Cross in Boston. And without knowing the date of my ordination, the Actor for Newman's cause notified me, on that same very day, that the Fathers at the Birmingham Oratory had voted to formally initiate the process for the beatification of their founder, the Venerable John Henry Cardinal Newman, and to take my case to Rome.

Was this notification a providential sign from God that my prayer to Cardinal Newman was miraculously answered or merely another coincidence? I don't know. But what I do know is that it was a beautiful

For private consultation and not distribution without the consent of E Ondrako

sign, affirming not only that my remarkable healing came from God at Cardinal Newman's intercession, but also by persevering in faith through my suffering, some greater good, some higher purpose, might be achieved. That Cardinal Newman would soon be counted as one of the Blessed in Heaven!

Reflection after the Beatification

After the beatification of Cardinal Newman by Pope Benedict XVI on September 19, 2010, Deacon Jack mused further and offered these thoughts. Although there was a light rain and fog hovering over Crofton Park in Birmingham, still 70,000 people were expected to attend this celebration, the likes of which had not been seen in 500 years. As I was walking to the sanctuary area that misty morning, I remember reading on one of the large screens the following message: The United Kingdom and City of Birmingham welcome Deacon Jack Sullivan, his wife Carol, son Brian, his wife Lauren, and their child, the Baby Nora Sullivan. I was overwhelmed and this feeling remained with Carol and me throughout the ceremony. Toward the beginning of the Mass, the Pope proclaimed his decree of beatification and a huge image of Cardinal Newman then appeared on the rear wall of the sanctuary. Carol was also asked to partici-pate in the Mass. At this moment she was given the relic of Bl. Newman and proceeded up the first tier of stairs leading to the Pope's chair. I then joined her from my place sitting with the bishops and cardinals to the side of the altar, and we both then ascended another flight leading to the Vicar of Christ. At that moment Carol said to me, "Jack, I can't talk," to which I responded, "Honey, you don't have to." I thought to myself how captivated we both were by the solemnity of that moment, for which she was largely responsible—although presently incapable of expressing herself. When we knelt before the Pope, Carol handed him Bl. Newman's relic for his blessing without a word. I then said, "Thank you Holy Father for beatifying Cardinal Newman and for coming to England. They surely need you!" I was thinking of the thousand years that the English people were fervently Catholic before the difficulties of Henry VIII, and how the Church had been suffering since. The Pope then said as best I could decipher from his strong German accent: "And the Church thanks you for persevering and making all of this possible." I am certain that the Holy Father was addressing his comments not just to me but to both of us. He was looking at both of us when he made them. After blessing Carol and me, we then withdrew and put the relic on the stand adjacent to the ambo.

For private consultation and not distribution without the consent of E Ondrako

The second most thrilling recollection was proceeding to the Pope and asking for his blessing before proclaiming the Holy Gospel in my office as Deacon. I thought, "He just blessed me!" I was so taken up by the exhilaration of this moment that I nearly forgot to retrieve the lectionary before proceeding to the ambo. I was completely terrified when I ascended it and for the first time really focused upon the faces of 70,000 people standing before me! Now, in my fright and apprehensiveness, would I become as speechless as Carol? My extreme nervousness immediately left me when I suddenly remembered that I had spoken to many English Catholics when touring England with Carol the year before. We started the year of Newman as the guest of Archbishop Nichols, the Archbishop of Westminster. I had many opportunities to speak with many English Catholics and marveled at their devotion and courage in the face of the ever present and obvious religious discrimination as it seemed to me. At that moment, I remembered all of this, and my apprehension immediately left me when I looked out at their faces again! I suddenly drew strength from their courage! And it was their courage which enabled me to "confidently proclaim the words of the Gospel." In my admiration and love for them I proclaimed: "THE LORD," and I paused, "BE WITH YOU!" meaning it with all my heart! I was then dumbfounded when this vast assembly of fervent Catholics responded in kind, "AND ALSO" and then they all paused, "WITH YOU!" I'm told that all who were gathered there were stunned at their response, including the Holy Father. At this moment, was not "Heart speaking to Heart" as it appears in the motto of Bl. Newman's Episcopal shield, "Cor ad Cor Loquitur?"

What I Think this May Mean for the Church and the Modern World

[Deacon Jack mused further about the meaning of his experiences and what it has to do for the Church in the modern world. He asked that this brief reflection might be included as his closing statement. Editor]

I believe that these events wherein I tried to persevere in faith and trust in God's loving providence especially amidst serious pain and suffering, setbacks and challenges was indeed rewarded by the occurrence of some greater good, and realization of some higher purpose. I had just been the recipient of a miracle! Many world renowned physicians attested to the fact that there was utterly no medical or scientific explanation for my healing! And I did not pray to a dead man! Therefore, my healing at Cardinal Newman's intercession convincingly points out the absolute reality of

For private consultation and not distribution without the consent of E Ondrako

this heavenly dimension, and the reality of God's love. So often we can mechanically recite the Nicene Creed without giving much thought to the following, "We believe in the Holy Catholic Church, the Communion of Saints…" More than anything else, these experiences dramatically reveal the utter reality of new life after death, as the Church professes it! God indeed is a reality and a most loving God! Our faith which must be constantly practiced and renewed embraces this truth! It is not a matter of subjective speculation or anyone's opinion! Nor is it a matter of philosophical abstraction! Although unseen, but tangibly experienced, God in His love for us is the ultimate reality! And if we possess Him, we possess all things. I therefore can identify with Simeon's inspired sentiments when reading night prayer: "My own eyes have seen the salvation which You have prepared in the sight of every people. A light to reveal You to the nations, and the glory of my people Israel." Who then should we fear? Why should we be anxious about ourselves? When reflecting on these issues shouldn't we all be brought to conversion, joy and peace, knowing that in our relationship with Almighty God, "Heart does continuously speak to Heart?"[1]

---

[1] On August 25 and 26, 2010, I had the rare privilege of spending time with Jack and his wife Carol as they prepared to travel to England. My superiors graciously consented to my journey to the beatification, a dream I have had ever since I began to study Bl. Newman's life and intuited that he was worthy of beatification and canonization as a role model for our time. On September 19, 2010, at Birmingham, U.K., during a State visit, Pope Benedict XVI beatified John Henry Cardinal Newman and Deacon Jack Sullivan proclaimed the Gospel with power, expression, and emotion, the likes of which I had never heard. The account he has given here was the core of his presentation at the Newman-Scotus Symposium on October 23, 2010 at Washington Theological Union. As he approached the podium, Jack defered to the theologians present. I commented with the words of Fr. Lethel, "the saints are the theologians and only the saints." Jack had the audience spellbound and, in his transparency, one could look into his soul. When he finished, he brought out a locket of Bl. Newman's hair which he had in a reliquary and the audience venerated it with reverence. Jack has lectured to countless groups and is always ready and willing to bring his deeply personal and inspiring account to anyone who cares to listen to the truth that miracles have always been, are now, and will be. Deacon Jack Sullivan delivered this talk: Please Cardinal Newman – Help Me to Walk at the Oratory of St. Philip Neri that Bl. Newman had built in Birmingham, England, on 20 September 2010, the day after Pope Benedict XVI had beatified him.

For private consultation and not distribution without the consent of E Ondrako

CHAPTER 14

Retrieving of Scotus and Newman by Imitating Gerard Manley Hopkins[1]

Edward Ondrako

Introduction. In 1870, Gerard Manley Hopkins thought that John Henry Newman's *Grammar of Assent* was written in an uninviting style. Newman was not under any pressure to write the *Grammar*, as he had been when he wrote the *Apologia*, so Hopkins may have thought: why didn't he write in a more readable manner? In 1872, Hopkins discovered the work of John Duns Scotus at the Bodleian. Within a decade, Hopkins offered to comment on the *Grammar* but Newman declined.[2] Why Newman may have declined the offer of one whom he received into the Church and who taught in his school in Birmingham, albeit for only a year, peeked my interest. The broader questions are: how acquainted with Scotus was Newman? Are there parallel streams of theological thought in their works? The narrower question is: if one understands and imitates Hopkins, might that be a means of retrieval of Scotus and Newman? May such retrieval help to answer the confusion about the radical autonomy of the will in its Kantian form and freedom of the will as taught by Christ, the one teacher of all? Might the imitation of Hopkins lead to the retrieval of the authentic doctrine on the Trinity?

---

[1] An initial foray into this topic of "retrieval" was the focus of my research at the Franciscan International Study Centre, Canterbury, U.K. in 2007 and 2008. On September 6, 2008 my first attempt at a public lecture was "Renewal, Christian Vitality, and Critical Thinking for an Emerging World." Scotus and his relation to Newman and Hopkins was the topic for the University College of Dublin lecture that I gave on December 8, 2008. This is an expanded version which is the fruit of research into the deeper problem of answering the confusion about freedom of the will in the West and its roots in Kantian and Hegelian thought.

[2] A hypothesis of why Newman declined the offer from Hopkins is suggested by Peter D. Fehlner in chapter 7 of this volume.

For private consultation and not distribution without the consent of E Ondrako

There is an implied bridge between two of the Oxford's greatest theological minds, Scotus and Newman, with the burning issue of freedom, will and intellect in the 21st century. The two towering figures whose lives graced Oxford and the British Isles inspired Hopkins's poetry and his precision in metaphysical English and theological thinking that may serve as a 'bridge.' There is a modern deformation in the exercise of freedom of the will and intellect. Their genius is in diagnosing the rationalism constitutive of the modern deformation. Scotus anticipated the deformation. Newman engaged it head on. To diagnose rationalism, one needs the discipline to master the more metaphysical style of Scotus and the implicit notional foundations of Newman's more phenomenological style.

This is true especially when dealing with the most fundamental Christian doctrine of the Trinity which grasps the realism and spirituality of Scotus's somewhat dry and abstract presentation. That is what Hopkins discovered in 1872 at the Bodleian and what Hegel, who was tied to German pietism in a Kantian strain, found in his interpretation of the mystical tradition. Kant had exiled the Trinity. Schleiermacher was a bit more subtle in his exile of the Trinity. Then Hegel came on the scene as the most Trinitarian of Trinitarian thinkers, except that his framework rejects being for becoming. Hegel's thought resembles Augustine on the Trinity, but he reverses it. That means that for Hegel, it is *in* and *through* creation, the fall, redemption, and eschatology that God becomes God. This is the key: God literally becomes in the order of the economy. Scotus and Newman answer that it is being as the criterion of theological truth and not what is coming to be or experienced or mystical.

Therefore, the main ideas are: a) to propose the imitation of the metaphysical English of Hopkins as a bridge between Newman and Scotus, especially their sense of being and becoming; b) to give a purview of 'what metaphysicians ask;'[3] c) to sketch Hopkins's life and formation as a metaphysician; d) to hypothesize freedom as the center of Hopkins's life work, especially freedom of the will in relation to the intellect. The conclusion follows with suggestions where one might continue to do research. Three short appendices are included, one on Franciscan metaphysics, one on "inscape" and "instress" (two of Hopkins's literary tools), and the views of four interpreters of Hopkins.

---

[3] ALLAN B. WOLTER, *The Transcendentals and Their function in the Metaphysics of Duns Scotus* (St. Bonaventure, N.Y.: The Franciscan Institute, 1946, rpt. Kessinger Publishing, 2008. Henceforth, *Transcendentals*.

For private consultation and not distribution without the consent of E Ondrako

Metaphysics and experience are not mutually exclusive.

St. Francis of Assisi and his theologian disciples differ profoundly in their thought about the theology of the cross from Luther and Calvin. The Francsican thesis centers on the radical goodness of God and of creation for its own sake which is guaranteed by the truth of the absolute primacy of Jesus and Mary. Luther and Calvin center their theology, their starting point on the reality of sin. The poetry of Gerard Manley Hopkins's is unintelligible without recognizing Christ and Mary as his theological center. In his poem, *As Kingfishers catch fire* Hopkins writes: "Christ plays in ten thousand placcs. Lovely in limbs, and lovely in eyes not his." In *The Blessed Virgin Mary Compared to the Air We Breathe*, Mary is really "our atmosphere." Moreover, Hopkins links experience and metaphysical thinking with knowledge that is in the service of love. His poetry does this successfully because his understanding of the will is its desire for union with Christ and Our Lady. Hopkins cannot be understood[4] without the Bonaventurian insight that in the journey of the mind to God, the activity of "the mind of the true contemplative, overflooded by the light of heavenly wisdom, is enabled to soar on high. In this passing over, if it is to be perfect, all intellectual activities ought to be relinquished and the most profound affection transported to God, and transformed into Him."[5] Scotus inherited this Bonaventurian tradition and Hopkins picked it up from Scotus.

Hopkins can be a bridge between Newman, Scotus and the modern sensibilities of freedom of the will in the West because of his gifted metaphysical English. Contrary to the views of some, it is arguable that both Newman and Scotus influenced Hopkins from their first encounter to his death. The more one becomes familiar with the thought of Newman and Scotus, the more that influence appears in Hopkins. For example, Hopkins's *Andromeda*, written at Oxford on August 12, 1879, could be an allegory of the Catholic Church attacked for centuries.[6] "Andromeda" is chained to a rock as a sacrifice to a sea monster, "doomed dragon food." She is rescued by Perseus in her seemingly forsaken state. Perseus is Christ, the final victor. In his fifth university sermon, the Anglican Newman recounted the

---

4 HAROLD WEATHERBY, *The Keen Delight* (Athens, Ga.: University of Georgia Press, 1975) , 96–98. Weatherby has many persuasive insights on Scotus, Newman and Hopkins in chapter four. However, he seems to miss the point about knowledge in the service of love, and, in my view, draws the wrong conclusions about Hopkins poetry. He seems to be Thomistic in his conclusions and does not mention Bonaventure who is the inspiration for Scotus.

5 BONAVENTURE, *Itinerarium Mentis in Deum, The Journey of the Mind to God*, chapter 7.1 and 4.

6 CATHERINE PHILLIPS, ed., intro., notes, *Gerard Manley Hopkins: The Major Works* (Oxford University Press, 2002), 363–64. This is the edition I am using throughout the essay.

For private consultation and not distribution without the consent of E Ondrako

struggles for truth and used the powerful image of a peaceful trust in 'slow paced truth.' Hopkins, no doubt, read that sermon and all of Newman's writings. There seems to be a connection. Another example is Newman's *'Biglietto,'* or acceptance speech when named a Cardinal by Pope Leo XIII. Given on May 12, 1879, it is a *tour de force* criticizing liberalism in religion meaning there is no positive truth in religion and that one creed is as good as another, the great *apostosia* of the day. Hopkins's *Andromeda* was written at Oxford four months after Cardinal Newman's *'Biglietto* Speech.'

Hopkins is not a subjectivist or modern idealist because he is intuitively aware that being is not becoming, that metaphysics and experience are not mutually opposed. Thomas Aquinas, Bonaventure and Scotus are consistent in their response to being, 'what is,' and becoming, 'what is coming to be.' Being is first. In 1216, upon this philosophical certainty, the Fourth Lateran Council condemned the works of Joachim of Fiore who taught that mystical experience is first. Joachim put 'what is coming to be,' first, or 'becoming,' first. Since, the young Fr. Joseph Ratzinger worked on St. Bonaventure's response to the thought of Joachim and it is no surprise that as Pope Benedict XVI, his concern, along with the other post-Vatican II Popes, is that future novelty not be the criterion of theological truth and vitality. Being, 'what is,' and not 'what is coming to be or experienced,' is the basis for a genuine hermeneutic of reform and adaptation in continuity with tradition.

Pope Benedict reflects the metaphysical understanding of being of Thomas, Bonaventure and Scotus. He recognizes what they did for the progress of doctrine in the Church and human science. Another way to say this is that metaphysics and experience are not mutually exclusive opposites. In *Laetare Colonia Urbs*, October 28, 2008, he said

> Combining piety with scientific research in accordance with his invocation: "May the First principle of things grant me to believe, to understand, and to reveal what may please his Majesty and may raise our minds to contemplate him" [7]—his refined brilliance penetrated the secrets of natural and revealed truths so deeply that he discovered a doctrine within them, earning him the titles of *Doctor Ordinis, Doctor Subtilis*, and *Doctor Marianus*, becoming a teacher and guide of the Franciscan School, and a light and example to the entire Christian people.

---

[7] BENEDICT XVI, *Laetere Colonia Urbs, Apostolic Letter on the Seventh Centenary of the Death of Bl. John Duns Scotus*, 28 October, 2008, Vatican. The quote in parenthesis is from the beginning of Scotus' *Tractatus De Primo Rerum Principio*, his proof for the existence of God. Henceforth, *De Primo Principio*.

For private consultation and not distribution without the consent of E Ondrako

Equally important as Scotus in the opening words for proving the existence of God that Pope Benedict quotes, is Newman's method for proving the existence of God from conscience. In brief, Newman's method prefers to take a view based on evidence, antecedent probability, and the cumulation of, or convergence of probabilities. That is not a metaphysical view strictly speaking, but, as in one's ordinary thinking, it reflects phenomenological and metaphysical elements. Evidence, for example, comes from Hopkins's journals and letters that clarify the intentions of his poems. It is an antecedent probability that from the time of his discovery of Scotus, a Scotistic sense runs deep within his poetry and writings. Another antecedent probability is that his correspondence and conversations with Newman shape Hopkins's thinking, without harming his individuality.[8] There is ample historical evidence of Newman's influence in their correspondence alone and a convergence or cumulation of probabilities to support the hypothesis of lifelong influence on Hopkins by both Newman and Scotus. Newman uses the image of many single wires wound together which make a strong cable as evidence.

Newman is not a scholastic metaphysician, but has metaphysical thought in his works as he answers the critical question of interiorization. The metaphysician[9] asks: 'why does being exist?' The late Scotist, Allan B. Wolter, wrote that Scotus's theory of the transcendentals is his metaphysics and his metaphysics are saturated with theological implications. Wolter's genial summary can help us to x-ray, so to speak, the Scotistic metaphysics in Hopkins's poetry. To the extent that we become familiar with the tools Scotus uses, to that extent we can put our finger on the pulse of what is happening in Hopkins's poetry, an intellectual effort with its own reward.

These Scotistic tools include the univocal notion of being, which a Scotistic metaphysician uses to analyze contingency, its limitation, its multiplicity, composition and more. He does this with the so called disjunctive transcendentals that are correlatives such as prior-posterior, cause-caused, and those which are contradictorily opposed such as infinite and finite. He is able to find a new knowledge of the more perfect member of each disjunction. "In those disjunctions contradictorily opposed, such as infinite and finite," namely God as infinite and we as finite, "the existence of the imperfect member," the finite, "implies the existence of the more perfect member but not vice versa." In other words, because God exists does not imply that we must exist. "With the correlatives such as cause-

---

[8] Weatherby, 74, takes a different view, that Hopkins suffered limitations due to Newman's influence, a view I find hard to substantiate.

[9] See Appendix A. This summary is based on Wolter, *Transcendentals*.

For private consultation and not distribution without the consent of E Ondrako

caused the existence of either member implies the other."[10] One may speak of parents who cooperate with God in begetting their children, which is the point of condetermination in the 17th century Scotists.[11] With Wolter the conclusion is: "In this sense, metaphysics is a truly existential science, and the theory of the transcendentals a genuine *theoria*—a contemplation of God."[12] It seems that Hopkins not only intuited these metaphysical tools but put them into practice in his contemplation of God and in his poetry.

Gerard Manley Hopkins was born on July 28, 1844 at Stratford, Essex, the first of eight children. His father was a marine adjustor and Ambassador for Hawaii in London. Gerard won prizes for his academic skills, including one for poetry and the Governor's Medal for Latin Verse. In 1863, he entered Balliol, Oxford. In 1866, he felt drawn to the Roman Church and, with no little trepidation, sought spiritual direction from Fr. John Henry Newman at Birmingham. His respect for Newman's reputation as a public ecclesiastical intellectual made him apprehensive. Sadly, by crossing the Tiber, he became estranged from his family. He stayed with Newman and the following year, 1867, accepted a teaching position in Newman's school for one term. In May 1868, he entered the Jesuit novitiate, and continued a lifelong correspondence with Newman. In July 1872 he made a fortuitous discovery of Scotus at the Bodleian. In 1877, he was ordained a priest, ministered in London, Oxford, Bedford Leigh, and Liverpool. In 1881 he began his tertianship at Roehampton and in 1882, moved to Stoneyhurst College to teach classics. In 1883, he wrote *The Blessed Virgin Compared to the Air We Breathe* that links him solidly with the Franciscan tradition. In 1884, he moved to Dublin as Fellow in Classics and Professor of Greek at Newman's School on St. Stephen's Green. In a letter to Newman he criticized the Irish. "If I were Irish," Newman replied, "I too would, at heart, be a rebel." In 1888, he wrote *That Nature is a Heracletian Fire and of the Comfort of the Resurrection*, a beautiful summary of Ignatian spirituality, Scotus, Newman and patristic thought. He wrote: "Man, how fast his firedint, his mark on mind is gone! Both are in an unfathomable, all is in an enormous dark Drowned." That darkness changes in a flash to make man an "immortal diamond."[13] On June 8, 1889, Fr. Hopkins died from typhoid and is buried in Dublin.

---

10 WOLTER, *Transcendentals*. 183–84.

11 See condetermination in chapter 2 and 7 in this volume.

12 WOLTER, *Transcendentals*, 183–184.

13 Several of my Jesuit teachers have pointed out that St. Ignatius was influenced by St. Bonaventure's writings.

For private consultation and not distribution without the consent of E Ondrako

If one looks back to 1870, when Hopkins began his philosophy formation as a Jesuit, his journals reveal his classical education at Oxford and contemplative mind and heart. "I do not think I have seen anything more beautiful than the bluebell I have been looking at. I know the beauty of the Lord by it."[14] He anticipated a very rich theme in contemporary theology, the beauty of the Lord.[15] On July 13, 1872, at the Bodleian Library, Hopkins found Scotus's *Opus Oxoniensis*, his *Ordinatio*, or *Commentary on the Sentences of Peter Lombard*. His journal entry[16] for August 3, 1872 shows the sustained excitement of discovery: "just when I took in any inscape of sky or sea I thought of Scotus." From that time, Hopkins breathed the air that Scotus breathed.

Scotus was not a new type of Franciscan. Rather his thought was in continuity with St. Francis of Assisi, who referred to himself as *simplex et idiota*, meaning without formal education in theology, but gave an original title for Mary in his "Salute to the Blessed Virgin," *Virgo ecclesia facta*, Virgin made Church. Reflecting on this experience of Mary by Francis of Assisi, Scotus "so accurately gave classic theological formulation into a Franciscan thesis, namely, the absolute predestination of Jesus and Mary for whom the entire universe was created and then redeemed."[17]

Moreover, Scotus abandons some of Bonaventure's terminology such as illumination and exemplarism, but his thought is even subtler and more correct. He knew Bonaventure's sermon, *Christus unus omnium magister,* 'Christ the one teacher of all,' as a veritable synthesis of the theologian son of Francis. Moreover, Bonaventure and Scotus's metaphysics is Marian, a help to the study of the light and understanding of what is above immediate experiences and beyond the experiences.[18] Understanding Francis, Bonaventure and Scotus is part of the reform and renewal of Franciscan theology today, which, at its root is re-discovering the inexpressible love of St. Francis for Christ and Mary.

---

14 HOPKINS, *Journal*, 221.

15 See HANS URS VON BALTHASAR, *Herrlicheit, The Glory of the Lord*, 1986, 7 vols. Balthasar has entries on Bonaventure, Scotus and Hopkins. Henceforth, BALTHASAR, *Herrlicheit*.

16 BALTHASAR, *Herrlicheit*.

17 RUGGERO ROSINI, *Mariology of Blessed John Duns Scotus* ed. and trans. Friars of the Immaculate (New Bedford, MA: Academy of the Immaculate, 2008), xv.

18 Bonaventure's theology begins where philosophy leaves off and constructs a ladder, so to speak, from earth to heaven. Scotus, as recognized by his contemporaries, was the subtle friar in continuity with that original Franciscan tradition. He completes and crowns the synthesis of Thomas Aquinas and Bonaventure. Scotus is the last teacher in the *via antiqua*, as, another Franciscan, William of Ockham is the first professor in the *via moderna*. There is a very significant difference. Ockham is a metaphysician-logician, while Scotus is a metaphysician-theologian.

For private consultation and not distribution without the consent of E Ondrako

Sometimes Scotus's famous axiom, "*potuit*, it is possible, *decuit*, it is fitting, *ergo fecit*, therefore, it is," as an axiom, is viewed as deducing certainty about something that is contingent from plausibility. However, the axiom reflects the broad view of theology of Bonaventure, for whom proper or scholarly theology is undertaken in order to be more virtuous, to be holy. Academic theologians assist the Magisterium in clarifying the intelligibility of any mystery. Scotus contributed the subtle reasoning for the intelligibility of the Immaculate Conception, the *potuit* in his argument. The example of St. Francis gave the *decuit*, the fittingness, which is the basis for incorporation of any idea into the Church's teachings. Scotus's metaphysics forms the substratum of his theology of love.

Contemporary Scotists, such as Olivier Boulnois, hold the independence of and interdependence of Scotus's metaphysics and theology.[19] The relationship to Newman is succinctly described: "the method of the *decuit*, a version of the illative sense of Newman, holds precedence over the notional involved in the theological method based primarily on the *decuit*."[20] What I understand this to be saying about making a judgment is that the more important meaning is fittingness, while the lesser important is the possibility. In this context, Newman's illative sense is a version of the higher level of judgment, which has both real and notional parts. Newman's real assent is a version of fittingness, *decuit*. Newman's notional assent is a version of possibility, *potuit*. No one lays down his or her life for a notion, however noble. Real assent comes from mind and heart. That is why a person can say, I believe. Notional assent is in one's mind as facts. These ideas will be explained as the independence and interdependence of metaphysics and theology takes on further clarity according to Boulnois.

The affinity of the more metaphysical method of Scotus to the more empirical and phenomenological method of Newman is visible in comparing Scotus's thought on the preservative redemption of Mary and the development of thought about her joint predestination with her Son, which is central in Franciscan theology. He humbly submitted his thought about the Immaculate Conception to the proper Church authority for its doctrinal definition. Newman, who knew almost nothing about Mary in his early life, gradually developed his understanding of Mary with the help of Hurrell Froude. His understanding of Mary demonstrates the steps from notional apprehension and assent to real apprehension and assent. They are inseparable, even if the notional may be more prominent or quantitative. In 1845, Newman resolved his personal questions about the

---

[19] OLIVIER BOULNOIS, *Duns Scot, La rigueur de la charité* (Paris: Les Éditions du Cerf, 1998), 149.

[20] PETER FEHLNER, "Sources of Scotus' Mariology in Tradition," *Mariologia Franciscana* III (New Bedford, MA: Academy of the Immaculate, 2009), vol. 3 in a series. See chapter 4 in this volume.

Roman Church with prayer and by formulating seven notes on the development of doctrine. Mary was already the pattern of his faith by 1843 and that growth continued so that he had no difficulty in accepting the solemn definition of the Immaculate Conception in 1854. At this time, one can see that Newman is very close to the thought of Scotus in his response to Protestant objections to his" Memorandum on the Immaculate Conception."[21] Newman explains doctrinal development as God, in his own time, enabling doctrines that are implicit to be made explicit. That is what Scotus held, a view fully in accord with being and not becoming.

There is no question that Newman held Scotus's primary motive for the Incarnation by December 1849, but it is a timely and useful topic for study to find Thomistic and Scotistic traces in Newman's works. Roderick Strange[22] holds that by 1835 Newman had a Thomist position. Cyril O'Regan holds a different view, that Newman gives a nod to Thomas in 1864. Peter Damian Fehlner holds that traces of Newman's sympathy for Scotus's teaching that even if Adam had not sinned, the Word would have become incarnate, is in Newman's *Lectures on the Doctrine of Justification* written in 1836. One can find the significant reference in Appendix one, where Newman refers to the Conventual Scotist, Cornelius Musso, who was present at the Council of Trent. In addition to this discovery, Fehlner notes that after studying Athanasius, by the early 1840's, Newman adopted the Scotist position and that is referred to in *Select Treatises of Athanasius* and *The Arians of the Fourth Century*.[23] This is a point where he agrees with Strange.[24] In 1849, Newman introduced Scotism into two of his Discourses to Mixed Congregations: "The Mystery of Divine Condescension"[25] and "The Infinitude of the Divine Attributes."[26] In a Letter to Frederick Faber, in 1849, his fellow Oratorian, Newman takes the Scotist view on the Incarnation.[27] Faber helped Newman to correct an apparent inconsistency that made it appear that in Newman's view, sin was

---

21 JOHN HENRY NEWMAN, "Memorandum on the Immaculate Conception" in *Meditations and Devotions*, (London, uniform edition, 1903), 79–86.

22 RODERICK STRANGE, *Newman and the Gospel of Christ*, (Oxford University Press, 1981), 110–115.

23 PETER DAMIAN FEHLNER, "Scotus and Newman in Dialogue," chapter 7 in this volume.

24 STRANGE, 111f.

25 JOHN HENRY NEWMAN, *Discourses to Mixed Congregations*, (London: uniform edition), 317.

26 NEWMAN, 309.

27 Newman wrote: "But as I understand the Scotist view it simply is, that he would have been incarnate, even had man not sinned—but when man sinned it was for our redemption; in matter of fact the end was to make satisfaction." *Newman, Letters and Diaries*, XIII (December 9, 1849), 335.

For private consultation and not distribution without the consent of E Ondrako

the cause of the Incarnation, in which case, one would refer to the relative primacy of Christ and not with Scotus as the absolute primacy of Christ.

In 1845, Newman resolved the question of how true developments can take place without letting private judgment or mystical experience, in any form, compromise truth. As it was for Scotus, the dogmatic principle was indispensible for Newman's seven comprehensive and creative notes on the development of doctrine.[28] The importance of his University Sermon on "The Theory of the Development of Doctrine," in 1843, Newman referred to Mary as the "pattern of faith," the key to understanding his answer about true and false development of doctrine. His seven notes on development link to his life long quest for certitude in the *Grammar of Assent*. Together, they offer a compelling theory for his *Apologia Pro Vita Sua*, the progressive illumination in his life. One enters into self with a sustained, humble search and arrives at free and firm assent to one's vocation in life and the mysteries of Christianity as Hopkins did.[29]

Hopkins took issue with the positivism, psychologism, and materialism of the time, a sign of his perceptive intellect and spirituality, especially his ecstatic love for Christ and Mary. Hans Urs Von Balthasar saw an advanced level of metaphysical thought in Hopkins already at the time of his conversion.[30] Hopkins wanted his poems to be experienced and heard by the spoken word, but never let any experience, however noble, overshadow being, 'what is,' in favor of 'what is coming to be.' Hopkins conveyed harmony and balance in his poetry. He rejected any self-contradiction, the principle both Scotus and Newman guarded against assiduously. In "The May Magnificat," May, 1878, Hopkins wrote:

> This ecstasy all through mothering earth
> Tells Mary her mirth till Christ's birth
> To remember and exultation
> In God who was her salvation.

---

[28] There may not be many citations other than the pivotal motive of the Incarnation, that prove that Newman was influenced by the writings of Scotus, but his epistemology of faith and theological activity in the *Essay on Development* and especially in the *Grammar of Assent* have close affinities to Bonaventure and Scotus. HAROLD WEATHERBY, *The Keen Delight*, 77–78. See chapter four for the further context.

[29] Scotus's idea of theology is not speculative but primarily practical. Practical is non-scientific, only in the sense, that knowledge does not lead towards doubt or skepticism but knowledge guides the will towards the free choice for sanctity, to be holy. See FEHLNER, Chapter 4 in this volume.

[30] BALTHASAR, *The Glory of the Lord*, vol. 3, 363.

For private consultation and not distribution without the consent of E Ondrako

Hopkins's achievement[31] is to demonstrate convincingly that being is prior to becoming. Truth comes from understanding the experience of people's real lives, from youth to old age, from religious, married, single, poet, scientist, or ploughman. Their experiences contribute to their becoming who they are in the eyes of God but being is first. All are made first to the image of God, to know, love and give glory to God. What we become is through free cooperation with God's graces.

Hopkins learned from Newman the meaning of certitude in religious matters, to respect the development of an idea and to be patient with truth for it comes out of shadows and images.[32]

> But whatever be the risk of corruption from intercourse with the world around, such a risk must be encountered if a great idea is duly to be understood, and much more if it is to be fully exhibited. It is elicited and expanded by trial, and battles into perfection and supremacy. In time … points of controversy alter their bearing; parties rise and around it; dangers and hopes appear in new relations; and old principles reappear under new forms. It changes with them in order to remain the same. In a higher world it is otherwise, but here below to live is to change, and to be perfect is to have changed often.[33]

Hopkins learned from Scotus:

> O God, you are supreme among beings, the only one of them who is infinite. Communicating the rays of your goodness most liberally, you are boundless good to whom as the most lovable thing of all every single being in its own way comes back to you as to its ultimate end.[34]

Even during his so called dark period, Hopkins never lost sight of the most lovable being as in his poem: *Patience, hard Thing.*

---

31 Alex Mizener observed that "ecstasy of interest" is every where in his poems, and worth examining carefully because his achievement is rare and especially rare in the late 19th century. To Mizener, Hopkins's great achievement was to see "the heart of reality as an acute sense of movement." Hopkins had "the kind of concentration and intensity which resulted from the combination of the exactitude of image with the precision of his thought and structure." ALEX MIZENER, *Gerard Manley Hopkins: A Critical Symposium*, original publication in (*The Kenyon Review*, 1944), rpt. as "Victorian Hopkins," (London, Burns and Oates, 1975), 118–122.

32 *Ex umbris et imaginibus in veritatem*, "out of the shadows and images to the Truth," is the epitaph which Newman chose for his tombstone.

33 NEWMAN, *Essay on the Development of Doctrine* (London: Longmans, Green, and Co., 1900), 39–40.

34 SCOTUS, *De Primo Principio*, 4.4.

For private consultation and not distribution without the consent of E Ondrako

We hear our hearts grate on themselves: it kills
To bruise them dearer. Yet the rebellious wills
Of us we do bid God bend to him even so.
And where is he who more and more distills
Delicious kindness?—He is patient. Patience fills
His crisp combs, and that comes those ways we know.[35]

If one compares Scotus and Newman on certitude, it warrants repetition that Scotus is not making the effort of deducing certainty about the contingent from mere plausibility. Rather, his is a subtle and original epistemology of faith, and theological thinking leading to certitude that comes from humble contemplation of truth. Some may dismiss this as 'unscientific,' in the sense that prayer accompanies one's search for truth vs. sole reliance on an empirical method. Nonetheless, Scotus's ideas are found in the official teachings of the Church.[36]

Newman's empirical method is unique, unlike any other nineteenth century empiricism. He argued the difference between certainty and certitude in the *Grammar of Assent*. Certainty requires logical proof. One may chose not to act because of the lack of certainty and potential to do harm, such as taking the wrong medicine. Certitude, however, deals with beliefs that are not logically demonstrable but require reasonable arguments. It is curious that in 1871, shortly after the *Grammar* was published, Hopkins criticized its style, but about a decade later, in 1883, he changed his mind. The change came after he discovered Scotus in 1872 and had a decade to deepen this Scotistic thought. Might Hopkins have wanted to write a commentary on the *Grammar of Assent* from a Scotistic perspective? It seems plausible. Might Newman have declined because of a concern that his intentions in the *Grammar* might be misunderstood? It is plausible because the *Grammar* has a tone of an apologetic text for Catholics and a retrospective for Protestants. Might Newman have worried that because he was not trained in scholastic metaphysics and was insisting on the personal nature of knowledge, the climate was not right in 1883 for such a commentary? It seems plausible that Newman wanted his thinking in the *Grammar* to be taken at face value. By 1883, Hopkins would have had ample time to integrate affinities between Newman and Scotus. Newman's unique realist-empirical method has a phenomenological and metaphysical dimension. Scotus was a scholastic metaphysician who inspired Newman to say that he was the greatest theological

---

[35] Catherine Phillips, *Gerard Manley Hopkins*, 170.

[36] *Ineffabilis Deus*, 1854, Pius IX; *Munificentissimus Deus*, 1950 Pius XII; Vatican II, *Lumen Gentium* 61; and *Redemptoris Mater* 8, of John Paul II, 1987.

For private consultation and not distribution without the consent of E Ondrako

luminary Oxford produced. Their epistemology of faith and theological thinking about the hierarchy of truths has much in common and brings them together on significant theological points. All of this augurs well to posit that Newman looked to Scotus as the one who inspired him the most by the time he was composing *The Idea of a University*, 1854–57 and, therefore, that much more by 1883.

In chapter nine of the *Grammar*, Newman explained the "illative sense"[37] as experiential and personal, a cultivated instinct that enables the mind to discover certitude in a mass of probabilities, to converge probabilities into a view, and to reach first principles. The instinct discerns data and ponders conclusions to accept and to reject. Newman is close to Bonaventure's idea of *dijudicatio*, a higher judgment of the mind and Scotus's theory of disjunctive transcendentals, which is an even more detailed account of the essence of a higher judgment of mind. In the concrete sense of apprehension, the operation of this higher judgment enables the person to see something that transcends the concrete, to find its timeless and abstract content, and from this, to be able to form an idea.

For Newman it is the proper use of the illative sense that brings certitude. He knew that if another person has a similar experience to one's own, that person may be more easily convinced by one's judgment. If logic fails, and certainty cannot be reached, an appeal to experience may be unable to convince another without a similar experience. Moreover, with many more being trained in scientific methods in his day, Newman knew that reliance solely on a scientific way of thinking might make it difficult for a person to acknowledge the certitude of the illative sense, which helps in making a judgment. That reality of scientific thinking is compounded today by a perceived conflict between science and religion. Perception is not knowledge. Perception is perception, a prejudgment or prejudice, which everyone has until it becomes knowledge. Newman rehabilitates perception in the *Grammar* so that it may lead to assent.

Newman's insights into the process of the illative sense includes being alert to the reasons one gives for the decisions of the illative sense, which may or may not persuade others. Certitude is not a passive impression on the mind from without, but an active recognition of a proposition as true for which one bears responsibility. Certitude has a sanction. There is no ultimate test of truth beyond the trustworthiness of the illative

---

37 I owe John Ford, historical theologian at the Catholic University of America a debt of gratitude for elucidating Newman's argument. Many have found the apparent dryness which Hopkins first encountered to give way to an exhilarating freshness. Bernard Lonergan commented that he found his scholastic studies dry then discovered and re-read Newman's *Grammar of Assent* five times. Reflection on experience today rightly occupies center stage. Newman brings the clarity of truth to human experience and religious decision making.

For private consultation and not distribution without the consent of E Ondrako

sense. When there is a temptation to misread Newman as unscientific, in the sense that his search for truth is 'on his knees in prayer,' one has to remember that Newman taught that the illative sense determines what science cannot determine, the limit of converging probabilities and the reasons sufficient for proof. Two persons may differ in interpreting the same facts because each person has one's own critical feeling, antecedent arguments or antecedent reasoning. Facts cannot be proved by presumptions. If one begins with universal doubt, as some philosophers, and the other partner in dialogue begins with faith seeking understanding, the point Newman is making is that there is no ultimate test of truth beyond the trustworthiness of the illative sense, but he had he integrity to admit that mistakes are possible when judgments are made about other people and events. Reality demands that one make judgments without seeing into the heart of another. Important decisions affecting the life of another person, judging innocence or guilt, and vocational decisions take time. The illative sense works at different speeds. In decisions about the past, historical interpretation, the pressing needs of the present as well as the future, prudential decisions must be made but they are subject to mistakes.

Assent that remains merely notional is very different from real assent. In chapter ten of the *Grammar*, Newman revisited inference and assent in religious matters. In the exact sciences, one is justified in withholding assent when one cannot strictly demonstrate a conclusion. An educated logical demonstration is expected. Christianity has doctrines, mysteries, a history with many judgments, personal experiences, much of which is expressed in symbol, not reducible to logical or natural inference. That is why a Catholic whose faith remains solely as notional assent will hardly have what it takes to imitate the saints and martyrs.[38] To accept Christianity, according to Newman, with a real assent involves the illative sense, but not the illative sense alone. It is the judgment of the illative sense in humble contemplation of unchanging revelation and dogma. However, the illative sense is not decisive in the attainment of real assent. Assent needs the *pietas fidei*, affective certitude, which is not the same as intellectual certitude. In the spirit of Scotus, Newman knew the balance between affective and intellectual certitude. Genuine piety is the key to the real assent of faith.

---

[38] *Grammar of Assent*, 353–54.

For private consultation and not distribution without the consent of E Ondrako

From Scotus's metaphysics to the metaphysical English in Hopkins's poetry.

At Oxford, Hopkins would have learned the British version of philosophy and classical philosophy when he began to study philosophy as a Jesuit. In 1874 his theological formation began at St. Beuno's and the combined Oxford and Jesuit foundation helps to explain the development of his evocative and precise metaphysical English, his theology, and poetry. Hopkins's metaphysical English is the key to the most profound meaning in his poetry.

In 1872, Hopkins discovered the Commentary on the *Sentences* of Peter Lombard, which is Scotus's *Ordinatio*. Scotus's metaphysical theology depends on Bonaventure who knew the disjunctive attributes of being. Scotus substitutes terminology of Bonaventure such as 'illumination' and 'exemplarism' with terms that may seem dry and less personal. That could be why some scholars posit a break between Bonaventure and Scotus. That is too facile a conclusion because, upon closer study, Scotus did not make any substantial change of position on the nature of philosophy and theology from Bonaventure. Rather, Scotus's terminology such as the univocity of the concept of being, the formulation of the cautious law of disjunction[39] (the disjunctive transcendentals), formal distinction *a parte rei*,[40] are, arguably, more correct. They enable a more rigorous analysis of the relation of metaphysics and experience centered on charity,[41] which is the foremost point in Hopkins's poetry.

Scotus's formulation of the cautious law of disjunctive transcendentals means that reasoning takes time to sort the disjunctions of finite and infinite, prior-posterior, independent-dependent.[42] There are many more. This is important because the differential notions of finite and infinite, which are used constantly by Hopkins, refer to the quantity rather than kind or quality of perfection. Quantity answers "how much?" Quality

---

[39] WOLTER, *Transcendentals*, has a concise explanation of Scotus's law of the disjunctive transcendentals, 137–38.

[40] Formal distinction *a parte rei* to Scotus seemed necessary to posit in being and its attributes. It is not a mere distinction made only in the mind. Each formality has its own proper entity or quiddity. For example, sensitivity cannot be separated from the rational soul. The intellect cannot be separated from the will. See WOLTER, *Transcendentals*, 22–24.

[41] PETER DAMIAN FEHLNER, "Neopatripassionism from a Scotistic Viewpoint," in *Quaderni di Studi Scotisti* (Frigento: Casa Mariana Editrice, 2006), n. 3, 40–41. This is a rare find by contemporary standards. Fehlner explains why it matters that being and not becoming is the criterion for reflecting on the truth. See BOULNOIS, *La Rigeur de la Charité*, 1998.

[42] *Finiens-finitum*, actual-potential, simple-composed, one-many, cause-caused, effecting-effect, exceeding-exceeded, substance-accident, same-diverse, equal-unequal. *Finiens*, finishing, *finitum* means being that is the object which is finalized, that is, which exists for the sake of another.

For private consultation and not distribution without the consent of E Ondrako

answers "what kind of being?"[43] *God's Grandeur* answers: what kind of being? "The world is charged with the grandeur of God." How much? "It will flame out like shining from shook foil; it gathers to a greatness, like the ooze of oil Crushed."[44]

After discovering Scotus in 1872, Hopkins learned that the disjunctive transcendentals may be used, as a cook learns how to use spices. In his sonnet, *Duns Scotus Oxford*, Hopkins recognized the one

> who of all men most sways my spirits to peace;
> Of realty the rarest veined unraveller; a not
> Rivaled insight, be rival Italy or Greece;
> Who fired France for Mary without spot.[45]

In March, 1300, Scotus, as Oxford bachelor, had the first opportunity to defend his thought on Mary. He engaged in the *questiones disputatae*, which were public debates open to everyone, to present his view in favor of the possibility of the Immaculate Conception. It would take until 1854 for his view to become incorporated into the official doctrine of the Church on Mary's Immaculate Conception, *Ineffabilis Deus*, written by Pope Pius IX. The process is the gradual explicitation of what is implicit in the Church's teaching according to God's time table.

The metaphysical substratum is the first key in Hopkins's theological reasoning, the fruit of humble contemplation of the Creator and Redeemer. The second key to understanding Hopkins is his reasoning about what Scotus said on freedom in relation to the will and intellect. Hopkins understood that he was created to praise, reverence and serve God and, by doing so, to save his soul. Hopkins coined the triple phrase 'freedom of pitch, freedom of play, and freedom of field.' Freedom of pitch is precisely that one can and must achieve 'self determination.' Freedom of play is that area of maneuver that nature grants it. Freedom of field is the logical range of objects from which to choose.[46] His words about self-determination, space to discover oneself, and logical clarity in life's decision making have a Kantian and contemporary ring, but there is one point that makes Hopkins very different from Kant on the meaning of freedom. For Hopkins this is not any freedom, or Kantian radical personal autonomy, but Scotistic freedom that tackles the toughest questions such as: Does God exist? Why was I created? Why be good? Scotus's proof for

---

43 Wolter, *Transcendentals*, 153.

44 Hopkins, *God's Grandeur*, 1877, 128.

45 Hopkins, *Duns Scotus' Oxford*, 1879, 142.

46 Christopher Devlin, ed., *The Sermons and Devotional Writings of Gerard Manley Hopkins*, (London: Oxford University Press, 1959), chapter 3. See the appendix on Scotus and Hopkins.

For private consultation and not distribution without the consent of E Ondrako

the existence of God in *De Primo Rerum Principio* starts with reflection on one's finite being (one's self) gifted with intellect and will.[47]

Hopkins's ideas about freedom are concise in his retreat notes on December 30, 1881. "It is the holiest that shows his freedom the most, the wickedest that is most the slave of sin and carried with the motion of the flesh and of the World wielder."[48] This ponderous note gives an insight into the poet's constant reflection on the human condition, personality, grace and free will which imbue his poetry. They radiate Scotus's thought on the motive of the Incarnation. Hopkins refused to accept that only the death of a God-Man could satisfy an offended God. He refused to accept that the Son assumed created nature contingent upon the sins of angels or men. The Fall was not the reason for Christ's predestination to glory. Even if no angel had fallen, nor any man, Christ would still have been predestined—yes, even if no others were to have been created save only Christ. He found the freedom of accepting this Scotistic view and wrote: "The worlds of angels and of men were created as fields for Christ in which to exercise his adoration of the father, fields for him to sow and work and harvest."[49]

A shipwreck in 1875 moved him very deeply to write *The Wreck of the Deutschland*.[50] The opening stanza conveys his ideas of freedom of pitch, play and field:

Thou mastering me God!
Giver of breath and bread World's strand, sway of the sea,
Lord of living and dead.
Thou hast bound bones and veins in me, fastened me flesh,
And after it almost unmade, what was dread,
Thy doing: and dost thou touch me afresh?
Over again I feel thy finger and find thee.

Stanza four:

I am soft-sift in an hourglass…Christ's gift.

The image of the hourglass and Christ's gift have layers of meaning, from recognition of one's origins and destiny, to the gift of life, time, talent and freedom to make decisions for or against God, all the while the finger of God points me towards truth and love.

---

47 DEVLIN, 122f. for Hopkins's reflection on being created to praise, reverence and serve God and, by so doing to save his soul, and 283.

48 DEVLIN, 157.

49 DEVLIN, 109.

50 HOPKINS, *The Wreck of the Deutschland*, 110–119.

For private consultation and not distribution without the consent of E Ondrako

Stanza thirty-one:

Startle the poor sheep back! Is the shipwreck then a harvest, does tempest carry the grain for thee?[51]

Stanza twenty-four:

O Christ, Christ, come quickly.

Hopkins placed these evocative words on the lips of one of the five Franciscan sisters who lost their lives. While the thirty-five short stanzas can be pondered individually for their weighty themes, they reflect Ignatian spirituality, Scotus's intuitive cognition,[52] and freedom of the will. *The Wreck of the Deutschland* is replete with Hopkins's spirituality of freedom of will in relation to intellect.

Hopkins's ideas on freedom seem to resonate with the luminous, lengthy, and comprehensive, response of Newman to the attack of the former Prime Minister, William Ewart Gladstone, on papal infallibility and the Catholic Church as an exercise in using 'rusty tools.' Newman's response to Gladstone, in the *Letter to the Duke of Norfolk*, was on authority and conscience, with chapter five explaining true freedom of conscience as not being a counterfeit for self-will. Freedom of conscience for Newman was intimately connected to one's personal quest for truth.[53]

Newman may seem to use Kant on the importance of 'personal autonomy,' but never as a disconnect from humble contemplation of God and the obedience of faith. Hopkins must have known Newman's thinking well on Kant's idea of 'personal autonomy.' What Newman and Hopkins understood is that if separated from contemplation of God, personal autonomy could lead to fatal errors, or at least in a post Lockian and post Humian world, skepticism about the existence of God. Bonaventure and Scotus, Newman and Hopkins have a common understanding of freedom of will in relation to intellect.[54]

When analyzing freedom in Hopkins, it helps to keep reflecting on Scotus's thought on the primacy of the will over intellect and the motive of

---

[51] HOPKINS, *Wreck*, stanza 31. Devlin suggests that the imagery of grain and barn in Hopkins's poetry is clearly from his acceptance of Scotus's thought on the motive of the Incarnation, 109.

[52] Intuitive cognition as distinct from abstractive cognition is another way of understanding conscience in Newman, according to Peter Fehlner, in a private interview, March 26–29, 2008, Cassino, Italy.

[53] I feel this sense throughout *The Wreck of the Deutschland*. Moreover, Newman's Letter to Norfolk shows engagement with Victorian writers for whom conscience was a major preoccupation.

[54] The one difference that needs research is that Hopkins may have had a larval Jansenist interpretation of freedom of will in relation to intellect, while Bonaventure, Scotus, and Newman did not.

For private consultation and not distribution without the consent of E Ondrako

the Incarnation as glorifying Christ, the first-born of creation, the absolute primacy of Christ. The Scotistic thesis that Christ was predestined before all other creatures generated hope throughout Hopkins's poetry even the severe trials towards the end of his life, which culminated in the accident of dying from contaminated water. It seems clear that Hopkins wanted the vivid image of ploughman to convey the demands of life, "by the sweat of your brow shall you get bread to eat" Gen. 3:19. Hopkins described *Harry Ploughman*, in 1887, as "the direct vision of a ploughman, without afterthought."[55] *Harry Ploughman* brings to mind, *The Windhover, to Christ the Lord*, the poem Hopkins thought was his best, written ten years earlier.

> Shear plod makes plough down sillion
> Shine.

This view of life, as the hard work of the manual plowman, whose plow, which gathers rust during the winter, and becomes shinny with new use in the spring, is an imitation of Christ's sacrifices which are like

> blue-bleak embers, …[that]
> Fall, gall themselves, and gash gold-vermillion.[56]

Scotus departs from Thomas about the ultimate reality of being, and coined the simple term *haecceitas*, which Hopkins translated as "thisness." The reason is that Scotus does not think of being purely in terms of essence as opposed to existence as Thomas does and Hopkins learned this pivotal principle of individuation from Scotus. The ultimate reason for the *haecceitas*, individuality, of everything, is its existence in the mind of God. Hopkins thinks as Scotus about the ultimate reality of being, a point worthy of explicitation in a world tainted by Hegelian thought patterns that eliminate being altogether in favor of change, or becoming. Devlin summarizes: "Scotus holds that individuality is inexplicable by any other element such as matter or form or quantity or even existence."[57] Rather, "the *haecceitas*, individuality of a being is a distinct intention both in God's mind and in his will."[58] That simple lesson from Scotus brought Hopkins freedom of the will in relation to the intellect, and a corresponding desire for sanctification of the intellect. *Haecceitas* helped Hopkins to answer the critical question about interiorization.

Mindful of the sensitive manner in which Pope Benedict XVI raised the question about freedom and the will in relation to the intellect, it is no

---

55 Letter to Robert Bridges, 28 September 1887.

56 HOPKINS, *The Windhover*, 1877, 132.

57 DEVLIN, 283. *Ultima realitas entis* and *ultima solitudo* are Scotus's descriptions of haecceitas. *Ratio ultima haecceitas non est quaerenda nisi in divina voluntate.* Scotus, Parisiensia, 2, 12, 5.

58 DEVLIN, 293.

For private consultation and not distribution without the consent of E Ondrako

small discovery to find that for Hopkins, in 1877, "after his ordination to the priesthood, his interest shifted increasingly from the presence of God's design or inscape (that is, Christ) in inanimate nature to the working-out of that design—by stress and instress—in the minds and wills of persons."[59] Christ is the exemplar in all of creation. Human beings use their minds and wills, to work out that design freely and with the gift of grace. For Hopkins, an 'instress' of the heart is towards God and goodness, while inscape is the pattern or form of a thing. There is an urge in the heart of everything, an instress, towards its proper function. For example, to buckle is to bring together. Instress is the energy or feeling or power in it, the energy of buckling a buckle.[60] *The Windhover: to Christ the Lord* uses buckle.

> Brute beauty and valour and act, oh, air, pride, plume, here
> Buckle! AND the fire that breaks from thee then, a billion
> Times told lovelier, more dangerous, O my chevalier!

Hopkins applies instress and inscape to Christ the Lord who brings all things together for those who freely chose to love God. The fire of love a billion times told lovelier breaks from the Resurrected Christ.

All things are charged with the Creator as in the poem, "As kingfishers catch fire, dragonflies draw flame."[61] The sensitive observer feels this urge or energy, 'instress,' leading to the revelation of God in the revelation of the *haecceitas*, 'self' of the trout swimming in clear, shallow, sunlit water, or as dragonflies are drawn to flame.[62]

In sum, Hopkins identifies 'inscape' as the pattern or form with nature which is distinct from 'pitch,' or 'self.' Self is identified with *haecceitas*. That view is affirmed in the conclusion of W.A.M. Peters: "Inscape precisely covers what Scotus calls *haecceitas*."[63]

Recapitulation

By using 'instress and inscape' Hopkins is able to touch the delicate area of mystery and problem, difficulty and doubt. He communicates metaphysical images in modern English as Scotus uses the metaphysical images that are fitting in the language of the scholastics. Hopkins learned

---

[59] DEVLIN, 109.

[60] See Appendix B for more on Hopkins's instress and inscape.

[61] HOPKINS, *As Kingfishers catch fire, dragonflies draw flame*, 129.

[62] JAMES HUNTER, *Gerard Manley Hopkins*, (Evans Brothers Ltd., London, 3rd ed. 1975), 21.

[63] W. A. M. PETERS, *Gerard Manley Hopkins*, Oxford, 1947, 23, quoted in DEVLIN, 293.

For private consultation and not distribution without the consent of E Ondrako

from Scotus how to express the independence and interdependence of metaphysics with his theology. Hopkins could say in modern metaphysical English that there is a link in the revelation of the Creator to creation, the *haecceitas* of everything. He replied to Robert Bridges "that mystery was not an 'interesting uncertainty' that held the mind only so long as one had not got to the bottom of it." Hopkins meant that Christians may have difficulties understanding some of the doctrines and may spend a lifetime balancing whether they have, for example, three heavenly friends or one, but they do not doubt the dogmatic truth of the mystery of the Trinity.[64] How close in pastoral understanding and sensitivity this answer of Hopkins is to Newman in the *Apologia*, "ten thousand difficulties do not make a doubt."[65] How far this answer is from the theologians who reject doctrine! How farther yet this is from Hegel who changes the landscape of the Trinity!

People treasure and retain insights from mentors who have touched their lives. They share their deepest longings with those who are trusted. Hopkins trusted Robert Bridges with explanations about his intentions in his poetry. For example, he explained to Bridges, who for some reason had become an unbeliever, that his poem *That Nature is a Heracletian Fire and the Comfort of the Resurrection*[66] was a distillation of Greek philosophical thought. One can speculate about the influence of Greek thought on his poetry. His Oxford education along with Scotus and Newman, who were as well versed in Greek thought, help to shape his poetry. From the initial sober look at nature, the human condition, and history, Hopkins switched to the comfort of the Resurrection. This is a far cry from the categorical imperative of Kant.

> …nature's bonfire burns on.
> …O pity and indignation.
> But vastness blurs and times beats level. Enough!
> the Resurrection,
> A heart's clarion! Away grief's gasping, joyless days, dejection.

Arguably, because of his close relationship with Hopkins, Bridges might have had a notional but not a real understanding of the comfort of the Resurrection. One can speculate about Hopkins and the critical influence of Newman who taught that the notional and real are meant to be linked together. Newman preached and exemplified the real and

---

[64] Leter to Bridges, 24.10.83 187f.

[65] NEWMAN, *Apologia Pro Vita Sua*, part seven. Balthasar pointed out that "Hopkins' language is a theological phenomenon and can be understood only in that way. In his view, Hopkins was unintelligible to a non-Christian like Bridges." See *The Glory of the Lord*, vol. 3, 392.

[66] HOPKINS, *That Nature is a Heracletian Fire and the Comfort of the Resurrection*, 1888, 180–181.

For private consultation and not distribution without the consent of E Ondrako

notional understanding of the comfort of the Resurrection. From Scotus's univocity of the concept of being, Hopkins learned that human beings have something in common with God, which brought him the greatest comfort. The genius of Hopkins leaps out in *The Windhover*.

> Across my foundering deck shone
> A beacon, an eternal beam. Flesh fade, and mortal trash
> Fall to the residuary worm; world's wildfire, leave but ash:
> In a flash at a trumpet crash,
> I am all at once what Christ is, since he was what I am, and
> This Jack, joke, poor potsherd, patch, matchwood, immortal
> diamond,
> Is immortal diamond.

These examples show a metaphysical substratum, the biblical, Ignatian, and Scotistic foundations[67] of Hopkins's walk with Christ. To reform, to renew, and to live a virtuous life is a constant challenge. Hopkins's affective, intellectual, and spiritual growth is an irresistible view of a noble life that desires to be holy. Hopkins was influenced by mentors such as Newman but never compromised his individuality. Devlin's take on his retreat notes suggest three stages, first, Hopkins's youthful affective will; second, his elective will that is found in the grace of the mature mind; third, being lifted from "one cleave of being into another and to a vital act in Christ."[68]

In these three stages, it is easy to trace a 'progressive illumination' first, from young Gerard's affective will towards the good, which he thought might be called natural grace; second, to his elective will, the free turning of his will from one direction to another which demonstrates the meaning of cooperating with grace as a mature mind; and third, to the power of election in taking the hand of God who lifts him from one level of being to another, into the work and love of Christ. Hopkins's writings express this 'progressive illumination' sustained by humble, contemplative, and receptive awareness that he had something in common with God. If one line may summarize the spirituality of Hopkins, it is from his poem *On the Portrait of Two Beautiful Young People*.[69]

---

[67] These Scotistic foundations, such as individuation, ought to be easier to understand at this stage of this essay. Individuation means that there are not two of the same beings. Intuitive cognition is used as conscience in Newman. There are formal distinctions a parte rei, for example, between memory, understanding and affective will in each person, but all three are inseparable in the person. Univocity of the concept of being is Scotus's logical extension of Bonaventure's theory of illumination. Univocity means that there is something that every person has in common with God. Disjunctive transcendentals are concepts that are very real and pertain to the metaphysical order of reality, e.g., the finite is not the infinite.

[68] DEVLIN, 158.

[69] HOPKINS, *On the Portrait of Two Beautiful Young People*, Christmas, 1886, 176.

For private consultation and not distribution without the consent of E Ondrako

Where lies your landmark, seamark, or soul's star?
There's none but truth that can stead you. Christ is truth.

Conclusion

In 1866, at the age of 22, the young Oxford graduate, Gerard Manley Hopkins, went to Newman for instructions and Newman received him into the Roman Catholic Church. A lifelong friendship began. Once Hopkins discovered Scotus in 1872, his life changed and a critical element for his on-going formation began. The first element was the privileged formation Hopkins had at Oxford. The second was the formation under Newman. The third was the formation under Scotus who gave Hopkins the insight that he incorporated into his life's work. "The more theology is distinguished from metaphysics, the more it is in need of it." It is on this foundation that I am making the thesis for retrieving Newman and Scotus by imitating Hopkins. Scotus established the independence of both theology and metaphysics within their interdependence. The three formative elements together are the key to my thesis of how three Oxford scholars came to understand freedom of the will in relation to the intellect.

The retrieval thesis has several dimensions. I identify ten.

First is the dialogical. All three Oxford scholars are resources for civil and noble Christians to engage in dialogue with the world religions and other cultures and to explain amicably why Christ is the one teacher of all, and his Mother is the second teacher and witness. Hopkins writes: She is really "our atmosphere." "Through her we may see him!"[70]

Second is the metaphysical. Metaphysical thinking does not have to yield to scientific thinking. The ontological does not have to yield to function in religious matters.[71] Theological criteria do not have to yield to novelty for genuine reform, renewal, and development. Rather, theology needs metaphysics, and Hopkins imbues his poetry with metaphysics. He incorporates Scotus on being, 'what is,' as the criterion of theological truth and not 'what is coming to be' or experienced or mystical. Hopkins follows Newman who identifies reality with truth, not with change, as in Hegel's thought.

Third is theoria. The metaphysics of Scotus is an existential science, a genuine *theoria*—a contemplation of God as Being, not Becoming. For Hopkins, the genuine *theoria* is the victor as Perseus, the Christ figure

---

70 HOPKINS, *The Blessed Virgin Compared to the Air We Breathe.*

71 Graham Leonard, former Anglican Bishop of London, and later Roman Catholic priest, held this view.

For private consultation and not distribution without the consent of E Ondrako

over the dragon of secularism or relativism. It is easy to apply this to the thought of Pope Benedict XVI, who knows the built in prejudices against living by conviction. The genuine *theoria* is the positive *laicité*, which is not a secular humanism[72] but a healthy secularity.[73]

Fourth is Newman's openness. He teaches: "The field of religious thought which the duty of faith occupies, is small indeed compared to that which is open to our free, though to our reverent and conscientious speculation."[74] Newman's personal quest for truth inspired Hopkins. How does is inspire contemporary teachers?

Fifth are the pure perfections. Scotus teaches about the pure perfections which the infinite God and finite human beings have in common: life, freedom, intelligence, wisdom, etc. How do preachers and pastors present the pure perfections in an attractive and persuasive way?

Sixth are the disjunctive transcendentals. Scotus explains the disjunctive transcendentals as the substratum for his theological metaphysics. Since human beings are inclined toward metaphysical thinking, how does Scotus renew the desire for metaphysical thinking?

Seventh is intuitive thinking. Scotus and Newman are guides to how the intuitive is liked to metaphysical thinking, and both to the contemplation of God. One of the most pressing questions is about human suffering in relation to God. The temptation is to buy into the patripassion thesis. It is not limited to those with Hegelian thinking. The consequences for modernity of Hegel's "template for a suffering God within a Trinitarian horizon" has a seductive appeal for Catholics.[75]

Eighth is language. Hopkins's translation of Scotus into precise metaphysical English is worthy of further exploration especially as a reply to the confusion about freedom of the will in the West. While their language differs, there are parallel streams of theological thought in Newman and Scotus for further discovery. The key is that it is certain that Newman accepted Scotus on the motive of the Incarnation.

Ninth is the decuit and illative sense. To place Scotus's *decuit* alongside Newman's 'illative sense' addresses freedom of the will and intellect.

---

72 Secular humanism has a contemporary appeal to so called 'neutrality' in public affairs, which can be a veil for atheism. See JOHN FINNIS, Address on Secularism and a Healthy Secularity, *Princeton University Colloquium*, October 23, 2003, n.p. Pope Benedict XVI used laicité in his visit to France, September 12, 2008. The Franciscans at Couvent Franciscains, Paris, offered their thoughts on the subtleties of laicité during a visit on November 22, 2008. It is a term to be engaged vis a vis Finnis's views that have purchase as part of the new natural law theoreticians.

73 See HOPKINS, *Andromeda*.

74 NEWMAN, Letter to Norfolk, 346.

75 CYRIL O'REGAN, *Theology and the Spaces of Apocalyptic, The Pere Marquette Lecture in Theology, 2009* (Milwaukee, WI: Marquete University Press, 2009), fn. 103.

For private consultation and not distribution without the consent of E Ondrako

To retrieve, to study and to understand Scotus and Newman in light of Hopkins's precise metaphysical English in his poetry has remarkable purchase for today's emerging world.

Tenth is how to deal with confusion. Freedom of will in the West is compounded by private judgment and autonomy as routine. Many educated young people recognize the deception. They learn from Newman in truth, from Scotus in charity, and from Hopkins in justice. They raise intelligent questions because the history of the Church is filled with those who unravel difficult questions. What Hopkins said about Scotus applies in part to Newman and to himself by extension. Scotus is the rarest veined of unravellers, "who sways my spirits to peace."[76]

> May the retrieval of Newman and Scotus[77] by imitating Hopkins, "ignite a fire a billion times lovelier."[78]

Supplemental Materials

Franciscan Metaphysics

Franciscan metaphysics is the study of being and not becoming alone. Allan B. Wolter wrote that being is the first and most important of the transcendental notions. There are as many concepts as different types of being. Scotus prescinded from the different elements of being and formed a common univocal concept, which is truly transcendental being. "It is an irreducibly simple concept. It represents the ultimate determinable element in everything that is not primarily diverse but only different."[79] Being "is predicable univocally as the common determinable note of all physical things or of any reality that is grasped by a concept that is not irreducibly simple." That is how one can reason that human beings have something in common with the Being that is first, whose name is "I am who am."

Higher attributes must coincide with a being that is first. That primacy is in eminence, finality and efficient causality. The Scotistic metaphysician

---

76 Hopkins, *Duns Scotus Oxford*.

77 Roderick Strange, *Newman and the Gospel of Christ*. This work from 1981 deserves to be expanded in light of further research as does the work of Arthur Burton Calkins, "Mary as Co-redemptrix in the Writings of Frederick William Faber" *Mary at the Foot of the Cross* 1 (New Bedford, MA: 2001), 317–343. Calkins identifies Faber as a Scotist and overlooks the popular controversy about the relationship between Faber and Newman.

78 Hopkins, *The Windhover*.

79 Wolter, *Transcendentals*, 182.

For private consultation and not distribution without the consent of E Ondrako

brings out the perfections of the highest being we call God as the solution to the question: 'why does being exist?' Whatever is a being is also one, true, and good, coextensive attributes. The realm of the pure perfections is substance, life, freedom, intelligence, wisdom and more. These are real concepts predicable of real beings, not just logical intentions. "It is by abstracting from the intrinsic mode of finiteness, which characterizes all creaturely perfections, that the mind forms its most important transcendental notions, namely, the notions of pure perfections which are common to God and to creatures. These common, imperfect and univocal notions must be distinguished from the proper composite concepts of God or of substance through which the mind conceives the formal perfection together with its intrinsic mode."[80] For example, the formal perfection of freedom is in God, but every human being is able to share something in common with God's freedom. I have tried to summarize to get a sense of what a Scotistic metaphysician such as Hopkins does. Wolter concludes: "In this sense, metaphysics is a truly existential science, and the theory of the transcendentals a genuine *theoria*—a contemplation of God."[81]

Instress and inscape

Balthasar's clear commentary is a help to understand these two essential points in Hopkins's poetry.[82] In 1868, Hopkins wrote an essay on Parmenides.

> His [Parmenides's] great text, which he repeats with religious conviction, is that Being is and Not-being is not—which perhaps one can say, a little over-defining his meaning, means that all things are upheld by instress, and are meaningless without it. His feeling for instress, for the flush and foredrawn, and for inscape is most striking.... But indeed I have often felt when I have been in this mood and felt the depth of an instress or how the inscape holds a thing that nothing is so pregnant and straightforward to the truth as simple *yes* and *is*.

Balthasar comments with the assistance of Hopkins's notes.

> A word has three terms: its prepossession of feeling, its definition; and its application. "The first moment of prepossession has clearly to do with instress. Instress, as in-stress, im-pression, intention in existing beings, is used by Hopkins for both the object and the

---

[80] WOLTER, *Transcendentals*, 181–82.

[81] WOLTER, *Transcendentals*.

[82] BALTHASAR, 364–65 with references to HOPKINS's *Journals*, 127–130, (18.5.70) 199, 125, and (13.7.74) 249.

For private consultation and not distribution without the consent of E Ondrako

subject: things express their instress, their deep, unique act, which establishes them, holds them together and holds them in tension, and there is required in the subject an answering stress, so that it can hold communion with the stress of things and experience them from within and can also through a feeling prepossession of their nature find the word that exactly expresses it. This communication is everywhere presupposed.

Balthasar continues:

The objective instress is taken up by the subject that is open to it, that is moved in its depths by the depth of the power of being. On seeing a comet, Hopkins says: 'I felt a certain awe and instress....

In sum, if *instress* refers to the power of a thing, then *inscape* refers to its form. Hopkins wrote to Patmore: "*Inscape* is species or individually distinctive beauty of style." He meant: if a person has eyes, *inscape* is everywhere in nature, something beautiful in itself.[83]

Views of four critics

One. John Robinson used Hopkins's notebooks and letters for his interpretation, as did the other three critics selected. Robinson quotes Hopkins about "the depth of an instress" and of feeling "how fast the inscape holds a thing." In 1879, Hopkins wrote to Bridges that "design, pattern, or what I am in the habit of calling 'inscape' is what I above all aim at in poetry." In 1886, to Dixon Hopkins wrote: "inscape is the very soul of art." Robinson's difficulty in interpreting these two words is the range of applications.[84] In his notebook Hopkins held that art exacts the energy of contemplation. His depth of feelings about art is an 'instress.' Instress is the depth of feeling about the quality of inscape holding the unity of things. Robinson suggests that Hopkins is able to use "inscape' widely because it "permanently holds out the possibility of an insight into the unity of things."[85] This is Scotistic. One may apply inscape as the form or pattern of matter. It is in the eye of the artist or sculptor or poet and goes off like a flashbulb. That moment of insight, creative imagination, and recognition of the form or pattern is reflective of God.

Robinson understood 'inscape' as the essential bridge between matter and the immaterial."[86] He is not clear on humble contemplation before

---

83 Balthasar, 366–67. Letter to C. Patmore, *Further Letters of GMH* (1938, 2nd ed. 1956). (7.11.86). See Ian Heuser, *The Shaping Vision of GMH* (Oxfor University Press, 1958).

84 John Robinson, *In Extremity: A Study of GMH*, 1978, 35.

85 Robinson, 30.

86 Robinson, 35.

For private consultation and not distribution without the consent of E Ondrako

truth in the life of a person. The final years of Hopkins's were particularly severe. He understood that Scotus's univocity of the concept of being did not mean human beings have the same nature as God, or that we are God, but that all of reality has something in common with God. The bridge between the material and immaterial is contemplation of God with mind and a heart that discerns God's plan for a person. To understand how Hopkins dealt with suffering of his last years and his life's purpose is by humble contemplation before truth. Newman's example was critical. Hopkins's life may have been short, but he had the gift for integrating in compelling poetry a very wide range of experiences for prayer and conscientious speculation in the spirit of Newman. He shows that one can be 'in extremity of mind' and find peace that surpasses understanding.

Two. Christopher Devlin makes Hopkins's sermons and devotional writings accessible.[87] His notes and commentary are indispensible for any serious study of Hopkins. The third chapter's appendix is: Scotus and Hopkins. Peter Damian Fehlner[88] is highly favorable to Devlin as a resource on Hopkins's Scotism, with some interpretive reservations. Devlin's research of the subtle doctor's thought strengthens the linkage with Newman. The next step is to explore their epistemology of faith in general and theological activity in particular. Fehlner's study in this volume is for those who desire a renewal of the study of theology with a Scotistic accent. The link is between metaphysics and Mary Immaculate, why and how Hopkins intuited this, and Mary as teacher of theology along with Christ, the primary teacher of theology.

Three. Harold Weatherby is critical of Hopkins as "suffering from that limitation of scope, from that curtailment of possession of keen delight, which is the consequence of modern skepticism's impinging on Catholic thought."[89] He blames Newman, in part. Weatherby wrote: "St. Thomas' confidence in the intellect and its capacity for metaphysical wisdom and his thorough supernaturalism which is the theological complement of that wisdom, give him [Hopkins] more to possess and to delight than Newman dreams of."[90] Fehlner's penetrating analysis is that Weatherby "confused affective certitude (piety) with intellectual.[91] Weatherby seems unfamiliar with the freedom of inquiry in Newman's *Letter to Norfolk*. Newman and Hopkins resisted Kantian thought that leads to skepticism. Weatherby's

---

[87] C. DEVLIN, *The Sermons and Devotional Writings of GMH*, 1959.

[88] FEHLNER, "Mary and Theology: Scotus Revisited," chapter 4 of this volume.

[89] HAROLD WEATHERBY, *The Keen Delight*, 1975, 74.

[90] WEATHERBY, 68. Weatherby's difficulty may stem from a too Thomistic reading of HOPKINS, 27–73, esp. 68.

[91] FEHLNER, *Mary and Theology: Scotus Revisited*.

For private consultation and not distribution without the consent of E Ondrako

view is that most of Hopkins's poems between 1876 and 1883 show the combined influence of Scotus and Newman, but ceases.[92] On the contrary, evidence shows their influence to the end of his life, June 8, 1889.

Four. Hans Urs Von Balthasar does not miss Hopkins' his humble contemplation before truth. After reading the evocative and condensed thought of Balthasar,[93] a must for any devotee of Hopkins, I was struck with the question: how might Hopkins answer Balthasar that theological aesthetics as a whole stands or falls with Mariology?[94] How do Balthasar, Devlin, and Fehlner converge in their understanding of Scotus? How do they differ? These questions call for further study. Peter Casarella from DePaul University, and Cyril O'Regan from Notre Dame are devotees of Balthasar, but scholars who recognize that Balthasar does not always understand Scotus as well as he might have.[95]

---

92 FEHLNER, *Mary and Theology.*

93 BALTHASAR, *The Glory of the Lord*, Vol. 3, 653–699.

94 BALTHASAR, 390f.

95 Peter Casarella shared these candid observations with me at the Catholic Theological Society of America meeting in Cleveland in June, 2010. Cyril O'Regan agrees, in general, with Casarella. He explained why in our private conversations at Notre Dame during the summer of 2010. Both are interested in engaging this promising area of research. Balthasar's take on Scotus is fertile ground for research.

For private consultation and not distribution without the consent of E Ondrako

CHAPTER 15

Uncoupling Scotus and Kant with the Help of Newman

Edward Ondrako

Précis

Scotus is a metaphysician-theologian whom Newman called the greatest theological luminary Oxford ever knew, a point worthy of further development. Newman is a help to understand Scotus properly. The beginning of a new structure in metaphysics can be traced from the thirteenth century, from Thomas Aquinas and Scotus to Kant who links logic, ontology and natural theology into a new focus of onto-theology.[1] Scotus, more than his predecessors, establishes independence within interdependence and allows metaphysics and theology to be united more profoundly.[2] The primacy of charity in Scotus is inseparable from the absolute primacy of Christ. Scotus's metaphysical-theological approach is poles apart from modern idealism and Kant's empirical-rational approach because Kant "redraws the map of the empire of reason."[3]

Introduction

Given the use of the term onto-theology by Kant, neither Scotus nor his predecessor, Bonaventure, fit the precise sense of onto-theology given by Kant. This is a subject of considerable controversy and the motivation for this modest contribution to lay to rest the idea that Scotus is Kant's projenitor. Ockham may be the more likely candidate for several reasons that will become apparent in the course of this essay. For example, the notion of development or evolution is often associated with the physical

---

[1] OLIVIER BOULNOIS, *Être et représentation* (Paris: Presses Universitaires de France, 2008), 504. Henceforth, *Être.*

[2] BOULNOIS, *Être*, 478.

[3] CYRIL O'REGAN, "Kant: Boundaries, Blind-Spots, and Supplements," in Christianity and Secular Reason: Classical Themes and Modern Developments, ed. Jeffrey Bloechl (Notre Dame, IN: University of Notre Dame Press, 2012), 87–126. Henceforth, Kant: Boundaries.

For private consultation and not distribution without the consent of E Ondrako

world and with the Kantian epistemology of science but its utility for metaphysics has to do with history, with voluntary causality, and with cultural growth where the Creator and rational creature are involved in establishing the rational character of contingent change. This is a critical point to correctly understand development of doctrine and theistic evolution[4] in creative fidelity to the thought of Scotus and Newman which is neither the nominalism of Ockham nor the neutralizing of religion by Kant. This step of uncoupling Scotus and Kant with the help of Newman is an invitation to further research into Ockham and Kant and a prelude to Hegel's writings on religion and their impact on contemporary theology.

The essay has three parts, an outer circle, inner circle and recapitulation. Ten general points form an outer circle and introduce several reasons to de-link Scotus from Kant.[5] Ten significant motifs form an inner circle of ideas present in Scotus and Kant which demonstrate their reply to the 'critical question' of interiorization. Finally a recapitulation emphasizes five pivotal points pertaining to a contemplative intuition of the goodness of being which becomes distinct in the light of the Incarnation.[6] A conclusion invites further thought about Ockham and Kant.

To begin, the position of Scotus dealing with being, the relation of the will to intellect, freedom, the absolute primacy of Christ, and redemption is not that of Kant's "duty" or moral imperative as interpretive key for what is meant by the will. Nor does Scotus posit the radical autonomy of the will, relation to nature, Christ and soteriology. Kant is a philosopher

---

[4] Evolution is almost always taken as a term exclusively used with the physical world and with the Kantian epistemology of science. The scotistic inspiration is not primarily with time in general, nor with natural causality, nor with physical growth, but with a theory of condetermination which takes into consideration efficacious grace and human freedom. I am grateful to Peter Damian Fehlner for drawing my attention to this theory which was popularized by BARTHOLOMEUS MASTRIUS, *Disputationes Theologicae De Divino Intellectu*, d. 3, q. 3, a. 8. See the work by the Spanish Jesuits, especially, SEVERINO GONZALEZ, *Sacrae Theologiae Summa* (Madrid: Biblioteca de Autores Cristianos, 1956, 3rd ed.), De gratia, vol. 3, n. 316, p. 680, n. 4. The idea of condetermination is under the section Concordia gratiae efficacis cum libertate in nn. 311–324, pp. 674–684. However in no. 322, González shows that he lacks familiarity with the Franciscan meaning of freedom, the will, and intellect by rejecting the Scotistic inspired idea of condetermination. Moreover, John of Napoli (a Sicilian) and Angelo Vulpes (Naples), two Conventual Franciscan scotists, used the term condetermination. Vulpes was a teacher of Mastrius. Mastrius produced a complete philosophical-theological synthesis of Scotus's teaching which was prepared for the intellectual formation of clerics. Luther's rebellion for one called for such formaion and the implementation of the Council of Trent was the other significant reason.

[5] Some in the contemporary school of Radical Orthodoxy at Oxford have made this erroneous connection.

[6] W. HOERES, *Kritik der transzendertalphilosophischen Erkenntnistheorie* (Stuttgard, 1969), 62–137. SCOTUS, *Opera Omnia, Ordinatio*, Prologus, Città del Vaticano, 1950, vol. I, pp. 1–237. See *Beato Giovanni Duns Scoto, Prologo dell'Ordinatio* (Frigento: Casa Mariana Editrice, 2006), xii. Peter Damian Fehlner's praemessa and Alessandro Apollonio's introduzione reflect the view of Hoeres.

For private consultation and not distribution without the consent of E Ondrako

of seventeenth and eighteenth century phenomenal empiricism with enormous purchase in the modern world, particularly for his notion of the will, its interpretation *via* the moral imperative, and freedom as the ultimate rational end of human beings. Paradoxically, he employs a hermeneutic of ingratitude[7] *vis a vis* the hermeneutic of trust in Scotus. Scotus teaches the unity of knowledge, while Kant separates faith from certitude of the speculative order, and has the view that knowledge is authentic to the degree that it is useful. Scotus teaches the unity in human consciousness and human experience, a unity in which the science of metaphysics may lead a person to the most important kind of realistic knowledge, nothing less than contemplation of the truth or light that is God. For Kant this is nothing more than mental fiction because one can only reach certitude through the sciences of phenomena, i.e., physical and natural science. On the positive side, Kant's appeal to freedom in works such as *Religion within the Boundaries of Mere Reason*[8] is a step toward the light or transcendence and away from a mathematical demonstration of Cartesian rationalism.

There is a problem that cannot be resolved between a definition of will in Kant based primarily on ethical concepts deriving from a miscegenist Protestant backdrop with strong Calvinist-Lutheran leanings, and one that is based on a metaphysics or metaethics as in the concept of the will of Scotus.[9] In brief, Kant takes the 'meta' out of metaethics, while Scotus's metaethics has been the center of controversy whether he accepts that the moral value of an action depends alone on the divine will. The debate has to take into consideration what Scotus says about natural law[10] in relation to revealed law and the relation of both to Christ and his absolute primacy. This debate centers on the meaning of divine goodness and divine freedom.

That seems to be the heart of a much debated question. In other words, Scotus views the Ten Commandments in relation to the promised

---

7 Hermeneutic of ingratitude is being used with the meaning that there is an anthropological and hermeneutical turn of Kant to the Bible and then failure to recognize its help. See Cyril O'Regan's course on 19th Century German Theology at the University of Notre Dame, Spring 2011. Henceforth, O'Regan, Spring 2011.

8 ALLEN WOOD and GIORGE DI GIOVANNI, trans. and eds., *Kant: Religion within the Boundaries of Mere Reason* (Cambridge: University Press, 1998, rpt 2006), 65–73. *The German edition of Kant's writings*, 6.44–6.53. Henceforth, Wood and di Giovanni.eds, *Religion*.

9 O'Regan, Spring 2011, offers parsed and persuasive reasons for this miscegenist view. His views complement those of PETER DAMIAN FEHLNER, "Scotus and Newman in Dialogue," in this volume. Henceforth, Fehlner, Dialogue.

10 RICHARD CROSS, "Natural Law, Moral Constructivism, and Duns Scotus' Metaethics: The Centrality of Aesthetic Explanation" in Jonathan Jacobs, ed., *Reason, Religion, and Natural Law: Historical and Analytical Studies* (Oxford: Oxford University Press, forthcoming). Cross's take on Scotus's view as some kind of divine command theory is groundbreaking, but it raises questions about the relations between natural law and revealed law that Cross does not develop.

For private consultation and not distribution without the consent of E Ondrako

Savior-Redeemer, which means that revealed law does more than repeat the natural law and makes possible modifications and adaptations by the lawgiver. This is a point that modern analytical philosophers may not develop sufficiently in fidelity to the original thought of Scotus on this critical point of relation between natural and revealed law,[11] but neither time nor the purpose of this essay allow for such a study. Rather, may it suffice that the definition of obligation first in God and then in rational human beings seems to be at the heart of the longstanding debate. Scotus defines the will as a pure perfection, a *perfectio simpliciter simplex*, something that cannot be reduced any further. A pure perfection is irreducibly simple and what is simple is more perfect because it lacks the notion of potentiality and act.[12] He holds that God's freedom cannot be restricted, that the first principle, or natural law, is that God should be loved, and suggests the importance of pondering in humble contemplation God's motivations. With a very different take on freedom, Kant makes a hermeneutical turn towards freedom in the transcendental realm, away from the phenomenon to the noumenon, in order to explain freedom as the highest rational end of the person.

General Points of Comparison

Necessity and contingency in Scotus vs. duty in Kant

For Scotus, necessity and contingency are pivotal concepts, disjunctive transcendentals.[13] Necessity is something that cannot be other than it is. Contingency is something that may or may not happen. Necessity is in relation to the infinite, or uncreated, and contingency is in relation to the finite, or created. That is why Scotus recognizes that there is a natural mode of acting which is to be moved by another as the intellect by what it contemplates. If one accepts this position, there is a logical outcome that is applicable to the primacy of the will in the spiritual order. God's perfect will always loves and acts in an orderly and rational manner. God's will is never absolute or arbitrary as one finds in Ockham's nominalist definition

---

[11] The thoroughness with which Cross refers to Thomas Williams supports this conviction that what is looming on the horizon is the recognition of the further debate on the natural law and revealed law in Scotus's metaethics.

[12] ALLAN B. WOLTER, *The Transcendentals in the Metaphysics of Duns Scotus* (St. Bonaventure, N.Y.: The Franciscan Institute, 1946, rpt., 2008), 159 and 174. See chapter 7, The Pure Perfections, 162–175 and St. Anselm's definition of pure perfection, 162–163. "In the unqualified sense of the term, it is one which, in anything possessing it, is better to have than not to have." Henceforth, Wolter, *Transcendentals*.

[13] WOLTER, The Transcendentals, ch. 6, The Disjunctive Transcendentals, 128–161. See Appendix A in this essay.

For private consultation and not distribution without the consent of E Ondrako

of God's arbitrary absolute will. A Kantian inspired reply that has its roots in Ockham is that God's "will has a duty to follow the good in every case. God can't fail to do this; creatures can, but in any case what counts as good for them is a matter of divine fiat."[14]

The Ockhamist-Kantian inspired reply opens up the debate seen in early Calvinism pervading the question of the power of God and God's duty. Scotus anticipates such a problem, so to speak, by using the disjunctive transcendentals to demonstrate that God is not obligated by duty, in the strict sense, but acts out of love, the primacy of love. Finite limitations on power for human beings are not the same for the infinite, because God's power has no restrictions. "Duty" or moral imperative is the identifying sign that the Ockamist-Kantian read above is in light of Kant's notion of the will. Such a read has no little consequence, for one finds it present as a concern in the Regensburg Address of Pope Benedict XVI, September 12, 2006. The brilliant theologian who occupies the Chair of Peter uses analogy or proportion to answer the questions which he raises as belonging to every thinking person.

What needs to be developed further in the Holy Father's erudite address to the faculty at Regensburg, in my humble view, is Scotus's thought on the pure perfection (*perfectio simpliciter*). For Scotus, the pure perfections have a distinct function in metaphysics as a theologic. The opposite of *perfectio simpliciter*, a perfection in the unqualified sense of the term, would be *perfectio limitata*, which contains the formal notion of the idea of limitation or imperfection. Perfections in a relative sense are not *simpliciter*.[15] This point cannot be stressed enough in the context of the modern question: does God learn from contemporary experience and gain new knowledge? This is a question which seems to be inspired by a Kantian form of modern idealism with the suggested answer that God does learn. Scotus anticipated Kant's 'question,' especially his use of abstractive and intuitive cognition.

There is a caveat for those who follow the logical structure of the Thomistic approach alone for they may unwittingly fall into a subtle trap of rationalism. Recognize the subtle trap of rationalism by understanding why Scotus's univocal concept of being is not a pure logical construct, but a unique, incomparable formulation of divine illumination in logical form! Recognize that univocal being may be a light guiding all of our thought, keeping logic securely linked to reality or being. The Scotistic unity of knowledge recognizes that proper use of the science of metaphysics may lead a person to the most important kind of realistic knowledge, contem-

---

14 Cross unpublished reply to the author. Henceforth, Cross replies.

15 WOLTER, *Transcendentals*, 162–163.

For private consultation and not distribution without the consent of E Ondrako

plation of the truth or light that is God. Nonetheless, Kant's Stoic inspired rationalist approach itself developed as he grew older to the point where he concludes that "happiness is the highest natural end of the human person, but freedom is an even higher rational end."[16]

Since 2006, the Holy Father has written on the seventh hundredth anniversary of the death of Scotus[17] and given a papal audience on the thought of Scotus on July 7, 2010, which show the development of his own understanding of the thought of Scotus in relation to the arbitrary voluntarism of Kant. His recent writings show that the Holy Father is being drawn to the thought of Scotus on the primacy of charity and the primacy of the will. The papal audience, given with the utmost sensitivity to anthropologists, philosophers, and theologians is his Holiness's invitation to address the question of using right reason in true liberty of will and intellect, the inseparability of the primacy of charity and the primacy of the will.

Aristotle, Scotus and Kant on the will

Scotus rejects the Aristotelian principle *omne quod movetur ab alio movetur*.[18] That step enables him to take the foundational metaphysical view that he teaches about the priority of the will in the order of cause and effect and supports his well known position on the primacy of the will and the primacy of charity. Scotus answers the questions:

How is it possible for the will to have priority?

How does the will, finite and divine, move itself?

What is the ultimate intelligible ground manifested in the fact that the will is not primarily an intellectual appetite, that it is a power of self-activation in love of the good for its own sake?

How is it possible for freedom to consist in this position? If God's love of himself is a necessary love, how is it possible and why is the ground of that fact the will?

The foundations of Scotus's priority of the will and Kant's sense of duty

Scotus and Kant are poles apart on the central concept of the will. A Kantian inspired reply to God's love of Himself as a necessary love is that

---

[16] IMMANUEL KANT, *Naturrecht Feyerabend*, 27:1321-2, trans. Paul Guyer, "Kant Autonomy and Modernity" Lecture at the Catholic University of America, October 15, 2010, unpublished.

[17] POPE BENEDICT XVI, *Laetare Colonia Urbs*, October 28, 2010.

[18] All that moves is moved by another. Scotus holds a different view from THOMAS AQUINAS, *Summa contra Gentiles*, bk. I, ch. 13.

For private consultation and not distribution without the consent of E Ondrako

"God follows his duties to himself irrespective of any additional motiva-tion. That's not so clear in the case of humans—if they follow their duty here, it might be despite strong motivations not to."[19] Scotus uses *affectio justitiae*, affection for justice, and *affectio commodi*, affection for happiness as the two affections of the will, a problem that from a Kantian standpoint seems that unable to be resolved. Kant uses the moral imperative, or duty, as the interpretive key for what is meant by the will, the reason for suggesting that following a sense of duty is Kantian on first impression. Scotus's position on the will as the affection for justice and the affection for happiness is comprehensive and not the same as the good will for Kant. For Scotus, the subject of God's motivations hinge on divine goodness and divine freedom, and human beings are invited to act in a similar manner. The good will of Kant hinges on the absolute autonomy of the human will.

Metaphysics in Scotus vs. the mathematical physics of Kant

My philosophy professor, Owen Bennett, often repeated that firm assent is found within faith, is free and is certain. This is a way of express-ing the independence and interdependence of metaphysics and theology of Scotus. Aquinas holds that God is the subject of metaphysics. Scotus does not. Rather, for Scotus, God is one of the subjects of metaphysics. He views metaphysics as the highest science because it gives the highest access to God.[20] Kant's philosophy is inspired by the mathematical physics of Newton; holding that metaphysics cannot reach certitude and therefore nothing can be said, while one remains in the speculative order, about the validity of God, freedom and the soul and its immortality.

To repeat, Scotus rejects the Aristotelian principle *omne quod movetur ab alio movetur*,[21] which he applies to the will, finite or infinite, and concludes that the will is a power of self-activation in love of the good for its own sake. For Scotus, it is in this primacy of the will that freedom consists. The will moves itself, but there is a natural mode of acting, to be moved by another, for example, when the intellect is moved by what it contemplates. Scotus holds that the divine will is always ordered and rational, never the arbitrary, absolute will of Ockham. It could be argued that Ockham's nominalism is linked to Kant, but not the primacy of the will of Scotus because for the subtle doctor, the will of God is the source of

---

19 Richard Cross, chairman of the philosophy department at Notre Dame, very kindly offered this reply to one of the most important of my many questions during the spring term, 2011. His unpublished reply is one reading of Scotus's distinction between the two affections, for justice and for happiness.

20 Boulnois, *Être*, 475.

21 All that moves is moved by another. The penetrating insight into the will's power of self-activation vs. the Kantian sense of duty is from Fehlner, Dialogue.

For private consultation and not distribution without the consent of E Ondrako

all order and rationality, and the divine will and intellect are one, though formally distinct.

The primacy of the will is related to the primacy of charity in the spiritual order, and is not the source of any anti-intellectual tyranny, or fideism. That is why Scotus risked all to defend the real presence in the Eucharist, the possibility of the Immaculate Conception, and papal primacy. Kant inherited a Lutheran inspired mode of thinking that had within and of itself a complex history of problems relating to the real presence, Mary, and papal primacy, via competing views from many of the reformers such as Zwingli, Calvin, and Leibnitz, who sincerely desired Christian unity and worked for it in the face of much opposition. Kant's philosophy of phenomenal empiricism followed in the wake of the non-metaphysical skepticism of David Hume.

It is noteworthy that Kant develops his idea of freedom with its stoical categorical imperative as a step towards the light, and away from the Cartesian inspired mathematical mindset. Scotus introduces the univocity of the concept of being as an incomparable way of keeping logic securely connected to being—securely connected to what is. That means that finite human beings share something in common with the infinite God, such as being, will, intellect and freedom. The Kantian view differs radically from Scotus's view of beatitude in that sharing freedom, will, intellect and being with God seems impossible on the face of it without contemplation.

The will as a pure perfection and the univocity of the concept of being vs. Kant's noumena

By comparing and contrasting the thought of Scotus to Kant, one gradually realizes that Scotus anticipated the momentums and currents underlying Kant's views and where such underpinnings might lead. The primacy of will in his thought presupposes the will as a pure perfection shared in common with God. The incomparable metaphysical discovery of Scotus, his formulation of the univocity of the concept of being, enables one to understand that the finite will is a pure perfection shared in common with the infinite will that always loves in an orderly manner. This gives the person the capacity to unite one's will perfectly with the will of God as did Mary. To subscribe to Scotus's perspective will not lead to the acceptance, but the rejection of many of the views of Kant. This is particularly true concerning Kant's exclusion of theology from the realm of theoretical knowledge. The result is the noumenal description of God as a concept or fact for Kant, and not a loving Creator in relationship with his creatures.

For private consultation and not distribution without the consent of E Ondrako

Kant denies that human beings may experience a personal relationship with God. His goal of freedom as the ultimate end of human beings competes with Scotus's freedom as a pure perfection. Scotus's thought on the disjunctive transcendentals is his metaphysics. This means that finite human beings share freedom in common with the infinite God, a freedom that invites the most profound personal relationship imaginable. Comparing and contrasting Scotus to Kant on freedom needs a bridge. The bridge is the metaphysical position of Newman in the *Idea of a University* and the sequel, the *Grammar of Assent*, the latter being the genuine phenomenology and metaphysical-epistemological thought underlying his theory of faith in the *Apologia*. Newman's theory of knowledge is in the *Idea of a University* but he first addressed many of the themes in his *University Sermons*, especially Sermons 10 to 14.

Newman uses many thomistic tools, but there is a difference between the thomistic and scotistic solution to the exercise of the will in making judgments about being, reality. Though always genial towards Thomas in his writings, in the *Idea of a University*, Newman refutes the utilitarian approach to learning of Locke and Hume and implicitly Kant, and seems to coincide more with the thought of Scotus on the unity of knowledge in all its parts, the place of theology, the principle of causality and the will, and knowledge as an end in itself. A key discovery is a scotistic character to "liberal knowledge" in Newman that comes to light when comparing the approaches to metaphysics of Thomas and Scotus.[22] The thomistic solution sometimes appears as more of an exercise in logic but not without some loose ends.

Freedom and the univocity of the concept of being

Kant and Scotus address a pivotal concept, freedom. Scotus's univocity of the concept of being may be easiest to understand in relation to the perfectly free and human consent of Mary, "freedom natural to the whole species, but is such as to render that freedom fully complete in itself and ontologically more suited to choosing the good given by God

---

[22] The view about comparing the approaches to metaphysics of Thomas and Scotus is summarized genially by Marino Gentile. He effectively puts to rest any anachronistic sparring between the two great schools of metaphysician-theologians, in favor of appreciating the complementarity, differences, and achievement of Aristotle and St. Thomas, and the works of the theologian disciples of St. Francis of Assisi, namely, St. Bonaventure and Bl. Scotus. Moreover, I am convinced that if one learns to read Newman in a manner that coincides with that of Scotus, one often finds a perfect description of the position of Scotus in modern English. For Gentile's summary of the differences regarding the unity of knowledge in a Thomistic and Scotistic view, see D. CORTESE, ed., *L'orazione della Immacolata* (Padua, 1985), 30–31, note 34.

For private consultation and not distribution without the consent of E Ondrako

in Christ, for the redemption of all mankind."[23]   This is very different from the categorical imperative of Kant, the idea of duty or the necessity to be moral, an ethical position that is disconnected from grace and the possibility of attaining true happiness in union with the beloved Creator.

Kant and Scotus deal with elements or a substratum of theistic evolutionary thought which, without caveats, may take an atheistic turn. This foundational point about theistic evolution takes into account three approaches: first, Aristotle-Aquinas; second, Ockham, Hume and Kant; and third, Bonaventure, Scotus and arguably Newman. Aristotle and Aquinas bring noble advances to human and Christian thought, and, notwithstanding some real and perhaps more of a perceived opposition, there is a deeper complementarity between Aquinas and Scotus. Second, Ockham's nominalism, a veil for agnosticism and voluntarism, may be put adjacent to Hume's skeptical voice and that of Kant during his agnostic period. Kant has been called a skeptic, whose pietism, with the notion of grace suspended, is in opposition to the metaphysical synthesis of Scotus. In the epistemology of Scotus, unity of knowledge presupposes the univocity of the concept of being. There are more reasons for including Newman close to Scotus in the third approach, rather than the first. Newman certainly does not belong in the second with its components of skepticism.

Scotus on revealed, natural and physical theology vs. Kant's anti-metaphysical take

In *The Idea of a University*, Newman identifies three forms of theology that can be discovered in Scotus. They are revealed theology based on supernatural or infused faith, natural theology and physical theology. Natural theology accents the anthropological, i.e., the person with an intelligent nature and free will as the central characteristic. Themes relating to natural theology abound in Newman's writings. However, the difficulties encountered when one makes an almost total reliance on scientific methodologies and the principles of physical cause and effect in the world of material are highlighted by Newman. He saw the problem in Paley's view of physical theology.[24]

Kant's view of natural theology and supernatural or infused faith differs radically from Scotus. Kant does not answer the critical question of entering into the heart as does Bonaventure with his theory of divine

---

[23] BENEDETTO IPPOLITO, "The Anthropological Foundation of Duns Scotus' Mariology," in *Acts of the Symposium on Scotus' Mariology, Grey College, Durham, England, September 9–11, 2008, Mariologia Franciscana III* (New Bedford, MA: Academy of the Immaculate, 2009), 170–171.

[24] FEHLNER, Dialogue. Scotistic affinities are in part two.

For private consultation and not distribution without the consent of E Ondrako

illumination and exemplarism. Scotus retains the essence of Bonaventure's theory and expands it to include the creative concept of the mind, finite and infinite as a pure perfection. To answer the alluring Kantian position, I do not grow tired of repeating that Scotus holds that the human mind has as its very center the unique concept of being as univocal, not a pure logical construct first, but a unique, incomparable formulation of divine illumination in logical form so that it can be the light guiding all our thought, keeping logic securely linked to reality or being. Univocity has the same role as divine light, as does a fontal object in Bonaventure. In other words, in the epistemology of Scotus, unity of knowledge presupposes the univocity of the concept of being.

Scotus is Newman's role model rather than Kant

In the *Idea of a University*, Newman refers to Scotus as the greatest theological luminary Oxford ever knew. As I study Newman, I grow more and more convinced that Newman went through several adjustments in his thinking as he strove to find the light of truth. Early in his Oxford career he seems to have discovered Scotus as a personal role model for what the essence of his thought concerning a university should be, and the kind of person it should form. Most of all, the creative formulation of the essence of a university brought his deepest longings into a tranquil order. A study of his *Oxford University Sermons*, writings on St. Athanasius, and *Lectures on Justification* strongly affirm the validity of his perception.[25] In brief, I am convinced that several factors lead Newman to gradually break from his early Calvinist inspired theology and that it was the example and thoughts of Scotus that he found attractive when learning about and testing several candidates.

Scotus and Newman differ radically from Kant on the issues already introduced. These issues, together with the changes in the meaning and use of words between the scholastic period of Scotus and 19th century Britain, makes it imperative to establish that Newman has contours with and puts the metaphysical and epistemological questions that Scotus was dealing with into modern English. The Scotistic question concerns the 'interiorization' or personalization of knowledge pointing towards the supernatural or holiness, a discernible and profound affective relationship to being as the supreme good, that is, the metaphysical aspect. The Kantian question is the epistemological or personalization as it is in itself autonomously. The Newmanian question accounts phenomenologically

---

25 FEHLNER, Dialogue. I concur with this view and suggest that there are references from Newman's works as early as 1832 to 1840.

For private consultation and not distribution without the consent of E Ondrako

for the correlation between the personalization and the sanctification of the intellect. Newman gives the apologetical dimension or justification of knowledge and assent

While Newman's metaphysics and epistemology may be put side by side with the approach of Scotus, Kant splits metaphysics with the logical reduction to autonomy and a radically autonomous will. The problem is the absolute autonomy of the transcendental 'ego' and will that is based on the arbitrary indifference of duty or Kant's categorical imperative. For the person who is convinced of the value of merit, who strives to practice virtue and to live a virtuous life oriented to holiness, the anti-metaphysical position of Kant may lead to skepticism rather than belief.

Firm assent in faith vs. the gap between the mental and extra-mental

The critical problem as defined by Kant is that one has to transcend the gap between the mental and extra-mental. The gap may be described as between the extremes of rigid traditionalism and trancendentalism. One will avoid them by coming to a progressive illumination as did Newman, who explains his theory of development (the *Essay on Development of Doctrine* in 1845) and theory of knowledge (the *Grammar of Assent* in 1870) in his theory of faith (in the *Apologia pro vita sua* in 1864). Having Scotus as an inspiration of an orderly thinker, is the strong antecedent probability that, in time, he became the indefatigable inspiration for Newman to answer the controversies of his day, and the model for exemplifying the purpose of and essence of a liberal education and holiness. Newman made a lasting contribution to the metaphysical essence of a university in *The Idea of a University*. In short, Newman's works are the prism by which to look back to Scotus, snipping any imagined threads that link him to Kant. I use the image of prism because Newman's works abound and bathe their refracted light in a myriad of colors onto Scotus's disjunctive transcendentals that are poised to receive all of the colors.

It cannot be stressed enough that firm assent that is found within faith, is free and certain. Scotus and Newman differ from Kant on the analysis and resolution of this critical question, but not on the need to personalize understanding and to make a judgment. Kant raises the question whether faith can bridge the notional and real. Kant's valid insights appear in Newman's thinking in another form. Unlike Newman, however, Kant seems to be unable to get beyond the agnostic as regards metaphysics and faith. Newman makes the 'leap of faith,' by the exercise of the illative sense. By bringing the illative sense into relation with Scotus on the further dimensions of the relation of the intellect and will, and the natural and supernatural in relation to divine illumination, one may reason to the

For private consultation and not distribution without the consent of E Ondrako

critical further question whether a metaphysics rooted in divine revelation is reasonable or arbitrary. Newman asks: is faith reasonable if it uses the illative sense or is it arbitrary? Newman answers that it is reasonable. Kant asks: does faith have anything to do with intelligibility, the relation between the notional and real? Kant searches for his answer in an autonomous sense of duty trancending all utilitarianism in an encounter with a Judge (first birth) and Savior (second birth or baptism). Kant's rationalism differs from a scotistic use of reason in metaphysics and Newman's argument with respect to conscience concerning the major point of the existence of God. Scotus's argument for the existence of God reflects help from Bonaventure his fellow metaphysician-theologian and disciple of Francis of Assisi. Both hold that personal judgment introduces something beyond a merely intellectual or notional-logical action. For Scotus, this transcends the scientific and remains intellectual, the incomparable formulation of the univocity of the concept of being.

Scotus and the epistemological-theological vs. Kant and the epistemological-scientific

Interiorization, humble obedience to truth, and preparation of heart characterize the approach of Scotus and Newman. They recognize that a genuine personal interiorization of faith that is apprehended notionally most often passes through a crisis, or problem of a judgment. This requires a person to enter into oneself. In the words of Augustine, it requires that a person apprehend and unconditionally affirm in a real assent of faith. This crisis is the heart of the critical problem in epistemology, the need to transcend the gap between mental and extra-mental, which can conclude in skepticism or hope. There is a deeply personal domain whose organization and conceptualization one needs to revise and to change often in order to relate to what is simple and unchanging in one's heart, nothing less than humble obedience to the truth.

An essential distinction is Newman's consistent emphasis on the preparation of heart. This key factor present in Scotus is noticeably absent in Kant. That is why a proper biblical, patristic, and scholastic perspective makes it easier to juxtapose the epistemological-scientific viewpoint of Ockham and Kant rather than an epistemological-theological viewpoint of Scotus and Newman. This significant difference has a bearing on two mysteries, the relation of the indwelling of the Holy Spirit and faith. Since the Newtonian discovery, these two mysteries cause difficulty for Kant. One way of studying them is through the emerging question of development of doctrine in Newman's *University Sermons* at Oxford. A second way is to relate natural and supernatural to the thesis on the primary motive

For private consultation and not distribution without the consent of E Ondrako

of the Incarnation for Scotus. It is by integrating that one will find the scotistic approach to indwelling and justification by faith. This is what Newman means by preparation of heart which situates him on the other side of the gap from Kant.

Special Points of Comparison

Ten significant motifs present in Scotus and Kant demonstrates their competing replies to the 'critical question' of interiorization. That question is perennial: in the context of faith and reason, what is the degree of 'interiorization' in a person? A second question is related: how is contemplating truth aided by the indwelling and faith viewed in contrast with reason? Newman helps to provide an insight into the complexity of answering the critical question and its corollaries about interiorization. First, for Newman faith is an assent with certitude. Second, faith includes a reasoning process which is its antecedent and is in a certain aspect an exercise of reason. Third, faith adopts the method of verisimilitude, and starts from religious first principles. Fourth, faith is kept from abuse, or superstition, by a right moral state of mind, by dispositions of religiousness, and by love of holiness and truth. In other words, Newman reasons in relation to religion with expertise in logical argument, a faculty of framing evidences, and starts from religious first principles.[26]

The seductive appeal of the Kantian form of modern idealism vs. Scotus's equilibrium

The world that gave rise to scholasticism had as well towering Christian theologians such as Aquinas, Bonaventure and Scotus, who gave priority to metaphysics over experience.[27] They provided the groundwork to engage modern idealism, its challenges to Christianity, and remain as lasting service to a post-Enlightenment environment. Scholasticism, properly taught, has a legitimate place for clear-headed thinking about contemporary problems. Taught poorly, it is better off in the dust bin or dismissed as an anachronism. German idealism, for example, tries to reconfigure modernity without a Christian code, into a religion of art, rather than incorporate both Christianity and art into the unity that it is. Although Kant and Hegel differ, both tried to reconfigure Christianity into a rational mode. For Kant, all knowledge is empirical and therefore anything else can not be validated as truth. Scotus anticipated the questions of Kant by his

---

[26] JOHN HENRY NEWMAN, *Oxford University Sermons* (London: uniform edition, 1871), Preface.

[27] This emphasis on contemplation of being rather than experience as it receives its due respect in psychology and sociology, is a critical juncture for a genuine hermeneutic of reform and adaptation in continuity with tradition.

For private consultation and not distribution without the consent of E Ondrako

revolutionary take on abstraction and intuition, the difference between the common concept and the singular reason for the divinity, and the autonomy of metaphysics.[28]

Kant feared a God forsaken universe and asked what kind of Christianity will survive in a rational world. He found his answer in freedom, the central philosophical conviction as the ultimate rational end of the human person. Friedrich Schleiermacher, the father of modern Protestantism, tried to counterbalance Kantian thought. German Catholics, lead by Ignaz von Döllinger, attempted to reply, but with mixed results. *Tuas Libenter* of Pope Pius IX, *Dei Filius* at Vatican I, and *Aeterni Patris* of Pope Leo XIII were a Catholic response to reaffirm the perennial validity of scholastic thought in new circumstances that included the Kantian definition of freedom in its highly individualistic form.

The form of modern idealism inspired by Kant and Hegel, although different from each other, has had a lasting influence into the twenty first century and is likely to remain for some time. Their thought finds a hearing among Catholic theologians, some called Transcendental Thomists, which may have an ambiguous connotation. Transcendental Thomists, of whom Karl Rahner and Bernard Lonergan may be the best known, intended to save Thomism from difficulties of neo-Thomism by following the inspiration of Joseph Marechal. The thought of the Transcendental Thomists and their philosophical substratum is complex and deserves its own comparison and contrast with Scotus, whom Richard Cross identifies succinctly as the one who was "the first to develop a strong libertarian account of freedom, one that applies to God too."[29] In a related way, Pope Benedict XVI frames this question as the relation of liberty to the will and intellect.[30]

I am convinced that as Vatican II engages modernity in a dialogical mode, a comprehensive Catholic reply to post Enlightenment challenges is in the practical theology of Scotus whose object is included in the object of metaphysics. Scotus's theology determines metaphysics by liberating it to allow it to accomplish its proper ends.[31] In that sense one can say that Scotus's is metaphysics of faith and freedom. The philosophy and theology of Scotus is a significant part of the reply[32] to Kant, who removes theology and theodicy from any effective means to help mankind to triumph over the root of evil and replaces it with his brand of anthropodicy, individualism, and Pelagian ideas. Kant is skeptical about the dogma of the Council

---

28 BOULNOIS, *Être*, 477, is emphatic and persuasive on this pivotal point.

29 R. Cross, Scotus' Metaethics.

30 POPE BENEDICT XVI, *Papal Audience on the Thought of Bl. John Duns Scotus*, July 7, 2010.

31 BOULNOIS, *Être*, 477.

32 POPE BENEDICT XVI, *Laetare Colonia Urbs*, Oct 28, 2008.

For private consultation and not distribution without the consent of E Ondrako

of Chalcedon. He rules out as supernaturalistic any expiation from Christ, and flattens the possibility and efficacy of grace as a help for human beings to make progress in virtue, and for their efforts to build a world of justice and charity. Kant substitutes an ambiguous view of progress with the help of Rousseau's social contract thinking and summarily replaces Catholic soteriology with heterodox thinking. He does, however, differ from some Protestant soteriology. Most of all, Kant is far removed from the authentic christo-centrism of Scotus, which is built on the primacy of charity and the primacy of the will. What makes Kant's thought a classic example of heteronomy, is his conclusion that if Christ saves a person, then, the person depends on another. For Kant, this is a slippery slope because it challenges the categorical imperative and freedom as the ultimate end of the human person.

The Church at Vatican II and attempts to 'Christianize' Kant

'Evolution' is a univocal, indifferent term for Scotus which could be atheistic or more properly theistic. Modernity may be studied from this point of view. The profundity of the Augustinian tradition and its interpretation by Anselm, the Victorines, and Bonaventure leads to Scotus. There was an evolution of metaphysics within a very short period of time which followed from Albert the Great and Thomas Aquinas who taught that God is the subject of metaphysics, to Roger Bacon and Giles of Rome who taught that God is one of the multiple subjects of metaphysics. The third wave included Siger of Brabant, Henry of Ghent, and Scotus who taught that God was one part of the subject of metaphysics. In this third wave, a new structure in fundamental concepts of metaphysics was born that has influenced the metaphysics of modernity. "Never had the autonomy of metaphysics been proclaimed with such force by a theologian,"[33] observes Olivier Boulnois, in reference to Scotus. Boulnois traces the contribution of Thomas Aquinas and Scotus on the metaphysics of Suarez, the intermediaries of Leibniz, Wolff and Baumgarten to Kant.[34] It is the Kantian discourse in *Religion within the Boundaries of Mere Reason* that looms on the horizon of contemporary discourse.[35]

At Vatican I, the Roman Catholic Church replied to many questions raised by the aforementioned developments. It was not until Vatican II that a sea change took place in reply to the critical question for every generation, that of 'interiorization' in continuity with the biblical,

---

[33] BOULNOIS, *Être*, 477.

[34] BOULNOIS, *Être*, ch. 9, 457–504.

[35] O'REGAN, Kant: Boundaries, 118. "It affects all discourses it comes in contact with and, depending on point of view, infects them."

For private consultation and not distribution without the consent of E Ondrako

patristic, scholastic and modern periods of thought. Given the metaphysical evolution sketched above, Scotus anticipated the modern questions at both Vatican Councils. It is no surprise that Newman considered Scotus his role model for academic excellence. "To live is to change," writes Newman in a balanced answer to the questions that Kant raises in *Religion within the Boundaries of Mere Reason.*

Good will and an initial flurry of change followed Vatican II, but only now, after a half of a century, can one see as dramatically how Scotus anticipated the Kantian achievement and the scholarly invitation to explain it to future generations who intuitively have competing views on the relation of freedom, the will and intellect. Scotus dealt more convincingly with the modern question, the critical question, with metaphysics as a distinct science and in freedom proper to its role. Theology and metaphysics determine each other and free themselves for their respective tasks. In this vital juncture, Newman expressly supports Scotus. Both support the thesis that evolution is creative and creation is evolutionary.

The dogmatic teaching on the Church at Vatican II took the world with surprise by its emphasis on the People of God.

> Christ is the light of all nations. The Holy Synod, which has been gathered in the Holy Spirit, eagerly desires to shed on all men and women that radiance of His which brightens the countenance of the Church, by proclaiming the Gospel to every creature. By an utterly free and mysterious decree of His own wisdom and goodness, the eternal Father, created the whole world. His plan was to dignify men and women with a participation in his own divine life. He did not abandon then after they had fallen in Adam, but ceaselessly offered them helps to salvation, in anticipation of Christ the Redeemer. All the elect, before time began, the Father "foreknew and predestined to become conformed to the image of his Son, that he should be the firstborn among many brethren (Rom. 8:29).[36]

Lumen Gentium continues: "We can say that in some real way they [who are consecrated by baptism recognize and receive other sacraments in their Churches or ecclesial communities] are joined with us in the Holy Spirit, for to them also He gives his gifts and graces and is thereby operative among them with his sanctifying power."[37] The continuity in reform and renewal at Vatican II reflects key themes in Newman's writings. *Lumen Gentium* said:

---

[36] Documents of Vatican II, *Lumen Gentium*, 1.

[37] *LG*, 2.15.

For private consultation and not distribution without the consent of E Ondrako

Those who have not yet received the gospel are related in various ways to the People of God. Nor is God Himself far distant from those who in shadows and images seek the unknown God, for it is He who gives to all men and women life and breath and every other gift (see Acts 17:25-28), and who as Savior wills that all men and women be saved. Those also can attain salvation who through no fault of their own do not know the gospel of Christ or His Church, yet sincerely seek God and, moved by grace, strive by their deeds to do His will as it is known to them through the dictates of conscience. Nor does Divine Providence deny the aids necessary for salvation to those who, without blame on their part, have not yet reached an explicit belief in God, but strive to lead a good life, under the influence of God's grace. Whatever goodness and truth is found among them is seen by the Church as a preparation for the Gospel.[38]

A century and a half after Kant and Hegel, the prophetic opening of the *Dogmatic Constitution on the Church* at Vatican II is replete with theological themes in reply to them, to nineteenth century philosophy and theology and its influence on the world. Newman would, in a sense, be an orphan without the controversies generated by and addressed by the many other great minds of his times, but he remained anchored in Scripture and the living Tradition from the Fathers to the present. Newman was called the absent father at Vatican II, the voice of a very significant English Catholic, and, therefore an English arc.[39] Examples of the German arc include those influenced by the rejection of Tradition as a source of revelation, the Reformers, and their subsequent influence on the thought of Kant, Hegel, and Schleiermacher, and by extension, Soren Kierkegaard.

The disjunctive transcendentals in Scotus and the phenomenal-noumenal in Kant

The point of departure for understanding the disjunctive transcendentals is with what Scotus notes. "This science which we call metaphysics and its name comes from "meta," that is to say "trans," and "ycos," which ought to say "science," in the sense of a transcendental (transcending) science, because it carries the transcendentals."[40] Boulnois notes that there is a significant evolution in metaphysics between Aquinas and Scotus, and

---

[38] *LG*, 2.16.

[39] E. ONDRAKO, *Freedom within the Church: The controversy between William Ewart Gladstone and John Henry Newman in 1874–1875 and its shadows and images over Vatican II* (Ann Arbor, MI: UMI, 1994).

[40] SCOTUS, in *Metaphysics*, Prologue, section 18, p.9.

For private consultation and not distribution without the consent of E Ondrako

Suarez, Leibnitz, Wolff, and Baumgarten which serve as steps to Kant. Therefore, it is not a surprise to expect an evolution in the thought of Kant from his *Critique of Pure Reason* (1787), to the *Critique of Practical Reason* (1788) and *Religion within the Boundaries of Mere Reason* (1794) with its anthropological turn and hermeneutical turn to the Bible. He discovered that his phenomenal or determined world has a noumenal aspect where the highest rational freedom as the end of the human person is found. Kant seems to secure that logic, ontology, and natural theology are centered on another focus, onto-theology.[41] In contrast, "the theory of transcendentals is not simply an important section of Scotus' metaphysics, it is his metaphysics. Like his metaphysics, it is saturated with theological implications."[42]

Boulnois's groundbreaking analysis of Scotus's thought as a step, in what he calls the new structure of metaphysics.[43] God is neither the subject of metaphysics nor one of the subjects of metaphysics. For Scotus, theology and metaphysics are distinct. Scotus produces a universal concept applicable to the divine essence, but in theology, this is known as singularity.[44] Scotus builds his argument that metaphysics is the highest science because it gives the noblest access possible to God, but it is not theology, nor is it part of its object, nor is it adequate for it. God is not the subject of metaphysics or its principle. The Aristotelian polarization of metaphysics with theology as a science is diminished because metaphysics is characterized as a transcendental science. It subject is being in general, which neither characterizes God, nor belief, but both in a common and indifferent way. The transcendental method must attain to God as included in the subject of metaphysics and conclude to his existence within the transcendental properties. Beginning with the possibility of a finite disjunctive transcendental, it attains to the existence of its correlation, the infinite disjunctive transcendental. God is attained as first, *primitas*, within a univocal concept, and is, therefore included in the most common object.

The opposition between being and nothing, that whatever is, is opposed to nothing, stands at the origin of Scotus's thought on the univocity of the concept of being, a concept and not a category. The disjunctive transcendentals, infinite and finite, necessary and contingent

---

41 Cyril O'Regan develops a definition of ontotheology and its pragmatic value in the current modern critical assessment of Hegel. See CYRIL O'REGAN, *The Heterodox Hegel* (Albany, N.Y.: State University of New York Press, 1994), 3.

42 ALLAN B. WOLTER, *Transcendentals*, 176–184. This quote is from 184. See p. 128–161 for Wolter's classification of Scotus's mentioning of illustrations of the disjunctive transcendentals. See page 138 for a synopsis.

43 BOULNOIS, *Être*, 472–475.

44 SCOTUS, *Ordinatio*, Prologue, 189 (I, 129).

For private consultation and not distribution without the consent of E Ondrako

have a simple difference. The pure perfection of the necessary infinite being is the source of the contingent. With this foundation, Scotus takes pains to demonstrate that our theology, as he calls it, requires autonomy from metaphysical knowledge without subalternating one to the other. The exegesis of "I am who I am " (Ex. 3:14) may be a purely rational meditation which conceives God as a being. This conception is oriented by theology but by right belongs to metaphysics alone.[45] The beginning of *De Primo Rerum Principio* is an excellent example of this kind of a metaphysical statement that enters a theological synthesis and reveals a double dimension: its terms are the object of *metaphysical* intelligence, but its composition in complex propositions set it in *theological* evidence. "Help me, Lord, when I seek to know how much natural reason can learn about that true being which You are if we begin with the being you have predicated of yourself."[46] Scotus's double dimension of using the disjunctive transcendentals is particularly helpful. On the metaphysical level, the mind abstracts to the Creator with eternal and immutable being, while affirming that the finite creature is subject to change. On a theological level, the creature comes to awareness of a relationship with the Creator and can change as he contemplates truth.

The disjunctive transcendentals complement what Scotus teaches about the first principle of the natural law, that God should be loved. "If God exists, He is to be loved as God alone, is a necessary consequence."[47] Every other precept of the natural law rests on this first principle. Scotus argues that the ultimate good of human nature is the beatific vision, which is grounded in the ego, the intellect, and the will.[48] Kant has difficulty with this because the concept of being is a pure product of the mind, without a bridge between the mental and extra-mental. The concept of being for Kant is a pure product of the mind which corresponds to nothing in reality. The univocal concept of being is not a pure logical construct first, but a unique incomparable formulation of divine illumination in logical form to keep logic securely linked to being. The final orientation of metaphysics for Scotus conceives of God, the subject of theology, under a more proper concept, which leads to a comprehension as mediated by the univocal concept of being.[49]

---

[45] BOULNOIS, *Être*, 476. He refers to SCOTUS, *De primo rerum principio*. ed. Allan B. Wolter, *A Treatise on God as First Principle* (Chicago: Franciscan Herald Press, 1966).

[46] SCOTUS, *De primo rerum principio*, 2.

[47] SCOTUS, *Ordinatio* 3.37.un., n.20 (Vatican, X, 280). See RICHARD CROSS, Scotus' Metaethics, fn. 28.

[48] BOULNOIS, *Être*, 2008), ch. 4, 151–221.

[49] *Être*, 477.

The nature of theology for Scotus differs from reason and Revelation in Kant

For Kant, "Revelation" means the empirical, historical sources of religious belief and practice. As to the essential doctrines, Kant does not think in terms of a hierarchy of truths as explained in Vatican II's *Decree on Ecumenism*,[50] but whatever constitutes "pure religious faith" for him does not depend on experience or history. Rather the source of these essential doctrines is *a priori* in pure practical reason. There is a difficulty to incorporate doctrines and revelation into the practice of a Church community. The Kantian difficulty is that revelation and doctrines do not determine the form of a church or ethical community. For Kant, three conditions must obtain to satisfy a "true" church.[51]

1. Its doctrines and practices must not contradict the principle of rational morality; it must be in that sense "within the boundaries of mere reason."

2. It must assign the pure religious faith of reason priority over its own historically conditioned doctrines and practices, regarding the later merely as a means or vehicle to the fostering and social embodiment of the former (*Religion* AK 6:178–82).

3. A "true" church must enshrine "a principle for continually coming closer to pure religious faith until finally we can dispense" with historical faith as a vehicle for religion (*Religion* AK 6:115).

Kant exalts the morally 'good will' meaning that the role of religion in history and human life is relegated to his very tight interpretation of good will as one finds in his demanding conditions to satisfy the definition of a true church.

The role of the will for Scotus is not Kant's 'good will.' A Bonaventurian metaphysical meaning and understanding of the desire for God, who is apprehended in Revelation, makes the difference for Scotus. The metaphysical dimension is paramount for theological knowledge because of its certainty. Metaphysics assists the study of the notions in dogmas. The study of the words in the creeds and the sacraments belongs to the dogmatic and authoritative part of theology. Christ is the teacher and Mary is teacher-witness.[52] Such proper study includes a relative freedom to experiment, hypothesize, and revise the formulations of dogmas without

---

[50] *Unitatis Redintegratio*, 11. This is the *Decree on Ecumenism*.

[51] ADAMS, xxxi, xxxii.

[52] PETER DAMIAN FEHLNER, *Mary and Theology: Scotus Revisited* (Rensselaer, N.Y., 1978, revised 2010), ch. 4, 157, 158, 163, 165 in this volume. Fehlner captures succinctly the Scotisic tone of metaphysics summarized in several paragraphs that follow. For a succinct view of the

For private consultation and not distribution without the consent of E Ondrako

changing their essential meaning, or, de-dogmatizing, a form of false eire-nicism. Finally, Bonaventure's schema includes prayer as the enjoyment of revelation in union with God.

The goal in the study of revelation for Bonaventure and Scotus is real knowledge and understanding of God. To this end, scientific knowledge alone is an intellectual exercise that has the power to make or to suspend definitive judgment in the form of a final assent. For Bonaventure and Scotus the correct use of scientific method does not begin with doubt that the definitive content of revelation can be known nor that the primary teacher can be trusted. In the absence of revelation that is dogmatically apprehended, the metaphysical aspect of theological activity becomes dry instead of a metaphysical aspect of theological activity identical with Christ's living in charity and faith in him as teacher.

As regards the nature of theology, the need for explicitation of the truths of faith, Bonaventure, Scotus and Thomas were mindful of the challenges, difficulties, and understood the possibility of development and error in any person who is engaging revelation, and seeking to make a judgment about God, namely, that God is. Newman continued this line of thinking about development with profound sensitivity to the personal quest for truth, which, in Bonaventure's formulation, is the journey of the mind to God. The scholastics use metaphysics in harmony with the light of the Holy Spirit. Thomas and Scotus have different but complementary approaches because they use metaphysics to study revelation while Kant does not. Thomas and Scotus agree that a direct understanding of God is not univocal but analogical, made known by proportions, or a way of knowing God and His will precisely in the way God has made himself known i.e., through revelation. Scotus holds that a person can appropri-ate and find theologically intelligible these proportions that convey direct understanding of God in the univocal concept of being. His argument from reason to the existence of God in *De primo rerum principio* is more cohesive than Thomas in the *Summa Contra Gentiles*.[53] Newman is close to Scotus in his argument for the existence of God from conscience.[54] Newman's argument is that of Anselm-Scotus in phenomenological form set forth in terminology with its psychological antecedents. In sum, there

---

framework for Thomistic metaphysics, see Robert Pasnau and Christopher Shields, *The Philosophy of Aquinas* (Boulder, CO: Westview Press, 2004), 49–80.

[53] Scotus, *De primo principio*, and Thomas Aquinas, *Summa contra Gentiles*, Book 1, ch 9–13.

[54] Adrian J. Boekraad, *The Argument for the Existence of God from Conscience according to J.H. Newman* (Louvain: Éditions Nauwelaerts, 1961). Boekraad does not mention Scotus but the similarities to one familiar with both Scotus and Newman are evident as he develops his thesis.

For private consultation and not distribution without the consent of E Ondrako

is a relation between the proof for God's existence from conscience, the *Itinerarium* of Bonaventure and *De Primo Rerum Principio* of Scotus.

Scotus uses metaphysical principles to understand the divinity of Christ as real even as it transcends the limits of human powers. Analogy helps him with the intelligibility of revelation. The theoretical grounds for intelligibility use proportion or analogy or the analogy of faith, that is, how truths form a harmony. In revelation, Christ is the teacher who teaches by intellectual analogy. Human understanding of what Christ is teaching is as a mirror reflecting divine harmony. Bonaventure, Scotus and Thomas use the method of the analogy of faith, i.e., sharing and comparing one article of faith with another. The teachings of Vatican I reaffirms this method and Vatican II adds the importance of the hierarchy of truths.[55] The inner consistency of this method is a rebuttal to Kant, i.e., that revelation and the analogy of faith help a person to make an assent that is certain, infallible and clear. The assent is with the help of the analogy of faith that is illumined by the light of faith. For Kant, illumination is the "presumed enlightenment of the understanding with respect to the supernatural (mysteries), the delusion of the initiates."[56] For Scotus, understanding in theology needs not only the teacher, Christ, but the influence of the Spirit and teacher–witness, Mary. Scotus's metaphysics has been called a Marian metaphysics, for this reason, that she is a teacher of Christian metaphysics because Mary understands the scotistic *decuit*, the fittingness of the Incarnation. To Kant, "dogmatic faith which announces itself to be *knowledge* appears to reason dishonest or impudent."[57]

The primacy of charity for Scotus and the categorical imperative for Kant

Kant's distinction between the mental and extra-mental reflects the concept of being as a pure product of the mind, which corresponds to nothing in reality. The univocal concept of being for Scotus enables him to employ the process of abstraction to form this concept of being in a manner that it is exactly the opposite of Kant. It warrants repeating that the univocity of being is not a pure logical construct only, but an incomparable formulation of divine illumination in logical form. Kant's distinction between mental and extra-mental plays out in his thought on duty, the categorical imperative. Scotus guides thought and keeps logic securely linked to 'what is.' The primacy of charity is open to individuation

---

55 *Unitatis Redintegratio*, 11.

56 WOOD and DI GIOVANNI, eds, *Religion*, 6.53, 72.

57 WOOD and DI GIOVANNI, eds., *Religion*, 6.52, 72.

For private consultation and not distribution without the consent of E Ondrako

and a creative exercise of freedom, will and intelligence. The categorical imperative is a heavy, depersonalized weight. The former has a metaphysical substratum and the latter, mathematical.

Scotus approaches the degrees of perfection in being in terms of the primacy of charity. Being is the metaphysical premise of psychology and ethics. The first examines the nature of pure or altruistic love, and the second, the norm of this love. Scotus formulates the primacy of charity and the will, not in psychological and ethical terms, but metaphysical, in terms of being. When he holds that the will has primacy over the intellect, he does not mean it in terms of selflessness or an ethical reason, nor of being that is oriented to communion with others, but in the metaphysical term of being as perfect act. It is not determined in any way by any concept of duty such as the categorical imperative of Kant. Perfect act is first, pure act, auto-initiated, voluntary as distinct from natural mode of action. The second act is totally contained in the first act. Without making these distinctions, one will never understand the difference between scotistic and ockhamistic voluntarism. This is a decisive point in offering a metaphysical view to uncouple Scotus from Kant and to suggest that a better coupling might be Ockham and Kant.

By using such traditional metaphysical principles, Scotus demonstrates how traditional metaphysics may contribute to reasoning about the primacy of charity, the dignity of the person, and meaning of freedom as the quality of voluntary action. This approach differs from Kant's rigid adherence to duty, the categorical imperative, and an accompanying arbitrary voluntarism. Scotus freely desires and pursues holiness. For Kant, the finite person cannot will or depend on the will, or love or grace of God revealed in the Incarnation.

The anthropology of Scotus, ethics, and hermeneutical turn for Kant.

Scotus's and Kant's anthropology are polarized. Scotus's anthropology builds on the premise that "the ontological change [from the causal capacity of our first parents] does not regard the nature of man, but his effective and existential condition."[58] The human person has a causal power that has been reduced because of sin, but the practical potential to achieve the objective proper to being human remains a practical potential

---

[58] Stephen Dumont, "Theology as a Science and Duns Scotus' Distinction between Intuitive and Abstractive Cognition" in *Speculum* 64, n.3 (July, 1989), 579–599. Benedetto Ippolito, "The Anthropological Foundations of Duns Scotus' Mariology" in *Acts of the Symposium on Scotus' Mariology, Grey College, Durham, England, September 9–11, 2008 Mariologia Franciscana II* (New Bedford, MA: 2009), 157–172.

For private consultation and not distribution without the consent of E Ondrako

in the person even with a lesser freedom. Kant places ethics in the realm of nature, or the phenomenal and not the noumenal.

As a realist philosopher, Kant recognizes the difference between meta-ethics or virtue ethics and his own philosophical convictions. He defines radical evil as choosing an evil maxim, the principle behind all moral actions, i.e., the means that a person chooses self and not the moral law. This is Kant's ground to explain the propensity of evil in a person. It is not a predisposition to good or it would be a holy will. Human beings over a period of time might be good, they might have a holy will, but that is an ideal because there are countless incentives not to behave morally.[59] Scotus, at the opposite pole, teaches that by contemplating truth, as it is revealed in metaphysics first, one is able to prepare to contemplate the one who claims to be the Way, the Truth and the Life. Kant misses this truth by separating the phenomenal from the noumenal world. He makes remote or takes away the joy that can come from the way of Scotus that humbly contemplates truth. Kant's freedom is the highest rational end of human beings, which is found in the noumenon, while Scotus's explanation is that finite freedom, which has something in common with God, will continue in heaven.

The surprising hermeneutical turn for Kant is in his *Religion within the Boundaries of Mere Reason*. The turn is to the Bible to draw out anthropological insights which contribute to his idea of freedom as outside the phenomenal order of determined freedom. Freedom in the noumenal order is not determined. Kant is raising a concern with Calvinist roots: I may be free if I do not have to contribute to my salvation, but how do I know if I am saved? The Lutheran answers *via* justification by faith, but Calvin epistemically qualifies that. The key questions are: is the person who has discovered the Calvinist or Lutheran kind of freedom, which is described in the noumenon of Kant now happy? What is the relation with the categorical imperative? In reply, there are many assumptions in Kant's ethics *sans* meta-ethics.

The difficulty has to do with assumptions and ideas that have been extrapolated and arbitrarily connected. For example, there is a problem, when a person who was held in esteem in a community for his or her virtue and moral rectitude, falls from virtue. The members of the community become victims of the assumptions they make about the person who may have done evil, and the assumptions contribute to outrage because they are assumptions that appear to be connected. Appearance is the Kantian way of describing commonplace happenings in a world of assumptions that

---

59 WOOD and DI GIOVANNI, eds., *Religion*, 65–73.

For private consultation and not distribution without the consent of E Ondrako

emerge as connected and may not be, yet outrage has been born. That is how a Kantian read of ethics differs from the virtue ethics of Scotus. Scotus recognizes that the person of virtue can fall from virtue, and the person who has been behaving immorally, can become virtuous. The Kantian dynamic of outrage caused by assumptions that have been extrapolated and arbitrarily connected is the Kantian trap that victimizes "persons of narrow views." Newman reflects the classical view of Scotus. "Persons of narrow view…show a secret misgiving about the truth of their principles. A state of uncertainty and distress follows. They who thought their own ideas could measure all things, end in thinking that even a Divine Oracle is unequal to the task."[60]

There is a wide divide between the outcomes of the hermeneutical turn of Kant and Scotus's thought on the will as a pure perfection, a *perfectio simpliciter simplex*. There are two affections of the will, the *affectio justitiae* (affection for justice and holiness) and *affectio commodi* (affection for happiness, self-preservation). The will is defined in relation to justice and holiness. By nature, the finite will has that affection, no matter if it strays by willful transgression from justice and holiness (virtue). Punishment is the sanction for guilt. The other part of finite will is its affection for what perfects its nature, for what is advantageous, the *commodum*. By defining the will in this manner, the will partakes of the character of an appetite, something that is in-built, a desire to perfect it. Love of what is advantageous, love of self, is not sinful or unjust *per se*. The main point is that metaphysics provides the premise for understanding all personal activity in and among finite human beings.

Without metaphysics, the psychological and ethical premises alone will not effectively answer the Kantian assumptions that appear connected and lead to bigotry or general skepticism. Scotus is a metaphysician-theologian who addresses virtue while Kant is a Protestant thinker with pietist leanings, but not a theologian. What Kant's ethics, *sans* meta-ethics, have done is to transfer a rule within Protestant theology into another horizon. Justification by faith is a critical concept for the Protestant thinking of Luther, and epistemically modified by Calvin. Strangely, this does not alleviate the anxiety of being saved, nor contribute to the happiness made possible by the virtue ethics of Scotus which leads to the conviction and happiness of those striving to be holy.

This is a key to how the primacy of charity and the primacy of the will of Scotus differ from Kant. Kant holds that the propensity to evil which remains inexplicable to humans and must be imputed to humans

---

[60] JOHN HENRY NEWMAN, *Oxford University Sermons* (London: uniform edition), sermon 14, no. 46.

For private consultation and not distribution without the consent of E Ondrako

is a supreme ground of all maxims that must in turn require the adoption of an evil maxim. Evil can have originated only from moral evil. When he tries to find the answer in Scripture, it represents the absolutely first beginning of all evil as incomprehensible, yet human beings, despite a corrupted heart, possess a good will and hope to return when they stray.[61] The hermeneutical turn for Kant to the Bible to draw out anthropological insights contributed to his discovery of freedom outside the order of determinism and within the noumenal. The reason for Christian hope and reply to the anxiety of not knowing about being saved is in knowing that one has a Savior-Redeemer who died for sins out of love and not out of necessity.

The absolute primacy of Christ in Scotus and Kant's Savior figure

Scotus describes the Savior-Redeemer as one who died for sin out of love not out of necessity. Prior to sin, Scotus identifies the divine plan and absolute primacy of Christ as Word Incarnate to be the Savior of the world and constructs a systematic elaboration of his mother to be the Mother of the Church. Scotus holds this as a revealed fact in the economy of salvation. This is a grace and every other consideration about creation is related to the motive and end of the primacy of Christ. In other words, the central premise for Scotus is the absolute predestination of Christ and the predestination of Mary.[62]

Kant follows a non-substitution theory where the Savior figure cannot substitute for human beings because each person has the moral duty to behave according to the categorical imperative. Salvation is prosecuted by the self that has sinned, which means that Kant's Savior figure suffered for sins but cannot save. Kant tries to explain suffering as ascribed to the self and notion of being redeemed. Here he is original because he offers an interpretation that makes substitution atonement something that is internal yet not a real process. The suffering of the Savior figure has been interiorized as suffering between the old and new person. Expiation is not what the Savior figure does on the behalf of humans but what the new person does on behalf of his old self.

Having made a hermeneutical turn by the time he is writing *Religion within the Boundaries of Mere Reason*, Kant set the stage for the allegorization of theological doctrine and biblical symbols. His strategy for interpreting the Bible is to set aside various symbols and helpful theological constructs while admitting some and moralizing or anthropologizing them. He uses

---

61 Wood and di Giovanni, eds., *Religion*, 64.

62 The predestination of Mary is not specifically mentioned by Scotus but by his immediate disciples in light of the theory of joint predestination of all of the elect in Christ.

For private consultation and not distribution without the consent of E Ondrako

philosophy to explain biblical symbols as a process of allegorization while assuming the position of *sola scriptura*, the literal sense, and distance from the allegorizing characteristic of Protestant interpretation. Ironically he includes a massive dose of allegorizing and, by doing so, set a pattern for theology and much of Protestant thought.

The historical Christ is not important within the Kantian heterodox freedom and the only way that Christ assists is by offering a degree of hope as archetype or exemplar. If a person undergoes conversion from following an evil maxim to choosing a good will, it is only because of Christ's example. The opposite is the exemplarist Christology that Scotus inherited from his theologian brother, Bonaventure, whose metaphysical exemplarism includes the hope to participate in a mystical element. This is not a Joachimite prioritizing of spiritual experience over metaphysics. Scotus qualifies Bonaventure's christocentrism because he thinks that a mathematical metaphor to communicate metaphysical truths runs the risk of the kind of misinterpretation of Joachim's errors which was affirmed by the Fourth Lateran Council. In a word, theology for Scotus is not a mathematical whole or system and bows humbly to the mystery of the love of the Trinity and the divine counsels that absolutely predestined Christ. Moreover, the natural law and revealed law are in relation both to Christ and his absolute primacy. The Ten Commandments are not simply a repetition of the natural law but Kant places it more explicitly in relation to the promised Savior in order not to constrain the divine lawgiver.[63]

The competing view is found in Kant's emphasis on experience, searching for the root of radical evil, and the possibility of change or conversion. If it occurs, it is without the help of any outside agent for conversion. It has to be internal to the person. Scotus's answer is in the necessary or immutable part of his theology with its center, the mystery of the Trinity, while the contingent part is what is known as the economy of salvation. In other words, the primary object of Franciscan theology is the Trinity, while the secondary object is the economy of salvation. Incarnational soteriology is contingent. For Scotus, the absolute primacy or predestination of Jesus and implicitly Mary are the point of contact for every person who cooperates with the graces given from a loving God who has *primitas*,[64] who wills all to be saved.

---

[63] There is much controversy around Hegel's trinitarian thought. However, *Lumen Gentium*, 61 affirms the position of Scotus about the limits of the mathematical metaphor. Moreover, in comparing the natural law with the divine revealed law, Scotus recognizes that nuances mean modifications or adaptations in relation to the lawgiver.

[64] ST. BONAVENTURE, *Questiones Disputatae de Mysterio SS. Trinitatis*, q. 8. PETER DAMIAN FEHLNER, "Neo-Patripassionism from a Scotistic Viewpoint" in *Quaderni di Studi Scotisti*

For private consultation and not distribution without the consent of E Ondrako

To recapitulate, it is by faith that we understand the divinity of Christ, not fully but partially. The understanding is real and transcends the limits of our native powers as humans which Scotus calls the metaphysical. What is in revelation and not easy to understand finds help towards intelligibility by analogy. What expresses the theoretical or possible grounds for intelligibility is also by analogy. Christ is the teacher who reveals the answers by intellectual analogy. This is as a mirror that reflects the divine in a way that human beings can understand the work of the Spirit to perceive the harmony and proportions reflected in the mirror. Bonaventure, Scotus and Thomas use the method of the analogy of faith (sharing and comparing one article of faith with another). Vatican I and Vatican II affirmed the analogy of faith and hierarchy of truths[65] at the heart of theological understanding, a reply to Kant, which has an inner consistency. The content of revelation and the analogy of faith helps a person to make an assent that is certain, infallible and clear, but the analogy of faith has to be illumined by the light of faith. For Scotus, understanding in theology needs not only the teacher, Christ, but the influence of the Spirit, and teacher–witness, Mary. Mary is a teacher of Christian metaphysics in this scotistic sense, because she understands the *decuit*, fittingness of the Incarnation, and shows how metaphysics reaches its proper end, to permit access to beatitude.[66]

The "meta-pedagogical ground" in Scotus and Kant's autonomous self

Kant has an agnostic (nominalist) period in his life when Descartes and David Hume and skepticism influence his signature strategy 'to deny knowledge in order to make room for faith.' Kant splits what should be united, that is, human consciousness and human experience. He separates faith from any certitude in the speculative order, or as Bernard Lonergan put it, dethroned speculative reason.[67] His hermeneutical turn leads to the discovery of finite autonomy to be the heart of human happiness as an even higher rational end. Scotus anticipates this turn by a position that unites and integrates the liberal knowledge between healthy secularity and freedom.

To unite liberal knowledge between secularity and freedom requires the cultivation of habits of knowledge, habits of virtue, and habits of right judgment along with the rigorous discipline of academic excellence. Scotus is Newman's greatest theological luminary at Oxford and the role

(Frigento: Casa Mariana Editrice, 2006), no. 3, 44, 45, 93. Henceforth, Fehlner, Neopatripassionism.

65 *Unitatis Redintegratio*, 11.

66 BOULNOIS, *Être*, 477.

67 BERNARD LONERGAN, *Insight* (New York: Philosophical Library, 1957, 1968), 373.

For private consultation and not distribution without the consent of E Ondrako

model for his academic excellence. The goal of a university is very different from a specialized academy. Healthy secularity is a free and personal choice to be happy, virtuous, and to seek holiness. Liberal intellectual formation teaches the love of knowledge and personal autonomy as the means to contribute to the building up of the world, hope for the cultivation of a civilization of love.

While Kant includes hope for immortality and other-world hopes, his empirical hope for this world through popular observance of the categorical imperative is cumbersome. His aspiration for progress based on an increase in good will in society is a false hope according to the thought of Scotus because it lacks sufficient metaphysical grounding.[68] The problem is caused by Kant's refusal to investigate hope using pure speculative knowledge, and to investigate only in the empirical order. Hope that is empirical alone is hope in progress that can bring great disappointment because the nature of progress is that it contains ambiguity. In contrast, the metaphysics of Scotus deals intelligibly with the relationship between the infinite and finite and enlightens the meaning of hope so that it can be understood and experienced.

To recapitulate, the meta-pedagogical ground, the idea of liberal knowledge in Scotus and Newman anticipate the hope in Vatican II that is humble and teaches the meaning of a universal call to holiness. The Church of Vatican II is unafraid of a university education as the soundest foundation in a person's life for the cultivation of the dogmatic principle of faith and basis for the cultivation of a life of faith. Vatican II sought the renewal of the whole Church, *ad intra* and *ad extra*, in continuity with its past, and according to the unity of knowledge, or scientific and eternal wisdom. On the other hand, Kant's view of organized religion and the Church affirms its necessity to promote a flourishing moral life, but his ideal Church is limited to an ethical function, without meta-ethics.[69] Worship is curiously important but futile because the attempt to please God by worship verges on a God with human vanity.[70] The result is depersonalized for Kant makes it impossible to find oneself in God. Rather the person stops at the 'self' with a form of vanity that accompanies the autonomy of a secularized person. Moreover, Kant's dethroning of the speculative reason leaves him anthropomorphizing God and the conclusion is that: "We create God in a way that we think we can easily win him

---

[68] WOOD and DI GIOVANNI, eds., *Religion*, xxv. See Introduction by ROBERT MERRIHEW ADAMS, vii–xxxii.

[69] ADAMS, xxix.

[70] Bonaventure warns about spiritual vanity when santification of the intellect is disregarded.

For private consultation and not distribution without the consent of E Ondrako

over to our advantage."[71] Therefore, dedication to God in this manner can be a mere delusion, an inclination to deceit and is to be condemned.[72] Scotus is poles apart.

Scotus, the intellectually mature person and holiness for the 21st century

The common insights of Scotus and Newman give a disciplined answer and are a powerful corrective for both secular modernist interpretations and rigid fideism. To this end, the cultivated judgment of the illative sense of Newman has affinities with the intuitive cognition works along with abstractive cognition in Scotus's thought. Notional and real apprehension and assent in Newman, and abstractive and intuitive cognition in Scotus are not meant to be separated. Together, they can deal effectively with the problem of Ockhamist inspired nominalism (agnosticism-voluntarism) which is veiled in pietism that Kant inherited. Agnosticism-voluntarism is Kant's Achilles heel which places him on the side of a secular modernist theory of interpretation. The Calvinist problem that Newman encountered in his early life as an Oxford curate had characteristics of rigid fideism. He extricated himself and avoided both extremes of fideism and the rationalism of the noetics by answering the critical question of interiorization, entering into the human heart. This problem if addressed by Kant's brand of pietism, without any place for grace,[73] leads to skepticism. If it is addressed by reason alone, it may lead to rationalism which is another version of skepticism.

In response to the scientific discoveries of Newton, Kant developed his view that Christianity's role in society is not erased and may continue, but with a contracted role. Newman was aware of the many currents relating to this typical Enlightenment response. Newman's metaphysical thought exudes from *The Idea of a University*. His epistemological thought follows in the sequel to the *Idea*, the *Grammar of Assent*. Newman specifically answers Locke and Hume and implicitly Kant. There is a trajectory of events in the life of Newman that identify his English form of theology and enable one to look back to his famous predecessor at Oxford, Scotus. His responses to the influence of the German theology of Kant and Hegel, in particular, coincide with a subtle development as a consistent systematic theologian that can be demonstrated as scotistic in orientation in the *Grammar of Assent*. His theory of education and metaphysical answers to the meaning

---

71 WOOD and DI GIOVANNI, eds., *Religion*, Section 6: 169–171, p. 167.

72 Section 6: 170, p.168.

73 WOOD and DI GIOVANNI, eds., *Religion*, pp. 168–171.

For private consultation and not distribution without the consent of E Ondrako

of the essence of a university implies that it is not by chance that he names Scotus as the greatest theological luminary Oxford ever knew and supports the theory that Scotus became the role model for Newman's definition of the essence of a university education, and his personal role model on the deepest level where the still waters of the soul run deep.

I think Newman held Scotus as his role model for academic excellence and exemplar for his deepest personal convictions on the meaning of holiness.[74] To Newman, Scotus is the model of a well-formed and intellectually mature person, one who is balanced in the speculative and practical use of reason, one who exercises prudence and all of the virtues. Such a person is one whose life and example could not do more for giving reasons to secular modernity why the Catholic faith is not only attractive but a far cry from unbelief or the heavy impersonal weight of Kantian moral duty. The Newmanian definition of holiness is "to do all things well." It may be as ascetic a definition as possible, but, it convinces me that the intention of achieving academic excellence, if one is so privileged, is integral to true holiness. Such a person takes his or her place in the public square and in family life as a subtle counterpoint to the atmosphere of secular modernity that is chronically inhospitable to those who live by conviction.

Uncoupling Scotus and Kant and the new structure of metaphysics

Evolution is creative and creation is evolutionary. This thesis is premised on the integration of divine transcendence and human development in the Incarnation of the Word. God the Word does not cease to be God when he becomes immanent in the world and related to it. With the Incarnation, God the Word does not merely transcend the world, neither by physical causality but maintains personal and transcendental relations to the world. This interpretation of theistic evolution is in creative fidelity to the thought of Scotus and Newman, which is neither the nominalism of Ockham nor a radical tendency in the Roman Church. That is the reason for devoting time to build an argument and sensitivity to uncoupling, should there have been a coupling of Scotus and Kant.

Boulnois[75] observes that "never before Scotus had the distinction between abstraction and intuition been so firm," but they are meant to be taken together. I add that never before Newman has the distinction between the nominal and real been so firm, and they are meant to be taken together.

---

[74] CYRIL O'REGAN, "The Call to Holiness," Lecture at the University of Notre Dame, January 24, 2011 (unpublished). O'Regan does not say this specifically but implies it in this lecture and a related lecture at the National Newman meeting in Pittsburgh, August 6, 2010, a position I fully support.

[75] BOULNOIS, Être, 477.

For private consultation and not distribution without the consent of E Ondrako

This is an important key for both, i.e., to be taken and used together, not separately. Boulnois observes that "never before Scotus had the common concept and the singular reason for the divinity been so neat." Fehlner observes that in Newman's *Grammar of Assent* the concept of univocal being and in particular the pure perfections, the *perfectio simpliciter simplex* rather than the thomistic act/potency analysis to explain the correlation of simple and complex in the human intellect and will fit as a phenom-enological discussion of conscience and assent-inference.[76] Boulnois adds that "never had the autonomy of metaphysics been proclaimed with such a force by a theologian." There is a nexus between inference-assent and the illative sense in Newman and mental activity and the natural judgment in the Franciscan theologian disciples of Francis.

These distinctions make a significant difference between scotistic and ockhamistic voluntarism. There is a decisive metaphysical point to uncouple Scotus from Kant and to suggest that a better coupling might be Ockham and Kant because Kant's voluntarism has affinities with Ockham's nominalism. For Scotus, perfect act has to be first. The second act, even if perfect and infinite, is totally contained within as content of the first.

> The first act defines what is meant be free action, the second what is meant by determined action. This is why voluntary action enjoys priority over natural, love over understanding. Both have the same object: being. But in the case of knowledge the object wholly determines the character of the action, whereas in love it is necessary and free, as well as free and rational, because knowledge or natural action, instead of being outside of and prior to willing act as its guide, is totally within it as its complement and joy.[77]

The subtlety of the *Grammar* which is the sequel to the *Idea of a University* is an epistemological work meant to illumine the metaphysical principles in the *Idea of the University*. Moreover, Newman's theory of knowledge illuminates the themes of faith, reason and development in the earlier *University Sermons* at Oxford, and *Essay on Development of Doctrine*. For Newman, besides the influence of Bishop Joseph Butler's *Analogy*, it is gradual deepening of his understanding of Mary and not Hegel, who becomes the first or primary influence on his ideas about development and change. For the same reason, she, and not Kant, becomes the first or primary influence on his epistemology in the *Grammar*, his cautious reply to Locke and Hume, and, implicitly, to Kant about the critical question of entering the heart in the quest for truth. The *Apologia pro vita sua* is the

---

[76] FEHLNER, Dialogue.

[77] FEHLNER, Neo-Patripassionism, 82.

For private consultation and not distribution without the consent of E Ondrako

answer to Newman's theory of faith. In sum, although Kant's philosophy demonstrates his worries about a religionless world, it is Newman and Scotus who are a *via media* between rigid fideism and secular modernism.

With the help of Newman, who serendipitously puts Scotus into modern English, I have been developing reasons to link Scotus and Kant in a linear historical sense only for what Boulnois calls the new structure in metaphysics that he has observed from the time of Albert the Great and his influence on Thomas Aquinas through Scotus and Thomas's influence on Suarez to Kant. In so doing, my purpose is to offer substantial reasons to delink Scotus from any misreprésentation of cause and effect on Kant's onto-theology. With the groundbreaking help of Boulnois, I cannot find a thread between them. Hence, is my solicitude about reading any form of Kantian thought into the thought of Scotus, and by extension, not reading Kantian thought into Newman.

Kant exemplifies a gifted mind in search of self-activation and autonomy but forgetful of God's invitation and help to cultivate a loving, personal, relationship with God. Kant puts God in brackets and can only find self and not God because the concept of God is based on morally transcendent ideas introduced into religion with effects on inner experiences (effects of grace) which is nothing more than *enthusiasm*. To the extent that there are alleged outer experiences, they are miracles and nothing more than *superstition*.[78] In reply, the primacy of will over intellect is an ancient traditional position about the will and conviction which in Bonaventure's chapter three and four of his *Itinerarium* unfolds in light of the journey of the mind to God

For Scotus, the intellect and will are *perfectiones simpliciter simplices* meaning that they cannot be broken down into any simpler reality. The Franciscans were not the first to reason that the primacy of the will leads will and intellect closer to God and that the intellect can be blinded to the light which leads it in the direction of agnosticism or skepticism. However, the formal distinction *a parte rei* between will and intellect is a powerful tool for Scotus, meaning one reality although formally distinct. This view is far from Kant's will in *Religion within the Boundaries of Mere Reason*. Kant's anthropological turn tries to explain how and why human beings can be perverse and concludes that human beings are noumenally free but phenomenally determined.

---

[78] WOOD and DI GIOVANNI, eds., *Religion*, 6.52, 72.

For private consultation and not distribution without the consent of E Ondrako

Recapitulation: personal convictions about de-linking Scotus and Kant

The first pivotal point is that the metaphysics and theology of Scotus depends on the univocal concept of being which is far from the logic, ontology and natural theology which makes up the onto-theology of Kant. Scotus recognizes that "every being without exception is either contingent or necessary, substance or accident, absolute or relative, and the like."[79] By his groundbreaking use of the disjunctive transcendentals, Scotus refines Bonaventure's theory of divine illumination with the univocity of the concept of being.[80] It is an incomparable formulation of divine illumination in logical form so that it can be the light guiding all our thought, keeping logic securely linked to reality or being. Not all are clear on the reasoning for this refinement by Scotus, but the answer to the correctness of this development is in Scotus's subtle use of the disjunctive transcendentals. He resolves the critical question or relationship between an object produced by the intellect and the reality it is intended to signify.

For Kant the critical question is to find a means to link what is mental to what is extra-mental. His *Critique of Pure Reason, Critique of Practical Reason*, and *Religion within the Boundaries of Mere Reason*, never address the idea of contemplating truth itself as it reveals itself. This is where the metaphysics of Scotus differs radically and offers the first light to help a person to freely take the step to believe that Truth was born in time and became Savior of all. As a finite human being, Scotus humbly contemplates his dependence on the love and grace of God manifested in the infinite will, a pure perfection, *perfectio simpliciter simplex*. Kant's concept of being is only in the mind, the noumenon, and has nothing corresponding in reality, the phenomenon. Scotus employs the process of abstraction to clarify that metaphysics is separate from experience without denying the reality at the heart of experience. The difference for Scotus is that metaphysics is distinguished from natural, conscious experience *a parte rei*,[81] while Kant separates irreconcilably what is in the mind (noumenon) from this reality (phenomenon).

The second pivotal point for Scotus is how he employs the formal distinction *a parte rei* which means one reality but formally distinct, *realiter*

---

[79] WOLTER, The Transcendentals, ch. 6, 128. Chapter treats the disjunctive transcendentals 128–161. Appendix A is a sketch of Wolter's treatment on p. 161.

[80] I am grateful to Fehlner's recent and extensive work on Scotus's thought, the significance of which I would not have comprehended without becoming familiar with several of his works that are now in print.

[81] OLIVIER BOULNOIS, *La rigueur de la charité* (Paris: Les Éditions du Cerf, 1998). See FEHLNER, Neo-Patripassionism, 40, fn. 3.

For private consultation and not distribution without the consent of E Ondrako

unum, formaliter distinctum. The intellect and will are formally distinct *a parte rei*, but one reality. Scotus helps the searcher for truth to comprehend something quite real, a mysterious reality *a parte rei*, a concept of experience which includes a supernatural element that the mind contemplates as the will desires truth. That reality may seem dim at the natural level, but together with the gift of supernatural faith, that dim natural light becomes more radiant. It is perfected as intuitive knowledge rather than conceptual knowledge and tends to merge with charity as perfect being. Intuitive knowledge leads to the understanding of experience that needs metaphysical and dogmatic guidance.

When one makes an act of faith in the Incarnation, for example, this act is no longer made up of only abstract concepts for Scotus. Rather, the abstract concepts together with intuition, contribute to a free and real profession of faith. Newman describes the desire and hard work of reasoning together with, at least a dim light of faith and the perdurance of humble contemplation, that is no longer notional alone, but together with the real [a mysterious reality *a parte rei*] as contributing to real assent of what the mind has been contemplating.

The third pivotal point is Scotus's thought on the will which is not that of Kant. From a Kantian standpoint, the two affections of Scotus, the *affectio justititae* and *affectio commodi* are incommensurable with freedom as the highest rational end of the human person in the Kantian noumenon. Kant is influenced in his definition of the will from a miscegenist Protestant backdrop, i.e., Zwingli, Calvin, Luther, and variations on their individualism and pietism. *Au contraire*, Scotus's will is based on a metaphysics of the univocal concept of being, the will as a pure perfection, and personal act as individuated, i.e., incommunicable existence. That is why Scotus defines the will in relation to justice. By nature, the will has an affection for justice, the *affectio justitiae*, no matter how unjust the finite will may act. Therefore, by nature there arises guilt for acting unjustly. By nature, the will also has an affection for what is advantageous to it, the *affectio commodi.* That means that by nature, the will, or what perfects the nature of the will has the character of an appetite for what perfects it. Therefore, suffering is only possible where the will has an appetite or desire for something that perfects it and does not get it.

The fourth pivotal point is that the absolute primacy of charity in Scotus is inseparable from the absolute primacy of Christ. The two affections, *affectio justitiae* and *affectio commodi* have everything to do with making intelligible the absolute primacy of Christ and the mystery of the Incarnation and explaining love that is willing to suffer, the mystery of the hypostatic union, a union of the divine and the human, a contingent

For private consultation and not distribution without the consent of E Ondrako

reality that provides the basis for Christian ethics that God should be loved and one's neighbor loved as oneself. For Scotus, the radical goodness of God and of creation for its own sake is guaranteed by the primacy of Jesus and Mary. There is an abyss between the theology of the cross of Scotus and that of Calvin and Luther and the pietists. One starts with the reality of love and the Incarnation while the other starts with the reality of evil and sin. Scotus's metaphysics serves authentic christocentrism. Scotus's "adequate object of theology is not Christ, but something common (univocal) to the Word, about whom articles (of the Creed) primarily pertain, and to the Father and Holy Spirit, with whom the remaining theological truths deal."[82]

The fifth pivotal point is that more than any of his predecessors, Scotus establishes the principle of independence within interdependence and allows metaphysics and theology to be united more profoundly. Each leans on the other to exist but both need the intellect with its transcendental powers to be sciences. Metaphysics is not a laicization of theology, no more than theology governs the development of metaphysics. The constitution of each is different and that implies autonomy. Scotus's *perfectio simpliciter simplex* means a pure perfection that is necessary and free in God. A pure perfection is irreducibly simple and what is simple is more perfect because it lacks the notion of potentiality and act.[83] The same pure perfection is contingent and free in the finite human being as it was for our first parents. Kant's logic, ontology, and natural theology as it plays out in his idea of onto-theology is current in that it gives insight into the logical categories of modern idealism, but it is not the contemplative intuition into the goodness of being that is distinctly found in the light of the Incarnation.[84]

Conclusion

The Enlightenment is very complex and any attempt to blame a single person or movement is doomed to failure. A valid question is to ask if Ockham may be a more likely candidate as precursor of Kant than Scotus. In reply, a fine argument can be made to posit Ockham for that title, but the primary intention in this essay is to offer several reasons to de-link any connection between Scotus and Kant. Three points stand out. First, Scotus distinguishes metaphysics *a parte rei* from natural human experience and that the end of theology is to love but in order to know what to love, one

---

82 SCOTUS, *Ordinatio* III p. 3, qq. 1–3, n. 174. See FEHLNER, Neo-Patripassionism, 38–39.

83 WOLTER, *Transcendentals*, 159 and 174.

84 W. Hoeres.

For private consultation and not distribution without the consent of E Ondrako

needs metaphysics. Second, Ockham's nominalism reduces the range of Christian philosophical intelligence to the point that one can understand almost nothing about what one believes. Third, Kant reduces the range of Christian theological intelligence. He "essentially changes the pregiven borders, and by so doing neutralizes religion, in general, and Christianity, in particular, as a potential and actual competitor."[85] What Ockham and Kant have in common is that the human intellect is reduced to an almost blind acceptance of everything. In Bennett's view, Ockham replaces "faith seeking understanding with faith rebuking understanding."[86] Ockham's thinking warrants a close study with Kant's development in the *Critique of Pure Reason, Critique of Practical Reason,* and the anthropological and hermeneutical turn in *Religion within the Boundaries of Mere Religion.* Such a study reveals why Kant's readers to this day may be moved by his take on faith and reason and his understanding of freedom.

What differs significantly from Kant in this essay, in my view, is that Scotus and Newman reflect the Bonaventurian metaphysical and theological synthesis *On the Reduction of the Arts to Theology.* Bonaventure is ascetic in his summary: "It is likewise clear how wide the illuminative way may be, and how the divine reality itself lies hidden within everything which is perceived or known."[87] Here is where Ockham rejects any universal knowledge and accepts that only knowledge of individuals is valid and reduces the universal concept of being to something logical, a product of the mind. His conclusion is that reality is individual and no human philosophical investigation may take place except for the empirical method. By thrusting aside universals, the analogical notion of the knowledge of God is impossible. The Ockhamist criticism of traditional Christian wisdom "makes any metaphysics worthy of the name impossible."[88]

This is a glimpse into the fourteenth and fifteenth century struggles between realists and nominalists in the universities and the breakdown in the relation of faith and reason that followed for centuries. Sadly, the quality of engagement between the metaphysical-theological approach and developing empiricism and rationalism did not seem to take advantage of resources such as the volumes of Scotus's philosophy and theology published by the Franciscans. The Conventual Franciscans Angelo Vulpes (d. 1647) and his pupil Bartholomeus Mastrius (d. 1673) were Scotists of particular note in the seventeenth century when there was a rich engagement and contrast with both the Dominican and Jesuit Thomism.

---

[85] O'REGAN, Kant: Boundaries, 87–126. See 108.

[86] BENNETT, 50.

[87] BONAVENTURE, *De Reductione Artium ad Theologiam,* 26.

[88] BENNETT, 50–51.

For private consultation and not distribution without the consent of E Ondrako

By the end of the eighteenth century Kant's reply to the relation between faith and reason and the neutralizing of religion in general made John Henry Newman 'worry.' He was persistent in challenging several dimensions of this split through his Oxford University Sermons, his metaphysical argument of the essence of a university, and epistemological amplification in the *Grammar of Assent*. More than a century later, Pope St. John Paul II wrote *Fides et Ratio* in a true Newmanian spirit, to counter the discursive colonization. Pope Benedict XVI knows the challenges and exemplifies the Bonaventurian-Scotistic-Newmanian conviction that "the fruit of all sciences is that faith may be strengthened, God may be honored, character may be formed, and consolation may be derived from union of the Spouse with the beloved, a union which takes place through charity."[89]

Future research calls for tracing a line of cause and effect from Ockham through Gabriel Biel, who taught Martin Luther, to significant influences on the reformers, through Francisco Suarez, Leibniz, Wolff, and Baumgarten to Kant. The Kantian theory of object is largely guided by the Suarezian tradition. Boulnois summarizes the structure of metaphysics in the evolution from Scotus to Kant as having a quadripart articulation, but it is easier to describe Kant's take on logic, ontology, and natural theology as recentered around an onto-theological focus.[90] Notably, the scotistic discussion of efficacious grace and human freedom is integrally related to the valid utility of the notion of evolution in metaphysics. Evolution[91] is used not as connected with time in general, nor natural causality, nor first with physical growth, but as primarily connected with history, with voluntary causality, with cultural growth where both Creator and human person are involved in establishing the rational character of contingent change.

I end with this caveat about using the notion of evolution and suggest that the theory of condetermination in the context of the scotistic discussion of efficacious grace and human freedom may be a further illuminating substratum to Cyril O'Regan's observation that Kant redraws the map of the empire of reason and neutralizes Christianity as a potential and actual contributor. It is no surprise that in his earlier work on Hegel, O'Regan calls onto-theology an ugly term, "but it can be justified on the pragmatic grounds that it is current in the modern critical assessment of Hegel.[92] The next step in this research is: "Being and Becoming: Hegel's Inversion and Newman's Consistency with Scotus."

---

89 *De Reductione*, 26.

90 Boulnois, *Être*, 493–504.

91 See fn.4.

92 O'Regan, *The Heterodox Hegel*, 3.

For private consultation and not distribution without the consent of E Ondrako

Appendix A[93]: The Disjunctive Transcendentals of Being

All of these attributes are in disjunction and are coextensive with being

Those which are primarily correlatives

Being either:

1. Is prior or posterior
2. Is a cause or is caused
3. exceeds or is exceeded

Those which are either materially or formally contradictories

Being is either:

1. actual or potential
2. independent or dependent
3. necessary or continent —
4. substantial or accidental
5. finite or infinite
6. absolute or relative
7. simple or composed
8. one or many
9. the same (equal) or different (not equal)

---

93 Wolter, *Transcendentals*, 161.

For private consultation and not distribution without the consent of E Ondrako

CHAPTER 16

Being and Becoming: Hegel's Inversion and Newman's Consistency with Scotus

Edward Ondrako

Précis.

The radical goodness of God and of creation according to John Duns Scotus competes with the view of absolute spirit in the thought of G. W. F. Hegel. By the time of his 1824 *Lectures on the Philosophy of Religion*, Hegel irrevocably inverts the unity of metaphysics and theology in Scotus and the coherent whole between the primary object of Franciscan theology, the Trinity, and the secondary object of that theology, the economy of salvation. John Henry Newman was a systematic consistent theologian at heart[1] and the system governing Newman's consistency resembles some of thomistic structure but was, arguably, scotistic at heart, in the sense that his thought echoes the definition of the will, freedom and necessity or independent being in the Franciscan school. After reading Bishop Joseph Butler's *Analogy* in 1823, Newman became an enthusiastic devotee. On his own and Butler's epistemological grounds, Newman found conscience to be the means by which human beings experience God. He gradually became drawn to Scotus who mirrors the mind of Christ as reflected in the one living, uninterrupted Tradition of the Church.

Prefatory Note

Several ideas, especially Butler's preference for natural theology and his teaching on the sacramentality of creation as inherited from the Alexandrines, Clement, and Athanasius, influenced Newman's philosophical view of the world. Contra Hegel, Butler influenced Newman's patristic

---

[1] Hermann Geissler, the director of the Internation Centre for Newman Friends, Rome, closed the International Conference on Newman, November 22–23, 2010 at the Gregorianum in an apodictic manner with the statement that Bl. John Henry Newman was not a systematic theologian but without defining what he meant. This essay takes a competing view that Newman had an overall consistent optic.

567

For private consultation and not distribution without the consent of E Ondrako

formation and is a step towards the views of Scotus on the relation of the natural and supernatural orders. Through Butler, Newman came in contact with aspects of the great scotistic tradition in England, although Newman had not read the works of Scotus. Hegel's inversion of Scotus centers on being and becoming, an indispensable distinction. It took time for Newman with his characteristic scholarly and scientific precision to understand the significance that liberal knowledge has theology and metaphysics as its center. This is a critical point to assessing the merit of the thesis about parallel thought patterns in Scotus and Newman.

There are two crucial presuppositions for this thesis. First, metaphysics is a transcendental science in preparation to engage thoughts about God. Second, there is an absolute character to metaphysical truth that takes precedence over any theory of inculturation or metaphysical subversion such as that of Hegel who changes the language to mean that the Trinity functions as a super explanation. This subversion serves as a logical conceptual apparatus to translate the Trinity into another idiom, one that serves as a massive conceptual step of smoothing, an explanation of all things, past, present, and to come.

The scholarly study of Christian metaphysics and theology which is 'the study of God and the relations between God and the universe,' depend on applying the contributions of the Hebrew Scriptures, the Greek and Latin Fathers, and the scholasticism of Thomas and Scotus to the study of the Trinity and Incarnational soteriology as the central point of reference. This Christian contribution enjoys a dialogical relationship with religious, intellectual and cultural history, but the focus is on the Trinity and Incarnational soteriology. The thought of Newman, especially his practical apologetics, is attentive to the character of metaphysics[2] and is no less systematic than the thought of Thomas and Scotus.

The doctrine of the Trinity was divisive in England from the seventeenth century and Newman seems to have had extraordinary pastoral sensitivity to people who could not affirm the Trinity but may have an experience of God and may use other terms than conscience as Newman prefers. Unlike his earlier works in defense of the doctrine of the Trinity, in *Select Treatises on St. Athanasius, Athanasius against the Arians,* and *Essay on the Development of Doctrine,* in the *Grammar of Assent,* Newman affirms the Trinity but distinguishes that the Trinity is not a subject of real apprehension. Every aspect of the Trinity may be open to real apprehension and real assent, but as a totality, the human person cannot take it all

---

2   JOHN HENRY NEWMAN, *Grammar of Assent* (London: uniform edition). Newman's convictions about the study of philosophy are succinct in his letter of gratitude, written on 14 December 1879, to Pope Leo XIII for the pastoral letter that encouraged the renewal of the study of philosophy, *Aeterni patris,* August 4, 1879. LD 23: 212.

For private consultation and not distribution without the consent of E Ondrako

in one view. In the *Grammar*, Newman is careful to depart from Locke's view about inference and entitlement. He avoids the Lockian trap of an illicit generalizing in religious matters, and uses an empirical method in the *Grammar* to teach about the Trinity, not as an object of real assent, but notional assent, on the mode of how everyone makes notional assents in everyday life.

The *ratio* of all contingent being is to participate in fellowship with the Father and the Son and the Holy Spirit. The study of the Trinity is the theology of necessity. The study of Incarnational soteriology is the *oikonomia*, the theology of contingency. The ascetic formulation is: "*theology* refers to mystery of God's inmost life within the Blessed Trinity and *economy* to all the works by which God reveals himself and communicates his life."[3] For Scotus, scholarly study requires the proper use of the disjunctive transcendentals and the *depositum fidei*, or orthodox Catholic teaching. For Hegel, the Trinitarian view is central but heterodox, with the final realization of the Incarnation as counter intuitive. Hegel holds that the death of Jesus is the death of God which is not a lament but something to celebrate because it is the death of the absolute transcendence of God. According to Hegel, eternity and time are collapsed. What is changeable and not changeable is collapsed. Hegel collapses the immanent Trinity into the economic Trinity which means that the Christian narrative of God's action in the world has no trace of contingency, accident or gratuity in order to rise to a higher order of syllogism and to give way to a concept that explains past, present and future. The circle is closed.

Newman's writings coincide with this post-Hegelian world, which saw the rise of right wing Hegelianism of an eclectic sort in Denmark and Kierkegaard's critique, and left wing Hegelianism in Germany in Marx, but, arguably, with a less than sufficient critique. Newman, ever alert to the controversies of his day, offers a substratum to help the theology of necessity and the theology of contingency to keep from being reconstructed by some form of idealistic spirituality or Hegelian influences. The thought of Newman and Scotus is a lens to view how Hegel substantively reverses the immanent and economic Trinity. The neo-Hegelian influences after Vatican II, in a sense, were anticipated by the two great Oxford theologians. Their insights are critical to interpreting Vatican II in fidelity to the intention of Pope John XXIII and his successors. Tradition, properly understood, and not future novelty is the criterion of theological truth. It is not what is coming to be or experienced alone that drives reform

---

3 *Catechism of the Catholic Church*, 1994, no. 236.

For private consultation and not distribution without the consent of E Ondrako

and adaptation, but continuity with tradition, based on and critiqued by being, that Scotus and Newman hold in exceptional balance.

Part I: The Problem of Being and Becoming

Introduction

Scotus reflects the Franciscan school that being is in flight from nothing.[4] Creator and creature share in whatever is, in reality, as opposed to nothing. Univocity is a concept that makes other concepts or categories possible. Univocity is a means of discussing that being is not becoming or change so that it may not be nothing. The Creator has immutable being. The creature is subject to change because of the love of the Creator. The difference between the infinite and finite, the necessary and contingent, to be and not to be, to act and not to act, comes from the pure perfection of the necessary infinite being as the source of all that is contingent. An application is to recognize why hate is not the same as love. *Eros* is not the same as *agape*. *Eros* for creatures is a point of reference for defining *agape* in the Creator. This scotistic view of being is predicated of the Trinity as being simply first and not being subject to succession. In support of this conclusion, Scotus demonstrates that human beings have a perception of self even before forming a concept of self, and that perception recognizes that the finite ego is not first, but that there is another supreme being that is first, a perception through synderesis or conscience, which Newman holds as well.[5]

Through memory, the perception leads to recognition that there is a difference between what is finite and what is infinite, the intrinsic modes of being,[6] and to at least a fundamental proof of divine existence which one may accept or reject or modify in the heterodox form as Hegel. Whether Hegel believed in the existence of God or is a skeptic is not clear because he depends on Spinoza's *Ethics* and concept of eternity as non-durational, a view that is mechanist and mystical as found in some forms of stoicism and in some Christian mystics. That Scotus and Newman prove the

---

[4] I can not adequately relate the profound influence that both Peter Damian Fehlner and Cyril O'Regan have had on my thinking in preparing this essay. Any shortcomings are mine and not those of two of the finest and most disciplined and open minds dealing with the challenging thought of Hegel in relation to Newman and Scotus.

[5] ADRIAN J. BOEKRAAD and HENRY TRISTRAM, *The Argument from Conscience to the Existence of God according to John Henry Newman* (Louvain: Éditions Nauwelaerts, 1961).

[6] OLIVIER BOULNOIS, *Être et Représentation* (Paris: Presses Universitaires de France , 1999, rpt. 2008), chapter four, 151–221. Henceforth, BOULNOIS, *Être*.

For private consultation and not distribution without the consent of E Ondrako

existence of God by entering into the self, or the heart, is not only their argument, but that of Augustine and Bonaventure. That is essentially how in his teaching on the Incarnation, Scotus is able to integrate metaphysics and experience and define theology as practical rather than the speculative psychologism of Hegel. It is a small step for Scotus to conclude that human beings are all predestined to glory before any consideration of sin and redemption, a view that includes the dignity of the person and genuine character of freedom.

For Hegel, the spirit is constitutive rather than Christ, the spirit is the community. That is why Hegel avoids the topic of the Resurrection, for the empty tomb is evidence that Christ is divine and cannot be human. The Resurrection and Ascension are minimized in favor of the real resurrection at Pentecost for the spirit is the community.

In Thomas and in Scotus, God has no becoming. God is pure act. Hegel's 'eternal history of the spirit' reverses this thomistic and scotistic opposition, and identifies being and nothing. This means that what is, reality, is identified with change. Hegel's conceptual understanding of the world is as an endless circle of becoming or change. Hegel suggests a giant religious syllogism moving from the Father to the Son and through the Son to the Holy Spirit. All of Christianity is summarized as a syllogism where there is no trace of contingency. Rather there is a self-mediating concept that all things past, present and to come are in a circle that is closed.

In diagnostic terms, Hegel has collapsed the theology of necessity into the theology of contingency but he does not see it that way. There are further dimensions. Hegel collapses metaphysics into psychology such as found in modern idealism, especially its German forms. Second, by taking the 'meta' out of metaphysics, Hegel collapses metaphysics into physics, into evolutionism, which means grounding thought into the empirical rather than the metaphysical. It is a small step for Hegel to reverse the position that metaphysics has priority over experience, the objective over the subjective. In this regard, it is critical to understand that metaphysics and experience are connected. What is real, though, is not identical with experience. In other words, all experience requires metaphysical or dogmatic guidance. In sum, it is unreality to identify reality with change because it is impossible to be and not to be, to be infinite and finite at the same time. That is the problem when Hegel identifies reality and unreality, or being and nothing, or love and hate.

Romanticism and modernity as a crisis

The following sketch contextualizes Hegel who assumes the view of Romanticism that modernity is a new crisis, a major division in the order

For private consultation and not distribution without the consent of E Ondrako

of history. As he reflects on the Enlightenment moving from being in the dark to the light, his is an eschatological feeling, that freedom is now really freedom. Moreover, reason and individuality are now real, but reason has a twofold effect. It gives both opportunity and causes a collective fear because there are no limits on reason. Hegel constructs himself as a child of the French Revolution which is an ideology made practical, a product of the Enlightenment. The extremes of the French Revolution provided Hegel the opportunity to use philosophy to show that sound values that have been given up need to be rediscovered. Correlatively, there is a crisis in Christianity caused by the way Christianity misunderstood itself. The rehabilitation of Christianity is possible but, even if it is changed, only confessional Protestantism needs to survive. Unfortunately, Hegel seems unfamiliar with Scotus's thought on spiritual vitality.

For Scotus, spiritual vitality must be rooted in being and not change or becoming as it is in Hegel. The intersection between will and being is proof of spiritual vitality. Vitality is rooted in goodness as the object of will and not in self-love which is objectless. Immutable metaphysical goodness is most personal. The opposite is depersonal which one finds in the profanation of love in modern times, with its cynicism that is depersonalizing. There is cynicism about 'being' as unholy, erroneous, and invidious. It is Hegelian inspired thought about modernity and the causes of the crisis that blames the unholiness of 'being.'

The dismissive view of 'being' as unholy needs analysis, i.e., to be read as a professional can read an x-ray. A person with skills reads x-rays. When in doubt, more sophisticated imaging is recommended. The metaphor of an injury or break that needs an x-ray illustrates the scotistic view of the will, his voluntarism that is not arbitrary. The crisis of modernity or the correlative crisis assumed in Christianity is exacerbated by the failure to formulate the primacy of the will in metaphysical terms of being. Scotus's emphasis on the primacy of the will and the primacy of charity is invaluable as a help to read the imaging of the crisis of modernity and assumed crisis of Christianity. The nobility of the will in respect to the intellect is one of being as perfect act, which means to determine the self to the good and not being determined. The perfect act must be first act and therefore auto-initiated which makes it voluntary and not merely the natural mode of action. However, even if the natural mode of action of the will is perfect and infinite, it is contained within the first act because the first act defines free action, while the second act defines what is meant by determined action.

In a few words, this is Scotus's voluntarism. Voluntary action has firstness, or priority over what is natural, whether that is love or under-

For private consultation and not distribution without the consent of E Ondrako

standing because voluntary action and natural action have the same object: being. Another way of saying this is that love is the action that determines itself and so attains its object. On the other hand, for knowledge, the object determines the character of the action. Love determines itself while knowledge determines the character of the action. The object and the power to act are the key ingredients. If the object of the action and the power are not really one, love will not be necessary and free, as well as free and rational. This is the critical juncture. Only if the object of the action and the power to act are really one may love be both necessary and free.

The difference with love is that the action determines itself and that is how it attains its object. Love will also be free and rational although the person can act irrationally. This is brought out convincingly in the realistic characters in the plays of Gabriel Marcel. In *Le Monde Cassé*, at the moment Christiane was about to declare her love for Jacques, he had decided to become a Benedictine, and she proceeded to make decisions that were a virtual suicide. The character profiles of Jacques and Christiane develop around the themes of love and freedom in making choices. Jacques's decision affects both of their lives and Marcel unfolds the consequences along scotistic lines and not Hegelian. In the end, Jacques's sense of spiritual responsibility for Christiane is discovered in his diary fragments after his death.[7] This play has several scotistic nuances of spiritual vitality rooted in goodness as object of the will and not in self-love which is objectless. The human drama and tension is visible in the changes taking place in all of the characters as their lives unfold. Being, and not what is coming to be or experienced, is the criterion for a good judgment.

Scotus discovered something that is at the core of his idea of this kind of spiritual vitality, an insight that makes him different but complementary to Thomas, who gives primacy to the intellect over the will. Scotus holds that knowledge or natural action is not outside of and prior to willing, but acts as its guide. Rather knowledge is totally within willing and acts as its complement and joy. Moreover, this definition of Scotus's view of the will may be considered as a complement of the scotistic definition of being: *ens est cui non opponitur esse* [being is that which has nothing opposed to being]. Scotus's univocity is not a genus with two different entities: God and man. Rather being is a common opposition to nothing. Being includes the order of what radically differentiates the disjunctive transcendentals.[8]

---

7 GABRIEL MARCEL, Le Monde Cassé, trans. Katherine Rose Hanley, *Gabriel Marcel's Perspectives on The Broken World* (Milwaukee: Marquette University Press, 1998). *Le Monde Cassé* was written by Marcel in 1932.

8 ALLAN B. WOLTER, *The Transcendentals and Their Function in the Metaphysics of Duns Scotus* (St. Bonaventure, N.Y.: The Franciscan Institute, 1946, rpt. 2008). Henceforth, WOLTER, *Transcendentals*.

For private consultation and not distribution without the consent of E Ondrako

Both Thomas and Scotus hold that God does not need human beings to love God in order to be God. This may appear very insensitive and why, with the help of traditional metaphysics, the disjunctive transcendentals for Scotus explain how creatures depend on the love of God and do not exist to fulfill something that is absent in God, a divine appetite, something that is becoming or changing in God. Traditional metaphysics helps one avoid the pitfall of thinking that the indifference of divine being to everything outside itself, i.e., the immanent Trinity, is not the definition of freedom or insensitivity. Rather, the indifference of divine being to all outside of itself is the basis for determining divine love as something outside itself, i.e., the economic Trinity. Human beings depend directly on divine love and are guaranteed to receive that love and guaranteed their dignity as persons, and guaranteed the genuine character of freedom, not the Kantian freedom that Kant postulates towards the end of his life. Pope Benedict XVI summarizes this question of Christian freedom as one that is most sensitive in modernity: the relation of liberty to the will and the intellect,[9] and Scotus is in the position to answer the Holy Father.

Here is where one may find the answer, in Scotus's spiritual vitality which is in full flight from Hegel's psychologism because Hegelian inspired thought is the identity between being and nothing. Moreover, Scotus's vitality is rooted in impassibility and not change. The Father, Son and Holy Spirit cannot change, suffer, sin or have fear. It is only the human nature of the Son, the Word Incarnate, who is able to suffer. When one refers to God suffering it is in a metaphorical sense and not a metaphysical sense.

Hegel and Kant vs. the theory of the person and the will in Scotus

At Vatican II, the deep realization that the Church was always in need of reform but in fidelity to Scripture, Tradition and the Magisterium emerged most convincingly with the history of the development of the Dogmatic Constitution on Divine Revelation, *Dei Verbum*. The split vote of the Council Fathers in November 1962 demonstrated that there was enormous confusion and Pope John XXIII paved the way with his authority for what became known as a total reform and renewal *ad intra* and *ad extra*. *Dei Verbum* was approved the day before the Council ended and remains a lasting example of Christianity with an accent on the personal, the supernatural, mystery and miracle. These key concepts do not insult reason or freedom of inquiry, of thought and of expression, are not merely institutional, dogmatic and legalistic, but scholarly. They recognize that

---

[9] BENEDICT XVI, *Papal Audience on the Thought of Bl. John Duns Scotus*, July 7, 2010.

For private consultation and not distribution without the consent of E Ondrako

there is a causal activity, the guidance by a divine agent, God the Holy Spirit. Hegel shares the assumptions with Kant that any rehabilitation of religion must recognize a turn to the subject and that is non-negotiable, as well as that Christianity cannot accent the supernatural, mystery, or miracle. If they were responding to *Dei Verbum*, Kant and Hegel would recognize the rich personalism and value of turning to the subject, but be critical that the turn was not far enough and that accent on the supernatural, mystery, miracle, and the causal role of the Holy Spirit, was proof that the Catholic Church was too constricting and that a renewed Protestant Christianity was the only hope for the future of Christianity. However, Hegel, unlike Kant, worried about what kind of religion would be the result if Christianity excluded revelation.

Hegel takes exception to Kant's epistemology. Kant has a more restrictive view of reason and Hegel replaces it with an expansive view of reason, his own brand of idealism that he is convinced brings one to God. *Verstand* or understanding for Kant is what is too restrictive and therefore *Vernunft* or reason is Hegel's interpretation of how to bring metaphysics and ontology back. Moreover, Hegel sees incoherence in Kant's epistemology, the obscuring of the relation between the theoretical and practical reason. In sum, Kant wants philosophy to take charge and Hegel agrees, but Hegel thinks that Kant fails to rehabilitate Christianity because his emphasis is on sin, the eschaton, and the Bible is not for Christianity's sake but for philosophy's sake. This is where Hegel convinces himself that he is interested in rehabilitating Christianity for Christianity's sake *and* for philosophy's sake. Kant provides a key to religion which Hegel capitalizes on with his take of symbol and narrative.

Looking back at the Romantics from the 1780's, Hegel wrestled with the dialectic of trying to explain evil and good and was influenced by the refined pantheism of Spinoza. God as God is an expressive reality and expresses himself in the world and as world. This kind of thinking and the lively debate in favor and against gave birth to a major move in history, for 'romanticism to supernaturalize nature and to divinize human beings.' In brief, Hegel saw himself as more of a narrative thinker than Kant in terms of rehabilitating Christianity, and that the Romantics underdeveloped the divine—human relationship, which opened the door for his thinking of how to ameliorate the chasm between the human and God. Hegel recognizes the cost of the newly constructed individualism and looks for a way to retain both the Romantic emphasis on individuality as inspired by the Enlightenment and the need to balance with a healthy notion of community. In sum, the Romantics maintain both autonomy and reason

For private consultation and not distribution without the consent of E Ondrako

as first, but not the primacy of will and primacy of charity in scotistic terms.

Hegel has no room for a *via negativa*, or form of negative theology, that is non-discursive, an apophatic or the theology of unknowing. Intuition and imagination are irrational to Hegel and he dismisses what is carefully analyzed in both Scotus and Newman and central to their theories of metaphysics and epistemology in favor of his own philosophical analysis which, notably, seems to overlook the disjunctive transcendentals as a science where the unity of being is flight from nothing. Intuitive and abstractive cognition for Scotus and real and notional apprehension and assent are meant to be taken together in the thought of each Oxford scholar. That is the key to how Scotus anticipates the main problems of Kant and Hegel. It is the key for how Newman subtly answers the post Kantian and Hegelian issues of his time.

For Kant, the concept of being is a pure product of the mind. That means that being corresponds to nothing in reality. Hegel steps in to rehabilitate metaphysics in his own manner, but forgets being and affirms becoming, change. This does not help because Hegel misses what the Franciscans do not, that perfect being is full flight from nothing. What Hegel misses is that Scotus uses the metaphysical process of abstraction to form the univocal concept of being. In reply, it cannot be said enough that Scotus's univocal concept of being is unique and incomparable with any other. Nonetheless every other concept is comparable to and made possible by this first concept of being. In a strikingly different take from Kant, the concept of being is not produced by the mind. Rather the concept of being is produced by a mysterious reality which Scotus describes as the formal distinction *a parte rei* which the mind contemplates. Kant and Hegel want nothing to do with the mysterious or supernatural, which makes a bridge impossible with Scotus for whom the mind contemplates the firstness of the univocal concept of being.

Often such contemplation of the univocal concept may begin dimly at the natural level and is more intense at the supernatural level meaning that supernatural faith brightens the light. Scotus's metaphysics is the study of the light that enables understanding of what is trans-experiential and trans-conceptual in experiences. This is critical for Scotus and Newman for the light of faith uses intuitive knowledge in pursuing faith. If the light of faith uses only the concept of experience, the merging with the charity of infused contemplation, and the light of glory, does not prevent metaphysics from playing a critical role, but perfects metaphysics in tending to merge with charity as perfect being. To deny this is to deny the necessity of faith and to affirm autonomy and reason alone. Even the

For private consultation and not distribution without the consent of E Ondrako

mystics including Eckhart, and Joachim of Fiore's followers, and Hegel's mystical insights have to acknowledge that in this life experience, even true mystical experience, will go awry without metaphysical or dogmatic guidance. Hegel's rejection of the division between the phenomenal and noumenal in Kant and worry about Christianity without revelation is a tip that he intuits something is wrong but flees from intuition. Hegel and Kant differ from Newman and Scotus in that they refuse to contemplate truth as it reveals itself in metaphysics and to believe the Truth. In sum, Scotus and Newman are not confused by the Kantian problem of trying to build a bridge between what is mental and extra-mental, the phenomenal and noumenal.

While Hegel objects to this Kantian distinction, he attempts his own dialectic to complete the narrative of Christianity in a marginally Trinitarian way. He reverses the Trinitarian theology of Scotus and depends on the theory of univocal being and its infinite and finite modes. Scotus's thought on the will with its being or nature is found in his anthropology. Scotus situates communicability in being by the term natural and incommunicability characteristic of the person by the term voluntary. This is a way of accenting the primacy of the will in Scotus's thought, his contribution that the most excellent degree of perfection in being is voluntary. Lest one roll one's eyes over this, or assume that this is a curious debate between Thomists and Scotists, the lack of distinctions and understanding between the communicability and incommunicability in being are the truth in contention in the controversy over patripassionism, ancient and new.

Patripassion connections: an attempt to reduce the gap between human and divine

Does God suffer? Do all three Persons in the Trinity suffer? In reply, there is an intimate relationship in the Trinitarian theology of Scotus and his theory of the hypostatic union that does not confuse what is substantially united. The hypostatic assumption of an integral human nature by the Second Person of the Trinity is defined as incommunicability. That is critical in distinguishing that it is the Son alone who is capable of suffering in his human nature alone. Scotistic metaphysics underscores the contribution of traditional metaphysics that there cannot be a succession or becoming in the human and divine natures. For Scotus the divine Person incarnate can suffer. Scotus defines the person as he defines being as related not to natural activity, but to what is nobler as a mode of acting. That is why voluntary activity, in distinction to finite limited voluntary activity that can sin, change, and be unloving, at the highest level cannot

For private consultation and not distribution without the consent of E Ondrako

sin, is immutable, and most loving. Personhood, independence, necessity, freedom and charity coincide in the mystery of the one and triune God.[10]

In sum, one can see that metaphysics and experience are related in taking this Scotistic position. Scotus does not subordinate metaphysics to experience, being to becoming. Rather the advocates of patripassionism fall prey to the appealing but erroneous position of subordinating metaphysics to experience, being to becoming. Why this matters is that such an error effectively profanes charity with cynicism. The error is that all love directed to an object can only be redeemed in suffering. If that love is self-love, all the more, it is selfish. That is why all love needs to be redeemed in suffering. On the finite level, this view of love is the most oppressive imaginable. In *Le Monde Cassé*, Christiane, a very beautiful woman, marries someone she does not love, and gerrymanders the truth of their relationship, to the point of deliberate suffering which is nothing less than extreme cynicism about love and freedom. On the infinite level, gerrymandering the truth translates erroneously to mean that all love can only be redeemed in suffering and that suffering has to be above all in God, Father, Son and Holy Spirit.

Scotus holds the primacy of the will over the intellect but that they are only formally distinct *a parte rei*. Although Thomas and Scotus have different views on the relation of intellect and will,[11] they do not hold the patripassion error. Nor does Newman subscribe to it in its neo-patripassion form, which means that in regard to the Trinity, the principle of subjectivism, *a la* Hegel, is the unconditional starting point to rework the theology of the Trinity. Thomas and Scotus offer carefully developed comprehensive arguments to demonstrate that the divine being is one.[12] The difficulty with abandoning the approach of Thomas and Scotus is sometimes identified as an example of semi-rationalism, or Hegelianism with a Catholic mask, a difficulty which Newman saw in those who seemed drawn to the Hegelian starting point. Anti-scholastic sympathies [13] were a *caveat* for

---

[10] BONAVENTURE, *Questiones Disputatae de mysterio SS. Trinitatis*, q. 7, a. 1–2.

[11] See THOMAS AQUINAS, *Summa Theologica* I, qq. 85–87 on the intellect and *ST* I qq. 82–83 on the will.

[12] Thomas Aquinas's later work, *Summa Theologica* III, qq. 1–59; and earlier work, *Summa contra Gentiles* IV, qq. 1–49 demonstrate the development of the thought of Thomas vis a vis competing views and heresies.

[13] Although Newman was critical of *Tuas Libenter*, the address of Pope Pius IX to the meeting of German Catholic theologians, the Munich Brief, for tying the hands of a controversialist, he seems to be clearly supporting the necessity of scholarly authorities to have the intellectual space to debate thoroughly any controversy. The intention of the Holy Father was to critique those who would disregard scholastic theology, a point Newman shared. Pope Innocent III did the same at the IV Lateran Council in warning about the anti-scholastic conclusions of Joachim of Fiore, a pre-Hegelian form of mystic.

For private consultation and not distribution without the consent of E Ondrako

Newman who had a sixth sense for misconceptions of the divine attributes that sought to explain the mystery of the Trinity solely in terms of created experience, or a psychological approach to theology alone, especially if it may have attempted to usurp what was the proper province of theology.[14]

Scotus teaches the radical goodness of God and of creation for its own sake. Scotus teaches that the love that moved the Father to send the Son to be born of Mary by the power of the Holy Spirit would have been as truly and perfectly love even if the Son had not become man capable of suffering in the flesh. The love of God is such that the suffering of the Son of God and not the Father nor Spirit is made possible for the redemption of all. The suffering of the sacred humanity and not the divine nature changes human suffering from punishment to a sign of the Father's love for the salvation of all. Fehlner formulates it in a manner most clear: "The wisdom of the Cross is not the experience of suffering; rather it is that love which in willing to suffer is not altered, and that in order to suffer must become incarnate."

Scotus conceives the will first as the power to self-determine, pure act, and not moved by something other than itself. In the case of the intellect, the intellect is moved by its object, truth. Second, the power to self-determine is the essential characteristic of the will. Third, voluntary action is essentially free, which is the basis of indifference towards contingent goods. However, voluntary action is not identical with this indifference. Scotus relies on Bonaventure who holds that the perfect will acts freely, even when necessarily, and always has total independence to love the perfect good. This does not eliminate profoundly personal sensitivity, nor suggest that the infinitely perfect divine will proceeds irrationally.

Here is where Thomas and Scotus have competing views. For Scotus, love is the characteristic act of the will. It is more excellent than knowledge. Love moves itself toward being which is perceived as good. Scotus distinguishes the perception in the perfect divine will and created will which is perfected by grace and glory. The perception in the perfect divine will is not something that is from outside of the will, but from the will itself, which is a pure perfection. To claim that the divine will is always just and holy, means that the divine will always wills in an orderly manner. This is a far cry from the thinking of an angry or punishing God by the Reformers or theories of penal substitution. For Scotus, the finite will is just and holy as divine grace is at work in it, but it can be disorderly or fall from grace, or return to the order of justice and holiness with the help of grace.

---

14 Newman's metaphysical argument on the essence of the university in *The Idea of a University* underscores a major difficulty with a liberal education that fails to offer a sound theology as part of the curriculum, i.e., another discipline will usurp what theology is expected to do.

For private consultation and not distribution without the consent of E Ondrako

Concentric circles of the key concepts in this essay underscore that the Scotistic view of metaphysics and experience are closely related with the priority given to metaphysics. Applying the principle correctly requires the finite spirit in the soul of a human being to have both a conscious perception of being and personhood prior to any understanding or expression, of being or personhood in conceptual form. That perception is in the soul's relation with God *via* synderesis and conscience. Prior to any attempt to conceptualize perception, the finite ego is not first but a supreme being is first. Newman's conversion at the age of fifteen, convincingly relates his "rest in the thought of two and two only absolute and self-evident beings, myself and my Creator."[15] Within the memory of the person there is a recognition of finite and infinite modes of being, a proof of divine existence, the possibility of love and suffering that links a person to God as holy and understanding that the Son of God too suffers out of love. This is the proof of God's existence by entering into the self, that of Augustine, Bonaventure, Newman and Scotus, but it is Scotus who links metaphysics and experience to the light of the mystery of the Incarnation most sensitively, with a bow of gratitude to Anselm. Sensitivity means that the contingent determination of the indifference of the will toward everything except the divine good does not remove love for a contingent good in the case of the infinitely perfect divine will in Christ and of any created will that is perfectly in accord with divine justice, his human will as united to the divine will made possible in the hypostatic union.

Scotus's formalitas, Butler's Analogy, Hegel's Lectures, Newman's Grammar of Assent

Besides Scotus's major contribution to the science of metaphysics of the univocity of the concept of being, his use of the formal distinction *a parte rei*, which is 'one reality with a formal distinction' is a very critical point which the English Friars defended and was not lost completely at the time of the Reformation. Butler recognized some aspects of the great scotistic tradition in England and their subtleties were passed on to Newman although he had not read the works of Scotus. When Newman was reading Butler's *Analogy* in 1823, he was under the influence of Whately and the noetics of Oriel, and breaking from the depersonalizing predestinationism of Calvinism and individualism. Newman's *Parochial and Plain Sermons* and later the Oxford *University Sermons* between 1826 and 1843 dealt with critical themes relating to personal changes taking

---

15 JOHN HENRY NEWMAN, *Apologia Pro Vita Sua* (London: Longmans, Green and Co., uniform edition, 1913), 4.

For private consultation and not distribution without the consent of E Ondrako

place through and in his devoted pastoral care. Moreover, the Sermons include the central theme of the development of an 'idea.'

In his 1824 *Lectures on the Philosophy of Religion*, Hegel refers to the 'idea' in the context of représentation as such or as appearance, the differentiation within the Divine Life and the World, in a manner that "God appears for the subjective consciousness in the shape of subjectivity."[16] It was not Hegel on 'idea' but Butler who provides the spark that ignited Newman's monumental theory of the development of doctrine. Newman was on the right track, thanks to Butler, that the analogical knowledge that we have of God leads to the interiorization that is vital to belief in the Trinity of divine Persons, which differs radically from Hegel.

While this essay focuses on Hegel and Scotus, the crucial connection to John Henry Newman cannot be overlooked. Bishop Joseph Butler's *Analogy* is the proximate source for his *Parochial and Plain Sermons*, several of the major themes in the *Oxford University Sermons* and for much of his *Grammar of Assent*. It is precisely in this sense that there is a connection with Scotus and Peter D. Fehlner points out the layers, so to speak, the subtleties of this connection. [17] From butler, Newman learned about the critical development of an idea and the importance of its inward understanding, and behind Butler, he discovered features of the significant earlier scotistic tradition in England, although Newman had not read the works of Scotus. Newman refers to Butler as inspiring his *Grammar of Assent* which was a phenomenology and genuine metaphysics-epistemology of the themes he treated in his *University Sermons*. Like Scotus, Newman carefully distinguishes natural and supernatural faith. That is critical to the claim that the *Grammar of Assent* gives the phenomenology and metaphysics-epistemology that is in the *Apologia* which is his theory of faith. Without these tools, metaphysical theology would not be equal to its task.

Thomas and Scotus differ in their teaching on the intellect and will. Scotus teaches the inherent rationality of the will as a *perfectio simpliciter simplex*, i.e., a perfection that is unable to be simplified. He is substantially the same as Bonaventure who teaches that free will is a power of reason and of will. The more perfect the powers of intellect and will are integrated, the more perfect is the discretion of the free will. The Franciscan approach holds that freedom is not a third power but the integration of intellect and will. Thomas analyzes the will as either an appetite of the intellect in itself which is radically irrational and natural. Scotus analyzes the will

---

16 HODGSON, 228–230.

17 P. D. FEHLNER, "Scotus and Newman in Dialogue," is chapter 7 of this volume. Henceforth, FEHLNER, Dialogue.

For private consultation and not distribution without the consent of E Ondrako

as radically rational and voluntary, a *perfectio simpliciter simplex*. There is constant study of the implications of these differences which Fehlner accomplishes most comprehensively and lucidly in his commentary on the following key quote in defining the meaning of Newman's illative sense.

> It is the mind that reasons, and controls its own reasoning, not any technical apparatus of words and propositions. This power of judging and concluding, when in its perfection, I call the Illative sense.[18]

The terms judging and perfection are intimately linked to the process of sanctifying the intellect and conscience, and bring Newman, unquestionably in relation to the theory of divine illumination of Bonaventure and its emendation in Scotus's metaphysics, the univocity of the concept of being and disjunctive transcendentals. When Newman writes that it is the mind that reasons, the term is close to Bonaventure's *Journey of the Mind to God*,[19] which means that mind is in common with the metaphysics of the person as taught in the Franciscan School. Newman's unity of knowledge rests on univocity of being. That is his substratum in his theory of education in the *Idea of a University*. Newman's unity of knowledge links all of reality to the firstness of the Creator and that link is through the Incarnation.[20]

In sum, Thomas and Aristotle hold that the will is an intellectual appetite with a necessary desire to know the truth and is free, but not in itself, rather in relation to goods that are contingent. The will is absolutely free for Ockham, Hume and Kant to do as it pleases and is indifferent to any prior intellectual assessment of good or evil. However, Scotus and Bonaventure disagree with both approaches because they hold that a rational act is primarily an act of discernment, one that makes possible a personal voluntary act which is ordered. Similarly, Newman's illative sense recognizes that reason is not simply reduced to strong or weak logic in a Lockian manner, nor is it separated from a personal character. Bishop Butler helped him to reach that conviction and neither Kant nor Hegel would sever that conviction, or prevent Newman from integrating knowledge and love. Most of all, Newman was alert to the deceptive process of knowing that is not different from any other physical process, which is knowledge as an instrument of absolute will separated from truth.

---

[18] *Grammar of Assent*, ch 9, 348.

[19] BONAVENTURE, *Itinerarium Mentis in Deum* (St. Bonaventure, NY: The Franciscan Institute, 1956).

[20] FEHLNER, Dialogue.

For private consultation and not distribution without the consent of E Ondrako

He chose Butler's preference for natural theology, which is a small step to Newman's argument for the existence of God from conscience.

How the will is defined in relation to the intellect and vice versa is the key to understanding the three approaches above, Thomas and Aristotle, Ockham, Hume and Kant, and Bonaventure, Scotus and arguably Newman. Newman's theory of the development of doctrine is not Hegel, but reflects the help of Butler's *Analogy*. Newman learned that ideas seem to remain stable at first then move progressively forward and lead to the fuller content of public revelation and then to its inward understanding. This critical interiorization, or balancing of what is extra-mental and inward, prepares Newman for Scotus's thesis on the absolute primacy of Christ. He had no difficulty accepting it. Underneath he saw instantly the pattern of growth and development with guidance from a proper metaphysical and dogmatic source.

In concluding part one, Scotus's theology and metaphysics helps to analyze the divine essence and human soul. Pure perfections are characteristic of spiritual being. When considered univocally they have no limitation. That is why, by essence, the pure perfections of intellect and will are identical in God although formally distinct or non-identical as perfections. The Franciscans hold that the will has a certain primacy because its mode of action is the key to the real identity found in the fullness of being or divine infinity. The human will can act apart from the truth about goodness and that is why only grace and the supernatural can lead to the integration we call sanctity as in God but all the while retaining freedom as the essential characteristic of voluntary action. Metaphysical necessity and freedom are not opposed in the Franciscan school. This is what Hegel misses dramatically, that the perfections in human beings, or what is common in finite human beings with the infinite God, provide the objective grounds for sharing in the circumincessory life of the divine Persons.

Part II: The theological center is the charity that is God

Introduction

Continuity and discontinuity is the question at the heart of change. The significance of the univocity of the concept of being and the contemplation of being in Scotus competes with the Hegelian substitution of becoming for being in metaphysics for being is the engine that drives the critiquing and not what is experienced or coming to be. Newman's axiom

For private consultation and not distribution without the consent of E Ondrako

"to live is to change," at first, may appear to support the Hegelian view, but on closer examination, is thoroughly scotistic. Given the recognition of the crises of modernity, a lasting and authentic change in persons, societies, cultures, and the Church is aided by contemplation of truth, critiqued by being.

Scotus's primacy, creation, and salvation vs. the non-being and becoming of Hegel.

Scotus primacy is an essential attribute of the Godhead and primacy in creation and in the economy of salvation gives the *ratio* of all contingent being. Scotus and Thomas hold that the transcendent perfection of the redemption is a certain truth of faith, but 'the metaphysical essence of perfect redemption' is a product of the Franciscan school. Our redemption and salvation is directly related to the purpose of the Incarnation, which God ordained as the purpose of creation. The primacy of charity and primacy of the will form the christocentrism of Scotus which centers on a metaphysics providing the substratum for a theology for believers based on what is immutable, or the theology of necessity, and deals with the contingent, or economy of salvation. The point of contact is the absolute predestination or primacy of Jesus, which places the redemption of the human race as subordinated to the greatest possible realization of the greatest glory of God, in any world God might create. The greatness of this glory is attained in the Incarnation. The Father had ordained the Incarnation as the purpose of creation which had its highest manifestation in the creation of Adam and Eve for the glory of God and the most perfect fruition of God by a creature. In other words, God foresaw the need to redeem a fallen mankind by an Incarnate Savior born of a Virgin Mother. This became the possibility for a most perfect Redemption by a most perfect Redeemer.

The Franciscan view of the metaphysical essence of perfect redemption is far removed from Hegel as the death of God meaning the death of the absolute transcendence of God. Creation and salvation are not equated with nothing as in the Hegelian synthesis. The key concepts in Scotus's theory of primacy, creation and salvation demonstrate what in fact actually has happened in the economy of salvation. Hegelianism is the inversion. Scotus's teachings are impossible to support without metaphysical premises, such as the univocity of the concept of being, the will as a pure perfection, and the concept of a personal act as incommunicable existence. A purely scientific or empirical exegesis or theory of the development of doctrine is impossible, which Newman demonstrates most convincingly in his classic work from 1845. The Franciscan School and Scotus illustrate

For private consultation and not distribution without the consent of E Ondrako

the principle of recapitulation- or recirculation of Ireneus that the intelligibility or meaning of history is discovered in the counsels of the one who created it, guided it and placed within its tradition 'types' and figures to help reach its fulfillment, or the glorification of time. This is not Hegel's closing of the circle of the Christian story of God.

Hegelianism and evolutionism tend to be synonymous meaning that change gets the primacy before the immutable, or, as this essay argues, becoming before being. The logic mediated by this Hegelian primacy is unable to accept the eternal Trinity as a glorification of time. Hegel, in effect, substitutes Satan, Adam and Eve, for the Father, Word Incarnate and Spouse of the Holy Spirit. The *solus Christus* theologies of the late Middle Ages and modern time set up an anti-economy, in which the presence or absence of divine maternity is critical. To deny the divine maternity is to lose sight of the ultimate victory of the Father through the mission of the Son and mission of the Holy Spirit and the role of the Virgin Mother, spouse of the Holy Spirit.

Hegel's use of the Incarnational principle is a far cry from the Franciscan School that holds the greatest of all God's gifts is the Incarnation. The heavenly Father and the Virgin Mother effect the Incarnation. It may seem counterintuitive, but the cross is willed by both. The wisdom of the cross, the tree of life where victory and defeat are defined, is that the love that is willing to suffer and in order to suffer must become incarnate. There is a mystery and supreme grace to the Incarnation, for the victim has the hypostatic union. The divine and the human in Christ form a unity of a pre-existing divine Person, the Word who became Incarnate. This grace from a theological perspective is a supremely contingent reality which should provide the meta-ethical basis of Christian ethics with the theology of the cross as the center. The hierarchical truth is supported by Scotus's metaphysics which depends on the univocal concept of being, on the will as a pure perfection, and the concept of a personal act as incommunicable existence. The clarification of his thinking is in the mystery and supreme grace of the Incarnation. Rather than a cynical conclusion, at the risk of profaning the greatest love, neither the heavenly Father nor Virgin Mother abandons the Victim at the moment of consummation. That is why the Mother stands at the foot of the Cross, sharing the suffering as the Father cannot. To deny that Mary has an active role in the oblation of Christ is to accept naturalism or evolutionism which is another word for Hegelianism.

For private consultation and not distribution without the consent of E Ondrako

Scotus's providence and predestination in Christ vs. Hegel's theory of history as mediated logic

Scotus holds the reasonableness of all divine Providence and predestination in Christ to share in the glory of God. At fifteen, the time of his first conversion, Newman believed that he was predestined to salvation. As he ministered to the faithful at Littlemore, and preached his *Parochial and Plain Sermons* and *University Sermons* from 1826–1843, he was gradually shedding his Calvinist thinking. In 1823, he read Bishop Joseph Butler's *Analogy* and that served as a precursor of much of Newman's future thought and the substratum of his ideas on the development of doctrine In 1849, with the help of F. Faber, Newman become familiar with Scotus's thought on the motive of the Incarnation and that convinced him on the meaning of the absolute predestination of Christ in Scotus's thought.[21] In contrast, Hegel views reason as the tool to conceptualize reality into a whole of self-generated concepts that form a history of mediated logic as a closed circle. This evolutionary view of history, logic, and all of reality gets mediated into this circle, with the complete absence of a sense of awe and personal relationship to the Trinity.

In recent times, the objection to the scotistic thesis on the absolute predestination of Christ, meaning without the fall of Adam and Eve, is that the salvation won for us would not be as perfect as Thomas and Scotus hold. The reasoning is that the absence of mercy means that the love of God for us would not be as perfect. The error is to think that God would not be truly good had man not sinned, for it is sin that brings out the merciful mediation of God. The answer is that any evolutionary interpretation is far removed from Scotus's theological metaphysics, the relationship between the intellect and the will, nature and the will, being and the person.

The concept of redemption in the Franciscan school is intimately linked to the scotistic thesis concerning the absolute primacy of the Word Incarnate and his Virgin Mother.[22] At the outset of examining this question of predestination, it is helpful to distinguish salvation and redemption. Had redemption not been necessary, salvation would still have been worked by Christ. Redemption is from sin in view of elevation to participation in the divine life, to share in the glory of God. This

---

[21] JOHN HENRY NEWMAN, *Apologia Pro Vita Sua* (London, uniform edition), 4. See *The Letters and Diaries of John Henry Newman*, ed. C. S. Dessain et al., (Oxford: Oxford University Press, 1961–2011), 13, 335. The letter is to Faber Dec. 9, 1849.

[22] Scotus himself does not use the term absolute primacy of the Virgin Mother but his first disciples do and that understanding at Vatican II has become incorporated into the teachings of the Church in Lumen Gentium, chap. 8. This is the Dogmatic Constitution on the Church.

For private consultation and not distribution without the consent of E Ondrako

participation was foreordained before the fall and independent of it. In the scotistic context, salvation means elevation from the nothingness of existence to supernatural happiness in existing. Therefore, redemption is relative to salvation. Christ is the Savior first and becomes Redeemer after the fall. However, even if Adam and Eve had not sinned, human beings would have to pass a test exercising the gift of freedom.

The scotistic thesis is opposite the view that the Incarnation was willed by God only after Adam and Eve's sin. Scotus holds that the Word Incarnate and Virgin Mother were jointly predestined in one and the same decree prior to any consideration of creation or of redemption. This scotistic view differs not only from the relative or consequent view of the fall but from the naturalist or Pelagian thought in its evolutionary form that the Incarnation was willed consequently on creation as its perfection. Some neo-Thomists, transcendental Thomists, and neopatripassions today seem inclined to interpret the scotistic thesis of absolute predestination of Christ this way that is far removed from his theological metaphysics. They do this in terms of the adoptionist pre-existence and prior predestination of Christ as an evolutionary process.

The error of the adoptionist and evolutionary tone will evaporate as the morning mist if the divine counsels are contemplated from a meta-physical perspective. This means that the concept of redemptive liberation from sin depends on a prior positive, the principal mediation of Jesus, and the subordinate mediation of Mary because of her preservative redemp-tion, i.e., preserved from original sin. To affirm with Scotus the absolute primacy of the Incarnation is to affirm that the definition of liberative redemption from sin [for all of humanity except Mary who is preserved and full of grace] depends on a prior positive or definition of the Immacu-late Conception in terms of the absolute predestination of Christ. Such a definition is prior to any consideration of sin, and clashes with the view of making redemption the primary motive of the Incarnation, that without sin, there would be lesser glory of God. That is the reason for suggesting an adoptionist tone to Christology that includes an evolutionary view, in a word, to hold that the perfection of the Incarnation is not at the virginal conception, but only at the term of the evolutionary process.

Newman makes no such mistake. He recognizes that if one does not reflect on the mystery of the Immaculate Conception as prior to original justice and original sin and in the saving counsels of the Father, one will not grasp the meaning of original and personal sin, nor redemption and liberation from original sin and its consequences.[23] This echoes the view

---

23 JOHN HENRY NEWMAN, "Memorandum on the Immaculate Conception" in *Meditations and Devotions* (Longmans Green and Co., uniform edition, 1903), 180–186.

For private consultation and not distribution without the consent of E Ondrako

of Scotus about the mercy and justice of the Father and underscores the perfection of our redemption that both Thomas and Scotus hold.

To recapitulate, Scotus holds that creation is for the glory of Jesus and his Virgin Mother.[24] It is a pure grace or gift of the Father to his Son, the Word Incarnate for whom as predestined the world was created, which means that He is predestined to be Savior of all of the elect, angels and human beings. Contrary to the non-mediation from non-being to becoming in Hegelian inspired thought, Scotus teaches that the elect are predestined in Him (Eph 1:3) in and through the merits of Christ. The work of salvation of the elect, from their absence of blessedness to sharing in his blessedness is a work of His role as Mediator.

The Hegelian inspired conclusion that the triune God suffered on the cross cannot be true for it annihilates salvation and creation by equating both with nothing. Kierkegaard's take re doubt about this comprises the entire *Philosophical Fragments* and is closer to the full flight from nothing of Bonaventure and Scotus. Newman's introduction to the *University Sermons* in the 1871 edition is a clear answer to the relationship between faith and reason. The encyclical, *Fides et Ratio*, of Pope St. John Paul II is a more recent *tour de force* in reply. Kierkegaard's concept of repetition applies here in the sense that the old being of a person is changed or converted, which is made possible by an encounter with Christ, and the new person has remnants of the old because the person is the same being but changed.

In terms of salvation and redemption, Scotus is both simple and profound for he argues that the lesser good, redemption, is ordered to the higher good. The basis of all rational willing is that the lesser is for the sake of the higher. Christ as Incarnate, according to Bonaventure, and a "quasi-infinite" according to Thomas,[25] means the greater than which nothing is possible. A perfect Creator is perfectly rational. Bonaventure and Scotus hold the principle of hierarchization as the progression from the lesser to the highest.[26] Scotus's simple and profound point is that the highest good is nothing less than the absolutely perfect good, the salvation and enjoyment of the supreme good in Christ Incarnate.

---

[24] BONAVENTURE, III *Sent.*, d.1, a. 2, q.2. See A. APOLLONIO and P. D. FEHLNER, "The Concept of Redemption in the Franciscan-Scotistic School: Salvation, Redemption, and the Primacy of Christ" in *Mary at the Foot of the Cross* VIII (New Bedford, MA: Academy of the Immaculate, 2008), 111–158.

[25] THOMAS AQUINAS, *ST*, I, q. 25, q. 4.

[26] SCOTUS, *Ordinatio*, III *Sent.*, d. 7, q. 3; II *Sent.*, d. 9, q. 7.

For private consultation and not distribution without the consent of E Ondrako

Scotus's sharing in the glory of the Blessed Trinity vs. the modern idealism of Hegel

For Scotus the triune God as such could not have suffered on the cross. His teaching on the two affections in the will, the *affectus justitiae* [justice] and the *affectus commodi* [advantageous] are the key to defining the will as a pure perfection and finite perfection. To put it simply, suffering is only possible where the will has an *affectus commodi* or affection for what is advantageous. The divine will does not have such a tendency and suffering is a radically negative entity, not a pure perfection, which demonstrates that there is a radical difference between being finite and infinite. To think that suffering is a pure perfection shared by the infinite and finite is to deny that there is difference and is a Hegelian denial of being in favor of change or of becoming.

For Hegel, to collapse the disjunctive transcendentals is to deny the difference from being finite and being infinite. The collapse leads to the conclusion that if God suffers by being rejected and abandoned and my sufferings are identical with his, then I am holy, I am God because there is no radical difference between being finite and infinite. Here is where, more than ever, the scotistic view of the will and of the cross competes with the Hegelian synthesis. To hold that salvation and creation are both equated with nothing, as being is equated with nothing, profanes love and the perfect love of the Redeemer. That is why the constant answer from the Franciscan School by Bonaventure and Scotus is to affirm the relation between being and the person, will and nature, will and intellect, by explaining that being is full flight from nothing. The inversion is a Hegelian inspired interpretation which equates justice with egoism and reduces being and justice along with God to non-existence, to nothing. This is a profanation of charity and substitution of a concept arbitrarily defined. One may ask: what kind of a Father would abandon his Son to condemnation? Scotus explains how the passion as willed by the Father is not cruelty. Rather it is an act of love for and union with the Son, suffering motivated by and endured in joy.

The onto-theology of Hegel has no connection with this scotistic view because it denies his metaphysics, the univocity of being, and formal distinction *a parte rei*, the metaphysics which provides the non-psychological and non-ethical premise for how Scotus understands the basis of all personal activity in finite creatures. Without this perspective, the idea of suffering in finite human beings and in the triune God can be very deceptive. Suffering is not a pure perfection but a negative entity, a contingency of personal life, either because they have sinned or are making reparation for sin. Scotus holds the will as a *perfectio simpliciter simplex*

For private consultation and not distribution without the consent of E Ondrako

with two affections which define the will as a pure perfection. Even if a person acts unjustly and is deserving of punishment, every will is defined in relation to justice, an *appetitus justitiae*. Second, because every finite will is finite, one must define the will in relation to what perfects nature. That means that the finite will has to be defined in relation to what is advantageous. This is best known as partaking in an in-built tendency or desire for what perfects it. In other words, the will partakes in the character of an appetite, an *appetitus commodi*.

Olivier Boulnois is a meticulous help in dealing with the key concepts of intuition and abstraction in Scotus, for Scotus brings a new epistemology which responds to theological exigency.[27] In the Prologue to the *Lectura*, Scotus states succinctly, *maxima pars theologiae est de contingentibus* [the greatest part of theology concerns what is contingent]. This means, creation, the Incarnation, and the beatitude of human beings. Everything created is contingent, to give to intuition a mode of knowing appropriate to be called a rule of the science of theology, in order to make the knowledge of the things of heaven available in ideas for this world of creatures. Intuition is an object in itself. This point cannot be stressed enough for it is precisely here that Kant and Hegel have difficulties, albeit slightly different from each other. Abstraction for Scotus is an object which is present in the intellect and made possible under a certain point of view. Intuition apprehends the object by a form in the intellect. Représentation is a sign which reflects directly to what it signifies. In abstraction, the représentation is considered what it is in itself: the concept constituted as a thing. The key to using intuition and abstraction in Scotus is that they are meant to be used together and not separate from each other. The same holds for the variation in Newman's phraseology, real apprehension and real assent. They are to intuition as notional apprehension and notional assent are to abstraction in Scotus, but are meant to be used together.

Knowledge, for Scotus, is an absolute and not a simple relation directed towards the object. He has a complex theory that situates intuition and abstraction in this context.[28] This is the case par excellence in beatific

---

[27] BOULNOIS, *Être*, 149–150.

[28] BOULNOIS, *Être*, 149. 150. Boulnois explains the theory of Scotus and how he situates intuition and abstraction into this complex theory. Scotus breaks with the Aristotelian correlation between intuition and the sensible, abstraction and the intelligible. Boulnois's explanation is very deep and technical but, it seems to me, in spite of an extraordinary study of Scotus, that in his conclusion, Boulnois does not necessarily appreciate the position taken and repeated continuously in this essay, i.e., why Scotus's univocal concept of being is not a pure logical construct first. That seems to be the heart of the debate about the light that guides all of our thought. Moreover, this problem is integrally linked to formal logic, strong or weak, according to Locke in the relation of an inference to its premises. Logic needs to be securely linked to being. That is why divine illumination gets refined by Scotus in logical form

For private consultation and not distribution without the consent of E Ondrako

intuition. Scotus wrote: "if I am able to have the operation of beatitude in this relation [to God] I would be happy, therefore I would not be happy if I have this relation without the operation [of the beatific vision]."[29] This is a very important difference between Scotus and Eckhart. Beatitude for Scotus is not the mystical interpretation of divinization as formulated by Eckhart, for knowledge is not the act of becoming identical with its object. For Scotus, it is a perfection, absolute and fundamental, to the insight that knowledge is desirable. It is a reality in us, subsisting and essential, distinct of the object which it retrieves.

Scotus's new epistemology, in Boulnois's phrase, is most capable of dealing with problems between Christianity and culture, the colonization[30] or impact any writer makes on a culture, or the deception of self-will and consequences of private judgment characteristic of modernity. Newman and Kierkegaard are contemporaries who know the Hegelian inspired thought as it manifests itself at home and feel compelled to reply. Examples of Newman's reply to problems of self-will and private judgment are in his "On Consulting the Faithful in Matters of Doctrine," *Grammar of Assent*, and *Letter to the Duke of Norfolk*.[31] Newman is less hyperbolic than Kierkegaard's *Philosophical Fragments*, but both reply to the colonization of the version of Hegelian thought that was making its way to Denmark and England. Kierkegaard and Newman wrote in a related manner about problems where conscience is auto-justified, unhealthy self-affirmation, and the primacy of an absolutely supreme and private judgment over and against the understanding of the teachings of Christ and that the future of Christian existence is made possible by Christ.

Kant's heterodox view of Christ, his example and teaching, recognizes Christ as the teacher who came to something of the possibility of reaching a holy will.[32] Hegel's heterodox view is more complex, for he concludes that one should pay more attention to the historical figure of Christ, but this is

---

so that it can be the light guiding all our thought, keeping logic securely linked to the reality of being.

29 Scotus, *Quodl.* XIII, [16] 49 (465); *Op. Ox.* IV, d.49, q. 2, section 27. Boulnois, *Être*, 149, fn. 3.

30 Colonization is a phrase used by Cyril O'Regan to identify such a comprehensive impact of a prominent writer on the culture.

31 John Henry Newman, "Letter to the Duke of Norfolk" in *Certain Difficulties Felt by Anglicans* 2 (London: uniform edition, 1910), ch. 5; Newman, "On Consulting the Faithful in Matters of Doctrine," *The Rambler*, May 1859, ed. John M. Coulson (New York: Sheed and Ward, 1961). The Catholic Bishops were not pleased with Newman's leadership in reigning in some of the Catholic thinking in the first Catholic periodical in England. Newman published this prescient essay in its final edition under his editorship and after he knew that he was being relieved of the position.

32 Immanuel Kant, *Religion within the Boundaries of Mere Reason*, eds. Allen Wood and George di Giovanni, intro. Robert Merrihew Adams. 6th ed. (Cambridge: Cambridge University Press, 1998, 2006).

For private consultation and not distribution without the consent of E Ondrako

deceptive. Hegel really means that in the last instance a person would not be a real Christian unless one breaks free of the historical figure of Christ. He dismisses the Resurrection as inconsequent in favor of Pentecost for what matters, because, in his view, the church is spirit as he defines spirit. Kierkegaard reacts to Hegel by the term "repetition," which he intends to be a constructive term. Repetition looks like memory, recollection but not the recapitulation-recirculation of Ireneus. Kierkegaard's "repetition" is important because it is not coming into being from non-being and challenges the Hegelian view by showing that Christian existence is made possible by Christ rather than identifying it as a form of a philosophical existence made possible by philosophical recollection.

Kierkegaard would agree with Newman and Scotus that the Incarnation is not a principle and that it occurs in a disturbed world, a world where original sin is a reality and not something morally neutral, in a world where there are many crises. Sin begets sin. Societies repeat themselves in their injustices. In this real world, the cross is the tree of life where the Incarnation bears fruit. From the Resurrection flows the power of reconciliation, of repetition, of conversion, of change from the old person to the new person, while remaining a new version of the old person. Only Christ is the means for this kind of change, of conversion, which is not to be domesticated by philosophical discourse. Rather than the Hegelian use of the principle of Incarnation, Kierkegaard identifies the possibility of a radically different self because of the Incarnation. That conviction brings him into proximity with Newman and Scotus.

Disputed Question:

"Human liberty in relation to the will and intellect" Condetermination in Scotus

Scotus's univocity of the concept of being is rooted in the study of being as being while Hegel's becoming is based on what is coming to be. Scotus's formal distinction *a parte rei* between the immanent and economic Trinity is the opposite of Hegel's collapse of the immanent Trinity into the economic Trinity and consequences for faith and the motivation to sanctify the intellect. To try to build a bridge between Scotus and Hegel in the post Vatican II dialogical era is noble but extraordinarily difficult. Being can never be equated with nothing. Ironically, Hegelian thought has much purchase long after his death in 1831. It is found in the contemporary tendency to think that novelty is the criterion of theological truth rather than proper understanding of tradition. Inspired by Bishop Butler's

For private consultation and not distribution without the consent of E Ondrako

Analogy, and behind him, some aspects of the great scotistic tradition in England, Newman discovered the religious epistemology that enabled him to explain the development of an 'idea.' The only satisfactory answer for him is found in his theory of true development of doctrine in his essay in 1845.

The English friars recognized Scotus as the end of the *via antiqua* and Ockham as the beginning of the *via moderna*. Newman worried when he came under the influence of Whately and the noetics of Oriel because he sensed that he was stressing academic excellence at the expense of striving for holiness. The influence of Ockham and his nominalism add to the difficulty of stressing scientific precision rather than striving for sanctity and wisdom. Newman and the leaders of the Oxford movement after 1833, were not far from the intentions of Popes St. John XXIII, Bl. Paul VI, St. John Paul II and Benedict XVI to foster a genuine hermeneutic of reform and adaptation in continuity with tradition. Newman and the reformers asked: is this reform and adaptation happening in step with the crises of modernity or not? By 1824, Hegel had a view of the object of theology as the eternal history of the spirit and a hermeneutic that is heterodox. He "brings the theologoumenon of the Trinity to the center of theology in a way unparalleled in modern Protestant thought."[33] Newman wanted nothing to do with extremes of Protestantism, nor what he perceived as the extremes of Catholicism, but rather, sought a *via media*.

The battle lines, on the one hand, are the definitive version of the commentaries on the *Sentences* of Peter Lombard by Bl. John Duns Scotus in the *Prologue* to the *Ordinatio*, which is his profound systematic introduction to dogmatic theology as a foundation to study the Trinity, and on the other hand, a "radical narrative character and Trinitarian essence" to Hegel's onto-theology, a radical philosophical mutation from the fifteenth century,[34] a rupture from mainline theological and philosophical traditions. The mutation into general and special metaphysics, include logic, psychology and theology. Scotus antedates and has nothing to do with this split but rather unifies metaphysics and theology in a manner that anticipates the deformation of freedom and reason of Kant. Scotus has nothing to do with the mystical affinities of Hegel's predecessors such as Joachim of Fiore, and anticipates the turn to the subject that is non-negotiable for Kant and Hegel. Their idea of the rehabilitation of Christianity is to disallow any accent of the supernatural, mystery, or miracle, and to deny any causal activity that might come from a divine agent.

---

33 CYRIL O'REGAN, *The Heterodox Hegel* (Albany, N.Y.: State University of New York Press, 1994, 21. Henceforth, O'REGAN, *Heterodox*.

34 BOULNOIS, *Être et représentation* is an extrordinary study of this mutation.

For private consultation and not distribution without the consent of E Ondrako

From a contemporary perspective, Cyril O'Regan recognizes the sincerity of Hegel's "Christian and Lutheran disposition, while acknowledging divergence; and wishes to configure a Hegel who belongs to the heterodox margins of the ontotheological tradition, but whose marginality is not such as to traject him extra-textually outside the tradition into a kind of hermeneutic free fall." [35] Like O'Regan, Peter D. Fehlner is cautious about the term hermeneutics as "the interpreter's theory of how a writer of the past, is conditioned by cultural circumstances no longer existent and to be understood, even by himself, needs to be "re-read" in terms of a current and diverse cultural ambient."[36] The deeper question for both O'Regan and Fehlner seems to be the absolute character of metaphysical truth *vis a vis* a reconstruction into a hermeneutic of inculturation.

Hegel's philosophy is sometimes called theosophy, or a philosophy or religious system that proposes to establish direct contact with divine principle through contemplation, revelation, etc., and to gain, thereby, a spiritual insight superior to empirical knowledge.[37] It is an example of the crisis of modernity, the begging of the question of the absolute character of metaphysical truth. In the midst of the crises of modernity, Pope Benedict XVI is an extraordinarily gifted theologian with a very broad and deep engagement with modernity. He invites an answer to his question which may be the most sensitive question of the day. Put forth with great modesty, sensitivity, and prompted by the thought of Scotus during his audience on Scotus, the Holy Father asks: what is the relation of liberty to the will and the intellect.[38]

This is a fertile field to cultivate. Scotus's disciples recognize that the problem of the intimate explication of the concordance of efficacious grace with liberty and that it has to be explained very carefully in order not to damage the concept of liberty.[39] The crux of the problem is to reconcile what is inspired by the theory of Scotus with those who hold a different view. They claim that Catholic teaching on the freedom of human will under grace, when explained scotistically, necessarily must will what God already wills necessarily and so is deprived of freedom. What is seriously

---

[35] O'REGAN, *Heterodox*, 25.

[36] PETER D. FEHLNER, *St. Maximilian Kolbe: Pneumatologist* (New Bedford, MA: Academy of the Immaculate, 2005), 12.

[37] *Websters New World Dictionary*.

[38] BENEDICT XVI, *Papal Audience*, July 7, 2010.

[39] SEVERINO GONZÁLEZ, et. al., *Sacrae Theologiae Summa* (Matriti – Madrid: Biblioteca de Autores Cristianos, 1956, 3rd ed.), De gratia, vol. 3, nn. 311–324, 674–684. In no. 322, González, who outlines the theory of condetermination correctly, flatly denies that it can be reconciled with Catholic teaching on the freedom of human will under grace, a view which the Franciscan scotists contest.

For private consultation and not distribution without the consent of E Ondrako

flawed with that conclusion has to do with the failure to understand that metaphysical necessity and freedom are not opposed in the theory of Scotus! It is only physical necessity and freedom that is opposed in the theory of Scotus. The key concept following the theory of Scotus is that the human will should be elevated by grace to the point where the human person via *condetermination* necessarily wills the absolute good which does not deprive the human person of freedom, but perfects it.

This discovery of the earlier work of Conventual Franciscans has implications to help answer the profound question of Pope Benedict XVI about "liberty in relation to the will and intellect," at the heart of modernity. The reply from a scotistic perspective is not apparent and not always agreed with. The concept of *condetermination*[40] is the original discovery of several seventeenth century Conventual Franciscan disciples of Scotus, John of Napoli a (Sicilian) and Angelo Vulpes (from Naples) who taught Bartholomeus Mastrius. They developed the scotistic inspired notion of condetermination. Condetermination is that it is not a predetermined idea of human liberty, but very much the kind of liberty that parents may intuitively understand when they cooperate with the Creator in bringing new life into the world. It is affective.

The defenders of the system of condetermination hold:

> *Efficacious grace is explained* by a divine condetermining decree, not a predetermining decree, in which the object is an act belonging to the will.

> This decree is *intrinsically efficacious*, because its efficacy does not depend on the determination of the will, nor any previous condition. On the contrary, what antecedes this determination is not in the priority of causality but of succession; to the extent, namely, that the decree of God virtually condetermining contains the free determination of the will.

> However, this *efficacy* of the condetermined decree is not effective, but *affective*; because the decree of God is connected infallibly with the determination of the created will, not as its cause, but as a pure affection.

> Here *liberty* is saved completely. Certainly the will determines its freedom in the same sense in which the decree of God set it in motion from all eternity; not because the determination of the will is caused by God, but because the will, according to the natural subordination and

---

40 I found this concept of "condetermination" to be richly rewarding about liberty in relation to the will and intellect and more urgent now than it was in the seventeenth century. I am indebted to Peter D. Fehlner for alerting me to engage it.

For private consultation and not distribution without the consent of E Ondrako

as it were sympathetic debt of the Creator, from the proper inclination and determination is continuous in the face of God.[41]

It should be readily apparent why I think that condetermination is a significant question for further research beyond what is possible here. Condetermination in an age when freedom is becoming more of a universal desire is interpreted according to the absolute character of metaphysical truth. The spectrum is from absolute autonomy of a Kantian sort to condetermination that necessarily wills the absolute good but does not deprive the human person of freedom, but perfects it. Condetermination has the potential of persuading the contemporary world that Scotus's take on freedom is the most noble imaginable. The onto-theology of Hegel does not have room for condetermination with such a Scotistic view on freedom. The real problem for Hegel is the notion of God. It is his most encompassing horizon. Hegel allows what Kant forbids and concludes that everything about Christianity is Trinitarian and the Trinitarian code of Christianity is almost the code of everything. Scotistic thought is surprisingly simple and attractive: every human being who willingly, knowingly and freely cooperates with supernatural graces to create, may do so as an act of condetermination because to will the absolute good does not deprive a person of freedom, but perfects it.

In closing part two, there are simply no connections between Scotus's definition of the will, freedom, and necessity or independent being as in the Franciscan school and Hegel's Trinitarian code of almost everything. First, Hegel's metaphysical point of departure is 'becoming,' change, the identity between being and nothing. Scotus's univocal concept of being is flight from non-being. Second, Hegel favors the view of Luther and the reformers in his take on the historical development of Christianity. To them, Christianity is realized for the first time in the Reformation and still remains to be carried out through the Enlightenment and Protestant Christianity. Third, the Ammerbach family of publishers, who were among the first to seriously promote Scotus's works, saw Luther as seriously digressing from fundamental Catholic doctrine. Fourth, Luther's contemporaries felt he had made a significant break with Catholic doctrine.[42] Fifth, there is an identifiable trail of difficulties caused by Ockham's nominalism, which denies universals. He leaves the *via antiqua*, of which Scotus is the last representative, and inaugurates a *via moderna*. Sixth, Luther picks up significant Ockhamist ideas, but not scotistic ideas, through steps *via*

---

[41] GONZÁLEZ, *De gratia*, no. 316, 680. This view, according to the leader B. Mastrius, the modern writers of Scotus's thought hold in common.

[42] C. DEL ZOTTO, La "via scoti" nell'epistolario di Johann Ammerbach (1443–1513), *Approfondimenti, in Via Scoti*, Roma 1995, vol II, pp. 1091–1108). Henceforth, Del Zotto, La via scoti.

For private consultation and not distribution without the consent of E Ondrako

Gabriel Biel, an eclectic, who was Luther's teacher. An Ockhamist tone plays out through complex historical developments of Lutheranism. Seventh, Hegel attributes to Luther what he could as easily have attributed to Calvin. Eighth, Hegel shares assumptions about the renewal of religion with Kant, but takes exception to Kant's epistemology. Ninth, Hegel brings metaphysics and ontology back to the fore, but instead of developing it into a healthy secularity, his philosophical and theological views take more of a narrative character and develop into a fully realized secularity with Trinitarian landscaping. Tenth, Newman would have nothing to do with this. Once he discovered the freeing spirit of Butler's *Analogy*, his preference turned to natural theology and the sacramentality of creation as handed down from the patristic period. It did not take long for Newman to recognize that scholarship alone was an incomplete and unfulfilling reason for his existence. He sought intellectual excellence along with moral and affective excellence, another name for holiness. There was nothing extraordinary to his personal quest for truth and for holiness, but, to do all things well. Newman may not have used the term condetermination, but operates with an understanding of the will as necessarily willing the absolute good and that does not deprive the human person of freedom, but perfects it.

Recapitulation

There are seven wide-ranging points about the Hegelian inspired thinking on becoming, as juxtaposed to the metaphysical theological position of Scotus on being and becoming, and the centrality of the Trinity in their thought. Each point aims to be ascetic, comprehensive, and an invitation for emendation about Hegelian inspired thought that has made its way into the mainstream of philosophical and theological work and appears to be well entrenched for some time to come. Of necessity, some points are more implicit than explicit, but all are intended to aid, to contextualize, and to inspire further research and the expression of competing views. For example, it is critical to understand why Scotus and Hegel both use the image of a 'closed circle' but with a radically different substratum and meaning.

First. The importance of the science of the transcendentals for theology.

Olivier Boulnois recognizes the monumental contribution of Scotus to the science of the transcendentals and why this science is required to do theology.[43] There are several 'edged tools' with which Scotus, anticipated the solution to many difficult problems about the nature, validity and

---

43 BOULNOIS, *Être*, ch. 7, 327–404.

For private consultation and not distribution without the consent of E Ondrako

scope, of theology. Seven of these 'tools' take pride of place and require effort to master in order to understand the Church's teaching on the mystery of the Trinity *vis a vis* Hegel's complete secularizing of the Trinity, with the tragic effect of eliminating a sense of awe in the presence of the mystery of the Godhead. This places the Creator on the same level as the one created. Scotus rescues us from a depersonalizing of the divinity with his metaphysical theology.

1. The notion of univocal being

2. The disjunctive transcendentals

3. Formal distinction *a parte rei*

4. The *perfectiones simpliciter simplex*[44]

5. The relation between the intellect and the will

6. The relation between nature and the will

7. The relation between being and the person

Olivier Boulnois, Allan B. Wolter,[45] and Ruggero Rosini[46] are three of a growing number of Scotists whose work is foundational. They represent only three of the most comprehensive senior writers who may help the students willing to do the work of establishing a sound intellectual foundation in the science of the disjunctive transcendentals of Scotus.[47] Without these skills, one may become taken by the deceptive thinking that Scotus's hypothesis is beautiful in theory but has nothing to do with the actual history of what happened especially which means that the Incarnation is a result of original sin, the exact opposite of Scotus's thought. Moreover, the Hegelian inspired teaching that God the Father can suffer precisely because God is a modern version of an ancient heresy, yet one that is charmingly deceptive.

Second. Theological metaphysics helps to make mysteries intelligible.

The answer to the problem of suffering raised above is that no divine person is capable of suffering except on the basis of the hypostatic union. Sacred Scripture and the Church's perennial Magisterium has affirmed

---

[44] *ST* I q. 82 a. 3, 4 may be compared to Scotus's primacy of charity and primacy of the will. There is a complementarity to the pure perfection of Scotus and meaning of simplicity for Thomas. See P. D. FEHLNER, Dialogue, chapter 7 in this volume.

[45] ALLAN B. WOLTER, *Transcendals*. See SCOTUS, *A Treatise on God as First Principle, De primo rerum principio*, ed. trans. and comm. Allan B. Wolter. (Chicago: Franciscan Herald Press, 1966).

[46] RUGGERO ROSINI, *Mariology of Bl. John Duns Scotus*, trans. and comm. Friars of the Immaculate. (New Bedford, MA: Academy of the Immaculate, 2008).

[47] There is a younger generation of Scotists whose works are readily available and helpful but, as Newman often cautioned, "time is our best friend and champion."

For private consultation and not distribution without the consent of E Ondrako

that teaching from as early as the Synod of Rome in 382. Moreover, Scotus's thought on the theology of the hypostatic union, the Immaculate Conception, and inhabitation of the Trinity in the souls of the just and in the Church builds on Scripture, Tradition, and the Magisterium. His metaphysical theology requires understanding of authentic notions of Trinitarian theology so as not to confuse them conceptually. Thomism and Scotism approach an explanation of the hypostatic union in competing ways, but the scholarly accent is to discover how they complement one another and by doing so, add to the *valor theologicus*.

To illustrate, Scotism explains the divine maternity without entailing a hypostatic union between Mary and the Holy Spirit, but respecting an analogous role in deference to the human nature of Mary, a finite person, consecrating and sanctifying her as full of grace, who cooperates freely with the Blessed Trinity in effecting the hypostatic union, not merely as an instrument of one or another divine person, but as a principal co-cause. Her proper relation is to the Word, and the Word to her. Mary is Spouse of the Holy Spirit, Mother of Jesus, and daughter of the Father. The historical and logical outcome can be traced in the true development of doctrine and repudiation of what was judged to be false.[48] Many current debates encouraged by Vatican II and the Magisterium sometimes are referred to as 'ecclesio-typical' and 'Christo-typical.' The terminology may be as helpful as it may mislead, but that is the work of development of doctrine.

For example, the key to understanding the developing theology of Marian coredemption and the mystery of the Church is that it is not an either/or, but a both/and. The title of *Lumen Gentium*, chapter eight, gets it right: the Blessed Virgin in the Mystery of Christ and of the Church. Moreover, the teaching that Mary is Mother of the whole Christ, head and body, from the first moment of the Incarnation and forever is from Bonaventure and carried forward by another theologian disciple of St. Francis, Scotus. Moreover, the Franciscan tradition is a "both/and" because the vocation of Francis and his Order is perfect conformity to Christ and repair and renewal of the Church.[49]

---

48 JOHN HENRY NEWMAN, *Essay on the Development of Doctrine* (London: uniform edition, 1900), is indispensible for its clarity of this charged issue in today's world.

49 BONAVENTURE, *Collations on the Seven Gifts of the Holy Spirit*, ch. 6. 20. See Friars of the Immaculate, ed. *Mary at the Foot of the Cross* IX (New Bedford, MA: Academy of the Immaculate, 2010) which addresses for the first time as a conference in this excellent series (2000–2010) the relation between Marian coredemption and the mystery of the Church. See E. ONDRAKO, "Mary in the Church in Newman with an Eye to Coredemption," 391–456, for a study of Newman's use of the term coredemptress in his "Letter to Pusey," 1865, and for a commentary on Newman's developing ecclesiology and use of theological typology. See NEWMAN, "A Letter Addressed to E.B. Pusey, D.D. on the Occasion of His Eirenicon," *Certain Difficulties of Anglicans in Catholic Teaching* 2 (London: uniform edition, 1907), 77–78.

For private consultation and not distribution without the consent of E Ondrako

The vocation of Francis and his Order leads to the theological meta-physics of the Franciscan school which is an approach to the mysteries such as the three central doctrinal truths that support the scotistic absolute primacy of Christ and Mary, the hypostatic union, Immaculate Concep-tion, and inhabitation of the Trinity in the souls of the just and of the Church. It is a small step to conclude that Mary has no other reason for existence but to be the Mother of God. Her divine maternity or maternal mediation is a total consecration of Mary so as to pertain to the order of the hypostatic union as no other person and that coincides with the Immacu-late Conception as the definition of her person, a maternal mediatory one. On scotistic grounds, this is the answer to the major objection to his thesis. In the tradition of the Church the divine maternity is the first principle of Mariology, while in the Franciscan school the answer is that the Immaculate Conception is the first principal of Mariology.[50] Hegel would have no such purchase.

Third. Thomas and Scotus differ regarding divine illumination.

Person and personality are examples of the content concerning the order of the hypostatic union, which is easy to misunderstand, to misrep-resent, or to misappropriate because of many complex philosophical and theological points within the development of the doctrines. Hegel's misappropriation about the hypostatic union effects his heterodox Trini-tarian thought.[51] In anticipation, Thomas Aquinas and Scotus are two, and some may say the only two, authentic approaches to the metaphysics and dogmatics of person and personality. Thomas teaches that we cognize kinds of things 'in' the divine ideas, not by having direct access to the ideas, but our agent intellect somehow participates in the divine ideas, and this enables it to abstract reliably.[52] Bonaventure holds a theory of divine illumination, a variation of Augustine's. For Bonaventure, "truth in the soul receives a relative certitude from below, and receives an absolute certitude from above."[53] Neither approach were completely convincing to all Dominicans or all Franciscans. Scotus chose not to use some of

[50] E. PIACENTINI, P. Leone Veuthey (1896–1974) e la visione francescana della Mariologia, *Miles Immaculatae* 39 (2003) 688–738. See P. D. FEHLNER, *St. Maximilian M. Kolbe, Pneumatologist* (New Bedford, MA, 2004), 74–78.

[51] HEGEL, *Phenomenology of Spirit and Lectures on the Philosophy of Religion*, ed. trans. and comm. PETER C. HODGSON. *G.W.F. Hegel: Theologian of the Spirit* (Minneapolis: Fortress Press, 1997). See *Phenomenology of Spirit*, 92–136, and *Lectures on the Philosophy of Religion*, 172–259 for a summary of Hegel's views that formed the foundation for his innovative and secularized trinitarian thought in later life. Henceforth, HODGSON, *Hegel*.

[52] THOMAS AQUINAS, *ST* I q. 84, art. 2–7, esp. art. 5. This critical chapter deals with abstraction and the origin of intelligible species.

[53] BONAVENTURE, *Disputed Questions on the Knowledge of Christ*, chapter 4, no. 23–26, Zachary Hayes, intro. and trans. (St. Bonaventure, N.Y.:The Franciscan Institute, 1992), 142–144.

For private consultation and not distribution without the consent of E Ondrako

the traditional Bonaventurian terminology such as illumination and exemplarism in favor of less personal terminology such as the univocity of the concept of being, disjunctive transcendentals, and formal distinction *a parte rei*. It is easy to conclude that Scotus disagrees with Bonaventure's divine illumination, but, another sustainable view, upon deeper reflection, is that univocity of the concept of being is not a pure logical construct first, but is a unique, incomparable formulation of divine illumination in logical form so that it can be the light guiding all our thought, keeping logic securely linked to reality or being. That is the position that I now find more convincing and it has extremely promising applicability.

For example, whatever the contribution of neo-Thomism and transcendental Thomism to the debate around the mystery of the Trinity, the complex theory of 'quasi-formal causality' of the transcendental Thomists and the particular form of an anthropological turn that usually accompanies it, seem to fall short of the definition of the univocity of the concept of being above. The jury is still out on how well the rigorous definitions and metaphysics characteristic of Thomas and Scotus, tried and tested, and handed down as effective replies to questions of their day apply to the theory of 'quasi-formal causality,' as it took shape in theologies that developed after the Second Vatican Council. Some senior scholars claim that there was too much of an uncritical 'rush' to eliminate the scholastic method before testing how applicable the newer theological methods with their rich anthropological and cultural content are to answering the difficult questions from modernity and post-modernity. There are mindful of the ecclesial vocation of the theologian, the perennial task of the anthropologist, philosopher and theologian to contribute to the development of doctrine.

The manner of exercising this perennial task varies. Kierkegaard[54] is not a metaphysician theologian, strictly speaking, as Thomas and Scotus, but analyzes and identifies the problem of doubt on the deepest level of the struggle between Christianity and culture *vis a vis* Hegel's influence. Kierkegaard has an epistemology that engages Newman's. Newman called himself a controversialist, meaning in touch with the debates of his day on as deep a level as possible, as was Kierkegaard. Adrian J. Boekraad[55] observes that Newman uses Hegelian terminology to imbue his arguments. As I take it, Newman, recognizes Hegelian underpinnings, addresses them

54 SOREN KIERKEGAARD, *Philosophical Fragments: Johannes Climacus*, ed. trans. intro. and notes. Howard V. Hong and Edna H. Hong (Princeton: Princeton University Press, 1987); and *Concluding Unscientific Postscript*. Vol. 1 (Princeton: Princeton University Press, 1992). Henceforth, KIERKEGAARD, *Fragments* or *Postscript*.

55 A. J. BOEKRAAD, *The Personal Conquest of Truth according to John Henry Newman* (Louvain: Éditions Nauwelaerts, 1955), 60.

For private consultation and not distribution without the consent of E Ondrako

subtly, and less polemically, although Newman was a gifted polemicist, as one reads in the *Tamworth Reading Room*, but his subtle replies seem to have more appeal, such as his epistemology in the *Grammar of Assent*. In some ways, both Kierkegaard and Newman may be likened to Socrates in the *Theatetus*, as Socrates likened himself to a midwife, helping the student to keep from delivering a phantom. In the Gospel, Christ is the way, the truth and the life, which Hegel deconstructs into a phantom such as Socrates warns his students to avoid.

Fourth. Fundamental premises from Scotus.

One has to be alert to any radical reinterpretation of Scotus or reconstruction in a new cultural ambient. Scotus holds that Christ would have been born even if Adam and Eve had not sinned because all creation is ordained for the glory of the Son. A caveat is in order concerning some contemporary commentators on Scotus because behind is Hegelian inspired thinking. They hold that if Adam and Eve had not sinned, Christ would still have become incarnate, and would still have been crucified to prove how great God's love really is. The error is to think that God would not be a loving and loveable God if he did not experience suffering. The error is to that the entire Trinity as divine suffered on Calvary. Hegel goes further and teaches that at the death of the Son on the cross, one ought not to lament but to celebrate that the death of God is the death of the absolute transcendence of God. It is a small step for him to marginalize the resurrection.

In reply to this Hegelian secularization of the Trinity, and contemporary neo-patripassionism, and some contemporary commentators on Scotus, the subtle doctor's fundamental premises are:

1. God as God can not suffer.

2. To claim sin as the necessary premise for the realization of God's most perfect love is irrational and depersonalizing.

3. God's supreme love, mercy and goodness is what it is regardless of sin and suffering.

4. The glory of Christ would be supreme whether he suffered or not.

5. The perfection of Christ's glory and grace is one question, and how he makes it attractive to us is another.

6. Christ might have redeemed us in many ways, and his self-emptying, or kenosis of the Incarnation would have been sufficient, but he chose the way of the cross to make his love most attractive.

For private consultation and not distribution without the consent of E Ondrako

7. His love for us would have been as great, whatever way he chose to effect our redemption.[56]

Fifth. Scotus is Newman's Oxford inspiration.

In the *Idea of a University*, Newman refers to Scotus as the greatest theological luminary Oxford ever had. The implications deserve further investigation, of Scotus's spiritual vitality, his thought on the primacy of the will, and the manner that his thought developed into condetermination by later Scotists. Pope Benedict XVI's recent question about liberty in relation to the will and intellect at the papal audience on the thought of Scotus invite investigation. Moreover, as I grow in familiarity with Thomistic arguments, I perceive that may of Newman's replies appear to be Thomistic at first, but on further reflection, there are Scotistic contours.[57] To recognize the potential complementarity of both approaches, of Thomas and Scotus, requires willingness to do the hard work of studying their overall corpus of writings and contemporary meaning while doing the same for Newman's works which are available on line.[58] One needs to read, analyze and lean to understanding subtleties in Newman, such as his replies to Hegelian inspired thought. An example is Newman's *Biglietto* speech on receiving the honor of being named a Cardinal. Newman deals with the problem of liberalism in religion and the great apostasy *vis a vis* Kantian and Hegelian philosophy of religion.

A related inspiring example of wrestling with Hegelian inspired thought is Kierkegaard[59] who is not a metaphysical theologian, strictly speaking, as Thomas and Scotus, but analyzes and identifies the problem of doubt on the deepest level of the struggle between Christianity and culture *vis a vis* Hegel's influence. Kierkegaard appears as a controversialist as Newman is a controversialist, meaning in touch with the debates of his day. Adrian J. Boekraad[60] observes that Newman uses Hegelian terminology to imbue his arguments. As I take it, Newman, recognizes Hegelian underpinnings, addresses them subtly, and less polemically, although Newman was a gifted polemicist, as one reads in the *Tamworth Reading*

---

56 See ROSINI, fn. 9, 271.

57 PETER D. FEHLNER, "Scotus and Newman in Dialogue," chapter 7 in this volume. As far as we know, this is the first scholarly attempt to develop such a thesis. One of the starting points is to understand Thomas and Scotus is to begin with Thomas on the intellect *ST* I qq. 85–87 and will *ST* I qq. 82–83. Then read the *Grammar of Assent* closely and see how Newman digresses and becomes more scotistic.

58 The web site is www.newmanreader.org. Newman's *Letters and Diaries* comprise thirty-three volumes but are not on line. Roderick Strange is preparing a compilation of selections of Newman's most important letters with Oxford University Press.

59 *Kierkegaard, Fragments, and Postscript.*

60 BOEKRAAD, *The Personal Conquest of Truth*, 60.

For private consultation and not distribution without the consent of E Ondrako

Room, but his subtle replies seem to have more appeal. In some ways, both Kierkegaard and Newman may be likened to Socrates in the *Theatetus*, as Socrates likened himself to a midwife, helping the student from delivering a phantom. In the Gospel, Christ is the way, the truth and the life, which Hegel deconstructs into a phantom.

Similarly, Pope St. John Paul II in *Fides et Ratio* and Pope Benedict XVI in *Deus caritas est* delicately counter the acerbic contemporary cynicism with faith, reason and love. Neither mentions Hegel but both address the implications of Hegelian thought at the heart of the crises of modernity. It seems that Pope Benedict's question about liberty in relation to the will and intellect is ingeniously asking the contemporary world to see through the brilliant philosophical ruse of Hegelian inspired thought.

Sixth. Scotus, the Holy Spirit, and Hegel's subversion of the Trinity.

Scotus only mentions the Holy Spirit in the context of the virginal conception of Jesus. The subversion of Trinitarian thought in Hegel first appears in the *Phenomenology of Spirit* in 1807 and is developed in his *Lectures on the Philosophy of Religion* in 1824, one of which is "Christianity: The Consummate Religion."[61] Hegel's metaphysical subversion is that the Trinity only functions as a super explanation, a logical apparatus to translate into another idiom, which functions as a massive conceptual step of 'smoothing.' Scotus's logical conceptual apparatus of the univocity of the concept of being anticipates Hegel. Scotus's teaching is behind his consideration of the elect in Christ before the foundation of the world and the reason for the world's creation. Hegel's Trinitarian landscape of the entire Christian narrative begins with creation. He holds experience as subjectivity as the point of departure for a meaningful theology. History for Hegel is proper to the mode of the creature and not the Creator. That is how he collapses traditional metaphysics into his psychologism or uses psychology in forming his theory of philosophy.

A caveat is in order concerning theories about Scotus as granddaddy of Kant and Hegel through his supposed influence on Luther. In reply, the English friars saw Scotus as the last of the ancients and Ockham is the first of the moderns. Hegel follows a Lutheran inspired line of thinking and deviates from it. Luther's contemporaries and the Ammerbach family of publishers, who were among the first to publish Scotus's works, saw Luther as radically rupturing the theological tradition.[62] This is a significant challenge to the hypothesizing about Scotus as begetting Ockham and therefore influencing Luther and ultimately the originator of the problems

---

[61] PETER C. HODGSON, *Hegel, Phenomenology of Spirit and Lectures on the Philosophy of Religion*.

[62] C. DEL ZOTTO, *La via scoti*.

For private consultation and not distribution without the consent of E Ondrako

of modernity. It is Ockham who is the better candidate, a theory to be investigated by appropriate ecumenical dialogue.

Seventh. The missions of the Son and Holy Spirit in the economy of salvation.

Scotus mentions the Holy Spirit as an appropriation[63] referring to the involvement of all three divine Persons in the work common to all three, the economic trinity. Scotus does not pinpoint the distinctive features of this appropriation but the singular mutual relation of Virgin Mother to her Son. Scotus nuances the contributions of Bonaventure on the missions of the Son and Holy Spirit in the economy of salvation.[64] Bonaventure reflects on Jesus as Word eternal, Word incarnate, and Word inspired. The first is how all things are created, second, saved from sin, and third that all the redeemed are animated in the economy of salvation. By Word inspired, Bonaventure means the Word dwelling in us by the mission of the Holy Spirit. As animator and sanctifier of the Church and her members, the Holy Spirit links with a kind of mediatory role found also in the Virgin Mary. In other words, the mission of the Spirit is the first fruit of the mission of the Word Incarnate. For Bonaventure, the mission of the spirit is occasioned by original sin. Creation in itself is independent of the Word incarnate.

Here is where the affirmation of the absolute predestination of Christ in Scotus's thinking considers the roles of the Word eternal and Word incarnate in relation to the world and redemption in a way so far removed from the self-mediating of the concept of the closed circle of Hegel to explain all things past, present and to come. Scotus holds that creation was brought into existence prior to any consideration of sin. Scotus views the Word Incarnate by whom all are saved and created as the basis for affirming how the Immaculate Conception is the Marian mode of the absolute predestination of Christ to be Head and Savior of the Church. The logical relation is between the Word inspired via the mission of the Holy Spirit and the mystery of the Immaculate Conception. It is the Word Incarnate for whom creation was brought into existence and her sinlessness from the moment of her conception which reflects her profounder relation

---

63 Appropriation in a traditional thomistic approach seems more cautious and to differ from contemporary Thomists so as not to suggest a second hypostatic union according to B. GHERARDINI, *La Chiesa, Mystero e Servizio* (Roma: 1991), 101–102. Appropriation in the Franciscan tradition means that Mary enjoys relations with each of the divine Persons because this union of charity is appropriated to the Holy Spirit. Mary is related to the Father as the Son and to the Son as the Father, because she is uniquely, though not exclusively related to the Holy Spirit. Because Mary is so related, we too can be. See FEHLNER, *Kolbe Pneumatologist*, (New Bedford, MA: 2004), 78–79.

64 BONAVENTURE, *Collations on the Six Days of Creation*, collation. 3.

For private consultation and not distribution without the consent of E Ondrako

to the Word Incarnate and her unique relation as a person to the Word inspired. This is the Word inspired dwelling in us by the mission of the Holy Spirit. In sum, this is deeper Franciscan reasoning behind St. Francis invoking Mary as Spouse of the Holy Spirit. It gives the ontological basis for what Francis intuited.

Conclusion

Scotus and Hegel use the metaphor of a closed circle, but with completely different meanings. Hegel's is a subjectivized kingdom of the absolute Spirit: "the first estate is that of immediate naïve religion and of faith; the second is that of the understanding, the estate of the so-called cultured, of reflection and the Enlightenment; and finally the third estate is the community of philosophy."[65] Such is Hegel's manner of smoothing the rough spots after creation and teaching that the beauty of Christianity which is on its way to tame the world by massage[66] and on its way to be a Trinitarian thinker. Compare this to Scotus's thought on the Trinity, his 'circle,' which builds on Bonaventure's thought.[67] Scotus teaches the primacy of charity which is behind the predestination of the elect in Christ, the very reason for the creation of the world prior to any consideration of sin. Scotus's teaching on the primacy of the will helps explain his view that the procession of the Holy Spirit from Father and Son is voluntary rather than natural.

In 1823, Bishop Butler's preference for natural theology, which is not the physical theology of W. Paley, and his teaching on the sacramentality of creation *via* the patristic sources, especially the Alexandrines, Clement, and Athanasius, had a profound effect on Newman's philosophical world. By looking back to the patristic influence on Scotus, one discovers a striking parallel in the thought of Newman on the natural and supernatural orders with Scotus. In 1870, by the end of the second chapter of the *Grammar of Assent*, Newman established the grammatical basis for an assent to the mystery of the Trinity. By the end of the fourth chapter, he laid the basis for the "illative sense." In the fifth chapter, the Trinity itself is paradigmatic for the assent of faith. This epistemological work can be read as a reply to Hegel's heterodox view of the Trinity in 1824.

---

[65] HODGSON, *Hegel*, "Christianity: The Consummate Religion," 259.

[66] O'Regan uses this poignant and fitting image.

[67] BONAVENTURE, *Disputed Questions on the Mystery of the Trinity*, trans. and intro. Zachary Hayes (St. Bonaventure, N.Y.: The Franciscan Institute, 1979); and, *Sermon: Christ the One Teacher of All*, trans. intro. and comm. Z. Hayes *What Manner of Man* (Chicago: Franciscan Herald Press, 1974), 21–56.

For private consultation and not distribution without the consent of E Ondrako

In 1879, Newman wrote a letter of gratitude to Pope Leo XIII for the pastoral letter *Aeterni Patris*. Newman was elated that the Holy Father wanted to make scholastic philosophy more intellectual for analyzing problems of modernity. He knew that the renewal of studies in philosophy could help to make the members of the Church more intellectual, more Catholic, and more holy. He voiced support and encouragement to scholars to become familiar and competent in the scholastic method as one of many methods to study and explain the Church's teachings, but with a purpose, to be holy. Newman's incorporation of Butler's natural theology is the anthropological argument of Bonaventure. Newman uses the term natural to qualify theology as anthropological, but a caveat is in order. The separating of the ways between Karl Rahner and the young Cardinal Ratzinger is apparently over this interpretation of the anthropological. To argue for the existence of God by Newman, is in the line of Bonaventure and Scotus where the human person is as image of God rather than as a vestige of God. Image of God is on the metaphysical level and not the psychological level. It is beyond the scope of this essay, but various versions of transcendentalism seem to follow the concept of the human person as image of God in the psychological sense.

This distinction between the metaphysical and psychological levels of interpretation of image of God is fully in accord with the teaching of Scotus that the human person possesses a *perfectio simpliciter simplex*, i.e., something the finite person has in common with the infinite God. Maximilian Kolbe, who was a Scotist, completes the thought of Scotus, that there is a coming forth of all things from the Father. Christ is the perfect work of the Father and Mary Immaculate is the most perfect fruit of Christ's work which was consummated on the Cross. Kolbe develops the idea of how a return begins with the work of the Spirit and Mary. The mission of the Holy Spirit in the economy of salvation uniquely terminates in the Virgin who is the Immaculate Conception.[68] It is their work that enables all of the rest of creation to be united to Christ and by Christ returned to the Father. In sum, Kolbe's is a further Franciscan explanation of the order to Scotus's primacy of the Incarnation and the primacy of charity which involves the missions of the Son and Spirit. The mode is set by the unique mediation of the Spouse of the Holy Spirit who is Mother of God and Mother of the Church. According to Scotus, such is the radical goodness of God and of creation.

---

[68] Scotus's Mariology is in chapter 8 of *Lumen Gentium* at Vatican II. The debate continues between what some call Marian minimizers and maximizers, ecclesio-typology and Christo-typology. From the sparks ignite greater understanding.

For private consultation and not distribution without the consent of E Ondrako

Finally, this perusal into the approaches on the metaphysics, human nature, or psychology, of Scotus suggests why it should differ from Thomas. The thomistic and scotistic approaches rest on the notion of the will as absolute and should differ. Rather than opening the door to Kant's agnosticism, and Hegel's inversions of Scotus, there is a corrective. One has to read the critical insights of Scotus, not as if, to be understood, he is to be re-read in terms of a current and diverse cultural ambient. This means that there is an absolute character to metaphysical truth. Parallels to Scotus are found in Newman's consistent systematic theological reflection, one of the reasons to advance the thesis that Newman, at heart, has an affinity to the scotistic school. For Scotus,

> the intellect as a natural rather than voluntary power is not distinguished from the will in terms of an object, but in terms of a mode of action concerning the same object, being. The formal character of intellect as a natural power is to be determined by that object as truth, whereas the formal character of the will is to determine itself in relation to the same object as good. By itself the intellect could not be discerning or critical; by itself the will would be merely arbitrary.[69]

For Scotus, God always loves in a most orderly way. The challenge of orderly willing is to give emphasis to the importance of the process of interiorization, of entering into the heart, the critical question where reason and will are in harmony with faith and the affectionate communion with God. There is a problem with the thomistic perspective that the will is not essentially free, but only marginally in relation to contingent objects. From a scotistic perspective, it is a mistake to conclude that the freedom of the human will under grace must will what God already wills necessarily and so is deprived of freedom. Rather, metaphysical necessity and freedom are not opposed, but only physical necessity, in the theory of Scotus. That the human will should be elevated by grace to the point where the human person by condetermination necessarily wills the absolute good does not deprive the human person of freedom, but, rather perfects it.

To finish, Hegel's rehabilitation of Christianity has no purchase for this scotistic perfection of human freedom. He takes exception to Kant's epistemology and replaces it with his own idealism. He inverts scotistic opposition between being and nothing. The result is that one cannot recognize the difference between infinite and finite, necessary and contingent, and that the source of the contingent is in the pure perfection of the necessary

---

69 FEHLNER, Dialogue, "Scotus and Newman in Dialog," ch. 7 in this volume, 265

For private consultation and not distribution without the consent of E Ondrako

infinite being.[70] I think there is a simple way to keep Scotus and Hegel apart and retain the noble goal of building a dialogical bridge between their thought. If Cyril O'Regan is right, it seems that the term "inclusive Trinity" may be a more adequate term for Hegel's Trinitarian elaboration than "economic Trinity." Inclusive Trinity may be a way of reading the peculiar turn in Hegel's attempt to identify the divine plenitude with absolute spirit.[71] For Scotus, the living Tradition of the Church alone can provide a permanent guarantee of theological metaphysics. The mediation of Mary, as *memory of the Church*,[72] provides the dynamic to bring the theological and metaphysical genius of Scotus to hearts in search of peace.

---

70 Newman's letter of gratitude was written on 14 December 1879 to Pope Leo XIII for the pastoral letter, *Aeterni patris*, August 4, 1879. LD 23: 212.

71 O'REGAN, *Heterodox*, 72–75.

72 See E. Ondrako, "Introduction: Key Concepts," 28, 31, 33; "Element 4. Mary as memory of the Church," 34, 35 in this volume.

For private consultation and not distribution without the consent of E Ondrako

CHAPTER 17

Scotus the Nefarious: Uncovering Genealogical Sophistications

Cyril O'Regan

Scotus is a thinker of sufficient philosophical and theological stature to command respect and to demand the kind of sophisticated analysis that is afforded other medieval figures such as Aquinas. Such work is ongoing, and there are attempts not only to lay bare but defend his metaphysics and theology. Equally, Scotus's elaboration of God and the relation between divine attributes has been found to be worthy of attention. Such also is the case with regard to his soteriology with its supralapsarian profile, and also of his Mariology.[1] This is simply to present a cross-section of what scholars have been exercised by over the past few decades. If the quality of this work is uneven, it is the case that some of it is very high. Still, the impression exists that this works belongs to particular enclaves variously affiliated to the Franciscans, and variously nostalgic about the production of a thinker whose day has long past and thus interest in whom is purely antiquarian. It is some aspects of this marginalization that I want to address, and address them precisely as an outsider. In particular I want to address the ways in which a whole series of constructions of Scotus impede his receiving a hearing outside a band of his devotees. In doing this I am neither suggesting that Scotus is right and the constructions wrong in every important respect, nor am I saying that the marginalization is not due in some part also to his defenders who have failed to make the case for his relevance in the contemporary philosophical and theological world. My point is that there are a surprising number of constructions and narratives that function to 'misprison' Scotus and essentially side-line him.[2] I intend to

---

1 Among the many good works on Scotus, see RICHARD CROSS, *Duns Scotus* (Oxford: Oxford University Press, 1999); OLIVER BOULNOIS, *Être et Représentation: Une généologie de la métaphysique moderne à l'époque de Duns Scot (xiii–xiv siècle)* (Paris: Presses Universitaire de France, 1999, rpt., 2008).

2 "Misprison" is a technical word in the vocabulary of the influential literary critic and theorist, Harold Bloom, where it has the meaning of offering readings of a literary oeuvre which are forceful, highly interested, and apparently definitive. Bloom borrows the word from the lexicon of Shakespeare. There is no reason to suppose that the concept does not have application in the areas of philosophy and theology. See among other books by Bloom, *The Anxiety of Criticism: A Theory of Poetics* (New York and Oxford: Oxford University Press, 1973); also *A Map of Misreading* (New York and Oxford: Oxford University Press, 1975).

For private consultation and not distribution without the consent of E Ondrako

touch on six such constructions in two sets of three, with the second set of three largely presupposing the first. I will give much greater attention to the second set, since not only are they more recent and there is much less written about them, but essentially these narratives enjoy sufficient authority to exacerbate an already bad situation for Scotus.

I begin necessarily with a brief outline of these six constructions, most of which have an explicit narrative genealogical code.

1. The first is the argument between Thomism and Scotism sponsored by the two great orders of the Dominicans or Franciscans. In the modern period Thomism has long held the upper hand and has been understood as the mode of medieval thought that can best engage with and resist the dominant discourses of modernity. Papal encyclicals in which Aquinas is recognized as the philosopher are but one reflection of this ascendancy.[3] A more proximate indicator is the way in which the major signature of Christian metaphysics turns out to be analogy. Scotus, who supports the univocity of being,[4] is consigned to the dark past and with him the rationalism and essentialism that it supports and that supports it.

2. The second construction is a variant of the first and is typical of reconstructed as opposed to unreconstructed Thomism. More nearly than the latter, the former separates out genuine Thomism from neo-Scholasticism, and suggests that from the time of Suarez on (16–17th c), Scotus is the second ingredient in a synthesis with Thomism that gets Scholasticism off track. To save Aquinas from neo-Scholasticism, it is felt that not only does one need to distinguish carefully between Aquinas's positions and that of his interpreters which are less labile and experimental than his own, but also identify and remove the Scotist elements of the synthesis which are blamed for obscuring the truly adequate positions of the historical Aquinas, which can speak in a way that Scotus cannot to the modern age.

---

[3] There exists an interesting relation between *Humani Generis* (Leo XIII) and *Fides et Ratio* (1998 by Pope St. John Paul II). Given the hermeneutical demands of encyclicals on the same—here faith and reason—not to contradict each other, not only is the 19th-century encyclical affirmed in *Fides et Ratio*, but Aquinas is in the end given pride of place. The difference is that in *Fides et Ratio* the language is more probative, on the one hand, and Aquinas is merely first among equals, on the other. See my article, 'Ambiguity and Undecidability in *Fides et Ratio*, in *International Journal of Systematic Theology*, vol. 2. No. 3 (2000), 319–29.

[4] See MARY BETH INGHAM and MECHTHILD DREYER, *The Philosophical Vision of John Duns Scotus* (Washington, D.C.: CUA Press, 2004), 38–51. A still useful account of univocity is provided by ALLEN B. WOLTER, O.F.M., *The Transcendentals and their Function in the Metaphysics of Duns Scotus* (New York: The Franciscan Institute, 1946, rpt. Kessinger, 2008), 31–57.

For private consultation and not distribution without the consent of E Ondrako

3. A third construction found in Thomism, but also in non-aligned historiography, links Scotus and Ockham such that the objection against the voluntarism and nominalism on the latter is taken to be an argument against Scotus who is seen to anticipate Ockham's positions.[5] Nominalism and Voluntarism in turn are regarded as harbingers of a degenerate modernity in which the ability to comprehend God, nature or ourselves is lost.

The first three constructions have been around for some time and have exerted sufficient influence as to be accepted as truisms which offer necessary and even sufficient incentives for not paying attention to the work of Scotus. The second group of three are different in kind and, arguably, have as much if not more influence in contemporary thought than the reservations of unreconstructed and reconstructed Thomists.

4. A particularly interesting way of putting Scotus out of philosophical circulation comes from Heidegger's reflections on metaphysical thought, which is understood to subvert the radical question of 'why is there something rather than nothing?' even as it raises it.[6] Although in one sense the metaphysics of Scotus is just one expression of the metaphysical tradition which has Plato and Aristotle at its roots, still Heidegger's lambasting of the view of being understood as the most general and abstract category does seem to recall the tradition of Scotus as much as it recalls the tradition of Hegel.

5. There are in addition two contemporary theological dispensations, which if they avoid deep engagement with his work, are very critical of it, and genealogically tend to cast his work in a bad light. The first of these two theological dispensations—and by far the milder of the two—is provided in and by the triptych of Hans

---

[5] Much of the literature on Scotus resists connecting Scotus too closely to Nominalism in general and Ockham in particular. The work of Richard Cross and Steven Dumont is illustrative of this. The literature on Ockham tends to have two different tracks. Along one track, Ockham has precursors, and although Scotus is not necessarily the main one (Peter of Spain and William of Sherwood are the two most often adduced), he is understood to be a precursor of some significance. On another track, the emphasis falls heavily on Ockham as an original, that while Scotus might anticipate him on some points, he enjoys no special status as an anticipator. For an expression of the former, see MEYRICH H. CARRÉ, *Realists and Nominalists* (Oxford: Oxford University Press, 1946). The books of Gordon Leff offer a good expression of the latter. See *William of Ockham: The Metamorphosis of Scholastic Discourse* (Manchester: Manchester University Press, Rowan and Littlefield, 1975); also *The Dissolution of the Medieval Outlook: An Essay on Intellectual and Spiritual Change in the Fourteenth Century* (New York: Harper & Row, 1976).

[6] For a typical expression of this, see *Introduction to Metaphysics*, tr. Ralph Mannheim (New Haven: Yale University Press, 1959), 6–7.

For private consultation and not distribution without the consent of E Ondrako

Urs von Balthasar and especially the first panel of the triptych, *The Glory of the Lord*.[7] Balthasar, who supports in a general way the view of the analogy of Being of his mentor Erich Przywara, casts Scotus's univocity of Being in a bad genealogical light whereby if it is not responsible for the henological forms of metaphysics that marks the modern age, nonetheless, makes a significant contribution to them.

6. The second of these theological dispensations, that is, Radical Orthodoxy is considerably more negative about Scotus. In its various representatives it argues that Scotus has the wrong epistemology (Blond), the wrong metaphysics, and anticipates Ockham, and is responsible for much that is wrong with modern metaphysics which went down the road that should not be travelled.[8] Arguably, Radical Orthodoxy provides the most chilling account of the influence of Scotus available.

As indicated already, I intend in this paper to say something about each of these constructions, my main focus will be the second band of constructions. There are a number of good reasons for this: (a) these constructions, which are all heavily genealogically inflected, have not had any critical attention; (b) correlatively, the first three are fairly well established positions which make value judgments and insinuate lines of connection between Scotism and other philosophical discourses that make it undesirable. I plan to spend as much time on each of the three constructions in the second band as I intend to spend on the first band of three. Still major elements of the three constructions which are within this first band tend to get recycled in the second band. Indeed, it is not going too far to say that the constructions in the second band—this is particularly true of Balthasar and Radical Orthodoxy—are determined almost totally by such recycling.

---

[7] See HANS URS VON BALTHASAR, *The Glory of the Lord*. Volume 5: *The Realm of Metaphysics in the Modern Age*, trans. Oliver Davies, Andrew Louth, Brian McNeil C.R.V., John Saward and Rowan Williams; ed. Brian McNeil C.R.V. and John Riches (San Francisco: Ignatius Press, 1991), 16–21 (Scotus); 21–29 (Suarez).

[8] If Philip Blond makes the point in an epistemological register, John Milbank and Catherine Pickstock make it in a metaphysical register. For Blond, see his *Introduction to Post-Secular Philosophy: Between Philosophy and Theology* (London and New York: Routledge, 1998), 1–66, esp., 33, 40. For John Milbank, see his essay 'Only Theology overcomes Metaphysics,' in *The Word Made Strange: Theology, Language, Culture* (Oxford: Blackwell, 1997), 36–52, esp. 40–9. For Pickstock, see *After Writing: On the Liturgical Consummation of Philosophy* (Oxford: Blackwell, 1998), 61–2, 122–25. The invidious comparison between Scotus and Aquinas is even more explicit in their co-authored text *Truth in Aquinas* (London and New York: Routledge, 2001).

For private consultation and not distribution without the consent of E Ondrako

Standard Misprisonings of Scotus and Scotism

In this the first of the four sections of this paper, I want to sketch three constructions of Scotus which hamper his thought being taken seriously, all three of which have something to do with the ascendancy of Thomist thought in Catholic intellectual life in the modern period, but especially since the end of the nineteenth century. My intention is by no means to refute any of these constructions, but rather turn the categorical mode of assessment into the hypothetical. The overall tendency here is deflationary: I wish to suggest that the constructions illegitimately function in an aprioristic fashion which is neither consistent with fair play nor good historiography. Thus, it would not be contradictory for me to prefer Aquinas, for example, on the most basic points of metaphysics and theology. My point here, however, is that it is not clear that the argument against Scotus and Scotism has actually been made, and that Scotus's wrongness has not been assumed from the very beginning.

As suggested at the outset the fates have been much kinder to Thomism than to Scotism. This was true in the time of the counter-Reformation and even more true in the past two hundred years as the Catholic church struggled with a secular modernity that questions ecclesiastical authority, sneers at traditional practices (prayer, devotions, Eucharist) and forms of life (especially religious life). The emergence of neo-Scholasticism in the second half of the nineteenth century goes hand in hand with the emergence to unchallenged eminence of Thomism over any and all forms of philosophy and theology not to mention his medieval rivals. This eminence is boldly stated in the encyclical *Aeterni Patris* (1879) which, in line with Vatican 1, attempted to conjugate the relation between faith and reason. Only later will it become a question as to whether Aquinas is fully understood even as he is raised to preeminence. But in the process of the elevation of Aquinas there is considerable collateral damage inflicted on the breadth of the Catholic tradition. Augustine is made a function of Aquinas; Bonaventure is made into a spiritual theologian without remainder and thus by definition a thinker who cannot compete with Aquinas when it comes to philosophy and systematic theology; and Scotus is simply—and reductively—the medieval philosopher who lost out in the battle with his great predecessor. If the Thomistic revival of the Twentieth century begins to take the neo-Scholastic covers off of Aquinas, this does not bode well for Scotus and Scotism. Here Etienne Gilson is the exception that proves the rule.[9] Gilson showed his openness to non-Thomistic forms of thought

---

9 Throughout his many general books on medieval theology, Gilson does not adopt a polemical tone against Scotus and tries to avoid making it a zero sum game between the Dominicans

For private consultation and not distribution without the consent of E Ondrako

by writing major books on Augustine and Bonaventure. But he also wrote a massive and not unappreciative book on Scotus also, which in principle helped further to validate the plurality of medieval thought. At the same time the narrative of philosophy to which he commits himself effectively cuts against the grain of the commitment to plurality. Despite the fact that Gilson shows no interest in reducing Scotus to inherited forms of rationalism (Averroes), his interest in championing the real distinction between *esse* and *essentia* and charting the metaphysics of Exodus which begins in Augustine and is crowned in Aquinas,[10] effectively construct Scotus as an essentialist and someone who does not get the relation between faith and reason quite right. At the very least God comes in much too late in that Scotus provides a general metaphysics in which God is a specific topic. An emblematic text in this regard is *Being and Some Philosophers* in which Scotus is effectively side-lined. In Gilson one finds no diatribe against the univocity of being or his uncoupling of discourse about being from discourse about God. This does not mean, however, that as he promotes the general study of medieval thought and promotes an understanding of its plurality that he does not enact preferences which in subtle ways repeat the neo-Thomist historiography he wishes to overcome.

Clearly there is plenty to object to here. The historical rise and fall of discourses are not validity tests. Validity tests would assess philosophical and theological systems as a whole, and ask among other things how coherent these systems are, analyze the price of such coherence since starting points may dictate either exclusion or inadequate treatment of particular kind of phenomena, and finally it would explore what compensatory mechanisms are in place to offset losses that accrue to starting points. In the case of the Aquinas –Scotus relation this would mean that all questions are asked of both. In the case of Scotus, for example, it would be behoove the interpreter, who is skeptical about the benefit of the univocity, to ask a number of questions: (i) what pitfalls are avoided by having a general covering concept for all being? It is not hard to see that the modern objection against the confounding the question of being with the question of the highest being has much more traction when it comes to Thomism than when it comes to Scotism, given that God is defined as *esse*

---

and Franciscans and especially between Aquinas and Scotus. Just how far this respect goes is evident in his *Jean Duns Scot, Introduction à ses positions fondamentales* (Paris: Vrin, 1952) Although the textual situation is now much clearer than it was in the middle of the twentieth century in terms of what texts are genuinely by Scotus and what texts derive from his School, it is nonetheless, the case that there has been no text in the modern period that rivals Gilson's account in terms of comprehensiveness and readability.

[10] For a good example of this drift in Gilson's thought, see *Being and Some Philosophers* (Toronto: PMS, 1952).

For private consultation and not distribution without the consent of E Ondrako

seipsum. (ii) Is the concept of being so absolutely constitutive that it relativizes all subsequent distinctions in the domain of reality? For example, is the subsequent distinction between infinite and finite modes (Oxon. 1, d, 8, q. 3, n. 16) entirely incapable of compensating for the unifying concept of being which begins reflection? In addition, why are Scotus's reflections on the infinite mode of being as being incommensurably intense, and thus a condition not only of transcendence but also of a significant degree of incomprehensibility, not given the minimum kind of credence that would warrant further investigation? Even if one was convinced that overall the analogy of being offers a better entry point and fulcrum of philosophical and theological inquiry, are there not some ways that the unbridgeable distinction between the infinite mode of being and the finite add an extra line of protection for divine transcendence? (iii) Notwithstanding the obvious merits of Aquinas's articulation of the coextensivity of reason and will in God, does Scotus's somewhat greater emphasis on divine will not correspond better to what is found in scripture and more nearly protect divine transcendence?[11] (iv) Are there conceptual features in Scotus's metaphysical system that not only compensate for the abstract point of entrance, but in the end better protect individuality? More specifically, can *Haecceitas* play this role?[12] Correlatively, are there conceptual features in Aquinas such as the parsing of the individual as a unity of matter and form that might be thought to compromise it? Now, all these questions need not be answered in the affirmative. In fact, none of them have to be. It is possible that the verdicts in all cases favor Thomism. But it is precisely my point that verdicts are not the same as assumptions. These questions are indicative of a requirement of understanding such that analogy does not function automatically as a salutation and univocity as an expletive.

I turn now to a second trajectory in Thomism in which if neo-Scholasticism—presumptively Thomist—is reproved, there is a real imperative to get back to the real Aquinas of the thirteenth century, a synthesizer but also an experimentalist, a theologian as well as a philosopher, a biblical exegete as much as a sifter of the theological tradition. At one level, this complex movement in equal part revision (Erich Przywara, Karl Rahner) and ressourcement (Pierre Marie Chenu) is intrinsically more open to philosophical and theological pluralism. There is some impatience with

---

11 One of the most thorough treatments of the relation of will and reason in God is provided by Walter Hoeres, *La Volontà Come Perfezione Pura in Duns Scoto* (Padova: Liviana Editrice, 1976).

12 This notion of 'thisness' is what distinguishes an entity from other entities in the genus of being (natura communis).This is crucial notion in Scotus and is articulated in the *Opus Oxoniense* and *Questiones Subtilissimae in Metaphysicam Aristotelis*. See, for example, See Ox. 2, d.3, q.6 and Meta. VII, q.13.

For private consultation and not distribution without the consent of E Ondrako

intra-Catholic polemics, which seems not to grasp the changed situation in which classical philosophy and theology are beset by a world that is uncomprehending at best, and skeptical at worst. Differences between Aquinas and Scotus then simply could not be those kinds of differences that make all the difference as is supposed by unreconstructed Thomists. At another level, however, this broad movement reinscribes the decision for Aquinas over Scotus in a quite specific genealogical account of the emergence and constitution of neo-Scholasticism. Some thinkers within this loosely affiliated Thomist group think of neo-Scholasticism as the kind of hardening and thus defacing of the historical Aquinas that follows in a thinker assuming preeminent status and being dubbed to be the thinker who has all the answers to all the questions. They are variously motivated by the question of whether neo-Scholasticism precedes its robust assertion in the nineteenth century, but in any event, its essential motivation is provided by the nineteenth century forms of neo-Scholasticism and the manual theology that results and against which an entire generation reacts. Other thinkers from this group are more interested in the genealogical issue, and are more anxious to trace nineteenth century neo-Scholasticism back to its roots in the counter-Reformation and especially to Suarez who is the period's preeminent theologian. For one subset of this group, it is here where something like a fall first occurs. If one group thinks of Suarez as a kind of sclerosis of Aquinas that gets repeated in a related but different form in the nineteenth century, another group offers a view of contamination from outside. On this account, Francisco Suarez (1548–1617) is not a Thomist all the way through, but rather attempts to effect a synthesis between Thomism and Scotism.[13] The synthesis is an unhappy one, and what makes it so is not simply the issue of incoherence—the lack of computability between these two systems—but the presence of Scotist features in the metaphysics and theology which can only bowdlerize because they are essentially inadequate. Neo-Scholasticism is fated to go wrong, then, because of a foreign element. None of this is to gainsay that this form of Thomism is less given to polemic than more hard line Thomism, but in its historiography of what went wrong in the articulation and appropriation of Aquinas, for some reconstructed Thomists Scotus becomes part of a plot in which Suarez is cast as the villain. In any event, this historiography continues to set an obstacle for Scotus and, as we shall see later with Balthasar and Radical Orthodoxy, come to function as something like a free radical that can be an item in other systems of

---

13 The key text of Suarez is *Disputationes Metaphysicae* (1597).

For private consultation and not distribution without the consent of E Ondrako

philosophical and theological discourse of a genealogical penchant that are not Thomist.

Thomism, of course, was not involved in one major battle in the medieval period but in two. Arguably, Thomism was engaged in a fiercer a battle with the nominalism and theological voluntarism of William of Ockham than it was with Scotus for the obvious reason that Ockham's anti-universalism, his emphasis upon will, and his separation of will and intellect in God constituted far more radical challenges to Thomism than the univocity of being and the merely offsetting emphasis on divine will in Scotus.[14] But in versions of modern Thomism in the battle between Aquinas and Ockham, whose thought is assumed either to have set the agenda for the Reformation or for the intellectual culture of modernity, Scotus gets implicated. Given Ockham's attestation of influence, and the presumption of association, Scotus gets constructed as pre-Ockhamite, and the philosophical and theological debilities of Ockham become the philosophical and theological debilities of Scotus. This has the peculiar effect that Ockham's revolutionary distinction between *potentia absoluta* and *potentia ordinata* is regarded as being grounded in Scotus's granting somewhat more status to will in the divine than Aquinas.[15] By dint of Scotus's presumptive anticipation of this Ockhamite distinction, Scotus becomes an anticipator of the Reformation emphasis on grace alone. On an even more generic level, Scotus is taken to anticipate as being Ockham *virtualiter* insofar as there is an absolutely general metaphysics indifferent to domain, and also an emphasis on sheer singularity in excess of what is found in Aquinas. Rarely mentioned are the differences in the two thinkers' treatment of the divine and the non-divine domains. Nor is there cognizance of the fact that Scotist *haecceitas* differs from nominalist singularity, in that in the former case, a general description of the particular is possible even if strictly speaking it is not conceptual. In the strict sense a singular in Ockham is unknowable; it has to be submitted pragmatically to schemes of thought as if it were an instance of a kind. There is no thought of another avenue of inquiry that would disclose the singularity that does not have to be merely idiosyncratic. Compounding the problem for those

---

14 Leff makes this point clear in the opening pages of *The Dissolution of the Medieval Outlook*, pp. 9–37; similarly in *William of Ockham: The Metamorphosis of Scholastic Discourse*, 2–14.

15 Of course, this distinction is a crucial one in Ockham, and has quite a career in the fifteenth century as it is taken up by theologians and eventually by Martin Luther. See HEIKO OBERMAN, *The Harvest of Medieval Theology: Gabriel Biel and late Medieval Nominalism* (Cambridge, MA: Harvard University Press, 1963). See also MARILYN MCCORD ADAMS, Ockham, 2 volumes (Notre Dame, IN: University of Notre Dame Press, 1987), 1151–1231, esp. 1234–35. Scotus definitely anticipates the distinction of *potentia absoluta* and *potentia ordinata* See *Ordinatio* 1.44. For a good discussion of divine will, see B. M. BONANSEA, O.F.M., *Man and his Approach to God in John Duns Scotus* (New York and London: Lanham, University Press of America, 1983), 187–205.

For private consultation and not distribution without the consent of E Ondrako

sympathetic to Scotus is that non-affiliated historiography has come to be extraordinarily infested in this narrative. We shall, in due time, point to its presence in both Balthasar and Radical Orthodoxy, but the connection between Scotus and Ockham has long tended towards indemnification even in secular circles. Mostly the relation is asserted in straightforward fashion. But even when there is interest in insisting upon the novelty of Ockham, even a revolutionary is in some way anticipated. In these cases Scotus usually finds himself on top of the list of anticipators.

My point in rehearsing this dispensation of interpretation in these three modalities or emphases is not intrinsic. A much more detailed and nuanced account of misprisoning is required than I have presented here. My aim was extrinsic or instrumental. I have aimed only to lay out as much of the Thomist misprisoning of Scotus as is necessary to set off three modern and/contemporary accounts that reinforce and even exacerbate the misprisoning of Scotus. They are in order the Heideggerian, Balthasar-ian, and Radical Orthodoxy constructions. I will treat them in order.

The story of the relation between Heidegger and Scotus is complicated. If it starts promisingly, it ends unhappily in that at best Scotus comes to be regarded as an instance of what is wrong with metaphysics. But perhaps more extrinsically than intrinsically Scotus's situation turns out to be more dire than that of Aquinas, who is also indicted, despite the fact that in the beginning Scotus has capital that Aquinas does do have, and possibly enjoys some constitutive advantages from a Heideggerian point of view. We begin with the very propitious beginning. Heidegger's *Habilitationshrift* (1915) was putatively on Scotus's doctrine of the categories.[16] As it turned out, however, the text that was the main subject of analysis, *De modis significandi sive Grammatica speculative*, was not in fact written by Scotus, but rather was the work of Thomas of Erfurt.[17] Obviously, this misidenti-fication complicates assessment of Heidegger' relation to Scotus. Yet there is a potential positive; in the case of Heidegger adopting a really negative attitude towards Scholasticism, the misidentification might be thought

---

[16] For two good accounts of Heidegger's Habilitation and what elements of Scotus continued to have currency and what elements did not, see Sean MCGRATH, *The Early Heidegger and Medieval Philosophy: Phenomenology of the Godforsaken* (Washington: CUA Press, 2006), 88–119; also PHILIP TONNER, *Heidegger, Metaphysics and the Univocity of Being* (New York: Continuum, 2011). See also THEODORE KISIEL, *The Genesis of Being and Time* (Berkeley, Cal.: University of California Press, 1993), 71, 81, 115; also 19, 20, 30, 32, 37.

[17] This was pointed out by Martin Grabmann in 1922. There is little mention of Scotus after the Habilitation, but Suarez is mentioned, especially in contexts in which Heidegger has an interest in refuting Leibniz's logic and metaphysics. For a good example of the latter, around the time of *Being and Time*, see *The Metaphysical Foundations of Logic*, tr. Michael Heim (Bloomington and Indianapolis: Indiana University Press, 1992), 29. This text was written in 1928.

For private consultation and not distribution without the consent of E Ondrako

to insulate Scotus against specific criticism. Looked at realistically, misattribution at best provides a very modest level of protection for two very obvious reasons. First, the reservations and hedges concerning medieval speculative grammar, which accompanies the praise, does not except Scotus since there are some obvious similarities between the thought of the two thinkers. Second, and even more importantly, while the main text under analysis is from Thomas of Erfurt, and is treated in part 2 of the text, Scotus's doctrine of categories also comes in for discussion and is treated in part 1. Heidegger demonstrates familiarity with the *Opus oxoniense* and Scotus's commentaries on Aristotle's *Categories* and *De sophisticis elenchis*. After the Habilitation Scotus is rarely mentioned by name and it is likely that within a matter of years Heidegger had relented of expressing anything positive about any of the forms of medieval Scholasticism, even as he showed interest in medieval mystics, for example, Bernard of Clairvaux, but also Meister Eckhart.[18] More of Eckhart later. Nonetheless, it should not be thought that Scotus entirely disappears from Heidegger's concertedly anti-metaphysical discourse. Heidegger claims throughout his career that Being has mistakenly come to be regarded as a most general and also empty category,[19] *Introduction to Metaphysics* provides just one of the many statements of this tendency—at the very least Scotus seems implicated in the fall of metaphysics which is at the same time the fall that is metaphysics. For the metaphysical formulation rejected seems to

---

18 Heidegger's early lectures series on philosophy of religion in which medieval mysticism plays a prominent role is now available. See *The Phenomenology of Religious Life*, tr. Matthias Fritsch and Jennifer Anna Gosetti-Ferencei (Bloomington, IN: Indiana University Press, 2004). While Augustine has pride of place (115–227), medieval mystics are mentioned. Even at this stage Meister Eckhart is prominent (239–41). See Theodore Kisiel, *The Genesis of Being and Time*, 81–4, 98–100, 112–15 (Eckhart); 523–24 (Bernard of Clairvaux); van Buren, *The Young Heidegger: Rumor of the Hidden King* (Bloomington and Indianapolis: Indiana University Press, 1994), 100–03, 113–25, 293–313 (Eckhart); 146, 149 (Bernard of Clairvaux).

19 For Heidegger's take on Being as the emptiest of all categories, see also *Identity and Difference*, tr. Joan Stambaugh (New York: Harper & Row, 1969). In the essays which make up the text, Heidegger speaks to the way that Hegel makes explicit was is implicit in the metaphysical tradition, that is, that the general category of Being is also the emptiest category. It is very important to point out, however, that despite Heidegger's scorn of Being as a general category (Being qua Being), he prefers it to identifying Being with God. In this sense he follows the lead provided by Scotus who, put in the position to chose between Being as a general category and Being as God, decides for the former. The locus classicus for this decision is the very first question in the Questiones on Aristotle's metaphysics. See *Questions on the Metaphysics of Aristotle*. Books 1–5, tr. Girard J. Etzkorn and Allan B. Wolter, O. F. M (St. Bonaventure, NY: Franciscan Institute Publications, 1997), 13–60. The motive for the question is provided by the tension in the Metaphysics between Book 4 which treats of metaphysics as the science of Being qua Being and Books 1 and 6 which treats metaphysics as the science of supersensible being. Scotus is being a good reader here. There is a sizeable commentary tradition on this tension in modern tradition of commentary. Pierre Aubenque and Joseph Owens are especially worth mentioning. For Owens, see *The Doctrine of Being in Aristotelian Metaphysics: A Study in the Greek Background of Medieval Thought* (Toronto: PIMS, 1951).

For private consultation and not distribution without the consent of E Ondrako

recall that of Scotus who spoke of the transcendental of Being as *primum objectum intellectus est uns, ut commune omnibus* (*Questiones subtillisimus super Metaphysicam Aristotelis*, bk. 4, q.1, 148 a).

It is true that Heidegger seems to have a much easier time with the univocity of Being than many Thomists who declare from the outset that God as *esse seipsum* is that to which all finite beings refer. If not in 1915, then later, the Thomist view can be classed by Heidegger as 'ontotheological,' that is, as confounding the question of being as such with the question of the highest being, and thus being with the highest being, the latter which thereafter functions as the explanatory ground of finite and temporal entities. Ontotheology, which receives a formal and modern exemplification in Leibniz's principle of sufficient reason,[20] is for Heidegger nothing but an explanatory myth or in fact the myth of explanation. In the *Habitationshrift* Scotus seems to fare better than other medieval and classical thinkers, but we should note the cost. As is well known in Scotus's articulation of universal category of Being, he defines Being as having two modes, an infinite and a finite mode. Commentators on the *Habilitationschrift* have observed that Heidegger confines himself exclusively to the analysis of the finite mode.[21] Heidegger is clearly offering an interested interpretation in which he reads the medieval texts before him for the way in which they correspond to, validate, and plausibly develop in an ontological direction phenomenology with its view of intentionality and its commitment to what is given. Heidegger does not accuse Scotus, then, of what he will accuse Augustine of in his lectures on Augustine five years later,[22] that is, the confusion of transcendence with the transcendent, which anticipates the charge of ontotheology that Heidegger will later level against the entire metaphysical tradition. But Scotus is surviving merely on the basis of a bracketing of constitutive aspects of his position. Heidegger's focus on the finite mode of being still does not gainsay that Scotus is suggesting relative cognitive competence with respect to Being, which troubles Heidegger in 1915 and will in due course become anathema. In addition, the infinite

---

[20] A good example of a text where Heidegger takes Leibniz to task is *The Principle of Reason*, tr. R. Lilly (Bloomington and Indianapolis: Indiana University Press, 1991). This text comes from 1955. It is clear, however, that in this text Heidegger articulates a position of long-standing. As Heidegger explores the Cartesian and non-Cartesian suppositions of Leibniz's thought in *The Metaphysical Foundations of Logic*, he takes aim at the principle of sufficient reason. See especially p. 58.

[21] For this point, see especially MCGRATH, *The Early Heidegger and Medieval Philosophy*, 102, 116–117.

[22] The Lectures were given in 1921. See *Phenomenology of Religious Life*, 115–227. For a good analysis of the Heidegger's reading of Augustine which explores the ways he opens up and closes paths beyond the metaphysical tradition, see KISIEL, *The Genesis of Heidegger's Being and Time*, 80–115, 149–219; VAN BUREN, *The Young Heidegger*, 113–30, 157–202.

For private consultation and not distribution without the consent of E Ondrako

mode of Being is identified with God and has attributed to it properties such as immutability and eternity which are comprehensively dismissed from philosophical language in the articulation of the existentials in *Being and Time* which have their root in temporality. From the point of view of Heidegger after *Being and Time*, any talk of infinity or any kind of God-talk compromises the mystery of the event of being. Of course, Scotus admits that the infinite mode of Being is not absolutely comprehensible. Yet this caveat would hardly suffice for the deep mystery at which Heidegger aims, where being is incomprehensible all the way down, and abysmal or anarchic in its disclosures. And again, at the risk of being anachronistic, one can easily think of the later Heidegger judging that Scotus has his own way of truly begging the question of why is there something rather than nothing?, since in the last instance the infinite mode is already in place as an answer. So, as in Scholasticism in general, Scotus at the very least is guilty on the ontotheological issue and manifestly derelict when it comes to preserving the prerogatives of the interrogative.

Scotus is no more granted a right of reply by Heidegger than any other medieval philosophical figure or for that matter any philosophical figure, ancient or modern. Heidegger puts up a systematic barrier against reply by implying that no answer to the question of being is possible, while also ruling out very specific answers of a theological or theiological kind,[23] that is, answers which point to a ontological or logical ground of beings that guarantees meaning, meaningfulness and, of course, truth. Of course, this does not mean, however, that there have not been replies to Heidegger. It is interesting, however, that it has been Thomists of various descriptions who have made the bulk of the replies. It is invidious to choose from what is now at least an eighty year history of reply, but names that especially stand out are Erich Przywara, Gustav Sivert, Bernard Welte, Cornelio Fabro, and latterly Jean-Luc Marion. While the emphasis fall differently in each of these thinkers, the real distinction between essence (*essentia*) and existence (*esse*), and especially the irreducibility of existence to essences regarded as constitutive of the way in which Aquinas escapes Heidegger's metaphysical censure. This line of argument, while it does not explicitly take exception to either Scotus's metaphysics or his theological reflections,

---

23 While Heidegger, undoubtedly, has serious reservations with respect to the mixing of philosophy and theology in the medieval period, and with God as creator being regarded as the answer to the question of why is there something rather than nothing?, he is much more interested in how philosophy behaves when it is in search of a ground to explain everything that is. This ground, whether logical or metaphysical, and whether or not it explicitly invokes God, functions as God would function in explanation. It functions in a divine-like way—thus theology—with an iota—rather than theology proper. See among other texts, "The Onto-Theo-Logical Nature of Metaphysics," in *Identity and Difference*, 35–67.

For private consultation and not distribution without the consent of E Ondrako

nonetheless seems to concede to various degrees Heidegger's narrative of betrayal of the mystery of being and the radical question. At the very least, Scotus goes down with the metaphysical tradition. The issue here is hardly whether Thomists succeed In saving Aquinas from the *massa damnata* of metaphysics. If the terms continue to be set by Heidegger, and are themselves not subject to revision, it is hard to see how this would be possible. Nonetheless, there is a twentieth century history of sophisticated Thomist engagement with Heidegger in which the case of exceptionality is made. An important set of questions is (a) whether there is a similar history of Scotist engagement? and (b) what features of Scotus's metaphysics would encourage the claim of exceptionality. The short answer with respect to the first question is that despite the favorable engagement of Heidegger with Scotus—albeit very early in his career—as far as I am aware there is no comparable tradition of engagement with Heidegger in commentators and defenders of Scotus. My point here is descriptive. It does not imply that Scotists should engage Heidegger and in the process concede in significant part his *Destruktion* of the metaphysical tradition. Indeed, I have already suggested that without revision of Heideggerian criteria the case is fairly hopeless. I simply mark that Scotists have not engaged Heidegger, who has enjoyed considerable intellectual cache, and revised his criteria for assessing philosophical systems in the way Thomists have. With respect to the second, although they have not been adduced, on the face of it there seems to be basically two lines of argument available to Scotists. I will treat each of these in turn.

The first of these concerns the philosophical question why there is something rather than nothing? Heidegger argues that this is the question (whether explicitly formulated or not) that motivates and sustains all philosophical inquiry. One finds in Scotus rather than Aquinas or Augustine, a much closer approximation to the most radical of questions, when he asks the question what kind of difference does something make relative to nothing and answers by saying an infinite difference.[24] In addition, by comparison with both Aquinas and Augustine, Scotus's thought is not so foundationally theological, and thus not as exposed to Heidegger's criticism of Christian philosophy, namely, that it amounts to a square peg in a round hole,[25] since it has already available God in his activity of creating as the answer. Having a general metaphysics, which has a real grasp of the basic philosophical question that validates wonder and mystery and in which

---

[24] For an interesting discussion of this point, see ALLAN B. WOLTER, "A Scholastic Approach to the Ultimate Why Question," in *Scotus and Ockham: Selected Essays* (Saint Bonaventure, NY: Franciscan Institute Publications, 2003), 63–83, esp. 63–4.

[25] This is Heidegger's judgment in the opening pages of *Introduction to Metaphysics*, 6–7.

For private consultation and not distribution without the consent of E Ondrako

God is not involved from the beginning, is obviously preferable to forms of philosophical thought in which there is neither explicit formulation of the question and which God is so involved. Such would be the case, for example, in Aquinas. Unfortunately, however, on Heideggerian grounds such advantages can be lost in the actual articulation of a philosophical conceptuality, for in the drive towards the answer the urgency of the question and the prospect of unanswerability are suppressed, and God or an analogue is allowed into radical thought. Any advantages Scotus enjoys over other figures in the Western tradition, especially Christian figures, therefore, has to be seen against the shadow of the prospect of offset, which itself has a tradition. In his *Metaphysics*, from Heidegger's point of view, Aristotle raises the radical question in a highly perspicuous way in his inquiry into the being as being as being (*to on he on*), but compromises this happy opening, first by making this question equivalent to the search for substance (*ousiology*), and second by making that this question is equivalent to the question about the highest being (*theology*). Whether metaphysics is compromised from the outset or during the course of its elaboration in the end is a matter of indifference. In this respect, Aristotle fairs badly in contrast with the gnomic Heraclitus,[26] who does not manage to formulate the radical question in an adequate form, but manages to avoid the kind of propositional taming of reality exhibited by the first of the great metaphysicians. There are other examples. In his interested and very much abbreviated history of philosophy, Heidegger identifies Leibniz as the figure who supplies the adequate form of the radical question; indeed, it is Leibniz's form of the question that is adopted by Heidegger himself. Still, once again Heidegger adduces a preference for a non-philosophical thinker, this time the late Baroque poetic religious thinker Angelus Silesius who shows in his rhyming couplets on the mystery of the rose that blooms "without why" (*ohne Warum*) just how overdetermined by answer Leibniz's system is which is founded on the principle of sufficient reason.[27] The question why does not merely evoke an answer, it demands it. Although Heidegger does not make the point this way, Scotus can become the object of an invidious comparison. Of course, the comparison here is not with Aquinas, with respect to whom Scotus could be thought to enjoy at least preliminary advantages, however likely they are to be forfeited given the judgment that the mystery of being is not preserved and that God

---

26 Once again, *Introduction to Metaphysics* is an illustrative text. Heraclitus is preferred to Aristotle in that text. See 126–34; also 61–2, 96–8.

27 Heidegger appeals to Silesius on a number of occasions. The most conspicuous is in *The Principle of Reason*, which represents one of Heidegger's most concerted engagements with Leibniz.

For private consultation and not distribution without the consent of E Ondrako

makes his way back into thought. The proper Heideggerian comparison would be with Meister Eckhart. In Heidegger's search to enlarge and deepen Phenomenology, Meister Eckhart becomes a favorite of Heidegger very soon after his Habilitation. He remains so throughout Heidegger's entire career. Heidegger thinks of Eckhart as a thinker who exceeds the metaphysical tradition in allowing being to disclose itself. The crucial Eckhartian concept or non-concept is *Gelassenheit*,[28] which captures in Heidegger's view the kind of non-grasping approach to reality that represents the cure of metaphysics rather than its perpetuation. Scotus may or may not be ultimately in a better position to avoid the constitutive metaphysical traps than Aquinas or Augustine, but he is certainly not in as good a position as Eckhart, the Dominican who absorbs the metaphysical thought of Aquinas and Augustine only to subvert their basic premises about analogy and the role of God in philosophical discourse. Needless to say, in order to make this kind of relative affirmation, Heidegger must bypass the fact that there are philosophical commitments in Eckhart that are deeply Neoplatonic, even Proclean. There are then some reasons for thinking that Scotus has some advantages over Aquinas (and Augustine) in a Heideggerian construction of what is valuable in philosophical thinking, even if it is not clear that they will be sustained. But these advantages cannot be sustained against the figure of Meister Eckhart who consistently is taken to exceed metaphysics and who is the main source for Angelus Silesius movement beyond 'why.'

A second vista for arguing the excess of Scotus over the metaphysical tradition in general, and the Scholastic tradition in particular, with their penchant for abstraction and vapid universality, can be found in Scotus's view of *haecceitas*, which is an object of simple apprehension (*simplex apprehendum*). In the *Habilitationshrift*, Heidegger found himself very attracted to this idea which got at the uniqueness and unrepeatability of individuals in a way that is useful for philosophy interested in overcoming Kantian Idealism, Hegelian speculation, and Husserl's increasing idealism. Scotus's famous formula that the full being of the singular is not contained by (under) the universal (*totia entitas singularis non continetur sub universal*) (*Opus oxoniense* 2, dist. 3, q. 11, no. 9) is in fact embraced by Heidegger (GA1, 351).[29] The fact that Scotus suggested that its excess relative to universality did not imply that it was absolutely resistant (or

---

[28] *Gelassenheit* is an important concept in Heidegger's later texts. The text by Heidegger in which it gets the most play is a text with *Gelassenheit* as its title (1959). See the English translation, *Discourse on Thinking*, tr. John M. Anderson and Hans Freund (New York: Harper & Row, 1966).

[29] I am indebted here to McGrath. See *The Early Heidegger and Medieval Philosophy*, 110–15, esp. 110–11.

For private consultation and not distribution without the consent of E Ondrako

repugnant) to thought was a plus rather than a minus for Heidegger who, if interested in combating rationalism, by no means embraces the view of total incomprehensibility which he judges to be rationalism's agnostic complement. This aspect of Scotus's thought strikes a chord in Heidegger who sees the potential alliance with Phenomenology's original inspiration whose cry of "back to the things themselves" ought, Heidegger believes, to favor individuals over universals or essences which are increasingly not the case in his teacher Husserl. Indeed, it is possible to see that Heidegger's favoring of poetry as a non-metaphysical discourse capable of opening up to and responding to the deliverances of reality represents a filling out of Scotus's gesture towards a non-categorical form of thought. Needless to say, Scotus's notion of *haecceitas* has even greater claims to prompt—if not necessarily shape—Heidegger's move in *Being and Time* to forsake categorical determination altogether and substitute for categories the various *existentials* which show a subject living in the world responding to phenomena as they truly present themselves.[30] Heidegger's interest at this point is not historiographical: specifically, he is not interested in what role—if any—*haecceitas* plays in the rise of Nominalism. The Scotus-Ockham relation is simply not his issue. Thus the praise of *haecceitas* does not involve a covert embrace of Nominalism with its loud rhetoric on behalf of the individual. We will see shortly how two other contemporary schemes differ from him in this respect. Once again, however, it is difficult to escape the sense that the exceptionality of Scotus on this point is potential rather than actual. It is not simply that after the *Habilitationsbrift* Heidegger stops referring to the notion, but perhaps also that the alternative means of access to the unrepeatable disclosures of being, provided by Heidegger, are viewed to be unimaginable within a medieval mind in general, and a Scotist mindset in particular. Scotus's *haecceitas* can be affirmed, but there are inbuilt limits to affirmation given the deployment of the concept within a system that so affirms conceptual formation that it is not at all clear whether the non-comprehensibility of the individual is understood truly positively or merely privatively. In terms then of chronology, but perhaps also in systematic terms, there are features of Scotus's thought that make possible arguments for exceptionality which, while different than the arguments made by the supporters of Aquinas, would have at least as much credibility. But Heidegger also offers us enough reasons to suppose that they would be no more sufficient in

---

30 My point here develops a point suggested in *The Early Heidegger and Medieval Philosophy*, 90–1. This is not to gainsay the role Heidegger's development and criticism of Kant's transcendental philosophy plays in the elaboration of the existential.

For private consultation and not distribution without the consent of E Ondrako

Scotus's case than in the case of Aquinas for similar—if not necessarily identical—reasons.

Balthasar and the Metaphysical Guilt of Scotus

I come now to the second major contemporary construction of Scotus which reinforces long-held prejudices against Scotus and discourages an open mind with respect to the prospects of Scotus being able to make a philosophical and theological contribution in and to contemporary thought. As already indicated, Hans Urs von Balthasar, who is both a revisionist reader of Aquinas and also a reader of Heidegger who takes seriously the diagnosis of the debilities of the metaphysical tradition, at an important point in the second of the two volumes on metaphysics in *The Glory of the Lord* (GL5) suggests that Scotus commences a line of metaphysical reflection that issues in and is crowned by a metaphysical system like the one we find in Hegel.[31] On the bases both of Przywara's *Analogia Entis* (1932)and Balthasar's own ruminations of truth in *Wahrheit* (1946),[32] which styles itself as being in significant part and interpretation of *de veritate* 2, one can infer that Balthasar is taking very seriously, indeed, the unreconstructed Thomist charge that Scotus's thought is fundamentally both rationalist and essentialist. Given the proximity of the praise of Aquinas and the blame of Scotus—the one ends volume 4 in the English translation, the other begins volume 5—Scotus suffers an invidious comparison with Aquinas. There is a second discussion of Aquinas at the end of volume 5 (613–27), which essentially involves a defense of Thomism against Heideggerian attack, a courtesy which quite conspicuously Scotus is not paid. This likely reflects the fact that from the thirties on the defense of Aquinas has a philosophical and theological currency lacking when it comes to the 'subtle doctor.'

Still, while it offers little solace to Scotists, the comparison of Aquinas and Scotus is not boilerplate. First, in his relatively brief treatment of

---

[31] See *The Glory of the Lord* 5, 17 for the connection between Scotus and Hegel through the univocity of Being and what is presumed to be a shared essentialism. Balthasar avails of Gilson's classic text, but he calls upon the Thomist Gustav Siewerth to make the connection between Scotus and Hegel. The texts he cites is Siewerth's great discussion of how Aquinas survives a Heideggerian critique of metaphysics, *Das Schicksal der Metaphysik von Thomas zu Heidegger* (Einsiedeln: Johannes Verlag, 1959).

[32] This text became in due course *Theologik: Erster Band: Die Wahrheit der Welt* (Einsiedeln: Johannes Verlag, 1985). The only difference between the earlier text and this is the addition of a second introduction. See the English translation, *Theologic: Volume 1: The Truth of the World*, trans. Adrian Walker. (San Francisco: Ignatius Press, 1998).

For private consultation and not distribution without the consent of E Ondrako

Aquinas in *The Glory of the Lord* 4,[33] Aquinas is constructed more nearly as a Neoplatonist with an interest in individuality than as a thoroughgoing Aristotelian; elsewhere Maximus the Confessor is described similarly in a treatment that is at once much more extensive and sophisticated than Balthasar's express treatment of Aquinas.[34] Second, favoring Aquinas over Scotus has little or nothing to do with favoring a Dominican ethos over a Franciscan ethos. For example, Bonaventure receives a considerably more extensive and richer treatment than Aquinas in *The Glory of the Lord* 2. In addition, it could be argued that it is Bonaventure rather than Aquinas who is more influential in the elaboration of the bases of Balthasar's theological aesthetic in volume 1 of *The Glory of the Lord*. And finally, even if Balthasar's description of God as Love is biblically rather than theologically based, specifically on 1 John 4:6, it is not an accident that Balthasar is a great admirer of Bonaventure's *Itinerarium Mentis in Deum* and prefers the designation of love over being or *esse ipsum*, although at the very least the Thomistic formulation is relatively adequate. Third, and most importantly in his essay on G. M. Hopkins in *The Glory of the Lord* 3 Balthasar seems to have stepped back in advance from the unreconstructed Thomist view concerning the univocity of Being when he actually affirms Hopkins's appropriation of *haecceitas*.[35] To be sure, one should not make too much of this in that the affirmation may be relative in that Scotus's *haecceitas* had for Hopkins, and for we who read Hopkins, the happy consequence of legitimating the irreducible particular while also suggesting a way of access to this singularity. This need not imply that Balthasar is systemically conflicted. It would be going too far to suggest that Balthasar is affirming this aspect of Scotus's thought in principle. And it should be noted that there is never a collateral affirming of God characterized as the infinite mode of Being. Still it is possible—although not necessary—that Balthasar is suggesting that the epistemic grasp of a singularity is more nearly prosecuted in and through symbolic than conceptual language. Thus one

---

[33] See *The Glory of the Lord: A Theological Aesthetics. Volume 4: The Realm of Metaphysics in Antiquity*, tr. Andrew Louth, Brian McNeil, C.R.V, John Saward, Rowan Williams, and Oliver Davies (San Francisco: Ignatius Press, 1989), 393–412.

[34] There is now an English translation of Balthasar's book on Maximus the Confessor, originally written in 1941. See *Cosmic Liturgy: The Universe According to Maximus the Confessor*, trans. Brian E. Daley, S.J. (San Francisco: Ignatius Press, 2003).

[35] See *The Glory of the Lord: A Theological Aesthetics. Volume 3. Studies in Theological Styles: Lay Styles*, trans. Andrew Louth, John Saward, Martin Simon and Rowan Williams; ed. John Riches. (San Francisco: Ignatius Press, 1986), 353–399, esp. 374–77 for the notion of individuality. A little later, Balthasar speaks approvingly of Hopkins's use of the Scotist idea of the sacrifice of the Son being the first thought of the world (380; also 381–82). It should be noted, however, that even as Balthasar approves of the strain of singularity in Hopkins that has its origin in Scotus, he still suggests links with Hegel. In GL5 Balthasar makes clear that the connection of Scotus and Hegel flatters neither.

For private consultation and not distribution without the consent of E Ondrako

element of the genius of Hopkins is to have shifted the epistemic register and to have suggested in and through the notions of inscape and instress how singularities become available in language and through language to thought. Balthasar does not dig deep in his Hopkins essay, but one senses that he grasps, however inchoately, the possibility that Scotus's suggestion about an alternative to a categorical mode of thought when it comes to the individual comes to fruition in the symbolic language of poetry. Perhaps here interpretively lies the excess of Balthasar over Heidegger.

Balthasar, it should be noted, also seems to be variously committed to two of the more popular genealogical constructions of Scotus outlined in the first section of the paper, and which are noticeably absent in Heidegger: (a) that it is Scotus rather than Aquinas who lays the foundation of neo-Scholasticism; (b) Scotus's specific form of rationalism is at the basis of Ockham's nominalism.[36] To these we might add the worry that Scotus's reflection on divine will is at the base of the theological voluntarism of Ockham, which influences Luther's own views, and which fatefully and fatally upset the proper relation between nature and grace, that is, grace completes nature rather than contradicts it. If the evidence for (a) and (b) is explicit, the evidence for painting Scotus as the precursor for Ockham when it comes to theological voluntarism is basically implicit.[37] The crucial text with respect to making arguments (a) and (b) is *The Glory of the Lord* 5. I will deal with (a) rather briefly and somewhat more expansively on (b). The Scotus-Suarez connection is made in the section at the beginning of *The Glory of the Lord* (21-9)where Balthasar is speaking to metaphysical systems that are injurious with respect to an openness to mystery and transcendence, the first Heidegger's complaint, the second a basic need for a viable theology. The hyphen between Scotus-Suarez describes an arc of discourse with unhappy rationalistic outcomes. Balthasar insinuates rather than states that Suarez is in turn a prime mover in the cause of neo-Scholasticism. Balthasar also repeats the common charge that Scotus's rationalism anticipates Ockham's nominalism. For Balthasar, this is by far the more consequential of the two genealogical moves he repeats. Through Ockham or together with him Scotus, he believes, has broad philosophical effect and no inconsiderable influence on modern metaphysical discourses despite their very different bases and tone.

Here, however, it is important to underscore the distinct Balthasarian inflection of the standard charges against Scotus. While undoubtedly indulging both Thomist readings of Scotus as a primogenitor of neo-

---

[36] For the connection between Scotus and Ockham, see *The Glory of the Lord* 5, 16, 19–21, 29.

[37] See, however, *The Theology of Karl Barth*, trans. Edward T. Oakes, S.J. (San Francisco: Ignatius Press, 1992), 317.

For private consultation and not distribution without the consent of E Ondrako

Scholasticism and a general historiography in which Scotus plays a role in the idealistic career of modern philosophy, Balthasar does not claim that Scotus is uniquely the source of modern rationalism either independently or in and through Ockham. In *The Glory of the Lord* 5, for example, Balthasar denies that Scotus is the source for the Enlightenment or German Idealism. Balthasar is not shy about making multiple genealogical suggestions especially when it comes to German Idealism. None of his many suggestions have anything to do with Scotus. Gnosticism or apocalyptic are sometimes invoked as root discourses for a resurgence of the kind of discourse exhibited by German Idealism. Balthasar also suggests that the Renaissance Neoplatonism of Nicholas of Cusa and Giordano Bruno function as sources. But perhaps most significantly he suggests Meister Eckhart as a source of German Idealism. Here Balthasar heads in a contrary direction to Heidegger. As we have already seen, Heidegger makes Eckhart the medieval exception to the fall of metaphysics. In contrast, in *The Glory of the Lord* 5, Balthasar not only does not make Eckhart the exception—the bouquet is handed Aquinas at the end of the volume 4—but Eckhart looks to be considerably more responsible than Scotus,[38] even if Scotus is hardly disimplicated. Balthasar shows himself to be unwilling to subtract the metaphysical commitments from thinkers such as Eckhart who have an existential base. And these commitments are even more vehemently henological than anything that can be found in Scotus: Eckhart offers a metaphysics which from the beginning is a theology, and this metaphysics is at least paradoxical—if not equivocal: it justifies simultaneously everything as divine or nothing.

To sum up: Balthasar reinforces a number of the standard constructions of Scotus especially when it comes to plotting Scotus in the history of Western thought. The constructions appear to be pre-given, in that Balthasar's synoptic discussion in *The Glory of the Lord* 5 does not indicate deep engagement with the texts of Scotus or his tradition. Still, there are alleviations, even if they are somewhat unfocused, in that whatever the debits of Scotus's univocity of being it only plays a role rather than the role in the emergence of modern rationalism and speculative philosophy. While this alleviation might appear mere tokenism to a Scotist, Balthasar looks positively generous when compared with the construction of Scotus in Radical Orthodoxy which repeats Balthasar's objections but in a much harsher key and without any alleviation. It is to this third and final form of modern/contemporary construction of Scotus that we now turn.

---

38 See *The Glory of the Lord* 5, 29–47. See also my essay on the complicated relation between Balthasar and Eckhart, "Von Balthasar and Eckhart: Theological Principles and Catholicity," in *The Thomist*, April (1996), 1–37.

For private consultation and not distribution without the consent of E Ondrako

In the movement that has come to be known as Radical Orthodoxy, the retrieval of the Christian tradition, and the Christian Neoplatonic tradition in particular, has as one of its dimensions a privileging of Aquinas over Scotus. Although Radical Orthodoxy is by no means a variety of neo-Thomism—and many Thomists think that the Aquinas retrieved by Radical Orthodoxy is thoroughly unfaithful to the historical Aquinas—in representatives such as John Milbank, Catherine Pickstock, and Philip Blond it resolutely favors Thomistic analogy over Scotist univocity. Moreover, in line with neo-Thomism in general, Radical Orthodoxy thinks of Scotism as the quintessential form of rationalism and essentialism. To the extent to which there is once again a quarrel between two of the most important philosophical and theological figures of the Middle Ages, the quarrel is again decided in favor of Aquinas and for similar reasons. Although Gilson is by no means a canonic figure for Radical Orthodoxy, having conceded, arguably, too much to philosophy, nonetheless, when it comes to a comparison between Aquinas and Scotus there is a similar judgment. Nonetheless, the *Tendenz* of Radical Orthodoxy is more nearly genealogical than analytic, which means that the preference for Aquinas over Scotus is connected with a reading of the history of effects of Scotus's thought with a particular eye on the thought of modernity, and more specifically on the intellectual backdrop of its skeptical and nihilistic tendencies. While nothing is essentially added to the arguments that are ready at hand in reconstructed Thomists concerning the role of Suarez as enabling Scotism to have less than salutary effect on philosophical and theological thought in the modern period, the level of rhetoric is accentuated to a point that Suarez appears to function as something like a Trojan horse in the Christian defense against an aggressive modernity. In addition, for this group of thinkers, there is only a minimal degree of separation between Scotus and Ockham. This is not good for Scotus, since Ockham is held accountable not only for the rampant skepticism of the modern period and correlatively its scientism, but is also held responsible for a form of theological voluntarism that stresses the lack of value in what is created, which in the post-Reformation period can be adapted by rationalists.

Although in Radical Orthodoxy quite generally, genealogy is often in excess of detailed analysis, this is more than usually the case with respect to Scotus who is seen as a huge dip in the history of metaphysics unfairly characterized as the 'forgetting of being.' The very definite exception to this rule is the complex work of Conor Cunningham. Cunningham's *Genealogy of Nihilism* represents an expansive investigation into Scotus's culpability in the emergence of a skeptical and nihilistic modernity. Cunningham is a sophisticated thinker and does not try to argue for a direct historical

For private consultation and not distribution without the consent of E Ondrako

influence of Scotus on the major figures of modern philosophy. He argues for a set of relations between Scotus and later thinkers, some elements of which are directly historical in that Scotus's views get transmitted and other elements which are more nearly dialectically related to those of the subtle doctor. It is not my brief to separate out these two different features of relation and to assess the measure of Cunningham's success or failure. Nor is my brief to lay forth Cunningham's core concern which has to do with how nothing, non-being and possibility are figured in Scotus and Ockham and affect and infect later thought, including the thought of Hegel who in his logical works speaks of Being in a manner almost identical to that of Scotus.[39] What I want to highlight in Cunningham's extremely interesting text is the fundamental basis of his genealogy which depends on and recycles long-standing judgments against Scotus : (a) the fateful set of metaphysical decisions made by Scotus that destroys the analogy of Being, ignores the distinction between essence and existence, and that puts possibility and actuality on the same plane;[40] (b) the linking of Scotus rather than Aquinas with Suarez;[41] and (c) the fundamental association of Scotus and Ockham despite acknowledgment of non-trivial differences.[42] All three fundamental judgments are laid out in the very first chapter and are followed through throughout. Given the thoroughgoing genealogical nature of his text which is not neutral on starting points, Cunningham thinks that the univocity of Being runs all kinds of mischief, both compromises the transcendence of the divine by including God under the concept of the most general category of Being, while also encouraging the essential nameability of reality in its finite mode. The Scotus-Suarez connection is reinforced throughout the text, even if it is not part of Cunningham's brief to assess the relative makeup of neo-Scholasticism against which much 20th-century Catholic theology and philosophy rebelled. The Scotus-Ockham connection laid down in chapter 1 is never reneged on, although it is not cashed in with regard to all the deviant forms of metaphysics discussed in the text. This is especially the case with Cunningham's treatment of Spinoza (ch. 3) and Hegel (ch. 5). In the case of Hegel, for example, the genealogical tandem is more nearly Scotus and a certain form

---

39 For Cunningham's elaboration of the relationship between Scotus and Hegel which is secured by the concept of the univocity of being, see *Genealogy of Nihilism*, 100–30, esp. 100–08.

40 See *Genealogy of Nihilism*, 20–3, 26–30. One interesting facet of Cunningham's analysis is his insistence on how much Scotus is dependent on Henry of Ghent (16). I am not suggesting that Cunningham is unique here, but he is quite pointed. The scholar who has most explored this aspect of Scotus's thought is Steven Dumont.

41 See *Genealogy of Nihilism*, 5, 24; 185, 211.

42 See *Genealogy of Nihilism*, 17–20, 23–5, 44–58.

For private consultation and not distribution without the consent of E Ondrako

of Neoplatonism than Scotus and Ockham. But then one of the more distinctive features of Cunningham's *Genealogy of Nihilism* is the pairing of Plotinus with Scotus. These are not thinkers usually thought together. Indeed, it is something of a commonplace in the interpretation of Aquinas to link him positively with Neoplatonism, whereas Scotus can only be linked negatively. This is something also fairly typical of other members of the Radical Orthodoxy, especially John Milbank and Catherine Pickstock.

Of the Radical Orthodoxy group, only Cunningham offers a decent measure of analysis when it comes to Scotus. Although Scotists are not likely to be happy, the amount of analysis does not fall below that found in Balthasar, even if it repeats in essence all of his genealogical moves. The difference is the level of emphasis on Scotus's role in derailing modes of thought that would assist Christianity rather than cannibalize it. As we saw in our treatment of Balthasar, while at some crucial points throughout his work he condemns Scotus's view of the univocity of being, acknowledges the connection between Scotus and Suarez and thereby suggests a Scotist ancestry for neo-Thomism, and links Scotus and Ockham, there are qualifications and a general lack of insistence on the point. Not so with Radical Orthodoxy in general and Conor Cunningham in particular. There is nothing probative about Scotus's philosophical and theological failures; nothing qualifying about the Scotus-Suarez relation in terms of making a causal claim about the implication of Scholasticism in aiding and abetting modern rationalism; and no self-conscious complicating of the relation between Scotus and Ockham, on the one hand, and their mode of influence on modern thought, on the other. Difference in emphases and difference in rhetorical inflection go hand in hand, and effectively harden and inflate positions that Cunningham is familiar with in Balthasar. Like other members of Radical Orthodoxy, Cunningham is interested in saving a broad swath of metaphysical discourse, which emphasizes analogy and participation, from Heidegger's condemnation of *Seinsvergessenheit*. At the same time, Cunningham reverses the charges: Heidegger's own thought is guilty of the forgetting of being on the terms adduced by Cunningham. Cunningham does not consider Heidegger's *Habilitationschrift* and does not consider any way in which Scotus might be exempted from Heideggerian critique. In fact, Cunningham makes Scotus responsible for the philosophical deformations that he sees in Heidegger's own thought.[43]

---

[43] See *Genealogy of Nihilism*, 131–54. Although the point of his reflections on Heidegger is to maintain that Heidegger continues Scotus's metaphysics of possibility and nothing, unlike McGrath, Cunningham does approach the issue of relation by tracing a line from Heidegger's treatment of Scotus to Heidegger's *Being and Time* and beyond.

For private consultation and not distribution without the consent of E Ondrako

Conclusion

This essay has provided a sketch of what amounts to a montage of negative constructions of Scotus which do not evince serious engagement with his thought and in fact discourage it (a) by suggesting that it is fatally flawed from the ground up and (b) implicating it in lines of modern discourse which are either demonstrated or assumed to be pernicious. My aim has not been so much to defend Scotus's actual positions as to protest against the apriorism of each of these individual schemes and their cumulative ideological effect which is to make impossible a hearing of what Scotus has to say. We are talking here about procedural fairness denied a thinker, but we are also talking about the way in which superficial engagements with a thinker's thought and superficial readings of the history of effects compromises the claims of the discourses being supported and in the process also serve to undermine the very enterprise of genealogy. Scotus's main philosophical and theological positions deserve to have much more sustained scrutiny, since he does address with rare scruple metaphysical questions about Being, nothing, possibility, actuality, finitude, infinity, individuality, and theological issues concerning the nature of the divine and divine causality, conjugations of divine will and reason etc. The questions are too important, the probing too deep, to be cast aside because of incitements to cease thinking. Gilson, whose Thomist leanings are unabashed, saw this well. In this essay I divided the constructions into two groups of three, with the first group being largely of Thomistic vintage and often serving as presuppositions for the second group. My interest lay mainly with this second group, especially given the fact that each of the three dispensations without formal allegiance to Thomism has constructed Scotus negatively and by dint of repeating long-established criticisms of Scotus effectively universalized them. The apriorism of this group is also unveiled. Nonetheless, where possible I tried to underscore those moments in these discourses, especially in Heidegger and Balthasar, where there is a counterthrust, and where there are the ingredients for making a case for something like exceptionality in Scotus's case in the brilliant career of Western rationalism and its careening towards nihilism.

Although indirectly, the essay is a form of plea for the unaligned for opening up the plurality of the tradition. This was the instinct of Gilson when he wrote his book on Scotus over sixty years ago. The fact that the instinct gets compromised in the performance is hardly unimportant, but it is not constitutive. What is needed is another Gilson in the very new situation, a new century with more derogatory discourses, a new century in which scholarship has considerably changed the textual landscape of

For private consultation and not distribution without the consent of E Ondrako

what belongs to the historical Scotus and what does not, a new century in which while there is much highly technical work done on Scotus, there is no book that takes a comprehensive look at the work of Scotus and shows its comprehensiveness, its seriousness, and its beauty.

Study Questions for Part Three

1. "Intuition is the blaze of certitude that tears the night of the senses.' When Gerard Manley Hopkins discovered the manuscript of Scotus at the Bodleian in 1872, he was struck by an intuition that never left him. In 1879, Hopkins wrote: "This air I gather and I release he lived on… who of all men most sways my spirits to peace." Why does the claim that Hopkins put Scotus into metaphysical English have purchase? When Newman refers to "the envious mischance that put an end to those halcyon days and revived the *odium theologicum*," what intuitions are at work? How does evidentialism, evangelicalism, British empiricism, the thought of Romanticism, Kant and Hegel influence his long and tranquil look at the meaning of certitude in the *Grammar of Assent*? Why are the positions of Newman and Scotus a happy medium between secular modernism and rigid fideism?

2. Scotus is a metaphysician-theologian, while Ockham, the next generation Franciscan, is a metaphysician-logician. Ockham is an innovator. If the two have any identifiable threads, it is because they are professed Franciscans. There it seems to stop because there is an essential difference in their thinking. Why is it misleading to assume that Ockham copies the thought of Scotus? Why is it invalid to say that Ockham puts the work of Scotus in a different package with the same form? Why does the innovative version of ancient nominalism by Ockham not have contours with Scotus and Newman? Although Newman lamented his lack of training in metaphysics and declined the title of theologian, his familiarity with metaphysics and recognition as a theologian is generally without challenge. Based on the material collected in this volume, why is this position viable?

3. The discipline to master the more metaphysical style of Scotus helps to uncover the implicit notional foundations of Newman's thought, such as what Newman says about the Trinity, and his hope that it would work for every dogma. Newman's more phenomenological style in dealing with the most fundamental Christian doctrine of the Trinity grasps the realism and spirituality of Scotus's somewhat dry and abstract presentation. At stake is belief in the doctrine of the Trinity and living by that belief. Why is a proper understanding of the doctrine of the Trinity critical for contemporary spirituality? Although not an answer to the doctrine of the Trinity, Newman's proof for God's existence from conscience, the *Itinerarium* of Bonaventure, and the *De Primo Rerum*

Principio of Scotus have obvious similarities. What are they? How do they relate to belief in the Trinity?

4. Immediately after Vatican II and its hope filled *Decree on Ecumenism*, Bl. Pope Paul VI wrote *Alma Parens* commemorating the birth of Bl. Scotus in 1265–66. Knowledge of the Anglican Tradition and the Incarnation surely inspired the Holy Father to express his hope that the thought of Scotus would "provide a golden framework for serious dialogue between the Catholic Church and the Anglican Communion as well as other Christian communities of Great Britain." Pope St. John Paul II broadened that hope to include all Christian denominations, and Benedict XVI included all people, Christian and non-Christian. His papal audience, on July 7, 2010, serves as a template and implies a dialogue about Bl. Scotus's thought on liberty in relation to the will and intellect. How might one incorporate this hope in inter-religious and intercultural dialogue? Does Scotus's primacy of the will and primacy of charity open the door to everyone to be free and loving in the spirit of true Franciscan anthropology? How does 'creative liberty' as the essence of the dignity of the person keep from obscuring the critical question of interiorization?

5. Scotus and Newman share the view that the human person is made for glory, a glory that is share in the unchangeable glory of the Creator. Even with human frailty, the human person retains the causal power of the will, and is able to make free decisions. Sin reduces the will in varying degrees within the person, but Scotus and Newman agree that it is the essence of the person for that causal power to remain free. Sin and sinfulness may be overcome by grace. How do Scotus and Newman defend that holiness is practical and achievable with their anthropology? How do the definition of the person and its relevance to the question of interiorization or preparation of heart relate in Scotus and Newman? How does their anthropology challenge the inadequacies of the anthropology of secular or liberal Christianity?

6. In *The Idea of a University*, Newman refers to the problem of contempt, and the union of intense hatred with a large toleration of theology. *Au contraire,* the similarities between Scotus and Newman in their view on holiness are a link between science and wisdom, the latter being the ultimate goal of all intellectual activity. Using Newman's definition of the essence of a university, what practical applications can you make for higher education today? "A university is a place of teaching universal knowledge. Its object is intellectual, not moral. If its object were scientific and philosophical discovery, or religious training, it

could not be the seat of literature and science." Newman knew that a
university is independent of its relation to the Church, but needs the
Church's assistance for its integrity. He taught that the Church steadies
the performance of the office of intellectual education in a university.
Discuss in light of the realities on today's university campuses.

7. Only divine love can open man's will to love God. Charity is the
intentional structure of the opening to God. Scotus defends true
intentionality as coming from the will and the intentionality of the
intellect as directed by the will. The will is what makes a person preeminently a self. Will is a transcendental perfection of being, both finite
and infinite. While all beings are endowed with intellect and will as
univocal perfections, the will is what 'desires' freely because it is will
and not because an object is presented to it as an aspect of what is
good. Further, supreme happiness is an act of will, a free act. That is
why we say that God delights in himself as an infinite beatitude and
his supreme happiness is the model of all beatitude which the blessed
imitate in proportion to their finished capacity. Should God be seen or
unseen, should we be here below or here after, our love for him remains
the same, as the supreme happiness which comes from him. Will is the
pivot on which presence and absence, intuition and abstraction express
themselves. In supreme happiness will passes from the mere state of
desire and absence to intuitive understanding and to the pleasure of
its object. This is how Boulnois (in chapter 17) helps to demonstrate
why Scotus concludes that "the highest form of freedom becomes the
necessity of the love of God." Discuss the similarities between Scotus
and Newman on the primacy of charity, the primacy of the will, its
relation to the intellect, and its relation to the principle of causality.

8. Scotus and Newman exemplify the complex pondering of human
knowledge which is ever unfolding. Its cause is the beauty of Truth
shining in the human mind. Why may one say that this development of
human knowledge is a reflection of the eternal generation of the Word
by the Father? Scotus and Newman exemplify the proposition: if the
human idea first formed is called a concept related to divine begetting,
there is no real abyss between the intra and extra mental. How do they
express their concern about how a person uses one's freedom, and
one's will? Why might cooperating with grace or not, create the abyss
between the intra and extra mental? How does Newman recognize this
freedom as foremost for every mind, the freedom to be holy, and the
perfection of freedom? Why is the choice every person makes from the
shadows and images of the natural order fully realized in our ability to
assent in faith which is aided by divine grace?

For private consultation and not distribution without the consent of E Ondrako

Conclusion

The Newman-Scotus Reader has two dimensions, an outer ring and an inner ring, the general and the specific elements to help to rethink ultimate questions in the context of the critical problem of modern theology which is the relation between faith and self-conscious experience in an evolving world. It is the search for wisdom, the relation between intellectual pursuits and prayer. The image of concentric circles describes the inaugural Newman-Scotus Symposium in October 2010, and to take a giant step forward in advanced study of both Oxford scholars. It is the first time that research has been set forth in a reader on Newman and Scotus to help shape more detailed studies by others. Their contribution to the ongoing work of theology in the Church and of the Church, as well as their influence in higher education, may redress fragmentation. For the first time, the Symposium brought together a diverse number of key Scotus and Newman scholars, students, and interested participants to explore reasons why there might be contours and to identify a systematic approach to the contours between the thought of the two great Oxford luminaries. At the Symposium the discussions were particularly animated. The responses, questions and answers were in accord with the general thesis and gave rise to this volume of contributed works by scholars who heard about the Symposium and were interested in contributing.

We discovered a global interest and interdependency. At the Paris meeting of Newman Friends on November 16–17, 2010, and again at the Gregorian University in Rome on November 22–23, the Anglican Bishop of Europe, Geoffrey Rowell, who is very knowledgeable in the thought of Scotus and Newman, responded enthusiastically with his eyes set on the centrality of the Incarnation and the Anglican Tradition. Dr. Cyril O'Regan from the University of Notre Dame, who is a very popular teacher and writer on the complex landscape of modern critical thinking, graciously accepted the invitation to parse the historical connections, especially with the backdrop of modern Romanticism, Kant and Hegel. He has the wide-ranging view that theology is a science that is more than a science. Dr.

For private consultation and not distribution without the consent of E Ondrako

Olivier Boulnois, emeritus professor at the Sorbonne, a revered Scotist, is following our progress and project, and gave permission for inclusion of a section from his work. Notre Dame's Institute for Advanced Study is following the progress of this original research.

The initial contributors and those who joined the project add to the thesis, the original idea, and the basis for the claim that there are striking similarities in the thought of John Duns Scotus and John Henry Newman without forcing the claim. The contributors freely developed their ideas in a scholarly manner. In retrospect, the image of outer circle and inner circle demonstrates a further dynamic in their work, that of a progressive illumination of the critical question. Of pivotal importance is the inspiring story of Deacon Jack Sullivan's miracle, for it narrates what it means to strive to be more intellectual, more Catholic, and more holy. In scotistic terms this is to will and to love in an orderly manner, the implicit and explicit purpose of our reader. The contributors engage themes that are emanations of orderly willing and loving. The inner circle relates to the outer, the specific to the general, with the scotistic center as the absolute primacy of Christ and Mary, the primacy of charity, and primacy of the will that unfold the most freeing meaning of *interiorization*, that is, to love in a most orderly manner. Scotus taught that God loves himself first and second loves himself in other beings which are a chaste love.

Outer circle: General Contributions

First, our contributors have shown that Scotus's and Newman's epistemology, that is, how they explain the complexity of human knowledge, has potential contemporary commerce with those who understand that the differences between one culture and set of assumptions and another does not mean that the truth is relative, that the truth changes from one age to another.

Second, Scotus and Newman are prototypes in the 14th and 19th centuries for a hermeneutical form of knowing that rehabilitates making judgments so as not to produce phantoms or illusions in the place of truth but uses the absolute character of metaphysical truth to make judgments.

Third, Scotus and Bonaventure explain the development of ideas as a pale reflection of the eternal generation of the Word by the Father, divine knowing, whereby the concept or interior word is begotten, not in the first instance in God in order to know, but because the Father knows. This is how the human idea which is first formed in order to know is related to divine begetting.

For private consultation and not distribution without the consent of E Ondrako

Fourth, Scotus and Newman are prophetic voices for the importance of learning to discern what is beyond language, which is a way of describing the preparation of the heart, interiorization, and the contemplation of truth in place of absolute autonomy and private judgment.

Fifth, the scientific or empirical is to be used along with the teachings of the Church to make prudential judgments in conjunction with one's own conscience, the voices of others influencing a person, and the course of world events and human life.

Sixth, there is a tacit dimension that is behind the mass of evidence related to intuition, perception, pre-judgment and a vague knowledge. The scientific process and tacit dimension work together with grace to collect data and to prepare to make judgments.

Seventh, the thesis of Scotus as a progenitor of Newman is not a zero sum game, but one that intrinsically merits discussion. Our goal is to step with and beyond Scotus and Newman, to broaden the lines of investigation and research, and to parse the faith-reason relation of their thought to the contemporary secularized world, the on-going work of theology in the Church and of the Church.

Inner Circle: Specific Contributions

Part One

Part one of three begins with an introduction of key concepts by the editor. In chapters one to four, John Ford, Timothy Noone, and Peter Damian Fehlner lay the foundations to support our thesis that there are contours between Bl. John Duns Scotus and Bl. John Henry Newman. The second chapter gives the historical foundation.

In chapter 1, John Ford identifies the key foundational insight that Newman's aim is for the middle ground between faith and reason—between "evidentialists," who considered reason supreme, and "existentialists," who wanted to create a fortress of faith. Always the realist in touch with the way people actually think, Newman identified three types of inference—formal, informal, natural—that lead people to make decisions. Informal inference, which is operative in the decisions of everyday life, serves as a paradigm for understanding how the human mind—particularly the illative sense—operates in religious matters; accordingly, Newman presents faith as a personal and reasonable inference.

The second chapter is an "overview of the Scotistic School" in reply to the inaugural Newman Scotus Symposium participants in October

For private consultation and not distribution without the consent of E Ondrako

2010 who requested it. As we discussed our project with many professed Franciscan religious and Secular Franciscans, they admit, with no little embarrassment, that they know very little about Scotus except that he had something to do with the definition of the Immaculate Conception. A judgment was made to include, not only a plausible reconstruction of his life, but to stress which works are authentic, and to demonstrate the perdurance of the Scotistic School and to place this in to the context of the challenges from modern secularism against the very Redemption itself. The heart of the Franciscan School is the contemplative theology of St. Francis of Assisi, which is translated into academic theology by Bonaventure and Scotus. Bonaventure summarizes: "Christ is our metaphysics."[1] The Scotistic School is built on that foundation.

At the dawn of the Enlightenment, J. Caramuel y Lobkowitz, a Spanish Cistercian of the common observance (died 1682), wrote about the spread of Scotism in Catholic Europe around 1650: "The scotistic school of theology counted more theologians than all the others put together." This is the time when there is a turn beginning that paved the way for Kant and his exercise of the hermeneutics of the Bible and an epistemological-metaphysical shift by his grammar. It remains a question for analysis of why Kant enjoys greater contemporary currency.

In chapter 3, Timothy Noone explains that intuitive and abstractive cognition opens the door to understand Scotus. He covers Scotus's formal treatments of our knowledge of God and the distinction between intuitive and abstractive cognition and makes it clear why the bulk of our work is before us. Scotus treats our knowledge of God by our ordinary informal awareness of God and its application to our everyday beliefs and judgments. This is how he argues for the reasonableness of Christian faith and belief. Noone identifies this feature of Scotus's works as unusual in reference to the common Scholastic pattern. Scotus's distinction between science in the strict sense and a broader notion of knowledge is tailored to fit everyday inference and historical knowledge. Noone comprehensively prepares us to study the looser notion of science or knowledge together with Scotus's treatment of faith, both acquired and infused, to be treated in chapter 6.

In chapter 4, Peter Damian Fehlner organizes several foundational insights to revisit the relationship between Scotus and Theology. He explains why Franciscans have a Marian metaphysics and why it is impossible for God to will in a disordered way. One timely application of this view is how Scotus deals with liberty in relation to the intellect and will. The answer

---

[1] ST. BONAVENTURE, *Sermons on the Six Days of Creation*, sermon 1, n. 17.

For private consultation and not distribution without the consent of E Ondrako

is in the truth that metaphysical necessity and freedom are not opposed. The definition of will, freedom and necessity or independent being in the Franciscan school is the heart of the debate and clarity seems as urgent today in the wave of Kantian voluntarism and Hegelian psychologism as it was in the beginning of the fourteenth century. What do we do with the freedom of the human will? What do we do with the freedom of the human will under grace? What is God's part in the salutary act of the human person acting under efficacious grace? To answer with Thomists that the human person must will what God already wills necessarily and so is deprived of freedom is a failure to see that metaphysical necessity and freedom are not opposed. To answer with the Franciscan school is to recognize that the human will should be elevated by grace to the point where the human person by way of condetermination necessarily wills the absolute good which does not deprive man of freedom, but perfects it, a major point that underlies chapter 7.

Part Two

Part two of three is a contextualizing of the theological consistency in our thought of the two Oxford giants. There is a certainty about how to engage the relationship between faith and reason that cannot be silenced at will. The radical autonomy of the will with its subtle and arbitrary voluntarism is far from the anthropology of Scotus, who recognizes ontological change, the weakening of the human person due to sin, but not the loss of causal power, practical potential and freedom. We wish to encourage research into the relationship between Scotus and Newman, not only because it is viable, but one will be pleasantly surprised to discover how Scotus anticipates the problems of modernity and answers many of the same questions as Kant. The valid and stimulating insights of Kant provide a challenge that can be met from a scotistic perspective while borrowing from Newman to restate this in a modern idiom. The critical problem of modern theology is the relation of faith and self-conscious experience in an evolving world and the Scotistic-Newmanian key has a very positive resolution of the concerns and multiple voices of modernity.

In chapter 5, Ford traces Newman's the attraction to, reflection upon, and decision to break away from rationalism. Newman, a person of faith, had reservations, both practical and theoretical, about philosophical proofs for the existence of God: in practice, he felt that most people are unlikely to investigate such proofs or, if they did, unlikely to be convinced by them; in theory, he objected to such proofs as leading merely to a notional or theoretical assent, not to a real assent of faith. Newman proposed an argument for the existence of God on the basis of conscience—an argument

For private consultation and not distribution without the consent of E Ondrako

which, theoretically considered, is defective both in its subjectivity and in supposing what needs to be proved. From an apologetical perspective, however, Newman's proof from conscience effectively challenges seekers to ask whether their conscience is truly the "voice of God" calling them not to take a philosophical position but to make a personal act of faith.

In chapter 6, Noone develops why Thomas and Scotus are systematic metaphysician-theologians with two levels of Christian discourse that influenced Newman. Their first level of Christian reference does not allow theology to substitute for the faith that is given; and their second level of Christian reference is to provide a set of guidelines of how not to get things wrong. Faith seeks understanding and theology is the understanding of faith and cannot replace it. Newman is no less a systematic theologian in this sense for he wisely kept away from any overclaims with respect to theological method. Although he regretted that he did not have the training of the *habitus metaphysicus* of the scholastics, he developed an intuitive phenomenological insight that any theory of evangelization or practical apologetics could never take precedence over the absolute character of metaphysical truth.

In chapter 7, Fehlner demonstrates thoroughly why the discipline to master the more metaphysical style of Scotus helps to uncover the implicit notional foundations of Newman's thought, such as what Newman says about the Trinity, and his hope that it would work for every dogma. Newman's more phenomenological style in dealing with the most fundamental Christian doctrine of the Trinity grasps the realism and spirituality of Scotus's seemingly dry and abstract presentation. Together, the two Oxford theologians exemplify the complex pondering of human knowledge which is ever unfolding with a cause that is the beauty of Truth shining in the human mind. This development of human knowledge is a reflection of the eternal generation of the Word by the Father. The human idea that is first formed is called a concept related to divine begetting. Therefore there is no real abyss between the intra and extra mental. It is how one uses one's freedom and one's will, whether cooperating with grace or not, that may create that abyss. Newman's recognizes this freedom as foremost for every mind, the freedom to be holy, and the perfection of freedom. It is a choice every person makes from the shadows and images of the natural order, and is fully realized in our ability to assent in faith which is aided by divine grace.

Part Three

Part three of three makes an 'arc' to include topics such as miracles and holiness, applications of theories of education, ethics and beauty, the iden-

For private consultation and not distribution without the consent of E Ondrako

tification of some misreading of Scotus, the role of the metaphysical poetry of Gerard Manley Hopkins, the Anglican Tradition and the Incarnation as the frame and context of Newman's understanding of the Incarnation, and contemporary theories of theological anthropology. This arc is fully in accord with the spirit of *Lumen Gentium, Unitatis Redintegratio, Nostra Aetate, Dignitatis Humanae,* and *Gaudium et Spes* at Vatican II that the task of theology is to remain open to the broadest possible standpoint, and not just magisterial. The *Newman-Scotus Reader* has many practical implications for the Church and Modern World. Behind this arc are the perennial assumptions about faith and reason as defined by Newman and the hubristic assumptions of Romanticism which defines modernity as a crisis, and dismisses theology as if it were something that is superstitious, and striving for holiness as superfluous, and living with conviction as pointless. Behind this arc are the differences between faith and reason as defined by Kant and Hegel, assumptions that Hegel shares with Kant such as the turn to the subject and denigration of any causal activity by a divine agent. Reason is assumed to be superior to faith because reason can prove by science. Today, Christianity is more ascetic about its truth claims for many reasons, but always in accord with God's self-gift in Christ as the way, the truth and the life and the Church whose mission is in creative tension for the world and to witness to the world.

In chapter 8, Olivier Boulnois brings us back to the center, the nobility of charity and of the will in Scotus. The emeritus professor at the Sorbonne explains the correlation between the primacy of the will and rationality and order in both Newman and Scotus. The primacy of the will obeys a structure, a metaphysical principle of Augustine, used by Bonaventure: "in spiritual beings, the base is in the peak."[2] What is most obvious is a reality less visible but the highest, which is why the base and peak imply themselves reciprocally. Boulnois shows how Scotus reuses the structure of Aristotelian metaphysics but shifts the primacy of the intellect to the primacy of the will. Aristotle, the authority, does not pose the problem of the primacy of the intellect or of the will. The fact that he does not speak of the primacy of the will does not prove anything against it. For Aristotle, the highest form of life is the speculative life, while the highest form of existence for Scotus lies in volition. Scotus's systematic plan is practical rather than speculative. Boulnois notices that the rule of organization changes from Aristotle's primacy of presence to Scotus's freedom towards the presence. The will remains free whatever the obviousness of an intuitive presence may be, whatever the perfection of the seen or abstract object

---

[2] AUGUSTINE, *Commentaries on the Psalms,* Ps. 29, 2, 10 (PL 36, 222); BONAVENTURE, *On the Six Days of Creation,* 22, no. 4. See BOULNOIS, *Être,* 214.

For private consultation and not distribution without the consent of E Ondrako

may be. "Whether its object may be presented or represented to it, by intuition or abstraction, it is given to it by charity."[3] With Scotus's description of metaphysics for the sake of theological demands, Boulnois brings us to a full hermeneutical circle, a strengthened metaphysics. Because the theology of charity surpasses the metaphysics of presence, this object is completed in the metaphysics of the will!

In chapter 9, "The Scotistic Doctrine of the Incarnation in the Anglican Tradition- Newman in Frame and Content," Bishop Geoffrey Rowell offers a not to be missed original insight into Scotistic elements in the Anglican and Reformed interpretations and their relation to the Orthodox about the motive of the Incarnation and the greatest work of God in creation. He unearths the Scotistic substratum about the Incarnation: what the Divine Architect planned first which was last in execution, for all of creation has its purpose, the glory of God. Jesus is the exemplar of all of Creation because all of creation exists through the Word-Incarnate. All of creation exists for Christ and the goal of all of creation is for the glory of God. Rowell centers on the motive of the Incarnation and recalls what has always been true and reflected on in the Anglican tradition and may be forgotten or never reflected upon. The Incarnation, hypostatic union, and person of the God-man reflect the axiom of metaphysics that operation follows on being (*operari sequitur esse*). The possibilities, fittingness and factual character of the Incarnation and its modalities is summarized in the scotistic formulation of theological method: and goal: *potuit, decuit, ergo fecit.*[4]

The reason for placing Rowell here rather than with chapter 2, the *Overview of the Scotistic School,* in this volume, is to present the broader ground of the theological formation and to encourage conversation with the depth and range of the *studium generale* of the thirteenth century on the motive of the Incarnation. The Bishop gives a hint at the broad historical understanding of the theological training at the time of Scotus and its development. From the time of the English friars, the pre-Reformation thought of Scotus finds its way into the eighteenth century work of Bishop Joseph Butler, *Analogy,* which was very influential on Newman's thought after 1823. Michael Ramsey saw the theological line of succession via the Incarnation as the center of the theological scheme concerning nature and man. Rowell invites creative adaptation for training in a broad theological range with a blessed familiarity with the motive of the Incarnation and its relation to the current concept of evolution. He demonstrates how such study includes the Greek and Latin Fathers, Augustine, Thomas Aquinas,

---

[3] BOULNOIS, *Être*, 216.

[4] It is possible, it is fitting, and, therefore, it is.

For private consultation and not distribution without the consent of E Ondrako

Scotus and Gerard Manley Hopkins, and some significant exponents of Scotistic doctrine which assists the faithful in what they already believe and enlightens study of the development of the Reformed and Orthodox Tradition.

Thanks to this careful and learned original contribution, the elasticity that is in the very nature of the Church comes forth in the thought of Scotus and Newman and opens the door to a new generation of research and dialogue among the Churches. The scotistic school prospered for centuries, a point often forgotten today, and Newman rediscovered it in his understanding of the Incarnation. It is part of our goal to give educators devoted to liberal higher education, searchers for Truth, not only Franciscans, a rich resource to mine for a forward looking response to the still to be developed authentic spirit of Vatican II, to the anthropological turn of recent decades, and contemporary spiritual problems and the ecumenical movement.

Chapters 10 and 11 continue the colonization with eminent practicality for the twenty-first century challenges to striving for holiness and growing in altruistic love. How do we live with recognition of the beauty of all of creation, without compromising right reason and moral living, with understanding the essence of a university, and the essentials in the curriculum? How do we live with creative liberty without marginalizing God and at the same time be able to critique modern secular society with the conviction that *Deus caritas est?* These topics are treated with a keen eye to the wisdom of the past, modern scientific thinking, the *via media* of perennial wisdom, and a lens to interpreting what being a Christian is all about.

In chapter 10, Mary Beth Ingham reframes the theme of the rationality of love, an ethics of beauty, and ethics of right loving with an eye toward inter-religious and inter-cultural dialogue. The challenge is to keep the meta in metaethics for modern critical thought jousts with the freedom to be holy and the perfection of freedom. Clarity in ethical and moral thought paves the way for the necessary engagement with the roots of modern secularity and secularism. Critical engagement welcomes scholarly retrieval of Scotus's subtle contributions to cultural growth where both the Creator and rational creature are involved in establishing the rational character of contingent change.

In chapter 11, Patricia Hutchison draws on her experiences in teaching in higher education, of evaluating and incorporating theories of education, and enthusiastically endorses the creative application of the range and development of the essence of the university as defined by Newman. She links this definition of the essence of a university to the essence of

For private consultation and not distribution without the consent of E Ondrako

the spirituality of Francis and Clare of Assisi as carried forward in the theologian disciples of Francis. Patricia calls for a lively, energetic, and creative continuation of the work begun at the inaugural Newman-Scotus Symposium.

In chapter 12, Robert Christie unfolds the validity of striving for holiness with many implications for sacramental and liturgical theology, for the hierarchical structure of the Church, for religious life and missionary labors, and for renewal in the life of the Church. He unfolds the genuine contributions to understanding miracles, holiness, faith and reason, and the nobility of the will, which are four burning themes since the Reformation. The unfortunate events, which had guilt on all sides, became a disunifying religious revolt in varying degrees that gave the Church many martyrs. These events and themes give insight into the development of doctrine in the centuries preceding Vatican II. Robert Christie does not suggest that Newman invents the concept of holiness, but develops why holiness has always been present in the great tradition of the Church with Christ as the source. He makes obvious how Newman grew in conformity to Christ and labored to repair and to renew the Church. Similarly, the great Franciscan tradition understands its founder's vocation to rebuild the Church. Vatican II set out to rebuild the Church by the centrality and universal call to holiness.

In chapter 13, Deacon Jack Sullivan gently and persuasively answers anyone who is opposed to the possibility and reality of miracles, a problem brought to the fore with the secular Enlightenment. If we leave aside many misleading criticisms of miracles, Jack shows, in a most straightforward manner, the practical meaning of living one's faith, the underlying dynamic of crying out in prayer with faith and with reason. It is not an either/or, but both/and. Moreover, Jack demonstrates why and how charity stands at the heart of the holiness of the Church's members. As a retired magistrate and permanent deacon for the Archdiocese of Boston, Jack's practical and moving account of devotion to Newman and his cry for help which resulted in the miracle that helped to raise Newman to the ranks of the Blessed radiates in "The Story of a Miracle." His free decision from the shadows and images of the natural order, his assent in faith which was aided by divine grace under the invocation of help from John Henry Newman brought a miracle. He lectures willingly to many who are seeking to counter and avoid skepticism in matters of religion.

In chapter 14, 15, and 16, Edward Ondrako tackles difficulties with what the light illumines and its intensity, i.e., as applied to terms such as development of doctrine or evolution. For example, neither theistic evolutionists nor creationists among Catholics get it exactly right. The

For private consultation and not distribution without the consent of E Ondrako

answer from Scotus is that he teaches us how to understand the divine plan of salvation and how history presupposes metaphysics, or what the light illumines. Development of doctrine and evolution are connected with history rather than time in general, with cultural growth which takes place where both the Creator and the rational creature are involved freely in establishing the rational character of contingent change. This is a critical link between the medieval synthesis and modernity. In chapter 14, Ondrako makes this application which includes the scotistic notion of grace as condetermined, the human will, and the freedom that perfects it, from examples in the life, poetry and metaphysical modern English of Gerard Manley Hopkins. In chapter 15, Ondrako takes up the challenge of uncoupling any misguided connections between Scotus and Kant with a close look at the difference between the metaphysics of Scotus and the mathematical physics of Kant. What comes into view gradually is how Scotus rather than Kant becomes Newman's role model. The primacy of charity and the creative freedom that it entails for Scotus is certain, quite different from the categorical imperative of Kant. How this influences Newman is very powerfully demonstrated in his seven notes on the true development of doctrine, the epistemological grounding in his Idea of a University and metaphysical grounding in his Grammar of Assent. In chapter 16, Ondrako engages the anti-metaphysical attempt to redesign the Trinitarian landscape by Hegel's psychologism. Scotus's thinking on divine providence and predestination in Christ is far from Hegel's theory of history as mediated logic. If properly prepared for contemporary purchase, he postulates that the thought of Scotus and Newman will be a sure win, a linkage between Thomas and Scotus and Newman, broadly, but more specifically with the problem of how God is present in history personally according to Scotus and the already-not yet Lutheran theology.[5] This is in line with the exhortations of Pope Benedict XVI to Dominicans and Franciscans that they not forget the proper intellectual component in their vocations. Ondrako offers a modest reply to the Holy Father's sensitive and open question about liberty in relation to the will and intellect. In sum, the limits of the Kantian epistemology of science and the importance of Scotistic inspired voluntary rather than natural causality enables terms as development or evolution to have significant purchase or substantial validity in metaphysics. A delicate dance between metaphysics-theology and experience-phenomenology is the underlying dynamic.

---

[5] I am deeply indepted to Peter Fehlner for guiding me to reflect upon the promise of linking this conviction of Scotus with the Lutheran theology of the already and the not yet for it has indescribable promise for the future of ecumenical dialogue and understanding evolution and doctrinal development.

For private consultation and not distribution without the consent of E Ondrako

Finally, in chapter 17, we find the genealogy of the 'misprisoning' of the works of Scotus for they are recognized as forceful, highly interesting and with their own definitiveness. Cyril O'Regan addresses a number of constructions and narratives that function to 'misprison' Scotus and essentially side-line him. His x-ray of the problems and wide lens to capture the changed textual landscape is a call for a new technical work on Scotus as timely. His analysis is challenging and effectively paves the way for exchanges among scholars at future Newman Scotus Symposia and scholarly writing about the subtle doctor. Scotus is the opposite of any cynicism which is the denial that love is possible, even divine love, that every act of charity is selfish. O'Regan offers an original and exciting analysis to explain how Scotus anticipated the underlying Romantic assumptions that Christianity is expected to continue to relinquish its authority in modernity, and that what reason and science say legitimates the perception of the inadequacy of faith in relation to reason. In reply to the secular air we breathe and to cynicism and its diabolical force, what emerges is the divine communion at the heart of the Church, which is the amazing foresight of Scotus on the Immaculate Conception *vis a vis* the popularizing of Hegel's less rigorous inventions about the Trinity. A Mariology whose ontological basis is the Immaculate Conception translates into Marian mediation.

O'Regan concretizes the goals of *The Newman Scotus Reader*: to blunt the appeal of absolute autonomy in intellectual and political affairs associated with modern secularity by giving the reader the breadth of information that does not suggest who is right and who is wrong in every important aspect of pre and post Vatican II theological architecture, but takes a view in the contemplative spirit of Scotus and Newman. O'Regan touches what may not seem obvious until one steps back to reflect on neo-Hegelian thinking that is alive and well in Western government, in secular universities, and one can find an increasing number of neo-Hegelian threads in the Catholic Church since Vatican II. Most of all, O'Regan helps one to begin to appreciate how Scotus anticipated Hegel's inversion of being and the consequences if people lose the tools to understand what gifted grace means and being a child before God.

Grace, Freedom and Bridge Building

The joint comprehensiveness of Scotus's and Newman's thought is the treasure to be found in The Newman-Scotus Reader: Contexts and Commonalities. By identifying misprisonings, the researcher is able to open the promising opportunity for dialogue that leads to mutuality and

For private consultation and not distribution without the consent of E Ondrako

a sure win in the future teaching and understanding of grace, the will, and freedom. An accurate revisit of the debate about scotistic *condetermination* with an answer from the Molinist or Banesian Thomist School and an answer from the scotistic Franciscan Mastrian School presents a compelling substratum to the thinking on grace and freedom. The Molinists in effect stress the immanentism of Pelagius. When one misses the profound understanding of human freedom and how it is perfected, one is prey to the deceptive Lockian argument of strong and weak. Newman rejected it and did not fall into the trap of the Lockian strong and weak argument for deciding whether to believe or not to believe. Every teacher of religion knows that this is a contemporary pastoral problem. Another way to say it is that if a student cannot give a clear answer for his or her being a Christian, the temptation is to leave it.

If there is a temptation for those who might interpret Thomas in terms of strong or weak, with Newman one has to recognizes that this Lockian argument is a subtle trap. Moreover, Newman does not buy into the Kantian understanding of freedom, nor Hegel's digression from the doctrine of the Trinity. Rather, Newman's fidelity to the true doctrine of the Trinity is based on how he answers the critical question of entering into the heart and resolving problems relating to the absolute autonomy of the will. After he died, the problem of modernism, with its gray but important history, needed his clear thinking in the *Grammar of Assent* to reply to the challenges from advocates of scientific form to certitude. Misunderstandings about modernism contributed many reasons that led to the papal call for Vatican II. From the time of St. John XXIII, it is easy to trace how the popes worry about the balance of holding to the deposit of faith. Novelty as the criterion for change is the ever present temptation which the popes counter with never tiring message of the universal call to holiness and true development of doctrine. The 'misprisoned' Scotus is the eager helper waiting to be invited to contribute to the search for meaning for the questions and preoccupations of the present and future.

Watching for the Shoals of an Evolutionary or pantheistic Unitarianism

The contributors to *The Newman Scotus Reader: Contexts and Commonalities* have been disentangling many threads in line with contemporary developments in theology. At the core as it was for Newman, is the ever present development of doctrine which makes clearer the great theological reflection of the past which have to be known well in order to explain and

For private consultation and not distribution without the consent of E Ondrako

to guide renewal. The references to the outstanding approaches of the past in this work are never so complete at the time in history when first written that one can imagine that the author has thought of all of the questions that may be encompassed within its frame of reference. One can imagine what our theologians might have said, but can never say what they would have said in light of new problems in modernity and post modernity. One question is articulated by Pope Benedict XVI. It is the sensitive and open question about liberty in relation to the will and intellect that embodies western culture today, but not only western, as recent international changes demonstrate, as well as to the anthropological turn to the subject.

Since a truly great theology is a living one, it must have meaning for the questions and preoccupations of future ages. The principles of the development of doctrine embodied in Newman's thought are a point of reference for interpreting the permanent works of a theologian of the past and for incorporating his thought in fidelity with faith and his genius. For example, ecumenical work, teaching, understanding grace, the will, and freedom in theological schools will benefit from revisiting accurately the debate and not merely be repeating the formulae of the past. Further inspiration from the work of Scotus and Newman is promising if one relates the fundamental themes that they researched with the great themes of theology that are a part of the history of the Church. Scotus and Newman were both geniuses who flowered at Oxford and the hope of the contributors to this volume is that the timeliness and timelessness of both geniuses will come to be better appreciated by the human endeavor they expended to put their convictions down for scholarly engagement while welcoming competing views. No doubt their views as expressed in *The Newman-Scotus Reader: Contexts and Comparisons* will inspire further research and request for clarification.

In *De Doctrina Christiana*, St. Augustine summarizes a frame of mind common to our contributors.

> Just as the person who knows how to read does not require another reader, when he gets hold of a volume, to tell him what is written in it, in the same way, those who have grasped the rules we are endeavoring to pass on will retain a knowledge of these rules, like letters, when they come across anything obscure in the holy books, and will not require another person who understands to uncover for them what is shrouded in obscurity. Instead, by following up certain clues, they will be able themselves to get the hidden meaning of a passage without any error—or at the very least to avoid falling into any absurdly wrongheaded opinion.

For private consultation and not distribution without the consent of E Ondrako

The outer and inner circles, the general and specific elements, are concentric around the critical question that arises along with interiorization or entering into the heart. The question has to do with freedom in choosing among contingent goods which presupposes freedom to love the perfect good for its own sake and the ability to think about that choice of a particular good in relation to goodness itself. Preparation of heart is linked to Newman and humble contemplation to Scotus, two sides of the same coin. Collectively, the contributors have endeavored to offer more than clues to suggest that two great Oxford theologians, separated by several centuries, have more than happenstance to link their names in a new century in which scholarship has changed the textual landscape but the future of Catholic theology may find their works offering a supporting part of its new architecture.

Beata vita, quae non est nisi gaudium de veritate.[6]

---

[6] Augustine, *Confessions*, 23. PL 794. Happiness is nothing but the joys of the truth.

For private consultation and not distribution without the consent of E Ondrako

Afterword: John Jukes, Bishop of Strathearn

To the Newman-Scotus Symposium
Washington Theological Union
October 22-24, 2010

October 3, 2010

Dear Participants,

In reflecting on the Scotus-Newman initiative, I commend this further exploration of the thought of these two eminent scholars. The inspiration of the Holy Spirit in leading us to truth cannot be anticipated with regard to which individuals or the social circumstances in which this gift is to be exercised. What is needed is that those blessed in this way have put the following of Christ first in their lives. From this base a secure start can be made to give us the inspiration that they have received. Thus we see how the Friar of the 13th and 14th centuries and the Cardinal of the 19th are linked in the service of the Lord to our great benefit.

May God bless your Symposium!

+ John Jukes, OFMConventual,

Bishop of Strathearn

For private consultation and not distribution without the consent of E Ondrako

Contributors

Boulnois, Olivier, Emeritus Professor, Sorbonne

Christie, Robert, Professor, DeVry University

Deferluc, Agnes, Doctoral Student, Montpelier University, France

Fehlner, F.I. Peter Damian, Emeritus Professor of Theology, Pontifical Collegium Seraphicum, Rome

Ford, C.S.C. John, Professor, The Catholic University of America

Hutchison, Patricia, Sr., Professor, Neumann University, Aston, PA.

Ingham, Mary Beth, Sr., Professor, Loyola Marymount, Los Angeles

Jukes, OFMConv. John, Bishop of Strathearn (RIP November 2011)

Noone, Timothy B., Professor, The Catholic University of America

Ondrako, OFMConv. Edward J., Doctoral Student in Theology, University of Notre Dame

O'Regan, Cyril, Huisking Professor of Theology, University of Notre Dame

Rowell, Geoffrey, retired Anglican Bishop of Gibraltar in Europe as of November 2013, Emeritus Fellow, Keble College, Oxford

Sullivan, Jack, Deacon, Archdiocese of Boston

Tasca, OFMConv. Marco, Minister General, Conventual Franciscan Order, Rome

For private consultation and not distribution without the consent of E Ondrako

Bibliography

Chambers English Dictionary. Edited by Rev. Thomas Davidson. Edinburgh: W. and R. Chambers, Limited, 1914.

Webster's Encyclopedic Unabridged Dictionary of the English Language 1996.

Aertsen, Jan and Andreas Speer. *Was Ist Philosophie Im Mittelalter?* Akten des X. Internationalen kongresses für mittelalterliche philosophie der société internationale pour l'étude de la philosophie médiévale, 25. bis 30. August 1997 im Erfurt. *Miscellanea Mediaevalia*. Berlin: W. de Gruyter, 1998.

Agnes, Michael and Charlton Grant Laird. *Webster's New World Dictionary and Thesaurus*. New York: Macmillan, 1996.

Apollonio, A. "Il contributo di Hugo Cavellus, OFM (+1626) alla teoria dell'intellezione dei singoli materiali." in *Quaderni di studi scotistic* 6. (Frident0: Casa Mariana Editrice, 2009.

Aquinas, Thomas. *De Rationibus Fidei contra Saracenos, Graecos, et Armenos, ad Cantorum Antiochenum*. Translated by Peter Damian Fehlner and Edited by James Likoudis. New Bedford, MA: Academy of the Immaculate, 2002.

———. *Summa Contra Gentiles*. Notre Dame [Ind.]: University of Notre Dame Press, 1975.

———. *Summa Theologica*.

Aquino, Frederick D. *Communities of Informed Judgment: Newman's Illative Sense and Accounts of Rationality*. Washington, D.C.: Catholic University of America Press, 2004.

Archa Verbi: Proceedings of the Quadruple Congress on John Duns Scotus Part 4. Mechtild Dreyer Edouard Mehl and Matthias Vollet, eds. St. Bonaventure, N.Y.: Franciscan Institute, 2013, Foreword.

Archer, Gleason L. *Reseña Crítica De Una Introducción Al Antiguo Testamento*. Rev ed. Grand Rapids, Mich: Editorial Portavoz, 1987.

Armstrong, Regis J., J. A. Wayne Hellmann, and William J. Short. *Francis of Assisi: Early Documents*. Vol. 1, The Saint. Hyde Park, N.Y.; London: New City Press, 1999.

For private consultation and not distribution without the consent of E Ondrako

Association of Catholic Colleges and Universities. "A United Endeavor" Washington, DC: ACCU, http://www.accunet.org/i4a/pages/index. cfm?pageid=3617.

Astin, Alexander W., Helen S. Astin, and Jennifer A. Lindholm. *Cultivating the Spirit: How College can Enhance Students' Inner Lives*. San Francisco: Jossey-Bass, 2011.

Augustine. *De libero arbitrio*, 2, 18, 50; 2, 19; *Retractationes*, 6.

———. *Commentaries on the Psalms*. PL 36.

Bacik, J. J. "Habits of Mind and Spirit: What Campus Ministers can learn from Blessed John Henry Newman." *AMERICA -NEW YORK-* 203, no. 6 (2010): 23–26.

Bak, Felix. "Scoti schola numerosior est omnibus aliis simul sumptis." *Franciscan Studies* 16, (1956), 144–165.

Balthasar, Hans urs von. *Herrlicheit: The Glory of the Lord. A Theological Aesthetics*. 7 Vols. Edinburgh: T and T Clarke, 1986ff. San Francisco : Ignatius Press, 1998.

———. *Liturgie Cosmique: Maxime Le Confesseur*. Paris: Aubier, 1947.

———. *The Moment of Christian Witness. Communio Books*. San Francisco: Ignatius Press, 1994.

Barrett, Cyril. "Newman and Wittgenstein on the Rationality of Religious Belief." in *Newman and Conversion*, edited by Ian T. Ker, 89–99. Notre Dame, IN: University of Notre Dame Press, 1997.

Barry, W. s.v. "Newman, John Henry (1801–1890)." in *Catholic Encyclopedia*. Vol. 10. Washington, D.C., 1911.

Beato Giovanni Duns Scoto. *Prologo dell'Ordinatio: traduzione italiana con testo originale a fronte. A cura del seminario teologico dei Frati Francescani dell'Immacolata. Premessa* di Peter Damian M. Fehlner; Introduzione e traduzione di Alessandro M. Apollonio. Frigento (AV): Casa Mariana Editrice, 2006.

Benedict XVI, Pope. *Values in a Time of Upheaval*. New York: Crossroads, 2005.

———. *Laetare colonia urbs. Apostolic Letter to Joachim Cardinal Meisner on the Seventh Centenary of the Death of Bl. John Duns Scotus*. October 28, 2008.

For private consultation and not distribution without the consent of E Ondrako

————. "Beatification Homily for Bl. John Henry Newman." http://www.zenit.org.

————. "Discourse at Lambeth Palace, September 7, 2010." , http://www.zenit.org.

————. "On Duns Scotus: Defender of the Immaculate Conception, Papal Audience." Vatican City, http://www.zenit.org/article-29826?l=english.

————. "Catechesis on St. Bonaventure, General Audiences March 3, 10, 17, 2010." http://www.vatican.va/holy_father/benedict_xvi/audiences/2010/documents/hf_ben-xvi_aud_20100317_en.html.

————. "Catechesis on William of Saint-Thierry, General Audience, Dec. 2, 2009." http://www.vatican.va/holy_father/benedict_xvi/audiences/2009/documents/hf_ben-xvi_aud_20091202_en.html.

————. "Christmas Discourse to Members of the Roman Curia on 22 December 2005." *L'Osservatore Romano*, 23 December, 2005, Rome.

————. "Homily for the Election of the Roman Pontiff, 8 April 2005," http://www.catholicnewsagency.com/document.php?n=272.

————. *Caritas in veritate*, Encyclical, June 29, 2009.

————. *Introduction to Christianity*. San Francisco: Ignatius Press, 1968, rpt. 2004.

————. *The Theology of History in St. Bonaventure*. Translated by Zachary Hayes. Chicago: Franciscan Herald Press, 1971.

————. *Jesus of Nazareth*, New York: 2007.

————. *Eschatology*. 2nd English ed. Washington, D.C.: The Catholic University of America Press, 2007.

Bennett, Owen. *Metaphysics of Faith and Freedom*. Rensselaer, N.Y.: Conventual Franciscan Publications, 1972.

Berardini, Lorenzo M. *La nozione del soprannaturale nell'antica scuola francescana*. Roma: Agenzia del libro cattolico, 1943.

Bergonzi, Bernard. *Gerard Manley Hopkins*. London: 1977.

Bernard. "Sermon 83." in *Opera Omnia*. Vol. 2 Editio Cisterciensis, 1958. 300–302.

For private consultation and not distribution without the consent of E Ondrako

Bettoni, Efrem. *Duns Scotus: The Basic Principles of His Philosophy*. Washington: Catholic University of America Press, 1961.

Blessed John Duns Scotus and His Mariology: Commemoration of the Seventh Centenary of His Death. Symposium on Scotus's Mariology 2008: Grey College, Durham, England, *Mariologia Franciscana* 3. New Bedford, MA: Academy of the Immaculate, 2009. Henceforth, Duram, Symposium, 2008.

Boekraad, Adrian J. *The Personal Conquest of Truth*. Louvain: *Editions Nauwelaerts*, 1955.

Boekraad, Adrian J. and Henry Tristram. *The Argument from Conscience to the Existence of God According to John Henry Newman*. Louvain: *Editions Nauwelaerts*, 1961.

Boethius of Dacia-James of Pistoia. *Ricerca della felicità e piaceri dell-intelletto*. Florence: Nardini, 1989.

Bonaventure. *Works of St. Bonaventure*. General Editor, Robert J. Karris. St. Bonaventure, N.Y.: The Franciscan Institute, 1996–2010. Fifteen volumes in a series with several contributions by Zachary Hayes.

———. *Itinerarium mentis in Deum*. Edited by Philotheus Boehner. St. Bonaventure, N.Y: The Franciscan Institute, 1956.

———. *Breviloquium*.

———. *Christus unus omnium Magister*.

———. *Collationes in septem donis Spiritus Sancti*.

———. *Collationes in Hexaemeron*.

———. *Commentarium in Quattuor Libros Sententiarum*.

———. *Questiones Disputatae de mysterio Ss. Trinitatis*.

———. *De Reductione Artium Ad Theologiam*. 2nd ed. Saint Bonaventure N.Y.: The Franciscan Institute Saint Bonaventure University, 1955.

———. *De Triplici Via*.

———. *Questiones Disputatae de scientia Christi*.

———. *Legenda Major*.

Bordoni, C M. "Cristologia: Lettura Sistematica." in *La teologia del XX secolo: un bilancio*, edited by Giacomo Canobbio, Piero Coda and Associazione Teologica Italiana. Roma: Città nuova, 2003.

For private consultation and not distribution without the consent of E Ondrako

Boulnois, Olivier. *Duns Scot: La Rigueur de La Charité*. Paris: Cerf, 1998.

———. *Être Et Représentation: Une généologie de la métaphysique moderne à l'époque de Duns Scot (XIII–XIV siècle)*. Paris: Presses Universitaires de France, 1999, rpt. 2008.

Bouyer, Louis. *Newman, His Life and Spirituality*. New York: P.J. Kennedy & Sons, 1958.

Boyer, Ernest L. "Creating the New American College." *Chronicle of Higher Education* A 48, (March 4, 1994).

Brechten, J. *Real-Erfahrung Bei Newman*. Bergen-Enkheim, 1973.

Brown, Stephen F. "Reflections on Franciscan Sources for Duns Scotus's Philosophic Commentaries." in *John Duns Scotus, Philosopher: Proceedings of "the Quadruple Congress" on John Duns Scotus Part 1. Archa Verbi*. Edited by Mary Beth Ingham and O. V. Bychkov. St. Bonaventure, N.Y.: The Franciscan Institute, 2010.

Brown, Raymond E. *Mary in the New Testament : A Collaborative Assessment by Protestant and Roman Catholic Scholars*. Philadelphia: Fortress Press, 1978.

Calkins, Arthur Burton. "Mary as Co-Redemptrix in the Writings of Frederick William Faber." MFC 2001, Vol. 1, 317–343.

Cardinal Matthaeus de Aquasparta. *Quaestiones Disputatae: De Fide et De Cognitione. Bibliotheca Franciscana Scholastica Medii Aevi*. Editio secunda. Vol. 1. Quaracchi: Florentiae, ex Typographia Collegii S. Bonaventure, 1957.

Casanova, Gabriel. *Cursus philosophicus ad mentem D. Bonaventurae et Scoti*. Matriti [Madrid]: ex typographia Aloysii Aguardo, 1894.

Catechism of the Catholic Church. Vatican City: Libreria Editrice Vaticana, 1994.

Cicero, M. T. "Chapter 27 n. 94." in *De Officiis* I, 97: Loeb, 1956.

———. "Chapter 40." in *De Officiis* I, 97: Loeb, 1956.

Colby, Robert A. "The Structure of Newman's Apologia Pro Vita Sua in Relation to His Theory of Assent." in *Apologia Pro Vita Sua: An Authoritative Text, Basic Texts of the Newman-Kingsley Controversy, Origin and Reception of the Apologia [and] Essays in Criticism*. Edited David J. DeLaura. 1st ed., 465–480. New York: Norton, 1968.

For private consultation and not distribution without the consent of E Ondrako

Congar, Yves. *True and False Reform in the Church.* Translated by Paul Philbert. Collegeville, Minn: 2011.

Conn, Walter E. *Conscience & Conversion in Newman: A Developmental Study of Self in John Henry Newman.* Milwaukee, WI: Marquette University Press, 2010.

Cross, F. L. and Elizabeth A. Livingstone. *The Oxford Dictionary of the Christian Church.* 3rd ed. New York: Oxford University Press, 1997.

Cross, Richard. "Natural Law, Moral Constructivism, and Duns Scotus's Meta-ethics: The Centrality of Aesthetic Explanation." in *Reason, Religion, and Natural Law: Historical and Analytical Studies.* Edited by Jonathan Jacobs. Oxford University Press, Oxford (forthcoming).

———. "Duns Scotus and Suárez at the Origins of Modernity," in *Deconstructing Radical Orthodoxy: Postmodern Theology, Rhetoric and Truth.* Wayne J. Hankey and Douglas Hedley, eds. Aldershot: Hants, UK: Ashgate Publishing Ltd., 2005, 65-80.

———. *Duns Scotus on Cognition.* Oxford: Oxford University Press, 2014.

———. *Duns Scotus. Great Medieval Thinkers.* New York: Oxford University Press, 1999.

Dean, Maximilian Mary. *A Primer on the Absolute Primacy of Christ: Blessed John Duns Scotus and the Franciscan Thesis.* New Bedford, MA: Academy of the Immaculate, 2006.

Del Zotto, C. "La "Via Scoti" nell'Epistolario di Johann Ammerbach (1443–1513), Approfondimenti " in *Via Scoti.* vol. 2. Rome: Edizioni Antonianum, 1995, 1091–1108.

Denzinger, Heinrich and Clemens Bannwart. *Enchiridion Symbolorum, Definitionum Et Declarationum De Rebus Fidei Et Morum.* 10. ed. emendata et aucta / quam paravit Clemens Bannwart ed. Friburgi Brisgoviae: Herder, 1908.

Déodat Marie de Basly, Joseph Léon. *Les deux grandes écoles catholiques du b. Duns Scot et de saint Thomas.* Paris : Le Havre, La bonne parole, 1907.

Dessain, Charles Stephen. *John Henry Newman.* Oxford: Oxford University Press, 1961, rpt. 1980.

Devlin, Christopher. *The Psychology of Scotus.* Oxford: 1950.

For private consultation and not distribution without the consent of E Ondrako

————. *The Sermons and Devotional Writings of Gerard Manley Hopkins.* Oxford: University Press, 1959.

Dettloff, W. *De Lehre von der Acceptatio Divina bei Johannes Duns Scotus mit besonderer Beruchsichtigung der Rechtfertigungslehre.* Werl in Westfalia, 1954.

Documents of Vatican II. Edited by Walter Abbot. New York : America Press, 1966.

————. *Dogmatic Constitution on the Church, Lumen Gentium.*

————. *Dogmatic Constitution on the Church in the Modern World, Gaudium et Spes.*

————. Dogmatic Constitution of Divine Revelation. Vatican: The Holy See, http://www.vatican.va/archive/hist_councils/ii_vatican_council/documents/vat-ii_const_19651118_dei-verbum_en.html.

————. *Declaration on the Relation of the Church to Non-Christian Religions Nostra Aetate.* Vatican: The Holy See, http://www.vatican.va/archive/hist_councils/ii_vatican_council/documents/vat-ii_decl_19651028_nostra-aetate_en.html.

————. *Decree on Ecumenism Unitatis Redintegratio.* The Vatican, http://www.vatican.va/archive/hist_councils/ii_vatican_council/documents/vat-ii_decree_19641121_unitatis-redintegratio_en.html.

Domanski O.F.M.Conv., Georges. "Lourdes Et Le Père Maximilien Kolbe (Esquisse de sa mariologie)." in *Miscellanea Francescana* 1958, 195–224.

Downey, Michael. *Alltogether Gift: A Trinitarian Spirituality.* Maryknoll, N.Y.: Orbis Books, 2000.

Dulles, Avery. *A Testimonial to Grace; and Reflections on a Theological Journey.* Kansas City, MO: Sheed & Ward, 1996.

Dumont, Stephen D. "Duns Scotus' Parisian Question on the Formal Distinction." *Vivarium* 43 (2005): 1, 7–62.

————. "Theology as a Science and Duns Scotus's Distinction between Intuitive and Abstractive Cognition." *Speculum* 64, no. 3 (Jul., 1989): 579–599.

For private consultation and not distribution without the consent of E Ondrako

Duns Scotus, John. *Opera Omnia*, ed. L. Durand, Lione 1639, referred to as the Wadding edition.

——. *Opera Omnia*, ed. Wadding-Vivès, 22 vols. Paris: 1891–1895, referred to as the Wadding Vivés edition.

——. *Opera Omnia*. Civitas Vaticana: Typis Polyglottis Vaticanis, 1950–2010, referred to as the Vatican edition.

——. *Libros Metaphysicorum Aristotelis Expositio*: in *Metaphysicam Quaestiones Subtilissimae*. Vol. XII. Hildesheim: G. Olms, 1968.

——. *Quaestiones Super Libros Metaphysicorum Aristotelis*. B. Ioannis Duns Scoti Opera Philosophica. Edited Robert Andrews. Vols. 3, 4. St. Bonaventure, N.Y.: The Franciscan Institute, 1997.

——. *Ordinatio*. Civitas Vaticana: Typis Polyglottis Vaticanis, 1950–2008.

——. *The De Primo Principio of John Duns Scotus: A Revised Text and a Translation*. Edited by Evan Roche. St. Bonaventure, N.Y.: The Franciscan Institute, 1949.

——. *A Treatise on God as First Principle*. Edited and translated with commentary by Allan B. Wolter. Chicago: Franciscan Herald Press, 1966,

——. *Commentary on the Sentences of Peter Lombard III*.

——. *Lectura*. I–III.

——. *Ordinatio* I, III, IV.

——. *Questiones Quodlibetales*.

——. *On the Will and Morality*. Selected and translated by A. B. Wolter, Washington, D.C.: Catholic University of America Press, 1986.

——. *On the Will and Morality*. Translation edition William A. Frank and by A. B. Wolter, Washington, D.C.: Catholic University of America Press, 1997.

——. *Lectura I 39. John Duns Scotus: Contingency and Freedom*. Edited by A. Vos Jaczn and research group at the University of Utrechtl. Dordrecht: Kluwer Academic Publishers, 1994.

——. *Duns Scotus on Divine Love: Texts and Commentary on Goodness and Freedom, God and Humans*. Edited by A. Vos, H. Veldhuis, E.

For private consultation and not distribution without the consent of E Ondrako

Dekker, N.W. Den Bok, A.J.Beck. Burlington, VT: Ashgate Publishing Co., 2003.

Effler, R. John Duns Scotus and the Principle 'omnequod movetur ab alio movetur.' St. Bonaventure, N.Y.: The Franciscan Institute, 1962.

Farrer, Austin Marsden. *Saving Belief.* London: Hodder, 1964.

Fehlner, Peter Damian. *Mary and Theology: Scotus Revisited.* 2nd ed. Rensselaer, N.Y.: privately published, 1978, revised 2010, ch. 4 in this volume. *The Newman Scotus Reader Contexts and Commonalities.* New Bedford, MA: Academy of the Immaculate, January, 2015, Epiphany.

————. "Mary, Mother of the Church According to the "Constitutio De Ecclesia." *Miles Immaculatae* 1 (1965): 31–40.

————. "Neopatripassionism from a Scotistic Viewpoint." in *Quaderni di studi scotisti* 3 (Frigento: Casa Mariana Editrice, 2006), 35–96.

————. "Redemption, Metaphysics, and the Immaculate Conception." in *MFC* 2005 Vol 5. 186–262.

————. *The Role of Charity in the Ecclesiology of St. Bonaventure. Pontificia Facultas Theologica S. Bonaventurae. Dissertationes Ad Lauream.* Selecta Seraphica. Vol 2. Rome: Editrice *Miscellanea Francescana,* 1965.

————. "Scotus and Newman in Dialogue." Chap. 7, in *The Newman Scotus Reader Contexts and Commonalities.* New Bedford, MA: Academy of the Immaculate, January, 2015, Epiphany.

————. "The Sense of Marian Coredemption in St. Bonaventure and Bl. John Duns Scotus." in *MFC* 2001, Vol 1, 103–118.

————. "Sources of Scotus's Mariology in Tradition" in *Durham Symposium,* 2008, 235–296.

————. *St. Maximilian M. Kolbe, Pneumatologist, His Theology of the Holy Spirit. Mariologia Franciscana* II. New Bedford, MA: Academy of the Immaculate, 2004.

————. *Letter to the Author* January 30, 2010. The meaning of general and special metaphysics in the context of ontotheology.

Fehlner, Peter Damian and A. Apollonio. "Redemption in a Franciscan Key." in *MFC* 2008, Vol. 8, 111–158.

For private consultation and not distribution without the consent of E Ondrako

Feuillet, A. *Jesus et Sa Mere*, Paris: Gabalda, 1974, 234ff.

Finigan, Timothy. "Belief and Devotion to the Immaculate Conception in Medieval England." in *MFC* 2005, Vol 5, 344–359.

———. "Immaculate Conception After Scotus. Scostistic Mariology from Scotus to the Dogma of 1854: The Formation of a Mariological Tradition Based on the Immaculate Conception." in Durham Symposium 2008. 297–320.

Finkenzeller, Josef. *Offenbarung und Theologie nach der Lehre des Johannes Duns Scotus*. Munster: 1960.

Finnis, John. "Address on Secularism and a Healthy Secularity." *Politics Department Colloquium*. Princeton University. 23 October 2003, unpublished.

Fletcher, Patrick J. "Newman and Natural Theology." *Newman Studies Journal* 5, no. 2 (Fall, 2008): 26–42.

Florovsky, Georges. *Collected Works of Georges Florovsky*. Belmont, Mass.: Nordland Pub. Co., 1972.

Fornero, Giovanni. *Laicità debole e laicità forte: Il contributo della bioetica al dibattito sulla laicità*. Milano: B. Mondadori, 2008.

Four, Vital du. "Quaestiones De Cognitione Anima" in *Le Cardinal Vital du Four: Huit Questions Disputées sur Le Problème de la Connaissance*. Edited by F. Delorme. AHDLMA 2 (1927), 156–336.

Francis of Assisi. *Early Documents of Francis of Assisi*. Edited by R. Armstrong, J.W. Hellmann, and W. Short. 3 volumes. Hyde Park, N.Y.: New City Press, 1999–2001.

———. "Regula Bullata." Turnhout Brepols Publishers; Centre Traditio Litterarum Occidentalium;, http://clt.brepolis.net.proxy.library.nd.edu/LLTA/pages/TextSearch.aspx?key=MFRASSF22.

Frank, William A. "John Duns Scotus's Quodlibetal Teaching on the Will," Ph.D dissertation. Washington, D.C. Catholic University of America, 1982), corrected version 1985.

———. *Duns Scotus on the Will and Morality*. Translation edition William A. Frank and A. B. Wolter, Washington, D.C.: Catholic University of America Press, 1997.

For private consultation and not distribution without the consent of E Ondrako

———. *Duns Scotus: Metaphysician*. Edited by William A. Frank and Allan B. Wolter. West Lafayette, IN: Purdue University Press, 1995.

Fraser, Hilary. *Beauty and Belief: Aesthetics and Religion in Victorian Literature*. Cambridge: Cambridge University Press, 1986.

Gardner, W. H. and N. H. MacKenzie. *The Poems of Gerard Manley Hopkins*. Edited by Catherine Phillips. 4th ed. Oxford: Oxford University Press, 1990.

Gerken, Alexander. *Theologie Des Wortes*. Vol 1 Düsseldorf: Patmos-Verlag, 1963.

Gilson, Etienne. *History of Christian Philosophy in the Middle Ages*. New York: Random House, 1955.

———. *Jean Duns Scot*. Paris: J. Vrin, 1952.

González, Severino. *Sacrae Theologiae Summa 4. De Sacramentis, De Novissimis*. Edited with Solà i Carrió, Francesco de P., José F. Sagüés, and José Antonio de Aldama. Matriti: Biblioteca de Autores Cristianos, 1956.

Grajewski, Maurice. *The Formal Distinction of Duns Scotus*. Washington, D.C.: The Catholic University of America Press, 1944.

Hart Research Associates. "Raising the Bar: Employers' Views on Colleges Learning in the Wake of the Economic Downturn." Washington DC: Hart Research Associates, http://www.aacu.org/leap/documents/2009_EmployerSurvey.pdf.

Haughey, John C. *Where is Knowing Going? : The Horizons of the Knowing Subject*. Washington, D.C.: Georgetown University Press, 2009.

Hayes, Zachary. *What Manner of Man? Sermons on Christ by St. Bonaventure*. Chicago: Franciscan Herald Press, 1974.

Heaney, J. J. "Modernism." in *National Catholic Encyclopedia*. Vol. 9, 991–991.

Hebblethwaite, Brian. *Philosophical Theology and Christian Doctrine*. Malden, MA: Blackwell Pub., 2005.

Hodgson, Peter C. *G.W.F. Hegel: Theologian of the Spirit*. Minneapolis: Fortress Press, 1997.

Heidegger, Martin. *An Introduction to Metaphysics*. Translated by Ralph Manheim. New Haven: Yale University Press, 1959.

For private consultation and not distribution without the consent of E Ondrako

Heuser, Alan. *The Shaping Vision of Gerard Manley Hopkins.* Oxford: Oxford University Press, 1958.

Hoeres, Walter. *Kritik Der Transzendentalphilosophischen Erkenntnistheorie.* Stuttgart: Berlin, Köln, Mainz, Kohlhammer, 1969.

———. *Die Wille als reine Vollkomenheit nach Duns Scotus.* Munchen: Verlag, Anton Pustet, 1962. *La volontà come perfezione pura in Duns Scoto.*Translated by Alfredo Bizzotto and Antonio Poppi. Liviana Editrice in Padova, 1976.

Honnefelder, Ludger. *Ens inquantum ens: der Begriff des Seienden als Solchen als Gegenstand der Metaphysik nach Der Lehre Der Johannes Duns Scotus.* Beiträge zur Geschichte Der Philosophie und Theologie des Mittelalters. n.f., Bd. 16. Münster: Aschendorff, 1979.

Hopkins, Gerard Manley. "The Blessed Virgin Compared to the Air We Breathe." in *Gerard Manly Hopkins: Selected Poetry.* Edited by Catherine Phillips. Oxford: Oxford University Press, 1998. References below are from the 1998 Phillips edition. She has a revision in 2002. An earlier edition is edited by W.. H. Gardner and N. H. MacKenzie. 4th ed. London, New York: Oxford University Press, 1967. Other editions do not change Hopkins's texts.

———. "Duns Scotus Oxford," 127.

———. "God's Grandeur," 114.

———. "On the Portrait of Two Beautiful Young People," 157.

———. "That Nature is a Heracletian Fire and the Comfort of the Resurrection," 163.

———. "The Windhover," 117.

———. "The Wreck of the Deutschland," 98.

———. "Letter to C. Patmore." in *Further Letters of Gerard Manley Hopkins,* 2d ed. London: 1938, 1956, 465. See reference to Balthasar, *Herrlicheit,* Vol 3, 364–365.

———. *Gerard Manley Hopkins: Selected Prose.* Edited by Gerald Roberts. Oxford: Oxford University Press, 1980.

Horan, Daniel P. *Postmodernity and Univocity: A Critical Account of Radical Orthodoxy and John Duns Scotus.* Lanham: Fortress Press, 2014.

For private consultation and not distribution without the consent of E Ondrako

Horne, Brian. "He Came Down from Heaven: The Christology of Charles Williams." in *The Person of Christ.* Edited by S. Holmes and Murray Rae. London: T&T Clark, 2006, 109–110.

Hubaut, Michael. "Christ our Joy: Learning to Pray with Francis and Clare." *Greyfriars Review* 9 Supplement (1995): 17–18.

Hunter, James. *Gerard Manley Hopkins.* London: Evans Brothers Ltd., 1975.

Ingham, Mary Beth. "Responding from the Tradition: Franciscan Universities in the Third Millennium." *The AFCU Journal: A Franciscan Perspective on Higher Education* 4, (2006): 7.

Ingham, Mary Beth. *Rejoicing in the Works of the Lord: Beauty in the Franciscan Tradition.* St. Bonaventure, N.Y.: The Franciscan Institute, 2009.

Ippolito, Benedetto. "The Anthropological Foundations of Duns Scotus's Mariology." in Durham Symposium, 2008, 157–172.

John Paul II, Pope. "Address." *L'Osservatore Romano* (22–23 March 1993, 1993).

————. "Address to the Members of the Scotus Commission of the Order of Friars Minor." Vatican: The Holy See, http://www.vatican.va/holy_father/john_paul_ii/speeches/2002/february/documents/hf_jp-ii_spe_20020216_frati-minori_en.html.

————. *Encyclical Letter, Fides et Ratio.* English. Washington, D.C.: United States Catholic Conference, 1998, http://www.vatican.va/holy_father/john_paul_ii/encyclicals/documents/hf_jp-ii_enc_15101998_fides-et-ratio_en.html.

Journet, C. "Scripture and the Immaculate Conception." in *The Dogma of the Immaculate Conception. History and Significance.* Edited by Edward O'Connor. Notre Dame, IN: University of Notre Dame Press, 1958.

Julian of Norwich. *Revelations of Divine Love of Julian of Norwich.* Wheathampstead: Anthony Clarke Books, 1973.

Kant, Immanuel, *Naturrecht Feyerabend: Kant Autonomy and Modernity."* Lecture by Paul Guyer, October 15, 2010. Washington, D.C.: The Catholic University of America, unpublished.

For private consultation and not distribution without the consent of E Ondrako

Kant, Immanuel. *Religion within the Boundaries of Mere Reason and Other Writings.* Edited by Allen W. Wood, and George Di Giovanni. Cambridge: Cambridge University Press, 1998.

Kerrigan, A. "The Predestination of Mary According to St. Cyril of Alexandria." in *Alma socia Christi.* Edited by Academia Mariana. Vol. 3 Roma: Academia Mariana, 1952, 34–58.

Kierkegaard, Søren. *Philosophical Fragments, Johannes Climacus.* Edited by Edna H. Hong and Howard V. Hong. Princeton, N.J.: Princeton University Press, 1987.

Kierkegaard, Søren. *Concluding Unscientific Postscript to Philosophical Fragments.* Edited by Edna H. Hong and Howard V. Hong. Princeton, N.J.: Princeton University Press, 1992.

King, Benjamin John. *Newman and the Alexandrian Fathers: Shaping Doctrine in 19th Century England.* Oxford: Oxford University Press, 2009.

Kovach, Francis. "Divine and Human Beauty in Duns Scotus's Philosophy and Theology." *Scholastic Challenges to some Mediaeval and Modern Ideas* (1987): 102–103. Originally in *Deus et homo ad mentem 1. Duns Scoti.* Rome: 1972, 445–459.

Knuuttila, S. "Review of the Philosophy of Duns Scotus." *Ars Disputandi: The Online Journal for Philosophy of Religion* (2007): paragraph 2.

Kuhn, Thomas S. *The Structure of Scientific Revolutions.* Chicago, University of Chicago Press, 1970.

Kung, G. "Nominalism." in *Catholic Encyclopedia.* Vol. 10. Washington, D.C., 1911, 483–486.

Lash, Nicholas. *Newman on Development: The Search for an Explanation in History.* Shepherdstown, W. VA: Patmos Press, 1975.

Leff, Gordon. *The Dissolution of the Medieval Outlook: An Essay on Intellectual and Spiritual Change in the Fourteenth Century.* New York: Harper & Row, 1976.

Lewis, C. S. and Walter Hooper. *Christian Reflections.* Grand Rapids: W.B. Eerdmans Pub. Co, 1967.

Lemieux, D. *She is Our Response. The Virgin Mary and the Church's Encounter with Modernity in the Mariology of Joseph Ratzinger.* New Bedford, MA: Academy of the Immaculate, 2011.

For private consultation and not distribution without the consent of E Ondrako

Lewis, C. S. Miracles: A Preliminary Study. New York: Macmillan Co, 1947.

Libera, Alain de. La Querelle Des Universaux: De Platon à La Fin Du Moyen Âge. Paris: Éditions du Seuil, 1996.

Locke, John. An Essay Concerning Humane Understanding. London: H. G. Bohn, 1695.

————. "The Reasonableness of Christianity, as Delivered in the Scriptures." Printed for A. Bettesworth and C. Hitch; J. Pemberton; and E. Symon.

Locke, John, J. R. Milton, and Philip Milton. An Essay Concerning Toleration and Other Writings on Law and Politics, 1667–1683. Oxford: Oxford University Press, 2010.

Loiret, François. Volonté Et Infini Chez Duns Scot. Paris: Kimé, 2003.

Lonergan, Bernard. Insight. New York: Philosophical Library, 1957, rpt. 1968.

MacIntyre, Alasdair. "The Very Idea of a University: Newman, Aristotle, and Us." British Journal of Educational Studies 57 December, (2009): 347–362.

Macquarrie, John. "Newman and Kierkegaard on the Act of Faith." in Newman and Conversion. Edited by Ian T. Ker. Notre Dame, IN: University of Notre Dame Press, 1997.

Mahoney, John. Christianity in Evolution: An Exploration. Washington, D.C.: Georgetown University Press, 2011.

Manteau-Bonamy, H. M. Immaculate Conception and the Holy Spirit: The Marian Teachings of Father Kolbe. 1st American ed. Kenosha, WI: Prow Books, 1977.

————. La Vierge Marie Et Le Saint-Esprit. 2nd ed. Paris: P. Lethielleux, 1971.

Marcel, Gabriel. Gabriel Marcel's Perspectives on the Broken World: The Broken World, a Four-Act Play: Concrete Approaches to Investigating the Ontological Mystery. Edited by Katherine Rose Hanley. Milwaukee: Marquette University Press, 1998.

For private consultation and not distribution without the consent of E Ondrako

Marcil, George. "Franciscan School." in *The History of Franciscan Theology*. Edited by Kenan B. Osborne. St. Bonaventure, N.Y: The Franciscan Institute, 1994, 313–316.

Marrone, Steven P. "The Light of Thy Countenance: Science and Knowledge of God in the Thirteenth Century." *Studies in the History of Christian Thought*. Vol. 98. Leiden; Boston: Brill, 2001, 439.

Martin, Robert Bernard. *Gerard Manley Hopkins: A Very Private Life*. Hammersmith, London: HarperCollins, 1991.

Mary at the Foot of the Cross. New Bedford, MA: Academy of the Immaculate, 2001–2010, vols. 1–9 in a series. Henceforth, MFC.

Mascall, E. L. *Theology and the Gospel of Christ: An Essay in Reorientation*. London: SPCK, 1977.

McGrath, Sean L. *Heidegger: A Very Critical Introduction*. Grand Rapids, MI.: W.B. Erdmans, 2008.

Merrigan, Terrance. "The Antropology of Conversion: Newman and the Contemporary Theology of Religions." in *Newman and Conversion*. Edited by Ian T. Ker. Notre Dame, IN: University of Notre Dame Press, 1997, 117–114.

Mettepenningen, Jürgen. *Nouvelle Théologie - New Theology: Inheritor of Modernism, Precursor of Vatican II*. London; New York: T&T Clark, 2010.

Miller, Lisa. "Harvard's Crisis of Faith: Can a Secular University Embrace Religion without Sacrificing its Soul?" *Newsweek* (February 11, 2010).

Minges, Parthenius. *Compendium Theologiae Dogmaticae Specialis*. 2nd ed. Ratisbon: Kösel and Pustet, 1921–1922.

Mizener, Alex. "Gerard Manley Hopkins: A Critical Symposium." *The Kenyon Review* 1944, rpt. Victorian Hopkins. London: Burns and Oates, 1975.

Mongrain, Kevin. "The Eyes of Faith: Newman's Critique of Arguments from Design." *Newman Studies Journal* 6, no. 1 (Spring, 2009): 68–86.

Morey, Melanie M. and John J. Piderit. *Catholic Higher Education: A Culture in Crisis*. New York: Oxford University Press, 2006.

For private consultation and not distribution without the consent of E Ondrako

Mühlen, Heribert. "Sein und Person nach Johannes Duns Scotus; Beitrag zur Grundlegung einer Metaphysik der Person." *Franziskanische Forschungen*. Vol. 11. Werl/Westf: Dietrich-Coelde-Verl, 1954.

Newman, John Henry. Primary material is in the uniform edition published by Longmans, Green and Co., London, New York, Bombay. Date { } year of composition; date in [ ] uniform edition; ( ) date in edition used.

———. *Apologia Pro Vita Sua*. {1864} {1873} (1905) (1913).

———. *Apologia Pro Vita Sua*. Edited by David. J. DeLaura. 1st ed. New York: W. W. Norton & Company, Inc, 1968.

———. *An Essay in Aid of a Grammar of Assent* {1870} (1898) (1903) (1909) (1913)

———. *An Essay on the Development of Christian Doctrine*. {1845} [1878] (1900).

———. *An Essay on the Development of Christian Doctrine*. Westminster, Md.: Christian Classics, 1968.

———. *Discourses to Mixed Congregations*. {1849} [1892] (1900) (1902).

———. *Essays, Critical and Historical*. 2 volumes [1872] (1895).

———. *Fifteen Sermons Preached before the University of Oxford*. {1826—1843} {1871} [1900] (1902) (1918).

———. *Fifteen Sermons Preached before the University of Oxford*. Notre Dame, Ind.: University of Notre Dame Press, 1997.

———. *Fifteen Sermons Preached before the University of Oxford*. Edited by James David Earnest and Gerard Tracey. Oxford: Oxford University Press, 2006.

———. *The Idea of a University, Defined and Illustrated*. {1852–1859} [1873] (1909)

———. *The Idea of a University Defined and Illustrated and Essays Addressed to the Members of the Catholic University*. Edited by Martin J. Svaglic. 1960.

———. *Lectures on the Doctrine of Justification*. {1838} {1874}.

———. *Lectures on the Doctrine of Justification*. Westminster: Md., Christian Classics, 1966.

For private consultation and not distribution without the consent of E Ondrako

————. "A Letter to the Duke of Norfolk." in *Certain Difficulties Felt by Anglicans in Catholic Teaching Considered.* Vol. 2{1874} [1895] (1900) (1907–1908)

————. "A Letter to the Duke of Norfolk on Occasion of Mr. Gladstone's Recent Expostulation in Certain Difficulties Felt by Anglicans in Catholic Teaching, Volume 2." B.M. Pickering, http://www.newmanreader.org/works/anglicans/volume2/gladstone/postscript.html.

————. "A Letter Addressed to the Rev. E.B. Pusey, D.D. on Occasion of His Eirenicon." in *Certain Difficulties Felt by Anglicans in Catholic Teaching Considered.* Vol 2. {1865} [1895].

————. *Letters and Diaries.* Oxford: Oxford University Press, 1961–2010.

————. *Meditations and Devotions.* [1893] (1903).

————. *The Rambler.* {1859–1860}

————. "On Consulting the Faithful in Matters of Doctrine." in *The Rambler.* Edited and introduction by John M. Coulson. New York: Sheed and Ward, 1961.

————. *Parochial and Plain Sermons.* 8 volumes {1834–1843} [1869] (1907–1909).

————. *Parochial and Plain Sermons.* San Francisco: Ignatius Press, 1997.

————. *Sermons Bearing on Subjects of the Day.* {1848} [1869] (1909).

————. *Sermons Bearing on Subjects of the Day.* Westminster, Md.: Christian Classics, 1968

————. *Discussions and Arguments on various Subjects.* [1872].

————. *Select Treatises of St. Athanasius in Controversy with the Arians.* 2 volumes. {1842–1844} [1897] (1903).

————. *The Via Media of the Anglican Church.* 2 volumes. {1837}[1877] (1908).

————. *The Arians of the Fourth Century.* {1833} (1908).

————. *The Arians of the Fourth Century.* Introduction and notes by Rowan Williams. Notre Dame: University of Notre Dame Press, 2001.

————. *Loss and Gain: The Story of a Convert.* [1903] (1906).

For private consultation and not distribution without the consent of E Ondrako

————. *Addresses to Cardinal Newman with his replies.* Edited by W.P. Neville. [1905].

Newsome, David. *The Victorian World Picture: Perceptions and Introspections in an Age of Change.* London: John Murray, 1997.

Nichols, Aidan. *From Newman to Congar: The Idea of Doctrinal Development from the Victorians to the Second Vatican Council.* Edinburgh: T & T Clark, 1990.

O'Dwyer, E.T. "Epistula, qua Pius PP X approbat opusculum Episcopi Limericiensis circa scripta Cardinal Newman, die 10a, Martii, 1908." in *Cardinal Newman and the Encyclical Pascendi Dominici Gregis.* London: 1908.

O'Malley, John W., et al. *Vatican II: Did Anything Happen?* Edited by David G. Shultenover. New York: Continuum, 2011.

Ondrako, Edward J. "Freedom within the Church: The Controversy between William Ewart Gladstone and John Henry Newman in 1874–75 and its Shadows and Images Over Vatican II." Ph.D., Syracuse University, 1994.

————. "Mary and the Church in Newman with an Eye to Coredemption." in *MFC* 2010 Vol. 9, 391–456.

O'Regan, Cyril. "John Henry Newman and the Argument of Holiness," *Newman Studies Journal* 9, no. 1 (Spring 2012).

————. *The Anatomy of Misremembering: Von Balthasar's Response to Modernity*, Volume 1, Hegel. The Crossroad Publishing Company www.crossroadpublishing.com, 2014.

————. *Gnostic Return in Modernity.* Albany, N.Y.: State University of new York Albany Press, 2001.

————. *The Heterodox Hegel.* Albany: State University of New York Press, 1994.

————. International Theological Commission. "Sensus Fidei in the Life of the Church." Paul McPartlan et al. eds. Vatican: 2014.

————. "Kant: Boundaries, Blind-Spots, and Supplements."In *Christianity and Secular Reason: Classical Themes and Modern Developments*, edited by Jeffrey Bloechl. Notre Dame, IN: University of Notre Dame Press, 2012).

For private consultation and not distribution without the consent of E Ondrako

———. "Bl. John Henry Newman: The Call to Holiness." Lecture at the University of Notre Dame, January 24, 2011 (forthcoming).

———. *Theology and the Space of the Apocalyptic, The Pere Marquette Lecture in Theology: 2009*. Milwaukee, WI: Marquette University Press, 2009.

Ortegat, P. and L. J. Walker. "Voluntarism." in *New Catholic Encyclopedia*. Vol. 14. Washington, D.C., 1967, 745–747.

Palmer, Parker J., Arthur Zajonc, and Megan Scribner. *The Heart of Higher Education: A Call to Renewal: Transforming the Academy through Collegial Conversations*. San Francisco: Jossey-Bass, 2010.

Pangallo, Don Mario. "La filosophia Cristiana come filosophia della liberta in Duns Scoto." in *Quaderni di studi scotisti*. 3 (2006), 21–34.

Parks, Sharon Daloz. *Big Questions, Worthy Dreams: Mentoring Young Adults in their Search for Meaning, Purpose, and Faith*. San Francisco, Calif: Jossey-Bass, 2000.

Pasnau, Robert. *Theories of Cognition in the Later Middle Ages*. Cambridge: Cambridge University Press, 1997.

Pattison, Robert. *The Great Dissent: John Henry Newman and the Liberal Heresy*. Oxford: Oxford University Press, 1991.

Peters, Wilhelmus Antonius Maria. *Gerard Manley Hopkins*. London: G. Cumberlege, 1948.

Paul VI, Pope. "Declaration of Mary as Mother of the Church." *Acta Apostolicae Sedis* 56 (1964), 1014–1018

———. *Apostolic Letter Alma Parens for the Seventh Centenary Celebration of Scotus's Birth*. AAS 58, 14 July 1966.

———. "The Task of Catholic Universities." in *Sermon at Milan Catholic University of the Sacred Heart*, April 5, 1964. *The Pope Speaks*. 10 (Fall, 1965), 44–45.

Pini, Giorgio. "Scotus on the Object of Cognitive Acts." *Franciscan Studies* 66, (2008): 281–315.

Pius XI, Pope. "Epistula, qua Pius PP X approbat opusculum Episcopi Limericiensis circa scripta Cardinal Newman, die 10a, Martii, 1908." in *Cardinal Newman and the Encyclical Pascendi Dominici Gregis*. Edited by E. T. O'Dwyer. London: 1908.

For private consultation and not distribution without the consent of E Ondrako

Prunieres, L. *Lexique Saint Bonaventure*. s.v. "contuition." Paris: 1969.

Ramsey, Arthur Michael. *From Gore to Temple: The Development of Anglican Theology between Lux Mundi and the Second World War, 1889–1939*. London: Longmans, 1960.

Ravera, M. and P. D. Bubbio. "Raccogliere e accogliere. Riflessioni sul Logos alla luce de la critica di R. Girard à Heidegger." *Filosofia e teologia*. (2006).

Richardson, Laurence. *Newman's Approach to Knowledge*. Herefordshire Leominster: Gracewing, 2007.

Risi, Francesco Maria. *Sul Motivo Primario della Incarnazione del Verbo, Ossia Gesù Christo Predestinato di primo invento*. Brescia: Mucchetti e Riva, 1897–1898.

Robinson, John. in *Extremity: A Study of Gerard Manley Hopkins*. Cambridge: University Press, 1978.

Roche, Evan. *De primo principio of Duns Scotus*. St. Bonaventure, N.Y.: The Franciscan Institute, 1949.

Rosini, Ruggero and Peter M. Felner. *Mariology of Blessed John Duns Scotus. Mariologia Franciscana* 2. New Bedford, MA: Academy of the Immaculate, 2008.

Rowell, Geoffrey. "Historical Retrospect: Lux Mundi 1889." in *The Religion of the Incarnation: Anglican Essays in Commemoration of Lux Mundi*. Edited by Robert Morgan. Bristol: Bristol Classical Press, 1989.

Saint-Exupéry, Antoine d., and Katherine Woods. *The Little Prince*. New York: Harcourt, Brace & World, 1943.

Scotus, See Duns Scotus

Sciamannini, Raniero. *La Contuizione Bonaventuriana*. Firenze: Editrice "Città di vita," 1957.

Shideler, Mary McDermott. *The Theology of Romantic Love: A Study in the Writings of Charles Williams*. New York: Harper, 1962.

Sillem, A. "David Hume." in *New Catholic Encyclopedia*. Vol. 7.

Sixtus IV, Pope. *L'Orazione della Immacolata: Discorso Tenuto Il 19 Marzo 1469 in Venezia*. A cura Dino Cortese. *Biblioteca apostolica vaticana editrice*. Manuscript: Cod. C46. Padova: Centro Studi Antoniani, 1985.

For private consultation and not distribution without the consent of E Ondrako

Solà i Carrió, Francesco de P., José F. Sagüés, José Antonio de Aldama, and Severino González. *Sacrae Theologiae Summa 4. De Sacramentis, De Novissimis.* Matriti: Biblioteca de Autores Cristianos, 1956.

Steel, Carlos. "Medieval Philosophy: An Impossible Project: Thomas Aquinas and the 'Averroistic' Ideal of Happiness." in *Was ist philosophie im mittelalter? Akten des X internationalen kongresses für mittelalterliche philosophie der société internationale pour l'étude de la philosophie médiévale.* August 1997, Erfurt. Edited by Jan Aertsen. Berlin: Walter de Gruyter, 1998.

Strange, Roderick. *Newman and the Gospel of Christ.* Oxford: Oxford University Press, 1981.

Sullivan, Deacon Jack. Sermon: "Please Cardinal Newman—Help Me to Walk." Oratory, Birmingham, England: 20 September 2010, unpublished.

Szabó, Titus. *De SS. Trinitate in Creaturis Refulgente: Doctrina S. Bonaventurae.* Bibliotheca Academiae Catholicae Hungaricae. Sectio Philosophico-Theologica.1. Roma: Orbis Catholicus; Herder, 1955.

Todisco, Orlando. *Il dono dell'essere: sentieri inesplorati del medioevo francescano.* Padova: Messaggero, 2003.

Tristram, Henry. *John Henry Newman, Autobiographical Writings.* Sheed and Ward, 1957.

Ullathorne, B. The Immaculate Conception. Ist ed. 1854. New York: Second edition, 1904.

Urritibéhéty, Christopher. *Christus Alpha Et Omega: Seu, De Christi Universali Regno.* Lille: R. Giard, 1910.

Veuthey, Léon. *St. Bonaventurae Philosophia Christiana.* Romae: Officium libri catholici, 1943.

Veuthey, Léon. *Dottrina Mariologica: Maria Immacolata Madre in Prospettiva Francescana.* Edited by Ernesto Piacentini. Roma: Ed. Miscellanea Francescana, 2003.

Veuthey, Léon. *Les Divers Courants De La Philosophie Augustino-Franciscaine Au Moyen-Âge.* Vol. 7. Romae: Pontificium Athenseum Antonianum, 1951.

For private consultation and not distribution without the consent of E Ondrako

Vier, Peter C. *Evidence and its Function According to John Duns Scotus.* Philosophy Series, no. 7. St. Bonaventure, N.Y: Franciscan Institute, 1951.

Vos, Antonie. *The Philosophy of John Duns Scotus.* Edinburgh: Edinburgh University Press, 2006.

—. *Lectura I 39. John Duns Scotus: Contingency and Freedom.* Edited by A. Vos Jaczn. H. Veldhuis, A.H. Looman-Graaskamp. E. Dekker, N. W. Den Bok at the University of Utrecht. Dordrecht: Kluwer Academic Publishers, 1994.

—. *Duns Scotus on Divine Love: Texts and Commentary on Goodness and Freedom, God and Humans.* Edited by A. Vos, H. Veldhuis, E. Dekker, N.W. Den Bok, A.J.Beck. Burlington, VT: Ashgate Publishing Co., 2003.

Walgrave, Jan Hendrik. *Newman the Theologian; the Nature of Belief and Doctrine as Exemplified in His Life and Works.* New York: Sheed & Ward, 1960.

—. *Newman: Le développement du dogme.* Paris: Casterman, 1957.

Walter, L. *Das Glaubenverstandnis bei Johannes Duns Scotus.* Paderborn: 1968.

Ward, Wilfrid Philip. *The Life of John Henry, Cardinal Newman, Based on His Private Journals and Correspondence.* New York: Longmans, Green, and Co, 1912.

Weatherby, Harold. *Cardinal Newman and His Age.* Knoxville, TN: Vanderbuilt Press, 1973.

—. *The Keen Delight.* Athens, GA.: University of Georgia Press, 1975.

Welch, Claude, Gottfried Thomasius, I. A. Dorner, and Alois Emanuel Biedermann. *God and Incarnation in Mid-Nineteenth Century German Theology.* Oxford: Oxford University Press, 1965.

Werner, Hans-Joachim. *Die Ermöglichung des endlichen seins nach Johannes Duns Scotus.* Bern : 1974.

Westcott, Brooke Foss. *The Epistles of St. John the Greek Text.* London: Macmillan, 1985.

Wiedmann, F. "Theorie Des Realen Denkens Nach John Henry Newman." *Newman Studien vierte Folgen.* Nürnburg: (1960), 144–248.

For private consultation and not distribution without the consent of E Ondrako

Williams, Charles. *He Came Down from Heaven, and the Forgiveness of Sins*. London: Faber and Faber, 1950.

————. *The Image of the City, and Other Essays*. London: Oxford University Press, 1958.

Williams, Charles and Charles C. Hefling. *Charles Williams: Essential Writings in Spirituality and Theology*. Cambridge, Mass.: Cowley Publications, 1993.

Williams, Thomas. *The Cambridge Companion to Duns Scotus*. Cambridge: Cambridge University Press, 2003.

Wolter, Allan Bernard. *The Transcendentals and their Function in the Metaphysics of Duns Scotus*. St. Bonaventure, N.Y.: The Franciscan Institute, 1946, rpt. Kessinger, 2008.

————. *Duns Scotus on the Will and Morality*. Selected and translated by A. B. Wolter. Washington, D.C: Catholic University of America Press, 1986.

————. *On the Will and Morality*. Translation edition William A. Frank and by A. B. Wolter, Washington, D.C.: Catholic University of America Press, 1997.

————. "Duns Scotus on the Will as Rational Potency." in *The Philosophical Theology of John Duns Scotus*. Edited by Marilyn McCord Adams. Ithaca, N.Y.: Cornell University Press, 1990.163–180.

————. *Duns Scotus: Metaphysician*. Edited by William A. Frank and Allan B. Wolter. West Lafayette, IN: Purdue University Press, 1995.

For private consultation and not distribution without the consent of E Ondrako

Index

abstraction, 8, 10, 101, 102, 221, 295, 314, 323, 356, 396, 411, 423, 433, 450, 459, 467, 510, 532, 577, 578, 581, 596, 715, 782, 793, 805, 810, 839, 857, 858, 885, 888, 910, 935, 947
   affection for happiness, 620, 621, 622, 771, 797
   affectus commodi, 304, 313, 321, 323, 338, 340, 342, 418, 424, 484, 516, 856

affection for justice, 316, 620, 621, 622, 771, 797, 811
   affectus justitiae, 304, 313, 316, 323, 338, 340, 342, 417, 424, 484, 516, 574, 856
   love of justice, 316

apprehension
   notional, 8, 10, 219, 234, 257, 296, 322, 434, 444, 448, 453, 470, 529, 536, 547, 727, 838, 858

being or nothing
   god, in full flight from nothing, 309
   infinite, xii, 6, 19, 20, 22, 23, 24, 90, 93, 94, 111, 112, 126, 130, 135, 138, 145, 146, 153, 217, 224, 226, 227, 237, 262, 272, 318, 319, 327, 345, 357, 360, 378, 402, 403, 414, 422, 425, 428, 430, 432, 436, 437, 446, 451, 452, 468, 489, 493, 494, 511, 526, 554, 555, 558, 559, 571, 576, 577, 580, 592, 655, 656, 657, 658, 659, 660, 661, 664, 668, 669, 670, 672, 677, 679, 681, 682, 723, 730, 736, 747, 761, 767, 768, 771, 772, 773, 774, 776, 788, 802, 806, 810, 816, 830, 832, 833, 840, 841, 844, 848, 855, 856, 879, 881, 898, 904, 907, 913, 935, 950
   personal, xv, 10, 13, 15, 18, 4, 5, 6, 9, 28, 41, 46, 47, 48, 52, 53, 54, 56, 57, 71, 88, 119, 122, 124, 125, 126, 128, 129, 132, 137, 139, 141, 143, 144, 148, 151, 155, 158, 162, 163, 164, 166, 169, 175, 177, 188, 194, 195, 196, 197, 199, 209, 213, 223, 226, 227, 231, 232, 234, 237, 240, 241, 242, 243, 255, 256, 257, 260, 262, 263, 264, 266, 268, 269, 270, 275, 277, 278, 280, 295, 308, 309, 312, 313, 314, 316, 317, 320, 321, 322, 323, 325, 329, 332, 333, 334, 336, 338, 339, 341, 342, 346, 348, 350, 351, 354, 356, 359, 361, 365, 369, 370, 371, 380, 388, 389, 403, 405, 406, 407, 413, 414, 418, 422, 423, 424, 426, 428, 430, 431, 433, 434, 435, 436, 437, 438, 442, 443, 446, 450, 451, 453, 460, 477, 478, 482, 490, 491, 494, 500,

PAGE NUMBERS ARE FROM THE WORD DOC.; THEREFORE, THEY DO NOT MATCH WITH THIS DOC'S PAGE NUMBERS

For private consultation and not distribution without the consent of E Ondrako

502, 504, 509, 511, 513, 519, 526, 529, 533, 556, 564, 590, 594, 623, 629, 634, 637, 639, 644, 649, 693, 696, 697, 698, 700, 704, 705, 717, 727, 732, 734, 735, 737, 739, 740, 747, 773, 777, 779, 780, 792, 797, 802, 804, 805, 808, 809, 811, 833, 836, 843, 844, 847, 850, 851, 852, 854, 857, 866, 870, 941, 944

univocity, xiii, xiv, 7, 8, 23, 11, 111, 112, 135, 153, 183, 205, 217, 236, 239, 240, 243, 246, 322, 327, 351, 360, 369, 389, 398, 399, 414, 425, 429, 432, 438, 445, 455, 468, 482, 499, 502, 526, 532, 536, 537, 543, 547, 551, 555, 558, 563, 575, 735, 744, 752, 772, 773, 774, 775, 776, 780, 788, 793, 809, 835, 844, 846, 849, 850, 857, 860, 870, 871, 875, 893, 895, 898, 901, 904, 913, 916, 918, 919, 923, 929, 931

independent, 7, 20, 69, 107, 112, 124, 138, 168, 214, 308, 309, 312, 339, 344, 381, 426, 433, 434, 438, 441, 448, 482, 483, 538, 597, 598, 599, 600, 601, 603, 736, 816, 826, 853, 865, 876, 935, 942

Esse:in fuga a non-esse, 308, 359

benevolence, 271, 484, 516

cognition
abstractive, 102, 104, 105, 107, 112, 114, 215, 219, 223, 233, 296, 315, 333, 423, 433, 451, 457, 502, 536, 544, 760, 803, 838, 941
intuitive, 21, 100, 102, 104, 105, 107, 190, 234, 296, 315, 333, 348, 362, 376, 406, 445, 448, 450, 457, 459, 482, 488, 497, 536, 547, 549, 739, 769, 803

contuition, 348, 350, 362, 488, 991
in speculo, 308, 347, 362, 406

discursive knowledge, 322, 347, 348, 436
per speculum, 308, 347, 362, 406

essentially rational, 25, 308

faith
infused, 9, 111, 129, 137, 288, 289, 290, 291, 292, 320, 325, 329, 334, 404, 414, 421, 433, 435, 482, 489, 491, 496, 500, 514, 533, 776
natural, viii, 9, 322, 324, 329, 331, 334, 351, 356, 369, 388, 406, 414, 417, 435, 437, 443, 467, 481, 489, 490, 493, 496, 513, 555

PAGE NUMBERS ARE FROM THE WORD DOC.; THERE-FORE, THEY DO NOT MATCH WITH THIS DOC'S PAGE NUMBERS

For private consultation and not distribution without the consent of E Ondrako

formal distinction, 7, 9, 11, 169, 230, 412, 414, 537, 558, 735, 761, 808, 810, 839, 844, 857, 860, 871

freedom, xii, 1, 7, 12, 13, 18, 20, 4, 6, 7, 11, 19, 23, 25, 30, 74, 77, 83, 84, 94, 122, 165, 178, 179, 189, 197, 198, 214, 218, 220, 226, 227, 240, 243, 246, 247, 272, 275, 282, 287, 304, 313, 315, 319, 320, 321, 337, 338, 339, 340, 341, 342, 349, 364, 365, 388, 412, 425, 426, 489, 507, 511, 515, 517, 537, 538, 543, 544, 545, 558, 572, 573, 574, 575, 577, 579, 583, 618, 619, 621, 622, 624, 627, 629, 635, 655, 656, 657, 658, 659, 660, 661, 662, 664, 665, 666, 667, 668, 669, 670, 671, 673, 674, 675, 676, 677, 678, 680, 681, 682, 683, 703, 718, 719, 721, 737, 738, 739, 740, 741, 746, 747, 748, 749, 753, 754, 760, 765, 766, 767, 769, 770, 771, 772, 773, 774, 782, 783, 785, 787, 791, 794, 795, 796, 798, 799, 801, 802, 811, 813, 815, 817, 826, 831, 832, 834, 835, 836, 841, 846, 848, 853, 862, 863, 864, 865, 880, 881, 886, 936, 942, 943, 945, 946, 949, 950, 952, 955, 957, 958
free will, viii, 8, 319, 404, 517, 574, 578, 737, 776, 846
liberum arbitrium, 25, 319

grace, 1, 7, 13, 16, 57, 61, 74, 86, 87, 89, 91, 94, 119, 120, 121, 129, 140, 148, 150, 151, 152, 153, 154, 155, 156, 157, 158, 165, 171, 174, 177, 191, 193, 195, 197, 228, 238, 241, 286, 319, 321, 328, 329, 337, 340, 345, 352, 355, 366, 370, 379, 383, 385, 386, 388, 390, 394, 422, 423, 429, 438, 484, 493, 494, 506, 517, 533, 538, 556, 601, 609, 622, 694, 698, 705, 737, 742, 745, 775, 783, 786, 795, 798, 804, 808, 809, 815, 817, 843, 848, 851, 854, 863, 864, 869, 873, 880, 886, 902, 914, 934, 936, 940, 942, 945, 951, 952, 954, 955, 957

ideas, xix, 10, 22, 25, 7, 25, 26, 37, 82, 215, 221, 257, 294, 295, 380, 409, 411, 443, 527, 551, 556, 605, 643, 646, 653, 660, 664, 719, 727, 731, 737, 738, 739, 765, 783, 796, 807, 808, 827, 848, 852, 858, 866, 870, 938, 939

illative sense, 4, 13, 22, 25, 5, 18, 19, 21, 41, 55, 56, 58, 62, 74, 129, 136, 162, 173, 217, 223, 236, 240, 242, 246, 293, 315, 324, 331, 334, 336, 343, 351, 353, 356, 359, 365, 378, 388, 401, 407, 413, 414, 423, 434, 435, 437, 441, 442, 450, 468, 469, 471, 472, 474, 475, 476, 479, 480, 481, 482, 490, 497, 502, 519, 532, 533, 537, 551, 554, 556, 561, 562, 625, 726, 732, 733, 734, 748, 779, 803, 806, 846, 847, 878, 941

For private consultation and not distribution without the consent of E Ondrako

illumination, theory of divine, 19, 130, 135, 218, 236, 239, 244, 246, 252, 321, 343, 344, 348, 353, 369, 389, 482, 499, 500, 503, 513, 563, 776, 809, 846, 870

image, 9, 16, 25, 20, 51, 80, 126, 131, 143, 275, 312, 314, 318, 323, 345, 348, 359, 369, 398, 404, 406, 421, 427, 428, 429, 430, 437, 438, 460, 488, 512, 518, 526, 545, 603, 628, 638, 640, 658, 661, 679, 681, 695, 706, 707, 713, 721, 723, 730, 738, 740, 757, 778, 785, 867, 879, 890, 937, 938

incommunicable existence, 339, 363, 385, 423, 425, 426, 811, 850, 851

inference, x, 8, 13, 23, 41, 44, 45, 46, 47, 52, 53, 54, 55, 59, 60, 62, 75, 114, 125, 128, 134, 236, 245, 295, 312, 315, 323, 331, 334, 336, 346, 348, 354, 356, 358, 365, 396, 417, 423, 424, 425, 429, 431, 432, 433, 434, 435, 436, 438, 439, 441, 442, 444, 446, 447, 450, 460, 467, 469, 470, 471, 472, 474, 475, 476, 478, 482, 490, 497, 527, 538, 541, 543, 545, 547, 562, 734, 806, 828, 885, 940, 942

judgment, vii, 4, 7, 8, 23, 24, 25, 5, 9, 19, 49, 73, 96, 101, 103, 126, 127, 128, 132, 139, 147, 162, 180, 181, 186, 188, 197, 223, 228, 229, 232, 236, 242, 243, 246, 272, 274, 295, 313, 314, 316, 321, 323, 326, 332, 335, 346, 350, 351, 365, 388, 403, 407, 408, 424, 435, 438, 453, 475, 477, 478, 482, 488, 491, 501, 504, 517, 530, 533, 546, 554, 556, 557, 619, 625, 626, 699, 726, 728, 732, 733, 734, 748, 779, 780, 791, 792, 802, 803, 806, 834, 859, 909, 917, 928, 939, 940, 941

dijudicatio, 4, 25, 236, 314, 323, 334, 343, 350, 351, 356, 423, 433, 472, 475, 490, 510, 519, 531, 533, 732

PAGE NUMBERS ARE FROM THE WORD DOC.; THEREFORE, THEY DO NOT MATCH WITH THIS DOC'S PAGE NUMBERS

knowledge, unity of, 25, 322, 329, 335, 351, 354, 390, 391, 398, 399, 401, 407, 645, 766, 769, 774, 775, 776, 803, 820, 847

liberality, 309, 315, 337

memory, iv, xx, xxi, 9, 7, 10, 12, 13, 33, 101, 104, 105, 107, 168, 170, 312, 331, 333, 349, 355, 379, 451, 454, 455, 518, 526, 529, 530, 531, 560, 570, 633, 667, 761, 830, 843, 859, 881

nature, xiv, 4, 6, 22, 25, 27, 13, 18, 22, 23, 25, 30, 49, 52, 57, 69, 81, 82, 106, 112, 119, 121, 122, 123, 129, 131, 141, 142, 143, 145, 150, 152, 153, 158, 161, 166, 168, 169, 170, 171, 173, 175, 182, 184,

For private consultation and not distribution without the consent of E Ondrako

185, 188, 192, 199, 203, 204, 210, 226, 230, 242, 260, 263, 271,
274, 275, 287, 296, 312, 314, 315, 319, 321, 326, 328, 329, 330,
338, 339, 340, 341, 342, 345, 354, 355, 363, 364, 382, 385, 386,
387, 388, 391, 394, 402, 403, 405, 408, 419, 425, 440, 443, 445,
446, 449, 451, 454, 461, 463, 464, 465, 466, 467, 470, 473, 475,
476, 477, 479, 484, 486, 487, 488, 489, 492, 496, 498, 511, 527,
533, 538, 541, 544, 554, 555, 558, 560, 571, 572, 573, 574, 575,
576, 577, 578, 587, 594, 595, 596, 600, 604, 608, 610, 626, 631,
638, 645, 656, 660, 661, 664, 665, 670, 671, 676, 677, 681, 683,
693, 696, 700, 732, 735, 737, 741, 742, 744, 751, 752, 765, 789,
790, 792, 794, 795, 797, 802, 811, 836, 837, 840, 842, 853, 856,
857, 867, 869, 879, 894, 914, 918, 921, 948, 950
  intelligent, 404, 776
  intelligible, 309

notions, 136, 180, 215, 257, 258, 259, 295, 442, 448, 449, 450, 452,
  453, 459, 472, 532, 596, 736, 749, 750, 791, 868, 913

origin, 125, 214, 246, 263, 284, 285, 312, 331, 333, 355, 358, 398, 400,
  448, 541, 546, 554, 573, 576, 585, 619, 684, 698, 788, 888, 930

perfections, 19, 112, 136, 226, 227, 242, 318, 319, 328, 340, 356, 370,
  417, 422, 438, 536, 571, 579, 747, 749, 768, 806, 848, 935
  *perfectio simpliciter simplex, 25, 315, 318, 319, 320, 321, 334, 336,
  359, 375, 378, 390, 397, 413, 421, 424, 437, 440, 460, 472,
  475, 484, 489, 491, 497, 501, 502, 509, 512, 767, 797, 806,
  810, 812, 846, 857, 879*
  *pure, vii, xiii, 31, 14, 19, 23, 26, 73, 82, 112, 125, 130, 136, 184,
  191, 219, 226, 227, 236, 239, 240, 242, 243, 246, 315, 322,
  328, 331, 334, 337, 339, 340, 342, 344, 348, 349, 351, 353,
  356, 370, 390, 395, 412, 417, 422, 441, 444, 459, 482, 490,
  510, 536, 537, 540, 551, 574, 590, 595, 606, 610, 667, 698,
  747, 749, 767, 768, 769, 773, 776, 788, 789, 790, 793, 794,
  797, 802, 806, 810, 811, 812, 819, 830, 831, 838, 842, 843,
  848, 850, 851, 854, 856, 857, 864, 871, 881, 885, 887*

power to be good, 25, 308

primacy, iv, vii, xiv, xv, xix, 3, 4, 6, 5, 12, 17, 22, 23, 24, 27, 30, 35, 80,
  81, 82, 83, 85, 88, 93, 94, 99, 122, 145, 151, 152, 153, 154, 156,
  159, 161, 167, 189, 193, 195, 227, 237, 241, 242, 303, 304, 311,
  312, 315, 317, 319, 321, 322, 327, 328, 329, 336, 341, 342, 348,
  349, 353, 359, 360, 361, 364, 365, 366, 368, 372, 374, 375, 376,
  381, 384, 385, 386, 389, 404, 412, 415, 420, 421, 437, 451, 460,

For private consultation and not distribution without the consent of E Ondrako

483, 485, 492, 497, 498, 499, 503, 507, 511, 517, 521, 528, 536,
540, 541, 542, 544, 574, 578, 579, 580, 588, 611, 619, 624, 626,
637, 646, 655, 656, 660, 669, 670, 671, 676, 720, 728, 740, 749,
764, 765, 766, 768, 769, 770, 772, 773, 783, 793, 794, 798, 800,
808, 811, 833, 835, 838, 840, 841, 848, 849, 850, 851, 853, 854,
859, 869, 873, 877, 879, 884, 887, 934, 936, 938, 946, 950, 952
firstness, 12, 834, 839, 847

purity, 138, 159, 309, 387, 484, 516, 668

ratio, vii, 17, 219, 230, 231, 242, 276, 288, 311, 314, 316, 319, 320, 331,
336, 343, 363, 370, 374, 412, 436, 479, 483, 498, 517, 534, 573,
574, 579, 582, 583, 584, 586, 601, 605, 617, 618, 619, 620, 621,
622, 623, 624, 627, 641, 656, 657, 673, 688, 691, 772, 828, 846,
849, 946, 949, 981

religion
    natural, 5, 326, 412, 486, 546, 554, 568

similitude, 348, 406, 427, 430

supernatural, 5, 18, 28, 52, 61, 80, 110, 111, 112, 127, 129, 130, 164,
233, 284, 285, 286, 287, 288, 289, 319, 324, 325, 327, 328, 329,
335, 351, 354, 355, 365, 369, 370, 371, 390, 404, 414, 418, 421,
422, 433, 435, 436, 437, 443, 451, 467, 469, 484, 485, 490, 491,
492, 493, 494, 500, 506, 512, 513, 533, 552, 553, 555, 556, 563,
604, 693, 696, 699, 775, 776, 777, 779, 780, 793, 810, 827, 836,
839, 845, 848, 853, 862, 865, 878

theology
    infused, 176
    *natural, 18, 19, 21, 42, 223, 225, 230, 352, 368, 369, 379, 404, 413,
    414, 415, 430, 458, 460, 484, 486, 526, 764, 776, 787, 809,
    812, 815, 827, 847, 866, 878*

transcendental, 20, 22, 97, 237, 239, 310, 329, 330, 343, 390, 436, 491,
492, 509, 512, 518, 526, 552, 570, 579, 749, 750, 767, 778, 787,
788, 805, 812, 827, 853, 871, 904, 929, 935
    *disjunctive transcendentals, xiv, 7, 24, 31, 14, 20, 22, 87, 217, 322,
    349, 353, 360, 414, 429, 431, 471, 482, 499, 545, 547, 723,
    732, 735, 736, 747, 758, 767, 768, 774, 779, 787, 788, 789,
    809, 822, 825, 829, 835, 838, 846, 856, 867, 868, 870*

transcendentals
    *disjunctive transcendentals, xiv, 7, 24, 31, 14, 20, 22, 87, 217, 322,
    349, 353, 360, 414, 429, 431, 471, 482, 499, 545, 547, 723,*

For private consultation and not distribution without the consent of E Ondrako

732, 735, 736, 747, 758, 767, 768, 773, 778, 787, 788, 789, 809, 822, 825, 828, 835, 838, 846, 856, 867, 868, 870

understanding, 9, 17, 20, 22, 25, 6, 12, 13, 14, 16, 18, 27, 28, 29, 30, 37, 41, 43, 74, 78, 83, 91, 95, 97, 99, 100, 110, 121, 125, 126, 127, 133, 136, 137, 139, 140, 142, 143, 144, 146, 149, 153, 159, 160, 161, 163, 165, 166, 168, 169, 170, 171, 174, 175, 179, 180, 181, 182, 183, 185, 186, 187, 188, 190, 191, 194, 196, 201, 203, 211, 219, 222, 226, 235, 249, 257, 262, 264, 273, 292, 296, 306, 310, 312, 326, 331, 333, 340, 354, 363, 365, 366, 371, 375, 390, 393, 399, 414, 425, 430, 444, 445, 447, 461, 469, 490, 501, 509, 513, 528, 530, 536, 538, 547, 549, 550, 557, 558, 559, 578, 594, 597, 605, 607, 608, 617, 618, 622, 633, 640, 645, 697, 704, 720, 722, 726, 727, 729, 734, 737, 740, 743, 744, 752, 754, 760, 761, 769, 779, 787, 791, 792, 793, 797, 800, 806, 807, 810, 813, 831, 834, 837, 839, 840, 843, 845, 847, 859, 861, 866, 868, 869, 874, 877, 884, 890, 898, 899, 933, 935, 941, 944, 945, 948, 949, 950, 951, 954, 955, 957, 959

vestige, 314, 323, 334, 348, 350, 369, 406, 422, 427, 430, 438, 512, 879

PAGE NUMBERS ARE FROM THE WORD DOC.; THEREFORE, THEY DO NOT MATCH WITH THIS DOC'S PAGE NUMBERS

NOTES

NOTES

18843017R20413

Made in the USA
San Bernardino, CA
02 February 2015